RELIGION
IN SCHOOLS

DEBATING ISSUES
in American Education

EDITORIAL BOARD

Editors-in-Chief

Charles J. Russo
University of Dayton

Allan G. Osborne, Jr.
Principal (Retired), Snug Harbor Community School, Quincy, Massachusetts

Volume Editor

Charles J. Russo
University of Dayton

Advisory Board

Francine DeFranco
Homer Babbidge Library, University of Connecticut

Ralph D. Mawdsley
Cleveland State University

Martha M. McCarthy
Loyola Marymount University and Indiana University

Mark E. Shelton
Monroe C. Gutman Education Library, Harvard University

RELIGION IN SCHOOLS

VOLUME EDITOR

CHARLES J. RUSSO
UNIVERSITY OF DAYTON

4 VOLUME

DEBATING ISSUES *in American Education*

SERIES EDITORS | CHARLES J. RUSSO
ALLAN G. OSBORNE, JR.

$SAGE reference

Los Angeles | London | New Delhi
Singapore | Washington DC

370
SA183R

Los Angeles | London | New Delhi
Singapore | Washington DC

FOR INFORMATION:

SAGE Publications, Inc.
2455 Teller Road
Thousand Oaks, California 91320
E-mail: order@sagepub.com

SAGE Publications Ltd.
1 Oliver's Yard
55 City Road
London EC1Y 1SP
United Kingdom

SAGE Publications India Pvt. Ltd.
B 1/I 1 Mohan Cooperative Industrial Area
Mathura Road, New Delhi 110 044
India

SAGE Publications Asia-Pacific Pte. Ltd.
3 Church Street
#10-04 Samsung Hub
Singapore 049483

Publisher: Rolf A. Janke
Acquisitions Editor: Jim Brace-Thompson
Assistant to the Publisher: Michele Thompson
Developmental Editors: Diana E. Axelsen, Carole Maurer
Production Editor: Tracy Buyan
Reference Systems Manager: Leticia Gutierrez
Reference Systems Coordinator: Laura Notton
Copy Editor: Matthew Sullivan
Typesetter: C&M Digitals (P) Ltd.
Proofreader: Lawrence W. Baker
Indexer: Mary Mortensen
Cover Designer: Janet Kiesel
Marketing Manager: Carmel Schrire

Copyright © 2012 by SAGE Publications, Inc.

All rights reserved. No part of this book may be reproduced or utilized in any form or by any means, electronic or mechanical, including photocopying, recording, or by any information storage and retrieval system, without permission in writing from the publisher.

Printed in the United States of America.

Library of Congress Cataloging-in-Publication Data

Religion in schools / volume editor,
Charles J. Russo.

p. cm. — (Debating issues in American education; vol. 4)

Includes bibliographical references and index.

ISBN 978-1-4129-8775-2 (cloth : alk. paper)

1. Religion in the public schools—United States.
I. Russo, Charles J.

LC111.R473 2012
379.2′8—dc23   2011051761

12 13 14 15 16 10 9 8 7 6 5 4 3 2 1

CONTENTS

About the Editors-in-Chief	x
About the Volume Editor	xii
About the Contributors	xiii
Introduction	xvii

1. Should Public Funds Be Used to Transport Students to Religiously Affiliated Nonpublic Schools?   **1**

OVERVIEW   1
Charles J. Russo, University of Dayton

POINT   4
James Van Patten, University of Arkansas, Fayetteville

COUNTERPOINT   9
Debra Miretzky, Western Illinois University

2. Should Public Funds Be Used to Provide Textbooks and Instructional Materials in Religiously Affiliated Nonpublic Schools?   **17**

OVERVIEW   17
Allan G. Osborne, Jr., Principal (Retired), Snug Harbor Community School, Quincy, Massachusetts

POINT   21
William E. Thro, Christopher Newport University

COUNTERPOINT   26
Debra Miretzky, Western Illinois University

3. Should Students Be Allowed to Include Prayer in Public School Graduation Ceremonies?   **35**

OVERVIEW   35
Allan G. Osborne, Jr., Principal (Retired), Snug Harbor Community School, Quincy, Massachusetts

POINT   38
Ralph D. Mawdsley, Cleveland State University

COUNTERPOINT   44
Martha McCarthy, Loyola Marymount University

4. Should Teachers Be Able to Pray in Public Schools?   53

OVERVIEW   53
Charles J. Russo, University of Dayton

POINT   56
William E. Thro, Christopher Newport University

COUNTERPOINT   60
Adam C. Hyde, Osceola School District, Florida

5. Should Moments of Silence Be Permitted in Public Schools?   67

OVERVIEW   67
Charles J. Russo, University of Dayton

POINT   70
Mario S. Torres, Jr., Texas A&M University

COUNTERPOINT   76
Luke M. Cornelius, University of North Florida

6. Should Public School Teachers Be Allowed to Read the Bible or Other Sacred Texts in Public Schools When Students Are Present?   85

OVERVIEW   85
Charles J. Russo, University of Dayton

POINT   88
Regina R. Umpstead, Central Michigan University

COUNTERPOINT   95
Brenda Kallio, University of North Dakota

7. Should School Officials Be Allowed to Use Religious or Sacred Music in Celebrations in Public Schools?   103

OVERVIEW   103
Charles J. Russo, University of Dayton

POINT   106
Allison S. Fetter-Harrott, Franklin College

COUNTERPOINT   112
Emily Richardson, Indiana University

8. Should Educational Officials Permit Displays of Religious Symbols in Public Schools?   120

OVERVIEW   120
Charles J. Russo, University of Dayton
Ralph D. Mawdsley, Cleveland State University

POINT 123
Courtney Hagele, Columbus, Ohio

COUNTERPOINT 129
Kathryn Shields, Columbus, Ohio

9. Should Students Be Encouraged or Required to Participate in Pledging Allegiance and Saluting the Flag If They or Their Parents Object to the Words "Under God"? 137

OVERVIEW 137
Charles J. Russo, University of Dayton
Ralph D. Mawdsley, Cleveland State University

POINT 140
William Jeynes, California State University, Long Beach

COUNTERPOINT 145
Amanda Harmon Cooley, South Texas College of Law

10. Should Public School Students Be Given Released Time for Religious Instruction? 152

OVERVIEW 152
Allan G. Osborne, Jr., Principal (Retired), Snug Harbor Community School, Quincy, Massachusetts

POINT 156
Kiera M. Sullivan, Elsass, Wallace, Evans, Schnelle & Co., LPA, Sidney, Ohio

COUNTERPOINT 161
Lindsey Swanson, Haller and Colvin, PC, Fort Wayne, Indiana

11. Should Public School Boards Be Allowed to Offer Courses on the Bible and Other Sacred Texts as Literature? 168

OVERVIEW 168
Charles J. Russo, University of Dayton

POINT 171
William Jeynes, California State University, Long Beach

COUNTERPOINT 175
Robert J. Safransky, Nova Southeastern University

12. Should Schools Teach Both Evolution and Creation Science/Intelligent Design in Science Classes? 184

OVERVIEW 184
Allan G. Osborne, Jr., Principal (Retired), Snug Harbor Community School, Quincy, Massachusetts

POINT William Jeynes, California State University, Long Beach	187
COUNTERPOINT Aaron Cooley, New England College	192

13. Should School Calendars Take Religious Holidays Into Account? — **201**

OVERVIEW Charles J. Russo, University of Dayton	201
POINT Amy M. Steketee, Baker & Daniels, South Bend, Indiana	204
COUNTERPOINT Allison S. Fetter-Harrott, Franklin College	209

14. Does the Equal Access Act Guarantee Religious Clubs Equal Access to Public School Facilities? — **216**

OVERVIEW Charles J. Russo, University of Dayton Ralph D. Mawdsley, Cleveland State University	216
POINT Michelle Gough McKeown, Indiana University	219
COUNTERPOINT Allison S. Fetter-Harrott, Franklin College	224

15. Should Nonschool Religious Groups Be Allowed to Use Public School Facilities? — **233**

OVERVIEW Charles J. Russo, University of Dayton	233
POINT Ralph D. Mawdsley, Cleveland State University	236
COUNTERPOINT James L. Mawdsley, Stark State College	242

16. Should Students and Others Be Permitted to Distribute Religious Materials in Public Schools? — **250**

OVERVIEW Charles J. Russo, University of Dayton	250
POINT Ralph D. Mawdsley, Cleveland State University	253
COUNTERPOINT James L. Mawdsley, Stark State College	259

17. Should Students Be Allowed to Wear Distinctive Religious Garb in Public Schools? **267**

OVERVIEW 267
Charles J. Russo, University of Dayton

POINT 270
Jane P. Novick, University of Dayton

COUNTERPOINT 276
Maureen Bridget Sexton, University of Dayton

18. Should Teachers Be Allowed to Wear Distinctive Religious Garb in Public Schools? **284**

OVERVIEW 284
Allan G. Osborne, Jr., Principal (Retired), Snug Harbor Community School, Quincy, Massachusetts

POINT 287
Ally Ostrowski, Rocky Mountain College of Art + Design

COUNTERPOINT 292
Luke M. Cornelius, University of North Florida

Index **300**

ABOUT THE EDITORS-IN-CHIEF

Charles J. Russo, JD, EdD, is the Joseph Panzer Chair in Education in the School of Education and Allied Professions and adjunct professor in the School of Law at the University of Dayton. He was the 1998–1999 president of the Education Law Association and 2002 recipient of its McGhehey (Achievement) Award. He has authored or coauthored more than 200 articles in peer-reviewed journals; has authored, coauthored, edited, or coedited 40 books; and has in excess of 800 publications. Russo also speaks extensively on issues in education law in the United States and abroad.

Along with having spoken in 33 states and 25 nations on 6 continents, Russo has taught summer courses in England, Spain, and Thailand; he also has served as a visiting professor at Queensland University of Technology in Brisbane and the University of Newcastle, Australia; the University of Sarajevo, Bosnia and Herzegovina; South East European University, Macedonia; the Potchefstroom Campus of North-West University in Potchefstroom, South Africa; the University of Malaya in Kuala Lumpur, Malaysia; and the University of São Paulo, Brazil. He regularly serves as a visiting professor at the Potchefstroom Campus of North-West University.

Before joining the faculty at the University of Dayton as professor and chair of the Department of Educational Administration in July 1996, Russo taught at the University of Kentucky in Lexington from August 1992 to July 1996 and at Fordham University in his native New York City from September 1989 to July 1992. He taught high school for 8½ years before and after graduation from law school. He received a BA (classical civilization) in 1972, a JD in 1983, and an EdD (educational administration and supervision) in 1989 from St. John's University in New York City. He also received a master of divinity degree from the Seminary of the Immaculate Conception in Huntington, New York, in 1978, as well as a PhD Honoris Causa from the Potchefstroom Campus of North-West University, South Africa, in May 2004 for his contributions to the field of education law.

Russo and his wife, a preschool teacher who provides invaluable assistance proofreading and editing, travel regularly both nationally and internationally to Russo's many speaking and teaching engagements.

Allan G. Osborne, Jr. is the retired principal of the Snug Harbor Community School in Quincy, Massachusetts, a nationally recognized Blue Ribbon School of Excellence. During his 34 years in public education, he served as a special education teacher, a director of special education, an assistant principal, and a principal. He has also served as an adjunct professor of special education and education law at several colleges, including Bridgewater State University and American International University.

Osborne earned an EdD in educational leadership from Boston College and an MEd in special education from Fitchburg State College (now Fitchburg State University) in Massachusetts. He received a BA in psychology from the University of Massachusetts.

Osborne has authored or coauthored numerous peer-reviewed journal articles, book chapters, monographs, and textbooks on legal issues in education, along with textbooks on other aspects of education. Although he writes and presents in several areas of educational law, he specializes in legal and policy issues in special education. He is the coauthor, with Charles J. Russo, of five texts published by Corwin, a SAGE company.

A past president of the Education Law Association (ELA), Osborne has been an attendee and presenter at most ELA conferences since 1991. He has also written a chapter now titled "Students With Disabilities" for the *Yearbook of Education Law*, published by ELA, since 1990. He is on the editorial advisory committee of *West's Education Law Reporter* and is coeditor of the "Education Law Into Practice" section of that journal, which is sponsored by ELA. He is also on the editorial boards of several other education journals.

In recognition of his contributions to the field of education law, Osborne was presented with the McGhehey Award by ELA in 2008, the highest award given by the organization. He is also the recipient of the City of Quincy Human Rights Award, the Financial Executives Institute of Massachusetts Principals Award, the Junior Achievement of Massachusetts Principals Award, and several community service awards.

Osborne spends his time in retirement writing, editing, and working on his hobbies, genealogy and photography. He and his wife Debbie, a retired elementary school teacher, enjoy gardening, traveling, attending theater and musical performances, and volunteering at the Dana Farber Cancer Institute in Boston.

ABOUT THE VOLUME EDITOR

Charles J. Russo, JD, EdD, is the Joseph Panzer Chair in Education in the School of Education and Allied Professions and adjunct professor in the School of Law at the University of Dayton. He has authored or coauthored more than 200 articles in peer-reviewed journals; authored, coauthored, edited, or coedited 40 books; and has more than 800 publications.

Before joining the faculty at the University of Dayton as professor and chair of the Department of Educational Administration in July 1996, Russo taught at the University of Kentucky in Lexington and at Fordham University in New York City. He earned a BA degree in classical civilization in 1972, a JD degree in 1983, and an EdD degree in educational administration and supervision in 1989, all from St. John's University in New York City. He also earned a master of divinity degree from the Seminary of the Immaculate Conception in Huntington, New York, in 1978.

ABOUT THE CONTRIBUTORS

Aaron Cooley received his PhD from the University of North Carolina at Chapel Hill. He teaches public policy at New England College. His work has been published in the *Southern California Interdisciplinary Law Journal, Law and Politics Book Review, Educational Studies,* and *Journal of Educational Policy.*

Amanda Harmon Cooley is an assistant professor of law at South Texas College of Law. She earned her JD and BA from the University of North Carolina at Chapel Hill.

Luke M. Cornelius is an associate professor of educational leadership at the University of North Florida. He teaches and researches in the areas of education law, school finance, educational policy and politics, and sports law.

Allison S. Fetter-Harrott is an assistant professor of political science at Franklin College, in Franklin, Indiana. Her research interests include public school anti-harassment measures, free speech, and the interplay between public schools and the First Amendment's religion clauses.

Michelle Gough McKeown is the assistant director of legal affairs at the Indiana Department of Education. She is currently at the dissertation stage of her graduate coursework in education policy and leadership at Indiana University School of Education. She earned her JD from Indiana University–Bloomington Maurer School of Law in 2006 and her BA in English literature from DePauw University in 2003. She has practiced education law at the law firm of Deatherage, Myers & Lackey in Hopkinsville, Kentucky.

Courtney Hagele graduated from The Ohio State University. In 2010 she received a JD from the University of Dayton School of Law. Hagele began her legal career at WilmerHale and continued on to practice law in Columbus, Ohio.

Adam C. Hyde is an educator from the School District of Osceola County, Florida. He received his BA from Southeastern University in Lakeland, Florida, and his MEd from the University of Dayton in Dayton, Ohio. In his spare time, he enjoys studying education law and politics.

William Jeynes, senior fellow at the Witherspoon Institute in Princeton, New Jersey, and professor of education at California State University, Long Beach, graduated first in his class from Harvard University. He has spoken for the

G. W. Bush and Obama administrations and several government departments. He was the architect of the economic and education stimulus package that passed the Korean parliament to recover from the 1997–1998 Asian economic crisis. He has more than 100 academic publications.

Brenda Kallio is currently an associate professor at the University of North Dakota where she teaches courses in public school law and special education law. Her research interests include legal/ethical decision making, the legal knowledge base of school administrators, and the First Amendment as it applies to teacher freedoms.

James L. Mawdsley received his BA from Yale University, an MA in English from Kent State University, and a JD from Cleveland-Marshall School of Law. He currently is an English instructor at Stark State College. He is a member of the Education Law Association and the Australia and New Zealand Education Law Association. He has authored or coauthored numerous publications, including the "Employees" chapter of the *Yearbook of Education Law*.

Ralph D. Mawdsley holds a JD from the University of Illinois and a PhD from the University of Minnesota. He has authored over 500 publications on the subject of education law. Mawdsley was president of the Education Law Association in 2001 and was awarded that organization's Marion A. McChehey Award in 2004. He has received two Fulbright Awards, one to South Africa and one to Australia.

Martha McCarthy is a professor in the School of Education at Loyola Marymount University and was former Chancellor's Professor and chair of the Educational Leadership and Policy Studies Department at Indiana University, specializing in educational law and policy. She has served as president of the Education Law Association (ELA) and the University Council for Educational Administration (UCEA) and as vice president for Division A of the American Educational Research Association. She has received ELA's McGhehey Award for Contributions to School Law and UCEA's Campbell Lifetime Achievement Award.

Debra Miretzky is an assistant professor in the Educational and Interdisciplinary Studies Department at Western Illinois University in Macomb, Illinois. She teaches education law and policy and social foundations courses for teacher candidates, and she is interested in the impact of such courses on teachers and their work in the classroom.

Jane P. Novick is a January 2012 graduate of the University of Dayton School of Law. Prior to entering law school she earned a BA from Barnard College and an MA in international affairs from Columbia University. She worked as an economist at the Federal Reserve Bank on New York. For the past 25 years, she has been an advocate for the disabled.

Ally Ostrowski is the director of institutional research and assessment at Rocky Mountain College of Art + Design (RMCAD) in Denver, Colorado. She is also an adjunct instructor of world belief systems as well as social psychology for the Department of Liberal Arts at RMCAD.

Emily Richardson is a PhD candidate in education policy at Indiana University–Bloomington School of Education. She received her JD from Indiana University Maurer School of Law.

Robert J. Safransky is adjunct professor of school law and American government at Nova Southeastern University. He received a BA from St. Francis, an MA from Stetson University, and a PhD from Florida State University. He has worked as a high school teacher, junior high school and adult vocational school principal, and central office administrator.

Maureen Bridget Sexton is coordinator of integrated learning and living and a lecturer in the Department of English at the University of Dayton, where she is also pursuing her doctorate in educational leadership. She taught high school for Miamisburg City Schools for 9 years, where she acted as the theater director.

Kathryn Shields began her legal career at the University of Dayton School of Law. In November 2010, she was admitted to practice law in the state of Illinois.

Amy Steketee is an attorney at Baker & Daniels in South Bend, Indiana, where she practices school law as well as labor and employment law. Steketee has authored or coauthored numerous articles on school law topics. Prior to working as an attorney, Steketee was a high school teacher and guidance counselor. She earned her MEd and her JD from Indiana University.

Kiera M. Sullivan has earned a BS in business administration from the University of Dayton and a JD from the University of Dayton School of Law. She is employed as an attorney at Elsass, Wallace, Evans, Schnelle & Co., LPA in Sidney, Ohio.

Lindsey Swanson is an associate attorney at Haller and Colvin, PC. Prior to working as an attorney, she was the judicial law clerk to Judge Nancy E. Boyer and Judge David J. Avery in the Allen County Superior Court in Fort Wayne, Indiana.

William E. Thro is university counsel and associate professor of constitutional studies at Christopher Newport University, a public liberal arts university in

Newport News, Virginia. In addition to serving as solicitor general of Virginia from 2004 to 2008, he has written extensively on constitutional law in educational contexts.

Mario S. Torres, Jr., is an associate professor in educational administration at Texas A&M University. He earned his PhD in educational administration from Penn State University and specializes in education law and policy. Torres has published in the field's premier journals including *Educational Administration Quarterly* and *Journal of Educational Administration*.

Regina R. Umpstead is an assistant professor at Central Michigan University where she teaches K–12 and higher education law. Her research interests are in K–12 law and policy and have included work on federal education funding, special education, charter schools, and teacher employment practices.

James Van Patten served as professor of education at Central Missouri State University, Warrensburg, and the University of Arkansas, Fayetteville, and adjunct at Florida Atlantic University. Currently an independent scholar, he has authored and coauthored a number of books and has published many articles in educational periodicals.

INTRODUCTION

The opening 16 words of the First Amendment to the Constitution have generated more litigation involving elementary and secondary schools, whether public or nonpublic, than any other words in the Constitution. According to the opening two provisions in the First Amendment, known as the Establishment and Free Exercise Clauses, respectively, "Congress shall make no law respecting an establishment of religion, or prohibiting the free exercise thereof...." The Supreme Court eventually applied the Free Exercise Clause to the states through the Fourteenth Amendment in *Cantwell v. Connecticut* (1940), wherein it invalidated the convictions of Jehovah's Witnesses who violated a state statute against soliciting funds for religious, charitable, or philanthropic purposes unless they had the prior approval of public officials. The Court subsequently extended the Establishment Clause to the states in *Everson v. Board of Education* (1947), a case that is discussed below.

As simple and straightforward as the words of the First Amendment Religion Clauses—as they are also often referred to—appear to be, the vast amount of litigation that they have spawned demonstrates that they are anything but clear. Further, turning to history for answers by reviewing the attitudes of the Founding Fathers is less than helpful because their attitudes ran the gamut. An intellectually diverse group of thinkers, the Founders included a range of views among their ranks. One group of Founders supported state aid to religious institutions as long as the nation did not establish a national church as in England. The other main group of Founders shared the perspective expressed in a metaphor made popular by Thomas Jefferson when he called for the erection of a "wall of separation," words that are not in the Constitution, between church and state in a private letter to the Danbury Baptist Convention in 1802. His association with this metaphor notwithstanding, Jefferson never challenged his native Virginia's practice of providing public funding for churches during his lifetime.

The Supreme Court, the final arbiter of all things constitutional in the United States, has often adopted the Jeffersonian perspective when dealing with matters of state-sponsored prayer and religious activities in public schools, issues occupying a prominent role in this volume. Yet, the Court has adopted a more flexible approach when examining cases involving aid to students who attend religiously affiliated nonpublic schools, the subject of the first two debates in this book and other essays scattered throughout this 10-volume set.

In its early opinions—most notably its first-ever case on religion and education under the Establishment Clause, *Everson v. Board of Education* (1947), involving transportation for students in nonpublic schools, an issue discussed below; and *People of the State of Illinois ex rel. McCollum v. Board of Education of School District No. 71, Champaign County* (1948), a controversy over religious instruction in public schools, subject of another debate in this volume—the Supreme Court chose not to develop precise judicial tests. Instead, the Court preferred to speak broadly of not permitting preferences in favor of or opposed to religion. However, as the Court continued to examine disagreements associated with religion and schools, it has typically applied one of three tests, the first of which stands out most prominently.

Under the test that the Supreme Court enunciated in *Lemon v. Kurtzman* (1971), a dispute involving government aid to religiously affiliated nonpublic schools,

> Every analysis in this area must begin with consideration of the cumulative criteria developed by the Court over many years. Three such tests may be gleaned from our cases. First, the statute must have a secular legislative purpose; second, its principal or primary effect must be one that neither advances nor inhibits religion; finally, the statute must not foster "an excessive government entanglement with religion." (pp. 612–613)

Although *Lemon* has been applied in well over two dozen Supreme Court cases, and a vast array of lower court judgments, it has created no end of controversy because its first two parts, or *prongs*, as they are typically called, were developed in a very different context from the third. The first two prongs of the *Lemon* test emerged in companion cases from Pennsylvania and Maryland, respectively, forbidding prayer and Bible reading in public schools (*School District of Abington Township v. Schempp* and *Murray v. Curlett*, 1963). The third prong of the *Lemon* test emerged in a nonschool dispute upholding New York's practice of granting state property tax exemptions for church property that was used in worship services (*Walz v. Tax Commission of New York City*, 1970). However, the *Lemon* test has been less than effective in many cases involving schools, not fitting squarely with the facts in disputes because, as school officials and legislators learned to develop policies and laws that can get past its first two prongs, they were often tripped up by its malleable third prong.

As the *Lemon* test became increasingly unworkable, the Supreme Court developed two other standards for use in cases involving religion. In *Lynch v. Donnelly* (1984), a nonschool case from Rhode Island upholding the inclusion of a nativity scene in a Christmas display on public property, a plurality of the Court—meaning that insofar as a majority of judges failed to agree on the same rationale, it is not binding precedent that must be followed in all cases—discussed what is known as *the endorsement test* when dealing with religious activity in public settings. This test considers whether governmental actions endorse or approve religion or religious activities. Later, in *Lee v. Weisman* (1992), another case from Rhode Island, this one prohibiting prayer at public school graduation ceremonies, the Court enunciated *the psychological coercion test* when addressing prayer in schools. Under this test, the actions of school officials can be invalidated if they coerce others, either directly or indirectly, to be exposed to or participate in religious activities.

Against this brief overview of the expansive issues involving religion and education in elementary and secondary schools, the debates in this volume can be grouped into five broad categories, the first of which focuses on aid to students in religiously affiliated nonpublic schools. The remaining four categories of debates examine issues of importance in public schools, especially in light of how they are becoming increasingly religiously diversified; these debates deal with prayer and devotional concerns, curricular and instructional questions, controversies surrounding access to facilities and the distribution of religious materials in schools, and religious dress by students and faculty.

ISSUES INVOLVING RELIGION AND EDUCATION
Aid for Students in Religiously Affiliated Nonpublic Schools

Transportation

Since the Supreme Court's first case on the merits of the relationship between the Establishment Clause and education involved state aid to students who attended religiously affiliated nonpublic schools, an examination of its parameters serves as a fitting start to a volume of debates about the relationship between religion and education. The first debate examines the controversy originating in *Everson v. Board of Education* (1947), a case from New Jersey. In upholding a state statute that permitted local school boards to develop policies to reimburse parents for the costs of transporting their children to religiously affiliated nonpublic schools, the Court created what is commonly referred to as *the child benefit test*, a legal construct. According to this test, aid is permissible because it flows to the students (and their parents), not their religiously affiliated nonpublic schools. Interestingly, Justice Black's majority opinion introduced the "wall of separation" metaphor as a kind of Trojan Horse because even though the Court upheld the program, this Jeffersonian reference has since been applied in a multitude of cases either denying aid to religiously affiliated nonpublic schools or forbidding what courts have identified as state-sponsored religious activities in educational settings.

Thirty years later, the Supreme Court addressed the related question of transportation for school field trips. In *Wolman v. Walter* (1977), the Court struck down a law from Ohio that allowed public funds to be used to provide transportation for field trips for children who attended religiously affiliated nonpublic schools. The Court was of the view that insofar as field trips were curricular in nature, they impermissibly focused on instruction, a matter that went to the heart of the missions of the religious schools, rather than the non-ideological secular service of transportation to and from school.

The debates on transportation adopt opposite positions on whether public funds should be used to help children travel to their religiously affiliated nonpublic schools. The point essay, in favor of transportation, maintains that in light of the value that religious schools have provided to the United States over the years, their students should continue to receive publicly funded transportation. The counterpoint essay relies on judicial analyses and public policy positions in arguing that providing transportation violates the Establishment Clause while placing unnecessary financial burdens on public school budgets.

Textbooks and Instructional Materials

Twenty-one years after *Everson*, the Supreme Court again relied on the child benefit test in *Board of Education v. Allen* (1968). Here the Court upheld the constitutionality of a law from New York that required local school boards to loan books used in instruction about secular subjects to children in grades 7 to 12 who attended religiously affiliated nonpublic schools. The Court subsequently upheld similar laws in *Meek v. Pittenger* (1975) and *Wolman v. Walter* (1977), cases from Pennsylvania and Ohio, respectively. Later, in a case from Louisiana, a plurality in *Mitchell v. Helms* (2000a) explicitly struck provisions in *Meek* and *Wolman* that had declared unconstitutional loans of various instructional materials such as library books.

The point essay argues that insofar as the Constitution does not bar such loans, coupled with the fact that programs of this type help reduce crowding in public schools while enhancing school choice, they should be permitted to remain in effect. Conversely, the counterpoint essay takes the position that allowing the use of public funds in this way should be discouraged because it assists in the religious missions of these nonpublic schools.

Prayer and Other Religious Activities in Public Schools

The remaining debates in this book address an array of contentious topics with regard to religion that have been litigated in connection with disputes in public schools.

Prayer-Devotional Issues

Student Prayer at Graduations. A controversial, but unresolved, topic that remains even after the Supreme Court prohibited school-sponsored graduation prayer in *Lee v. Weisman* (1992) is whether students can select individuals to pray at their public school graduation ceremonies. Later, a case from Texas involved a dispute over a policy that allowed prayer both at graduation and prior to the start of high school football games. Without explaining why, the Court declined the opportunity to resolve the lack of clarity about graduation prayer in *Doe v. Santa Fe Independent School District* (2000). Yet, the Court did invalidate prayer prior to the start of high school football games and, by extension, other school-related activities.

The point essay asserts that insofar as a great deal of the anti-prayer jurisprudence evidences hostility toward religion, it amounts to little more than public endorsement of disrespect and intolerance. This essay comments that completely removing student-initiated prayer from graduation ceremonies results in the total separation of public schools from their historic connection to religion with the message that religion is of no consequence. The counterpoint essay replies that insofar as the Establishment Clause prohibits religious influences in public schools, vulnerable students should not be made to feel uncomfortable or torn between adhering to their own beliefs and participating in activities where prayers are from faiths other than those which they profess. It would be better, the counterpoint concludes, for students to exercise their rights by freely practicing their faiths outside of public schools.

Teacher Prayer. Absent a controlling precedent from the Supreme Court, the next set of debates spars over whether teachers should be able to pray in public schools. The point essay contends that insofar as there are no constitutional prohibitions against teacher prayer, it is sound public policy to permit teachers to pray in their schools as a means of helping foster a sense of appreciation for religious diversity. The counterpoint essay retorts that in light of the Court's having largely adopted the Jeffersonian metaphor calling for a wall of separation between church and state in public schools, teacher prayer both violates the First Amendment and may coerce students to accept religious beliefs with which they do not agree.

Moments of Silence. In its only case on the merits of the issue, *Wallace v. Jaffree* (1985), the Supreme Court invalidated a statute from Alabama calling for a period of silence at the start of the school day for meditation or voluntary prayer on the basis that it lacked a secular legislative purpose. However, four federal circuit courts have since upheld laws calling for moments of silence because they were able to avoid placing too much emphasis on prayer in their provisions.

With both sides of the debate essentially having relied on the same cases, the point essay is satisfied that carefully crafted moment of silence laws should be permitted because they are valid secular activities that have passed Establishment Clause analysis in serving legitimate secular purposes in helping to prepare students for their school days. At the heart of its response, the counterpoint essay declares that moments of silence should not be permitted because they are more likely to be legal or political statements rather than activities designed to enhance the quality of public education.

Teacher Bible or Sacred Text Reading in Schools. In the only reported case of its kind to date, the Tenth Circuit, in *Roberts v. Madigan* (1990), affirmed that a public school teacher in Colorado had to refrain from silently reading his Bible as he walked around his classroom while his students were quietly reading their own materials. In a debate that is expanded to include the Bible and other sacred texts, the point essay argues that public school teachers should be free to read the Bible or other sacred texts in their public schools as long as they are doing so of their own free will. Conversely, the counterpoint essay indicates that public school teachers should not be allowed to read their sacred texts in the presence of students because their doing so runs the risk of coercing children to share their beliefs in violation of the First Amendment.

Religious or Sacred Music and Celebrations in Public Schools. A potentially explosive topic that has generated a fair amount of litigation but has yet to reach the Supreme Court concerns whether officials in public schools can use religious or sacred music and celebrations in public schools. The point essay opines that religious or sacred music should be allowed in public schools because it can contribute a great deal to their secular educational mission by helping students learn valuable lessons about significant historical periods and events as well as about different cultural and national groups. On the other hand, the counterpoint essay rejects the use of religious music. This essay maintains that using religious music would protect the rights of students of minority religions while not devoting valuable time for religious rather than academic purposes, thereby making schools more inviting for all, regardless of their religious beliefs or lack thereof.

Religious Symbols in Public Schools. In its only case directly involving schools, *Stone v. Graham* (1981), the Supreme Court employed Establishment Clause analysis to invalidate Kentucky's practice of displaying the Ten Commandments in all public schools in the commonwealth. The Court subsequently reached mixed results in nonschool cases even as lower courts continue to struggle with this issue.

The point essay supports the position that officials in public schools should be able to allow displays of religious symbols because they can have the legitimate secular goal of promoting respect for diverse cultures. Yet, the counterpoint essay posits that such displays should be prohibited because they violate the Establishment Clause by typically advancing the beliefs of the majority religions without taking the values of minority faiths or nonbelievers into consideration.

"Under God" in the Pledge of Allegiance. Controversy over whether students should be required to participate in the Pledge of Allegiance to the flag, without the words "under God," made its way to the Supreme Court twice. In a third case, the Court sidestepped the merits of whether students can be expected to participate if they or their parents object to the inclusion of the words "under God."

In *Minersville School District v. Gobitis* (1940), the Supreme Court initially upheld a school board in Pennsylvania's punishment of students who refused to participate in the Pledge because doing so violated their beliefs as Jehovah's Witnesses. However, 3 years later, in another case involving Jehovah's Witnesses, *West Virginia State Board of Education v. Barnette* (1943), the Court upheld an injunction prohibiting the board from enforcing a state statute requiring all students to participate in the recitation of the Pledge in interpreting as preventing the state from requiring citizens to do so. After the words "under God" were introduced into the Pledge, a series of cases that reached mixed results led to the Supreme Court's ruling *Elk Grove Unified School District v. Newdow* (2004). In *Elk Grove*, the Court avoided the Constitutional question in finding that insofar as a non-father lacked standing, or the ability to file suit under California law, to make educational decisions for his daughter, his case could not proceed. The Ninth Circuit, from whence *Elk Grove* originated, has since joined other federal courts in upholding the constitutionality of the disputed words, apparently placing the legal controversy to rest for the present (*Newdow v. Rio Linda Union School District*, 2010).

The fact that the courts seem to have agreed about the constitutionality of the words "under God" in the Pledge does not mean that controversies ended in school settings. The point essay thus posits that insofar as the inclusion of the words "under God" in the Pledge is not an assertion of faith in God or religion, students should participate in its recitations as part of their American heritage. The counterpoint essay answers that the mandatory daily recitation of the Pledge of Allegiance violates the First Amendment rights of students such that they should be free not to participate in its recitation if they object on religious or other grounds.

Curricular-Instructional Issues

Released Time for Religious Instruction

In its first case directly involving religious activity in public schools, *People of the State of Illinois ex rel. McCollum v. Board of Education of School District No. 71, Champaign County* (1948), the Supreme Court invalidated a local school board's practice of allowing Roman Catholic priests, Protestant ministers, and Jewish rabbis to enter public schools to provide religious instruction for children whose parents consented to having their children attend such classes. The Court ruled that this practice violated the Establishment Clause because allowing tax-supported public school buildings to be used to disseminate religious doctrine impermissibly gave religious groups invaluable aid in violation of the Establishment Clause.

The point essay maintains that insofar as Americans are a religious people, public school boards should accommodate the wishes of parents by allowing their children to be released from classes so that they could have the opportunity to receive religious instruction. Echoing *McCollum*, the counterpoint essay disagrees in contending that the practice of released time should be forbidden because it violates the Establishment Clause not only by entangling public schools with religion but also by aiding in its advancement.

Bible and Other Sacred Texts as Literature

In *School District of Abington Township v. Schempp* and *Murray v. Curlett* (1963), the Supreme Court forbade educational officials from starting school days with Bible readings and prayer. Yet, even as it prohibited Bible reading, in nonbinding dicta the Court left the door open for later controversy in conceding that

> [i]t certainly may be said that the Bible is worthy of study for its literary and historic qualities. Nothing we have said here indicates that such study of the Bible or of religion, when presented objectively as part of a secular program of education may not be effected consistently with the First Amendment. (p. 225)

As could have been expected, the Supreme Court's remark led to additional litigation, the subject of which is the topic of this debate over whether public school boards should be able to offer courses on the Bible and other sacred texts as literature. The point essay focuses almost exclusively on the Bible because it has been in the topic of all but one of the cases on this issue, taking the position that school boards should be free to offer such classes. In acknowledging that many of its arguments could be used to justify teaching about other sacred texts, the point observes that given its influential place in history, one cannot be considered well educated or well-rounded without knowledge of the Bible that could be gained from such classes. Conversely, in a largely legal response, the counterpoint essay notes that in addition to the weight of litigation forbidding teaching of the Bible and other sacred texts, related concerns can arise over such issues as teacher certification and course content. The counterpoint essay contends that these legal issues, plus concerns for students whose faiths were not studied, should lead to the result that public school boards not be allowed to offer classes on the Bible or other sacred texts as literature.

Evolution—Creation Science/Intelligent Design

A dispute that has generated litigation since *Scopes v. State* (1925), otherwise known as the Scopes Monkey Trial in Dayton, Tennessee, the question of the origins of humankind has twice made its way to the Supreme Court. In *Epperson v. Arkansas* (1968), the Court invalidated a state statute because it failed to comply with the recently created judicial test from *Abington*, which not only required the state to avoid any practice that aids or opposes any religion but also cautions it to avoid any enactment that has a purpose and primary effect that neither advances nor inhibits religion. Of course, these points became the first two prongs of the *Lemon* test. Subsequently, in *Edwards v. Aguillard* (1987), the Court struck down a law from Louisiana that forbade the teaching of "evolution-science" in public elementary and secondary schools unless accompanied by instruction on "creation-science." The Court reasoned that the law was unconstitutional because it violated the first prong of the *Lemon* test insofar as it lacked a secular purpose. Even after these cases were litigated, controversy about the origins of humankind continues.

Faced with this ongoing controversy about human origins, the point essay writes that as long as the goals of public education include teaching students to be open-minded and exposing them to a variety of perspectives, then teachers should be able to present competing theories about the origins of humankind. The point essay argues that educators should allow students to think for themselves and make up their own minds.

The counterpoint essay takes the opposite position, relying on two points. First, the essay acknowledges that case law has long interpreted such teaching as violating the Establishment Clause as a form of religious belief. Second, the essay points out that insofar as creation science and intelligent design are not science, teaching these theories would undercut strong science and technology pedagogy in schools.

School Calendars and Religious Holidays

An issue that has generated some litigation and that is likely to become increasingly contentious as the United States becomes more religiously diverse is whether school systems accommodate the requests of parents of minority religions to modify their academic calendars to allow their children to celebrate the religious holidays of their faiths.

Mixed results in litigation give rise to differing perspectives in these debates. The point essay asserts that as long as educational officials can demonstrate that taking religious holidays into account in developing school calendars is in response to legitimate secular purposes such as addressing religious diversity, then they should be able to do so under Establishment Clause analysis. Conversely, the counterpoint essay is of the view that in light of their duty to focus on students' educational needs, combined with the chance that taking some, but not all, religions into account when setting school calendars can lead to strife, educators should ignore religious holidays when devising school calendars.

Access to and Distribution of Literature in Public Schools

Access by Religious Clubs

In *Board of Education of Westside Community Schools v. Mergens* (1990), a case from Nebraska, the Supreme Court resolved the split between the federal circuit courts and upheld the constitutionality of the Equal Access Act. Under this act, student-sponsored religious clubs are free to meet in public secondary schools that receive federal financial aid during noninstructional time but that they are subject to an array of limitations, such as being nondisruptive and limiting the involvement of adults from outside of their schools. Even so, controversy remains over the issue of access by religious groups.

The point essay takes the position that insofar as the act is working as it was designed to, in granting religious clubs equal, but not greater, access to public facilities than other organizations, it should not be changed. Conversely, the counterpoint essay examines the gaps in the Equal Access Act, suggesting that it has, in fact, significantly limited the access right of religious clubs to public school facilities.

Access by Nonschool Religious Groups

An issue that has led to two Supreme Court cases in elementary and secondary school settings is whether nonschool religious groups should be allowed to use public school facilities. In two cases from New York, *Lamb's Chapel v. Center Moriches Union Free School District* (1993, 1994), which involved a group that sought to rent facilities to show a religious film series, and *Good News Club v.*

Milford Central School (2001), wherein a mother started a religious club for students after school hours had ended, the Court held that officials could not deny them access to facilities on the same basis as other groups.

The point essay agrees with the Supreme Court's position in these cases, explaining that granting such access is pedagogically important and constitutionally required because it helps demonstrate that religious believers, including students, are not second-class citizens. The counterpoint essay responds that pursuant to constitutional principles, board officials must be careful not to appear to sanction religious activities lest they find themselves embroiled in controversies from critics on both sides of the issue.

Distribution of Religious Materials

In addition to access to facilities, as reflected by the two debates in this chapter (Chapter 16), litigation has raged over whether religious groups can distribute their materials in public schools. The point essay maintains that the religious speech contained in the materials that groups wish to distribute on campuses should be entitled to the same protection as other kinds of speech. The counterpoint essay responds that insofar as school officials should focus on their duty to educate their students rather than allow them to be treated as captive audiences for those wishing to distribute religious materials, this practice should be forbidden.

Religious Dress

Should Students Be Allowed to Wear Distinctive Religious Garb in Public Schools? In the first of two sides of the same coin over distinctive religious garb in public schools, the point essay posits that students should be able to express their religious faiths in what they wear to their public schools. The essay remarks that students should be free to dress as they wish because allowing them to do so would be consistent with the constitutional rights to freedom of religion and speech that go to the heart of what it means to be American.

The counterpoint essay begins by noting that American schools have not always been welcoming to religions other than Christianity. Aware of this situation, coupled with the need to avoid religious intolerance that can lead to strife, the essay maintains that public schools should be religion-free zones to help ensure student safety, and thus students should not be able to wear distinctively religious garb to their schools.

Should Teachers Be Allowed to Wear Distinctive Religious Garb in Public Schools? As to whether school personnel ought to be permitted to wear distinctively religious garb to public schools, the point essay maintains that teachers should have the right to do so. This essay concedes that statutes and case law forbidding teachers from wearing religious garb in public schools have a noble purpose, namely, protecting children from indoctrination while encouraging religious neutrality. Even so, the debate questions whether these prohibitions really accomplish their goals absent evidence to the contrary, concluding that teachers should be free to dress as they wish.

The counterpoint essay responds that the need for school boards to preserve religious neutrality and nonendorsement, meaning that they should neither favor one religion over another nor seek to endorse one as the official religion, restricts public school teachers, such that school boards can forbid teachers to wear distinctively religious garb. According to this essay, since public employment is a privilege and not a right, and since teachers lack the same range of rights as children, teachers cannot use their positions to interfere with the rights of their students by engaging in activities that may evangelize or proselytize specific faiths.

CONCLUSION

As with so many topics involving constitutional questions, disputes over the relationship between religion and education, particularly concerning aid to religiously affiliated nonpublic schools and religious activities in public schools, are likely to continue to multiply as the United States becomes an increasingly religiously diversified nation. Of course, it should not be surprising that many seek to avoid conflict and controversy to establish schools as relatively tranquil places where students can learn. Yet, as reflected by the central role that religion played, and continues to play, in the history and development of the United States and the American people, some conflict on such a core national value is inevitable. Still, the topics that are debated in this volume and other volumes in the *Debating Issues in American Education* series reflect one of the many strengths of the American way of life, namely, that members of various communities may disagree strongly with one another on an array of topics, with this volume focusing on the role of religion in schools, and often make their way to court to seek redress. Yet, as strongly as individuals and communities may disagree over these crucial questions, they ultimately follow the rule of law to resolve their differences. As legal controversies over the place, if any, that religion might occupy in public education are bound to continue, perhaps the only certainty is that litigation is unlikely to abate on this important topic in the foreseeable future.

Charles J. Russo
University of Dayton

FURTHER READINGS AND RESOURCES

Mawdsley, R. D. (2004). Access to public school facilities for religious expression by students, student groups and community organizations: Extending the reach of the Free Speech Clause. *Brigham Young University Education and Law Journal, 2004*(2), 269–299.

Mawdsley, R. D. (2005). The profane, the offensive, and the religious: The use of *Hazelwood* to prohibit religious activity in public schools. *Education Law Reporter, 195,* 425–441.

Mawdsley, R. D. (2009). The rise and fall of constitutionally protected religious speech in the United States. *International Journal of Law and Education, 14,* 71–91.

McCarthy, M. M. (2000). Religion and education: Whither the Establishment Clause? *Indiana Law Journal, 75,* 123–166.

McCarthy, M. M. (2001). Preserving the Establishment Clause: One step forward and two steps back. *Brigham Young University Education and Law Journal, 2001*(2), 271–298.

McCarthy, M. M. (2004). Religious influences in public schools: The winding path toward accommodation. *St. Louis University Public Law Review, 23,* 565–596.

Russo, C. J. (2000). Prayer and public school activities: An enduring controversy. *Religion & Education, 27*(1), 46–52.

Russo, C. J. (2006). Of Baby Jesus and the Easter Bunny: Does Christianity still have a place in the educational marketplace of ideas in the United States? *Education and Law Journal, 16*(1), 61–81.

Russo, C. J. (2008). Judicial "hostility to all things religious in public life" or healthy separation of religion and public education? *Religion & Education, 35*(2), 78–94.

COURT CASES AND STATUTES

Board of Education of Westside Community Schools v. Mergens, 496 U.S. 226 (1990).
Board of Education v. Allen, 392 U.S. 236 (1968).
Cantwell v. Connecticut, 310 U.S. 296 (1940).
Doe v. Santa Fe Independent School District, 530 U.S. 290 (2000).
Edwards v. Aguillard, 482 U.S. 578 (1987).
Elk Grove Unified School District v. Newdow, 542 U.S. 1 (2004).
Epperson v. Arkansas, 393 U.S. 97 (1968).
Everson v. Board of Education, 330 U.S. 1 (1947), *reh'g denied*, 330 U.S. 855 (1947).
Good News Club v. Milford Central School, 533 U.S. 98 (2001).
Lamb's Chapel v. Center Moriches Union Free School District, 508 U.S. 384 (1993), *on remand*, 17 F.3d 1425 (2d Cir. 1994).
Lee v. Weisman, 505 U.S. 577 (1992).
Lemon v. Kurtzman, 403 U.S. 602 (1971).
Lynch v. Donnelly, 465 U.S. 668 (1984).
Meek v. Pittenger, 421 U.S. 349 (1975).
Minersville School District v. Gobitis, 310 U.S. 586 (1940).

Mitchell v. Helms, 530 U.S. 793 (2000a), *reh'g denied*, 530 U.S. 1296 (2000b), *on remand sub nom.* Helms v. Picard, 229 F.3d 467 (5th Cir. 2000c).
Newdow v. Rio Linda Union School District, 597 F.3d 1007 (9th Cir. 2010).
People of the State of Illinois ex rel. McCollum v. Board of Education of School District No. 71, Champaign County, 333 U.S. 203 (1948).
Roberts v. Madigan, 921 F.2d 1047 (10th Cir. 1990), *cert. denied*, 505 U.S. 1218 (1992).
School District of Abington Township v. Schempp and Murray v. Curlett, 374 U.S. 203 (1963).
Scopes v. State, 289 S.W. 363 (Tenn. 1925).
Stone v. Graham, 449 U.S. 39 (1981).
Wallace v. Jaffree, 472 U.S. 38 (1985).
Walz v. Tax Commission of New York City, 397 U.S. 664 (1970).
West Virginia State Board of Education v. Barnette, 319 U.S. 624 (1943).
Wolman v. Walter, 433 U.S. 229 (1977).

Should public funds be used to transport students to religiously affiliated nonpublic schools?

POINT: James Van Patten, *University of Arkansas, Fayetteville*
COUNTERPOINT: Debra Miretzky, *Western Illinois University*

OVERVIEW

In *Everson v. Board of Education of Ewing Township* (1947), the Supreme Court reviewed its first case on the merits of education and the Establishment Clause in the First Amendment to the Constitution. At issue in *Everson* was a statute from New Jersey that permitted local school boards to reimburse parents for the cost of transporting their children to not-for-profit nonpublic schools, all of which were Roman Catholic in the district in dispute.

The Supreme Court rejected a taxpayer's claim that the statute violated the Fourteenth Amendment to the Constitution because it was a public taking for a private good. A closely divided Court rebuffed the plaintiff's claim, responding that facilitating secular education is clearly a public purpose. In permitting the statute to remain in effect, the Court reasoned that the First Amendment did not prohibit a state from extending general benefits to all of its citizens without regard to their religious beliefs. In its analysis, the Court placed student transportation in the same category as other public services such as police, fire, and health protection. Justice Hugo Black's majority opinion also introduced a Jeffersonian metaphor into the lexicon of the Court's First Amendment jurisprudence, writing, "The First Amendment has erected a wall between church and state. That wall must be kept high and impregnable. We could not approve the slightest breach" (p. 18). In light of Justice Black's earlier membership in the Ku Klux Klan, an organization that opposed such groups as Roman Catholics, Jewish people, and African Americans, coupled with how later courts applied the wall metaphor to invalidate a wide array of interactions between church and state ranging from aid to religious activities, its critics view it as something of a Trojan Horse that ultimately reduced aid to religious schools and their students (Russo, 2008).

Following *Everson*, lower courts, relying on state constitutional provisions and statutes, reached mixed results on the legality of providing publicly funded transportation to students who attend religiously affiliated nonpublic schools. For example, on the one hand, courts in Washington (*Visser v. Nooksack Valley School District No. 506*, 1949), Alaska (*Matthews v. Quinton*, 1961, 1962), Oklahoma (*Board of Educ. for Independent School District No. 52 v. Antone*, 1963), Idaho (*Epeldi v. Engelking*, 1971, 1972), Missouri (*Luetkemeyer v. Kaufmann*, 1973, 1974), and Iowa (*Americans United for Separation of Church and State v. Benton*, 1975) forbade states from providing transportation to students in religious schools. Conversely, the federal trial court in Connecticut (*Cromwell Property Owners Association. v. Toffolon*, 1979) and the First Circuit (*Members of Jamestown School Committee v. Schmidt*, 1983a, 1983b), both of which explicitly rejected the case from Iowa, along with the Supreme Courts of Pennsylvania (*Pequea Valley School District v. Commonwealth of Pennsylvania Department of Education*, 1979a, 1979b) and Kentucky (*Neal v. Fiscal Court, Jefferson County*, 1999), upheld laws permitting students to be transported to their religiously affiliated nonpublic schools.

In *Wolman v. Walter* (1977), the Supreme Court addressed the related question of field trips. In a case from Ohio, the Court invalidated a statute permitting public funds to be used to provide transportation for field trips for children who attended religiously affiliated nonpublic schools. The Court maintained that the law was unconstitutional because insofar as field trips were curricular oriented, they were in the category of instruction rather than permissible nonideological secular services such as transportation to and from school.

Against this backdrop, the essays in this chapter, like the courts, reach different judgments over the constitutionality of providing transportation for children who attend religious schools. In the point essay, James Van Patten (University of Arkansas, Fayetteville) takes the position that public funds should be used to provide transportation to children who attend religiously affiliated nonpublic schools. In his rationale, he relies on litigation upholding the constitutionality of providing transportation as well as on his belief that religious schools provide educational choice and diversity in American education. Van Patten concludes that in light of the great value that religiously affiliated nonpublic schools have provided over the years, their students should continue to receive publicly funded transportation.

On the other hand, in the counterpoint essay, Debra Miretzky (Western Illinois University) takes the opposite position. In stressing that public funds should not be used to provide transportation to children who attend religiously affiliated nonpublic schools, she relies on judicial opinions and public policy positions. At the heart of Miretzky's essay are her concerns that providing transportation not only violates the Establishment Clause but also places an unnecessary financial burden on public school budgets at a time when there are insufficient funds to meet the needs of their own students.

As you read these debates about whether public monies should be used to pay for transportation for students who attend religious schools, ask yourself two questions. First, is it a good use of public funds to provide transportation for children to travel to and from their religious schools? Second, what impact might the discontinuation of publicly funded transportation have on the quality of education in states that provide it for students who attend religiously affiliated nonpublic schools?

Charles J. Russo
University of Dayton

POINT: James Van Patten
University of Arkansas, Fayetteville

In recognition of its importance, the authors, or framers, of the Constitution addressed religious freedom in its very first amendment. According to the relevant language in the First Amendment, "Congress shall make no law regarding an establishment of religion, or prohibiting the free exercise thereof."

As part of their deliberations regarding the use of public funds for private and private religious schools, federal and state courts regularly refer to the Establishment Clause of the First Amendment for guidance. Even though more than three fifths of the states prohibit the use of public funds for religious purposes, three fourths of the states provide some form of aid to private and religious schools. The primary types of public aid are transportation, state-required testing programs, special education for students with disabilities, and counseling. In addition, states work to ensure that safety programs are present in all schools to assist children in areas of safety and protection such as ensuring plans for fire emergencies and ensuring sanitary standards in cafeterias.

Since religious schools have contributed much to the fabric of American life, and education, this essay maintains that in light of the Supreme Court's holding in *Everson v. Board of Education of Ewing Township* (1947), public funds should be used to pay for the costs of transporting children to their religiously affiliated nonpublic schools.

EDUCATIONAL DIVERSITY AND CHOICE

Recent Supreme Court cases on education, albeit involving higher education, recognized that diversity is a compelling state interest. To this end, in both *Gratz v. Bollinger* (2003) and *Gutter v. Bollinger* (2003), the Court highlighted the importance of a diverse student body. Moreover, American democracy is premised on consensus building to achieve unity within diversity. Accordingly, religiously affiliated (and other) nonpublic schools provide choice and diversity in educational opportunities. In fact, universities such as Harvard, Yale, Columbia, Princeton, and other leading institutions of higher learning had religious origins that provided avenues for choice and excellence in the teaching learning process.

As evidence of how contentious a topic this is, every year, a variety of cases reach different outcomes on federal and state funding for various aspects of religious schools. Each state and each community views the role of religiously affiliated nonpublic schools from very different perspectives, even amid current discussions about alternative educational approaches. Florida, for example, has joined other states that have initiated distance learning programs to allow students, including those in religious schools, to acquire their education through the Internet. In recent years, voucher programs have become more popular. Economist Milton Freedman proposed vouchers to provide poor parents with an opportunity for private education. In some inner-city private religious schools, children receive more individual attention, with positive outcomes, than is possible in public schools. Thus, advocates of economic and social justice, after receiving assurances that religiously affiliated nonpublic schools are nondiscriminatory with regard to race, class, and gender, might tend to support more federal and state funding for these schools.

LITIGATION

As noted in the overview essay that introduced this debate, one can cite an array of cases in favor of or in opposition to the use of public funds to transport children to and from their religiously affiliated nonpublic schools. Rather than revisit all of those cases, this part of the essay reviews *Everson* because of its importance to this debate. However, before, and after, examining *Everson*, it is worth briefly examining leading litigation illustrating how the Supreme Court has permitted the use of state and federal funds to provide public services primarily to students in religiously affiliated nonpublic schools.

In an early case, *Bradford v. Roberts* (1899), the Supreme Court was satisfied that there was nothing sectarian in the use of state funds for a Catholic hospital to serve the sick in the District of Colombia. The Court was of the opinion that city commissioners in the district were within their powers in offering financial support to the hospital even though it was operated by Catholic Sisters of Charity.

Turning specifically to K–12 schooling, in *Cochran v. Louisiana State Board of Education* (1930), the Supreme Court presaged the child benefit theory that it would enunciate in *Everson*. In its unanimous judgment, the Court ruled that a state plan to furnish textbooks to all students, regardless of whether they attended religious or public schools, did not run afoul of the Fourteenth Amendment to the Constitution.

Everson, the Supreme Court's first case on the merits of the Establishment Clause of the First Amendment and education, involved a law from New Jersey that provided reimbursement for the transportation costs that parents incurred in sending their children to and from school. The law was designed to provide transportation funding for all school children as long as the institutions were nonprofit. The Court likened free transportation to other state benefits such as fire prevention, police patrols, public highways, roads, and bridges, all of which provided benefits for students who attended religious schools. The Court concluded that it was not the purpose of the First Amendment to cut off religiously affiliated nonpublic schools from government benefits but to ensure neutrality of the state toward religion.

In creating what has come to be known as the child benefit test in *Everson*, the Supreme Court pointed out that providing support in the form of transportation for students who attended religiously affiliated nonpublic schools was constitutional. More specifically, the Court reasoned that insofar as that aid primarily benefitted the children, who needed safe, dependable, reliable school buses so that they could get to their schools, rather than the institutions that they attended, it was constitutionally acceptable.

Twenty-one years later, in *Board of Education of Central School District No. 1 v. Allen* (1968), the Supreme Court essentially extended *Cochran*, this time under the First Amendment and the child benefit test. The Court upheld a state law from New York that required local school boards to loan all children textbooks for secular instruction, regardless of where they went to school.

In *Lemon v. Kurtzman* (1971), arguably its most important case on the Establishment Clause and K–12 schooling, the Supreme Court tightened the parameters for the use of public funds for religious institutions. In striking down statutes from Pennsylvania and Rhode Island that offered salary supplements for science teachers in religious schools, the Court created a tripartite test. Under what is now known as the *Lemon* test, when issues involving religion and the state converge, governmental action must have a secular legislative purpose, a principal or primary effect that neither advances nor inhibits religion, and must avoid excessive government entanglement with religion. The judicial system has used this test often to deny aid to religious schools.

Two years later, in *Levitt v. Committee for Public Education and Religious Liberty* (1973), the Supreme Court determined that using federal and state funds to help nonpublic schools in data collection and maintenance violated the *Lemon* test because insufficient safeguards were in place to ensure that none of the public funding aided religion. However, after the New York state legislature modified the law, the Court upheld the revised version in *Committee for Public Education and Religion Liberty v. Regan* (1980).

Wolman v. Walter (1977) was the Supreme Court's only other case directly addressing transportation for students who attended religiously affiliated nonpublic schools. Here the Court struck down a law from Ohio that would have provided public transportation for students in religious schools to attend field trips because of an inability to monitor such activities to ensure that they served a secular purpose.

In *Mueller v. Allen* (1983), the Supreme Court upheld a law from Minnesota that allowed all taxpayers, regardless of where their children went to school, to take a state income tax deduction. The deduction covered expenses paid for "tuition, textbooks, and transportation" not exceeding $500 for children in grades K–6 and $700 for those in grades 7–12. The Court explained that nothing in the Establishment Clause requires the exclusion of pervasively sectarian schools from otherwise permissible aid programs.

Agostini v. Felton (1997) departed from the Supreme Court's traditional post-*Lemon* Establishment Clause analysis in permitting Title I teachers to enter religiously affiliated nonpublic schools to provide remedial instruction. The Court pointed out that where adequate safeguards were in place, the instruction was permissible because it did not necessarily result in state-sponsored indoctrination of religion or constitute a union between government and religion.

In *Mitchell v. Helms* (2000), the Supreme Court found that the use of federal funds to pay for instructional and educational materials did not violate the Establishment Clause. Perhaps more importantly, before the case made its way to the Supreme Court, a federal trial court rejected a challenge to a program that provided transportation to children from religiously affiliated nonpublic schools.

Most recently, in *Zelman v. Simmons-Harris* (2002), the Supreme Court upheld the use of publicly funded vouchers under which the majority of parents sent their children to religiously affiliated nonpublic schools in Cleveland, Ohio. In the part of its analysis that is most relevant to the issue of transportation, the Court noted that a substantial body of scholarship reveals that some state statutes and constitutional provisions banning aid to religious schools are rooted in 19th century religious prejudice under so-called Blaine Amendments. Acknowledging that these laws, which can trace their origins to the failed federal constitutional amendment proposed by U.S. Senator James G. Blaine (R-Maine) in 1875, were a reflection of anti-Catholic bigotry, the Court hoped that they would soon be repealed.

PROVIDING TRANSPORTATION

As debate continues over transportation (and other forms of aid), the cases just reviewed highlight the fact that in more recent years, the courts have looked favorably on many forms of school choice, such as vouchers and charter schools, that afford parents more alternative education options while enhancing America's diverse democratic and pluralistic society. At the same time, administrators in public schools can look to innovations, experimentation, and agendas from their nonpublic counterparts for ideas about closing the achievement gap between students in the high- and low-performing groups while improving the quality of education for all. Of course, nonpublic schools may not be able to operate if their children are unable to access transportation to attend their classes.

Using public funds to provide transportation for children to and from their religiously affiliated nonpublic schools continues to be a subject of controversy. Yet, student safety and protection in getting to and from school ideally ought to be viewed as nonsectarian. Bridging the gap of school–state–religious controversies entails a spirit of compromise and good will in meeting the needs of America's most precious resources—its future generations. In the spirit of sharing resources in difficult economic times, public and nonpublic school facilities could be shared by students according to need and location.

Transportation could be a shared process with public school buses being used for students who attend religious schools when they are not being used by the public schools. Although controversial during economic down cycles, the Boston school district covers the transportation costs of 2,000 private and religious elementary and middle school students while providing free public transportation for high school students. Under state law, school systems are required to provide transportation for students who attend their nonpublic schools that are located more than 2 miles from their homes (Vaznis, 2009). Part of the rationale for this transportation support is the safety of a large number of children as well as supporting low-income, at-risk, marginalized populations in need of such assistance. Further, in New York City, for example, because all students have the opportunity to take public transit, at no cost, to get to school, little direct cost impacts public school budgets.

There can be no doubt that the current controversies over funding that the counterpoint essay identifies are very real financial concerns. Yet, it is important to keep in mind that religious schools help save the public billions of dollars annually by carrying some of the enrollment load of public schools. In this regard, it is unfair to threaten to or actually eliminate transportation for parents who send their children to religious schools even as they continue to pay local, state, and federal taxes because this cost typically has minimal impact on public school budgets. Thus, it is fair to ask what would happen if nonpublic schools closed their doors because parents could not receive the limited form of public aid that allows them to send their children to school. One probably does not wish to consider the financial nightmare that might ensue as public school budgets increased.

As the pendulum swings in judicial interpretations, the federal courts continue to support the child benefit theory. This is revealed in the long-term support that the federal courts have provided for public funding for transportation because it is content free, a concern voiced by supporters of Jefferson's wall of separation metaphor.

With religious diversity firmly established over the years, public support for private and private religious schools in the form of transportation certainly poses no threat in the development of a powerful church society that Jefferson feared. The need to support children who attend religiously affiliated nonpublic schools is reflected in the large number of disadvantaged, at-risk, and marginalized students who are taught in religious schools. In fact, there appears to be no threat to either the Establishment Clause or to the rights and privileges according citizens under the Fourteenth Amendment.

CONCLUSION

The courts have relied on both the Establishment Clause of the First Amendment and the Fourteenth Amendment to both prevent and provide support for children who attend religiously affiliated nonpublic schools. Yet, as noted in the review of litigation in this point essay, along with related arguments, there should be no doubt that it is constitutionally permissible, and desirable, for states to continue to provide public aid to transport children to and from their religiously affiliated nonpublic schools under the child benefit theory.

COUNTERPOINT: Debra Miretzky
Western Illinois University

In *Everson v. Board of Education of Ewing Township* (1947), the Supreme Court rather schizophrenically reaffirmed the notion of "a wall of separation between church and state" while at the same time upholding the constitutionality of a law from New Jersey that allowed reimbursements to parents for their transportation costs in getting their children to and from their Roman Catholic schools. *Everson* was based largely on the Court's assessment that transportation was a public service, like fire and police protection, sidewalks, or sewage disposal, and as such could not reasonably be withheld, in the same way that the fire department must respond to a call from a burning church. In *Everson*, the Court observed that withholding transportation would have positioned the state as an active opponent of religion, thereby violating the Free Exercise Clause of the First Amendment to the Constitution.

As it turns out, *Everson* opened the door to an ever-expanding role for government to play in providing services and support to religious schools (although, ironically, the statute in question in *Everson* authorized reimbursement only for public and Catholic school parents) and their students, a perhaps unintended consequence of which at least some of the justices were aware. As Justice Wiley B. Rutledge wrote in his dissent, "Nor is there pretense that [busing] relates only to the secular instruction given in religious schools" (p. 46). He added that since the "purpose of the state's contribution is to defray the cost of conveying the pupil to the place where he will receive not simply secular, but also and primarily religious, teaching and guidance . . . there is undeniably an admixture of religious with secular teaching in all such institutions" (pp. 46–47).

In light of the preceding, this counterpoint essay agrees with the dissent in *Everson*. Accordingly, this essay stands for the proposition that public funds should not be used to pay to transport students to their religiously affiliated nonpublic schools.

WHY PUBLIC FUNDS SHOULD NOT BE USED FOR RELIGIOUS SCHOOLS

The public service argument that *Everson* raised is problematic if one considers the reality that it is foolish to expect churches, or other religious institutions, to have their own fire departments or cement-laying businesses. The United States does not have competing fire departments selling their services to the highest bidders. However, there is a choice for parents, and the default choice is the local public schools, which are there to serve any students within their geographic boundaries. If parents decide not to take advantage of this available option, they can send their children to private or religious schools, secure in the knowledge that the fire trucks will pull up in the event of emergencies. Even so, there is no reason to expect that the general public, while contributing its monies to a common fire protection system, should also contribute to the means of getting those students to their religious schools.

Think of it this way: As illustrated by Paul Freund (1969), in a situation that is now in flux, every state had required legal ceremonies to certify marriages as valid and provided the publicly funded representatives to perform the ceremonies as well as the setting (City Hall). Yet, the state is not obligated to compensate couples who feel the need to conduct religious ceremonies in addition to or instead of the civil events.

Justice Rutledge, possibly the most vigorous dissenter in *Everson*, conceded that "religious property or activities" could not be excluded from "protection against disorder or the ordinary accidental incidents of community life" (p. 61, n. 3). Yet, even Justice Rutledge wisely pointed out that the First Amendment "forbids support, not protection from interference or destruction."

Every society has a public obligation to intervene to prevent harm. Of course, the government should provide basic services when needed, but providing transportation is very different from actively sustaining the mission of institutions such as churches or religiously affiliated nonpublic schools. Despite this distinction, the public service argument remains compelling to many. In addition, the child benefit theory, bolstered by the Supreme Court's analysis in *Everson*, suggests that aid is defensible when the primary beneficiary is students (or their parents) rather than their schools. For example, one might argue that hot lunches for students does not benefit their schools but rather benefits children who might otherwise be hungry.

In terms of transportation, one might see the financial underwriting of bus systems for religious schools as direct and therefore indefensible aid, even as reimbursement for the costs of the use of public buses is indirect and permissible. This essay thus rejects the Court's argument in *Everson* that the state's "legislation, as applied, does no more than provide a general program to help parents get their children, regardless of their religion, safely and expeditiously to and from accredited schools" (p. 18).

If the safety and well-being of children is more likely to be assured by transporting students to schools on buses, rather than have them walk or hitchhike, then the aid appears to be benign and even desirable. Who, after all, could offer objections to keeping school children out of danger? Still, Justice Robert Jackson's dissent in *Everson* pointed out that the town of Ewing, New Jersey, was not going to be creating a school bus system; rather, he remarked, "All school children are left to ride as ordinary paying passengers on the regular busses operated by the public transportation system" (p. 19). In other words, he recognized that under the system at issue, children were going to be riding the same busses they always rode, and as a result, reimbursements had "no possible effect on the child's safety or expedition in transit. As passengers on the public busses they travel as fast and no faster, and are as safe and no safer" (p. 20).

The *Everson* Court offered no evidence at all in support of the child benefit theory in deciding that the students who attended religious schools were walking on dangerous streets or hitchhiking. Nor did the Court provide evidence that the reimbursement to parents would prevent their children from walking or hitchhiking (Strasser, 2009). So, ironically, transportation reimbursement could potentially be used to defray other unrelated costs and did not necessarily provide any more safety than what children previously enjoyed.

INDIRECT AID AND ITS DIVERSION

There remains the argument one can make about many forms of aid to religious schools, that money not spent on secular costs is money available for other, possibly religiously based, expenditures. In *Committee for Public Education v. Nyquist* (1973), the Supreme Court struck down state subsidies for janitorial and snow-removal services in religious schools in New York. The Court rejected the argument that "since janitorial functions and snow removal obviously are not the teaching of religion, their neutral character permits a benevolent grant for these purposes from the tax raised funds in the State Treasury" (p. 763). To have adopted this argument would have required the Court to accept the wrongful assumption that in a religiously affiliated nonpublic school, a budget is divisible. If anything, the Court indicated that once a public subsidy is provided for a nonpublic school, it lightens the burden on the rest of the budget, even permitting more private money to be freed for use for religious instruction and related purposes.

In the Supreme Court's leading case on the Establishment Clause, *Lemon v. Kurtzman* (1971), wherein the Court struck down salary supplements for teachers in religious schools in Pennsylvania and Rhode Island, Justice William O. Douglas, in a concurring opinion, wrote that it should not matter whether teachers teach religion part or all of the day. Rather, he was of the view that a "school is an organism living on one budget. What the taxpayers give for salaries of those who teach only the humanities or science without any trace of proselytizing enables the school to use all of its own funds for religious training" (p. 641).

One might argue that if school officials would not have had to pay for services such as fire protection, to begin with, then it cannot be claimed that their institutions are benefitting financially from having these services provided. This raises another question, for as Andrew Stark (2001) argues, if the public aid that is provided skews parents' choices in such a way as to persuade them to send their children to religious schools, this financial incentive introduces an element of state persuasion that would seem to make such aid public rather than private. It is true that it may be difficult to "prove" whether parents have made an honestly independent decision. Absent such a test, though, it seems reasonable to conclude that incentives of this nature factor into decision making and may indeed be a deciding factor as to where parents choose to send their children to school.

WE DO NOT HAVE ENOUGH MONEY FOR PUBLIC SCHOOLS

Today, as the United States continues to struggle from the economic effects of the recession, it is clear that education has been particularly hard hit and may feel the reverberations for years to come. As reporters for the *Christian Science Monitor* wrote in spring 2010, even though the economy seemed to be improving, a situation that is not at all clear more than a year and a half later, officials in public schools are worried about their future budgets. As many teachers have lost their jobs and children face the prospect of crowded classrooms, parents scramble to purchase supplies that their children may otherwise have received free of cost in their public schools (Khadaroo & Paulson, 2010).

State and local funding cuts are lessening the impact of stimulus dollars that some states have been awarded via the Race to the Top competition, and, as a result, the *Monitor* reports that many school boards cut funding for textbooks, technology, extracurricular activities, and yes, transportation. The article notes that, according to the American Association of School Administrators, 43% of respondents reported budget cuts of 10% or less, and 21% reported cuts of 11% to 25% for the 2009–2010 school year, with projections of 48% and 30%, respectively, for 2010–2011 (Khadaroo & Paulson, 2010). Who knows what the future will bring?

This, of course, raises the question of how funding transportation for students who attend religiously affiliated nonpublic schools can possibly be justified. Some states are reconsidering or have eliminated this aid; the state of Illinois, for example, had a budget of $11.95 million for its Parental Transportation Reimbursement Program for the 2007–2008 school year, which resulted in a reimbursement of up to $101 per qualifying pupil, but the state eliminated funding beginning in fiscal year 2009. It is hard to imagine that such funding will be possible any time in the near future, leaving aside constitutional considerations.

Inevitably, those who support indirect aid, especially in times of budget cuts, argue that parents who send their children to religiously affiliated nonpublic schools pay twice to support both the public systems they do not use and the private education they have chosen. However, as noted, parents make the choice to forego public schools, as is their right. It is important to keep in mind that citizens pay for common services such as parks, libraries, and roads, regardless of whether they use these facilities. As a society, Americans do not offer financial incentives for individuals who do not use libraries to stock their own bookshelves with classics and best sellers, or to buy weed killer and grass seed for the backyards of those who avoid public green spaces. Thus, there is no obligation to provide financial support for alternative educational experiences.

RELIGIOUS SCHOOLS' CONTRIBUTION?

The point essay offers the argument that publicly funded transportation for students to attend religious schools advances diversity and the kinds of educational choice that provide an important contribution to a democratic pluralistic society. If fewer students were able to attend religiously affiliated nonpublic schools because their parents could not afford to transport them to school, their supporters might claim that American education would suffer, not having the opportunity to develop innovative methods to maintain and preserve high expectations in our schools.

There may be evidence that some minority students do perform better academically in religious schools (which do not have to be held to accountability standards and are under no obligation to take or keep every student who walks in the door). Even so, it is unclear that, for example, Catholic schools, which historically educated the majority of minority children in religious schools (National Center for Education Statistics [NCES], 2010), are telling educators much that they do not already know about successful schooling experiences.

Religious schools may be better able to require and enforce expectations for parent involvement and accountability, rigorous teacher selection and retention policies, and well-articulated nonacademic goals, including character education programs, along with strong ties to community and content-rich as opposed to test-based curricula, but they did not invent these factors. Indeed, it might be argued that most schools could, given the resources and time, develop these same standards, and some public schools already have done so.

In addition, there does seem to be evidence that religious schools reflect diversity, but more in terms of serving specific groups of children such as inner-city African American children than in terms of the diversity represented by a given school population. Recent statistics from NCES reveal that religious schools overall consistently enroll about 75% White and 25% minority students. If these percentages were representative of the majority of individual religious schools' demographics, it would be impressive. However, it is not likely that this is the case. If it were, this would buck trends experienced by public and charter schools alike.

CONCLUSION

Overall, the public funding of transportation for students who attend religiously affiliated nonpublic schools has been one of the "thousand cuts" that finally may result in the death of public education as we know it. In and of itself, while support for transportation seems benign and reflective of a generous people, it should be discontinued. *Everson* laid the foundation for the continued financial enmeshment of church and state, and more than 60 years later, America continues to pay the price as states continue to divert funds that could be used to educate students in public schools to assist children whose parents prefer that they attend religious schools.

Further Readings and Resources

Barker, M. (2004). From *Everson* to *Zelman*: The advent of "true private choice" and the erosion of the wall between church and state. *Santa Clara Law Review, 44,* 529–559.

Esbeck, C. H. (2007–2008). The 60th anniversary of the *Everson* decision and America's church–state proposition. *Journal of Law and Religion, 23,* 15–41.

Freund, P. (1969). Public aid to parochial schools. *Harvard Law Review, 82,* 1680–1692.

Khadaroo, S. T., & Paulson, A. (2010, April 20). School budget cuts across the US projected for next academic year. *Christian Science Monitor.* Retrieved November 16, 2010, from http://www.csmonitor.com/USA/Education/2010/0420/School-budget-cuts-across-the-US-projected-for-next-academic-year

Mawdsley, R. D. (2006). *Legal problems of religious and private schools* (5th ed.). Dayton, OH: Education Law Association.

National Center for Education Statistics (NCES). (2010). *The condition of education: Private school enrollment.* Retrieved December 8, 2010, from http://nces.ed.gov/programs/coe/2010/

Russo, C. J. (2008). Judicial "hostility to all things religious in public life" or healthy separation of religion and public education? *Religion & Education, 35*(2), 78–94.

Stark, A. (2001). Moving the baseline: The contradiction at the core of constitutional discourse over state aid to parochial schools. *William & Mary Law Review, 42,* 1437.

Strasser, M. (2009). Repudiating *Everson*: On buses, books, and teaching articles of faith. *Mississippi Law Journal, 78,* 567–636.

Vaznis, J. (2009, November 18). Opposition grows to education reform bill. *The Boston Globe.* Retrieved from http://www.boston.com/news/local/breaking_news/2009/11/opposition_grow.html

Court Cases and Statutes

Agostini v. Felton, 521 U.S. 203 (1997).

Americans United for Separation of Church and State v. Benton, 413 F. Supp. 955 (S.D. Iowa 1975).

Board of Education for Independent School Dist. No. 52 v. Antone, 384 P.2d 911 (Okla. 1963).

Board of Education of Central School District No. 1 v. Allen, 392 U.S. 236 (1968).

Bradford v. Roberts, 175 U.S. 291 (1899).

Cochran v. Louisiana State Board of Education, 281 U.S. 370 (1930).

Committee for Public Education and Religious Liberty v. Regan, 444 U.S. 646 (1980).

Committee for Public Education v. Nyquist, 413 U.S. 756 (1973).

Cromwell Property Owners Association. v. Toffolon, 495 F. Supp. 915 (D. Conn. 1979).

Epeldi v. Engelking, 488 P.2d 860 (Idaho 1971), *cert. denied,* 406 U.S. 957 (1972).

Everson v. Board of Education of Ewing Township, 330 U.S. 1 (1947), *reh'g denied,* 330 U.S. 855 (1947).

Gratz v. Bollinger, 539 U.S. 244 (2003).

Grutter v. Bollinger, 539 U.S. 306 (2003).
Lemon v. Kurtzman, 403 U.S. 602 (1971).
Levitt v. Committee for Public Education and Religious Liberty, 413 U.S. 472 (1973).
Luetkemeyer v. Kaufmann, 364 F. Supp. 376 (W.D. Mo. 1973), *aff'd.*, 419 U.S. 888 (1974).
Matthews v. Quinton, 362 P.2d 932 (Alaska 1961), *cert. denied*, 368 U.S. 517 (1962).
Members of Jamestown School Comm. v. Schmidt, 699 F.2d 1 (1st Cir. 1983a), *cert. denied*, 464 U.S. 851 (1983b).
Mitchell v. Helms, 530 U.S. 793 (2000).
Mueller v. Allen, 463 U.S. 388 (1983).
Neal v. Fiscal Court, Jefferson County, 986 S.W.2d 907 (Ky. 1999).
Pequea Valley School District v. Commonwealth of Pa. Dept of Educ., 397 A.2d 1154 (Pa. 1979a), appeal dismissed for want of a substantial federal question, 443 U.S. 901 (1979b).
Title I of the Elementary and Secondary Act, 20 U.S.C.A. §§ 7301–73.
Visser v. Nooksack Valley School Dist. No. 506, 207 P.2d 198 (Wash. 1949).
Wolman, v. Walter, 433 U.S. 229 (1977).
Zelman v. Simmons-Harris, 536 U.S. 639 (2002).

Should public funds be used to provide textbooks and instructional materials in religiously affiliated nonpublic schools?

POINT: William E. Thro, *Christopher Newport University*
COUNTERPOINT: Debra Miretzky, *Western Illinois University*

OVERVIEW

The Constitution's First Amendment gives all citizens basic freedoms and as a result has been the focus of much litigation in education. Even though the text of the First Amendment states that it applies to Congress, the Fourteenth Amendment has extended its reach to the states and, consequently, to local governmental entities. The First Amendment provides that

> Congress shall make no law respecting an establishment of religion, or prohibiting the free exercise thereof; or abridging the freedom of speech, or of the press; or the right of the people peaceably to assemble, and to petition the Government for redress of grievances. (U.S. Constitution, Amendment I)

The Establishment Clause of the First Amendment has been interpreted as creating a "wall of separation" between church and state, even though those words are not found anywhere within the Constitution itself. Rather, the phrase comes from a letter Thomas Jefferson wrote to the Danbury Baptists Association in 1802. Since then, the expression has often been quoted by the Supreme Court, most significantly in a series of cases beginning in 1947 with *Everson v. Board of Education*. In *Everson*, the justices agreed that the First Amendment required a distinct separation between government and religion, but nevertheless, a 5–4 majority found that a New Jersey law that allowed local school boards to provide transportation to private school students, the majority of whom attended a religiously affiliated school, did not violate the Constitution.

Much of the First Amendment litigation in an education context has involved the use of public funds to benefit students attending private religiously affiliated schools. Of particular significance to the debate in this chapter is what has come to be known as *the child benefit theory*. Using the child benefit theory, the Supreme Court has ruled that students in nonpublic schools may receive services that have the effect of helping individual pupils as long as they do not provide direct financial aid to religiously affiliated institutions. Following this standard, in addition to the transportation allowed by *Everson*, the Court has approved the loan of textbooks to students in sectarian schools as long as they address secular subjects that are not adapted to religious purposes (*Cochran v. Louisiana State Board of Education*, 1930; *Board of Education v. Allen*, 1968; *Meek v. Pittenger*, 1975; *Wolman v. Walter*, 1977). Furthermore, the Court has allowed states to use funds to benefit students in religiously affiliated schools by way of providing diagnostic and health services and administering commercially developed and scored standardized tests as long as those tests are the same ones given to students in the public schools (*Wolman v. Walter*, 1977).

In 1971, in *Lemon v. Kurtzman*, the Court established what has become known as *the tripartite test* for Establishment Clause challenges. In *Lemon*, two Pennsylvania and Rhode Island statutes that provided aid to nonpublic schools in the form of salary supplements or reimbursements for the teaching of secular subjects were held to be unconstitutional. In striking down both laws, the Court stated that to pass constitutional muster, state actions must have a secular legislative purpose, must have a primary effect that neither advances nor inhibits religion, and must not foster an excessive entanglement between government and religion. In *Zobrest v. Catalina Foothills School District* (1993), however, the Court held that the on-site provision of a sign-language interpreter for a hearing-impaired student who attended a religiously affiliated high school did not offend the Constitution, even though the interpreter would transmit the religious as well as nonreligious content of the student's classes. The Court found that this type of aid was neutral in that it provided benefits to a broad class of citizens and provided no financial incentive for parents to enroll their children in nonpublic schools (Osborne, 1994).

Zobrest set the stage for a significant reversal of the Court's prior jurisprudence. Three years later, the Court held that the provision of on-site Title I remedial services to students enrolled in religiously affiliated schools did not violate the Establishment Clause. The Court's decision in *Agostini v. Felton* (1997) explicitly abrogated its earlier 1985 *Aguilar v. Felton* opinion that providing on-site services at sectarian schools was not in keeping with the separation of church and state doctrine. In its ruling, the Court acknowledged that not all government aid that directly affects religiously affiliated schools is forbidden (Osborne & Russo, 1997). Although such aid may be allowed under the Constitution according to the prevailing Supreme Court interpretations, it may be forbidden by state constitutions that have more explicit bans on the degree to which government entities can aid religious institutions.

The debates in this chapter examine the important question of whether public funds should be used to supply students who attend private religiously affiliated schools with textbooks and other learning materials. Although providing materials to students may fall within the acceptable parameters of the child benefit theory, opponents of the practice are concerned that by relieving the schools of the burden of purchasing these materials, and subsequently freeing up monies for other purposes, public funds may aid the religious mission of the schools. Opponents also contend that monitoring the kinds of materials purchased with public funds to make sure their content is strictly secular could foster the type of entanglement forbidden by *Lemon*. On the other hand, those who favor a policy of purchasing such materials with public funds argue that doing so helps to ensure a well-educated populace and is in the best interests of society.

In the point essay, William E. Thro, university counsel and associate professor of constitutional studies at Christopher Newport University in Virginia, and a leading expert in the field of education law, emphasizes that since the Constitution does not prohibit the use of public funds to purchase textbooks and other materials for use in religiously affiliated schools, the debate is essentially one of public policy. After presenting a thorough review of the constitutional issues, Thro argues that there are many sound public policy reasons for providing secular textbooks and materials to religious schools. In particular, Thro contends that providing textbooks and other materials promotes educational quality, facilitates the exercise of constitutional rights, alleviates overcrowding in the public schools by helping private schools succeed and remain in operation, and, by promoting competition with the public schools, helps them improve.

Debra Miretzky, assistant professor in the Department of Educational and Interdisciplinary Studies at Western Illinois University, takes the opposite view in the counterpoint essay. Miretzky contends that providing textbooks and materials can indirectly aid the religious mission of sectarian schools. Miretzky is particularly concerned that without proper oversight, public funds could be used to purchase textbooks that contain religious viewpoints. Thus, Miretzky argues that in spite of recent Supreme Court cases that allow for public funds to be used for supplying textbooks and materials to religiously affiliated schools, such aid should not be encouraged.

As the essays in this chapter make clear, the debate over whether public funds should be used to provide learning materials to students in religiously affiliated schools is over the direction public policy should take, since most of the constitutional issues have been settled. Thus, as you read these essays, you should think about how public funds can best be spent. Is it in the public interest for funds to be expended on students whose parents have elected to send them to nonpublic schools? Will indirect support of nonpublic schools help or erode public schools? Are there efficient means of monitoring funds once they have been channeled to nonpublic schools without creating the excessive entanglement that the Supreme Court has forbidden? In the final analysis, should we be more concerned with what is in the best interests of children and less concerned with the indirect benefits nonpublic schools may receive?

Allan G. Osborne, Jr.
Principal (Retired), Snug Harbor Community School,
Quincy, Massachusetts

POINT: William E. Thro
Christopher Newport University

Public funds should be used to provide secular textbooks and instructional materials to religiously affiliated nonpublic schools for two reasons. First, the Constitution does not prohibit the use of public funds to provide secular textbooks and instructional materials to religiously affiliated private schools. Indeed, *Board of Education v. Allen* (1968) explicitly holds that the government may loan secular textbooks to private religious schools. While the Supreme Court's Establishment Clause jurisprudence has undergone significant changes since *Allen*, the Court's current jurisprudence confirms, rather than undermines, the *Allen* holding. In short, providing secular textbooks is inherently constitutional. Thus, the question of whether secular textbooks should be provided is entirely a policy issue. Second, there are sound public policy reasons for providing secular textbooks and other materials to religious schools. Specifically, providing textbooks and other materials promotes educational quality, facilitates the exercise of constitutional rights, alleviates overcrowding, and promotes competition.

CONSTITUTIONALITY

The Constitution does not require that in every and all aspects there must be a separation of church and state (*Zorach v. Clauson*, 1952), but simply mandates "a freedom from laws instituting, supporting, or otherwise establishing religion" (Hamburger, 2004, p. 2). As the Supreme Court has stated, the Establishment Clause must be viewed "in the light of its history and the evils it was designed forever to suppress" (*Everson v. Board of Education*, 1947, pp. 14–15) and must not be interpreted "with a literalness that would undermine the ultimate constitutional objective as illuminated by history" (*Walz v. Tax Commission of New York*, 1970, p. 671). That constitutional objective is clear:

> Neither a state nor the Federal Government can set up a church. Neither can pass laws, which aid one religion, aid all religions, or prefer one religion over another. Neither can force nor influence a person to go or to remain away from church against his will or force him to profess a belief or disbelief in any religion. No person can be punished for entertaining or professing religious beliefs or disbeliefs, for church attendance or nonattendance. (*Everson v. Board of Education*, 1947, pp. 15–16)

Nearly 2 decades later, the Court put it another way:

> Government in our democracy, state and national, must be neutral in matters of religious theory, doctrine, and practice. It may not be hostile to any religion or to the advocacy of no religion; and it may not aid, foster, or promote one religion or religious theory against another or even against the militant opposite. (*Epperson v. Arkansas*, 1968, pp. 103–104)

The Establishment Clause

> does not prohibit practices which by any realistic measure create none of the dangers which it is designed to prevent and which do not so directly or substantially involve the state in religious exercises... as to have meaningful and practical impact. (*School District of Abington Township v. Schempp*, 1963, p. 308)

It permits "not only legitimate practices two centuries old but also any other practices with no greater potential for an establishment of religion" (*County of Allegheny v. ACLU*, 1989, p. 670). Indeed, "there is nothing unconstitutional in a State's favoring religion generally, honoring God through public prayer and acknowledgment, or, in a nonproselytizing manner, venerating the Ten Commandments" (*Van Orden v. Perry*, 2005, p. 692).

However, the Establishment Clause's mandate of neutrality is not absolute. Insofar as the state is not required "to be oblivious to impositions that legitimate exercises of state power may place on religious belief and practice" (*Board of Education v. Grumet*, 1994, p. 705), the state may extend benefits to religion that are not extended to nonreligion (*Cutter v. Wilkinson*, 2005). Similarly, while the state may not designate a particular religious sect for special treatment (*Board of Education v. Grumet*, 1994), there is no requirement that a state's policies have the same impact on all religious sects (*Varner v. Stovall*, 2007). Thus, a neutral definition of conscientious objector that has the effect of favoring Quakers and Mennonites is constitutional (*Gillette v. United States*, 1971). Similarly, the Establishment Clause does not prohibit a neutral definition of the clergy communications privilege even though that definition has a disparate impact on some denominations (*Varner v. Stovall*, 2007).

When courts interpret the Establishment Clause, there is no single mechanical formula that can be used to precisely demarcate the constitutional contours in all cases (*Myers v. Loudoun County Public Schools*, 2005, p. 402). Although the three-part test of *Lemon v. Kurtzman* (1971) has been used to decide several Establishment Clause cases for many years, the factors identified in *Lemon* serve as "no more than helpful signposts" in Establishment Clause analysis (*Van Orden v. Perry*, 2005, p. 686) Indeed, the *Lemon* test frequently is ignored by the Supreme Court. Nevertheless, the *Lemon* test offers the best guidance for predicting how the courts will address Establishment Clause issues. Under the *Lemon* test, a statute or program is constitutional if it has a secular purpose, its principal or primary effect neither advances nor inhibits religion, and it does not foster an excessive entanglement with religion.

Secular Purpose

The requirement that the law serve a "secular legislative purpose" does not mean the law's purpose must be unrelated to religion, as "that would amount to a requirement that the government show a callous indifference to religious groups, and the Establishment Clause has never been so interpreted" (*Corporation of Presiding Bishop of Church of Jesus Christ of Latter-day Saints v. Amos*, 1987, p. 335). Indeed, the judiciary is reluctant "to attribute unconstitutional motives to the states particularly when a plausible secular purpose for the state's program may be discerned from the face of the statute" (*Mueller v. Allen*, 1983, pp. 394–395). Even if some policymakers were motivated by a desire to promote religion, "that alone would not invalidate [the statute] because what is relevant is the legislative *purpose* of the statute not the possibly religious *motives* of the [policymakers] who enacted the [statute]" (*Board of Education v. Mergens*, 1990, p. 249).

Rather, the objective of the secular legislative purpose requirement is to prevent the relevant governmental decision makers from abandoning neutrality and acting with the intent of promoting a particular point of view in religious matters. Although "[t]he eyes that look to purpose belong to an 'objective observer,' one who takes account of the traditional external signs that show up in the 'text, legislative history, and implementation of the statute,' or comparable official act" (*McCreary County v. ACLU*, 2005, p. 862), a policy "that is motivated in part by a religious purpose" may still satisfy the first part of the *Lemon* test (*Wallace v. Jaffree*, 1985, p. 56). This is a fairly low hurdle. Indeed, the Supreme Court "has invalidated legislation or governmental action on the ground that a secular purpose was lacking, but only when it has concluded there was no question that the statute or activity was motivated wholly by religious considerations" (*Lynch v. Donnelly*, 1984, p. 680). Thus, the first prong of the *Lemon* test is to be contravened only if the action is entirely motivated by a purpose to advance religion (*Lambeth v. Board of Commissioners*, 2005).

Given that schoolchildren will benefit from the textbooks and instructional materials, there clearly is a secular purpose. Indeed, the Supreme Court has repeatedly upheld public expenditures that directly benefit children while indirectly benefiting religious schools. For example, in *Zelman v. Simmons-Harris*

(2002), the Court approved the use of school choice vouchers by private religious schools. Similarly, in *Zobrest v. Catalina Foothills School District* (1993), the Court held that a hearing-impaired student at a private religious school could receive special education services.

Advancement or Inhibition of Religion

"For a law to have forbidden 'effects' under *Lemon*, it must be fair to say that the *government itself* has advanced religion through its own activities and influence" (*Corporation of Presiding Bishop of Church of Jesus Christ of Latter-day Saints v. Amos*, 1987, p. 337). Evaluation of the primary effect prong turns on whether government defines recipients by reference to religion and whether the government's action results in indoctrination (*Agostini v. Felton*, 1997). Evidence of the impermissible government advancement of religion includes "sponsorship, financial support, and active involvement of the sovereign in religious activity" (*Walz v. Tax Commission of New York*, 1970, p. 668).

Funding secular textbooks and other instructional materials does not actively involve the government in religious activity. Nor does it result in government indoctrination. Moreover, assuming that the textbooks are available to all religious schools, it does not express a preference among religions.

Excessive Entanglement

The excessive entanglement inquiry often is coextensive with the primary effect inquiry. In other words, because a policy of providing secular textbooks does not have the primary effect of advancing or inhibiting religion, there is no excessive entanglement.

Moreover, any entanglement between the state and religious sects is minimal. In the past, the Supreme Court held that there was no excessive entanglement in the requirement that state officials examine textbooks to determine if they qualify for tax deduction so that deductions for sectarian books could be disallowed (*Mueller v. Allen*, 1983). Similarly, the Court found that administrative cooperation, by itself, is insufficient to create excessive entanglement (*Agostini v. Felton*, 1997).

PUBLIC POLICY

Of course, the fact that it is constitutional for the government to provide textbooks does not mean that the states must do so. Within the gap between what the Establishment Clause prohibits and the Free Exercise Clause requires, the states retain substantial sovereign authority to make religious policy. Indeed, the text and history of the Establishment Clause strongly suggest that it is a federalism provision intended to prevent Congress from interfering with the states' religious policy choices (*Elk Grove Unified School District v. Newdow*, 2004). As one scholar noted,

> Congress has no power to dictate a position on religion . . . for states. It has no power to dictate church-state relations at all—where 'state' refers to the governments of the several states. This is the core meaning of the Establishment Clause. (Rubenfeld, 1997, p. 2357)

Of course, the mere fact that something is constitutional does not make it wise. Conversely, the mere fact that something is sound public policy does not make it constitutional. Yet, there are a number of sound public policy reasons for providing textbooks and instructional materials.

First, it is in the state's best interest to promote quality education. Because an educated populace is vital to the preservation of democracy, every state constitution recognizes the importance of education. Thus, education is a constitutional value, albeit at the state level. Although the state constitutions do not require assistance to private religious schools, providing secular textbooks and other materials is consistent with the state's core value of ensuring that the populace is educated. If textbooks and other materials are not provided, students in nonpublic schools may not have access to the best curricular materials.

Second, providing secular textbooks and other instructional materials to religious schools facilitates the exercise of constitutional rights. In *Pierce v. Society of Sisters* (1925), the Supreme Court declared, "The child is not the mere creature of the state; those who nurture him and direct his destiny have the right, coupled with the high duty, to recognize and prepare him for additional obligations" (p. 535). In reasoning that parents in the case had the right to send their children to a religiously affiliated nonpublic school, the Court emphasized that the state, acting through local school boards, may not "unreasonably interfere with the liberty of parents and guardians to direct the upbringing and education of children under their control" (pp. 534–535). The Constitution protects "the fundamental right of parents to make decisions concerning the care, custody, and control of their children" (*Troxel v. Granville*, 2000, p. 66). Because "the custody, care and nurture of the child reside first in the parents" (*Prince v. Massachusetts*, 1944, p. 166), there is a parental right to send their offspring to nonpublic schools. Similarly, to the extent that the parents' religious beliefs compel them to send their children to private religious schools, providing textbooks and other instructional materials thereby facilitates the free exercise of religion.

Third, to the extent that private religious schools alleviate overcrowding in the public schools, it is in the state's interest to help such schools succeed. If a private school enrolls 1,000 students and then closes, those 1,000 students may well have to be absorbed into the public schools. The cost of educating 1,000 additional students is far less than the costs of subsidizing textbooks and other instructional materials.

Finally, by competing with public schools for students, private religious schools force public schools to become better. In other words, the public schools and society as a whole benefit from educational competition. By providing limited assistance to the private religious schools, the public schools ensure that the competition will continue—a result that is beneficial to both public and private schools.

CONCLUSION

States should provide secular textbooks and other instructional materials to private religious schools. Such assistance is constitutional under both earlier and contemporary analysis of the Establishment Clause. More significantly, such programs are in the state's best interest. Providing textbooks and other materials promotes educational quality, facilitates the exercise of constitutional rights, alleviates overcrowding, and promotes competition.

COUNTERPOINT: Debra Miretzky
Western Illinois University

To the average American, it may seem benign for states to provide instructional materials, including textbooks, to religiously affiliated nonpublic schools. After all, as has been argued, such largess reflects a child benefit theory (*Cochran v. Louisiana State Board of Education*, 1930) and merely makes available to all children the benefits of a general program (*Board of Education v. Allen*, 1968). While it may seem as though the barn door has closed behind the horse, after 4 decades of cases that led to Supreme Court approval of ever-increasing levels of indirect aid, this essay argues the importance of recognizing the troubling path these decisions have put our democracy on and reminds the reader that such aid continues to blur the lines between our secular government and sectarian organizations—in this case, religious (and private) schools. Such aid should not continue to be encouraged in the 21st century.

A BRIEF OVERVIEW OF RELEVANT CASES

In *Board of Education v. Allen* (1968), the Supreme Court approved a New York state law that allowed public school authorities to loan textbooks to all students in grades 1–12 whether they attended public or private schools. The justices relied on an earlier ruling, *Everson v. Board of Education* (1947), where the Court ruled that reimbursement by the state for busing expenses incurred by either public or private school parents was constitutional, despite the Court's vigorous defense of a wall of separation between church and state that must be kept high and impregnable. The Justices in *Allen* found that there was no reason to believe, provided that the textbooks in question were strictly secular in nature, that such resources supplied by the public were in fact instrumental in the teaching of religion.

Allen and *Everson* were instrumental when the Supreme Court later ruled that Pennsylvania and Rhode Island statutes authorizing direct aid in the form of contributions to teacher salaries and reimbursement for textbooks and instructional materials in religious schools were unconstitutional. In the landmark *Lemon v. Kurtzman* (1971), the Court articulated the three-pronged test to determine constitutionality: A statute or program must have a secular legislative purpose, must have a principal or primary effect that neither advances nor inhibits religion, and must not foster an excessive entanglement with religion. With this decision, the Court presumably clarified the differences between direct and indirect aid, noting that *Allen* simply approved the loaning of secular textbooks to students in religious schools, and finding that the type of aid the statutes in *Lemon* would provide would foster impermissible administrative and political entanglement between church and state.

Since *Lemon*, however, decisions made by the Court have eroded the wall of separation between church and state in many ways—certainly in terms of the subsidization of textbooks and instructional materials for religious schools. In *Meek v. Pittenger* (1975), the Court curiously reaffirmed the constitutionality of the loan of secular textbooks to religious schools, but struck down the loan of instructional materials such as maps, films, charts, and lab equipment, reasoning that these items could potentially advance religion in a way that secular textbooks presumably would not. In *Wolman v. Walter* (1977), the Court reiterated this finding, again claiming that textbooks were permissible, but additional aid in the form of instructional materials was not because it would foster excessive entanglement as the state sought to determine the nature of the use of such materials.

Everson's legacy was a paradoxical view of church–state relations—a ruling that reinforced the notion of a wall of separation while upholding the right of parents to be reimbursed by the state for transportation costs for religious school attendance—that opened the door for the inconsistent rulings that followed. *Aguilar v. Felton* (1985), while clear, had the unintended consequence of sparking a backlash that paradoxically contributed to the lowering of the wall. In *Aguilar*, the Supreme Court considered a New York City case in which Title I remedial support in areas such as English and math were provided to students in religious schools. This effort foundered constitutionally, in the Court's eyes, because of the administrative entanglement necessary to ensure that these secular services remained secular. In essence, if there was a need to monitor the use of resources or services to make certain secular and religious aims continued to be separate, this monitoring fit the description of entanglement; as David Futterman (1993) put it, the steps taken to ensure that the Establishment Clause was not violated, violated the clause themselves.

After *Aguilar*, some members of the Court began to view this type of expectation as unnecessary and untenable, especially when used to strike down a program that had done so much good and little harm. Led by Chief Justice William Rehnquist, the Court began to be more likely to approve the types of aid it saw as indirect, meaning that if aid were channeled through a student's parents, instead of being furnished directly to a school, it was permissible.

This shift was advanced in *Mueller v. Allen* (1983), which allowed parents to deduct the costs of tuition, textbooks, and transportation, no matter the school's orientation, from their income tax. Additionally, the *Mueller* Court's ruling never spelled out that public money must support only secular activities in religious schools. Essentially, from this point on, Court rulings reflected the belief that when there was a middleman (read, parent) between the secular government's disbursement of funds and the religious school's receipt of said funds (whether the end result was services, tax credits, or textbooks and instructional materials), the aid was constitutionally permissible, even if it ended up supporting religious activities. And finally, 17 years later, *Mitchell v. Helms* (2000) effectively overruled *Meek* and *Wolman* in allowing aid in the form of instructional materials, partly based on the indirect aid categorization that had already been assigned to textbooks.

Since *Mueller*, as Marci A. Hamilton (2001), Futterman (1993), Mark Strasser (2009), and others have pointed out, the Supreme Court has continued to move in a direction allowing for greater public funding for assistance as varied as remedial services for students and tax exemptions, notwithstanding legitimate questions about the difference between typical secular services, on the one hand, and the enhancement of a school's capacity to provide religious education, on the other. Hamilton (2001), noting with alarm the increasing connections between government and religious organizations of all kinds, warns,

> The most successful grabs for power are those that are hard to detect, e.g., incremental additions. A stream of financial advantages has been flowing from government to religion since the Court decided its first Establishment Clause case, *Everson v. Board of Education*.... The current has picked up speed in recent years and has turned a trickle of government benefits into a torrent. (p. 8)

HOW CAN AID NOT ADVANCE THE MISSIONS OF SCHOOLS?

In terms of textbooks and other instructional materials, what are the salient issues? The Supreme Court has split hairs over the potential impact of providing one type of aid versus another in various cases since *Meek*, as justices sought to argue that services or resources might or might not end up contributing to the teaching of secular curriculum. As already noted, some felt strongly that indirect aid was constitutional given the boundaries provided by the lack of direct contact with the school itself, but it was not unusual for the Court—or even individual justices—to issue seemingly contradictory opinions depending on the case (Futterman, 1993; Strasser, 2009).

Other observers are not as sanguine as the justices who throughout the years presented variations on the neutrality theme articulated in *Mitchell v. Helms* (2000):

> In distinguishing between indoctrination that is attributable to the State and indoctrination that is not, we have consistently turned to the principle of neutrality, upholding aid that is offered to a broad range of groups or persons without regard to their religion. If the religious, irreligious, and areligious are all alike eligible for governmental aid, no one would conclude that any indoctrination that any particular recipient conducts has been done at the behest of the government. (p. 794)

Such assertions would seem to coexist uncomfortably with the acknowledgement by the Supreme Court in both *Allen* and *Meek* that it becomes more likely that children will attend religious schools, as a function of a possible financial barrier being eased, when the state provides free textbooks. If children are to attend public school because their parents cannot afford to send them to a private school, but the easing of a financial burden opens the door to a religious education, how can we plausibly claim that the work of the school has not been assisted, perhaps even fostered, for these types of students, by the financial advantage a perquisite like free textbooks provides?

Parents of children in religious schools have lobbied for years for financial support from state governments and, in the area of textbook loan programs, have been quite successful. Currently, many states contribute significant funding to districts to support the purchase of textbooks for nonpublic school students; parents may or may not have to formally request to be included to take advantage of this benefit. Religious organizations logically believe that the availability of free textbooks is a drawing card for families considering religious schools. It is clear that the money that goes into the religious school's pot all serves to further the mission of the school: to provide a religious education to students who have the option of attending a public school but choose not to exercise that option. What does not need to be spent on books or materials, or any other bills that accrue to religiously affiliated nonpublic schools, for that matter, is money that may be available to schools to spend elsewhere.

While we may split hairs over who touches the money as it moves from government coffers to the tuition and fees statements parents receive, it is incontestable that whatever is subsidized by the state does not have to be subsidized by the family. Laura Underkuffler (2001) argues that indirect aid cannot be separated, whether in terms of curriculum delivery or revenues, at the school level, and therefore results in a radical departure from the Supreme Court's previous Establishment Clause doctrine. Underkuffler adds that direct aid and indirect aid are similar in very significant ways because they pay for expenses that religious schools would otherwise incur, thereby freeing the resources of those schools for use in other, perhaps religious, activities.

WHAT IS PUBLIC MONEY SUPPORTING?

Justice David Souter's dissent in *Mitchell v. Helms* specifically addressed the majority claim that state funding of instructional materials was constitutional since assistance was provided to "recipients who provide, so to speak, a broad range of indoctrination" (p. 809):

> If we looked no further than evenhandedness, and failed to ask what activities the [state] aid might support, or in fact did support, religious schools could be blessed with government funding as massive as expenditures made for the benefit of their public school counterparts, and religious missions would thrive on public money. (p. 885)

Souter's observation raises an important question and underscores how critical this ruling was in terms of relinquishing any pretense of concern about

Lemon's primary effect prong: How do we know, exactly, what is in the textbooks and instructional materials being used by religious schools? As Strasser (2009) points out, Justice Clarence Thomas's assertion in the *Mitchell* plurality about the neutralizing effect of "the religious, irreligious, and areligious [being] all alike eligible for governmental aid" (p. 838) means that religious content in textbooks or other instructional materials would no longer matter as far as deciding constitutionality. As a result, states could pay the costs of textbooks in public and private schools, without regard to content, as no one would assume that the sectarian texts chosen by officials in the religious schools were chosen at the behest of the government. The state is therefore protected from accusations of promoting religious indoctrination, and it is left to school administrators to be on their honor in their choice of materials.

Is there reason to be concerned? F. R. A. Paterson (2000) examined the context of textbooks and other curricular materials used by many Christian schools, including schools in publicly funded voucher programs in Milwaukee and Cleveland, and found highly conservative values that resulted in materials that resembled partisan, political literature more than they resembled the textbooks used in public schools. In Paterson's opinion, these were Christian school textbooks that made no pretense of being secular in orientation. Paterson presented examples from these materials of strong conservative perspectives on social and economic issues, politics and government, and foreign affairs—information that went beyond religious perspectives and were clearly ideologically oriented. Paterson's point is clear, and relevant: If states no longer need to monitor where indirect aid goes in private and religious schools, as seems to be the case per *Mitchell*, how do we know that students are not being indoctrinated in religious—or political—ideologies, courtesy of public funds? Just recently, the Supreme Court refused to hear an appeal from California Christian schools that wanted the University of California (UC) system to grant credit for high school classes required for admission that contained strong religious viewpoints. Critics argued that the addition of religion might have required students, for example, to reject any scientific evidence that contradicted the Bible in biology classes and to adhere to specific interpretations of excerpted works of literature. The Court refused to reconsider a lower court's ruling that such curricula did not meet academic standards as outlined by the UC system.

Many have argued that parents have every right to pass on their beliefs, morals, and values to their children and that the state, especially in a society that holds individual liberty and freedom as pillars of its foundation, should not be an obstacle to this transmission. However, since the inception of public schools—which have long been expected to act as parental surrogates—we have lived with the tensions that exist between the stakeholders: the family, the state, and educators.

Parents are free to choose private or religious schooling as one means of handling this tension. Yet, this does not necessarily mean that our society cannot consider the implications of these choices in the context of the types of support such choices deserve. Many citizens might rightfully take issue with providing textbooks and instructional materials, or funding support for these, to schools that have an obvious investment in the indoctrination of students in an ideologically charged religious context. Further, we must recognize that *Mitchell* opened the door for less-than-obvious contexts that are troubling; we have no way of knowing, for example, if a school that takes part in a textbook loan program for the purpose of lowering costs for existing students and attracting new ones uses the books as the basis for a sectarian or conservatively based revisionist curriculum.

A SLIPPERY SLOPE?

So far, the largest beneficiaries of public funds for textbooks and instructional materials are Christian and Catholic schools. What happens when schools—existing or future—of other faiths decide that they, too, want to be part of, for example, a textbook loan program? Or they request funding for instructional materials? Are states ready to fund Scientologists, or the Nation of Islam, or Hare Krishnas? If so, it will be very difficult for courts to claim neutrality if they elect to deny aid to some groups and not others. What about religions or sects that espouse religious hatred or bigotry, or advocate practices—like polygamy—that most Americans would find difficult to support in general, let alone with their tax dollars? As Underkuffler (2001) points out, Americans tend to be more tolerant of mainstream religions such as Christianity, Judaism, and Islam (though this last tolerance is certainly under attack in the wake of the Ground Zero mosque controversy) and less tolerant of religions perceived to be on the fringes.

Cleary, *Norwood v. Harrison* (1973) reinforced a clear understanding that schools that discriminated on the basis of race should not be eligible for inclusion in any type of state-funded textbook program; such aid would certainly reinforce the notion of a government that turns a blind eye to racism. Race as an admissions criterion, we can agree, is fairly simple to monitor. How, though, would the state monitor what content is provided to students, in every classroom, every day, supplemented or perhaps fostered by classroom materials underwritten by public funds?

FURTHER READINGS AND RESOURCES

Futterman, D. (1993). School choice and the religion clauses: The law and politics of public aid to private parochial schools. *Georgetown Law Journal, 812,* 711, 723.

Hamburger, P. (2004). *Separation of church and state*. Cambridge, MA: Harvard University Press.

Hamilton, M. A. (2001, January). *Free? Exercise* (Cardozo Law School, Public Law Research Paper No. 33). Retrieved from the Social Science Research Network website: http://ssrn.com/abstract=257480

Jefferson, T. (1998, June). Jefferson's letter to the Danbury Baptists. *Library of Congress Information Bulletin, 57*(6). Retrieved from http://www.loc.gov/loc/lcib/9806/danpre.html (Original work published January 1, 1802)

Osborne, A. G. (1994). Providing special education and related services to parochial school students in the wake of *Zobrest*. *Education Law Reporter, 87,* 329–339.

Osborne, A. G., & Russo, C. J. (1997). The ghoul is dead, long live the ghoul: *Agostini v. Felton* and the delivery of Title I services in non-public schools. *Education Law Reporter, 119,* 781–797.

Paterson, F. R. A. (2000, October). Building a conservative base: Teaching history and civics in voucher-supported schools. *The Phi Delta Kappan, 82*(2), 150–155.

Rubenfeld, J. (1997). Antidisestablishmentarianism: Why RFRA really was unconstitutional. *Michigan Law Review, 95,* 2347–2393.

Strasser, M. (2009). Repudiating *Everson*: On buses, books, and teaching articles of faith. *Mississippi Law Journal, 78,* 567–636. Retrieved from the Social Science Research Network website: http://ssrn.com/abstract=1393747

Underkuffler, L. S. (2001). Public funding for religious schools: Difficulties and dangers in a pluralistic society. *Oxford Review of Education, 27,* 577–592.

U.S. Department of Education, Office of Innovation and Improvement. (2009). *State regulation of private schools.* Washington, DC: Author. Retrieved November 22, 2010, from http://www.ed.gov/admins/comm/choice/regprivschl/index.html

COURT CASES AND STATUTES

ACLU Nebraska Foundation v. City of Plattsmouth, 419 F.3d 772 (8th Cir. 2005).
Agostini v. Felton, 521 U.S. 203 (1997).
Aguilar v. Felton, 473 U.S. 402 (1985).
Board of Education of Westside Community Schools v. Mergens, 496 U.S. 226 (1990).
Board of Education v. Allen, 392 U.S. 236 (1968).
Board of Education v. Grumet, 512 U.S. 687 (1994).
Cochran v. Louisiana State Board of Education, 281 U.S. 370 (1930).
Corporation of Presiding Bishop of Church of Jesus Christ of Latter-day Saints v. Amos, 483 U.S. 327 (1987).
County of Allegheny v. ACLU, 492 U.S. 573 (1989).
Cutter v. Wilkinson, 544 U.S. 709 (2005).
Edwards v. Aguillard, 482 U.S. 578 (1987).
Elk Grove Unified School District v. Newdow, 542 U.S. 1 (2004).
Epperson v. Arkansas, 393 U.S. 97 (1968).
Everson v. Board of Education, 330 U.S. 1 (1947).
Gillette v. United States, 401 U.S. 437 (1971).

Lambeth v. Board of Commissioners, 407 F.3d 266 (4th Cir. 2005).
Lemon v. Kurtzman, 403 U.S. 602 (1971).
Locke v. Davey, 540 U.S. 712 (2004).
Lynch v. Donnelly, 465 U.S. 668 (1984).
McCreary County v. American Civil Liberties Union of Kentucky, 545 U.S. 844 (2005).
Meek v. Pittenger, 421 U.S. 349 (1975).
Mitchell v. Helms, 530 U.S. 793 (2000).
Mueller v. Allen, 463 U.S. 388 (1983).
Myers v. Loudoun County Public Schools, 418 F.3d 395 (4th Cir. 2005).
Norwood v. Harrison, 413 U.S. 455 (1973).
Pierce v. Society of Sisters, 268 U.S. 510 (1925).
Prince v. Massachusetts, 321 U.S. 158 (1944).
School District of Abington Township v. Schempp, 374 U.S. 203 (1963).
Troxel v. Granville, 530 U.S. 57 (2000).
U.S. Constitution, Amendment I.
Van Orden v. Perry, 545 U.S. 677 (2005).
Varner v. Stovall, 500 F.3d 491 (6th Cir. 2007).
Wallace v. Jaffree, 472 U.S. 38 (1985).
Walz v. Tax Commission of New York, 397 U.S. 664 (1970).
Wolman, v. Walter, 433 U.S. 229 (1977).
Zelman v. Simmons-Harris, 536 U.S. 639 (2002).
Zobrest v. Catalina Foothills School District, 509 U.S. 1 (1993).
Zorach v. Clauson, 343 U.S. 306 (1952).

Should students be allowed to include prayer in public school graduation ceremonies?

POINT: Ralph D. Mawdsley, *Cleveland State University*
COUNTERPOINT: Martha McCarthy, *Loyola Marymount University*

OVERVIEW

Until the early1960s, it was not uncommon for students in the public schools to begin their day with opening exercises that included Bible reading and a prayer. That practice was curtailed after it was banned by a pair of Supreme Court decisions. In New York, pursuant to state law, school boards could require public schools students to recite daily a nondenominational prayer composed by the state's Board of Regents. Children who did not want to recite the prayer were excused. Nevertheless, parents in a school district that required the daily recitation of the Regent's prayer brought suit challenging the constitutionality of the law. In *Engel v. Vitale* (1962), the Court struck down the practice, ruling that the recitation of prayer in the public schools violated the Establishment Clause of the First Amendment to the Constitution.

One year later, in *School District of Abington Township v. Schempp* (1963), the Supreme Court struck down state laws in Pennsylvania and Maryland that required Bible reading and the recitation of the Lord's Prayer at the beginning of the school day in all public schools. As in New York, students in Pennsylvania and Maryland could be excused from the opening exercises on parental request. The Court once again held that it was unconstitutional for a state law to promote Bible reading and prayer recitation on schools grounds, during the school day, and under the supervision of school personnel. In each decision, the Court noted that the Establishment Clause requires states to be neutral when it comes to religion and that requiring the recitation of prayer in schools amounted to an impermissible establishment of religion. These decisions were reinforced again in 1964 in *Chamberlin v. Dade County Board of Public Instruction* when the Court struck down a Florida statute that required prayer and Bible readings in public schools.

In spite of the decisions banning prayer during the school day, many schools continued to officially sponsor prayers at school events such as athletic contests and graduation ceremonies. Even so, it was not until 3 decades later that the Supreme Court heard its first challenge to a Rhode Island school board's practice of inviting local clergy to offer invocations and benedictions at public school graduation exercises. In *Lee v. Weisman* (1992), the Court found that nondenominational invocations and benedictions offered by clergy at official ceremonies also violated the Establishment Clause. Although attendance at these ceremonies was voluntary, the Court noted that they are so much a fabric of our society that they had a coercive effect. Eight years later, following up on *Lee*, the Court declared that a policy allowing student-led and -initiated prayers to be offered over a public address system prior to an athletic contest also violated the Establishment Clause (*Santa Fe Independent School District v. Doe*, 2000).

Following *Lee*, many school boards have allowed graduating students to offer prayers at their graduation ceremonies without any imprimatur on the part of the school. The debate in this chapter, between two recognized experts on First Amendment jurisprudence, examines the issue of whether this practice is constitutional and should be allowed. Ralph D. Mawdsley, a professor in the College of Education and Human Services at Cleveland State University, argues in the point essay that students should be allowed to offer prayers at their graduation ceremonies. Martha McCarthy, a former professor at Indiana University and currently a professor in the School of Education at Loyola Marymount University, takes the opposite view in the counterpoint essay.

Mawdsley begins his defense of student-initiated prayers at graduation ceremonies by noting that *Lee* left ambiguity as to whether the decision banned all prayers or only those that were arranged by school officials. To further complicate matters, Mawdsley observes that lower courts have been inconsistent in their interpretations of the Supreme Court's opinion. After providing a comprehensive review of the lower court decisions, Mawdsley emphatically states that much of the antiprayer jurisprudence is nothing more than hostility toward religion and that by allowing speech at graduation ceremonies to be determined by those who object to showing respect for, or tolerance of, religious differences amounts to little more than public endorsement of disrespect and intolerance. He also expresses the view that completely removing student-initiated prayer from graduations seals the complete separation of public schools from their historic connection to religion and sends the message that religion doesn't matter. This, Mawdsley insists, is not required by the First Amendment.

Providing a contrary view of the First Amendment than that espoused by Mawdsley, McCarthy argues that the Establishment Clause prohibits religious influences that appear to represent the public schools. Noting that children are vulnerable and compelled to be educated, she contends that they should not be made to feel uncomfortable or torn between adhering to their own religious beliefs and participating in school activities where a prayer of a different religious faith is said. McCarthy states that it is a stretch to find a secular purpose for allowing student-led prayers at school assemblies, such as graduation ceremonies. Further, she posits that the Free Exercise Clause and Free Speech Clause arguments offered to justify student-led prayers are also unpersuasive because students can freely practice their religious beliefs outside of school during nonschool hours.

The question addressed in this chapter is controversial, as evidenced by the fact that the courts are in disagreement as to whether student-led prayers at graduation ceremonies are constitutional. The debate will continue until the Supreme Court addresses the issue. In reading the essays in this chapter, you may want to think about two questions. First, if the practice of allowing students to offer prayers at graduations is constitutional, does it have a purpose and place at such ceremonies? Second, if school boards establish policies allowing students to offer prayers, should they make provisions for students of all religions to offer prayers?

Allan G. Osborne, Jr.
Principal (Retired), Snug Harbor Community School,
Quincy, Massachusetts

POINT: Ralph D. Mawdsley
Cleveland State University

Lee v. Weisman (1992) is the beginning point for discussing prayer at public school graduation ceremonies. In one fell swoop, the Supreme Court in *Lee* invalidated a practice that had been part of many public school graduations for 150 years. In *Lee*, a dispute from Rhode Island, the Court invoked a new test, psychological coercion, to protect persons in attendance at a middle school graduation from being exposed to religious content in an invocation and benediction by a cleric who was selected by the school principal from the list of those clerics who expressed an interest in praying at graduation. The rabbi's two prayers, each not more than a minute in length, contained one reference to "Lord" and two references to "God." Treating this prayer as a "state-sponsored religious exercise" (p. 592), the Court majority held that the role of school district officials in arranging for the prayers amounted to a form of psychological coercion, using "peer pressure . . . on attending students at graduation to maintain respectful silence during the invocation and benediction" (p. 593). In his blistering dissent in *Lee*, Justice Antonin Scalia, referring to "the Court's psycho-journey" (p. 643) as "psychology practiced by amateurs" (p. 636), observed that the psychological coercion test would become "as infinitely expandable as the reasons for psychotherapy itself" (p. 644). Scalia's poignant conclusion reflects the missed opportunity of the majority to view the graduation experience as one

> inclined to foster among religious believers of various faiths a toleration—no, an affection—or one another. . . . The Baptist or Catholic who heard and joined in the simple and inspiring prayers of Rabbi Gutterman on this official and patriotic occasion was inoculated from religious bigotry and prejudice in a manner that cannot be replicated. To deprive our society of that important unifying mechanism, in order to spare the nonbeliever what seems to me the minimal inconvenience of standing or even sitting in respectful nonparticipation, is as senseless in policy as it is unsupported in law. (p. 646)

In light of the opportunity that the Supreme Court missed to teach about religious tolerance, this point essay examines the litigation on the contentious issue of prayer at public school graduation. In so doing, this essay stands for the proposition that students should be allowed to include prayer as part of their public school graduation ceremonies.

LITIGATION

Despite the Supreme Court's sounding the death knell of school-organized graduation prayer in *Lee*, what was unclear was whether its rationale prohibited all graduation prayers or applied only to those arranged by public school officials. Put another way, would the result in *Lee* reach graduation prayers where students, rather than school officials, made the decision to have prayer at graduation?

Supreme Court Decision on Prayer at Athletic Events

The Supreme Court has not heard another graduation prayer case since *Lee*. However, the Court followed *Lee* in *Santa Fe Independent School District v. Doe* (2000) in invalidating a policy of a school board in Texas setting forth a student election procedure for determining whether to have a message prior to football games and then selecting the student to deliver the message. In *Santa Fe*, the Court fulfilled Justice Scalia's "infinitely expandable" prediction, observing that a "student election does nothing to protect minority views but rather places the students who hold such views at the mercy of the majority" (p. 304).

In reaching its decision in *Santa Fe*, the Supreme Court ignored the language of the school board's most recent policy that permitted "messages," "statements," as well as "invocations" (p. 298) at football games. Without remanding to consider whether the policy would be implemented in a manner consistent with the Establishment Clause of the First Amendment to the Constitution, the Court used its ever-expandable authority to invalidate the policy, prompting Chief Justice William Rehnquist's acerbic rejoinder in his *Santa Fe* dissent that "the tone of the Court's opinion ... bristles with hostility to all things religious in public life" (p. 318).

Federal and State Court Decisions on Prayer

With the kind of hostility toward religion demonstrated in *Lee* and *Santa Fe*, one should not be surprised that federal circuits lack consistency in their approaches to public school graduation prayer. In the first post-*Lee* case, the Fifth Circuit, in 1992, upheld student choice and graduation prayer in *Jones v. Clear Creek Independent School District* (1992), another case from Texas, maintaining that a voluntary policy allowing nondenomination and nonproselytizing student prayer as means of solemnizing graduation had a secular purpose, did not have the primary effect of advancing religion, and, by limiting school examination of the content of the prayer to only one event during the school year, did not present excessive entanglement. In covering all of its constitutional bases, the Fifth

Circuit also pointed out that a student decision about graduation prayer did not amount to school endorsement, and, with regard to psychological coercion, found the effect less (than in *Lee*) on students who would realize that the prayer "represent[ed] the will of their peers," and, in terms of others present at graduation, the effect "is more analogous to the innocuous "God save the United States and this Honorable Court" stated by and to adults" (p. 971).

In 1995, the Third Circuit invalidated a student choice process to select graduation prayer in *ACLU v. Black Horse Pike Regional Board of Education*. Taking an opposite approach to a student vote on prayer at graduation in a case from New Jersey, the Third Circuit rejected the notion that solemnization of such a ceremony could have a secular purpose where students faced "a Hobson's choice" of casting their votes based on religious preferences. Pursuant to the policy, student voting to decide whether prayer would occur had the effect of advancing religion because the longstanding history of the school district having prayer at graduation created a tradition that would likely have favored the approval of graduation prayer.

In 1998, the Ninth Circuit upheld student choice and graduation prayer in *Doe v. Madison School District No. 321*. While technically not a graduation prayer case, the court initially upheld as facially constitutional a school board policy in Idaho that permitted four student speakers chosen on the basis of class standing to each deliver "an address, poem, reading, song, musical presentation, prayer, or any other pronouncement" and prohibited the school administration from "censor[ing] any presentation or requir[ing] any content" (p. 833). The Ninth Circuit, in essence, found the policy to be "neutral on its face" because the students are selected by academic criteria and the school exerts no control over the speech content. Although not detracting from the rationale here for the purpose of support for graduation prayer, the Ninth Circuit later vacated its earlier judgment in decreeing that a parent lacked standing to challenge the policy because insofar as the students graduated, injunctive relief was no longer an appropriate remedy.

In 1999, the Eleventh Circuit, in *Chandler v. James*, upheld a voluntary, student election process in Alabama for evaluating whether student prayer at graduation would occur, declaring that "genuinely student-initiated religious speech must be permitted ... [as] fully protected [speech]" (*Chandler*, 1999, p. 1264). In 2001, the Eleventh Circuit again, this time in *Adler v. Duval County School Board*, held that the graduation policy of a school board in Alabama, which provided an opportunity for student-selected, student-initiated private expression through a neutral selection criterion, did not violate the Establishment Clause simply because the venue was equally available for religious or secular expression.

On the other hand, the Tenth Circuit, in *Corder v. Lewis Palmer School District No. 38* (2009), rejected the free speech claim of a recent high school valedictorian in Colorado who had been refused her diploma until she publicly apologized for including a religious comment that had not been in the version of her speech approved in advance by the principal. The comment, while clearly religious in content, represented the personal convictions of a student who had excelled in her academic program: "Jesus Christ died for you on a cross over 2,000 years ago, yet was resurrected and is living today in heaven. . . . If you don't already know Him personally I encourage you to find out more about the sacrifice He made for you so that you now have the opportunity to live in eternity with Him" (p. 1222).

In finding that that graduation speech was school-sponsored speech, the Tenth Circuit in *Corder* applied free speech pedagogical concern analysis in determining that "[t]he question whether the First Amendment requires a school to tolerate particular student speech . . . is different from the question whether the First Amendment requires a school affirmatively to promote particular student speech" (p. 1227). In essence, finding that "a valedictory speech at graduation is school-sponsored speech" (p. 1229), the school board's control over the content of the valedictory speeches of 15 speakers was reasonably related to educators' pedagogical concern of "preserv[ing] neutrality on matters of controversy within a school environment" (p. 1230).

A more recent decision by the Supreme Court of Montana in *Griffith v. Butte School District* (2010) suggests that school boards cannot disregard their own district policies concerning graduation speeches. In *Griffith*, the state supreme court assessed the refusals of a high school principal and the district superintendent to permit a high school senior to deliver a valedictory speech with references to "God" and "Christ" in light of a board policy. According to the policy, "[T]he school administration shall not censor any presentation or require any content" (p. 197). In addition, the policy provided that the graduation program was required to contain a disclaimer stipulating that student speeches represented

> private expression of the individual participants and does not necessarily represent any official position of the District. . . . The Board . . . does not endorse religion, but recognizes the rights of individuals to have the freedom to express their individual political, social or religious views. (p. 197)

In reasoning that the officials and boards violated the student's free speech rights, the Supreme Court of Montana rejected their claims that their refusal to permit the students' religious content was consistent with Supreme Court guidelines in *Tinker v. Des Moines Independent School District* (1969), *Morse v. Frederick* (2007), and *Hazelwood School District v. Kuhlmeier* (1988). Instead, the Supreme Court of Montana noted that the school officials presented no evidence of disruption within the school to bring the case within *Tinker*, presented no evidence that the speech promoted drug use so as to bring the case within *Morse*, and presented no evidence that the use of "God' and "Christ" could have been perceived under *Hazelwood* as demonstrating that the religious content bore the imprimatur of the school board. The court thus remanded the dispute for further proceedings to determine the damages due the student as a result of violating her constitutional right to free speech.

WHY PRAYER SHOULD BE ALLOWED

The challenge in addressing prayer in public schools is that the result will generally depend on the prevailing legal theory that a court applies. The argument that school boards and educational officials can limit graduation fora to comments that are not religious raises the question whether such a restriction constitutes prohibited viewpoint discrimination under *Lamb's Chapel v. Center Moriches Union Free School District* (1993). At the same time, while *Lamb's Chapel* granted free speech protection to religious expression, it did not prohibit school boards from prohibiting such expression under the concept of government speech or under the Establishment Clause of the First Amendment.

Government speech permits school boards to control speech content where they have clearly articulated interests and where those interests are narrowly defined. The difficulty with applying government speech analysis to the religious content of graduation speeches is in reviewing whether graduation furthers the interests of school boards in controlling their curricula as suggested in *Corder*. Yet, if the purpose of graduation speeches is to further interest of school boards in managing such areas as curricula, one can query as to why educational officials bother at all in permitting students to deliver their own graduation speeches.

If, as indicated in *Corder*, a graduation speech is about the school's pedagogy, namely, curriculum and instruction, are we permitted to read into the school board's refusal in this case to permit personal religious comments in a graduation speech that the district's curriculum and instruction, in fact, had not allowed for any religious content? It would seem that a public school board cannot have it both ways—it cannot claim that it advocates tolerance for, and respect of, differences and then penalize those persons at graduation whose expression represents those differences.

If the purpose of graduation speeches is to advance a school board's interests rather than furnish a window into the interests of successful students, a simpler approach would seem to be to have students read speeches prepared by school district officials. Such a practice is not likely to occur because, while school boards and their officials may be in control of graduation ceremonies, the focus of these events is the students and not the school systems. Indeed, one can question whether student graduation speeches or prayers serve any legitimate purpose if the primary, if not sole, purpose of the speeches is to present viewpoints agreeable to school boards and their administrative officials.

The disclaimer used in *Griffith* reflects the reality of graduation speeches and allows for students to reflect on their past success while, at the same time, anticipating their future challenges. Where the student in *Griffith* restricted her comments to what "I learned," or "my faith," such comments the Supreme Court of Montana noted were "unmistakably directed to her personal life and beliefs" (p. 209).

A more formidable challenge to religious content in student graduation speeches arises under the Establishment Clause that allowing such content can be viewed as an endorsement of religion. The approach in *Doe*, *Adler*, and *Jones*, all of which upheld the rights of students to include religious content in graduation messages, is countered by the approach in *Corder*. In *Doe*, *Adler*, and *Jones*, the courts agreed that school board policies permitting students to choose their speech content was constitutionally permissible because they were considered to be neutral. As such, the courts were of the opinion that these neutral policies could not reasonably have been viewed as public school endorsements of the students' religious speech content.

In *Corder*, though, the notion that public school policy concerning graduation prayer or religious-content speeches is to be determined by those who object to showing respect for, or tolerance of, religious differences amounts to little more than public endorsement of disrespect and intolerance. If the student, as in *Corder*, could not make her religious comments at graduation, would she have been permitted to include in her speech statements to the effect that the high school had been intolerant of her religious expression during her time in high school? More appropriately, could students in their graduation prayers ask guidance and direction that the high school adopt in the future a more tolerant and respectful approach to religious differences?

The final insult in *Corder* was the Tenth Circuit's upholding the school board's requirement that part of the apology must include the following statement: "I realize that, had I asked ahead of time, I would not have been allowed to say what I did" (p. 1223). Insofar as the Tenth Circuit asserts, since graduations are school sponsored, boards are free to set students before the audience to mouth only that which the district has determined is not offensive. Religion simply no longer counts in the equation as a factor that the public needs to be aware of concerning the reason for a student's success.

CONCLUSION

Both Justice Scalia's dissent in *Lee* and Chief Justice Rehnquist's dissent in *Santa Fe* have exposed the core problem of school prayer at graduation for what it really is—hostility toward religion. To assume that a school board's control over religious content in its curriculum entitles it to frame a graduation speaker's personal comments is hostility at its virulent worst.

The suggestion that a school board's excising personal religious comments and prayer from graduation is neutral because the district also controls for profanity, lewdness, vulgarity, and obscenity reflects how distorted has become our viewpoint of religion. To suggest that the solution to the challenge of graduation prayer or speech content is simply to abolish all prayer and student speeches is to seal the complete separation of public schools from their historic connection to religion and send the clear message that religion doesn't matter. The message, I can well imagine, will not be lost on the graduates.

COUNTERPOINT: Martha McCarthy
Loyola Marymount University

The First Amendment to the Constitution provides in part that "Congress shall make no law respecting an establishment of religion or prohibiting the free exercise thereof." The Establishment Clause reflects the sentiment that interests of the government and of religion are best served when the two are kept discreet. Since our nation's founders knew well the pain of religious persecution, discrimination, and conflict, they attempted to incorporate these lessons in the Establishment Clause. Indeed, our nation was unique among countries in adopting a constitutional antiestablishment provision.

This prohibition on religious establishment, originally directed toward Congress, was subsequently made applicable to states through the Supreme Court's interpretation of the Fourteenth Amendment, which specifically places limits on *state action*. In the mid-20th century, the Court reasoned that Fourteenth Amendment liberties incorporate the guarantees of the First Amendment and safeguard them against state interference (*Cantwell v. Connecticut*,

1940). This is particularly important regarding church–state controversies involving schools because education is not mentioned in the Constitution and is, therefore, primarily a state function.

The Supreme Court rendered its first significant Establishment Clause decision in 1947 over state aid to religious schools. In *Everson v. Board of Education*, the Court introduced Thomas Jefferson's metaphor of a wall of separation between church and state in a school case even though it had appeared in church–state litigation for much longer. Since the mid-20th century, schools have provided the setting for some major church–state decisions rendered by the Supreme Court.

Interpreting the Establishment Clause in the early 1960s, the Supreme Court ruled that public schools are prohibited from sponsoring daily prayer and Bible reading. The Court reasoned in *School District of Abington Township v. Schempp* (1963) and *Engel v. Vitale* (1962) that school sponsorship of devotional activities abridged the First Amendment regardless of the voluntary participation of students. Yet, these decisions did not end the church–state controversies involving schools. Judicial decisions since then have addressed various aspects of government aid to religious schools and religious influences in public schools, and few issues have evoked more volatile legal disputes and responses from the citizenry than church–state issues involving public education. School prayer has generated more than 4 decades of legislative, administrative, and judicial responses to the Court's decisions barring such state-sponsored religious activities, and numerous constitutional amendments have been proposed, but not enacted, to authorize prayer in public schools.

This essay focuses on a specific aspect of religious influences in public schools: the constitutionality of student-initiated prayers in public schools. Many recent judicial decisions have turned on what is considered "private" religious expression and thus is not subject to Establishment Clause prohibitions that are applied to school-sponsored devotionals.

The position expressed in this essay is straightforward. The Establishment Clause prohibits religious influences that appear to represent the public school, and this constitutional guarantee is independent from the Free Exercise and Free Speech Clauses. Religious liberties deserve special protection in public schools because of the vulnerability of children who are compelled to be educated, and for most students that means attending a public school through at least part of high school. These students should not be made to feel uncomfortable or torn between adhering to their own religious beliefs and participating in school activities, such as a sporting event or graduation ceremony, where a prayer of a different religious faith is said. Educators' overriding concern should be to protect students from religious indoctrination by school personnel or classmates and to ensure that school policies do not unduly interfere with students' practice or expression of their beliefs. Moreover, the First Amendment demands such vigilance.

LITIGATION

In 1992, the Supreme Court, in *Lee v. Weisman*, invalidated a Rhode Island school board's policy that permitted principals to invite clergy members to deliver invocations and benedictions at middle and high school graduations because of its coercive effect. The Court reasoned that students felt peer pressure to participate in the devotionals during the school-sponsored ceremony.

Some school boards proposed creative ways to include prayers in graduation ceremonies and other public school activities in response to *Lee*. Incorporating some type of student-led prayer has been the most popular strategy, and these practices have often been challenged under the Establishment Clause. The federal judiciary has been called on to distinguish school-sponsored devotionals from private religious expression that does not abridge the Establishment Clause.

A number of school boards responded to *Lee* by designating the graduation ceremony a forum for student expression, allowing students to select their graduation messages that may include prayers. This practice has been upheld if school authorities do not review the students' speeches and if student speakers are selected based on secular criteria, such as their class rank (*Doe v. Madison School District No. 321*, 1998). However, if school authorities retain control over the content of graduation ceremonies, they have the right to censor proselytizing messages, and the Establishment Clause may require them to do so (*Lassonde v. Pleasanton Unified School District*, 2003). The main consideration is whether educational officials created a forum for student expression or have kept the graduation ceremony under the school's control. In a case from Colorado, the Tenth Circuit upheld the board's requiring a student to issue a public apology by e-mail for making a religious speech at the graduation ceremony after submitting different remarks for the principal to review (*Corder v. Lewis Palmer School District*, 10th Cir. 2009).

The most controversial post-*Lee* strategy to return devotionals to public schools has been to allow students to vote whether to include student-delivered prayers in graduation ceremonies and other extracurricular activities. Courts are unlikely to uphold school boards' actions allowing students to make such decisions that school authorities could not lawfully make. In short, delegating the decisions to students does not eliminate the Establishment Clause violation. Invalidating a Texas school board's policy authorizing elections to determine that student-led devotionals would be delivered before public school football games (*Santa Fe Independent School District v. Doe*, 2000), the Supreme Court concluded that such expression at a school event and representing the student body under the supervision of school personnel could *not* be considered private speech. The Court recognized that the purpose of the Bill of Rights is to remove certain subjects from the political process and concluded that student elections to determine if prayers will be said silences minority views. The Court reasoned that "while Santa Fe's majoritarian election might ensure that *most* of the students are represented, it does nothing to protect the minority; indeed, it likely serves to intensify their offense" (p. 305). Still, the Court emphasized that only *state sponsorship* of devotionals abridges the Establishment Clause and that truly private expression of religious views does not.

Subsequently, the Eleventh Circuit broadly interpreted the Free Speech Clause protection of student-initiated private religious expression, recognizing that all student speech in public schools cannot be equated with expression *representing* the public school (*Adler v. Duval County School Board*, 2001; *Chandler v. Siegelman*, 2000). The court decided that messages that were not invocations and were prepared by student volunteers could be delivered at the school-sponsored graduation ceremony even though parts of the messages were religious in nature. Also, the Eighth Circuit uncovered no Establishment Clause violation in a school board member's unscheduled recitation of a prayer in the graduation ceremony, reasoning that the board member's expression was private and thus constitutionally protected, even though it took place at a school-sponsored event (*Doe v. School District of City of Norfolk*, 2003).

In more recent cases, federal courts seemed inclined to equate student-initiated devotionals in graduation ceremonies and other school events with school-sponsored religious activities that are barred from public schools by the Establishment Clause. For example, a federal trial court in West Virginia enjoined the practice of senior students voting to have an invocation during the graduation exercises (*Deveney v. Board of Education*, 2002). Also, a federal trial court in Kentucky struck down the practice of having a student chaplain elected by classmates for the sole reason of giving a prayer in the graduation ceremony (*Doe v. Gossage*, 2006). The court ruled that such voting practices always allow the religious will of the majority to be imposed. In 2010, a federal trial court similarly struck down a board's practice of having the senior class vote as to whether to have a student-led prayer at graduation (*Workman v. Greenwood Community School Corporation*, 2010).

Prayers through religious music also have been controversial. The Third Circuit in 2009 upheld a school board's policy prohibiting the performance of celebratory religious music at school-sponsored events including the graduation ceremony (*Stratechuk v. Board of Education*, 2009). The court observed that the policy did not convey a message of disapproval toward religion. Earlier, in 2004, a student was not successful in requesting that she be allowed to sing "The Prayer" at her public high school graduation (*Ashby v. Isle of Wight County School Board*, 2004). The court viewed it as reasonable to prohibit religious presentations in graduation exercises to respect the Establishment Clause. Similarly, the federal trial court in Iowa maintained that it was immaterial that the majority of the students wanted the Lord's Prayer to be sung at graduation; there was no secular purpose in having a prayer recited or sung during the ceremony (*Skarin v. Woodbine Community School District*, 2002). And in 2007, a federal trial court in Washington state upheld the superintendent in denying a high school wind ensemble's request to play "Ave Maria" in the graduation ceremony (*Nurre v. Whitehead*, 2007). The court found no hostility toward Christianity, explaining that the prohibition was based on a decision to keep religion out of the graduation exercises rather than to discriminate against a particular religion.

LEGAL ISSUES AND STANDARDS

It seems clear that overt prayers and other religious observances during the public school day, even if initiated by students, violate the Establishment Clause. Applying the three-part test articulated in *Lemon v. Kurtzman* (1971), challenged government action can satisfy the Establishment Clause only if it has a secular purpose, neither advances nor impedes religion, and avoids excessive government entanglement with religion. Student-initiated devotionals in public schools and school-sponsored events cannot satisfy this standard. It certainly is a stretch to find a secular purpose for including a student-led prayer in a school assembly, at a school athletic event, in the graduation ceremony, or at other school activities. Therefore, consideration of the second and third prongs of the *Lemon* test would not be required.

The free exercise and free speech arguments offered to justify student-led prayers are unpersuasive. The assertion that individuals' free exercise rights are impaired if their religious views are not allowed in public schools strips the Establishment Clause of any meaning. Students are in school for 6 hours a day, and they can freely practice their religious beliefs before or after school and on weekends in their homes or places of worship. If public school officials make such accommodations to the religious views of the majority by allowing student-led prayers in school events, students holding minority beliefs will always be disadvantaged.

Assuming that the federal judiciary should conclude that students have a free speech or free exercise right to advance their religious views in public schools, all religions cannot possibly be promoted, so in effect, the preferences of the community's dominant sect would be endorsed. This practice contradicts the purpose of the Bill of Rights, which is to remove certain subjects from majority rule. In essence, there is no burden on students' exercise of their religious beliefs to keep 6 hours of the day, while they are attending public school, free of religious observances. When children of minority faiths feel peer pressure to attend school assemblies, sporting events, or graduation ceremonies where prayers of the community's majority sect are said, such practices cannot be defended as reasonable religious accommodations. What rationale can be mounted to make students choose between honoring their religious tenets and participating in important public school events, such as the graduation ceremony, where the dominant religious sect is promoted? Absolutely none comes to mind.

Similarly, there is no Free Speech right for students to say prayers at school events—such expression is restricted by the Establishment Clause. Even though the Supreme Court, in *Good News Club v. Milford Central School* (2001), upheld the right of a proselytizing group to meet in an elementary school immediately after school because other community groups were allowed to use the building at that time, this decision did not authorize student devotionals during the school day or at school-related events. Further, under the First Amendment standard to assess the constitutional protection afforded to student expression in public schools, expression that interferes with the rights of others or threatens a disruption can be curtailed (*Tinker v. Des Moines Independent School District*, 1969). Prayers delivered during the graduation ceremony, for example, may cause some students to miss the event because of their religious beliefs, which certainly interferes with their rights.

Of course, students always can pray silently in schools, and it would be impossible for school personnel to monitor whether such silent prayer was taking place. About one half of the states have laws authorizing a minute at the beginning of the public school day for students to engage in silent meditation or prayer. In 1985, the Supreme Court invalidated a 1981 Alabama silent prayer statute under the Establishment Clause because the law's legislative history exhibited an impermissible intent to encourage students to pray (*Wallace v. Jaffree*, 1985). Yet, the Court indicated that provisions calling for silent meditation or prayer in public schools *without* such an intent might survive an Establishment Clause challenge. Subsequent litigation in lower courts reached mixed results, with some courts upholding and others striking down state laws calling for a moment for silent reflection or prayer in public school classrooms at the beginning of the school day.

In the most recent federal appellate ruling, the Seventh Circuit reversed the court below and ruled that the Illinois law specifying a mandatory period of silence for reflection or prayer in public schools was designed to calm children at the beginning of the day and satisfied all prongs of the *Lemon* test (*Sherman v. Koch*, 2010). The key to the decisions seems to be whether the provisions' legislative history indicates a governmental intent to advance religion, such as having only members of the clergy speak in favor of the bill.

Students might assert that under the federal Equal Access Act (EAA), they are entitled to say prayers in the public school graduation ceremony and other extracurricular events. However, the EAA's reach is limited to student-initiated groups meeting in federally supported secondary schools that create a forum for student expression during noninstructional time. The EAA authorizes student religious meetings only in such a forum, and the meetings must be student initiated. School assemblies, sporting events, and graduation ceremonies are not student-initiated meetings, so the EAA would not apply to them. If school authorities distribute diplomas during the graduation ceremony, it would be difficult to bill the ceremony as student initiated and thus subject to the EAA.

An argument has been made, but not generally endorsed by the courts, that students are saying a prayer in public schools in violation of the Establishment Clause when they recite the Pledge of Allegiance with the phrase "under God." To date, only the Ninth Circuit had held that the words "under God" were inserted in the pledge in 1954 to promote religion rather than to advance the secular goal of encouraging patriotism. The Supreme Court in 2004 reversed the Ninth Circuit's decision but avoided the Establishment Clause issue by ruling that the noncustodial parent did not have standing to challenge his daughter's recitation of the pledge (*Elk Grove Unified School District v. Newdow*, 2004). Other lower courts, including the Ninth Circuit, subsequently found no Establishment Clause violation in saying "under God" in this patriotic observance. Of course, it is well established that students do not have to recite the pledge if such participation violates their religious or philosophical beliefs (*West Virginia State Board of Education v. Barnette*, 1943).

CONCLUSION

Public schools should be places that are free of religious influences and where students can learn *about* various religions throughout the world but not be indoctrinated with particular sectarian beliefs. The Supreme Court has emphasized that it is permissible and even desirable in public schools to teach the Bible and other religious documents from a literary, cultural, or historical perspective (*School District of Abington Township v. Schempp*, 1963). Such religious *education*, in contrast to *indoctrination*, can promote religious tolerance, and few people are critical of that type of religious instruction.

In the late 1980s and 1990s, federal courts seemed to go further in allowing religious *observances* in public schools. It appeared that the concepts of equal access for religious groups and equal treatment of religious expression were replacing the metaphor of a wall of separation between church and state in public school controversies as they had in other contexts. The Supreme Court and many lower courts seemed disillusioned with the *Lemon* standard and more inclined toward accommodation of religious influences in public schools. In some cases, free speech rights seemed to prevail over the Establishment Clause in protecting religious as well as other private expression.

Recent court decisions, though, have been more mixed, with some favoring church–state separation. Federal courts have seemed more inclined to conclude that student-led devotionals in graduation ceremonies and other school events are not private expression but represent the public school in violation of the Establishment Clause. Thus, perhaps the Establishment Clause has more life in it than it appeared to have a decade or so ago, which is a welcome and appropriate development.

Further Readings and Resources

Cambron-McCabe, N., McCarthy, M. M., & Thomas, S. B. (2009). *Legal rights of teachers and students* (2nd ed.). Boston: Allyn & Bacon.

Mawdsley, R. D. (2009). One minute of required silence in Texas classrooms: The Fifth Circuit upholds the state's moment of silence amendments. *Education Law Reporter, 246,* 589–606.

Mawdsley, R. D. (2011). Religious viewpoint discrimination in public elementary schools: Lessons from the Fifth Circuit. *Education Law Reporter, 269,* 29–52.

Mawdsley, R. D., & Russo, C. J. (2009). Hostility toward religion and the rise and decline of constitutionally protected religious speech. *Education Law Reporter, 240,* 524–545.

McCarthy, M. M. (1991). Student religious expression: The Supreme Court sends mixed messages. *Education Law Reporter, 64,* 1–13.

McCarthy, M. M. (2000). "A wink and a nod" to student-initiated devotionals in public schools. *Education Law Reporter, 139,* 1–16.

Russo, C. J. (2009). *Reutter's The law of public education* (7th ed.). New York: Foundation.

Russo, C. J., & Mawdsley, R. D. (2001). The Supreme Court and the Establishment Clause at the dawn of the new millennium: "Bristl[ing] with hostility to all things religious" or necessary separation of church and state? *Brigham Young University Education and Law Journal, 2001*(2), 231–269.

Court Cases and Statutes

ACLU v. Black Horse Pike Regional Board of Education, 84 F.3d 1471 (3d Cir. 1995).
Adler v. Duval County School Board, 250 F.3d 1330 (11th Cir. 2001).

Ashby v. Isle of Wight County School Board, 354 F. Supp. 2d 616 (E.D. Va. 2004).
Cantwell v. Connecticut, 310 U.S. 296, (1940).
Chamberlin v. Dade County Board of Public Instruction, 377 U.S. 402 (1964).
Chandler v. James, 180 F.3d 1254 (11th Cir. 1999).
Chandler v. Siegelman, 230 F.3d 1313 (11th Cir. 2000).
Corder v. Lewis Palmer School District No. 38, 566 F.3d 1219 (10th Cir. 2009).
Deveney v. Board of Education, 231 F. Supp. 2d 483 (S.D.W.Va. 2002).
Doe v. Gossage, 2006 U.S. Dist. LEXIS 34613 (W.D. Ky., May 24, 2006).
Doe v. Madison School District No. 321, 147 F.3d 832 (9th Cir. 1998).
Doe v. Madison School District No. 321, 147 F.3d 832 (9th Cir. 1998), *reh'g granted, opinion withdrawn*, 165 F.3d 1265 (9th Cir. 1999), *vacated*, 177 F.3d 789 (9th Cir. 1999).
Doe v. School District of Norfolk, 340 F.3d 605 (8th Cir. 2003).
Elk Grove Unified School District v. Newdow, 542 U.S. 1 (2004).
Engel v. Vitale, 370 U.S. 421 (1962).
Everson v. Board of Education, 330 U.S. 1 (1947).
Good News Club v. Milford Central School, 533 U.S. 98 (2001).
Griffith v. Butte School District, 244 P.3d 321 (2010).
Hazelwood School District v. Kuhlmeier, 484 U.S. 260 (1988).
Jones v. Clear Creek Independent School District, 977 F.2d 963 (5th Cir. 1992), *reh'g denied*, 983 F.2d 234 (5th Cir. 1992), *cert. denied*, 508 U.S. 967 (1993).
Lamb's Chapel v. Center Moriches Union Free School District, 508 U.S. 384 (1993).
Lassonde v. Pleasanton Unified School District, 320 F.3d 979 (9th Cir. 2003).
Lee v. Weisman, 505 U.S. 577 (1992).
Lemon v. Kurtzman, 403 U.S. 602 (1971).
Morse v. Frederick, 551 U.S. 393 (2007).
Nurre v. Whitehead, 520 F. Supp. 2d 1222 (W.D. Wash. 2007).
Santa Fe Independent School District v. Doe, 530 U.S. 290 (2000).
School District of Abington Township v. Schempp, 374 U.S. 203 (1963).
Sherman v. Koch, 623 F.3d 501 (7th Cir. 2010).
Skarin v. Woodbine Community School District, 204 F. Supp. 2d 1195 (S.D. Iowa, 2002).
Stratechuk v. Board of Education, 587 F.3d 597 (3d Cir. 2009).
Tinker v. Des Moines Independent School District, 393 U.S. 503 (1969).
Wallace v. Jaffree, 472 U.S. 38 (1985).
West Virginia State Board of Education v. Barnette, 319 U.S. 624 (1943).
Workman v. Greenwood Community School Corporation, 2010 WL 1780043 (S.D. Ind. 2010).

Should teachers be able to pray in public schools?

POINT: William E. Thro, *Christopher Newport University*
COUNTERPOINT: Adam C. Hyde, *Osceola School District, Florida*

OVERVIEW

Teacher prayer is a topic that could readily generate legal controversy. Yet, to date, there have been no reported court cases explicitly addressing whether individual teachers in public schools can pray in their places of work. Still, because two related controversies involving teachers and religion, neither of which directly addressed the question of educator prayer, have been litigated, they are worth examining at the outset. Even though these two cases do not directly involve teacher prayer in their own schools, the way in which they were resolved can shed some insight on judicial thinking with regard to this potentially contentious, yet confusing, topic.

On the one hand, the Tenth Circuit ruled that a school board in Colorado could prevent a fifth-grade teacher from silently reading his Bible as he walked around his classroom while his students were quietly reading materials of their own choice (*Roberts v. Madigan*, 1990). The court also prevented the teacher from hanging a poster with a religiously themed message in his classroom. At the heart of its analysis, the court was of the opinion that insofar as the teacher's actions could have unduly influenced his students, he simply could not read the Bible as he walked around the class. If one were to rely on this rationale in the debate at hand, it appears that teachers are unlikely to prevail should they wish to pray in their schools.

On the other hand, the Eighth Circuit affirmed that school officials in South Dakota violated the free speech rights of an elementary school teacher by refusing to allow her to join a Good News Club, a forum for student prayer and

Bible study that met in her building after the completion of the school day (*Wigg v. Sioux Falls School District 49–5*, 2004a). The court reversed an earlier order that would have allowed the teacher to meet with the club, but only at schools other than the one where she taught. Reasoning that the teacher's after-school participation amounted to private speech over which the school board had no control, the court pointed out that the after-school participation did not put the board at risk of violating the Establishment Clause. In light of this case, then, an argument can be made that if teacher prayer is silent or unobtrusive, it can be viewed as private speech beyond the authority of school officials.

Faced with these paradoxical results, educational leaders must take two sets of putative, conflicting rights into account, those of teachers and those of students in conjunction with their parents. Since it is well-settled law that insofar as teaching in public schools is a privilege and not a right, educators can be forced to leave some of their rights at the school house gate. Broadly in line with the holding in *Madigan*, among the rights that public school teachers have had to forego are the ability to wear politically expressive buttons or to freely offer their opinions on matters that are not of public concern because of the impact that they might have on their impressionable students who may be unable to distinguish between the views of their teachers and school boards. Yet, if teachers seek to assert their rights to pray, as in *Wigg*, their being able to do so can conflict with the rights of parents who may want their children to be educated in public school settings where they are free from teacher-imposed religious influences such as prayer.

Against this backdrop, the debates in this chapter have adopted two distinctly different approaches to the thorny question of whether teachers should be able to pray in their public schools. In the point essay, William E. Thro (Christopher Newport University) takes the position that it is not constitutionally impermissible for teachers to pray in public schools. To this end, he writes that even if one puts aside constitutional concerns based on the Federal Constitution and its state counterparts, coupled with state laws, then it is sound public policy to permit public school teachers to pray in public schools because doing so can help foster a sense of appreciation for religious diversity in the United States.

Conversely, the counterpoint essay by Adam C. Hyde (Osceola School District, Florida) asserts that teachers should not be able to pray in public schools. He bases his position on the notions that insofar as the Supreme Court has adopted a position largely calling for "separation of church and state" in public schools, teacher prayer not only violates the First Amendment but also runs the risk of coercing, however unintentionally, students to accept religious beliefs that they and their families do not share.

As you read these essays, ask yourself the following questions. First, do you think that public school teachers should be allowed to pray in their classrooms or other locations in public schools? Second, if public school teachers are allowed to pray, should there be any restrictions in place such as limiting their prayers to a form of silent expression? Third, would allowing public school teachers to pray run the risk of making students who may not share the same faiths as their teachers generate controversies such as the fears of children (and their parents) that they will not be accepted if they have different beliefs or that their grades will suffer if they do not participate?

Charles J. Russo
University of Dayton

POINT: William E. Thro
Christopher Newport University

Before answering the question of whether teachers should be able to pray in the public schools, it is first necessary to define the scope of the question. The question is not whether teachers may force students to join them in prayer. Supreme Court precedent is clear that students may not be coerced into prayers (*Engel v. Vitale*, 1962). Nor is the question one of whether teachers should encourage students to join them in voluntary prayer. Rather, the question is whether public school teachers should be able to pray in the public schools. Phrased differently, if teachers wish to practice their religions by engaging in prayer, may the state, through local school board policies, forbid teachers from doing so?

This point essay argues that government may not deny public school teachers the right to pray while in their schools. In advancing this position, this point essay makes three points. First, as a matter of federal constitutional law, particularly the First Amendment, officials in public schools may not deny teachers the right to pray freely. Second, regardless of what the federal Constitution requires, state law, whether in the form of statutes or provisions in their state constitutions, may require the government to respect the right of teachers to pray in their schools. Third, constitutional and statutory questions aside, it is sound public policy to allow teachers to pray.

FEDERAL CONSTITUTION REQUIRES THAT TEACHERS BE ABLE TO PRAY

The government in the American democracy, whether state or national, must be neutral in matters of religious theory, doctrine, and practice. At the same time, the government may not be hostile to any religion or to the advocacy of no religion; further, the government may not aid, foster, or promote one religion or religious theory against another or even against the militant opposite (*Epperson v. Arkansas*, 1968). To this end, the Supreme Court has declared that "the Free Exercise Clause requires government respect for, and noninterference with, the religious beliefs and practices of our Nation's people" (*Cutter v. Wilkinson*, 2005, p. 719). The Court added,

> [T]he door of the Free Exercise Clause stands tightly closed against any governmental regulation of religious beliefs as such. Government may

neither compel affirmation of a repugnant belief, nor penalize or discriminate against individuals or groups because they hold religious views abhorrent to the authorities nor employ the taxing power to inhibit the dissemination of particular religious views. (*Sherbert v. Verner*, 1963, pp. 402–403)

Indeed, the Supreme Court had specified that "religious beliefs need not be acceptable, logical, consistent, or comprehensible to others in order to merit First Amendment protection" (*Thomas v. Review Board of Indiana Employment Security Division*, 1981, p. 714). Because the government is not required "to be oblivious to impositions that legitimate exercises of state power may place on religious belief and practice" (*Board of Education of Kiryas Joel Village School District v. Grumet*, 1994, p. 705), governmental officials, including those in public schools, may treat religious organizations more favorably than nonreligious groups without violating the Establishment Clause. Consequently, officials of public school boards may not penalize teachers because of their religious beliefs (*Corporation of Presiding Bishop of Church of Jesus Christ of Latter-day Saints v. Amos*, 1987).

While belief is absolutely protected, "the right of free exercise does not relieve an individual of the obligation to comply with a 'valid and neutral law of general applicability on the ground that the law proscribes (or prescribes) conduct that his religion prescribes (or proscribes)'" (*Employment Division, Department of Human Resources of Oregon v. Smith*, 1990, p. 879). Thus, "a law that is neutral and of general applicability need not be justified by a compelling governmental interest even [if] the law has the incidental effect of burdening a particular religious practice" (*Church of the Lukumi Babalu Aye v. City of Hialeah*, 1993, p. 531). Consequently, board officials in public school systems could force teachers to comply with neutral and general applicable policies even though such policies may burden teachers' rights to the free exercise of religion.

In determining whether school board officials may prohibit teachers from praying, the critical inquiry becomes whether policies are neutral and of general applicability. "In order to determine whether a law is neutral, as the Court used the term in *Smith*, we must examine the object of the law" (*St. John's United Church of Christ v. City of Chicago*, 2007, p. 631). The Supreme Court explained, "[A] law is not neutral" if "the object of the law is to infringe upon or restrict practices because of their religious motivation" (*Lukumi*, 1993, p. 533). Moreover, the related principle of "general applicability" forbids the government from "impos[ing] burdens only on conduct motivated by religious belief" in a "selective manner" (p. 543). Of course, "[n]eutrality and general applicability are interrelated, and failure to satisfy one requirement is a likely indication that the other has not been satisfied" (p. 531).

School board policies prohibiting public school teachers from practicing their religions are neither neutral nor generally applicable. The effect of such policies would be to force individual teachers to compromise their core religious beliefs by refraining from prayer. To the extent that government designs such policies to target only religious actions, namely, the practice of prayer, the policies impose unique burdens on religious groups. Therefore, such policies could be upheld as constitutional only if they are "justified by a compelling interest and [are] narrowly tailored to advance that interest" (*Lukumi*, 1993, p. 533). As a practical matter, since it is up to the courts to apply this strict scrutiny standard, it is highly likely that the judiciary would uphold policies of this nature.

STATE LAW MAY REQUIRE THAT TEACHERS BE ABLE TO PRAY

Even if the federal Constitution allows public school boards and their officials to prohibit teachers from engaging in prayers, state constitutional provisions or state laws may require that governments permit teachers to pray in their schools. Because state constitutions often are more protective of individual liberty, teachers may have state constitutional rights to pray in their schools.

Indeed, since the decisions of the Supreme Court under the leadership of Chief Justice Warren E. Burger prompted a revival of state constitutional law in the early 1970s, "it would be most unwise these days not also to raise the state constitutional questions" (Brennan, 1977, p. 502). Although the issue apparently is one of national first impression, meaning that it has not yet been litigated, it would not be surprising if a state court determined that its state constitution prohibited public school boards from restricting teacher's religious free exercise.

In fact, after the Court diminished religious freedom in *Smith* when it ruled that the state could limit the free exercise rights of Native American drug counselors to ingest peyote, a recognized sacrament in their faith, at the risk of losing their jobs, some state courts held that their state constitutions provided greater protection for religious freedom. In addition, state religious freedom restoration acts prohibit state and local governments from imposing a substantial burden on the free exercise of religion unless there is a compelling governmental interest pursued through the least restrictive means. To the extent that as policies prohibiting teacher prayer impose burdens on the free exercise of religion, such policies would be invalid.

PUBLIC POLICY FAVORS ALLOWING PUBLIC SCHOOL TEACHERS TO PRAY

Even if the federal Constitution and state laws permit public school boards to restrict the free exercise rights of their teachers, there are sound public policy reasons why educators should be allowed to pray freely.

First, allowing teachers to pray will send a broader message of inclusion and tolerance for religion and differences of opinion. Christianity no longer dominates American society. In fact, a significant part of America embraces no religion or embraces a religious tradition dramatically different from our Judeo-Christian heritage. In such an environment, it is essential that everyone respect and tolerate other beliefs. Permitting teachers of all faiths to pray would help to demonstrate such respect and tolerance. Adopting policies that allow teachers of different faiths to pray would send the implicit message that people are free to believe as they wish even if others do not share such beliefs. In addition, treating prayer in the same manner as other forms of expression reinforces the constitutional principle that religious speech is at least as valuable as nonreligious speech, a concept that the Supreme Court has upheld. Conversely, banning public school teachers from praying sends a message of hostility toward religious expression.

Second and similarly, allowing teachers to pray will make people of faith feel welcome in public schools. In contemporary America, employers and educational institutions make extraordinary efforts to ensure that persons from different cultures or ethnic groups feel welcome. While such efforts are, of course, laudable and necessary, they should not be limited to ethnic and cultural minorities. These efforts must include people of faith.

Third, as long as there is no interference with the educational process, school board policies should afford teachers broad discretion to behave as they wish, including praying, while on the job. Indeed, school board officials rarely, if ever, try to regulate every aspect of the behaviors of teachers regardless of whether they are in class or other parts of their school buildings. The decision to allow teachers to engage in prayer should be no different from other activities.

Fourth, as a general matter, teachers can participate in prayer without disrupting the educational process. As long as there are no disruptions, teachers should be allowed to pursue whatever activities, including prayer, they wish to pursue while in their schools. Put another way, teacher prayer should be no different from other activities. To the extent that prayer causes disruptions, then public school boards should be free to impose restrictions to prevent the disruption. Still, there is a significant difference between minimal restrictions on teacher prayer and an outright ban on teacher prayer.

Fifth, the mere fact that teachers engage in prayer does not mean that school boards are endorsing prayer. Students, even young children, can recognize that teachers' views and actions are separate and distinct from those of their school boards. Board officials do not worry about perceptions of district endorsements when teachers support particular organizations such as their unions, political candidates, or a sports team. In the same way, school boards should not worry unduly about perceptions of endorsement if teachers happen to engage in prayer. Moreover, teachers can participate in prayer without coercing or even encouraging students to join them in prayer. Of course, to the extent that the prayer conveys an appearance of endorsement or to the extent that there is coercion or encouragement of students, then school board policies should be free to impose restrictions. In an important distinction, any such restrictions should be designed to regulate the context of the prayer, not banning or prohibiting the prayer itself.

CONCLUSION

As the counterpoint essay correctly notes, the federal Constitution prohibits mandatory prayer by teachers and prohibits public school–sponsored prayer in specified other contexts such as graduation exercise or athletic contexts. Still, those cases deal with the Establishment Clause, which has been interpreted as meaning that the government may not endorse or express its disapproval of a particular religion. However, the right of individual teachers to engage in prayer does not implicate the Establishment Clause. Rather, teacher prayer implicates the Free Exercise Clause. Although the Supreme Court has reinterpreted the Free Exercise Clause in a manner that diminishes protection for religious liberty, the Constitution still precludes public school boards from banning teacher prayer. Moreover, even if the federal Constitution allows such a policy, state constitutional provisions and state law may well protect the teacher's religious liberty. Finally, there are sound public policy reasons for allowing teachers to pray because doing so would demonstrate respect not only for religion but also for diversity of belief in the American public education system.

COUNTERPOINT: Adam C. Hyde
Osceola School District, Florida

Teacher prayer is a debated, but nonlitigated, issue in the United States. Perhaps this issue has not been litigated because the Supreme Court has forbidden school-sponsored prayer beginning with *Engel v. Vitale* (1962) and *School District of Abington Township v. Schempp* and *Murray v. Curlett* (1963).

American judicial attitudes toward religion in general, and prayer in schools in particular, are largely shaped by Thomas Jefferson's notion of separation of church and state; this is the position that the Supreme Court has most often adopted in this area. Even though this phrase is not in the Constitution, it is what many base arguments on regarding prayer and the place of religion in public schools.

Amid debate over the place of religion in schools and appeals to the Founding Fathers, it is important to recall that they were about as divided as present-day Americans. Accordingly, resorting to history is not entirely helpful. Moreover, allowing teacher prayer in public schools opens the door for the inclusion of many forms of religions that may leave educational leaders with no way of differentiating between and among them. Although students already have multiple opportunities to pray and may do so on their own, teacher prayer would be in direct violation of the First Amendment. Teacher prayer should remain impermissible because it may improperly expose students to religious beliefs that can lead to their indoctrination. Thus, this counterpoint essay stands for the proposition that a combination of judicial analyses, policies, and the need for respect for diversity of religions, or beliefs, mandates that teachers should not be allowed to pray in American public schools.

THE SUPREME COURT HAS CONSISTENTLY DISALLOWED SCHOOL-SPONSORED PRAYER
Student Prayer

This debate focuses on prayer by teachers in public schools. Even so, it is important to begin with a review of the cases addressing student prayer because they provide a necessary background for the topic of teacher prayer.

The first Supreme Court case dealing with school prayer was *Engel v. Vitale* (1962). Parents in New York alleged that their religious views were being ignored when the State Board of Regents composed and recommended a teacher-led prayer to be used at the start of each school day. In light of the prayer's reference to an "All Mighty God," the parents charged that it violated the Establishment Clause in the First Amendment to the Constitution.

When *Engel* reached the Supreme Court, the justices reversed earlier judgments to the contrary by ruling in favor of the parents. In its analysis, the Court reviewed the history of state-approved prayer from England through the Colonial Period, acknowledging that the prayer would have essentially established a state religion in violation of the Establishment Clause. The Court noted that insofar as prayer is too personal of a matter to allow state officials to interject themselves, even the potential that students might have felt coerced to join in the prayer meant that it had to be struck down as unconstitutional. Applying this same kind of rationale, how can the practice of a teacher praying in a class be any less a risk of coercion?

The Supreme Court's companion cases in *School District of Abington Township v. Schempp* and *Murray v. Curlett* (1963), from Pennsylvania and Maryland, respectively, moved away from solely prayer in public education to include a challenge to reading of the Bible. The plaintiffs claimed that these practices violated the First Amendment.

The Supreme Court invalidated the practices in both cases. The Court explained that public school officials cannot force students, who are a captive audience, to endure religious readings or prayers. More specifically, in examining the practices, the Court declared that

> [t]he test may be stated as follows: what are the purpose and the primary effect of the [legislative] enactment? ... [T]o withstand the strictures of the Establishment Clause there must be a secular legislative purpose and a primary effect that neither advances nor inhibits religion (*Abington*, p. 222)

In 1971, the Court added to this test a prong forbidding excessive entanglement between religion and government in *Lemon v. Kurtzman*, creating what is often referred to as the *Lemon* test that has been important in many cases involving religion.

The issue of prayer at graduation made its way to the Supreme Court in 1992 in *Lee v. Weisman*. In *Lee*, in a dispute from Rhode Island, a divided Court affirmed that school-sponsored graduation prayer was unconstitutional by relying on two major points. First, the Court thought that prayer was unacceptable because the state, through school officials in the form of a principal here, played a key role both by selecting who would pray and by directing its content insofar as the principal gave those who would pray a set of suggested guidelines. Second, the Court feared that governmental activity of this nature could be psychologically coercive to students. The Court maintained that because students were a captive audience who may have been forced, against their wishes, to participate in ceremonies, they were not genuinely free to be excused from attending.

Finally, in *Santa Fe Independent School District v. Doe* (2000), a typically divided Supreme Court affirmed that a board policy from Texas permitting student-led prayers prior to the start of high school football games violated the Establishment Clause. In striking down this policy, the justices first rejected the board's claim that the policy advanced the free speech rights of students.

Second, the Court rebuffed the board's claim that the policy was neutral. Third, the Court disagreed with the board's assertion that the case was premature since no one had offered a prayer at a football game under the policy.

Teacher Prayer/Religious Activity

The only case directly involving a teacher and religious issues in class, although not concerning prayer directly, was *Roberts v. Madigan* (1990). In a case from Colorado, the Tenth Circuit affirmed that school officials did not violate the rights of a fifth-grade teacher when they limited his use of the Bible in his class. The teacher often read his Bible silently as students sat at their desks reading books of their choice. The teacher always kept a copy of the Bible on his desk and he displayed a poster with the message "You have only to open your eyes to see the hand of God." At the same time, the court upheld the actions of the principal who removed two books about the Bible and life of Jesus from the teacher's classroom library of "about 239 books of varying content that [he] had compiled over his nineteen-years of teaching" (p. 1047). Yet, the court permitted books on Buddhism, Greek gods and goddesses, and Indian religions to remain in the in-class library. In an aspect of the case that is not directly relevant to this debate, the court did order the principal to return copies of the Bible to the school library.

In the part of its analysis that is most relevant to the question of whether teachers can pray in public schools, the Tenth Circuit focused on the fact that the teacher worked with a class full of impressionable children. As such, the court held that insofar as the teacher may have impermissibly communicated the school board's approval for his reading of the Bible, it had the authority to prevent him from doing so. If it is appropriate for a court to prevent a teacher from reading the Bible in front of impressionable children, then how much more so is it constitutionally impermissible for a teacher to pray in class or around students?

STUDENT PERCEPTIONS AND POLICIES TOWARD TEACHER PRAYER

As American society diversifies, students in today's public schools are becoming exposed to many other cultures and religions. This transition to an increasingly multicultural society impacts all public school systems. Moreover, there is an outcry for religious tolerance and teaching about different religions to help students inculcate respect for faiths not their own.

In light of this, it is worth noting that Supreme Court cases on religion have dealt almost exclusively with Christianity. In fact, the Court has rarely addressed a case about any other religion. Thus, an argument can be made that the best way to eliminate religious intolerance among school children would be a ban across the board with regard to any type of prayer, particularly by teachers. As noted, the Supreme Court has disallowed any form of school-sponsored prayer even though it has failed to address student-initiated prayer at public school graduations, a topic admittedly beyond the scope of this essay, but which is addressed in another essay in this volume (Chapter 3).

Turning to teacher prayer, if board policies cannot permit school-sponsored prayer, then it is illogical for them to permit teachers to pray. As such, there should be no teacher prayer in schools. Teachers can teach, present their material, or, as the Supreme Court has recognized, even lecture about different religions. However, teacher prayer should not be allowed in public schools because allowing this practice can only give rise to clashes between and among various religious, cultural, and ethnic groups in schools as they vie to ensure supremacy for their beliefs, as expressed by having their prayers recited. Accordingly, preventing teacher prayer in schools can help to reduce, if not eliminate, related religious or cultural/ethnic difficulties. The best way to promote tolerance in school is to have no religion at all, including teacher prayer.

As authority figures who might indirectly coerce students to join them, even if they do so unintentionally, teachers should not have the right to impose prayer or religion in public schools or in their individual classrooms. Public school classrooms are four walls of separation between church and state. Classrooms should be seen as safe havens for those who want to shelter themselves from any type of religion and theocratic thoughts. Teachers need to provide instruction of state-prescribed curricula and not depart from their duties by venturing into religious activities such as prayer. More strident critics than this author might even argue that allowing teacher prayer could be detrimental to students, as it could cloud the judgments of young minds. These critics might assert that any type of exposure to religious influences (what they would describe as indoctrination) such as teacher prayer would violate the trust that parents and the government have placed in a teacher's hands. The appearance of any type of religious indoctrination or even prayer, particularly by teachers, would, from this perspective, impermissibly coerce children to deal with issues that have no place in today's classrooms.

Teachers are expected to teach their secular curricula without regard for religious controversies such as those that might arise should they pray in front of students. Parents should be able to trust that all instruction follows state-prescribed curricula. Teachers who depart from the prescribed curricula not only disobey their school boards but violate parental trust. Parents should be able to send their children to public schools with the expectation that they will receive well-rounded educations free from religious influences such as teacher prayer. The thought of teachers praying in school contradicts the need for educators to perform their duties free from (religious) bias.

As the Tenth Circuit recognized in *Madigan*, students can be impermissibly influenced, if not coerced, by viewing a classroom display of religious materials or by observing a teacher reading a religious text. Recognizing that being a public school teacher is a privilege and not a right, courts have upheld limits on the free speech rights of teachers. Courts have, for example, prevented teachers, as authority figures, from wearing political buttons because their doing so could influence their students. Similarly, teachers should not be permitted to pray in public schools because of the impact that doing so can have on their students. Furthermore, since teachers are rightfully looked on as being persons in authority or in charge, if they pray in schools, they run the risk of creating discomfort for students whose values are different. These students may feel coerced to share the same belief systems as those of their teachers. When teachers act out their beliefs through prayer, they risk making students feel as though they must participate to ensure that they receive favor in class. Because of such concerns, school boards have rightfully adopted policies preventing teachers from praying in public schools.

CONCLUSION

Teacher prayer is inappropriate on two important levels. First, teacher prayer violates the rights of students not to be coerced to pray. Second, teacher prayer violates the rights of parents to direct the upbringing of their children free from external influences. In other words, by keeping teacher prayer out of classrooms, school boards protect both students and their parents in pursuit of unbiased educations.

The Supreme Court's modern jurisprudence has relied on the "wall of separation" as the best way to ensure that no one religion or set of beliefs trumps those of another. Thus, while schools certainly can pursue the academic study of religion, insofar as allowing teachers to pray in public schools may impermissibly influence students, it is a practice that school boards simply should not permit.

FURTHER READINGS AND RESOURCES

Brennan, W. J. (1977). State constitutions and the protection of individual rights. *Harvard Law Review, 90,* 489.
Howard, A. E. D. (1976). State courts and constitutional rights in the day of the Burger Court. *Virginia Law Review, 62,* 873.

Howard, A. E. D. (1988). The renaissance of state constitutional law. *Emerging Issues in State Constitutional Law, 1,* 14.

Laycock, D. (2004). Theology scholarships, the Pledge of Allegiance, and religious liberty: Avoiding the extremes. *Harvard Law Review, 118,* 155.

Lund, C. C. (2011). Religious freedom after *Gonzales*: A look at state RFRAs. *South Dakota Law Review, 55,* 467–496.

Mawdsley, R. D., & Russo, C. J. (1996). Religious expression and teacher control of the classroom: A new battleground for free speech. *Education Law Reporter, 107,* 1–14.

McCarthy, M. (1992). Is the wall of separation still standing? *Education Law Reporter, 77,* 1–13.

Russo, C. J. (2004). The religious free speech rights of public school teachers: *Wigg v. Sioux Falls School District 49–5*. *Religion & Education, 31*(2), 98–106.

Wheeler, T. E. (1997). Religious expression by teachers: Whose classroom is it? *Education Law Reporter, 118,* 571–589.

Wright, J. W., Jr. (2010). Note, making state religious freedom restoration amendments effective. *Alabama Law Review, 61,* 425.

COURT CASES AND STATUTES

Board of Education of Kiryas Joel Village School District v. Grumet, 512 U.S. 687 (1994).
Cantwell v. Connecticut, 310 U.S. 296 (1940).
Church of the Lukumi Babalu Aye v. City of Hialeah, 508 U.S. 520 (1993).
Corporation of Presiding Bishop of Church of Jesus Christ of Latter-day Saints v. Amos, 483 U.S. 327 (1987).
Cutter v. Wilkinson, 544 U.S. 709 (2005).
Employment Division, Department of Human Resources of Oregon v. Smith, 494 U.S. 872 (1990).
Engel v. Vitale, 370 U.S. 421 (1962).
Epperson v. Arkansas, 393 U.S. 97 (1968).
Lee v. Weisman, 505 U.S. 577 (1992).
Lemon v. Kurtzman, 403 U.S. 602 (1971).
Roberts v. Madigan, 921 F.2d 1047 (10th Cir. 1990), *cert. denied,* 505 U.S. 1218 (1992)
Santa Fe Independent School District v. Doe, 530 U.S. 290 (2000).
School District of Abington Township v. Schempp and Murray v. Curlett, 374 U.S. 203 (1963).
Sherbert v. Verner, 374 U.S. 398, 402–03 (1963).
St. John's United Church of Christ v. City of Chicago, 502 F.3d 616 (7th Cir. 2007).
Thomas v. Review Board of Indiana Employment Security Division, 450 U.S. 707 (1981).
Wigg v. Sioux Falls School Dist. 49–5, 382 F.3d 807 (8th Cir. 2004a), *reh'g and reh'g en banc denied* (2004b).
Wisconsin v. Yoder, 406 U.S. 205 (1972).

Should moments of silence be permitted in public schools?

POINT: Mario S. Torres, Jr., *Texas A&M University*
COUNTERPOINT: Luke M. Cornelius, *University of North Florida*

OVERVIEW

Arguably somewhat less controversial than the related practice of prayer in public schools, a significant number of cases have been litigated over the constitutionality of whether educational officials can permit moments of silence in public schools. In the first round of litigation, after lower federal courts reached mixed results in disputes over the constitutionality of moments of silence in public schools, the Supreme Court addressed its first and only case on the merits of this topic in 1985 in *Wallace v. Jaffree*.

In *Wallace*, the Supreme Court invalidated a law from Alabama that authorized a period of silence at the start of the school day for meditation or voluntary prayer. In its review of the law's legislative history, the Court held that the law violated the Establishment Clause of the First Amendment to the Constitution because it lacked a secular legislative purpose. Subsequently, after lower federal courts struck down a statute from New Jersey as unconstitutional (*May v. Cooperman*, 1985), the Court dismissed an appeal without addressing the constitutionality of the debated statute (*appeal dismissed sub nom. Karcher v. May*, 1987). The Court was of the opinion that the former speaker of the state general assembly and former president of the state senate who intervened and participated in the litigation to uphold the law's constitutionality could no longer participate in the suit because they lacked standing by virtue of having lost their leadership positions.

Four circuit courts have since upheld statutes permitting silence in public schools. The Eleventh Circuit affirmed that a statute from Georgia allowing a moment of silent reflection in school was constitutional since it passed all three prongs of the *Lemon v. Kurtzman* (1971) test insofar as it had a valid secular legislative purpose, a principal or primary effect that neither advanced nor inhibited religion, and did not excessively entangle the government and religion (*Bown v. Gwinnett County School District*, 1997). Also, the Fourth Circuit upheld a law from Virginia mandating a minute of silence in schools that included the word "pray" in listing an unlimited range of permissible mental activities (*Brown v. Gilmore*, 2001a, 2001b). The court affirmed that the statute did not violate the Establishment Clause because even though it had two purposes, one clearly secular and the other an accommodation of religion, it satisfied the *Lemon* test's requirement of a secular purpose. The court reasoned that the statute neither advanced nor hindered religion and did not result in the state's becoming excessively entangled with religion.

The Fifth Circuit reached the same outcome in a case from Texas (*Croft v. Governor of Texas*, 2009), affirming that a law calling for a minute of silence following the recitation of the Pledge of Allegiance during which students may, if they choose, reflect, pray, meditate, or engage in any other silent activity that is unlikely to interfere with or distract others was constitutional. The court was satisfied that the law met all three prongs of the *Lemon* test.

Most recently, the Seventh Circuit reversed an earlier order to the contrary in upholding the Illinois Silent Reflection and Student Prayer Act (*Sherman ex rel. Sherman v. Koch*, 2010, 2011). The court ruled that the law neither was unconstitutionally vague nor did advanced or inhibited religion.

Against this backdrop, the debates on moments of silence in this chapter rely on essentially the same case law in reaching divergent outcomes on their constitutionality. In the point essay, Mario S. Torres, Jr. (Texas A&M University), takes the position that moments of silence should be permitted in public schools because they are valid secular activities that have passed Establishment Clause analysis. More specifically, he is of the view that in light of recent circuit court precedent, it should be clear that carefully constructed moments of silence are not treated as a form of religious endorsements by the state such that officials should be free to permit this practice because it serves legitimate secular purposes in helping prepare students for their school days.

Conversely, the counterpoint essay by Luke M. Cornelius (University of North Florida) opposes moment of silence statutes because he thinks that they are more likely to be legal or political statements rather than activities designed to enhance the quality of public education. He thus makes the case that rather than being seen as benign moments designed for structured moments of silent prayer, these laws may actually have the effect of proscribing when students are free to pray on their own, a reason why school officials should not be able to institute policies calling for this practice in public schools.

As you read these essays about moments of silence in public schools, ask yourself the following two questions. First, is it a good idea to include moments of silence in public schools? Second, in a related inquiry, are moments of silence legitimate secular activities that help students focus on the tasks of the day, or are they designed to bring prayer back into public schools via an indirect route?

Charles J. Russo
University of Dayton

POINT: Mario S. Torres, Jr.
Texas A&M University

In the United States, there is a reticence to engage in frank discussions about religion. Since religion tends to arouse intense emotions, it is usually not addressed outside of homes and places of worship. For this reason, the notion of a moment of silence in schools seems to spark strong viewpoints that are both expected and understandable. These feelings, however intense, are likely influenced by factors bearing some link to political orientation, ethnic diversity, economics, and culture.

Regardless of where one stands, it is difficult not to appreciate, as least in terms of historical significance, the role religion has played in safeguarding fundamental American rights in general. Any depiction of the origins of the United States should probably include religion as a focal point. Often overlooked are the varying motivations of the early colonists who settled here for reasons other than fleeing religious persecution and intolerance. As James W. Fraser (1999) notes, some colonists, like the Massachusetts Puritans and the Dutch Reformers, came to the new world committed to ensuring the survival of their faith and engaged in a fair amount of proselytizing. Massachusetts' Old Deluder Act of 1647 also serves as an example of the tight coupling between religion and social goals in early America.

With growing diversity and the emergence of compulsory education laws, the role of religion in American public schools formed into an intensely contested issue of legal import. The courts were eventually asked to respond to constitutional questions that would more precisely outline the contours limiting the relationship of the state and religion as well as the liberties entitling citizens to some control over the upbringing of their children, such as the decision to opt for religious education. Despite years of legal challenges, religious case law taken together demonstrates support for individuals and groups to engage in religious activity free from state hostility, which appears to encompass the moment of silence. For this reason, this point essay primarily relies on an examination of the rationales in case law rather than separate arguments in support of the proposition of allowing public school officials to permit moments of silence. The essay bases this position on the belief that moments of silence are constitutionally permissible because they are fundamentally secular activities through which students may choose freely to exercise their religious freedom under the First Amendment.

SUPREME COURT CASES AND ANALYSIS

The Due Process Clause of the Fourteenth Amendment to the Constitution, as well as the Establishment, Free Exercise, and Speech Clauses of the First Amendment, together establish a legal basis supporting moments of silence in schools. *Wallace v. Jaffree* (1985) laid the legal groundwork for the formalization of secular occasions for students to engage in independent prayer, meditation, and thought. While the Supreme Court ruled that the law lacked a secular legislative purpose and was, as such, unconstitutional, its judgment ironically established clarity as to what circumstances constituted legal moments of silence. In *Wallace*, the Alabama legislature attempted to design a statute authorizing school officials to institute a moment of silence. The legislature thus created three separate versions. One encouraged prayer to "Lord God" and allowed teachers to "lead" the willing students in devotional exercises. The version scrutinized by the High Court involved "a period of silence not to exceed one minute in duration [which shall be used for] meditation or voluntary prayer" (p. 40). While the religious motives appear far less obvious in the latter version, the Court remained troubled by the legislation's intent because its lead supporter expressed his desire that the law would lead to the return of school prayer.

The 6–3 majority opinion authored by Justice John Paul Stevens rejected the assertion that states had the power to establish a state religion. As the Supreme Court argued, due process applies equally to the states as it does to Congress in "prohibiting any State from depriving any person of liberty without due process of law [as well as placing] the same substantive limitations on the State's power to legislate" (p. 49). The Court largely anchored its analysis in the First Amendment which reads in relevant part that "Congress shall make no law respecting an establishment of religion."

Using the criteria established in *Lemon v. Kurtzman* (1971), the Supreme Court had to evaluate whether the legislation carried a secular purpose, such that the "government's actual purpose is to endorse or disapprove of religion" (*Lynch v. Donnelly*, 1984, p. 690). According to the Court, the purpose was not secular. The opinion then turned to the bill's motives. The state senator sponsoring the legislation, Donald Holmes (D-Alabama), commented in legislative hearings that the singular intent of the period of silence was to "return voluntary prayer" (p. 57) to public schools. Senator Holmes expressed that by enacting the law, the legislature in Alabama would allow children the opportunity to share in the spiritual heritage of the state and country because both were founded by people who believed in God.

The High Court decided that the statute's purpose was religious. Aside from textual revisions of the bill such as switching the term "shall" for "may" or "meditation" for "meditation or voluntary prayer," the expressed intent captured in the legislative record sufficed the Court to conclude that the bill's intent was to "convey a message of state endorsement and promotion of prayer" (p. 59). Regardless of the modifications, the High Court thought the statute was a purposeful support for prayer in the schools and that the state failed to demonstrate neutrality. In the end, the legislation was found unconstitutional.

The narrative in *Wallace* is not extraordinary. In truth, similar case storylines played out extensively in other legal areas, such as desegregation. As the aftermath of *Brown v. Board of Education* (1954) demonstrates, issues of "broad social concern" (Johnson, 1967) are most susceptible to drawing a wide variation of responses from local agencies. Supreme Court rulings related to religion in schools reveal this similar tendency. Robert H. Birkby (1973) observed that despite *School District of Abington Township v. Schempp, Murray v. Curlett's* (1963) prohibiting school prayer, a legal issue that would be further clarified by subsequent Supreme Court rulings, 70 of the 121 districts studied operated in compliance with Tennessee state law allowing devotional exercises. Further, officials in another 50 of the districts surveyed made changes in the form of making prayer a voluntary choice for the student or giving teachers discretion to incorporate prayer into daily classroom practice. Only one district surveyed reported ending all forms of devotional exercise. Finding no significant correlation between the manner of implementation and demographic factors, Birkby concluded that implementing agencies tended to superficially adhere to the rulings and generally sustained the religious practices.

What should not be overlooked despite implementation challenges are the policy clues *Wallace* yields to governing bodies interested in legislating constitutionally valid moments of silence. *Wallace* offers a previously unavailable roadmap and indirectly provides tangible legislative and policy advice. Its logic is both practicable and realizable. First, moments of silence must be legislated without intentional pursuit of returning religion back to the public schools. Second, the wording of the statute should avoid all explicit and implicit religious intentions. To this end, the legislative action and language of the statute must not indicate purposeful support for state religious advancement. States have proven that thoughtfully designed moment of silence bills can be legislated constitutionally in view of the lessons provided in *Wallace*. Be that as it may, the language and terminology in state laws governing moments of silence may still vary considerably. Some states actually mention the term "prayer" in their statutes. For instance, the Illinois state law passed in 2007 requires teachers to "observe a period of silence for silent prayer or reflection on the anticipated activities of the day" (National Conference of State Legislatures [NCSL], 2011).

Virginia's 2000 law

> requires school boards to establish daily moments of silence for meditation, prayer or other silent activity in every classroom in the public schools of Virginia. No other activities may be allowed during this time. The Office of the Attorney General must provide legal counsel for the defense of this law. (NCSL, 2011)

Others simply mention the period of silence and make no mention of prayer but allow local educational agencies greater control over how the statute is implemented; for example, the law in Arkansas states that "a teacher may, or if so directed by the district board of directors, shall, conduct a brief period of silence at the start of each day with the participation of all students who desire to do so" (NCSL, 2011). Indiana, Kansas, New York, and Pennsylvania have similar statutes. Despite differences in statutory language, the laws in and of themselves cannot be legally construed as having sectarian purposes or advancing religion if intent cannot be clearly established.

By the same token, implicit state motives for the advancement of religion should not be tolerated or encouraged. Supreme Court rulings like those in *Engel v. Vitale* (1962), *School District of Abington Township v. Schempp* and *Murray v. Curlett* (1963), and *Lee v. Weisman* (1992), all of which prevented prayer whether in class as in the first two cases or at graduation in the third, are unambiguous in their denouncement of state-sponsored prayer, even when parties argue that the state is hostile to free exercise. In *Lee*, the Court stressed that "the free exercise of religion does not supersede the fundamental limitations imposed by the Establishment Clause" (p. 587). Hence, as stated in *Lee*, permitting prayer at graduation equals a "choice attributable to the State, and from a constitutional perspective it is as if a state decreed that the prayers must occur" (p. 587). Even in circumstances when school involvement is far more subtle, such as board endorsement of a policy guiding the selection of a student to offer the pregame invocation at football games, as in *Santa Fe Independent School District v. Doe* (2000), the Supreme Court has decided that such activities invite religious messages and reach a critical level of state endorsement. As expressed in *Santa Fe*, "Contrary to the District's repeated assertions that it has adopted a 'hands-off' approach to the pregame invocation, the realities of the situation plainly reveal that its policy involves both perceived and actual endorsement of religion" (p. 305).

Logic suggests that the Establishment Clause does not cancel out the provisions of the Free Exercise Clause. Pursuant to the First Amendment, citizens are entitled to freely exercise their religion. Further, government agencies must make reasonable accommodations for religious exercise. The High Court proved in *Wisconsin v. Yoder* (1972), which through a very narrow ruling allowed Amish parents to educate their children at home after eighth grade, that states cannot ignore free exercise even when its interests may be compelling. With respect to schooling, the Free Exercise clause touches on aspects akin to the moment of silence, such as the creation of religious clubs and other forms of voluntary student religious expression.

Board of Education of Westside Community Schools v. Mergens (1990) signifies yet another pivotal legal victory for free exercise supporters. In *Mergens*, a student unsuccessfully asked to form a religious club for Bible study and prayer because officials feared a breach of the Establishment Clause. The Supreme Court dismissed the allegation that the Establishment Clause was violated by a school's official recognition of a religiously themed club and further found that the denial of the club's request violated the tenets of the Equal Access Act (1984). The act has been largely instrumental in curbing administrative hostility against students who wish to coalesce for religious reasons in public secondary as well as postsecondary institutions. In short, the act forbids officials in public secondary schools that receive financial assistance and have created limited open fora from denying "equal access or a fair opportunity to, or discriminate against, any students who wish to conduct a meeting within that limited open forum" that may be religious in nature (20 U.S.C. § 4071a).

Circuit Court Cases and Analysis

Without question, Supreme Court case law and federal legislation form a strong defense for legislated moments of silence. Similarly, lower federal court cases, starting with the Eleventh (*Bown v. Gwinnett County School District*, 1997) and Fourth Circuits (*Bown v. Gwinnett County School District*, 2001), have upheld statutes calling for moments of silence as part of larger laws.

Two later circuit court cases addressing the constitutionality of moments of silence deserve mentioning. The Fifth Circuit, in *Croft v. Governor of Texas* (2009), addressed a challenge to the Texas moment of silence statute that permits students, as they wish, to "reflect, pray, meditate, or engage in any other silent activity that is not likely to interfere with or distract another student" (p. 738). The opponents claimed that the statute was an unconstitutional endorsement of religion in violation of the secular purpose prong of the *Lemon* test. Affirming an earlier order upholding the law, the Fifth Circuit agreed that the statute's intent of advancing three secular purposes of "fostering patriotism, providing a period for thoughtful contemplation, and protecting religious freedom"

(p. 746) was not facially unconstitutional in light of *Wallace*. The court preferred to focus exclusively on the "plain text" (p. 749) of the statute and refrain from interpolating the religious motives expressed by a few legislators.

The Seventh Circuit's decision in *Sherman v. Koch* (2010) reveals the most current judicial posture toward moments of silence. In *Sherman*, opponents argued that the Illinois statute was unconstitutionally vague and consequently violated the Establishment Clause of the First Amendment. A federal trial court held that the law authorizing silence "not be conducted as a religious exercise" but rather an "opportunity for silent prayer or for silent reflection on the anticipated activities of the day" (p. 505) in violation of the first prong, dealing with the secular purpose, of the *Lemon* test. The opponents argued that the statute violated the Establishment Clause based on *Wallace*. However, the state responded that the intent of the law was to "calm students and ready them for the school day" (p. 508) while the opponents asserted that the "stated secular purpose is not sincere—that it is a sham—and that the real purpose is to promote prayer" (p. 508). The court was not persuaded that the statute demonstrated the same legislative intent established in *Wallace*. Referring to extensive legislative debate, which resulted in an amendment, and an override of the Illinois governor's veto, which led to more debate, the court concluded that the statute along with the accompanying legislative activity represented no motivations to bring prayer back into the schools and as such was a "stark contrast to the *Wallace* case" (p. 510). Together, *Sherman* and *Croft*, both of which support moments of silence, may be persuasive in the final constitutional analysis of intent with regard to moments of silence.

WHY MOMENTS OF SILENCE SHOULD BE PERMITTED

This essay agrees with the law as a whole, particularly as reflected in the four most recent circuit court cases, which appear to indicate that moments of silence are not facial religious endorsements by the state and thus fulfill legitimate secular purposes. Nonetheless, as evidenced in the counterpoint essay, opponents will continue to attack the practice on what it theoretically implies or endorses rather than the legislated intent. For instance, it has been argued that the ends for justifying a moment of silence are inherently religious when considering the cumulative and individual effects concerning the impressionability of the child and the unmistakable religious solemnity of reflecting in silence (Kaminer, 2002). There is criticism as well that moments of silence are simply veiled attempts to maintain prayer in the schools and purposely seek to offset the 1960s wave of Supreme Court cases prohibiting audible prayer.

In truth, one may never really know the true motives for seeking moments of silence. Perhaps, a fair level of distrust stems purely from the strong emotional valence attached to religion. As Linda D. Lam (2003) suggests,

> Encouraging youth to reflect upon matters, or merely allowing them a moment of quiet, is a legitimate, secular purpose, and one that should not be disregarded simply because earlier statutes had the express legislative purpose of introducing religious activities in the public school arena. (p. 936)

Policymakers must be conscientious of their language and actions and give thoughtful consideration to the proposed benefits of policy, especially when religion is involved. This requires state legislatures to be especially sensitive to diverse religious values and beliefs and fully commit to statutory policy with unambiguous secular intents.

CONCLUSION

As long as local educational agencies act with due diligence to ensure that moments of silence comply with and do not undermine their carefully written statues, then there is no reason for the courts to invalidate their actions. To the contrary, this essay argues that denying students the opportunity to have moments of silence in their schools would impermissibly infringe on their freedom of religion.

COUNTERPOINT: Luke M. Cornelius
University of North Florida

A "moment of silent reflection" in the context of American public schools represents either an egregious waste of time or a daily political statement made at the expense of our school children. In either event, moments of silent reflection represent more of a legal and political exercise than anything truly designed or likely to advance American education. Moments of silence also represent a vestigial and increasingly irrelevant artifact in the development of First Amendment litigation concerning schools. Objections to these moments can be found not merely in law, but also in philosophy, history, and sound educational practice. Even religious objections to school moments of silence are cognizable. Accordingly, this counterpoint essay takes the position that moments of silence should not be permitted in public schools.

JUDICIAL BACKGROUND

At the outset, it must be recognized that moments of silence are neither traditional nor authentic in school settings. Regardless of their stated purposes and intents, mandated school moments of silence only began to appear in the decades following major adverse school prayer precedents that forbade school-sponsored prayer, such as *Engel v. Vitale* (1962) and *School District of Abington Township v. Schempp* and *Murray v. Curlett*. (1963). More recently, rulings such as *Lee v. Weisman* (1992) and *Santa Fe Independent School District v. Doe* (2000) reiterated that school employees, when acting in their official capacities, are not allowed to encourage or facilitate student prayer and religious observances whether at graduations or sporting events, respectively. Taken as a whole, these cases agreed that for school boards or their officials to organize or lead daily prayers was a *prima facie* violation of the Establishment Clause of the First Amendment to the Constitution. Such activities put public officials in the position of not only proselytizing religious beliefs to captive audiences of impressionable children, but also essentially subjected all students at schools to the dominant religious beliefs of school officials or the majority of the community with little regard to their own and their families' own spiritual beliefs or lack thereof. To many citizens and politicians, the so-called school prayer cases represented nothing less than an active judicial effort to end the tradition of religious instruction in public schools and to expel God from the schoolhouse.

Of course these interpretations, as noted by the Supreme Court and subsequent litigation, are not only simplistic but thoroughly erroneous as well. The Court never intended, nor attempted, to remove prayer from public schools. Indeed, such a result does not seem even remotely achievable, much less desirable or constitutional. Rather, all the Court did in the school prayer cases was to clarify that whatever prayer or religious expression that occurred in public schools could not be led, initiated, or facilitated by public employees in their official capacities. The principle at issue in the school prayer cases was not the right of children to pray in public schools but merely the involvement of school officials in such prayer.

Since the school prayer cases, the courts have repeatedly upheld the right of students to pray and express their faith in a multitude of fora, from gatherings at flag poles, to lunchrooms, to extracurricular clubs and organizations. Far from banishing religion and prayer from public schools, the consistent evolution of Establishment Clause jurisprudence has noted that the sole constitutional concern with school prayer has been the question of the involvement of the state, in the form of its employees, in directing, selecting, or controlling such prayer. Nor did the school prayer cases reverse or overturn any precedent in this regard. School-sponsored prayer and religious instruction was a relic of an era where nonsectarian texts were relatively scarce and a less litigious and heterogeneous population had simply never challenged the practice. As such, the school prayer precedents neither deprived educators and citizens of a constitutionally protected right, nor did they overturn established precedent. They merely addressed a tradition born of centuries of legal benign neglect and a limited development of First Amendment law.

School prayer did not really end in 1962 or 1963. Despite this apparent fact, some elements of society and politics perceived an attack on student religious expression and community norms. The origin and motives of the earliest moment of silence laws are difficult to ascertain, although it is clear that such statutes were on the books by the end of the 1960s, mere years after the school prayer cases. These laws might well have benefitted from legal neglect as well had it not been for an Alabama law enacted in 1982. During a debate on overtly returning prayer and religion to public schools, a legislator in Alabama proposed a law mandating a period of silent meditation or prayer as a "first step" to returning prayer to the public school program.

Given the intent of the law's author and the notably sectarian tone of the legislative debate, to say nothing of the state's clear attempt to evade the Supreme Court's school prayer decisions, it is not surprising that in *Wallace v. Jaffree* (1985), the justices ruled that the Alabama statute was unconstitutional. The Court observed that since the clear intent of the moment of silence law and its backers had been to "restore" organized prayer to the public school day and the legislative history was replete with the indisputable intent of the law's backers, it violated the secular legislative purpose prong of the 1971 *Lemon v. Kurtzman* test.

Unlike the school prayer cases, *Wallace* instead spawned a spate of alternative efforts. Other states either enacted or amended school laws to allow for "moments of silent reflection" or similar wordings. These laws, somewhat suspiciously, usually passed with little significant discussion and almost no public mention of the word "prayer." These laws either provided purely for an undifferentiated moment of silence or one in which students could engage in any number of silent ruminations, including prayer. When legislative intent was announced or elicited, sponsors would claim a variety of secular and nonsectarian justifications for these measures. For example, in the instance of the adoption of Georgia's Silent Reflection and Student Prayer Act, the bill's sponsor asserted that the measure would, in some way, ameliorate the rising rate of violence in the state's public schools. At present, roughly a third of states now have some form of moment of silence law. Most notably, the circuit courts have upheld these secular-purpose moments, under the *Lemon* test, in Georgia, Texas, Virginia, and, most recently, Illinois. Only in New Jersey did the Third Circuit strike down a moment of silence law for which no legitimate secular purpose was advanced; the Supreme Court then refused to hear an appeal (*Karcher v. May*, 1987). In the absence of further Supreme Court intervention in these disputes, the legality of such secular-purpose moments appears to be confirmed.

Judicial willingness to look the other way when statutes are challenged notwithstanding, a strong case can be made against state-mandated, or even allowed, moments of silence. In the most recent case, from Illinois, *Sherman v. Koch* (2010), the Seventh Circuit allowed that such enactments were presumed to have a legitimate secular purpose absent clear evidence that the proffered purpose was a "sham." Further, proponents of these measures offered little more than vague, unsupported rationales. In over 40 years of "silence," no studies or even pedagogically well-grounded theories have been advanced in support of these laws. Apparently the courts are willing to accept untested and unsubstantiated aspirations as something more credible than a sham. Still, the fact remains that the legitimacy of claimed secular justifications for these moments of silence remains untested, unproven, and, largely, unspecified. The "sham" in the secular justification of daily moments of silence lies in a complete and total official lack of curiosity into their efficacy. In a period of intense legislative interest in measuring standards and accountability in education, this total lack of oversight or evaluation stands as an even starker evidence of the pretextual nature of these enactments.

MOMENTS OF SILENCE SHOULD NOT BE PERMITTED

Aside from not providing any demonstrable educational benefit, moments of silence themselves raise questions of good educational practice. It must be remembered that the entire crux of the school prayer debate is not whether children may pray in school, but rather whether public employees and representatives of the state can be involved in such prayers. To this end, mandating moments of silence simply serves to once again place school personnel in a constitutionally precarious position. Since the original school prayer cases concerned the potentially coercive effects of public employees leading and directing student prayer, how should school officials handle moments of silence? Are teachers allowed to also bow their heads in prayer or will this eventually give rise to future litigation about teachers "modeling over-reverent behaviors"? Will administrators be forced to design and enforce staff policies regarding proper body language and posture during silent moments? Or will devout parents complain about teachers who use their moment to silently complete paperwork and attendance reports instead of some more solemn contemplation?

At the same time, far from facilitating the school day, such moments of silence may actually serve to merely disrupt educational activities. Consider that a full implementation of the Georgia law would actually amount to 3 hours of lost instructional time for every student each academic year. This may not represent an unreasonable loss of time, but it still represents a significant investment in an awkward moment.

Legally, these moments of silence represent nothing more than a relic of an outdated legal argument a half century in the past. As such, moments of silence are neither necessary nor relevant in modern schools. Contrary to the fears of the backers of school prayer and moments of silence, students in public schools remain free to pray and express their beliefs throughout the school day and beyond. Consider that today students may legally gather daily at their school flagpoles for a pre-school devotional activity. Students may freely say grace and spend a 20- to 30-minute lunch period with prayer or Bible study. Even as courts debate the constitutional boundaries of their ability to do so, students are seeking to demonstrate their faith through clothing and symbols. Students can meet after school, for hours, and engage in constitutionally protected religious activities and meetings. Students can even pray silently at almost any time they are not otherwise actively engaged in class activities, and such moments no doubt compose a considerably greater amount of time daily than even a maximum 20-second period of officially sanctioned contemplation.

Against this backdrop, all of which has been established or upheld by subsequent legal precedents in light of *Engel* and *Jaffree*, the much ballyhooed "official" moments of silence seem less like a desperately needed and precious exercise to preserve a besieged tradition of student free exercise and more like a diminished, inauthentic, and extraneous activity that seeks to restore some inappropriate and unnecessary governmental role into matters that the Constitution significantly leaves to the private individual and not the state. Taken as such, these legislatively enacted moments of silence can be seen as less than authentically preserving student prayer, silent or vocal, which is clearly unnecessary, and more as an increasingly anachronistic protest by voters and state legislatures against what were once, and wrongly, deemed attacks on the free exercise of religion and community norms. Seen within this context, legislatively mandated moments of silence are simply the expenditure of public school instructional time in an ongoing, and largely pointless, protest against long-settled precedents and long-retired justices.

Moments of silence are a protest that ignores decades of developing Supreme Court jurisprudence. For instance, cases such as *Westside Community Schools v. Mergens* (1990) and *Good News Club v. Milford Central School* (2001) that permit student-organized Equal Access Clubs in secondary schools and Christian Clubs in lower grades, respectively, have strengthened the free exercise rights of public school students and, in accordance with the American legal tradition in other areas of the public square, transferred the right to conduct religious observances from the state and its agents to the individual worshipper. Taken to its fullest extent, statutes seeking to impose moments of silence for prayer or other enumerated purposes reveal a desire to continue to impose public control and influence over activities that are constitutionally presumed to be the free exercise of the citizen and not the state. To even suggest the need to create a publically protected time for religious or other silent contemplation inaccurately suggests that such activities cannot occur in schools without government sanction, a proposition that the culmination of legal precedent demonstrates clearly is false.

Additionally, these state-created periods for silent contemplation, meditation, preparation, and *prayer* seem to harken back to the entire *raison d'être* of the school prayer cases in the first place. To a somewhat lesser extent, this approach recalls a day when a child's spiritual instruction was not solely the province of the family and their preferred denomination, but when the state, in the offices of local school officials, sought to impose the importance of devotion and faith, usually with a majoritarian emphasis. Although moments of silence, presumably, eliminate most denominational influences, they can still be claimed to represent, much like the universal school prayer struck down in *Engel*, a governmental preference for religion and religious activities. It can be argued that even the subtle peer pressure of classmates engaged in silent but clearly spiritual exercises, exercises facilitated by the state and the school officials, still constitute a symbolic endorsement and preference for religion by the government itself.

Finally, there are considerable philosophical and theological implications of state-defined moments of silence, at least to the extent that they facilitate student prayer. It must be recalled that the thin veneer of "secular purpose" that makes the moment of silence, thus far, legal proposes that the moment may be used for secular activities other than prayer. What does it say to persons of faith that laws inspired, at least in a significant part, to restore a solemn and even sacred practice to the public school day provide equal treatment and protection to activities such as counting the ceiling tiles of the classroom or contemplating the attractive classmate in the third row? Further, to the extent that these laws accommodate the religious interest of the more devout students, what message do they send to those pupils whose faith requires expression not accommodated in a brief and silent legally defined moment?

It must be remembered that contrary to the view of some supporters of moment of silence laws, such as expressed in the point essay, a major purpose of the Establishment Clause is not merely to insulate government agencies and activities from sectarian influence, but also to protect religious institutions and traditions from governmental influence and control. In America, constitutionally, the government has no interest in whether a given religion or place of worship requires from its adherents a single hour of worship on a Sunday morning or several hours of devotion a day, 7 days a week. Yet, all of the state laws regarding moments of silence in public schools clearly indicate that the government is willing to accommodate, among other activities, student prayer, but only so long as this particular expression of faith can be performed in utter silence and condensed to a legally delimited period of 60 seconds, or less.

The second prong of the *Lemon* test, which is customarily an essential standard in the evaluation of moments of silence and similar enactments, is that a statute shall not have the primary effect of either advancing or inhibiting religion. And, no doubt, these brief moments of silent reflection and prayer may be more than sufficient to accommodate the religious needs and practices of many, if not most, child adherents of America's most popular religions. Still, what of the free exercise of those children whose religious traditions cannot be accommodated in either an unvoiced or artificially truncated manner? It can be argued, persuasively, that these laws, which are intended, at least in part, to accommodate the religious observances of some students, may actually have the effect of inhibiting, by either artificially abridging or altogether preventing, spiritual exercises that do not conform to the limitations of the legally constrained moment of silence enshrined by legislative acts,

CONCLUSION

When the government, no matter how benign its intention, simultaneously seeks to both enable and then delineate the form and duration of religious expression, silent or spoken, it is engaging in the type of control and interference in religion that the Establishment Clause was designed to prevent. Although most litigation addressing educational moments of silence argue, in part, that such laws violate the *Lemon* test by seeking to advance religion, it can be equally argued that they also actually serve to inhibit it as well. Indeed, taken to another extreme, it is conceivable that such formally sanctioned and structured moments of silent worship might have a chilling effect on other constitutionally protected student religious activities in schools by implying that their religious expression may be limited to a single, legally established minute at the start of school days.

Further Readings and Resources

Birkby, R. H. (1973). The Supreme Court and the Bible belt: Tennessee reaction to the "Schempp" decision. In T. L. Becker & M. M. Feeley (Eds.), *The impact of Supreme Court decisions* (2nd ed., pp. 110–118). New York: Oxford University Press.

Fraser, J. W. (1999). *Between church and state: Religion and public education in a multicultural America.* New York: St. Martin's Griffin.

Goldberg, S. S. (1985). The Supreme Court remains silent on moments of silence: Karcher v. May. *Education Law Reporter, 43,* 849–853.

Harvard Law Review. (1983). The unconstitutionality of state statutes authorizing moments of silence in public schools. *Harvard Law Review, 96.* (Original work published 1874)

Johnson, R. M. (1967). *The dynamics of compliance: Supreme Court decision-making from a new perspective.* Evanston, IL: Northwestern University Press.

Kaminer, D. (2002). Bringing organized prayer in through the back door: How moment-of-silence legislation for the public schools violates the Establishment Clause. *Stanford Law & Policy Review, 13,* 267–322.

Kirakofe, C. R. (2009). Pretending not to pray: A historical overview of moment of silence legislation and why Illinois' statue clearly violated the *Lemon* test. *Education Law Reporter, 241,* 1–21.

Lam, L. D. (2003). Silence of the lambs: Are states attempting to establish religion in public schools? *Vanderbilt Law Review, 56,* 911–937.

Mawdsley, R. D. (2009). One minute of required silence in Texas classrooms: The Fifth Circuit upholds the state's Moment of Silence Amendments. *Education Law Reporter, 246,* 589–606.

National Conference of State Legislatures. (2011). States with moment of silence or school prayer legislation [data file]. Retrieved from http://www.ncsl.org/IssuesResearch/Education/MomentofSilenceandSchoolPrayer/tabid/12828/Default.aspx

Rabe, L. A. (2004). A rose by any other name: Prayer defined as a moment of silence is still unconstitutional. *Denver University Law Review, 82,* 57–78.

Strasser, M. (2009) Religion in the schools: On prayer, neutrality, and sectarian perspectives. *Akron Law Review, 42,* 185–241.

Walsh, E. A. (2004). Shh! State legislators bite your tongues: Semantics dictate the constitutionality of public school "moment of silence" laws. *Catholic Lawyer, 43,* 225–254.

Court Cases and Statutes

Board of Education of Westside Community Schools v. Mergens, 496 U.S. 226 (1990).
Bown v. Gwinnett County School District, 112 F.3d 1464 (11th Cir. 1997).

Bown v. Gwinnett County School District, 258 F.3d 265 (4th Cir. 2001), *cert. denied,* 533 U.S. 1301 (2001).
Brown v. Board of Education of Topeka, 347 U.S. 483 (1954).
Brown v. Gilmore, 258 F.3d 265 (4th Cir. 2001), *cert. denied,* 533 U.S. 1301 (2001).
Croft v. Governor of Texas, 562 F.3d 735 (5th Cir. 2009).
Engel v. Vitale, 370 U.S. 421, 434 (1962).
Equal Access Act, 20 U.S.C. §§ 4071 *et seq.* (1984).
Good News Club v. Milford Central School, 533 U.S. 98 (2001).
Karcher v. May, 484 U.S. 72 (1987).
Lee v. Weisman, 505 U.S. 577 (1992).
Lemon v. Kurtzman 403 U.S. 602 (1971).
Lynch v. Donnelly, 465 U.S. 668 (1984).
May v. Cooperman, 780 F.2d 240 (3d Cir. 1985); *appeal dismissed sub nom.* Karcher v. May, 484 U.S. 72 (1987).
Santa Fe Independent School District v. Doe, 530 U.S. 290 (2000).
School District of Abington Township v. Schempp and Murray v. Curlett, 374 U.S. 203 (1963).
Sherman ex rel. Sherman v. Koch, 623 F.3d 501 (7th Cir. 2010), *cert. denied,*—U.S.—, 132 S.Ct. 92,—L.Ed.2d.—(2011).
U.S. Constitution. Amendment I.
Wallace v. Jaffree, 472 U.S. 38 (1985).
Wisconsin v. Yoder, 406 U.S. 205 (1972).

Should public school teachers be allowed to read the Bible or other sacred texts in public schools when students are present?

POINT: Regina R. Umpstead, *Central Michigan University*
COUNTERPOINT: Brenda Kallio, *University of North Dakota*

OVERVIEW

The Bible, more than any other sacred text, has played a major role in the history and development of American public education. In fact, as reflected by the discussion of litigation that follows, even as the United States is becoming increasingly religiously diverse, all but one of the cases dealing with sacred texts focused on the Bible. Moreover, the Bible was in the forefront of the major companion cases of *School District of Abington Township v. Schempp* and *Murray v. Curlett* (1963), disputes from Pennsylvania and Maryland, respectively, that played a major role in helping shape the Supreme Court's modern Establishment Clause jurisprudence.

In *Abington*, the Supreme Court created a two-part test in ruling that prayer and Bible reading, as part of the opening of a school day, violated the Establishment Clause. The Court ruled that insofar as the Bible is a sectarian document, the government, including public school officials, must be neutral with regard to religious matters in schools. The Court explained,

> The test may be stated as follows: what are the purpose and the primary effect of the [legislative] enactment? . . . [T]o withstand the strictures of

the Establishment Clause there must be a secular legislative purpose and a primary effect that neither advances nor inhibits religion. (p. 222)

Eight years after *Abington*, in its most significant case ever involving the Establishment Clause and education, *Lemon v. Kurtzman* (1971), the Supreme Court added a third prong to this test, forbidding excessive entanglement between religion and government. The Court has since applied the seemingly ubiquitous, and difficult to interpret, tripartite *Lemon* test in the vast majority of its cases involving religion and public education. Eventually, the Court devised additional tests that prohibit states, and their officials, from endorsing religion or coercing individuals to participate in religious activities.

As much litigation as American courts have resolved over issues involving religion and education, there has been only one reported case in which a teacher was forbidden from reading a Bible, his sacred text of choice, in his classroom. At issue in a dispute from Colorado was a poster that a fifth-grade teacher hung on a wall in his classroom displaying the message "You have only to open your eyes to see the hand of God," an in-class library collection he developed for his students, and his practice of leaving a Bible on his desk and reading from it as he walked around his classroom during silent reading time. As part of the controversy, the school's principal also removed copies of the Bible from the school library.

In a split 2–1 judgment, the Tenth Circuit affirmed that school officials did not violate the teacher's rights primarily under the Establishment or Free Speech Clauses. The court agreed that school officials had the authority to forbid the teacher's use of the Bible, however indirect, as he walked around his class; to remove the poster from the classroom wall; and to remove two books about the Bible and life of Jesus from the teacher's classroom library of "about 239 books of varying content that [he] had compiled over his nineteen-years of teaching" (*Roberts v. Madigan*, 1990, p. 1049). Yet, the court allowed other books in the classroom library dealing with Buddhism, Greek gods and goddesses, and Indian religions to remain on the shelves.

The Tenth Circuit affirmed not only that officials did not violate the teacher's rights but also that the Establishment Clause required them to take such actions. The court was of the opinion that insofar as the teacher walked around the room with his Bible, he could have unduly influenced his students. As such, the court decided that the teacher could not read the Bible as he walked around the classroom because his doing so might have had led the students to believe that he did so with the approval of the school board. However, the court agreed that the principal had to return the copies of the Bible to the school library since there was no basis for having them removed.

OVERVIEW: Chapter 6

In light of the dearth of litigation directly on the issue that could serve as guidance, it is not surprising that the essays in this chapter reach different outcomes over whether public school teachers should be allowed to read the Bible or other sacred texts in public schools when students are present. On the one hand, the point essay of Regina R. Umpstead (Central Michigan University) supports the position that public school teachers should be free to read the Bible or other sacred texts in their public schools. In her analysis, she examines American history and judicial decisions weighing the conflicting interests of teachers to free speech and religion against those of students and their parents to be free from potentially coercive activities. In balancing the equities, Umpstead concludes that as long as they are doing so of their own free will, teachers should have the right to read their Bibles or other sacred texts in public schools even if students are present.

On the other hand, in her counterpoint essay, Brenda Kallio (University of North Dakota) takes the position that teachers in public schools should not be permitted to read the Bible or other sacred texts in their public schools while students are present. In elucidating her position, she relies on a review of the history and development of the United States through its founding documents, most notably the federal Constitution, and case law in which the Supreme Court and lower courts have agreed that there can be no state-sponsored religious activities in public schools. Reiterating their right to do so as private citizens, Kallio adds that allowing teachers to read Bibles or other sacred texts while they are on duty as public school employees runs the risk of coercing children to share their beliefs in violation of the First Amendment.

As you read these essays, ask yourself the following three questions. First, is it appropriate for public school teachers to read the Bible or other sacred texts in their schools when their students are present? Second, does allowing teachers to read the Bible or other sacred texts in public schools run the risk of their unduly influencing or coercing students? Third, what do you think that teachers hope to accomplish as they read the Bible or other sacred texts while in their public schools?

Charles J. Russo
University of Dayton

POINT: Regina R. Umpstead
Central Michigan University

The idea that teachers should be allowed to read from the Bible or sacred texts of their religions during the school day seems self-evident to proponents of this view, who believe that such rights are guaranteed by the Constitution's First Amendment declaration that "Congress shall make no law respecting an establishment of religion, or prohibiting the free exercise thereof, or abridging the freedom of speech." Yet, the actions of teachers reading from their holy literature during the school day pits educators' freedom to exercise two of their First Amendment rights, religious beliefs and speech, against a third First Amendment principle, a school's concern over a potential Establishment Clause violation. The conflict between these principles creates the controversy at the heart of this debate.

This point essay asserts that proponents are correct in their understanding that teachers should be allowed to read from their holy literature of their religions during the school day. Contributing to this understanding is a healthy respect for America's commitment to protect religious freedoms from its foundation and the notion that religious literacy is crucial to developing an educated citizenry. This essay examines all three of the relevant clauses from the First Amendment that encourage religious freedom and freedom of speech while preventing school officials from promoting specific religions or religious views and requiring neutrality between those who believe in religion and those who do not believe in religion.

RELIGION'S CONTRIBUTIONS TO AMERICAN LIFE

Religion has played a major role in both the foundation of the United States and its educational system. To this end, the Free Exercise Clause is designed to protect the rights of individuals to exercise their religions freely within the boundaries of the law. Many of the initial British colonial inhabitants came to Colonial America to pursue religious autonomy and to have the ability to practice their own faiths. The Christian Calvinist beliefs held by many of the early settlers required that each person have an individual relationship with God. This belief motivated many to promote literacy among the colonists, so each person could read the Bible and interpret it for him- or herself. This desire was evident in the 1647 Massachusetts law, known as the Old Deluder Satan Act, that required towns of 50 families or more to establish schools. It was also apparent in the Northwest Ordinance of 1787 that was promulgated by the Second Continental Congress to charter the government for the Northwest Territory. This ordinance declared, "Religion, morality, and knowledge, being necessary to good government and the happiness of mankind, schools and the means of education shall forever be encouraged" (Baron, 1994, p. 86).

Religion continues to play a crucial role in the lives of Americans. The United States is a diverse nation as represented by the varied racial, ethnic, cultural, and religious backgrounds of its people. The nation thrives on the free exchange of ideas and a respect for differing opinions. Many of these divergent viewpoints are based on individuals' religious convictions. One of the major ways people make sense of the world is through religion. It influences how people think and act. It shapes the way people live their lives in their attitudes and expectations for community, work, marriage, and family life. This is also true for people around the world, and so as our world becomes more interconnected, it becomes increasingly important to understand the diversity of the nations and cultures with which we interact.

American public schools are the places where children are taught shared civic values and where they are prepared to assume their roles in society as adults. The key goals of our educational system include preparing students to become adults who possess an understanding of basic academic subjects such as mathematics, science, and history; teaching them about the world around them; and training them to interact with others in a complex and rapidly changing society. Schools have embraced these goals by introducing 21st century skills and by implementing a diversity focus in their curricula to build the awareness and acceptance of different cultures. Some schools have also adopted this approach toward religious diversity.

To develop an educated citizenry, it is important that all citizens acquire basic knowledge of the key tenets and stories of the world's major religious faiths. Knowledge of other religions is important for three reasons: History is replete with events motivated by religion and religious works and references; America's democratic government is based on understanding and interacting with diverse viewpoints; and the global community consists of peoples with various national, ethnic, and religious backgrounds.

National and world histories contain numerous events that were motivated by religion, many classical works are based on religion, and our popular culture continues to reflect religion's influence. References to the Bible are common in classic art and literature and in popular culture. The work of Rembrandt, Da Vinci, Shakespeare, John Milton, Herman Melville, and Ernest Hemingway all contain references to the Bible. Biblical references are evident in movies such as *Red Dragon*, *Magnolia*, *Mission Impossible*, *Pulp Fiction*, and *Deep Impact*. Similarly, depictions of the Islamic faith are present in the films *My Son the Fanatic*, *Robin Hood: Prince of Thieves*, and *The 13th Warrior*. Thus, being familiar with religious texts provides the person viewing these works with a deeper understanding of their meaning.

By affording citizens the right to practice differing faiths, the Constitution created an environment for a strong, pluralistic democracy, but this requires citizens who are able to listen to and respect the voices of those with whom they differ and disagree. The laws governing American society could not be made, followed, or enforced if citizens were unable or unwilling to examine the viewpoints of others and compromise in matters of governance. These differing voices and viewpoints represent the various racial, cultural, and religious backgrounds of the American people. This commitment to a democratic form of government, initiated at the founding of our nation, specifically includes the notion that respecting religious voices is vital. As evidenced by the religion clauses of the First Amendment, this commitment should be reflected in the education of our nation's children so that they become citizens who are able to participate fully in our civil society.

Living in our global community expands our need for understanding different cultures as we interact with other nations in business and political matters. The post-9/11 world is increasingly interconnected, and many significant events that take place both around the world and in the United States are religiously motivated. Students should have at least a summary knowledge of the world's five major religions—Judaism, Christianity, Islam, Hinduism, and Buddhism—to better understand the world's sociopolitical climate and foster respect and understanding among peoples. When dealing with religion, as with many other topics in life, knowledge is power because it provides individuals with the ability to engage in constructive dialogue while seeking to avoid religious misunderstanding and conflicts, which continue to plague our multifaith world.

LEGAL FRAMEWORK

Now that the importance of including religious literacy as an aspect of established curricula has been acknowledged, this essay turns its attention to the legal framework of this debate. As mentioned, teachers' religious expression is governed by three prominent clauses of the First Amendment: the Establishment Clause, the Free Speech Clause, and the Free Exercise of Religion Clause. These clauses are the framework under which the question of whether teachers should be allowed to read from their religion's holy literature during the school day would be subject to judicial scrutiny.

Free Exercise

The Free Exercise Clause was intended to prevent governmental regulation of religious beliefs. The Supreme Court explained the scope of the Free Exercise Clause in *Employment Division, Department of Human Resources of Oregon v. Smith* (1990) as follows:

> The government may not compel affirmation of religious belief, punish the expression of religious doctrines it believes to be false, impose special disabilities on the basis of religious views or religious status, or lend its power to one or the other side in controversies over religious authority or dogma. (p. 877)

Yet, in *Smith*, the Court ruled that the state could limit the Free Exercise rights of Native American drug counselors to ingest peyote, a recognized sacrament in their faith. To this end, the Court concluded that public officials could fire the counselors even though they were exercising their deeply held religious beliefs because the latter conflicted with state law.

The Free Speech Clause protects individuals' right of expression. Moreover, it is well established that teachers do not "shed their constitutional rights to freedom of speech or expression at the schoolhouse gate" (*Tinker v. Des Moines Independent Community School District*, 1969, p. 506). Even so, the extent to which the First Amendment protects the religious rights of teachers while working in the public schools may be limited to further a compelling government interest.

School boards use their concern over potential Establishment Clause violations to justify the actions they take to limit teachers' religious expression. The Establishment Clause requires public school boards, as arms of their states, to be neutral toward religion. It is commonly described as creating a "wall of separation" between church and state, a metaphor borrowed from Thomas Jefferson and a principle that was introduced in school settings in *Everson v. Board of Education* (1947).

The *Lemon v. Kurtzman* (1971) test, one that courts typically employ in disputes over religion, declares that schools must have a secular or nonreligious purpose for their actions, may neither advance nor inhibit religion, and cannot be excessively entangled with religion. Courts also consider whether students could view the actions of teachers as endorsements of religion or whether children are coerced to participate in religious exercises in evaluating claims under the Establishment Clause.

Teachers who oppose these limitations argue that their free speech and free exercise rights should not be restricted. These teachers rely on the Free Exercise Clause to prevent the government from discriminating against them because of their religious practices and beliefs.

Freedom of Speech

Teachers also rely on the Free Speech Clause to guard their right to express their opinions and ideas. Free exercise claims arise when the actions of a school board burden the religious conduct of teachers. Courts thus balance the interests of school boards against the extent that their actions impair the sincere and legitimate religious beliefs of teachers. Courts must evaluate whether boards can regulate the expressive conduct of teachers by considering whether the actions of officials are "reasonably related to legitimate pedagogical concerns" as described in *Hazelwood v. Kuhlmeier* (1988, p. 273). Alternatively, courts address whether the interests of boards in promoting the efficiency of educational services outweighs the interests of teachers in speaking on matters of public concern as explained in *Pickering v. Board of Education* (1968).

The courts have rendered numerous judgments about religious speech in public schools. From these judicial decisions, it is clear that school boards cannot conduct schoolwide prayer or Bible reading as part of opening exercises or invite clergy members to offer nonsectarian prayers at graduation since these activities are religious in nature and thereby violate the Establishment Clause by promoting or endorsing religion or coercing students to participate in religious exercises. However, despite earlier case law to the contrary, more recent litigation has upheld minute-of-silence statutes that have allowed students to reflect quietly in the wake of high-profile violent acts in public schools as permissible even if students choose to use the time for silent prayer because it has a secular purpose and does not promote religion.

While the courts generally frown on schoolwide statements of faith by teachers or administrators, individual expressions of faith have received a warmer reception. Yet, the courts have permitted teachers to opt out of the Pledge of Allegiance because of their religious beliefs as long as arrangements are made for the students to participate in the pledge. Courts have reached mixed results over whether teachers can wear religious garb to work. For instance, one court ruled in favor of an instructional assistant who wore a cross necklace to school while another forbade a teacher from wearing a shirt with a religious message to school. Further, in a case discussed below, the Eighth Circuit reasoned that a teacher was able to attend an after-school religious group in the library of the elementary school where she taught. However, the courts have consistently rejected teachers' attempts to alter curricula by adding religious components or ignoring aspects that conflict with their religious beliefs.

At the same time, school boards have introduced courses that teach students about world religions and examine the Bible as literature. These courses, when objectively presented as part of a secular course may, subject to judicial review, be consistent with the schools' goals of creating an educated citizenry. Justice Robert Jackson, in his concurring opinion in *McCollum v. Board of Education of School District No. 71* (1948), wherein the Supreme Court invalidated a policy that allowed religious leaders to enter public schools to provide religious instruction, noted, "The fact is, for good or for ill, nearly everything in our culture worth transmitting, everything which gives meaning to life, is saturated with religious influences" (p. 236). He went on to add, "One can hardly respect a system of education that would leave the student wholly ignorant of the currents of religious thought that move the world society for a part in which he is being prepared" (p. 236).

A case of some relevance to teacher Bible reading arose in South Dakota. It involved the interplay between freedom of speech and freedom of religion. A teacher challenged a trial court order that she could not participate in the meetings of a Good News Club, an organization devoted to student prayer and Bible study, that gathered in her school after the class day had ended. The court had allowed the teacher to take part in meetings but not at her own school. Reversing in favor of the teacher, the Eighth Circuit held the teacher's after-school participation amounted to private speech over which the school board had no control. The court pointed out that the after-school participation in her own school did not put the board at risk of violating the Establishment Clause (*Wigg v. Sioux Falls School District 49–5*, 2004). In the same way, private reading from religious texts should be so protected.

Balancing First Amendment Rights

Having examined the legal landscape of the First Amendment and the decisions governing teachers' rights of free exercise and free speech in public schools, this point essay returns to the question of whether teachers should be allowed to read from their religion's holy literature during the school day. What is known is that school boards are concerned that teacher references to religion may create the appearance that the school is violating the Establishment Clause by promoting or endorsing either that specific religion or religion in general. What is also clear is that the Free Exercise Clause may allow teachers the right to wear religious symbols such as a Star of David necklace and religious clothing depending on the factual circumstances because not all courts agree on whether doing so can pass constitutional muster. The question then becomes whether teachers may silently read religious text during their lunch periods, student recesses, or even silent reading time while school is in session as an acceptable form of religious expression. This essay advances the position that the Free Exercise and Free Speech Clauses afford teachers this individual right.

As reflected in the counterpoint essay, opponents of this view claim that this question has already been answered by the Tenth Circuit in *Roberts v. Madigan* (1990). Here, the Tenth Circuit affirmed that school officials could require a fifth-grade teacher to remove a Bible from his desk and refrain from reading it during silent reading time based on the fear of a potential Establishment Clause violation. Yet, *Madigan* involved more than just the silent reading of a religious text at school. In reaching its decision, the court looked to the totality of the environment established in the classroom, which included two Christian books that the teacher placed in his in-class library, a poster referencing God, and the fact that he always kept the Bible on his desk. Therefore, *Madigan* is distinguishable from situations where teachers merely read religious texts during the school day.

Permitting teachers to read from sacred texts during school days is merely a private choice of reading material, not a government endorsement of religion. This fact is clear when teachers choose to engage in this activity outside the presence of students such as in the teachers' lounge or when students are not present in classrooms. However, it is still true when students are in classrooms as teachers silently read religious texts. This situation is similar to the silent expression wherein supporters of such an approach might argue the teachers should have the right to choose their manner of dress including the wearing of religious symbols.

What is more, students are allowed to read religious texts during the school day, and, in fact, they are even encouraged to do so in specified courses because of the significant role religion has played in American history and culture as well as its importance in preparing students to participate both in our pluralistic society and our complex, multifaith world. Teachers who choose to read from religious texts are selecting one of the world's most influential texts as they model reading to their students. This is an important and legitimate value to advance.

CONCLUSION

Since public school teachers retain their free exercise and free speech rights while serving in their professional roles, and since religious literacy is a significant educational goal, a compelling argument can be made that teachers' reading of sacred texts without additional religious activities should be considered an individual choice, not a school's promotion of a specific religious viewpoint. Thus, teachers should be allowed to read from their sacred literature of their religions during the school day even if students are present.

COUNTERPOINT: Brenda Kallio
University of North Dakota

Insofar as many of the Europeans who immigrated to the Americas did so to avoid the religious persecutions that raged in their native countries, the role that religion was to take in the lives of the fledgling country's government was a matter of critical importance. Among these early immigrants, some colonists, the Erastians, held the position that government should assume a position of authority and that ecclesiastical matters should not promote governmental action. While the Erastian point of view was held by the majority of the colonists, a group known as Theocrats strongly believed religion should be the primary consideration and that government should serve the purpose of the church.

From this brief description of the tension between these two philosophical positions in the early days of what became the United States, it should be evident that religion has played a significant role in the development of our country from its very inception. In light of the role that religion continues to play in American life and its public schools, the question at issue in this essay is whether teachers should be allowed to read from the Bible or other sacred texts during the school day in the presence of children. This issue goes to the very core of the rights of American citizens to either express their own religious beliefs or be exempt from the governmental expressions of religion.

This counterpoint essay supports the proposition that teachers should not be allowed to read from their sacred texts of their religions during the school day when students are present. To definitively prove this position, one needs to establish parameters and develop the argument step by step. In doing so, this essay reviews the nation's early history and selected legal documents created by the Founding Fathers. Then, by applying those early legal premises, the essay responds appropriately to the validity of the statement that teachers should not be allowed to read from sacred texts in public schools when students are present.

ARGUMENT PARAMETERS

To clarify the parameters of this argument, it is important to agree on the following points. "Teachers should not be allowed to read from their religion's sacred texts during the school day when students are present" means that teachers should not be allowed to have sacred texts visibly in their possession during the school day. It also means that teachers should not be permitted to read from sacred texts when students are present even during such times as lunch in the school cafeteria or silent reading segments of class periods.

EARLY HISTORY

To prove that teachers should not be allowed to read from their religion's sacred texts during the school day, it is important to consider the historical development of the U.S. legal framework. While in school, most Americans should have learned how the colonial delegates set about developing our country's legal framework, which, as discussed below, addressed the place of religion. Initially, most students were taught about the First Continental Congress in 1774, where delegates, claiming the British government had violated citizen's inalienable rights, developed a list of complaints against the British government. Americans also learned about the Second Continental Congress in 1775, where delegates from the 13 colonies developed the Articles of Confederation, the document that served as this country's Constitution until 1789. Next, students learned that in May 1787, 55 delegates met in Philadelphia to create the document that ultimately replaced the Articles of Confederation and became the United States' second, and current, constitution. That newly created document, the Constitution, has been the bedrock of the country's legal jurisprudence since its adoption.

The development of the Constitution was not without controversy, as the delegates divided into two philosophically diverse groups. One group, the Federalists, believed that a Bill of Rights was implied within the Constitution. As such, they favored ratifying the Constitution without additions or changes. The second group, the Anti-Federalists, claimed that, as exemplified by recent British violations of individual civil rights, any constitution that specified the powers held by the central government but did not outline the powers denied to that government would ultimately lead to tyrannical government. An example of the strong Anti-Federalists' position and their fear of government intervention can be seen in correspondences between Thomas Jefferson and James Madison in which they agreed that citizens are entitled to a bill of rights and that no just government should refuse to specify those rights.

Anti-Federalist sentiments were so strong that the colonies of Virginia, Massachusetts, South Carolina, New Hampshire, and New York openly opposed ratifying the Constitution until it included a Bill of Rights. However, the delegates reached a gentlemen's agreement that following ratification of the Constitution, they would reconvene and add a Bill of Rights. Largely inspired by Jefferson and Madison, and after 4 years of arduous debate, the American Bill of Rights was adopted in 1791. Because of the power and influence of the

Anti-Federalists, the American people have a guarantee that governmental power over specified individual rights is prohibited.

APPLICATION OF LEGAL PREMISES

Having established that the Constitution grants power to a central government and the Bill of Rights, contained in its first 10 amendments, is designed to limit the government's ability to inhibit specified individual rights, this essay returns to the assertion that teachers should not be allowed to read from their religion's sacred texts during the school day when children are present. This limitation can be seen clearly within the first of the Constitutional amendments, wherein the Founding Fathers clearly stated, "Congress shall make no law respecting an establishment of religion." This clause forms the framework under which the position that teachers should not be allowed to read from their religion's sacred texts during the school day has been analyzed by the American judicial system for hundreds of years.

In other words, the First Amendment, one of our country's most seminal, historical documents, clearly declares that the federal government is not allowed to engage in activities to establish a national religion. In addition to the First Amendment limits on the government's ability to establish religion, the Ninth Amendment states, "The enumeration in the Constitution, of certain rights, shall not be construed to deny or disparage others retained by the people." Thus, by placing limitations on the ability of the federal government to establish a national religion, coupled with the wording of the Ninth Amendment, which states that the rights contained within the Constitution are not to be used to deny or disparage individual rights, it appears the creators of the Bill of Rights believed very strongly in the need to protect citizens from mandatory, governmentally imposed religion at the federal level.

Since the Tenth Amendment relegates public education to the states, one must ask whether the restrictions imposed by the Bill of Rights on the federal government apply to the states. More importantly for this discussion, one must consider whether the protections of the Bill of Rights apply to state agencies such as public schools. To begin analysis of these questions, it is important to examine the implications of the Fourteenth Amendment, according to which in pertinent part,

> No State shall make or enforce any law which shall abridge the privileges or immunities of citizens of the United States; nor shall any State deprive any person of life, liberty, or property, without due process of law; nor deny to any person within its jurisdiction the equal protection of the laws.

In the late 1800s, the courts entertained the question of whether the Fourteenth Amendment was intended to make the freedoms guaranteed in the Bill of Rights applicable to state governments. Since the lower courts were not in agreement about the legal relationship between the Fourteenth Amendment and the Bill of Rights, the Supreme Court agreed to hear *Twining v. State of New Jersey* (1908) in which Justice William Henry Moody wrote, "The 14th Amendment withdrew from the states' powers theretofore enjoyed by them to an extent not yet fully ascertained, or rather, to speak more accurately, limited those powers and restrained their exercise" (pp. 16–17). Later, in *Adamson v. California* (1947), the Supreme Court ruled that insofar as state and national citizenship coexist within a person, a state does not have the authority to remove protections guaranteed at the national level. While these two cases provided insight into judicial interpretation, it was in the landmark cases of *Cantwell v. Connecticut* (1940) and *Everson v. Board of Education* (1947) that the Supreme Court clearly asserted that just as the First Amendment limits the federal government's rights to restrict individual freedoms, the First Amendment is also binding on state governments.

The question, then, is answered in the affirmative. The First Amendment prohibits the federal government from establishing a national religion and it applies to the states through the Fourteenth Amendment. Ergo, the Bill of Rights, as applied through the Fourteenth Amendment, prohibits public schools from establishing religions. Even so, there is one more step to consider to be sure that the position asserting that teachers should not be allowed to read from the Bible or sacred texts during the school day in the presence of students is legally correct.

A review of Supreme Court cases demonstrates its consistent stance that governmental advancement of religion is strictly forbidden. For example, in the 1962, in *Engel v. Vitale*, at the behest of parents, the Court struck down a state-sponsored prayer on the basis that school officials lacked the authority to require students to participate in such an activity.

In the 1963 companion cases of *School District of Abington Township, Pennsylvania v. Schempp* and *Murray v. Curlett*, the Supreme Court agreed that it was inappropriate for school officials to conduct morning ceremonies that included readings from the Bible and the recitation of the Lord's Prayer or Our Father. Focusing on the first of these disputes for the moment, the facts revealed that schools in the Abington Township school district that did not have a public address system. Consequently, the teachers either read the Bible verses and led the students in the Lord's Prayer/Our Father or asked a student to lead the class in the activities. In both *Abington* and *Murray*, the Court reiterated that the schools' involvement in the religious activities exceeded what was permissible under the Establishment Clause. In *Abington*, the Court pointed out that any interpretation that the Establishment Clause is limited to forbidding the government to establish a religion is faulty, as that interpretation does not include the second, and critical, component that the government may not participate in activity that promotes one religion or prefers one religion over another. Thus, since 1963, the Supreme Court has made it clear that teachers' leading or participating in religious activities in the presence of students is a direct violation of the Establishment Clause.

It is this promotion of religion that proves to be the final nail in the proverbial coffin for teachers' rights to read from the Bible or sacred texts in the presence of students. Further, a review of litigation to the present day demonstrates the Court's position that teachers, as government employees, are forbidden to participate in religious activities during the school day and in the presence of students.

In 1971, the Supreme Court noted in *Lemon v. Kurtzman* that a determination as to whether there is a violation of the Jeffersonian "wall of separation" between church and state was to be based on a three-prong test that some courts continue to apply: Every analysis in this area must begin with consideration of the cumulative criteria developed by the Court over many years. Three such tests may be gleaned from our cases. First, the statute must have a secular legislative purpose; second, its principal or primary effect must be one that neither advances nor inhibits religion; finally, the statute must not foster "an excessive government entanglement with religion" (pp. 612–613).

Even a cursory understanding of *Lemon* shows that if school boards allow teachers to read from their sacred texts during the school day and especially in the presence of children, they violate, at a minimum, two of the *Lemon* prongs, namely, the lack of a secular purpose and the ban against advancing religion.

Over time, the Supreme Court relied less and less on the *Lemon* test. In *Lee v. Weisman* (1992), in invalidating school-sponsored graduation prayer, the Court began using the concept of "coercion" as its basis for decision making in religion cases. Adopting the philosophy of coercion, the Court was of the opinion that it was inappropriate that persons be, even minimally, required to participate in religious activities to receive a governmentally guaranteed entitlement. For example, requiring students to participate, even passively, in adult-delivered prayers at graduation to receive their diploma is coercive and in violation of the Establishment Clause. If the Court has adamantly avowed that adult-led religious liturgy at graduation ceremonies is coercive, it is reasonable to understand their position on teachers' reading religious literature in the direct presence of students would be equally as so. After all, what could be more coercive than requiring a child to watch (or listen to) a role model read religious materials to get a public education?

Reading the Bible during the school day in the presence of students was one of the primary questions posed in *Roberts v. Madigan* (1990), a case from Colorado. The Tenth Circuit affirmed the unconstitutionality of a fifth-grade teacher's practice of reading from the Bible he kept on top of his classroom desk while he walked around the room as students silently read at their desks. The court decided that the teacher's actions violated the Establishment Clause because they had the effect of promoting Christianity to a group of students who were required to be present during the time he read from his Bible. The court added that the teacher's act was coercive and created the appearance the he was advancing his personal religious views.

In responding to the point essay's belief that teachers should be able to read the Bible in the presence of their students, it is important to once again review American history. Although American history is laden with discussions regarding the positions of both the Erastians and the Theocrats, our forefathers ultimately chose to build our country on Thomas Jefferson's philosophy of separatism. This position supports the belief that the function of government and the practice of religion play two entirely different roles in citizens' lives. Although the case was decided almost 100 years after the founding of our country, the Supreme Court's support of separatism can be seen in *Reynolds v. United States* (1879), the first time that the Court applied the Jeffersonian metaphor. Here, in rejecting a challenge to a federal antipolygamy statute, the Court found that it was unconstitutional to allow individual states to permit the professed doctrines of their religious beliefs superior to the law of the land because this would have permitted citizens to create their own set of laws thus rendering government nonexistent. Looking back at the more than 200 years since the inception of the United States, it takes little imagination to see the regressive path that the country would have taken had Americans allowed themselves to neglect the tenets of the Establishment Clause and separatism.

When the point essay tries to make the argument that teachers should be allowed to read from their Bible based on the outcomes of cases that are only tangentially related to the act of reading the Bible or other sacred texts during the school day in the presence of children, readers must be cautioned not to be taken in. Readers should go back to the basics, to the Constitution as a whole, the Bill of Rights, and the Fourteenth Amendment, and remember that those who created the United States strongly believed in (and created laws aimed at) preventing state and federal governments from establishing or promoting religion.

Teachers are, of course, free to read their Bibles and other sacred texts in their roles as private citizens. However, during their contract time as public employees, the law specifically forbids teachers from proselytizing or promoting their faiths, however indirectly they may be doing so. Thus, teachers should put down their Bibles or other sacred texts and adhere to the secular curricula they were hired (and agreed) to teach.

CONCLUSION

The Anti-Federalists fought for, won, and created a Bill of Rights that soon became part of the Constitution. The First Amendment of the Bill of Rights prohibits the federal government from establishing a national religion. The Fourteenth Amendment extends the First Amendment to apply those same prohibitions to the states. *School District of Abington Township Pennsylvania v. Schempp* iterates that in addition to prohibiting the establishment of a governmentally supported religion, the First Amendment also prohibits states from promoting religion. The principles of the *Lemon* test require that the actions of educational officials must have a secular legislative purpose, a principal or primary effect that neither advances nor inhibits religion and avoids excessive entanglement between religion and the state, while other measures forbid the endorsement of religion or coercing others to believe. In addition, *Roberts v. Madigan* demonstrates the judicial system's commitment to prohibiting state-sponsored activities that are either coercive or that provide the imprimatur of government support of religion.

Based on the foregoing analysis, permitting teachers to read from the Bible or other sacred texts during school hours in the presence of students is the quintessential example of what some of the Founding Fathers and judicial system have fought diligently to stop. More specifically, in light of American legal history and tradition, the government, in the form of public school board officials, cannot impose religion on this country's citizens, particularly those who are most vulnerable to being influenced: impressionable students who are little more than members of captive audiences in their public school classrooms, should their teachers wish to read from sacred literature in their presence.

FURTHER READINGS AND RESOURCES

American Civil Liberties Union (ACLU). (2002). *The Bill of Rights: A brief history.* Retrieved from http://www.aclu.org/racial-justice_prisoners-rights_drug-law-reform_immigrants-rights/bill-rights-brief-history

Baron, R. C. (Ed.). (1994). *Soul of America: Documenting our past: Vol. 1. 1492–1870.* Golden, CO: North American Press.

Mawdsley, R. D. (1996). Religious issues and public school instruction: The search for neutrality. *Education Law Reporter, 167,* 573–588.

Mawdsley, R. D., & Russo, C. J. (1996). Religious expression and teacher control of the classroom: A new battleground for free speech. *Education Law Reporter, 107,* 1–14.

Nash, R. J., & Bishop, P. A. (2010). *Teaching adolescents religious literacy in a post-9/11 world*. Charlotte, NC: Information Age Publishing Inc.

Nord, W. A., & Haynes, C. C. (1998). *Taking religion seriously across the curriculum*. Alexandria, VA: Association for Supervision and Curriculum Development.

Russo, C. J. (2004). The religious free speech rights of public school teachers: *Wigg v. Sioux Falls School District 49–5. Religion & Education, 31*(2), 98–106.

Witte, J. (2003, January 3). *Overview: Religious liberty in America*. First Amendment Center. Retrieved from http://www.firstamendmentcenter.org/overview-religious-liberty-in-america

COURT CASES AND STATUTES

Adamson v. California, 332 U.S. 46 (1947).

Cantwell v. Connecticut, 310 U.S. 296 (1940).

Employment Division, Department of Human Resources of Oregon v. Smith, 494 U.S. 872 (1990).

Engel v. Vitale, 370 U.S. 421 (1962).

Everson v. Board of Education, 330 U.S. 1 (1947), *reh'g denied*, 330 U.S. 855 (1947).

Hazelwood School District v. Kuhlmeier, 484 U.S. 260 (1988).

Lee v. Weisman, 505 U.S. 577 (1992).

Lemon v. Kurtzman, 403 U.S. 602 (1971).

McCollum v. Board of Education of School District No. 71, 333 U.S. 203 (1948).

Pickering v. Board of Education, 391 U.S. 563 (1968).

Reynolds v. United States, 98 U.S. 145 (1879).

Roberts v. Madigan, 921 F.2d 1047 (10th Cir. 1990), *cert. denied*, 505 U.S. 1218 (1992).

School District of Abington Township v. Schempp and Murray v. Curlett, 374 U.S. 203, 300 (1963).

Sherbert v. Verner, 374 U.S. 398 (1963).

Tinker v. Des Moines Independent Community School District, 393 U.S. 503 (1969).

Twining v. State of New Jersey, 211 U.S. 78 (1908).

Wigg v. Sioux Falls School District 49–5, 382 F.3d 807 (8th Cir. 2004).

Should school officials be allowed to use religious or sacred music in celebrations in public schools?

POINT: Allison S. Fetter-Harrott, *Franklin College*
COUNTERPOINT: Emily Richardson, *Indiana University*

OVERVIEW

In light of the long-held notion that "one who sings prays twice," it should come as no surprise that the use of religious or sacred music in American public schools has spawned controversy that has led to litigation. As reflected in the following debate in this chapter, discussion on whether officials in public schools can permit religious or sacred music must be contextualized in the broader picture of the place of religion in public education.

Beginning with its first case forbidding public school officials from allowing religious leaders to enter public schools to conduct religious education classes for members of their own faiths in *People of State of Illinois ex rel. McCollum v. Board of Education of School District No. 71, Champaign County* (1948), the Supreme Court has largely prohibited school-sponsored use of prayer and religious activities in public schools. Yet, even though the Court prohibited such activities as prayer and Bible readings in public schools as impermissible forms of religious activity, it has yet to address the place of sacred music. As such, lower courts continue to grapple with the constitutionality of using religious or sacred music as part of public school celebrations.

During an initial round of litigation that ended in the 1990s, a federal trial (*Clever v. Cherry Hill Township Board of Education*, 1993), joined by the Fifth (*Doe v. Duncanville Indep. School District*, 1993), Eighth (*Florey v. Sioux Falls School District*, 1980a, 1980b), and Tenth (*Bauchman v. West High School*, 1997, 1998) Circuits, permitted the officials to use religious or sacred music in public schools. These courts generally agreed that the religious music could be used under policies that satisfied the three-part *Lemon v. Kurtzman* (1971) test. Under this test, governmental actions or policies must have a secular legislative purpose, must have a principal or primary effect that neither advances nor inhibits religion, and cannot result in excessive entanglement between government and religion. More specifically, the courts were content that uses of the music were acceptable since religious or secular music was part of a class or activity on the history of music or was designed to teach about choral singing. Earlier, the Supreme Court of Florida (*Chamberlin v. Dade County Board of Public Instruction*, 1962) affirmed the constitutionality of a state statute that permitted the singing of religious hymns in public schools.

Starting in the late 1990s, though, the judiciary interpreted the use of religious or sacred music as violations of the Establishment Clause in the First Amendment to the Constitution under the *Lemon* test. To this end, a federal trial court (*M.D. v. St. Johns County School District*, 2009), joined by the Second (*Marchi v. Board of Cooperative Educational Services of Albany Schoharie, Schenectady, and Saratoga Counties*, 1999a, 1999b), Third (*Stratechuk v. Board of Education, South Orange-Maplewood School District*, 2009, 2010), and Ninth (*Nurre v. Whitehead*, 2009, 2010) Circuits, forbade the use of religious or sacred music in public schools.

In light of this ongoing controversy, the point essay by Allison S. Fetter-Harrott (Franklin College) stands for the proposition that educational officials should be allowed to use religious or sacred music in celebrations in public schools. After tracing the application of the tripartite *Lemon* test in the earlier cases, Fetter-Harrott maintains that religious or sacred music should be allowed in public schools because it can contribute a great deal to public schools' secular educational mission by helping students to learn valuable lessons about significant historical periods and events as well as about different cultural and national groups.

Conversely, the counterpoint essay of Emily Richardson (Indiana University) responds that educational officials should not be allowed to use religious or sacred music in celebrations in public schools because doing so violates the Establishment Clause. Relying on a combination of judicial review and policy analysis, Richardson concludes that forbidding the use of such music not only protects the rights of minorities but allows valuable time to be used for academic purposes rather than religious ends while making schools more inviting places for all, regardless of their religious beliefs or lack thereof.

As you read these essays about the use of religious or sacred music in public school celebrations, ask yourself the following questions. First, do you think that public school officials should be able to allow religious or sacred music to be used in celebrations in public schools? Second, if religious music is excluded from public schools regardless of the context, such as music history classes, can one make a persuasive argument that doing so communicates a message of hostility, under the guise of neutrality, to religion that children, and their parents, can sense? Third, should anything be done to restore a sense of religious neutrality apart from excluding sacred or religious music from public schools, especially where the music has essentially become secularized from its widespread use in popular culture?

Charles J. Russo
University of Dayton

POINT: Allison S. Fetter-Harrott
Franklin College

There is a significant place for the appropriate and educational inclusion of religious or sacred music in celebrations in public school. During many periods in history, religious and sacred music have been the prevailing genre or have provided unique cultural reflections of specific times, movements, or cultures. Moreover, the religious musical tradition of various historical and contemporary groups, even nations, provides unique perspective on the beliefs, characters, and practices of peoples. Additionally, some religious music typifies specific musical styles or offers unique opportunities to young students to build musical skills. As such, religious and sacred music can contribute a great deal to the educational mission of today's American public schools.

It is understandable that in today's context, many educational leaders might be unsure about the extent to which, if at all, religious and sacred music can be integrated into public school celebrations. Even so, school administrators should keep in mind the tightrope that our public schools walk daily. On the one hand, school leaders have a duty to respect appropriate separation between the missions and functions of religious and governmental institutions, a responsibility arising under the Establishment Clause of the First Amendment to the Constitution, which states, "Congress shall make no law respecting an establishment of religion." On the other hand, educational officials likewise have a duty to respect the rights of students to believe in and practice the religious faiths of their choice, a right that emerges from the First Amendment's Free Exercise Clause: "Congress shall make no law . . . prohibiting the free exercise thereof."

Conflict thus arises when religious music is included in school curricula to further legitimate nonreligious educational aims as there is debate over the constitutional place for such material in public schools. This point essay explains how courts have analyzed and found constitutional the inclusion of religious music in schools in cases challenging such action under both the Establishment Clause and the Free Exercise Clause of the First Amendment. This essay concludes that educational officials should be allowed to use religious or sacred music in celebrations in public schools.

ESTABLISHMENT CLAUSE JURISPRUDENCE

The Establishment Clause doctrine established by the Supreme Court has been anything but a straight and predictable path. Rather, even the justices themselves acknowledge that decisions on the meaning and contours of the Establishment

Clause have trod a winding and sometimes uncertain terrain. At the same time, the Court has never had occasion to rule directly on the question of whether the performance of religious music violates the religion clauses of the First Amendment as does school-sponsored prayer. Analysis of the Court's opinions on similar questions and of federal appellate and trial court opinions as well as the limited state litigation on religious and sacred music in schools reveals that if presented in a context of valid secular curricular aims, the inclusion of such music in school performances and celebrations may likely be entirely in line with the spirit and letter of the First Amendment.

THE *LEMON* TEST

In *Lemon v. Kurtzman* (1971), the Supreme Court considered whether state statutory programs permitting public aid to support students in religiously affiliated nonpublic schools violated the Establishment Clause. Finding that these plans did, in fact, run afoul of the Constitution, the Court articulated its most enduring and criticized Establishment Clause test to evaluate whether the actions of public school officials abridge the boundaries of church–state relations established by its interpretation of the First Amendment. Under the *Lemon* test, to pass Establishment Clause scrutiny, government acts must have a secular legislative purpose, must have the principal or primary effect of neither advancing nor inhibiting religion, and cannot excessively entangle the government with religion.

The *Lemon* test is the most often applied standard that the Supreme Court, and lower courts, apply in addressing Establishment Clause disputes in the context of public schools. In addition, the *Lemon* test is widely considered the most searching standard applied in Establishment Clause jurisprudence, perhaps the least friendly to intermingling of religious and secular activities. Yet, in the disputes reviewing Establishment Clause challenges to the use of religious music in school celebrations, judicial analyses under *Lemon* have differed. Some courts have affirmed that the inclusion of such music under the right sets of circumstances is well within the boundaries of the First Amendment, while others have disagreed.

SECULAR PURPOSE

Some might argue that the inclusion of a piece of religious music in public school celebrations reveal the intent to use schools to proselytize in a manner prohibited by the Constitution. However, such a view ignores the significant role that religious pieces have in the field of music. In its opinion in *Bauchman v. West High School* (1997, 1998), rejecting a student's Establishment Clause challenge to a high school choir in Utah's use of religious music, the Tenth Circuit observed that its inclusion could be justified by a variety of secular purposes such as the fact that

> it is recognized that a significant percentage of serious choral music is based on religious themes or text. . . . Any choral curriculum designed to expose students to the full array of vocal music culture therefore can be expected to reflect a significant number of religious songs. (p. 554)

The court went on to add that

> a vocal music instructor would be expected to select any particular piece of sacred choral music, like any particular piece of secular choral music, in part for its unique qualities useful to teach a variety of vocal music skills (i.e., sight reading, intonation, harmonization, expression). (p. 554)

Earlier, the Fifth Circuit ruled that allowing a school choir in Texas to adopt the same song as was disputed in Utah as its theme song did not violate the Establishment Clause. The court was satisfied that allowing the song to be used did not violate the Constitution since officials had legitimate secular reasons for doing so insofar as it was useful to teach students to sight read music and sing a cappella. The court also agreed that the actions of educators neither advanced nor endorsed religion and that reaching any other outcome would have demonstrated hostility rather than neutrality on its part toward religion (*Doe v. Duncanville Independent School District*, 1993).

Accordingly, while the Establishment Clause might prohibit school officials from including religious music in celebrations if the intent is to proselytize to students, it is clear that there is a wide range of entirely secular and appropriate aims for including such music. The Establishment Clause does not require public schools to close their ears to the volumes of historically, culturally, and musically significant pieces simply because they happen to have religious context or hail from sacred beginnings. Rather, many may choose to include religious music in school celebrations for its cultural or musical value, and presentation of religious music for these reasons does not violate the "purpose" prong of the *Lemon* test.

EFFECT

As with the purpose inquiry of the *Lemon* test, it is entirely possible for officials in public schools to include religious or sacred music in school celebrations in a manner that does not have the primary effect of advancing (or inhibiting) religion. Recognizing the significant cultural and historical significance of religious-themed music to the field of music generally, the Eighth Circuit's decision in *Florey v. Sioux Falls School District* (1980a, 1980b) held that educational officials may include religious music in school performances without violating the "effects" prong of the *Lemon* test. Where such a performance is emblematic of a "genuine 'secular program of education'" (p. 1316), the court explained, such performances do not run afoul of the Establishment Clause.

At the same time, many kinds of religious or sacred music have gained value beyond solely religious perspectives and instead are observed as having cultural, patriotic, or other significances. Educational officials thus may present religious music as part of secular programs where it is used to teach students about musicianship, building capacity and skill. Additionally, religious or sacred music might be included in secular educational programs as ways of teaching students *about* religion from a secular world religions perspective. Religious music likewise might be used to illustrate the tone and arts of a given historical period, national tradition, or cultural group. Religious music might demonstrate for students a celebration of a diversity of cultures around the world or in a school community. When presented in this manner, religious music does not have the effect of advancing impermissibly one religion over others or even of advancing religious ideals over secular values. Rather, the inclusion of religious music in a school celebration that does so as a way of teaching students about important technical, historical, cultural, or other secular educational values provides a valuable lesson to students and does so in a manner entirely consistent with the Establishment Clause. To find otherwise would be unnecessarily to sacrifice the tremendous potential that such music can offer students.

EXCESSIVE ENTANGLEMENT

The final prong of analysis under the *Lemon* test requires consideration of whether presentations of religious music in school celebrations excessively entangle the government with religion. This argument is principally made in cases involving government aid to religiously affiliated nonpublic schools or where schools exert restrictions on the content of prayers made in school settings. This was the view of the federal trial court in New Jersey in *Clever v. Cherry Hill Township Board of Education* (1993). In *Clever*, the court upheld a policy from New Jersey permitting secular inclusion of religious music and other symbols in school holiday celebrations. The court was of the opinion that the policy did not create excessive entanglement between religion and the state because educational officials must make a bevy of content-specific curricular choices on religious and nonreligious topics. Finding that a policy permitting secular inclusion of religious music is unconstitutional would have the undesired effect of requiring schools to bolt their doors to *any* inclusion of such music. Such a reaction has not been required by any court.

FREE EXERCISE

There may be instances when the inclusion of religious music in a celebration might raise questions as to whether such performance violates the free exercise rights of students whose religious beliefs are different from those reflected in sacred musical pieces that they are about to study, perform, or be exposed to. In fact, in *Bauchman*, discussed earlier, the Tenth Circuit rejected the student's opposition to being exposed to a religious song.

Under the proper circumstances, then, the inclusion of religious or sacred music in school holiday celebrations may very likely comply with the Free Exercise Clause liberties of students and other members of educational communities. Admittedly, as with the Establishment Clause, some ambiguity exists in jurisprudence interpreting the Free Exercise Clause. Courts continue to debate which set of standards apply to Free Exercise challenges to school actions.

Even without resolving the question of exactly which test applies, some common guidelines can be discerned. First, courts have made clear that school officials are not compelled to remove all materials from curricula materials that might conflict with some religious doctrines. The Supreme Court long ago observed in its opinion in *People of State of Illinois ex rel. McCollum v. Board of Education of School District No. 71, Champaign County* (1948) that if we as a society burdened schools with the obligation to remove all references to religion, then "we will leave public education in shreds" (p. 235). Courts have generally agreed that the First Amendment forbids governmental entities such as school boards from taking actions targeted at suppressing religious exercise for its own sake. Yet, where apparently neutral school practices or rules are challenged under the Free Exercise Clause, at least one federal appellate court has applied a test that considers "'whether government has placed a substantial burden on the observation of a central religious belief or practice and, if so, whether a compelling governmental interest justifies the burden'" (*Altman v. Bedford Central School District*, 2001, p. 79, citing *Jimmy Swaggart Ministries v. Board of Equalization*, 1990, pp. 384–385).

Second, courts have ruled that permitting students to opt out of celebrations or ceremonies that they believe conflict with their religious beliefs can alleviate Free Exercise Clause challenges to school choir performances of religious pieces of music. Where religious music is performed as part of school celebrations designed to serve secular educational aims, it may indeed pose no true burden or little burden to the religious exercise of either audience members or performers.

Yet, even where such objections are raised, school officials may serve the interests of the community and the Free Exercise Clause by permitting students to opt out where performances interfere with their religious practice.

STATE CONSTITUTIONAL CHALLENGES

As the preceding discussion explains, the Federal Constitution has, until recently, typically been interpreted as permitting educational leaders in public schools to include religious or sacred music in nonproselytizing manners in celebrations for secular and educational reasons. In some cases, students or parents have asserted challenges to the inclusion of religious aspects into celebrations or curricula under state constitutional provisions as well.

In many states, but not all jurisdictions, state constitutional provisions limiting involvement between religion and government or prohibiting government intrusion into individual free religious exercise are coextensive with the Establishment Clause and the Free Exercise Clause of the First Amendment to the Constitution. However, since this is not always the case, educational leaders should work with counsel to understand the unique implications of their state's constitutions, if any, to the inclusion of religious or sacred music into a school's celebration or other curricular event. In fact, in one notable, early case, *Chamberlin v. Dade County Board of Public Instruction* (1962), the Supreme Court of Florida affirmed the constitutionality of a state statute that, among other practices, permitted the singing of religious hymns in public schools.

CONCLUSION

Educational leaders in public schools should be permitted to include religious or sacred music in school celebrations as long as doing so serves important secular educational aims. In fact, it is worth noting that religious music serves a variety of such aims. For an array of reasons, school leaders should be driven by the desire to unite their communities and to advance the educational aims of their programs. This means that educational leaders should foster environments that encourage knowledge of world history and cultures and that helps students understand the pluralist nature of our democracy. Inclusion of religious or secular music in public school celebrations that advances one or only a couple of faiths or that advances belief over nonbelief may very well pose a risk of divisiveness that the drafters of the First Amendment sought to avoid. Accordingly, teachers and other school leaders must thoughtfully proceed when determining whether to include religious or sacred music in the public school context.

The inclusion of religious or sacred music in school celebrations can help students learn valuable lessons about historical periods, significant events, and cultural and national groups. Additionally, across continents and cultures, the history of music itself is inextricably tied to the history of religious music. Of course, it is essential for educational officials to respect the appropriate boundaries between public schools and religious entities by avoiding the inclusion of religious music for proselytization. Still, educators should not be required to shut their eyes to the existence of the historical links between music and religion. Doing so might rob public school music students of valuable lessons regarding the history and body of music. While school boards may, therefore, avoid the use of religious or sacred music in celebrations and performances in an effort to serve the important aims of the Establishment Clause, a view that seeks to eradicate completely religious music from the domain of the public school, it may indeed be overly prophylactic and may assert a course of action that would deprive students of the secular pedagogical value of religious music. Thus, an overly prophylactic view does not serve the interests of the Establishment Clause since it would remove nonproselytizing musical performances and fall short of serving the teaching and learning interests of schools that including religious or secular music as appropriate would certainly advance.

COUNTERPOINT: Emily Richardson
Indiana University

Religious or sacred music and religious celebrations have little place in the public schools. Even though the Supreme Court has not yet ruled on this issue, its precedent indicates that the practice of allowing religious music and celebration may be disallowed. This counterpoint essay first explains the Supreme Court's Establishment Clause precedent, including the three tests that courts use to assess whether state action is a violation of the Establishment Clause in the First Amendment to the Constitution. The essay then applies these tests to show that the use of religious or sacred music in school celebrations is unconstitutional. This essay ends by offering policy arguments to support its position that celebrations in public education should not include religious or sacred music.

THE ESTABLISHMENT CLAUSE IN SCHOOLS

Litigation surrounding the role of religion in public schools has increased in recent years. Starting in the 1940s, the Supreme Court developed a line of precedent regarding the Establishment Clause's prohibition on religion in public schools. The Establishment Clause requires that "Congress shall make no law respecting an establishment of religion." Courts are more cautious about Establishment Clause violations in public schools because of the very nature of that setting. Courts have recognized that compulsory attendance laws, which do not apply to students who are homeschooled or who are in nonpublic schools, create a captive audience of children. Additionally, students are impressionable and likely to be influenced by teachers and other school officials.

To evaluate whether a state action violates the Establishment Clause, the Supreme Court developed three tests: *Lemon*, endorsement, and coercion. The judiciary continues to use all three of these tests, though the Supreme Court has questioned their use in various opinions, and lower courts often apply all three when evaluating potential Establishment Clause violations.

The *Lemon* test, first enunciated by the Supreme Court in *Lemon v. Kurtzman* (1971), requires that the state action have a secular legislative purpose, have a principal or primary effect that neither advances nor inhibits religion, and not create excessive government entanglement with religion. State action must meet all three prongs; if even one prong is not met, the state action constitutes an Establishment Clause violation. The Supreme Court applied the *Lemon* test in *Stone v. Graham* (1980), holding that the Kentucky legislature could not require schools to display the Ten Commandments in every classroom. The Court found that the first prong was violated because "[t]he preeminent purpose for posting the Ten Commandments on schoolroom walls is plainly religious in nature" (p. 42). The Court did not give credence to the fact that the documents were purchased with private donations or that they included a disclaimer that explained the secular nature of the Ten Commandments.

In a nonschool case, *Lynch v. Donnelly* (1984), the Supreme Court held that the display of a crèche or manger scene annually did not violate the Establishment Clause. In applying the *Lemon* test, the Court reasoned that there was a secular purpose for the crèche and that it did not excessively entangle religion with the state action. Further, the Court dismissed the argument that the crèche advanced religion, calling any advancement indirect, remote, and incidental.

The endorsement test is similar to the *Lemon* test; indeed, courts have sometimes incorporated it into the *Lemon* test. Under the endorsement test, a state actor violates the Establishment Clause if its actions have the purpose or effect of endorsing religion. In *Wallace v. Jaffree* (1985), Justice Sandra Day O'Connor first described the endorsement test in her concurring opinion, analysis she later expanded. Justice O'Connor wrote that the inquiry was "whether an objective observer, acquainted with the text, legislative history, and implementation of the statute, would perceive it as a state endorsement of prayer in public schools" (p. 76).

A majority of the Supreme Court first accepted the coercion text in its 1992 decision in *Lee v. Weisman* striking down school-sponsored graduation prayer. A student and her father challenged the board's practice of allowing local religious leaders to deliver nonsectarian prayers at junior high graduations. Acknowledging that

> [w]hat to most believers may seem nothing more than a reasonable request that the nonbeliever respect their religious practices, in a school context may appear to the nonbeliever or dissenter to be an attempt to employ the machinery of the State to enforce a religious orthodoxy. (p. 592)

The Court held that the practice violated the Establishment Clause because it coerced students to participate in the prayer. Further, the Court thought that the fact that a graduation ceremony is voluntary did not remove the coercion. Even though the event was voluntary, the Court commented that students should not have to decide between attending an important event and respecting their personal religious beliefs.

RELIGIOUS MUSIC AND CELEBRATIONS IN SCHOOLS

Case law supports the proposition that the use of some religious celebrations and songs in public schools may violate the Establishment Clause. Although there may be some exceptions to the claim that religious or sacred songs at celebrations violate the Establishment Clause, often these practices lack secular purposes or advance religion. To evaluate whether a practice violates the Establishment Clause, the three tests will be applied to the issue at hand.

Religious and sacred songs in public schools are likely to violate the *Lemon* test's mandates for a secular purpose and against the advancement of religion. Teaching and performing religious music may have the purpose of exposing students to the rich cultural and historical underpinnings of this type of music; the music may also be used for merely entertainment reasons. Similar justifications have been used to justify impermissible religious celebrations. However, courts are less likely to find a secular purpose if schools are using religious music in a devotional manner. Religious celebrations are more likely devotional, depending on the context of the celebration.

The use of religious or sacred music may also be interpreted as an advancement of religion in violation of the *Lemon* test. If public school choirs perform only traditional Christmas carols, they appear to advance the Christian faith. Or if public school officials only recognize Jewish holidays while ignoring the holidays of other faiths, they may advance Judaism. Further, the advancement of religion may be found in the repetition of religious celebrations and music. Although conducting an Easter assembly one year would likely be treated as advancing religion, an Establishment Clause violation would be even more likely if the assembly were an annual event.

As noted above, Establishment Clause doctrine has paid special attention to religion in schools. Insofar as children are both impressionable and a captive audience (as the Supreme Court noted in *Lee*), courts are more likely to strike down state action as unconstitutional in these settings. Younger students are particularly unable to distinguish between secular and religious activities. Celebrations using religious or secular music in public schools may be designed for secular purposes, but students may not be situated to understand the nonreligious purposes. For example, although the Supreme Court did not find an Establishment Clause violation in the crèche challenge in *Lynch*, its analysis would have likely been different if the crèche had appeared in front of a public school. The Court would have been less likely to find the advancement of religion indirect, remote, and incidental (Hartenstein, 1992).

The endorsement test's reasoning on these issues mirrors the *Lemon* test's analysis with one important exception—the explicit reliance on the objective observer. Although *Lemon* test analysis takes into account the context of state action, the contextual factors may play a larger role in the endorsement test when analyzing whether Establishment Clause violations have occurred. For instance, when deciding whether singing religious or secular songs at school concerts violates the Establishment Clause, courts applying the endorsement test may inquire as to whether objective observers would see the songs as having purposes or effects of endorsing religion. Again, the answer to this inquiry depends on the context in which the religious or sacred song is used.

Whether the use of religious or secular music violates the Establishment Clause is a complex issue, a complexity that may confuse school officials. By way of illustration, in *Sechler v. State College Area School District* (2000), a federal trial court in Pennsylvania allowed a "winter" display and program, reasoning that both were designed to celebrate religious diversity rather than advance a particular faith. The contested display included multiple faith perspectives, including a menorah, a Kwanzaa candelabra, and holiday books, as well as a banner proclaiming "Happy Holidays." The program included myriad songs celebrating holidays, including Hanukkah and secular Christmas songs, and a Kwanzaa chant. The court concluded that the program and display were secular in nature and did not advance a religion. However, school officials should be cautious about including the celebration of multiple religious holidays along with the majority-preferred holiday. The upshot is that merely including multiple religious perspectives will not inhibit Establishment Clause claims without further judicial inquiry.

The final Establishment Clause measure, the coercion test, may provide the most support that the incorporation of religious songs and celebrations in public schools violates the Establishment Clause. As explained above, the coercion test prohibits officials from coercing students into practicing or engaging in a religious activity. In *Lee*, the Court concentrated on the coercive nature of the graduation prayer even though the ceremony was an optional activity. Oftentimes, the singing of religious and sacred songs at celebrations of religious holidays can be similarly coercive. Students, especially those who are young, may not have the option to remove themselves from participating in singing or listening to religious or sacred songs. Further, this type of activity could be considered similar to prayer, which was at issue in *Lee*. Religious songs often include elements of prayer such as adoration (such as "O Holy Night" and "My God Is an Awesome God") and thanksgiving (such as "For the Beauty of the Earth" and "Hava Nagila"). Often, these songs, as well as others, are performed in a solemn manner as is prayer in many traditions.

Whether religious or sacred songs in celebrations in public schools violate the Establishment Clause is context specific. If school officials do not have secular purposes for the religious activities they are sponsoring, those activities are unconstitutional. Further, if religion is advanced or appears to be endorsed by religious or sacred songs, the actions of educational leaders are similarly unconstitutional. School officials could also be found to violate the coercion test if their religious song or celebration is required, either explicitly or implicitly.

RECENT LITIGATION

More recently, two federal appellate courts upheld judgments excluding religious music from public school activities. In *Stratechuk v. Board of Education, South Orange-Maplewood School District* (2009, 2010), the Third Circuit affirmed that the policy of a school board in New Jersey, which prohibited the use of religious music in holiday celebrations, did not violate the First Amendment because its actions satisfied all three parts of the *Lemon* test. In addition, the court was satisfied that the board's action did not demonstrate governmental disapproval of or hostility toward religion.

In like manner, the Ninth Circuit, in *Nurre v. Whitehead* (2009, 2010), affirmed that a superintendent in Washington did not violate a high school student's rights to freedom of religion or speech in forbidding the wind ensemble in which she participated from performing the instrumental version of a religious song at her graduation. The superintendent forbade the music from being played in light of worries that permitting it might have been viewed as violating the Establishment Clause by endorsing religion. The court agreed that the superintendent's action passed all three prongs of the *Lemon* test.

Earlier, in *M.D. v. St. Johns County School District* (2009), a federal trial court in Florida prevented educational officials from including a country music song about the place of God in America. The court granted an injunction against the use of the song because it was convinced that the plaintiffs presented sufficient evidence that they were likely to succeed on the merits of their claim. The court explained that the plaintiffs would have suffered a greater irrevocable harm by allowing the song to be used than if it failed to intervene to keep the wall of separation between church and state in place.

POLICY ARGUMENTS

Even if courts agree that the Establishment Clause does not forbid specified types of religious instruction, celebrations, and songs, school officials should not allow these types of religious activities. Instead, these activities should be reserved for the home and places of worship. In other words, to protect the rights of minorities and to reserve time for academics, school officials should refrain from initiating activities that enter into the religious realm.

Schools already retain the enormous responsibility of educating children. The students that they educate are from diverse backgrounds and exhibit relative levels of proficiency in educational subjects. Instead of spending valuable time celebrating religious holidays by singing religious songs, school leaders should focus on academic subjects. Indeed, academic success, measured through high-stakes testing, increasingly is vital to the success of schools.

At the same time, school boards and educational leaders would be wise to avoid religious songs and celebrations to limit, if not eliminate, the threat of litigation. The Establishment Clause has been one of the most thoroughly litigated constitutional amendments, and these activities often spur litigation. Since the Supreme Court has not yet issued an opinion on this subject and because the line drawing involved in parsing an Establishment Clause claim is difficult, school officials may be wise to avoid the issue entirely and pursue academic subjects.

Even if a claim disputing the religious song or celebration is not filed, the practice itself might damage relationships with parents and students who are not represented by the practice. School events and classroom celebrations should be welcome places for everyone. The United States is a multicultural society with multiple religions being widely represented. Moreover, an increasing number of people do not associate with religion. It is often argued that Christian religious celebrations should be allowed in majority Christian school systems. However, protection for those in the minority is a staple of the American educational system, which is illustrated by federal legislation protecting the rights of students with special needs and homeless children.

School officials may unintentionally make some children and parents uncomfortable when they choose to incorporate religion in their schools. For example, Jewish students may not feel welcome in classrooms that color Christmas trees and make ornaments while singing Christmas songs. Some may argue that these students could simply opt out of the activities, but this would more likely isolate them and perhaps even lead to a major problem in schools today—bullying. The singing of religious songs may also make students and parents feel uncomfortable. If religious songs are sung at school concerts or in school assemblies, some students may feel the need to opt out and parents may choose not to attend. Educational officials should instead focus on being inclusive societies.

Finally, some may argue that if multiple religions are represented, as described in *Sechler*, educators should be allowed to incorporate religion into curricula. While this type of presentation may limit Establishment Clause concerns, it is difficult in practice. The school board in *Sechler* recognized three specific holidays, but there are myriad other holidays that were omitted, such as those relating to Islam and Buddhism. Line drawing regarding the number of holidays represented and the extent of representation creates questions about not only the constitutionality of school practices but also the potential emotional impact on students and staff. Indeed, school boards may be tempted to simply tack on a little information about minority religions to decrease the likely success of potential litigation.

CONCLUSION

The Establishment Clause doctrine does allow some space for the use of religious or sacred music in school celebrations. However, the Establishment Clause does not allow school officials to permit these practices in a devotional manner. Thus, educational officials should avoid engaging in using religious or sacred music in school activities because of the limited time for instruction already allowed and the potential impact these types of activities will have on students with minority faiths or no faiths at all.

FURTHER READINGS AND RESOURCES

Hartenstein, J. M. (1992). A Christmas issue: Christian holiday celebrations in the public elementary schools is an establishment of religion. *California Law Review, 80,* 981–1026.

Kasparian, F. D. (1997). Note: The constitutionality of teaching and performing sacred choral music in public schools. *Duke Law Journal, 46,* 1111–1168.

Knowlton, M. (2009). Religious music in public schools: The disappointing analysis in *Stratechuk v. Board of Education, South Orange-Maplewood School District. Rutgers Journal of Law & Religion, 10,* 17–31.

Mangrum, C. M. (2005). Shall we sing? Shall we sing religious music in public schools? *Creighton Law Review, 38,* 815–870.

Mawdsley, R. D. (1994). *Clever v. Cherry Hill Township Board of Education:* Recognition of religious diversity in public schools. *Education Law Reporter, 90,* 533–545.

Russo, C. J. (2010). Tone deaf? The courts turn a deaf ear to religious music in schools. *Education Law Reporter, 257,* 1–22.

Seidman, L. N. (1997). Note: Religious music in the public schools: Music to Establishment Clause ears. *George Washington Law Review, 65,* 466–505.

Whitaker, B. A. (2003). Religious music in the public schools: A guide for school districts. *Brigham Young University Education and Law Journal, 2003,* 339–362.

COURT CASES AND STATUTES

Altman v. Bedford Central School District, 245 F.3d 49 (2d Cir. 2001).

Bauchman v. West High School, 132 F.3d 542 (10th Cir. 1997), *cert. denied,* 524 U.S. 953 (1998).

Chamberlin v. Dade County Board of Public Instruction, 143 So. 2d 21 (Fla. 1962)

Clever v. Cherry Hill Township Board of Education, 838 F. Supp. 929 (D.N.J. 1993).

Doe v. Duncanville Independent School District, 70 F.3d 402 (5th Cir. 1993).

Florey v. Sioux Falls School District, 619 F.2d 1311 (8th Cir. 1980), *cert. denied,* 449 U.S. 987 (1980).

Jimmy Swaggart Ministries v. Board of Equalization, 493 U.S. 378 (1990).

Lee v. Weisman, 505 U.S. 577 (1992).

Lemon v. Kurtzman, 403 U.S. 602 (1971).

Lynch v. Donnelly, 465 U.S. 688 (1984).

Marchi v. Board of Cooperative Educational Services of Albany Schoharie, Schenectady, and Saratoga Counties, 173 F.3d 469 (2d Cir. 1999a), *cert. denied,* 528 U.S. 869 (1999b).

M.D. v. St. Johns County School District, 632 F. Supp. 2d 1085 (M.D. Fla. 2009).

Nurre v. Whitehead, 580 F.3d 1087 (9th Cir. 2009), *cert. denied,* 130 S. Ct. 1937 (2010).

People of State of Illinois ex rel. McCollum v. Board of Education of School District No. 71, Champaign County, 333 U.S. 203 (1948).

Sechler v. State College Area School District, 121 F. Supp. 2d 439 (M.D. Pa. 2000).

Stone v. Graham, 449 U.S. 39 (1980).

Stratechuk v. Board of Education, South Orange-Maplewood School District, 587 F.3d 597 (3d Cir. 2009), *cert. denied,* 131 S. Ct. 72 (2010).

Wallace v. Jaffree, 472 U.S. 38 (1985).

Should educational officials permit displays of religious symbols in public schools?

POINT: Courtney Hagele, *Columbus, Ohio*
COUNTERPOINT: Kathryn Shields, *Columbus, Ohio*

OVERVIEW

Whether religious symbols and displays can be permitted in public schools depends on three interrelated issues: the extent to which the control of school officials over the religious symbols or displays constitutes school sponsorship under the Establishment Clause in the First Amendment to the Constitution; the nature of the fora that public school officials created; and the degree to which displays or symbols fit within categories such as disruptive or curricular material over which public school officials are accorded greater control. Although these categories have discrete legal differences, the reality is that they tend to be merged together.

Before turning to forum analysis, it is helpful to complete a brief review of Supreme Court cases involving religious symbols in schools and public areas. In *Stone v. Graham* (1981), the Supreme Court invalidated, under Establishment Clause analysis, the display of the Ten Commandments in public schools, a result that the justices later extended to a courthouse in *McCreary County, Kentucky v. American Civil Liberties Union of Kentucky* (2005), declaring that allowing such displays amounts to impermissible endorsement of religion. Yet, on the same day, in *Van Orden v. Perry* (2005), a plurality, meaning that a majority of justices could not agree on the same rationale, affirmed that a display of the

Ten Commandments, including 17 monuments and 21 historical markers spread out over the 22 acres of the Texas State Capitol, was constitutional. The plurality was satisfied that including the Ten Commandments was constitutional because even though they continue to have religious significance, the monument was a far more passive display than that in *Stone.*

In two earlier cases, the Supreme Court did permit some displays of religious symbols in public places. In *Lynch v. Donnelly* (1984), a plurality allowed a nativity scene in a Christmas display to remain on public property. The Court relied largely on its newly created endorsement test, which considered whether the purpose of governmental action was to endorse or approve a religion or religious activity in deciding that the display was constitutional.

The Supreme Court's next case, *County of Allegheny v. American Civil Liberties Union* (1989), involved two displays. The Court invalidated the display of a crèche in a county courthouse that included an angel bearing a banner with the message *Gloria in Excelsis Deo*, meaning "Glory to God in the Highest," along with a sign indicating that the scene was donated by a private religious organization. The court found that the display had the impermissible effect of endorsing religion. The Court allowed the second display, on the property of a county-owned office building, consisting of a 45-foot Christmas tree, an 18-foot menorah, and a sign proclaiming that the city saluted liberty during the holiday season. The Court found that insofar as the Christmas tree and menorah were placed in the broader context of the season, they did not endorse a particular religious faith.

Determining a public school's forum for free speech purposes has become, at best, an uncertain science. The Supreme Court has recognized three kinds of fora for expressive purposes in public settings: traditional, including streets and parks; designated, also referred to as *limited*, and including a forum opened to use by specific designation or by practice; and nonpublic, where school officials retain control over the setting. Of these three categories, only limited public fora have clear free speech application to public schools. Accordingly, the questions for school officials are, for the purposes of free speech, the extent to which the nature of a school's forum may require a display of religious items and, on the other hand, for purposes of the Establishment Clause, the extent to which a display may be permitted or prohibited.

Lower courts have not been sympathetic to the presence of religious symbols or displays in public schools. For example, in *Bannon v. School District of Palm Beach County* (2004), the Eleventh Circuit upheld a principal's ordering a student to take down a mural with religious symbols and messages she painted in a school hallway. In rejecting the student's claim, the court was of the view that school officials had a legitimate pedagogical concern in avoiding the disruption, albeit minimal, to the school's learning environment caused by the student's religious mural/display. Earlier, the Sixth Circuit ordered educational officials to remove a portrait of Jesus that was painted by a graduate and that had been hanging in a school hall for many years as violating the Establishment Clause (*Washegesic v. Bloomingdale Public Schools*, 1994a). The court maintained that the portrait had to be removed because it lacked a secular purpose, advanced religion, and was not integrated into any course of study as it hung in an area controlled by school officials.

Against this backdrop, the following essays rely on largely the same Supreme Court opinions, not addressing lower court cases, in debating the constitutionality of religious symbols in public schools. In the point essay, Courtney Hagele, an attorney in Columbus, Ohio, adopts the position that officials in public schools should be able to allow displays of religious symbols in public schools. Hagele is of the opinion that insofar as religious symbols can have the legitimate secular goal of promoting respect for diverse cultures, such displays should be permitted. On the other hand, Kathryn Shields, also an attorney in Columbus, Ohio, takes the position that educational leaders in public schools should not permit displays of religious symbols. More specifically, Shields asserts that allowing such displays violates the Establishment Clause insofar as they typically advance the beliefs of the majority religions without taking the values of minority religions or nonbelievers into consideration.

As you read these essays, ask yourself the following questions. First, is it possible that religious displays, especially during the Christmas season, can or do evidence a secular purpose? Second, would the presence of religious displays advance or inhibit students' understandings not just of religions other than their own but also of the role that religion has played in shaping history and American society?

Charles J. Russo
University of Dayton

Ralph D. Mawdsley
Cleveland State University

POINT: Courtney Hagele
Columbus, Ohio

Since displays of religious symbols in public schools typically have the secular goal of promoting respect for diverse cultures, they should be permitted under an accommodationist approach to the Constitution's First Amendment Religion Clauses. In applying this approach, school officials must reconcile the tension between the twin objectives of preventing the unnecessary intrusion of either the church or the state on the other in addition to the reality that total separation of the two is not possible in contemporary America.

In adopting the accommodationist approach, this point essay takes the position that religious beliefs, as expressed in symbols, should be accorded the same treatment as nonreligious beliefs, which comport with the requirements of the prohibition of laws respecting the establishment of religion under the Establishment Clause in the First Amendment. While an accommodationist point of view considers the proper balance between church and state, advocates for separation demand a strict separation between the two. If schools officials adopt an approach of separation, they would not only be inappropriately limiting the free exercise of religion but also violating the free speech provisions of the First Amendment.

WHY RELIGIOUS SYMBOLS SHOULD BE ALLOWED

The inclusion of religious symbols in public schools does not violate the Supreme Court's *Lemon v. Kurtzman* (1971) test or the endorsement test from *Lynch v. Donnelly* (1984). Under the *Lemon* test, when government and religion come together, a statute or policy must have a secular legislative purpose; its principal or primary effect must be one that neither advances nor inhibits religion; and the action must not foster an excessive government entanglement with religion (pp. 612–613). If any of these principles is violated, then the Court will strike down the statute as violating the Establishment Clause of the First Amendment.

Under the endorsement test of *Lynch*, the focus is on whether one could view a public school's display of a religious symbol as approval or allowance of a particular religion. To answer whether actions endorse a particular religion, courts must make inquiries into the intent of officials who permit displays of symbols as well as the messages they actually convey.

As indicated, displaying religious symbols for the advancement of diverse knowledge of world culture serves a secular purpose and therefore does not violate either the *Lemon* or the endorsement test. If anything, to adopt a blanket ban on religious symbols would violate the First Amendment's Free Speech Clause and Establishment Clause. The next sections advance these points.

THE *LEMON* TEST

Displays of religious symbols do not violate the *Lemon* test as long as they are used to promote respect for diverse cultures in a passive manner. In other words, religious displays in public schools are proper when they lack a predominantly religious purpose. Since displaying the Ten Commandments, for example, teaches children the fundamental values of Western civilization as well as the common law of the United States, this essay maintains that doing so does not violate the *Lemon* test. Religious symbols should be permitted in schools because the Constitution mandates accommodation, not mere tolerance of religions, and forbids hostility toward any religion. Schools officials have the responsibility of fostering mutual understanding and respect among the beliefs, values, and customs of all students who come from diverse backgrounds.

When the purpose of school officials in displaying symbols is to aid not only in teaching the history of the American legal system but also as a means of instilling values in children, a secular purpose exists. Further, the mere overlap between a secular purpose and a religious objective does not render a symbol unconstitutional under the Establishment Clause. For instance, the Ten Commandments, of course, is a sacred text that remains an integral part of different faiths yet undeniably had a significant impact on the development of the secular legal codes of the Western world. To this end, when a display of the Ten Commandments, for example, is presented to students as part of a larger display including other, similar sets of religious teachings, students should be instructed about its secular significance. What is significant in the secular purpose analysis is whether the display, or symbol, as a whole has a secular impact.

The Establishment Clause prevents school officials from adopting specific religions but does not require educators to shelter students from all things that may have religious value. To the contrary, the Supreme Court has recognized that throughout American history, religion has been closely identified with history and government. The Court has also acknowledged that "the history of man is inseparable from the history of religion" (*Engel v. Vitale*, 1962, p. 434). Thus, in the example of the display of the Ten Commandments, the Court's ruling to the contrary in *Stone v. Graham* notwithstanding, such a display may foster awareness of the traditions and customs associated with the Ten Commandments and demonstrate a secular purpose: educating students about the effect that the Ten Commandments have had on Western culture.

Completely separating what some observers may regard as religion and secular education is an insurmountable task. While some subjects such as science and mathematics can be completely secularized (aside from debates about the origins of humankind), teaching past customs, practices, or appreciations of the arts would be impossible if educators were required to implement teaching lessons void of any religious influences. In this regard, "Music without sacred music, architecture minus the cathedral, or paintings without the scriptural themes would be eccentric and incomplete, even from a secular point of view" (*Stone v. Graham*, 1981, p. 46, citing *McCollum v. Board of Education*, 1948, pp. 235–236). Nearly all culture is entrenched with religious influences, derived from several different faiths, from paganism to Christianity. Permitting educational leaders to forbid displays of religious symbols that have the effect of leaving students wholly ignorant of the religious cultures that shaped American society would do a great injustice to the education of our children.

When displays of religious symbols, such as the Ten Commandments, are integrated into school curricula, they satisfy the second part of the *Lemon* test that forbids governmental actions from having a principal or primary effect of advancing (or inhibit, not at issue here) religion. If the purpose of religious displays in schools is to educate students by fostering an understanding of history, civilization, ethics, or comparative religion, then they should be permitted.

Public schools play an important role in educating and guiding our youth through the marketplace of ideas and in instilling national values. Under the doctrine of *parens patria*, literally "father of the country," the state has an interest in ensuring the well-being of its citizens. In fulfilling this role, public school officials have the responsibility of educating our youth on such important topics as the diverse religious views and cultures of others. Schools thus have the duty to prepare and teach children how to deal with the challenges of facing perspectives different from their own rather than promoting a view that shelters them from the beliefs of others.

To further this principle and not offend the Constitution, purported historical displays must present religious symbols objectively and integrate them with secular messages. A variety of factors are relevant when assessing whether religious symbols have been presented objectively and integrated with secular messages so that they are consistent with the Establishment Clause of the First Amendment. These factors include the content of the displays, the physical setting in which the religious symbols are displayed, and any changes made to displays since their inception (*ACLU v. McCreary County*, 2003). Here, the Supreme Court observed that an evaluation of purpose must be made by an "objective observer" who takes the whole picture into account. Applying these principles, the primary effect of a religious display can be to advance the history of American culture rather than religion.

In addition, there must not be an excessive government entanglement with religion. School officials must not be required to interact on a daily basis with religious leaders in an extensive manner. For example, the government must not be required to monitor religious activities. As such, the mere integration of displays into school curricula should not require governmental oversight.

Even if one were to analyze a display of religious symbols without using *Lemon*, their presence in schools still does not violate the Establishment Clause. When, by way of illustration, the Ten Commandments were displayed over 22 acres of the Texas State Capitol among 17 other monuments and 21 other historical markers commemorating the state's history, a plurality of the Supreme Court upheld the display as constitutional in *Van Orden v. Perry* (2005). Relying on the passiveness of the monument, the Supreme Court pointed out that the *Lemon* test was not useful in this controversy. Instead, the Court focused on both the nature of the monument and its history. Rather than advancing religion, the Court was convinced that the monument had a dual purpose of representing the state's political and legal history through religion and did not violate the Establishment Clause.

THE ENDORSEMENT TEST

Another example of the proper application of the *Lemon* test includes permitting officials in public schools to establish holiday observances such as Christmas, a federal holiday, along with appropriate seasonal displays. This observance involves promoting the secular purpose of advancing the knowledge and appreciation of students of the role of religions in the social, cultural, and historical development of civilization through their symbols.

In *Lynch v. Donnelly* (1984), the Supreme Court rejected the claim that the government endorsed a religious display, although the city's display comprised many of the figures and decorations traditionally associated with Christmas, such as a Santa Claus gingerbread house, reindeer pulling Santa's sleigh, candy canes, a Christmas tree, carolers, and the crèche. The Court reiterated that the Constitution does not require complete separation between church and state. Rather, the Court explained that the Constitution affirmatively mandates accommodation. Even though a display such as this may lead some to conclude these symbols could be considered religious, the Court held that the city satisfied the *Lemon* test.

In making this determination, the *Lynch* Court relied on the three reasons. First, even if there were a benefit to one faith or religion, the Court held that it was indirect, remote, and incidental. The Court agreed that the city's desire to commemorate the origins of Christmas met the secular purpose requirement of the *Lemon* test by characterizing the display as acknowledging the existence of a significant historical religious event that has long been celebrated.

Second, the Supreme Court did not think that the display of the crèche was more of an advancement or endorsement of religion than the congressional and executive recognition of the origins of Christmas itself as "Christ's Mass," or the exhibition of literally hundreds of religious paintings in governmentally supported museums. Further, the Court observed that the crèche benefited religion no more than other debated activities that have not necessarily violated the First Amendment, such as legislative prayer by chaplains paid with public funds, released time for religious training, or advancing public funds for transporting children to religious schools.

Third, the Supreme Court decided that city officials included the crèche under the secular purpose of celebrating Christmas. Consequently, the Court concluded that the city's display did not impermissibly advance religion, and including the crèche did not create excessive entanglement between church and state.

CONSTITUTIONALITY OF RELIGIOUS DISPLAYS IN PUBLIC SCHOOLS

The display of religious symbols in public schools does not fail either the *Lemon* or endorsement tests. School officials who allow displays of religious symbols are not endorsing religion merely by displaying symbols that may have religious underpinnings. Using the endorsement test, the *Lynch* Court rejected the argument that the city endorsed and promulgated religious beliefs when the city displayed the crèche in the manner discussed in the preceding section.

In its analysis, the *Lynch* Court properly viewed the crèche in light of the entire Christmas season rather than focusing solely on the nativity scene, a valuable lesson for educational leaders. This emphasis supports the view that a religious connotation is not dispositive on the issue of whether the government is endorsing religion. Instead, an observer must take into account the context in which the symbol is displayed. Focusing solely on the religious component of any symbol would inevitably lead to its invalidation under the Establishment Clause. However, the context of this type of display in *Lynch* negated any message of endorsement of religion even though its context did not neutralize the nativity scene's religious significance. In school settings, teachers' use of displays as teaching tools negates the religious component because the displays are merely historical symbols embodying the rich traditions for three reasons.

First, the display of a crèche, for example, does not constitute promotion of religious content but is a celebration of the public holiday through its traditional symbols. While a display may have religious significance, the celebration of a public holiday has cultural significance with a secular purpose. Thus, symbols reflecting other public holidays are permissible when they have both cultural and religious meanings.

Second, a display does not communicate the message that the government intends to endorse the religious belief represented by the display. When a display celebrates a public holiday, it cannot be understood as an endorsement of religion insofar as government commemoration of a holiday is not considered an endorsement of a particular religion. In other contexts, governmental recognition of religion, such as the phrase printed on a coin "In God We Trust," serves the secular purpose of encouraging the recognition of what is worthy of appreciation in our society. Therefore, because a religious display can serve the secular purpose of celebrating a public holiday with traditional symbols, as in the case of the crèche, it cannot be interpreted as an endorsement of religion.

Third, because it is unlikely that an observer would conclude that school officials or the government supports a particular ideology, a holiday display consisting of both religious and secular symbols in a school does not violate the Establishment Clause.

FREE SPEECH PROTECTIONS

Briefly stated, the Free Speech Clause of the First Amendment prohibits the suppression of speech when a regulation is based on its content. To accomplish a school's task of educating and guiding youth through the marketplace of ideas and instilling national ideals, students must be permitted exposure to a rich diversity of backgrounds and opinions held by faculty.

The courts must permit teachers, under free speech principles, to provide displays that some observers may perceive as "religious" in their classrooms. In this regard, the Supreme Court reasoned that educational officials cannot make content-based restrictions in a setting where "[t]he vigilant protection of the Constitutional freedoms is nowhere more vital than in the community of American Schools" (*Shelton v. Tucker*, 1960, p. 487). Since patriotic banners stating messages such as "In God We Trust" or "God Bless America" displayed by teachers in their classrooms cannot be perceived as endorsements of a single religion, their suppression would be impermissible one-sided censorship.

Those opposing the display of symbols that may be interpreted to some as religious fear that students are incapable of dealing with diverse viewpoints that include the role of God and religion in American history and culture. Yet, religion is deeply entrenched in society's history. The Constitution permits some latitude in recognizing and accommodating the central role religion plays in our society. As such, silencing the role religion has played in American history would promote hostility toward religion, which is not permitted by the Constitution.

CONCLUSION

Insofar as educators have the duty to foster open-mindedness and critical thinking in their students, they must be permitted to fulfill their function without being silenced. Particularly, teachers should be permitted to use a display that references religion when it is apparent that a wide range of ideas is permitted to be expressed. Banning the display of patriotic themes is impermissible when opposition is based merely on speculative fear of endorsement. When the focus of a symbol is merely patriotic rather than religious, it is simply a historic symbol used to highlight that Americans live in a nation founded by those escaping religious persecution. As a nation dedicated to religious freedom, educators cannot escape incidental references to religion.

Educational leaders can preserve their neutrality and still teach students that as a society, Americans must tolerate divergent views without suppressing them. Therefore, the elimination or removal of symbols that observers may interpret as religious would do a disservice to students as part of a society grounded in tolerance of divergent political and religious views.

COUNTERPOINT: Kathryn Shields
Columbus, Ohio

The display of religious symbols in public schools has long been a debated issue in the United States. Yet, in recent years, the gap between advocates and opponents of posting religious symbols in public schools has widened dramatically. For many, the display of religious symbols is an important way in which to identify with their corresponding beliefs. Others, of course, disagree. A question that arises concerns what can or should be done when displays representing a specific religion or two are permitted in public schools. In other words, if displays representing one or two religions are permitted, then must all groups be granted equal access to post their religious symbols? In the ever-expanding amalgam of American society, these religious symbols take on new meaning. The absence of religious symbols representing all cultures in schools can be interpreted as showing favoritism toward some cultures and intolerance toward others.

Aware of the potential conflict that displays of religious symbols can have, this counterpoint essay stands for the proposition that officials in public school systems should not be responsible for shifting the focuses of students from general education topics to religion. Put another way, since American public schools educate a wide array of students, it would be inequitable to display only one or two religious symbols since the world of religion is not one dimensional and includes many different faiths. Insofar as it would be unbalanced to display the symbols of only one or two religions, the only way to represent the masses would be to flood the public school system with every depiction of religious symbol available. Instead of opening the symbolic flood gates, why not erect a dam? The public schools are a tool designed to educate America's children. While education includes religious education, it is not the public school system's responsibility to dispense such information. Standardized tests and proficiency tests do not test religious aptitude. Since the responsibility for religion falls on the shoulders of parents, religious symbols have no place in American public schools.

BACKGROUND

Historically, there has been an unflinching resolve to guarantee religious freedom in the United States. In fact, based on the experiences of their ancestors in Europe, the Founding Fathers knew well the dangers and repercussions of religious persecution and kept that very issue in mind when drafting the Constitution and its Amendments. This pertinent issue of religious freedom resulted in the First Amendment to the Constitution, consisting of the Establishment and Free Exercise Clauses, both of which protect freedom of religion. According to these clauses, which serve as the foundation to the arguments for and against religious separation, "Congress shall make no law respecting an establishment of religion, or prohibiting the free exercise thereof."

Individuals often cite the importance of separation of church and state in the United States. In this regard, Thomas Jefferson used the phrase "wall of separation between church and state"—admittedly in a private letter to a committee of the Danbury, Connecticut, Baptist Association in 1802—to describe what he maintained should be the relationship between religious institutions and the government. This Jeffersonian perspective is the position that the Supreme Court has most commonly adopted with regard to religious activities, prayer, and related issues in public schools. The Supreme Court first used this phrase in 1947 in *Everson v. Board of Education*, a dispute over the constitutionality of providing transportation for students who attended religiously affiliated nonpublic schools. Separationists share this Jeffersonian view. On the other hand, accommodationists argue that religious influences should not be completely separated from the government, only that the state should not have the ability to endorse any one, single religion.

American culture is riddled with religious undertones. As such, there is no possible way to separate these undertones from the government completely. For example, those in roles of governmental authority, including officials in public schools, are, more likely than not, affiliated with some religion in their private lives. These representatives of the citizens of the United States are charged with the impossible task of separating their own personal beliefs while carrying out the wills of their constituents, many of whom are also religious believers. This intricate web of religious connections makes separatism, at best, a daunting task for American leaders, whether in schools or other arenas in the public marketplace of ideas. Regardless of how daunting the task before them is, it is necessary for educational leaders, in particular in the context of this debate, to, at the very least, strive for separation since the task of accommodation is nearly impossible.

LITIGATION

The accommodationist versus separationist conundrum in American public education has surfaced in litigation since 1947 in *Everson*. In an attempt to resolve the question of the appropriate relationship between church and state, the Supreme Court devised the seemingly ubiquitous *Lemon v. Kurtzman* (1971) test to evaluate whether governmental actions violate the Establishment Clause. This three-pronged test asks whether the government's action has a secular legislative purpose, has a principal or primary effect that neither advances nor inhibits religion, and manages to avoid an "excessive government entanglement" with religion (pp. 612–613).

One may ask how displays of religious symbols in public schools in the United States possibly have secular purposes. This is the very same question that many courts and educational leaders have struggled to answer. Among these cases, there is an overwhelming majority ruling in the negative.

At issue in *Stone v. Graham* (1981), the Supreme Court's first case on religious symbols, was a statute from Kentucky that required the posting of the Ten Commandments on the walls of each public school classroom in the commonwealth. The copies of the Ten Commandments were paid for by private funds. Opponents of the statute obtained a permanent injunction ordering that the displays be discontinued, arguing that the statute violated the Establishment

Clause. On further review, in a brief unsigned opinion, the Supreme Court agreed that the statute violated the Establishment Clause. The Court rejected the notion that the Commandments were part of the fundamental legal code of Western civilization and American common law. In *Stone*, the Supreme Court addressed the inescapable tension between the objectives of preventing unnecessary intrusion of either church or state on the other and the reality that total separation of the two is not possible.

Three years later, in *Lynch v. Donnelly* (1984), a nonschool case, opponents challenged the inclusion of a nativity scene in a city's Christmas display. The Supreme Court found that although the display had a religious significance in and of itself, city officials had not violated the Establishment Clause, thereby adopting a position of accommodation rather than separation. Since it was the Christmas season, the Court decided that the context of the display was appropriate.

In its analysis, the *Lynch* Court noted that regardless of whether the key word is *endorsement*, *favoritism*, or *promotion*, the essential principle remains the same. In other words, the Supreme Court explained that the Establishment Clause, at the very least, prohibits the government from appearing to take a position on questions of religious belief or from "making adherence to a religion relevant in any way to a person's standing in the political community" (p. 687). According to this test means, if a governmental action or statute can be construed by others as endorsing one religion over another, or any religion at all, then it has violated the Establishment Clause. However, the Court pointed out that an exclusive focus of a religious component on a display would not have passed muster under the review mandated by the Establishment Clause. Lower courts have since turned to this endorsement test to evaluate the validity of religious display in the public sector. To reiterate, this test focuses on whether the public schools' allowance of the religious display would also be viewed as an endorsement of that particularly displayed religion.

Five years later, in a similar case, again not involving a school, *County of Allegheny v. American Civil Liberties Union* (1989), a civil liberties union challenged the placement of two displays. The first was a crèche that was in the county courthouse. The second display, which was on the grounds of city and county buildings, was a Chanukah menorah next to the city's 45-foot decorated Christmas tree; there was also a sign at the foot of the tree bearing the mayor's name and text declaring the site to be the city's salute to liberty. The Supreme Court ruled that the display of the crèche violated the Establishment Clause because of its religious nature, observing that the words *Gloria in Excelsius Deo*, literally "Glory to God in the Highest," were posted below the crèche. The Court allowed the second display to remain because it had a secular purpose insofar as it merely signified the holiday season. Specifically, the Court noted that "the Constitution mandates that the government remain secular, rather than affiliating itself with religious beliefs or institutions, precisely in order to avoid discriminating among citizens on the basis of their religious faith" (p. 610).

In its two most recent cases, neither of which was school related, both resolved on the same day in 2005, the Supreme Court reached different results. In *McCreary County, Kentucky v. American Civil Liberties Union of Kentucky*, the Court found that the display of the Ten Commandments at a county courthouse failed the purpose prong of the *Lemon* test. Conversely, in *Van Orden v. Perry*, a plurality of the Supreme Court upheld the display of the Ten Commandments on the 22-acre grounds of the Texas State Capitol that included 17 monuments and 21 historical markers commemorating the state's history as constitutional. Without addressing *Lemon*, the plurality was satisfied that including the Ten Commandments in the display was constitutional because even though they continue to have religious significance, the monument was a far more passive display than that in *Stone*. Unfortunately, viewed together, these two cases shed little light on the issue since the Court seemed unwilling to develop a clear and specific "bright line" test for the question of religious display.

These cases demonstrate that the judiciary is careful not to inhibit religious freedom. Even so, there is an extremely fine line dividing inhibition and advocacy of religion. Aware of this close distinction, in some of the cases discussed above, the Supreme Court found that the displays did not violate the Establishment Clause as long as they were used as part of larger holiday collages. The Court did not find the displays alone to be proper, at least in these cases. However, the *Lynch* Court added that the inclusion of an exclusively religious display would have violated the Establishment Clause. If, as is the case, well-educated judges have a difficult time with these fine-line distinctions, one can only wonder about the confusion that is likely to be present in the minds of educational leaders, let alone school children, especially those who are not members of the dominant faith.

DISPLAYS OF RELIGIOUS SYMBOLS IN PUBLIC SCHOOLS

As the Supreme Court has noted in litigation involving the Establishment Clause, religion is, by its very nature, too personal and important to individual believers to be left to state officials, particularly in public schools where their actions could impact impressionable young minds. At the same time, religion is a way in which to relate to others, to converge as a group, or to invoke self-reflection. Clearly, Americans practice many different religions even as

Christianity remains the single largest, and majority, faith in the nation. Of course, in the cases that have been litigated, the religions most often mentioned in the public school cases are Christianity and Judaism.

Against this background of religious diversity, imagine for a moment that an individual practicing the Wiccan religion would like to display a horned god or a pentagram as part of a display in a public school. There would unquestionably be a discussion of the symbol's appropriateness, especially when many people, not knowledgeable about the Wiccan religion, would find a pentagram synonymous with satanic worship. In another scenario, what if there is a satanic worshipper in the community wishing to display a satanic symbol? This would undoubtedly leave many uncomfortable and public school officials in a bit of a quandary. Would those parents who were attempting to have their religious displays made public have the same attitudes toward these individuals?

Those advocating accommodation in this context tend to throw out words such as *fear* and *religious hostility* as motives for those advocating separation between the government and religion in public schools and elsewhere. It is all too clear from history and the present that the issue of religion in a public atmosphere is a hotly debated topic. Yet, such a single-minded approach in terms of wishing to permit displays of the dominant religion in public schools fails to take into account that there are many different perspectives, reasons, and motives behind advocacy and opposition to religious displays. With so many different perspectives on the issue, it is necessary for educational leaders to act prudently. Caution is simply the approach that should be used when dealing with the intensely personal issues associated with religion in public schools.

Some argue that the role of public schools is, in part, to educate students about the different cultures and religions present in American society. This argument is valid, if and only if the goal is to teach the broad subject of diversity. In a world cultures or social studies class, where students are taught about different cultures around the globe, it seems logical that religion would need to be examined. Religion is the cornerstone to many societies, and as such, it may be necessary to discuss religion simultaneously with the culture. While this essay in no way advocates a society free of religion from the public eye, it implores readers to acknowledge that the display of religious symbols may not be in line with the Constitution.

A dominant theme in contemporary America is tolerance. Since there are so many different cultures in American society, all must approach different cultures with impartiality. Tolerance can broadly be defined as respecting someone else's position while not necessarily approving of the other person's beliefs. Yet, religious intolerance is prevalent in many parts of the world. Fortunately, the lack of tolerance, religious and otherwise, that has been a catalyst for war, prejudice, and a multitude of other negative happenings in other nations has not visited the United States to the same degree as elsewhere. Perhaps the United States has not had such religious strife because of the healthy separation between religion and the state in public schools as evidenced by not permitting religious displays. In a society where tolerance is a needed characteristic for cohesive living, it is necessary to encourage it in American public schools. As such, one must ask whether the best way to encourage tolerance is through the display of limited religious symbols. This essay maintains that the answer is no. That any display would likely be limited in its representations magnifies an already present bias against those who are not represented and may well have a negative impact on students of minority religions or no faith at all.

By way of response to the point essay, a ban on religious symbols in public schools does not violate the free speech rights of students or others. More specifically, insofar as educational officials have the duty to limit the kind of speech that occurs in schools, as long as their actions are reasonably related to legitimate pedagogical concerns such as maintaining neutrality by maintaining separation of government and religion, then they will not have violated the Free Speech Clause.

CONCLUSION

As noted, this counterpoint essay stands for the proposition that religious symbols should not be displayed in American public schools because of the myriad issues that they would create. For example, what types and how many different kinds of religious displays would be appropriate in public schools? Are public schools the appropriate setting for religious images? Designing a so-called bright line test about religious symbols is not an easy feat. American history has taught that the law is ever changing, as is our culture and religious makeup. In a not so black-and-white world, it is hard to find an answer that is not gray.

Until the Supreme Court develops a clear test in line with the Establishment Clause and remainder of the Constitution, it is necessary to prohibit religious displays in public school systems. As the Supreme Court has noted on numerous occasions, this issue is far too important to begin down the road of permitting one-way religious displays supported by the majority, especially when dealing with impressionable children in American public schools.

FURTHER READINGS AND RESOURCES

Horner, J. J. (2005). Let's take "Bah humbug" out of Christmas: A guide to permissible activities at public schools during Christmas season. *Education Law Reporter, 207,* 831–837.

McCarthy, M. M. (2005). The Ten Commandments on trial. *Education Law Reporter, 194,* 473–487.

Russo, C. J. (2006). Of Baby Jesus and the Easter Bunny: Does Christianity still have a place in the educational marketplace of ideas in the United States? *Education and Law Journal, 16*(1), 61–81.

Russo, C. J., & Mawdsley, R. D. (2002). December dilemmas: The celebration of Christmas in American public schools. *Education and the Law, 13*(4), 381–387.

Russo, C. J., & Raisch, C. D. (2005). Posting religious student art in public schools. *School Business Affairs, 71*(1), 39–41.

Smith, D. G. (2007). The constitutionality of religious symbolism after *McCreary* and *Van Orden*. *Texas Review of Law and Politics, 12,* 93–136.

COURT CASES AND STATUTES

ACLU v. McCreary County, 354 F.3d 438 (6th Cir. Ky. 2003).
Bannon v. School District of Palm Beach County, 387 F.3d 1208 (11th Cir. 2004).
County of Allegheny v. American Civil Liberties Union Greater Pittsburgh Chapter, 492 U.S. 573 (1989).
Engel v. Vitale, 370 U.S. 421 (1962).
Everson v. Board of Education, 330 U.S. 1 (1947a), *reh'g denied*, 330 U.S. 855 (1947b).
Lemon v. Kurtzman, 403 U.S. 602 (1971).
Lynch v. Donnelly, 465 U.S. 668 (1984).
McCollum v. Board of Education, 333 U.S. 203 (1948).
McCreary County, Kentucky v. American Civil Liberties Union of Kentucky, 545 U.S. 844 (2005).
Shelton v. Tucker, 364 U.S. 479 (1960).
Stone v. Graham, 449 U.S. 39 (1981).
Van Orden v. Perry, 545 U.S. 677 (2005).
Washegesic v. Bloomingdale Public Schools, 33 F.3d 679 (6th Cir. 1994a), *reh'g and suggestion for reh'g en banc denied* (1994b), *cert. denied*, 514 U.S. 1095 (1995).

Should students be encouraged or required to participate in pledging allegiance and saluting the flag if they or their parents object to the words "under God"?

POINT: William Jeynes, *California State University, Long Beach*
COUNTERPOINT: Amanda Harmon Cooley, *South Texas College of Law*

OVERVIEW

The seminal Supreme Court case addressing student participation in the Pledge of Allegiance and parental objections is *West Virginia State Board of Education v. Barnette* (1943). In *Barnette*, the Court upheld an injunction prohibiting the board from enforcing a state statute requiring all students to participate in the recitation of the pledge. The Court essentially reversed its own decision from 3 years earlier, *Minersville School District v. Gobitis* (1940), wherein it had upheld a school board's disciplinary punishment of students who refused to participate in the pledge. *Barnette* is best remembered for the Court's assertion,

> If there is any fixed star in our constitutional constellation, it is that no official, high or petty, can prescribe what shall be orthodox in politics,

nationalism, religion, or other matters of opinion or force citizens to confess by word or act their faith therein. (p. 642)

In neither of these cases, though, were the now contested words "under God" in the pledge. Congress added the words "under God" to the Pledge of Allegiance in 1954 at the behest of a religious organization due to concerns about the spread of "godless communism." With the addition of these two words, the legal issues focused on the Establishment Clause of the First Amendment to the Constitution as well as the role of parents in making decisions on behalf of their children.

In *Elk Grove Unified School District v. Newdow* (2004), resolving a split in the lower federal courts, the Supreme Court sidestepped a noncustodial father's Establishment Clause challenge to the State of California's requirement that students participate in the daily recitation of the pledge. Since the custodial mother in *Newdow* had not objected to her daughter's participation in the pledge and was not a party to the suit, the Court reasoned that to the extent that the father lacked standing under California law as a noncustodial parent to make educational decisions for his daughter, he lacked standing, or the legal basis, for addressing the merits of his Establishment Clause challenge. As such, the Supreme Court did not reach the substantive question over the constitutionality of the words "under God" in the pledge.

On remand, the Ninth Circuit (*Newdow v. Rio Linda Union School District*, 2010) ultimately rejected the noncustodial father's claim on the merits after he was joined by like-minded plaintiffs. The Ninth Circuit thus joined the Seventh Circuit (*Sherman v. Community Consolidated School District 21 of Wheeling Township*, 1992, 1993) in reaching this outcome. The Fourth Circuit (*Myers v. Loudoun County Public Schools*, 2005) also upheld the words "under God" as not violating the Establishment Clause. Thus, it is unlikely that this debate will soon reach the Supreme Court. Even so, this is a debate that is likely to continue to linger in public schools as parents seek to assert their rights not to participate in the pledge and flag salute.

The Third Circuit did, in fact, address the role of parents in the participation of their children in the pledge, albeit in a private school, in *Circle Schools v. Pappert* (2004). The court invalidated a Pennsylvania statute requiring school officials to notify parents if their children did not participate in the pledge. The court held that the parental notification provision "unconstitutionally tread[s] on students' First Amendment right [not to speak as well as] . . . school plaintiffs' First Amendment associational rights" (p. 180). Having found the statute unconstitutional based on the rights of students, the Third Circuit avoided addressing the claim of whether it violated the parents' "fundamental liberty interest . . . in the education of their children, [s]pecifically [the state's] infringe[ment] of the rights of parents . . . by imposing restrictions unrelated to legitimate educational concerns" (p. 183).

Against this background, the two essays in this chapter take different perspectives on what children should be expected to do during the daily recitation of the Pledge of Allegiance and flag salute. On the one hand, the point essay of William Jeynes (California State University, Long Beach) takes the position that insofar as the inclusion of the words "under God" in the pledge is not an assertion of faith in God or religion, students should be encouraged to participate in its recitation and the flag salute as part of their American heritage. On the other hand, the counterpoint essay by Amanda Harmon Cooley (South Texas College of Law) is of the view that since the mandatory daily recitation of the Pledge of Allegiance violates the First Amendment rights of students, then they should be free not to participate in the Pledge of Allegiance and flag salute if they object on religious or other grounds.

As you read these essays, ask yourself the following two questions. First, does the inclusion of the words "under God" in the Pledge of Allegiance amount to a statement of belief in religion such that it violates the Establishment Clause? Put another way, can an argument be made that insofar as the inclusion of the words "under God" in the pledge is an acknowledgment of the role that religion has played in American history, then the words do not violate the Establishment Clause? Second, should students be required to participate in the daily recitation of the pledge?

Charles J. Russo
University of Dayton

Ralph D. Mawdsley
Cleveland State University

POINT: William Jeynes
California State University, Long Beach

Consistent with the position of the Supreme Court that school officials cannot force students to participate in the flag salute or Pledge of Allegiance, this essay acknowledges that individuals certainly have the freedom not to participate in this daily patriotic activity. However, the essay takes the position that, case law aside, students should voluntarily join in the recitation of the pledge and salute to the flag as a means of enhancing national unity.

The Supreme Court first decided in 1940 in *Minersville School District v. Gobitis* that students had to participate in the pledge. However, 3 years later, in *West Virginia State Board of Education v. Barnette* (1943), the Court essentially reversed itself in holding that students were free not to participate in the pledge. Lower courts have reached similar results. By all means, this decision should be upheld. Requiring students to recite the pledge would be inconsistent with the Supreme Court's ruling and the underlying values of liberty and freedom of conscience. At the same time, though, this essay argues that American students and their parents should reexamine the value of the pledge and flag salute in the hope that they will join in these patriotic activities as a sign of sharing national values.

WHY THE PLEDGE SHOULD BE RECITED

To comprehend fully the value of the Pledge of Allegiance and accompanying flag salute, one should consider its contents and, in so doing, come to appreciate its enduring significance and worth. What many people overlook is that in reciting the Pledge of Allegiance, Americans commit themselves to one another, not God or religion.

> I pledge allegiance to the flag of the United States of America,
>
> And to the republic for which it stands,
>
> One nation, under God,
>
> Indivisible, with liberty and justice for all. (4 U.S.C. § 4 (1954))

What students assert in the pledge is that Americans should care about the welfare of all U.S. citizens. When it comes to the welfare of fellow citizens, Americans should not be divided but instead devoted to "liberty and justice for all." For example, Americans should care about those who suffer as a result of regional disasters, such as Hurricane Katrina and the BP oil spill catastrophe. The adherence to the Pledge of Allegiance, combined with the flag salute, and the internalization of its values is one of the primary means Americans have to express love and commitment to one another—again, not to God or religion. Through American history, this spirit of commitment to one another has given rise to antislavery initiatives, the civil rights movement, and the willingness of brave men and women to lay down their lives for one another. Out of this spirit, firefighters and rescue squads on 9/11 ascended the towers of the World Trade Center, as they heard it creak and felt it wobble, cognizant of the phenomenal risks that they were incurring.

UNDERLYING PRINCIPLES

Those supporting participation in the pledge and flag salute by all students have difficulty understanding why parents and others object to children's choosing to participate in honoring the following principles asserted in the Pledge of Allegiance and accompanying flag salute by joining in their daily recitation. This point essay takes the position that the pledge reiterates key principles as Americans, which students honor by joining in the daily recitation of the Pledge of Allegiance.

Unity

The Pledge of Allegiance encourages students to have compassion and be concerned about the welfare of all of the nation's people. It declares that Americans are to function as the United States and that the nation is to be "indivisible." The nation needs more compassion, not less of this quality. When Americans are killed as a consequence of crime, for example, the remainder of the population should care. Yet, there is evidence that compassion stemming from a sense of unity is a quality that the nation needs in greater doses than it possesses now. Polls and surveys indicate that the United States, contrary to its name, is, in many respects, a divided country. Tensions exist between people living in the inner city versus the suburbs, between Democrats and Republicans, as well as among races. By joining in the pledge, children and adults can work their way through these divisions and help the nation to become one people.

Liberty and Justice for All

The Pledge of Allegiance involves a commitment to liberty and justice for *all*; it is not merely liberty and justice for oneself. One is reminded of the famous quote by the German Evangelical pastor, Martin Niemöller (1892–1984), an anticommunist who initially supported German dictator Adolf Hitler, but who later vigorously opposed Hitler when he realized that he was both anti-Jewish and anti-Christian. In his often-quoted words, Niemöller expressed the fear that because he remained silent when he said nothing after the Nazis came for the communists, social democrats, trade unionists, and Jews because he was not one of them, there was no one left to speak on his behalf when they came for him.

It is wise to remember that even the founders of this country did not consider democracy as inherently good and self-sustaining, In this regard, in his Farewell Address, President George Washington warned of an unbridled democracy that is out of control. Washington believed that such a development was almost inevitable unless democracy was accompanied by the practice of morality. In essence, what Washington was stating is that democracy tends to lead toward self-centeredness, unless it is accompanied by moral restraint. President Ronald Reagan also averred that human beings have a proclivity toward self-centeredness, especially when economic factors are in play. He asserted that the tendency was for persons to define recessions as occurring when their neighbors were unemployed and depressions as transpiring when they themselves were unemployed.

There is a natural propensity for human beings to be self-centered. Loyalty to the Pledge of Allegiance will help students to instead become "other-centered." Students can make this declaration as an assertion that they are not merely committed to seeking liberty and justice for themselves, but that they are committing themselves to pursuing liberty and justice for all Americans.

The Pledge of Allegiance and flag salute are designed to lead each individual to reflect on the injustices that confront their neighbors and citizens across the great spans of the United States. If one sees a lack of justice because the government or a bank has taken away the land of an individual, Americans should care. If religious expression is impeded or a community affords more compassion toward adolescent perpetrators of crimes than for the victims, Americans should care. For any citizenry to survive, there must be an understanding that the attitude "it is all about me" is not in the nation's best interest.

An argument can be made that nations thrive where there is love and concern for other people. When citizens decide to live in self-imposed isolation from one another, purposely removed from the hurts and tribulations that others experience, the ultimate decline and fall of that civilization has already been set in motion. If anything, history is replete with examples, starting with the Roman empire, of how a loss of common values led to national decline. If all do not work together, then it may only be a matter of time before social disorder, rioting, and inexplicable shooting rampages take place. Where there is no love, people die from within. When Americans refuse to lovingly commit themselves to the experience of "liberty and justice" of those around them, America begins to die. To cease to care is indeed to begin to cease. One would thus hope that as Americans, students and their parents should express solidarity for all through participation in the pledge and flag salute.

When students pledge a heightened level of commitment to the principles of "liberty and justice for all," they also express a willingness to be concerned with these issues for people around the world. It appears that all nations are not committed to these issues to the same degree that Americans are. Unfortunately, oppression is all too common in many parts of the world. Today, in many nations, large numbers of people cannot vote, go to college, or serve in high positions in government because of their faiths or ethnicities. In many nations, only one faith is allowed and only one or a select few ethnicities are recognized as possessing any inherent value. When American students declare their commitment to "liberty and justice for all," it is a promise not only to care about people in the United States, but also to embrace the cares, concerns, and the sufferings of people all over the world. Reciting the pledge may help to awake the feelings of compassion for these people, not only in the United States but also around the globe.

The Flag

It is valuable for students to become cognizant of the qualities the American flag represents. What do red and white stand for? "White signifies purity and innocence, Red, hardiness & valour, and Blue, the color of the Chief (the broad band above the stripes) signifies vigilance, perseverance & justice" (Streufert, 2005). An understanding of the flag will help students comprehend and honor the nation's roots, which include justice, loyalty, community, love, and mutual commitment. Participating in the Pledge of Allegiance and flag salute can lead teachers and students to reflect on this symbolism.

One Nation, Under God

The assertion of the Pledge of Allegiance and flag salute is that U.S. citizenry is to act as one nation. Although there are well over 300 million inhabitants dwelling between the nation's shores, people should not think of themselves as isolated and alone within this nation. Although Americans may differ from one another in appearance, ethnicity, and location, Americans must not feel alone in this country. Americans have each other.

In recent years, though, the phrase "under God" in the pledge has become controversial. Nevertheless, the words "under God" in the pledge need not be interpreted as seeking to sway Americans into adhering to a particular set of religious tenets. Rather, supporters of these words interpret the phrase as acknowledging that, consistent with the approach taken in the Declaration of Independence, all have been endowed with inalienable rights from the Creator as a form of civic or ceremonial religion, the recognition of the place that the Founders saw for God in the creation of this nation, not a statement of belief in God or of adherence to religion. They are included to affirm that the freedoms and rights that Americans cherish and enjoy are eternal in nature and are not guaranteed by the unpredictable ways of humanity that could eradicate them with a simple coup d'état.

These words are also included to remind Americans that the nation's founders cited God frequently as the basis on which they could assert that these freedoms and rights were a birthright. However, the inclusion of references to God in America's founding documents, and later inclusion in the pledge in 1954, is an integral part of the nation's heritage. As noted, Thomas Jefferson argued in the Declaration of Independence that it was the Creator who had endowed people with certain "unalienable rights." In other words, Americans could call for the free exercise of certain rights because they were God-given. Jefferson and the founders of the United States believed that Americans must understand that the rights guaranteed under the Constitution are God-given and not spawned by humans. If human beings are the source of the rights of the citizenry, then at a moment's notice, these rights can be taken away. In this case, human rights—whether they are the right to vote, civil rights, the right not to be discriminated against, the right to act by one's conscience, and so forth—are only relative rights that are not eternally applicable and enduring. In contrast, if these rights are divinely inspired and from God, or the Creator as noted in the Declaration of Independence, then they are eternal and absolute and cannot rightfully be pillaged by human beings.

At the same time, it should be clear that this essay is not suggesting that it is un-American to criticize the inclusion of God in the pledge or to opt out of participating in its daily recitation. However, the essay supports the position that students should participate in reciting the pledge because the inclusion, and retention, of the words "under God" represent the recognition of the place that the Founders saw for God in the creation of this nation. It is, as noted, not meant to be a statement of belief in God or of adherence to religion. To this end, it might be helpful to think of the words "under God" as a form of what has been described as civic or ceremonial religion, meaning that doing so acknowledges that the Founders believed that God played a key role in guiding American history rather than as the establishment of a specific religion. From this perspective, it is hoped that all will share this view and support the pledge and flag salute as forms of sharing American values, not a profession of faith.

CONCLUSION

If parents or children themselves desire not to participate in the Pledge of Allegiance and flag salute, as it stands now they certainly have that right as Americans to refrain from doing so. However, students should consider joining in the recitation of the Pledge of Allegiance and flag salute, not as a sign or prayer of worship, but as a reminder that they are Americans.

COUNTERPOINT: Amanda Harmon Cooley
South Texas College of Law

One of the purposes of American public education is to introduce students to the political institutions, constitutional rights, and civic values of the United States. This educational objective is manifest in the required history and civic curriculums that are mandated by state legislatures. This goal is an important one for helping to maintain national unity and for teaching students about their basic civil liberties. Many educators and political leaders argue that a required daily recitation by all students of the Pledge of Allegiance in American schools is an innocuous form of accomplishing civic education. Yet, such an argument, if transformed into practice, is a direct infringement of the legal rights of students.

Based on well-settled Supreme Court case law, this essay stands for the notion that students should not be required to participate by saluting the flag during the recitation of the Pledge of Allegiance at public schools if they or their parents object to the inclusion of the words "under God" or other words in the pledge insofar as such a requirement would clearly violate students' First Amendment freedom of speech rights. Further, this essay adds that students should not be required to obtain parental permission to refrain from saluting the flag during the pledge since such a requirement also violates the students' First Amendment rights. Finally, this counterpoint essay advances the position that along with the constitutional argument, any governmental requirement to compel students to recite the Pledge of Allegiance or salute the flag during it would undercut the vital political value of dissent that has been central to the democratic tradition in the United States. Arguments to the contrary, such as those raised in the point essay, undercut the foundational tenents of American civic values.

ESTABLISHED SUPREME COURT PRECEDENT

Since the landmark *West Virginia State Board of Education v. Barnette* (1943), the Supreme Court has firmly established that states do not have the power to force citizens to speak. This applies to students in the classroom. Specifically, *Barnette* struck down as unconstitutional a regulation from the West Virginia Board of Education requiring students to salute the flag while reciting the Pledge of Allegiance and classifying a refusal to do so as punishable insubordination. In the majority opinion of the Court, Justice Robert Jackson declared,

> We think the action of the local authorities in compelling the flag salute and pledge transcends constitutional limitations on their power and invades the sphere of intellect and spirit which it is the purpose of the First Amendment to our Constitution to reserve from all official control. (p. 642)

Barnette is important for many reasons. First, the justices essentially overruled *Minersville School District v. Gobitis* (1940), wherein the Supreme Court found that public school officials in Pennsylvania could constitutionally compel students, despite the religious or philosophical objections that they or their parents had, to salute the flag and say the Pledge of Allegiance. Further, in *Barnette*, the Supreme Court determined that the state regulation from West Virginia compelled speech in violation of the First Amendment freedom of speech rights of students. The Court explained that school children, like all citizens, have the right to both speak and the right to refrain from speaking. This is true despite external political circumstances that were reaffirmed by the timing of *Barnette* as the United States was then in the midst of World War II. Consequently, it is clear that students cannot be required to salute the flag during the recitation of the Pledge of Allegiance at public schools if they or their parents object to the inclusion of the words "under God" or other words since such a requirement would run contrary to clearly established Supreme Court First Amendment case law.

Given the longstanding precedent of this case, to reject the fundamental holding in *Barnette* at this point, one would either have to find a fault in the reasoning of the Supreme Court or assert that social, political, or other circumstances have changed to such an extent that a different interpretation of the Constitution when applied to a new set of facts is needed. Yet, such an argument, at either level, would be misguided. Simply, there is not a compelling case to be made that would suggest a need to overturn the basic democratic values of freedom of speech, dissent, protection of minority views, and religious pluralism that are supported by the opinion in *Barnette*. These values have been examined in several other federal cases that have involved students and the Pledge of Allegiance; time and time again, in these cases, the core *Barnette* principles have been upheld and affirmed.

STUDENTS' CONSTITUTIONAL RIGHTS

In 1973, in *Goetz v. Ansell*, the Second Circuit expanded *Barnette*. In this case, Theodore Goetz, an honor student and president of his senior class in Latham, New York, attempted to assert his right not to speak by remaining seated at his desk during the recitation of the Pledge of Allegiance, even though school policies required him to stand in silence or to leave the classroom. The court found that Goetz should be allowed to remain seated without punishment during the pledge as forcing him to stand would be in conflict with his First Amendment rights regarding compelled speech.

Similarly, in *Lipp v. Morris* (1978), the Third Circuit was of the opinion that a state law from New Jersey requiring all students to either salute the flag or stand at attention during the Pledge of Allegiance was unconstitutional. The rationale of the Third Circuit was based in large part on *Barnette* and *Goetz*. Each of these decisions correctly apply the Constitution and reflect the rightful proposition that students should not be required to salute the flag during the recitation of the Pledge of Allegiance at public schools if they or their parents object to the inclusion of the words "under God" or other words in the pledge.

A more contemporary example of this balancing between majority and minority rights involved the passage of a Colorado statute in 2003, which mandated the daily recitation of the Pledge of Allegiance by students and teachers in public schools. The only opt-out provisions for students that were incorporated into the law were those based on religious grounds or if students' parents filed written objection with the school principal. After this legislation became effective, the *Lane v. Owens* case was filed in the federal trial court in Colorado. The judge, citing the established precedent of *Barnette* and its progeny, ruled that the statute did not pass constitutional muster and granted the plaintiffs' motion for a temporary restraining order, forbidding the enforcement of the statute. As a result, in the following year, the Colorado legislature amended the statute by making the Pledge of Allegiance voluntary rather than mandatory. Here, the judiciary and the legislature acted in accordance with the constitutional rights that are granted via the First Amendment.

What is interesting about each of these cases, which reaffirmed the guiding principles of *Barnette*, is that many state legislatures and school boards continue to pursue policies that compel students to participate in the Pledge of Allegiance, salute the flag, or stand at attention even when the courts continue to strike down such policies. In essence, the famous words of *Barnette*, which assert that some rights are beyond the reach of the legislatures, are still heavily contested by those very branches of government:

> The very purpose of a Bill of Rights was to withdraw certain subjects from the vicissitudes of political controversy, to place them beyond the reach of majorities and officials and to establish them as legal principles to be applied by the courts. (p. 638)

The *Barnette* Court deemed the right to free speech to be one of these fundamental rights that are not dependent on either elections or votes. Consequently, the tension between the political arena and judicial chambers on this issue has not ceased even in the face of continued court decisions that allow students to dissent from the majority views of their states and schools. Hence, the courts that reinforce the foundational principles of *Barnette* in student Pledge of Allegiance cases are correctly interpreting the law; legislatures that strive to pass statutes that contravene *Barnette* are likewise contravening the Constitution. A closer examination of state Pledge of Allegiance statutes demonstrates that future inquiry on the scope of students' First Amendment rights in public schools will likely involve the opt-out provisions that are included in these statutes.

CONSTITUTIONALITY OF OPT-OUT PROVISIONS

Although it appears that most state legislatures are willing to acknowledge and follow the bright line rule of *Barnette* that students cannot be compelled to salute the flag and recite the Pledge of Allegiance, many state statutes have been passed requiring parental consent as the only way for students to opt out of saluting the flag during the pledge. These statutes, just like the regulation that was at issue in *Barnette*, are unconstitutional and should be struck down as a violation of students' First Amendment free speech rights.

An example of this type of statute was at issue in *Frazier v. Winn*, which was decided by the Eleventh Circuit in 2008. Here, the court was asked to examine the Florida Pledge of Allegiance statute, which required civilians to stand at attention to respect the flag during the daily recitation of the Pledge of Allegiance in public schools and written parental consent as the only means for a student to opt out of reciting the pledge. A high school student challenged the constitutionality of these two provisions of the Florida law. The trial court maintained that insofar as the student's argument had merit, both of these provisions were unconstitutional. On appeal, the Eleventh Circuit affirmed that requiring students to stand during the Pledge of Allegiance violated the First Amendment. At the same time, the court reversed the trial court's order in pointing out that the parental consent requirement violated the student's constitutional rights.

Frazier is problematic insofar as it asserts that the fundamental rights of parents to determine how to bring up their children outweigh the fundamental free speech rights of students to not be compelled to speak. This case sets a dangerous precedent for the evaluation of other state statutes that premise the rights of student to opt out of mandatory recitation of the Pledge of Allegiance while saluting the flag solely on parental consent. This case runs contrary to *Barnette* and should not be followed by other courts that will likely soon address this issue.

The *Frazier* determination not only conflicts with the decisions of *Barnette* and its progeny; it also chips away at the solid bedrock principles that the Supreme Court enunciated in its famous 1969 judgment in *Tinker v. Des Moines Independent Community School District*, a case that arose out of the contentious Vietnam era when students sought to wear black arm bands to school as a form of political protest:

> First Amendment rights, applied in light of the special characteristics of the school environment, are available to teachers and students. It can hardly be argued that either students or teachers shed their constitutional rights to freedom of speech or expression at the schoolhouse gate. (p. 506)

In an era where states and schools are increasingly narrowing the legal rights of students and teachers, it seems that core principles like freedom of speech should be held inviolate within the schoolhouse door. Therefore, state statutes requiring parental consent in opt-out provisions for students during the Pledge of Allegiance should be deemed as an unconstitutional end run around the rightfully decided *Barnette*.

Still, it is worth noting that not all courts agree on parental notification. To this end, the Third Circuit, in *Circle Schools v. Pappert* (2004), reached the opposite result. Here, the court invalidated a statute that required school officials in Pennsylvania to notify parents if their children did not participate in the daily recitation of the pledge. The court ruled that the statute violated the free speech rights of students and the association rights of the private school by seeking to compel their speech in having to recite the Pledge of Allegiance.

CONCLUSION

By way of conclusion, one of the primary articulated purposes of American public education is to provide students with an introduction to government, civics, and the law. However, some educators and legislators are choosing to confront students with a forced recitation of the Pledge of Allegiance, despite students' religious, philosophical, or moral objections, instead of promoting a vibrant and rich social studies, civics, and history curriculum. The fact that almost 90% of the states have some type of Pledge of Allegiance statute is telling in the nation's desire to promote civic engagement, which is inarguably an important cause.

If these statutes do not contain provisions allowing for students to not participate in the Pledge of Allegiance based on their religious, philosophical, or other beliefs, then these laws should be struck down as unconstitutional. Additionally, if these opt-out provisions are expressly conditioned on parental consent, then these laws should also be struck down as unconstitutional. Although these may seem like difficult cases, educators will best illustrate the true meaning of civic values by upholding the legal and constitutional rights of their students. In sum, America's democratic values of free speech and dissent require that students have the option not to salute the flag during the recitation of the Pledge of Allegiance at public schools if they object to the inclusion of the words "under God" or other words in the pledge.

FURTHER READINGS AND RESOURCES

Ellis, R. J. (2005). *To the flag: The unlikely history of the Pledge of Allegiance.* Lawrence: University Press of Kansas.

Falconer, B. (2003, November). Murder by state. *The Atlantic Monthly,* pp. 56–57.

Haynes, C., Chaltain, S., Ferguson, J., Jr., Hudson, D., Jr., & Thomas, O. (2003). *The First Amendment in schools: A guide from the First Amendment Center.* Alexandria, VA: Association for Supervision and Curriculum Development.

Hudson, D., Jr. (2003). *The silencing of student voices: Preserving free speech in America's schools.* Nashville, TN: First Amendment Center. Retrieved from http://www.firstamendmentcenter.org/PDF/Silencing.intro.pdf

Mawdsley, R. D., & Russo, C. J. (2006). *Myers v. Loudoun County Public School Board:* The Fourth Circuit upholds the Pledge of Allegiance. *Education Law Reporter, 205,* 1–18.

Russo, C. J. (2004). The Supreme Court and Pledge of Allegiance: Does God still have a place in American schools? *Brigham Young University Education and Law Journal, 2004*(2), 301–330.

Russo, C. J. (2010). Pledge of Allegiance causes more controversy. *School Business Affairs, 76*(6), 34–36.

Russo, C. J., & Mawdsley, R. D. (2004). Trumped again: The Supreme Court reverses the Ninth Circuit and upholds the Pledge of Allegiance. *Education Law Reporter, 192,* 287–299.

Russo, C. J., & Mawdsley, R. D. (2007). *Elk Grove Unified School District v. Newdow:* The Supreme Court and Pledge of Allegiance. In W. Jeynes & E. Martinez (Eds.), *Christianity, education and modern society* (pp. 93–106). Charlotte, NC: Information Age Publishing.

Streufert, D. (2005, February 10). *What do the colors of the Flag mean?* Retrieved from http://usflag.org/colors.html

Whittaker, K. (2009). Gay–straight alliances and free speech: Are parental consent laws constitutional? *Berkeley Journal of Gender, Law & Justice, 24,* 48–67.

COURT CASES AND STATUTES

Circle Schools v. Pappert, 381 F.3d 172 (3d Cir. 2004).
Elk Grove Unified School District v. Newdow, 542 U.S. 1 (2004).
Frazier v. Winn, 535 F.3d 1279 (11th Cir. 2008).
Goetz v. Ansell, 477 F.2d 636 (2d Cir. 1973).
Lane v. Owens, No. 03-B-1544 (D. Colo. Aug. 15, 2003). Retrieved from http://www.aclu-co.org/docket/200309/200309_309pledge_Courts_Oral_Ruling_8-15-03.pdf
Lipp v. Morris, 579 F.2d 834 (3d Cir. 1978).
Minersville School District v. Gobitis, 310 U.S. 586 (1940).
Myers v. Loudoun County Public Schools, 418 F.3d 395 (4th Cir. 2005).
Newdow v. Rio Linda Union School District, 597 F.3d 1007 (9th Cir. 2010).
The Pledge of Allegiance to the Flag, 4 U.S.C. § 4 (1954).
Sherman v. Community Consolidated School District 21 of Wheeling Township, 980 F.2d 437 (7th Cir. 1992), *cert. denied,* 508 U.S. 950 (1993).
Tinker v. Des Moines Independent Community School District, 393 U.S. 503 (1969).
West Virginia State Board of Education v. Barnette, 319 U.S. 624 (1943).

Should public school students be given released time for religious instruction?

POINT: Kiera M. Sullivan, *Elsass, Wallace, Evans, Schnelle & Co., LPA, Sidney, Ohio*
COUNTERPOINT: Lindsey Swanson, *Haller and Colvin, PC, Fort Wayne, Indiana*

OVERVIEW

Released time is the practice of allowing public school students to participate in religious education during normal school hours by releasing them from secular studies for a period of time. Many school boards in the first part of the 20th century began to allow students to be released from secular classes for this purpose. Generally, released time religious classes were held off campuses and were not taught by public school employees. Giving students released time is not as widespread today as it was in the 1940s and 1950s when legal challenges placed some restrictions on the practice. Even so, many school boards in the United States still offer students the option of being released from classes to attend religious education programs. In two major challenges to the practice, the Supreme Court struck down a program that allowed religious instruction to take place on school property during the school day but approved a program in which the religious classes were held off campus, even though they were also conducted during the school day.

The first major challenge to released time arose when a parent filed suit alleging that the practice violated the Establishment Clause of the First Amendment and Equal Protection Clause of the Fourteenth Amendment to the Constitution. The suit was filed after the parent complained, without avail, to school officials in Champaign, Illinois, that one of her children was being ostracized for not participating in released time classes. Among other things, she insisted that even though participation in released time classes was supposed to be voluntary, students were, in fact, coerced into attending the classes. In this instance, religious education classes were taught during school hours in public school buildings by teachers employed by private religious groups, subject to the approval and supervision of the superintendent of schools. Students attending religious education classes did so with parental permission and were excused from attending secular classes. Those who chose not to participate in the religious education program remained in their regular classes, presumably continuing with their secular studies. After being unsuccessful in the state courts, the mother appealed to the Supreme Court.

In *People of State of Illinois ex rel. McCollum v. Board of Education of School District No. 71, Champaign County* (1948), the Supreme Court ruled that the practice of permitting religious education to take place in the public schools during normal school hours and excusing students from their secular schedule to attend religious classes was unconstitutional. The Court was convinced that using public property for religious instruction along with using the compulsory attendance system to assist with the religious education instruction amounted to using the tax-supported public schools to aid religious groups in spreading their religious faith. Noting that the First Amendment prohibits the establishment of religion by states and requires a strict separation of church and state, the Court held that using state property for religious classes and providing state support for students' attendance in such classes was unconstitutional.

Four years later, the Supreme Court reached a different result in reviewing a New York law that allowed for students to be released from classes at their parents' request to attend religious education classes held at religious centers. Insofar as school attendance was compulsory, personnel from the religious centers reported their attendance to public school officials, and students who were not released remained in their public school classrooms. No public funds were spent, and no public facilities were used in running the program. Even so, a group of taxpayers and parents filed suit claiming that the program was unlawful under *McCollum*. After the plaintiffs succeeded in state courts, the board of education appealed to the Supreme Court.

In *Zorach v. Clauson* (1952), the Supreme Court decided that allowing public school officials to release children early from their schools so that they could receive religious instruction elsewhere was constitutional. The Court explained that this arrangement did not violate the First Amendment because it did not involve the use of public facilities or state financial support. Thus, the Court determined that the statute neither respected the establishment of religion nor prohibited its free exercise within the meaning of the First Amendment. It is also important to note that the Court did not see any evidence that students were coerced into attending the religious classes. In distinguishing *McCollum* from *Zorach*, the Court observed that in *McCollum*, public school classrooms were used for religious instruction, and the authority of the public schools was used to support the program. By contrast, in *Zorach*, the Court acknowledged that public school officials only accommodated their schedules, at the request of parents, so that the religious instruction could take place.

Even though *McCollum* and *Zorach* established the constitutional parameters for released time programs, there has been some additional litigation. In a more current case also challenging a released time program in New York, the Second Circuit ruled that the program did not violate the Establishment Clause because it did not use public funds, religious instruction was not on site, participation was voluntary, and nonparticipants were not coerced or pressured to participate (*Pierce ex rel. Pierce v. Sullivan West Central School District*, 2004). A federal trial court in South Carolina rejected a challenge to a released time program that awarded students academic credit for participating in religious classes (*Moss v. Spartanburg County School District No. 7*, 2011). The court was convinced that the program was constitutional because it did not have an impermissible religious motive, its principal effect neither advanced nor inhibited religion, and it did not create excessive entanglement because it gave students credit without regard to a particular religion or denomination (citing *Lemon v. Kurtzman*, 1971).

The two essayists in this chapter have divergent views on the question of whether public school boards should provide released time for religious education. Although each acknowledged that the courts have allowed the practice, they differ on many of the fundamental legal and policy issues involved with released time. In the point essay, Kiera M. Sullivan, of Elsass, Wallace, Evans, Schnelle & Co., LPA (Sidney, Ohio), argues that since we are a religious people, boards should accommodate religious beliefs by giving students the opportunity to receive religious instruction during released time with parental consent. As long as the religious education classes do not take place on school grounds and meet other constitutional requirements, Sullivan contends that giving students released time follows the best of our religious traditions.

In contrast, in the counterpoint essay, Lindsey Swanson, of Haller and Colvin, PC (Fort Wayne, Indiana), strongly disagrees with allowing public school boards to grant released time to students. In spite of current jurisprudence, Swanson insists that when public school boards allow released time, they entangle themselves with religion. By structuring their schedules around the released time, Swanson maintains that boards aid in the advancement of religion. Thus, Swanson disagrees with the courts that have ruled that providing released time does not violate the Establishment Clause.

As you read these essays, ask yourself the following questions. First, do you think that released time programs should be permitted? Second, are released time programs pedagogically sound? Put another way, is it wise to allow students to miss some of their state-mandated curricular subjects to go and study religion?

Allan G. Osborne, Jr.
Principal (Retired), Snug Harbor Community School,
Quincy, Massachusetts

POINT: Kiera M. Sullivan
*Elsass, Wallace, Evans, Schnelle & Co., LPA,
Sidney, Ohio*

Supreme Court Justice William O. Douglas, in the majority opinion in *Zorach v. Clauson* (1952), wrote,

> We are a religious people whose institutions presuppose a Supreme Being. We guarantee the freedom to worship as one chooses.... When the state encourages religious instruction or cooperates with religious authorities by adjusting the schedule of public events to sectarian needs, it follows the best of our traditions. For it then respects the religious nature of our traditions. For it then respects the religious nature of our people and accommodates the public service to their spiritual needs. To hold that it may not would be to find in the Constitution a requirement that the government show a callous indifference to religious groups. That would be preferring those who believe in no religion over those who do believe. (p. 313)

Released time programs afford parents the opportunity to have their children who attend public schools be released from classes during the school day to attend religious education classes of their choice. As long as these classes are not conducted in public school buildings during normal school hours, then the Supreme Court has ruled that the practice does not violate the Constitution's First Amendment jurisprudence. Although public schools are not required to participate in any sort of released time program, the Court has held that such programs in public schools are constitutional as long as public funds and facilities are not used to support the religious instruction. This principle is based on the constitutional right of parents to direct the religious education of their children. As such, this point essay argues that public school students should be released from classes to participate in religious instruction and that more public schools should accommodate the religious beliefs of their students by affording them the opportunity to participate in released time programs.

BEGINNING OF RELEASED TIME PROGRAMS

The idea of releasing public school students for devotional religious study off school premises was first discussed in the United States in 1905 at a conference in New York City. The proposal was for public elementary schools to close one day a week in addition to Sunday so those parents who so desired could have their children attend religious instruction outside of the school building. However, released time programs were not officially created until 1914 when William Wirt, an educator and superintendent of the Gary, Indiana, schools, enacted the first program. The released time program quickly caught on, and by 1922, released time programs were active in 23 states. In 1932, 30 states had active released time programs in 400 communities with enrollment of 250,000 students. By 1942, participation reached 1.5 million students in 46 states. In 1947 released time reached its peak with enrollment totals of 2 million students in approximately 2,200 communities. During this time, legislation favoring released time was adopted by 12 states (Bible Education Released Time, 2011).

There are approximately 1,000 released time programs operating today, with about 250,000 students enrolled nationally (Bible Education Released Time, 2011). These released time programs involve students ranging from kindergarten through high school. Generally, these released time programs allow students to have a free daily class period, which may be used for extracurricular religious studies.

LITIGATION

The constitutionality of released time programs was clearly established by the Supreme Court in *Zorach v. Clauson* (1952), a dispute from New York City. In *Zorach*, the Court was of the opinion that released time programs in public schools are constitutional so long as students are released on the written permission of their parents; all religious groups are treated equally and are allowed to participate; and students leave school grounds for the religious instruction and devotional exercises. Therefore, under *Zorach*, states can allow released time programs as long as they meet those conditions. Most states, though, leave it up to individual school boards to decide whether to offer released time for their students.

Long after *Zorach* was settled law, two lower federal courts reached similar results in upholding programs. In a case from New York, the Second Circuit affirmed that a program satisfied Establishment Clause analysis because it did not use public funds or on-site religious instruction, was purely voluntary, and school officials did not impose any specific coercion or pressure to bear on nonparticipating students (*Pierce ex rel. Pierce v. Sullivan West Central School District*, 2004). More recently, the federal trial court in South Carolina denied the claims of opponents who challenged the constitutionality of a released time program that granted students the opportunity to earn academic credit for participating in off-campus religion classes. The court found that the program was constitutional because it satisfied all three prongs of the *Lemon* test since there was no impermissible religious motive, its principal or primary effect did not advance religion, and it did not create excessive entanglement because it allowed students to earn credit without considering the specific religions or denominations of the courses they completed.

OPPOSITION TO RELEASED TIME

There are more than 13,000 school districts in the United States but, as noted, only about 1,000 participate in released time programs. This raises the question of why more school boards choose not to make arrangements for students to participate in such programs if there is no constitutional bar to their doing so.

As reflected in the two more recent cases, some opponents of released time argue that despite *Zorach*, such programs violate the Establishment Clause of the First Amendment to the Constitution. The First Amendment reads in relevant part, "Congress shall make no law respecting an establishment of religion, or prohibiting the free exercise thereof." Some educators, and perhaps parents, fear that if they allow released time programs in their public schools, then, in effect, they will be establishing or promoting a religion. Yet, judicial opinions simply do not support this proposition. The courts have agreed that as long as released time programs are privately run and the only involvement of public school officials is to accommodate the schedules of their students, there are no constitutional infirmities.

ARGUMENTS FOR RELEASED TIME

There are four arguments why released time programs should be permitted to continue to operate. First, when students participate in released time programs, they are not forced to attend religious instruction or prayer. The decision of whether to participate in released time religious instruction is entirely up to students and their parents. If school boards have released time programs in place, those students who choose not to attend any outside religious instruction can remain behind in their school buildings to attend elective secular classes or study halls.

Second, religious instruction or devotional activities are not brought on to the public school grounds. Since students must leave their campuses, this ensures that there is no religious influence on those children who choose not to become involved or those who participate in programs run by different religious groups.

Third, all religions, large and small, are supposed to be treated equally under such released time programs. Public school officials are not allowed to favor one religion over another, nor can they favor religion in general over no religion at all.

Fourth, no federal or state funds are, or can be, used to support released time programs. Released time programs are entirely funded by the individual religious groups themselves. Therefore, released time programs, wherein officials in public schools allow for students to be released to religious instruction, do not translate to the establishment of any particular religion, or even religion in general, and thus, there is no violation of the First Amendment.

Free Exercise of Religion

The First Amendment provides that the government cannot establish a religion, but it also provides that the government cannot prohibit the free exercise thereof. When school boards fail, or refuse, to allow released time programs, they are essentially prohibiting students from freely exercising, practicing, or continuing their religious instruction or prayer at any time during school. It is true that the country's founders wished for church and state to be separate, but again, the programs allowing for released time do not take place on school grounds, they treat all religions equally, they do not promote any one religion or even religion in general, and no tax dollars are spent on the programs. Further, released time programs simply do not promote the entanglement of church and state. Officials in public schools that participate in such released time programs are merely accommodating the religious needs of our society.

Even the minimum involvement of public school officials in making sure that released students actually show up for their religious education classes does not amount to the excessive entanglement banned under the Supreme Court's *Lemon v. Kurtzman* (1971) standard. In *Lemon*, the Supreme Court established a three-part test for determining if statutes, policies, or practices violated the First Amendment. According to the Court, to be constitutional, state statutes or actions must have a secular legislative purpose, must have a principal or primary effect that neither advances nor inhibits religion, and may not foster an excessive entanglement between government and religion.

Moreover, there is no doubt that the First Amendment reflects the philosophy that church and state should be separated, but the First Amendment does not say that in *every* and *all* respects there shall be a separation of church and state or that the government needs to be hostile toward religion. Rather, it means that there shall be no concern, union, or dependency of one or the other. Otherwise, the state and religion would be aliens to each other. For example, municipalities would not be permitted to render police or fire protection to religious groups. Policemen who help parishioners into their place of worship would violate the Constitution. Prayers in our legislative halls, the proclamations making Thanksgiving Day a holiday, "so help me God" in our courtroom oaths—all would be unconstitutional. Surely this is not the type of atheist or agnostic society that our country wants to turn to, and surely this is not what our forefathers had in mind when they drafted the Constitution.

Therefore, just because the First Amendment provides that there should be "no law respecting an establishment of religion," there is nothing in the First Amendment or in the way courts have interpreted the Constitution to suggest that there should be a complete separation of church and state in every way imaginable. Released time programs do not violate the First Amendment or in any way entangle church and state.

Benefits of Religious Instruction

At the same time, as a whole, American society has unfortunately reached a point where many people are afraid to outwardly promote, encourage, or endorse any sort of religion. American society has become very secular, especially when it comes to religion in schools. This is somewhat understandable, especially because of much criticism and scrutiny certain religious groups are currently under due to the negative actions of religious figures, but what our society is forgetting is that not all religion is bad. If not extremist, most religions throughout time have been fundamentally good. People often forget that beyond the basic religious instruction, religion also often teaches discipline, morals, and values. Religion helps people learn how to think and to think about things in a different way than just what they are taught in school. Religion often promotes friendship and a sense of community, and it often gives many people something to look toward. These are all positive things that more of our schoolchildren need to be exposed to. As such, released time programs may be able to help foster such aims.

If more school boards participated in released time programs, and thus, if more students were allowed to be released from school to attend religious instruction or religious prayer, then more school children and adolescents might have something else to focus on, something else to think about, and somewhere else to meet friends and mentors to grow both intellectually and spiritually. This would be especially good for school districts in which children have little parental guidance and parental involvement in schools is minimal, or those that struggle with drugs, gangs, hazing, or any number of other problems.

Why Schools Should Accommodate Released Time

Some opponents, such as the counterpoint essayist, argue that if parents wish for their children to attend some sort of religious education or devotional programs, then it should be their responsibility to take their children to such religious activities off of school time. However, this is often very difficult for many parents, especially those who are single or work in the evenings and on weekends, those who have multiple children for whom they need to help with homework and prepare dinner, or those who have children who participate in after-school sports and curricular activities. This can become very demanding for many parents, and often the evenings and weekends are the only time when parents get to spend quality time with their children. Again, the question becomes, why would school boards not want to participate in released time programs if they can? These programs would help parents and students participate in religious instruction and devotion, when they may not otherwise have the opportunity to do so.

CONCLUSION

As a whole, the United States is made up of religious people who presuppose a supreme being. We guarantee all citizens the freedom to worship as each chooses. We make room for as wide a variety of religious beliefs and creeds as necessary. When the state accommodates religious instruction and devotion, it follows the best of our traditions. In this regard, when the state works with religious authorities and not against them, it respects the religious nature of our people, accommodates the public to their spiritual needs, and ultimately suggests that it does not necessarily prefer an agnostic or atheist society over those who believe in some religion or a higher being. Clearly, government cannot prefer one religion, finance religious groups, undertake religious instruction, blend secular and sectarian education, or use secular institutions to force one or some religion on any person; however, there has never been a constitutional requirement that makes it necessary for government to be antireligion or even hostile to religion. So long as schools do not prefer one religious sect over another, do not use government aid to fund released time programs, and hold such programs off school campus, why would they not try to accommodate the religious and spiritual needs of the next generation of our society?

COUNTERPOINT: Lindsey Swanson
Haller and Colvin, PC, Fort Wayne, Indiana

In *Zorach v. Clauson* (1952), the Supreme Court ruled that public school officials can honor parental requests to release their children during the public school day to receive private religious instruction off of their campuses. Of course, to reiterate, students may do so only if their parents consent. In contrast to an earlier decision where the Supreme Court struck down a released time program that was offered in a public school building (*People of State of Illinois ex rel. McCollum v. Board of Education of School District No. 71,*

Champaign County, 1948), the *Zorach* Court was satisfied that programs that were conducted off campus did not violate the Establishment Clause of the First Amendment to the Constitution. The Court held that the programs were constitutional as long they were held off school grounds, no school funds were expended, and students were not forced to attend. Even so, in light of possible constitutional and liability issues associated with released time programs during the school day, this essay contends that students should not be allowed to leave their public schools early to receive religious instruction at the religiously affiliated nonpublic schools selected by their parents.

ORIGINS

The notion of released time can be traced back to 1905 when it was discussed in a conference in New York City. At the conference, supporters proposed that public elementary schools should close one extra day of the week, other than Sunday, so that children could receive additional religious instruction outside of their school. In 1914, at a school in Indiana, the proposal was implemented into practice. In the program's first year, more than 600 students participated in the released time. Released time popularity began to grow with every year (Released Time Education, 2011).

In 1922, about 40,000 students from 200 districts in 23 states were enrolled in released time programs. The highest number of participants was seen in these programs in 1947 when 2 million students were enrolled in about 2,200 communities (Bible Education Released Time, 2011).

Currently, about 1,000 released time programs are in operation in the United States. The programs, which range from kindergarten to high school, include approximately 250,000 students (Released Time Education, 2011). The programs are not limited to one religion or another; instead, any religion can establish a released time program through the public schools. For example, there is a multidenominational Christian organization that supports Released Time Bible Education across the country known as School Ministries, Inc., a program that was designed to assist local communities in the creation of Released Time Bible Education. Additionally, there are programs in New York City, the most common two being the Jewish Education Program and the Jewish Released Time Program of Greater New York.

CONSTITUTIONALITY OF RELEASED TIME EDUCATION PROGRAMS

The Supreme Court first dealt with the issue of religious instruction in public schools in *People of State of Illinois ex rel. McCollum v. Board of Education of*

School District No. 71, Champaign County (1948). Although the Court struck down the program challenged in this litigation, it established principles that guided later rulings on the First Amendment and public schools. The *McCollum* Court held that the released time program at the schools in this case were unconstitutional because the religious instruction was conducted on tax-supported government property. According to the Court, the program violated the First Amendment's prohibition against the state's establishment of a religion.

The Supreme Court directly addressed the issue of released time programs 4 years later in *Zorach v. Clauson* (1952). This time, the Court held that a statute that provided for the release of public school students from school to attend religious classes off campus was constitutional. Following *Zorach*, some general rules were established regarding the operation of released time programs. It is now well-established that in released time programs, the religious classes must be conducted off of school grounds and public funds cannot be expended, even indirectly, to support these programs. Classes that meet on school grounds during school hours could create the impression that the school is supporting the program and, thus, endorsing religion. Such an impression would be a violation of the separation of church and state doctrine. Additionally, school officials or teachers cannot promote program attendance through coercion or other means. In addition, public school officials cannot be required to create released time programs; they are only permitted to allow parents to choose to have their children released from their public schools to attend these religious classes.

ARGUMENTS AGAINST RELEASED TIME PROGRAMS

There are key arguments to be made against the allowance of released time programs in the public school systems. Even though the Supreme Court has held that released time programs are constitutional as long as they meet the guidelines established in *Zorach*, the first argument centers on constitutional issues. The Constitution prohibits the state from establishing churches or otherwise entangling itself with religions. It is important to keep in mind that public schools are the creation of the state. Accordingly, when officials in public schools allow released time programs to be established, they inevitably entangle themselves with religion. Even though public school boards do not spend government funds on released time programs, the instruction takes place off of school grounds, and educational officials do not encourage or discourage student participation, this essay maintains that public schools are still promoting religion by making provisions for the programs to operate. More specifically, public schools are aiding religion by structuring daily schedules around time blocks set specifically for religious instruction. Further, educational officials are permitting the religious groups to take their students out of the public schools for a portion of a day.

Simply stated, released programs in public schools do not preserve separation of church and state. If anything, these programs lead to an impermissible entanglement of church and state. In such programs, states, through public school mechanisms, are providing aid for the religious groups by using their compulsory public school attendance laws as a vehicle for promoting and encouraging the religious instruction. All states require that children attend school and have compulsory attendance policies in place to ensure their attendance. The religious groups then benefit from the required attendance because students must be present for a set number of school days and hours out of the school year. If the children have to be at school as required by compulsory attendance laws, then they are being made available to attend the religious instruction during the school day. As the Supreme Court observed in *McCollum* through the attendance requirement, the religious groups are receiving aid from the state because students are at school, where they can more easily attend the religious instruction. This is not separation of church and state.

Released time programs also create the risk of indirectly using state funds to support the programs. This form of entanglement also violates the Establishment Clause of the First Amendment to the Constitution. Even if funds are not directly going to the religious programs and the school buildings and buses are not being used for the instruction, there are still state funds being expended on the programs. For example, school officials, who are paid by their public school systems, need to interact with the organizations conducting the religious classes to make sure that students who have been released show up and attend the classes. While such monitoring is required for safety purposes and to make sure the compulsory attendance laws are being enforced, it has the effect of aiding the program while entangling the state with the church.

The promotion of religion may not be through direct support, but the public schools are still affording students a break from a school day to attend certain religious classes, tailored specifically to the religion of their parents' choice. The other students whose parents do not give them permission to attend the religious instruction are usually required to attend a study hall. To some children, especially younger students, getting out of school, even for an hour or two, is such a treat. With this thought in mind, some children may feel as though they are being punished because they do not practice that particular religion and are required to remain behind. Children and teenagers already struggle with their identity and fitting into a social circle, and the released time programs create just another group that has the potential to exclude some students. At the same time, the exclusion would be based on something that the child most likely did not choose, religion. The younger the children, the more likely it is that they would not understand why they have to stay at school while others get to leave. Students likely will not understand what the other children are doing while they leave school. Additionally, the students who are left behind may think that there is something wrong with them because they are not privileged enough to leave school with their classmates. Moreover, the students who are left behind may feel stigmatized or think that there is something wrong with their religion because it is not important enough to allow them to leave school in the middle of the day.

Another difficulty may arise when one considers how it is decided which religions offer released time programs. Even if outside entities are the ones to make such decisions, it is unclear whether public school officials have any responsibilities in ensuring that every religion has a program if students or families so desire. It does not seem fair that only the most "popular" religions are represented through the programs. Again, this runs the risk of having young students believe that their religions are not good enough. Whose responsibility is it to decide which religious programs are permitted and which are not? It would seem that if this was the school's decision, it again would create the risk of entanglement between church and state in violation of the Establishment Clause.

On the other hand, it also does not seem practical to have a variety of religious instruction programs being offered for students through one school. If this were the case, then students could be sent to many different locations during the school day to receive their religious instruction. For instance, there could be 10 different locations where the students could be during the released time from school. Are public school officials required to keep track of where the children are once they leave? Again, monitoring where all of the children are during released time causes further entanglement between school and religious officials. Another similar issue is whether officials in public schools must release students to a verified or registered religious program or whether parents are permitted to pick up their children for one-on-one instruction in their homes.

An additional argument against allowing released time programs to continue is the problem of civil tort liability. Since programs must take place off of public school property, students must relocate to other premises for classes. While some of the schools where religious instruction occurs may have the classes right next door to public schools, down the block, or across the street, most likely they are not that close. When these students are in transit to their classes, questions emerge about who is liable if they fall, get hit by cars, or are injured. Who is responsible for ensuring their safety, officials in the public or religious schools? Although parents have to provide their permission for their child to attend the program, are they also releasing the schools of liability when they leave the property? In some released time programs, parents come to the schools to assist with the transportation of children between their public schools and the programs. Do these parents have any liability? In short, since many issues of civil liability remain, when coupled with potential constitutional challenges, public school boards just should not permit children to participate in released time programs.

Released time programs simply do not have a place in public schools since other options are available to parents who wish their children to receive religious instruction. If parents wish to have their children receive religious instruction, such as that received via released time programs, then they should send their children to religiously affiliated nonpublic schools. At religious schools, the children would most likely get more intensive religious instruction than they would in released time programs. Moreover, while at the religious schools, the children would also be around others who think that religion is important. If parents are unable to send their children to religious schools due to the lack of availability or lack of money, there are still other options for students to receive religious instruction. For example, weekend or evening classes are often available through religious institutions and communities where children can become involved. There is no need to have the released time programs in public schools because there are plenty of other opportunities for children to receive religious instruction.

CONCLUSION

By highlighting all of the problems with implementing released time programs in public schools, this counterpoint essay has demonstrated that these programs create unnecessary difficulties for public school officials and their students. Released time programs are inappropriate because they aid in the advancement and sponsoring of religions, in violation of the Establishment Clause of the First Amendment. Further, dividing students based on religious affiliation and liability can create issues for school boards, educators, and parents.

Looking at the numbers of released time programs currently in place, compared to when they first began, it appears that their use has been on the decline. Thus, it is likely that some of the reasons for the decline in the existence of the programs that have been discussed above have influenced public school officials to the extent that they no longer want to deal with the associated and possible problems with the released time programs. Public school boards are not required to operate released time programs; they are only permitted to allow them to exist. The decline in numbers also demonstrates that most school systems have opted out of having the programs, rather than permit them to continue. There simply are too many challenges surrounding released time programs in today's public schools to allow them to continue to operate.

FURTHER READINGS AND RESOURCES

Bible Education Released Time. (2011). *History*. Retrieved from http://www.released time.org/sitert/besthtml/best_history.htm

Gordon, D. (2006). A constitutional res gestae: Ending the dueling histories of *Everson* and *McCollum* and the Nazi state. *Widener Law Review, 16*, 1–42.

Released Time Education. (2011). *Released time history: How long has released time education been around and how did it get started?* Retrieved from http://www.rtce.org/pages.asp?pageid=32778

Zucker, J. E. (2007). Better a Catholic than a communist: Reexamining *McCollum v. Board of Education* and *Zorach v. Clauson. Virginia Law Review, 93*, 2069–2118.

COURT CASES AND STATUTES

Lemon v. Kurtzman, 403 U.S. 602 (1971).

Moss v. Spartanburg County School District No. 7, 775 F. Supp. 2d 858 (D.S.C. 2011).

People of State of Illinois ex rel. McCollum v. Board of Education of School District No. 71, Champaign County, 333 U.S. 203 (1948).

Pierce ex rel. Pierce v. Sullivan West Central School District, 379 F.3d 56 (2d Cir. 2004).

Zorach v. Clauson, 343 U.S. 306 (1952).

11

Should public school boards be allowed to offer courses on the Bible and other sacred texts as literature?

POINT: William Jeynes, *California State University, Long Beach*
COUNTERPOINT: Robert J. Safransky, *Nova Southeastern University*

OVERVIEW

The first reported case involving the use of the Bible in public schools appears to have been *Board of Education of Cincinnati v. Minor* (1872). In *Minor*, the Supreme Court of Ohio invalidated an 1852 rule directing educational officials to open school days with Bible reading. Since then, the use of the Bible, more than any other sacred text, in public schools has generated its fair share of legal controversy.

Bible reading, in the context of prayer rather than the study of literature, reached the Supreme Court in the companion cases of *School District of Abington Township v. Schempp* and *Murray v. Curlett* (1963), disputes from Pennsylvania and Maryland, respectively. In *Abington*, the Court held that prayer and Bible reading as part of the opening of a school day violated the Establishment Clause in the First Amendment to the Constitution. In its analysis, the Court created twin tests that were destined to become the first two prongs of the *Lemon v. Kurtzman* (1971) test, the primary measure used to evaluate the constitutionality of religious practices in public schools. Under this test, "First, the statute must have a secular legislative purpose; second, its principal or primary effect must be one that neither advances nor inhibits religion; finally, the statute must not foster an excessive government entanglement with religion" (pp. 612–613).

In *Abington*, though, the Supreme Court laid the groundwork for future strife with its comment, "It certainly may be said that the Bible is worthy of study for its literary and historic qualities. Nothing we have said here indicates that such study of the Bible or of religion, when presented objectively as part of a secular program of education," would violate the First Amendment (p. 225). Later litigation would pick up on disputes over whether public school boards could offer courses using sacred texts, most often the Bible, in literature classes.

A brief sequential review of key cases reveals that the first dispute on teaching about the Bible arose in Alabama when it was still in the Fifth Circuit (due to a change in the court structure, it is now in the Eleventh Circuit). The court invalidated a "Bible as Literature" course because it was taught essentially from a Christian religious perspective as part of fundamentalist or evangelical doctrine (*Hall v. Board of School Commissioners of Conecuh County*, 1981).

Conversely, federal trial courts in Tennessee (*Wiley v. Franklin*, 1980) and West Virginia (*Crockett v. Sorenson*, 1983) suggested guidelines to govern teaching about the Bible in public schools. These recommendations focused on the use of certified teachers who are employed in the same manner as other staff, vesting complete control of course content and materials in school boards, supervising courses to assure objectivity in teaching, and requiring that no part of courses be mandatory for students.

The Eighth Circuit affirmed the unconstitutionality of a program in Arkansas that permitted students to leave their regular classrooms to learn about the Bible in voluntary sessions during regular school hours because the classes had the principal effect of advancing religion (*Doe v. Human*, 1990). Later, a federal trial court in Mississippi forbade a school board from offering a Bible study class that was taught in a rotation with music and other courses, including one supposedly on the history of the Middle East because it failed the *Lemon* test (*Herdahl v. Pontotoc County School District*, 1996).

In a case with a bit of a different twist, a federal trial court in Florida reviewed the constitutionality of a two-semester Bible history class that was supposed to divide time equally between the Old and New Testaments (*Gibson v. Lee County School Board*, 1998). The court allowed the Old Testament class to proceed but enjoined the course on the New Testament because it was convinced that the plaintiffs were likely to prevail on the merits of their claim that it failed the *Lemon* test.

In a case from Tennessee, the Sixth Circuit affirmed that a school board could not permit students from a Christian college to teach regular weekly religion classes. In acknowledging that the instructors presented the Bible as religious truth, the court agreed that this failed all three prongs of the *Lemon* test.

The only case involving religious literature other than the Bible arose in Idaho. The Ninth Circuit affirmed that officials in a charter school could not use such works as the Bible, the Koran, the Book of Mormon, and the Hadith as primary source texts (*Nampa Classical Academy v. Goesling*, 2011). The court explained that doing so would have violated a provision in the state constitution against using religious books or documents in public schools.

Aware of the fact that American public schools are becoming increasingly diversified based on religion, the authors of the essays in this chapter reach opposing conclusions regarding whether public school boards should be able to respond to the increasingly religiously diverse student population by offering courses on the Bible and other sacred texts as literature. In the point essay, William Jeynes (California State University, Long Beach), focusing primarily on the Bible because it has been in the forefront of all but one of the cases on this issue, answers in the affirmative. He thus posits that one cannot be considered well educated or well rounded without knowledge of the Bible, given its influential place in history. Conversely, relying primarily on legal analysis, the counterpoint essay of Robert J. Safransky (Nova Southeastern University) takes the opposite stance. He is of the opinion that insofar as the weight of litigation forbids teaching of the Bible and other sacred texts, combined with a host of logistical difficulties, such as teacher certification and course content, and the possibility that students who do not participate in the classes could feel left out, boards should simply not be allowed to do so.

As you read these debates, ask yourself the following three questions. First, should public school boards be able to offer classes on the Bible and other sacred texts as literature? Second, would these classes help enhance appreciation for other faiths or would they essentially serve as backdoor entries permitting public schools to teach religion? Third, would offering classes of this nature be good for public schools and their students or might they lead to religious strife?

Charles J. Russo
University of Dayton

POINT: William Jeynes
California State University, Long Beach

This point essay argues that public school boards should be allowed to offer courses that teach the Bible and other sacred texts as literature. Insofar as all but one of the cases in the United States dealing with teaching sacred texts as literature deal solely with the Bible, this essay focuses largely on the Bible. Still, many of the same arguments that this essay uses in support of the Bible can apply to other sacred literatures.

It is wise to teach the Bible and other sacred texts as literature in public schools for three reasons. First, knowledge of major faith traditions is an important part of education, given the religious diversity that exists both within the United States and globally. Knowledge of the Bible, the key document in the Judeo-Christian tradition, for example, provides an understanding of history and an awareness of religiously based content and themes in Western literature. Other sacred texts serve the same purpose in their faith traditions. Second, the Supreme Court has ruled that teaching the Bible as literature is acceptable as long as it is "presented objectively as part of a secular program of education" (*School District of Abington Township v. Schempp* and *Murray v. Curlett*, 1963, p. 225). Since the Constitution dictates equal protection under the law, absent a compelling interest not to do so, sacred texts of other faiths must be treated in the same manner such that they should also be studied as literature in public schools. Third, knowledge of the Bible and the sacred texts of other religions can generally help to enhances one's understanding of other people of faith.

FUNDAMENTAL KNOWLEDGE

It is unlikely that one would receive much of an argument in declaring that the Bible, along with its Judeo-Christian principles, has been the most significant religious document that helped to shape the development and history of the United States. Since the Bible is one of the most published books in the world each year, it is difficult to imagine that persons would be regarded as educated if they were devoid of knowledge of it or, for that matter, other sacred texts. Myriad people believe that the Bible possesses an unfathomable degree of wisdom and guidance for life, and about 65% of the world's population regards it as a holy book that is one of the most influential books in history. At the same time, the influence of other sacred texts on history and current events may also be cited as a basis for their being worthy of study. For example, in light of how the Koran seems to be shaping world events today, some advocate for its being taught as literature in public schools.

It is becoming increasingly clear that a fundamental knowledge of sacred texts is important to understand history, and the Bible, in particular, to understand American history. Christians, led by the Puritans and Quakers, were the largest group to settle the New England and Mid-Atlantic states. George Washington's own writings, specifically those that describe his miraculous eschewing of certain death during the French and Indian War that had such a dramatic impact on his Christian commitment, communicate the faith of a man who was strongly religious. Unless one has fundamental knowledge of the Bible, one cannot fully understand many historical events and movements in the United States, including the fight against slavery; the Underground Railroad, supported by the Quakers; the education of African Americans by Puritans and Quakers; the women's suffrage movement; and the civil rights movement. Knowing the Bible is essential to comprehending American history.

For centuries, authors wrote with the assumption that readers would have a fundamental knowledge of the Bible. As a result, many of the great books of the world have themes, titles, and references to the Bible. William Shakespeare, for example, cited the Bible about 1,300 times. The works of authors as diverse as Charles Dickens, Fyodor Dostoevsky, John Steinbeck, Leo Tolstoy, and Ernest Hemingway are difficult to understand without a thorough knowledge of the Bible.

In addition, recent research confirms that Bible literacy is strongly associated with higher academic outcomes and better social behavior among students. As David Van Biema notes in his 2007 *Time* magazine article, "The Case for Teaching the Bible," "The 'new consensus' for secular Bible study argues that knowledge of it is essential to being a full-fledged, well-rounded citizen" (p. 42). Recent studies estimate that the gap in achievement in the United States between those instructed in Bible literacy and those who are not is about a full grade point. Thus, one can understand why many academics believe that an adequate knowledge of the Bible is essential for a complete education, at least as it relates to the Western world. Certainly, such an approach should also apply to the study of other sacred texts as literature in light of the religious diversification occurring in the United States and throughout the world. Having a greater understanding of the sacred texts of faiths such as Islam, Buddhism, and Hinduism will provide well-educated Americans with deeper insights into developments in the non-Western world. Moreover, as the United States becomes more religiously diverse, educated Americans will need to have fundamental knowledge of these other sacred texts because their precepts undoubtedly impact the actions of the followers of individuals who subscribe to their teachings.

CONSTITUTIONALITY

A second reason why the teaching of sacred texts as literature should be allowed is because the Supreme Court has suggested that teaching the Bible is constitutional. As noted earlier, in light of the legal principle of equal protection under the law, to the extent that the Bible can be offered in a course on sacred literature in public schools, there is no reason why this same protection would be denied other sacred writings. Refusal to permit such courses equally would, simply, violate the law.

This essay has relied heavily on the Bible by way of example because, other than one case wherein school officials in Idaho were not permitted to use such works as the Bible, the Koran, the Book of Mormon, and the Hadith as primary source texts because doing so would have violated the state constitution (*Nampa Classical Academy v. Goesling*, 2011), all of the cases to date have focused on the Bible.

In this regard, even the American Civil Liberties Union, which is not always friendly toward religious perspectives in public schools, acknowledged this fact, as states have initiated statewide public school programs of the Bible as literature or history. Further, in *Abington*, although forbidding educational officials in Maryland and Pennsylvania from beginning the day with Bible reading and prayer, the Court did address the status of the Bible. According to the Court, "Nothing we have said here indicates that such study of the Bible or of religion, when presented objectively as part of a secular program of education, may not be effected consistently with the First Amendment" (p. 225).

In *People of the State of Illinois ex rel. McCollum v. Board of Education of School District No. 71* (1948), Justice Robert Jackson's concurring opinion stated, "One can hardly respect a system of education that would leave the student wholly ignorant of the currents of religious thought that move the world society for . . . which he is being prepared" (p. 236). Jackson warned that making faith off limits in classrooms would leave public education "in shreds."

The analysis of these decisions sparked an effort to reintroduce the Bible into public schools both for its historical value and as a tome of great literary import. Certainly, the same can be said about an array of different sacred texts that have influenced other regions of the world. As such, those who dismiss the importance of knowing about the Bible or other sacred texts would be marginalizing much of human history because religion has played a central role in most nations. In addition, opponents of the study of the Bible and other sacred texts would appear to be asserting that all of history is worth learning except the Bible and other religious works.

UNDERSTANDING PEOPLE OF FAITH

This issue of understanding people of faith is particularly important because in recent years, the United States has developed friction with nations who highly value religious faith. In a sense, this should come as no surprise, because as the United States has become increasingly secularized, it may be difficult for some in the United States to understand and relate to people of faith, especially to those who believe religion should be integrated into all aspects of society, including politics. This dearth of understanding is most ostensible in the case of the relationship between the United States and Islamic countries, but it is creating friction with a variety of other nations as well. For example, many nations where Christianity is practiced, such as South Korea, the Philippines, and various African nations, consider American television programs to be immoral and offensive, inciting lust and violence. For this reason, South Korea, for example, has made it a priority to develop its own television programs to serve as an alternative to American productions.

Many Americans have little notion about the primary reasons Islamic extremists are angry at the West. If one were to ask most Americans if they have ever read one of Osama bin Laden's speeches, they would probably respond that they had not done so. Clearly, this point essay is not stating that one should agree with the essence of bin Laden's hate-filled speeches; nevertheless, bin Laden made several points that reflected why many of his followers had associated the United States with evil practices.

In addition to the United States' insistence on protecting Kuwait after it was invaded by Iraq in 1990 and also defending Israel, there are certain actions of the United States that some Muslims and extremists among them are especially grieved by. Such grievances include what they insist is an American obsession with sexuality, ranging from pornography to using beautiful women to sell cars. They also believe that Americans have little regard for what is holy. Some Muslims have considered the presence of American military bases in Saudi Arabia a direct affront to their religion, because they deem that land to be holy. Indeed, it may well be that some Americans support the policies of the U.S. government with regard to the Middle East and Israel. In light of this mix of political-religious issues related to the Middle East and other parts of the world, an argument can be made that Americans, and others, on different sides of such political-religious questions would be well served to have a better understanding of the religious sensitivities of all involved. To the extent that offering courses on the Bible and other sacred texts as literature can help members of different faiths to understand the backgrounds of others, then they would serve a valuable function in American public schools. Offering courses on sacred texts as literature can help bridge gaps in knowledge and understanding by providing students with deeper insights into the nature of other faiths as reflected in their sacred texts.

If Americans do not develop a deeper understanding of the Bible and other sacred texts, they may not be able to comprehend what is happening in other countries with regard to religion. For example, according to a Gallup Poll, China has experienced a growth in Christianity that is unparalleled in modern history. Many Chinese have observed, as sociologist Max Weber (1905/1930) noted, that where Christianity surges, so does economic prosperity. Thus, the Chinese government considers the growth of Christianity as one of the keys to becoming a dominant superpower. If well-educated Americans are to understand China, Islamic countries, and other nations where faith is prominent, then they should know about the sacred texts that influence those cultures and countries as well.

CONCLUSION

The Supreme Court has indicated that the teaching of the Bible, and by extension, other sacred texts, as literature and history is permissible in the public schools. Yet, as reflected in the counterpoint essay, litigation continues over the extent to which the Bible and, in at least one reported case, other sacred texts can be taught as literature, even though several American leaders and academics have lauded the merits of their use in instruction in the public schools. To allow public school students to continue in their ignorance of the world's most published book, not to mention of other sacred texts, is anti-intellectual and serves to condone unnecessary misunderstanding of and friction with much of the world's population. Such an insular mindset may serve to undermine America's place of leadership as well as the promise of world peace and would be remedied by allowing the Bible, and other sacred texts, to be taught in American public schools.

COUNTERPOINT: Robert J. Safransky
Nova Southeastern University

The roots of the controversy over whether public school boards should be allowed to offer classes on the Bible or other sacred texts as literature are embedded in early American history. From the earliest days in American history, there have been deep differences of opinion on which religions would be accepted by the state and which would be considered heretical with the result that their members should be punished by the state. The establishment of the colonies in New England and other parts of the New World by members of English religious minority groups was a direct result of the persecution that they suffered at the hands of the state during the 16th and 17th centuries.

When the new American republic, the United States, was founded, Congress was mindful of safeguarding religious freedom. To this end, after adopting the Constitution, to safeguard the rights of Americans from having a central government that was too strong, it adopted the Bill of Rights. Following contentious struggles over what should be included in the Bill of Rights, the First Amendment begins with the words "Congress shall make no law respecting an establishment of religion, or prohibiting the free exercise thereof." Clearly, this indicated strong congressional desire to protect freedom of religion. The Supreme Court later applied this provision to individual states.

Over the years, there have been countless disputes over religion in education, one of which dealt with the place of the Bible in public schools. Turning to this specific topic, this counterpoint essay emphatically stands for the proposition that public school boards should not be allowed to offer classes on the Bible and other sacred texts as literature. This essay adopts this stance both because allowing such classes would violate the Establishment Clause of the First Amendment and because such an approach risks harming students who do not share the religious beliefs of those who promote the inclusion of such classes.

BACKGROUND AND HISTORY

The Puritans, as an example of but one group of religious refugees seeking religious freedom, were forced to leave England because of religious persecution and lived in Holland until they decided that they wanted to go to the New World and set up their own state. Their success in establishing their own colony led other religious dissenters from England and the continent to come to the New World to set up their own religiously controlled state.

In light of the developments in the early colonies and their impact on religion in schools, it is necessary to take a brief look at the history of public education in the United States to see why it took decades for the teaching of the Bible as literature to become an issue. The Massachusetts Bay Colony began the first public school system when it enacted the Massachusetts Education Act of 1642. Then in 1647, the "Ye Olde Satan Deluder Act" was passed, which created the first public schools in towns with 50 or more families. The act relied on the teaching of the Bible to help keep people from eternal damnation at the hands of the devil. Officials would hire and pay persons to teach the children and when the number of families reached 100, they were to start grammar schools to prepare students for the universities.

Eventually, U.S. Representative Horace Mann (Free-Soil, Massachusetts) led the movement to establish public education at the elementary level when the first compulsory education law was passed in Massachusetts in 1852. Compulsory elementary education was achieved in the remaining states by 1918. As public schools developed, they largely adopted the Protestant ethos, which included the use of the Bible as central in educating children. Then, as time passed, litigation ensued over whether the Bible, as a Christian religious document, could have a place in public schools.

ARGUMENTS AGAINST CLASSES ON THE SACRED TEXTS AS LITERATURE

In light of American history and the desire of the Founding Fathers to have freedom of, or some would say freedom from, religion, this counterpoint essay contends that public school boards should not be allowed to offer classes on the Bible and other sacred texts as literature. The essay proceeds with an examination of case law before offering related policy/legal arguments why school boards should not be able to do so.

Case Law

Allowing school boards to offer classes on the Bible and other sacred texts as literature is inconsistent with the vast majority of litigation that addressed this issue. The Supreme Court's first case directly involving the Bible, *School District of Abington Township v. Schempp* and *Murray v. Curlett* (1963), involving disputes from Pennsylvania and Maryland, respectively, admittedly did not involve its use or that of any other sacred text as part of a class on religious literature. Rather, in creating a measure that would be included in the tripartite *Lemon v. Kurtzman* (1971) test, the Court invalidated the practices of Bible reading and prayer in public schools on the basis that these practices violated the Establishment Clause. Moreover, as noted in the point essay, the Supreme Court, in nonbinding dicta, did write that "the Bible is worthy of study for its literary and historic qualities . . . when presented objectively as part of a secular program of education" (p. 225). Yet, since this is not part of the Court's holding, it is inappropriate to interpret this language as allowing unfettered teaching of the Bible in public schools.

Insofar as many later cases, including those discussed below, relied on the *Lemon* test, it is worth noting that the Court ruled, "First, the statute must have a secular legislative purpose; second, its principal or primary effect must be one that neither advances nor inhibits religion; finally, the statute must not foster "an excessive government entanglement with religion" (pp. 612–613). As simple and straightforward as this test appears to be, lower courts, and school officials, continue to struggle in applying this test in an array of disputes, including those wherein plaintiffs sought to introduce classes on the Bible as literature.

In the earliest case involving a class on the Bible as literature, the Fifth Circuit invalidated such a course that a school board in Alabama hoped to offer. The court was of the opinion that the class would have violated the Establishment Clause because it was taught essentially from a Christian religious perspective as part of fundamentalist or evangelical doctrine (*Hall v. Board of School Commissioners of Conecuh County*, 1981). Also, the Eighth Circuit struck down a program that allowed students to leave their regular classrooms to learn about the Bible in voluntary sessions during regular school hours because it violated the *Lemon* test insofar as it had the effect of advancing the Christian religion (*Doe v. Human*, 1990). Later, a federal trial court in Mississippi reached a similar result because the school board's actions failed the *Lemon* test (*Herdahl v. Pontotoc County School District*, 1996). A federal trial court in Florida allowed a class on the Old Testament to proceed but enjoined the course on the New Testament based on its belief that the plaintiffs were likely to prevail on the merits of their claim that it violated the Establishment Clause insofar as it failed all three prongs of the *Lemon* test (*Gibson v. Lee County School Board*, 1998).

More recently, the Ninth Circuit addressed the first case involving materials other than the Bible. The court affirmed that a charter school in Idaho and two of the teachers could not use religious documents such as the Bible, Koran, the Book of Mormon, or the Hadith as textbooks because doing so would have violated a provision in the state constitution against using religious books or documents in public schools (*Nampa Classical Academy v. Goesling*, 2011).

Policy/Legal Reasons

Eight overlapping reasons explain why public school boards should not be allowed to offer courses on the Bible or other sacred texts as literature.

The first reason to oppose such courses is the concern that there would no longer be true public schools but "religious schools" operating under the guise of "public schools." There really can be no other way to say it but to say it bluntly: Under such an approach, religion would impermissibly be the controlling power if school boards offer courses on the Bible or other sacred texts.

Second, concerns can be raised about what religious groups would be operating "public schools" and want their sacred texts taught. The United States is becoming increasingly religiously diverse with an array of branches of Christianity, Judaism, Islam, Buddhism, and Hinduism, to name a few faiths, not to mention other sets of beliefs such as those espoused by Wiccans, New Age Religion proponents, and atheist groups. This partial listing of religions and nonreligious bodies in the United States should be sufficient to demonstrate the point that there are different groups with different sacred texts. While about 85% of Americans are Christians, they are spread across many different organized groups that may use different versions of the Bible or sacred texts. This multiplicity of religions leads to the next reason to oppose courses using sacred texts as literature.

In a closely related third point with multiple dimensions, if boards were to offer classes on sacred texts in public schools, it is unclear which versions of the Bible or works should be used. The three largest religions in the United States—Judaism, Christianity, and Islam—all use sacred texts. Further, all three are grounded in the Hebrew scriptures, while Christianity and Islam also rely on the New Testament. At the same time, some Muslims believe that their sacred text, the Koran or Qu'ran, should not be translated from Arabic into another language. Will officials select the Hebrew Torah or Tanakh? Will educators choose the Protestant version of the Old Testament or the Catholic translation? Which version of the Old Testament will students use as their textbook: Hebrew, Protestant, Orthodox, or Catholic?

These questions raise another question that can readily cause legal disputes over whether state school boards, local boards, teachers, or parents have the authority to select which version of Bibles or sacred texts to be used in classes. If any of those groups become involved in text selection, then, as reflected in the litigation reviewed earlier, opponents could file suit claiming violations of all three prongs of the *Lemon* test. A related point that could also involve *Lemon* concerns the question of who must purchase the sacred texts: school boards or students? If boards buy these texts, will such expenditures be using public money to advance religion?

The fourth question is the first of three related concerns about qualifications of the teachers of Bible or sacred text courses. Who would determine whether instructors who teach courses about the Bible, for example, have had adequate educational backgrounds in such subject areas as Hebrew and Greek and are familiar with the Bible's various versions? In this regard, the American Civil Liberties Union (ACLU, 2007a) cites a passage from *The Bible in Public Schools: A First Amendment Guide*, which deals with teacher preparation for Bible course instruction: "[T]eachers should possess the relevant academic training and should teach the course as a proper academic subject" (p. 9). This means that the educational backgrounds of teachers should not be limited to that of a particular religious tradition, but should include serious academic study of the Bible. This document adds that in such classes, boards

> should look for teachers who have some background in the academic study of religion. Unless they have already received academic preparation, teachers selected to teach a course about the Bible should receive substantive in-service training from qualified scholars before being permitted to teach such courses. (p. 9)

While teachers are completely free to have deeply felt religious beliefs, it is inappropriate, and unconstitutional, for them to use classrooms to advocate their religious beliefs to public school children.

In addition, when dealing with sacred texts, questions can arise about whether teachers have knowledge of the languages, geography, history, and empires that ruled the lands in which the texts originated. A study of Bible teachers in Texas found that there were serious deficiencies in educator knowledge since individuals had no undergraduate or graduate courses in the Bible or theology and did not know applicable constitutional law dealing with religion. The lack of knowledge of constitutional law among classroom teachers is high because school law is not required in most undergraduate programs. If teachers earn advanced degrees in their content areas rather than education-related areas per se, then they are unlikely to have studied school law and have gained an understanding of the American legal principles addressing how to deal with the religious rights of students, an approach that can help head off controversies.

Fifth, related issues can arise over whether classes are to be taught by teachers or volunteers who are proselytizing for their religions, and whether those classes would be offered as required academic subjects or electives—issues that have resulted in litigation. How will parents and administrators know that instructors are not teaching the courses from distinctly religious perspectives? Will the students be encouraged to put down other faiths? Will students be encouraged to convert to other faiths other than their own depending on the course? Will teachers be hostile to those students in the class who do not follow the beliefs of the sacred text being taught?

If school boards can offer classes as electives, it is unclear what will happen since courts have reached mixed results. For instance, as noted earlier, the Eighth Circuit affirmed the unconstitutionality of a program in Arkansas that allowed students to leave their regular classes to attend voluntary sessions about the Bible because doing so advanced religion (*Doe v. Human*, 1990). However, more recently, the federal trial court in South Carolina upheld a law that allowed students to receive academic credit for released time studies of Christianity that undoubtedly included some focus on the Bible (*Moss v. Spartanburg County School District No. 7*, 2011). There are many questions that school boards and administrators must answer before they can start classes on sacred texts.

If school boards lack clear plans to prepare teachers and to focus on the nonreligious elements of the Bible or sacred texts in their course curricula, they will likely be visited with a summons to appear in court. This is precisely what happened in May 2007 when the ACLU and others sued the school board in Odessa, Texas, over courses at two high schools that used the curriculum of the National Council on Bible Curriculum in Public Schools (ACLU, 2007b). The suit also alleged that the schools were using the King James version of the Bible, which is typically not used in many Christian traditions or in Judaism. The board avoided potentially costly litigation by agreeing to stop using the disputed curriculum.

Although one could argue that ensuring that teachers should have the proper educational background concerning sacred texts should be the same as that for such secular subjects as mathematics or science, it is not clear that this is so. For example, would teachers with degrees from Catholic institutions be deemed qualified in schools dominated by evangelical Christians? Would officials hire teachers to teach religion classes if they were well-credentialed atheists or agnostics?

Sixth, where are the parents who want their children to know about the Bible and its influence on history, music, and literature? Why do these parents not take the time to teach their children at home? Why are the parents shifting many of the duties and responsibilities of inculcating values and morality in their children to the public schools? If parents are so concerned with having classes taught about the Bible or other sacred texts, they have the option of enrolling their children in nonpublic schools or seeking other options as discussed in the next point.

Seventh, if parents wish to have their children study their sacred texts, why have they not turned to their churches and youth ministries? Why are the churches and other houses of worship not developing classes for children? Putting aside the topic of released time, the subject of another debate in this volume (Chapter 10), in systems with such a practice in place, why is this not sufficient? Why must parents involve public schools in teaching classes about religious texts as literature when the underlying values about religion are essentially private family matters?

Eighth, what would school boards say to students and parents whose religious traditions were not represented in literature classes about sacred texts? It is certainly possible that offering such classes could lead to feelings of exclusion among those whose faiths were not studied, thereby unnecessarily creating difficulties by breeding resentment and possible conflict in and around schools. School boards should thus think twice before permitting classes that can give rise to strife in their communities.

CONCLUSION

As interpreted by voluminous litigation, the First Amendment has made it clear that there can be no teaching of religion, including the Bible, in public schools. The point essay and those who support allowing public school boards to offer courses on the Bible and other sacred texts should refer to "Federalist No. 51":

> It is of great importance in a republic, not only to guard the society against the oppression of its rulers; but to guard one part of the society against the injustices of the other part. Different interests necessarily exist in different classes of citizens. (Madison, 1788/2000, p. 333)

Rather than run the risk of injustice to members of minority religions, public school boards should not be allowed to offer courses on the Bible or other sacred texts in public schools since doing so would risk violating the First Amendment.

Further Readings and Resources

American Civil Liberties Union (ACLU). (2007a, May 9). *The Bible in public schools: A First Amendment guide*. Retrieved from http://www.aclu.org/cpredirect/29618

American Civil Liberties Union (ACLU). (2007b, May 16). *Texas parents challenge unconstitutional Bible class in public schools*. Retrieved from http://www.aclu.org/religion-belief/texas-parents-challenge-unconstitutional-bible-class-public-schools

Biblica. (2010). In what language was the Bible first written? *Bible FAQs*. Retrieved November 20, 2011, from http://www.biblica.com/bibles/faq/11

Chancey, M. A. (2009). The Bible, the First Amendment, and the public schools in Odessa, Texas. *Religion and American Culture: A Journal of Interpretation, 19*, 169–205.

Madison, J. (2000). "Federalist No. 51." In R. Scigliano (Ed.), *The Federalist: A commentary on the Constitution of the United States* (pp. 330–335). New York: Modern Library. (Original work published 1788)

Smith, M. C., & Hartneti, R. A. (1986). Teaching Bible in the public schools. *Education Law Reporter, 32*, 7–19.

Van Biema, D. (2007, April 7). The case for teaching the Bible. *Time*, p. 42.
Weber, M. (1930). *The Protestant ethic and the spirit of capitalism* (T. Parsons, Trans.). New York: Charles Scribner's Sons. (Original work published 1905)

Court Cases and Statutes

Board of Education of Cincinnati v. Minor, 23 Ohio St. 211 (Ohio 1872).
Crockett v. Sorenson, 568 F. Supp. 1422 (W.D. Va. 1983).
Doe v. Human, 923 F.2d 857 (8th Cir. 1990), *cert. denied*, 499 U.S. 922 (1991).
Doe v. Porter, 370 F.3d 558 (6th Cir. 2004).
Gibson v. Lee County School Board, 1 F. Supp. 2d 1426 (M.D. Fla. 1998).
Hall v. Board of School Commissioners of Conecuh County, 656 F.2d 999 (5th Cir. 1981).
Herdahl v. Pontotoc County School District, 933 F. Supp. 582 (N.D. Miss. 1996).
Lemon v. Kurtzman, 403 U.S. 602 (1971).
Moss v. Spartanburg County School District No. 7, 775 F. Supp. 2d 858 (D.S.C. 2011).
Nampa Classical Academy v. Goesling,—Fed.Appx—, 2011 WL 3562954 (9th Cir. 2011).
People of the State of Illinois ex rel. McCollum v. Board of Education of School District No. 71, Champaign County, 333 U.S. 203 (1948).
School District of Abington Township v. Schempp and Murray v. Curlett, 374 U.S. 203 (1963).
Wiley v. Franklin, 497 F. Supp. 390 (E.D. Tenn. 1980).

12

Should schools teach both evolution and creation science/intelligent design in science classes?

POINT: William Jeynes, *California State University, Long Beach*
COUNTERPOINT: Aaron Cooley, *New England College*

OVERVIEW

Insofar as public education is a function of the states, control of the curriculum is left to the state legislatures, which, in turn, delegate decisions regarding the specifics of curricular implementation to local school boards and educational officials. State and local education officials, therefore, have significant discretion in determining what is to be taught and how it is to be taught in public schools. Even so, there are limitations on the authority of the states and local school boards. For example, state and local school officials cannot make decisions that would contravene federal law or constitutional principles on an array of issues.

The teaching of evolution, and more recently creation science and intelligent design, by way of illustration, has been one of the more controversial curricular issues subject to litigation during the past century. Proponents of the approach known as *creation science* try to provide scientific support for the biblical account of the creation as presented in the Book of Genesis. At the same time, many of these proponents attempt to disprove commonly accepted scientific theories of biological evolution. Moreover, supporters of *intelligent design* refer to the hypothesis that the universe and all living things were created by an intelligent cause as opposed to natural selection.

OVERVIEW: Chapter 12

One of the earliest and more well-known legal battles involving the teaching of evolution took place in Tennessee in 1925. Commonly known as the Scopes monkey trial (*Scopes v. State of Tennessee*, 1925), the case garnered much attention at the time but entered the annals of popular culture when it was fictionalized years later in the movie *Inherit the Wind* (Kramer, 1960). In this case, John Scopes, a science teacher, was convicted and fined $100 for violating a state statute prohibiting the teaching of evolution. The fine was later reversed on a procedural irregularity when the trial court's decision was appealed, but the state law was never struck down or rescinded until much later.

Forty-three years after the Scopes trial, the Supreme Court overturned a statute from Arkansas that was essentially an adaptation of the Tennessee law, forbidding the teaching of evolution in public schools and universities (*Epperson v. State of Arkansas*, 1968). The Court ruled that the statute was contrary to the Freedom of Religion Clause of the First Amendment and further violated the Fourteenth Amendment of the Constitution. In particular, the Court ruled that the purpose of the law was to prevent teachers from discussing evolution because evolution was contrary to the religious belief of many in the divine creation of humans. The Court declared that the First Amendment did not permit a state to mandate teaching tailored to the principles or prohibitions of any particular religious sect or dogma.

In a move to counter the impact of the Supreme Court's opinion in *Epperson* striking down the Arkansas antievolution statute, legislatures in a variety of states passed laws requiring school systems to provide teaching based on the biblical version of the creation along with the scientific theory of evolution. In 1987, in *Edwards v. Aguillard*, the Supreme Court held that one such statute violated the First Amendment. A statute from Louisiana, known as the Creationism Act, forbade the teaching of evolution in public schools unless it was accompanied by instruction in creation science. Although public schools were not required to include instruction in either theory, the law mandated that if one was taught, the other theory also had to be presented. In nullifying the statute, the Court was of the opinion that it served no identified secular purpose, but rather, its purpose was to promote a particular religious belief. Thus, the Court concluded that the statute from Louisiana was unconstitutional because it impermissibly endorsed religion in contravention of the First Amendment.

In the point essay, William Jeynes (California State University, Long Beach) contends that if the goal of public school systems is to teach students to be open-minded and expose them to a variety of perspectives, then they should be presented competing theories of the origins of the universe so that students can think for themselves and make up their own minds. Currently, according to Jeynes, schools present one theory as fact and dismiss alternative explanations. As such, Jeynes maintains that the teaching of all theories on the origin and development of the universe should be much more comprehensive and should give students more information about each theory.

In the counterpoint essay, Aaron Cooley (New England College) takes the opposite position, namely, that evolution and creation science or intelligent design should not be taught side by side in public school science classrooms. Cooley argues that current federal law and constitutional interpretations prohibit the teaching of creation science or intelligent design. In addition to violating principles of church and state, Cooley asserts that insofar as creation science and intelligent design are not science, teaching these theories would undercut strong science and technology pedagogy in schools.

In reading these essays, it might be helpful to reflect on the following questions: Can creation science or intelligent design be taught outside of a religious context? Are schools presently teaching evolution as fact rather than theory? Do creation science and intelligent design constitute legitimate scientific theories?

Allan G. Osborne, Jr.
Principal (Retired), Snug Harbor Community School,
Quincy, Massachusetts

POINT: William Jeynes
California State University, Long Beach

In the United States, teachers supposedly teach students to have open minds and to be exposed to a variety of perspectives. One clear exception to this trend is the teaching of the origin of the universe and life in science classes. The origin of the universe and of life is one of those occurrences that cannot be absolutely proved one way or the other.

For years, before Charles Darwin's *Origin of Species* (1859) and the *Scopes v. State of Tennessee* trial of 1925, most schools in the United States taught that a divine intelligent being created the universe and life. When this changed, public school textbooks and teachers taught students that this approach did not leave room for competing perspectives and was therefore closed-minded. In contemporary American public schools, evolution is now the dominant theory that educators teach as fact. Ironically, it is now the theory of intelligent design that is the competing perspective that is left out. Somehow the concept of open-mindedness has been disregarded, and only one theory is taught. This essay asserts that students should be exposed to the beliefs of evolution in conjunction with the theory of intelligent design. Schools should encourage students to think for themselves and evaluate competing theories to arrive at their own conclusions. In theory, this is what education should be about, but in reality students are inculcated in just one theory, evolution, which is generally taught as an irrefutable fact.

THEORIES OF EVOLUTION AND INTELLIGENT DESIGN

Evolution is a theory worthy of consideration, but it is just that: a theory. It should not be taught as absolute fact, but as a possible explanation of the origins of the universe and the development of life. Students need to be exposed to the theory of evolution; there is no question about that. Nevertheless, evolutionary theory has some pronounced weaknesses that even advocates of this theory acknowledge. It is largely because of these weaknesses that, according to a Gallup poll, only about half of the American people believe in the theory of evolution. Three issues emerge in this regard.

First, evolution has real problems with explaining how the universe was created. Those who espouse Darwin's theory aver that it was an act of chance. Yet, some find such an explanation capricious and devoid of any attempt to explain where the elements or materials came from to produce an act of creation. The problem of "first cause" has been one of the primary reasons that many graduates find evolution at best an incomplete and insufficient explanation of the origins of the universe and its subsequent development.

Second, evolution has not been able to produce any evidence of change from one species into another. They have been able to demonstrate that there has been change within species, but those who espouse intelligent design also insist there are changes that take place within a species. They just simply assert that one species does not change into another.

Third, evolution has had problems with dating fossils. Not only have there been embarrassing hoaxes, most famous among these being the Piltbeam and Nebraska man fiascos, but some have questioned the assumptions on which dating techniques are based. For example, major floods may negate the accuracy of dating. And given that most archaeologists believe there was a widespread flood that came upon much or all of the earth, there is reason to suspect that dating fossils may not be reliable or accurate.

Of course, the theory of intelligent design has issues that have caused others to question whether it is the best theory of origins and development. First, there are some who are disinclined to believe in this approach because they resist the idea of a deity, which intelligent design might appear to suggest. Second, some would feel more comfortable with intelligent design if religious works gave a more specific and agreed-upon sense of dating. In reality, the Bible and other religious tomes do not give a specific time for the formation of the earth, especially since the sun, the earthly measure of time, was not created until the third "day." Nevertheless, students ought to be exposed to each theory and arrive at their own conclusions.

Why should educators stifle access to particular theories? Many Americans are not raised in homes in which intelligent design theory is even discussed. Teachers cannot assume students will receive this knowledge outside the school. For example, I was raised in a home totally devoid of religion, where evolution was sacrosanct and antireligious attitudes inundated my family's thinking. There was never any talk of intelligent design in high school or in the college classroom. I did not learn of the theory until I attended a debate at one of the foremost Big Ten universities that involved an intelligent design advocate and one of the foremost evolutionist professors in the country. Many individuals that day, myself included, entered the auditorium as evolutionists and comfortably sat next to biology or other science professors from the university.

Approximately 75–90 minutes into the debate, it appeared to many of us that the intelligent design scientist was clearly winning. When we questioned science professors in the audience about the outcome, they responded that the problem was that the evolution scientist was holding to pure evolutionary theory. They further explained that most biologists and scientists believe that change occurred as a result of a combination of evolution and divine intervention and that there are many gaps in evolutionary theory. Upon further questioning, these professors acknowledged that they did not teach this in their classes because the university would not allow them to do so and they feared not getting tenure or losing their jobs if they did.

Does such an approach prepare people to interact with people in the real world? The reality is that, according to a Gallup poll, 50% of Americans believe in intelligent design, and 40% believe in some combination of intelligent design and evolution. One needs to ask the question of why, after decades of evolutionist teaching, this is still the case. Certain church or house of worship attendance figures cannot explain these results. A primary reason, which was declared by those Big Ten university scientists, is that the theory of evolution just simply has too many holes.

FOUR ISSUES THAT NEED TO BE ADDRESSED

The presentation of theories on origin and subsequent development should be more comprehensive and give students a more complete sense of what is involved in each of the theories. Specifically, teachers should address four issues.

First, whether due to ignorance or other reasons, there are too many facts that students are not told, which are vital to make intelligent conclusions on this debate. For example, increasingly, proponents of intelligent design point to major holes in the theory of evolution that are becoming more conspicuous as advances in DNA emerge (*New York Times* News Service, 1997). For example, one issue that has been raised by proponents of intelligent design is, if there were all these transitional forms of species, as evolutionists suppose, there should be vast numbers of examples of these in the fossil record—and yet there appear to be none or close to none at all. Evolutionists replied to this objection by stating that although these transitional forms rarely if ever occur in the fossil record, one could be certain of a recent transitional form that unquestionably supported the existence of this process in the past: Neanderthal man.

Unfortunately for this perspective, a major turn occurred in 1997, 1999, and 2004 when in three separate studies German, English, and French evolutionary scientists performed DNA testing in an attempt to divulge the extent of the biological relationship between modern humans and Neanderthals (Serre et al., 2004; Wade, 2000). In the piece titled "DNA Analysis Knocks Neanderthals Out of the Human Evolutionary Tree," the *New York Times* News Service (1997) reports that the short strip of genetic material retrieved from the Neanderthal specimen "indicates that Neanderthals did not interbreed with the modern humans who started to supplant them from their ancient homes about 50,000 years ago." Swedish biologist Svante Pääbo of the University of Munich, who worked on the study, notes that the DNA testing concluded that Neanderthals were "a distinct species that contributed nothing to the modern human gene pool." Both sets of studies produced the same set of results. Each set of studies yielded results that indicated that the DNA structure between Neanderthal and modern humans was significantly distinct so that it could not possibly be related to one another. What had appeared to be the most reliable part of evolutionary theory had now been undermined.

Students are often not taught about the cofounder of evolution, Alfred Russell Wallace, and the racism that is inextricably connected with Darwin's evolutionary theory. Instructors often are ignorant of the fact and therefore do not communicate with students that the full title of Darwin's famous treatise is *On the Origin of the Species by Means of Natural Selection or the Preservation of the Favoured Races in the Struggle for Life*. And yes, Darwin's writings make it patent that he means exactly what the title indicates. He views the White race as the superior one, as the last that will go extinct. Darwin was quite specific in his claims, asserting that the smallest gap between ape and humankind was between the gorilla and Blacks (Gould, 1981). Darwin (1871) states,

> The break will then be rendered wider, for it will intervene between man in a more civilized state, as we may hope, than the Caucasian, and some ape as low as a baboon, instead of at the present between the Negro or Australian and the gorilla. (p. 201)

Therefore, Darwin predicted that various groups of Blacks would be the first to go extinct (Darwin, 1871; Gould, 1981).

Second, currently public school students are taught to be closed-minded rather than open-minded regarding the origins of the universe. By not even acknowledging the existence of an alternative theory of origins to that of evolution, by forfeiture, students are being taught that intelligent design scientists are not to be taken seriously. Does this dismissal of alternative theories prepare people to interact with people in the real world, in which there is a wide variety of beliefs? One needs to ask the question of why, after decades of evolutionist teaching, there is still such a wide variety of opinions. Many Americans dismiss intelligent design not on the basis of science, but rather because of antireligious stereotypes.

Third, theories of origins as they are presently taught in the United States do not allow for any middle ground. They assert that one essentially must believe in the theory of evolution without leaving any room for the intervention of God. However, some people believe that the best perspective is to have a combination of the two views. Some believe that because there are no transitional species to support Darwin's assertions, the diversity of species and their similarities can only be explained by the creativity of an "intelligent designer" being involved. As Albert Einstein, perhaps the greatest intellect of the 20th century, stated, the more he studied science, the more he became convinced of a divine order (Calaprice, 2005).

Fourth, intelligent design, as a theory, has a vast variety of scientific points, made by academics who are professors at and graduates of some of the nation's leading universities, that are worthy of consideration. Unfortunately, students are not told that the main proponents of intelligent design come from universities such as University of California, Berkeley; Yale University; Manchester University; Lehigh University; Baylor University; and a variety of other institutions. They are not told that a large number of French biologists rebelled against evolutionary theory because of its many inadequacies, culminating in the publication of the article "Should We Burn Darwin?" (Litynski, 1961). In addition, students are not told that most of those who advocate intelligent design do so not on the basis of theological belief, but on the foundation of scientific conclusions.

RESPONSE TO COUNTERPOINT ESSAY

The essence of Aaron Cooley's argument surrounds the issue of the separation of church and state. Unfortunately, Cooley evades the essence of the issue, which is scientific and educational in nature. First, the German, English, and French scientists, who in three separate studies undermined evolution's connection between modern humans and Neanderthals, are secular scientists. Second, Zygmunt Litynski (1961), who wrote the article "Should We Burn Darwin?" is a secular scientist. Third, the primary scientists who are attacking evolution for its inaccuracy, lack of support in the fossil records, and racism are from secular universities such as Harvard, Yale, Manchester, and UC Berkeley. Fourth, statements regarding intelligent design have been made by people such as Einstein. Fifth, according to the British Council (2009) and Evolution Space (2007), adults raised under atheistic communism in the former Soviet bloc have rates of disbelief in evolution just slightly less than the American rates (e.g., Russia, several other nations in the former Soviet Union, Bulgaria, Romania, and Poland).

In addition, Cooley's church and state argument is puzzling because he omits other quotes from the very sources that he cites that give a totally different picture of what is actually stated. First, he cites Thomas Jefferson, but for reasons that are enigmatic, and makes no reference to Jefferson's second inaugural address as president. In this speech, Jefferson (1805/2001), consistent with his emphasis on the power of the states, asserts that "religious exercises" should be "under the direction and discipline of state or church" (p. 11). President Jefferson affirmed this belief in a letter that he wrote to Rev. Samuel Miller in which he stated "religious matters" were "reserved to states" (Jefferson in Hutson, 2008, p. 80). Jefferson believed governors, rather than presidents, should be the ones to declare days of fasting, religious proclamations, and prayer for schools and society; and as governor of Virginia, Jefferson acted accordingly. Among the founders, Jefferson's interpretation of the First Amendment was the most liberal, and yet even he believed that governors should address these issues. In addition, Cooley quotes *School District of Abington Township v. Schempp* (1963) but makes no mention of the following statement: "Nothing we have said here indicates that such study of the Bible or religion, when presented objectively as part of a secular program of education, may not be effected consistently with the First Amendment."

Education should be a means of encouraging students to be exposed to diverse viewpoints rather than a monolithic assertion that a theory such as evolution is an absolute truth. Evolution has some real problems and weaknesses, as divulged by many secular scientists. To ignore this fact and pretend that there are no alternative theories presents an incomplete picture and discourages America's youth from having open minds.

CONCLUSION

Supposedly, the American education system is designed to foster the development of inquiring minds in children and to teach them to reach their own conclusions. In reality, however, the American education system hardly operates this way. It tends to present one theory as unassailable fact and dismiss all other explanations. It really does not prepare American children to function in the real world or give them the opportunity to reach their own conclusions.

COUNTERPOINT: Aaron Cooley
New England College

One of the most important innovations of modern thought and politics is religious tolerance. The United States has a long and turbulent history of supporting both religious freedom and de facto conformity to Judeo-Christian traditions. The politics around religion have become even more contentious over the centuries due to the advances in science and technology that have challenged beliefs about the origins of life and humanity. When these spheres of human inquiry collide, there are often few arguments that can persuade the other side, and rightly so, as the basic right of religious or rational belief is fundamental. Yet, these systems of thought have regularly come into conflict in the arena of government and specifically in public schools.

This counterpoint essay contends that evolution and creation science/intelligent design should not be taught side by side in public school science classrooms. This is not a judgment about the theological assertions of either side. Rather, it is a simple assessment of current federal law as well as constitutional interpretation. At present, *Kitzmiller v. Dover* (2005), a case from Pennsylvania, struck down a school board's attempt to allow teaching of creation science/intelligent design. This is a correct holding because creation science/intelligent design was determined to not be science. Therefore, teaching it in science classrooms makes as much sense as teaching literature in math classrooms. However, given the nature of this volume and the nature of this public debate, it is useful to fully explore the background on the topic more generally with attention to the history of science and religion.

The body of this essay begins with a discussion of the tradition of separating church and state through the Constitution and case law. The next section moves to cases and controversies having to do with religion, science, and the public schools, with a focus on the *Dover* case as the binding precedent. The concluding section speaks to the pragmatic rationales for why teaching creation science/intelligent design in public school science classrooms does not benefit students or the country's long-term interests, because it undercuts strong science and technology pedagogy.

SEPARATION OF CHURCH AND STATE

The constitutional foundation for keeping public governmental affairs and private religious functions separate derives from the First Amendment to the Constitution. Many casual observers would assert that the First Amendment should have additional merit or maintain the first place among equals when compared to the following amendments. Yet, this "common sense" notion does not hold with the historical fact that it was the third article listed in the initial batch of amendments. So, the elevated place it has based on its number is somewhat misplaced. This being said, it was a central part of the Bill of Rights and was incorporated into the Constitution upon having been adopted September 25, 1789, and ratified by the states on December 15, 1791.

The text of the First Amendment was written in a way that has created a tremendous amount of ambiguity in the meaning and voluminous amounts of litigation over the past 60 or so years, all of which have substantial import for teaching creation science/intelligent design in public schools. The First Amendment states,

> Congress shall make no law respecting an establishment of religion, or prohibiting the free exercise thereof; or abridging the freedom of speech, or of the press; or the right of the people peaceably to assemble, and to petition the Government for a redress of grievances. (Amendment 1, 1791)

The First Amendment has been widely interpreted by opposing scholars and jurists as the prohibition of any intermingling of religious practice with public enterprises, on the left, to any practice that does not result in the establishment of an official state religion being constitutional, on the right. These varying perspectives are the result of the doctrines of constitutional interpretation that have solidified since the end of the Warren Court as originalism or strict construction and the so-called living Constitution view of the document. Insofar as these positions have become more entrenched, the debates around science, religion, and government have continued to spark debate.

Another core notion of American political belief comes from Jefferson's letter to the Danbury Baptists. In this piece, he uses the phrase *wall of separation* between church and state, which would become as famous as it is controversial:

> Believing with you that religion is a matter which lies solely between Man & his God, that he owes account to none other for his faith or his worship, that the legitimate powers of government reach actions only, & not opinions, I contemplate with sovereign reverence that act of the whole American people which declared that their legislature should "make no law respecting an establishment of religion, or prohibiting the free exercise thereof," thus building a wall of separation between Church & State. (Jefferson 1802, para. 2)

This statement adds clout to the constitutional provision and further lays the political foundation for the demarcation between public and private affairs when it comes to religion.

The next step in discussing the background in this area is to engage in a brief review of the holdings of the most influential Supreme Court cases on religion in public education. The first case of note is *Engel v. Vitale* (1962). Here, the Supreme Court invalidated New York's attempt to permit daily prayer in public schools. The Court explained,

> We think that by using its public school system to encourage recitation of the Regents' prayer, the State of New York has adopted a practice

wholly inconsistent with the Establishment Clause. There can, of course, be no doubt that New York's program of daily classroom invocation of God's blessings as prescribed in the Regents' prayer is a religious activity. It is a solemn avowal of divine faith and supplication for the blessings of the Almighty. (*Engel v. Vitale*, 1962, p. 424)

The next dispute of substantial importance came only a year later in the companion cases of *School District of Abington Township v. Schempp* and *Murray v. Curlett* (1963). What is significant in this case is the way in which the Court frames the issue of government being neutral in matters of religion. This is an aspect that was certainly a hallmark of our constitutional founding as well as integral part of a modern pluralistic and diverse society.

In striking down prayer and Bible reading in public schools, the Court devised a two-part test:

> The test may be stated as follows: what are the purpose and the primary effect of the [legislative] enactment? . . . [T]o withstand the strictures of the Establishment Clause there must be a secular legislative purpose and a primary effect that neither advances nor inhibits religion. (p. 222)

The last of these cases, and the most prominent in setting the precedential tests for future cases, is *Lemon v. Kurtzman* (1971). The so-called *Lemon* test has three parts, which are laid out as follows:

> Three such tests may be gleaned from our cases. First, the statute must have a secular legislative purpose; second, its principal or primary effect must be one that neither advances nor inhibits religion; finally, the statute must not foster "an excessive government entanglement with religion." (pp 612–613; internal citations omitted)

Each element of the test must be used to evaluate the constitutionality of governmental action when it comes into contact with religion. This cabining off of spheres of influence and behavior is crucial to having public schools that reflect secular viewpoints and a multicultural society.

RELIGION, SCIENCE, AND PUBLIC SCHOOLS

Of course, there have been broader struggles with science and religion from the times of Ptolemy to Copernicus to Galileo to the present day, but Charles Darwin's *The Origin of Species* prompted the most widespread backlash against scientific thought when it clashed with religion. As Darwin's ideas filtered through the mainstream of colleges and universities, it was only a matter of time before the public schools would become a battleground between belief and science. The most well-known example comes from Tennessee in the form of the Scopes Monkey Trial, *Scopes v. State of Tennessee* (1925, 1927). Here, a teacher was accused of violating a state law that made it

> unlawful for any teacher in any of the Universities, Normals and all other public schools of the State which are supported in whole or in part by the public school funds of the State, to teach any theory that denies the story of the Divine Creation of man as taught in the Bible, and to teach instead that man has descended from a lower order of animals. (Butler Act, 1925)

Even though the conviction was overturned, the act remained in effect until 1967.

The Supreme Court eventually entered the fray in 1968 when it struck down a law from Arkansas that was similar to the one from Tennessee. The law from Arkansas prohibited the teaching of evolution in public K–12 schools and institutions of higher learning at the risk of being fined up to $500. The dispute arose in 1965 when officials assigned a teacher to use a biology textbook that relied on evolution even though state law prohibited her from doing so. A trial court obtained a court order that invalidated the statute and prevented the board from terminating her employment. Even so, the Supreme Court of Arkansas subsequently upheld the statute as a legitimate exercise of the state's authority over the public school curriculum (*State v. Epperson*, 1967). On further review in *Epperson v. Arkansas* (1968), the Supreme Court unanimously invalidated the statute as unconstitutional.

In *Epperson v. Arkansas*, the Supreme Court declared that the statute was unconstitutional because it violated the Establishment Clause to the First Amendment of the Constitution by breaching the "wall of separation" between church and state. The Court ruled that the law was unacceptable because it ran afoul of the two-part test that it recently created in *Abington*. More specifically, the Court invalidated the statute on the basis that it sought to impose a religious perspective in place of a generally accepted scientific theory.

It is now crucial to move to the most relevant cases on the teaching of creation science/intelligent design in public schools. In *Edwards v. Aguillard* (1987), the Supreme Court struck down the ability of a public education system in Louisiana to teach creation science, because it implies nonscientific causes to events. In short, science curricula cannot rely on forces or notions that are outside of scientific and empirical inquiry explanations. The statute at issue prohibited instruction about evolution in public schools unless it was accompanied by teaching about creation science. Moreover, even though public schools were not obligated to include instruction in either theory, the law mandated that if one was taught, the other theory also had to be presented. The Court explained its rationale in this manner:

> The Act impermissibly endorses religion by advancing the religious belief that a supernatural being created humankind. The legislative history demonstrates that the term "creation science," as contemplated by the state legislature, embraces this religious teaching. The Act's primary purpose was to change the public school science curriculum to provide persuasive advantage to a particular religious doctrine that rejects the factual basis of evolution in its entirety. Thus, the Act is designed either to promote the theory of creation science that embodies a particular religious tenet or to prohibit the teaching of a scientific theory disfavored by certain religious sects. In either case, the Act violates the First Amendment. (*Edwards v. Aguillard* 1987, citing the Syllabus at p. 579)

The most recent case in this area is *Kitzmiller v. Dover* (2005). In this instance, the text that was being offered for use in science curricula was shown to have adapted creation science to intelligent design in the wake of the *Edwards* decision. This transparent changing of the rhetoric was the missing link in the case and provided solid ground for the holding that prevents the teaching of intelligent design in science classrooms. A federal trial court in Pennsylvania made clear that public school boards and officials cannot advance nonscientific explanations that leave the realm of science and enter the realm of religion. Barring a constitutional revolution on the courts from the district level to the Supreme Court or a scientific consensus that embraces intelligent design, there seems little likelihood that courts will undo the decades-old precedent of *Edwards* and the more recent finding in *Kitzmiller v. Dover.*

Beyond this legal conclusion, there is the broader point about what this debate has done to science education in the United States. Here, the facts are clear and not positive. Sadly, the United States ranks near the bottom of the list of developed countries' belief in evolution. From a recent article in *Science*, the numbers come through:

> Over the past 20 years, the percentage of U.S. adults accepting the idea of evolution has declined from 45% to 40% and the percentage of adults overtly rejecting evolution declined from 48% to 39%. The percentage of adults who were not sure about evolution increased from 7% in 1985 to 21% in 2005. After 20 years of public debate, the public appears to be divided evenly in terms of accepting or rejecting evolution, with about one in five adults still undecided or unaware of the issue. (Miller, Scott, & Okamoto, 2005, p. 765)

So, for whatever the merits of the debate and legal outcomes of the cases are, the pushback against evolution seems to have been working on the public at large. This would not be a problem if it were exclusively a loss of scientific understanding to theology alone, but one cannot so easily separate knowledge and understanding of evolution from other parts of science. It is here that the United States risks undermining its place as a leader in science and technology.

To conclude, it is vital to reiterate that evolution and religion do not have to be at odds. Indeed, many of the world's religions as well as Christian denominations accept evolution or aspects of it. Further, if proponents of creation science and intelligent design want to see it taught in schools alongside evolution, then it needs to provide a similar level of advancement of scientific knowledge. At this point, it has not and therefore should not be taught on an equal footing to evolution even if the legal prohibitions were lifted.

RESPONSE TO POINT ESSAY

The point essay's intent to further open-minded thinking in public education by suggesting ideas that are controversial or not fully proven should be discussed by students and teachers is appreciated. This type of educational attitude is all too infrequent these days given the pressures of standardized testing and accountability regimes that require drill-and-kill clinics before end-of-year exams. Even so, the argument in favor of academic freedom to discuss issues in schools must have some bounds. Just because an idea exists does not mean that it belongs in a public school curriculum. Some people still believe in a flat earth. Should that be taught in public schools? Clearly, the answer is no, as this belief is not supported by scientific evidence. Therefore, the decision to put a subject in the curriculum should not be an issue of anything other than the consensus of the academic community that researchers and teachers in that field and the constitutional guidance from the federal courts.

A few of the themes of the point essay deserve attention, consideration, and then rejection. The first issue that needs to be addressed is the questioning of carbon dating and other methods judging the age of fossils. Quite simply, these are the best practices of science. Denying the accuracy of these processes goes against the consensus of the global scientific community and will inhibit student success in learning science that is not related to evolution.

The next topic that must be discussed is that schools are not in the business of exposing students to every idea that exists in the public domain. There are numerous religious faiths and organizations that would gladly educate students about intelligent design. They can do this at community centers and other venues. There is no need for this to be taught in schools given the resources of these faith communities.

A discussion of selected studies on the relationship of modern humans to the Neanderthals does not disprove evolution. The relationships between and among different groups of humans and possible ancestors or related populations are still being researched. What is clear is that humans and primates have common ancestors who share nearly all of their DNA. Of course, this is all immaterial to the debate at hand, which should remain a debate about education law and policy and not the well-established merits of evolution.

Moreover, the painting of supporters of evolution as possibly racist and antireligious is specious on its face. Few groups of researchers know more about race and its social consequences than anthropologists. Further, many of these supporters teaching evolution are not atheists or agnostics and believe in theistic evolution.

The ideas expressed in the point essay advance several ideas passionately, but the essay neglects the crucial issues of guiding legal precedents and best practices in science classrooms. Without addressing these areas, one would probably have a difficult time convincing school boards or parents why creation science/intelligent design should be taught to their public school children.

FURTHER READINGS AND RESOURCES

British Council. (2009). *Darwin survey shows international consensus on acceptance of evolution* [Press release]. Retrieved May 4, 2011, from http://www.britishcouncil.org/darwin_now_survey_global.pdf

Calaprice, A. (2005). *The Einstein almanac.* Baltimore: Johns Hopkins University Press.

Darwin, C. (1871). *Descent of man.* London: Murray.

Evolution Space. (2007). *Not only in America: Evolution science endangered worldwide.* Retrieved May 4, 2011, from http://evolutionspace.wordpress.com/2007/04/24/not-only-in-america-evolution-science-endangered-worldwide

Gould, S. J. (1981). *The mismeasure of man.* New York: Norton.

Hutson, J. H. (2008). *Religion and the new republic.* Lanham, MD: Rowman & Littlefield.

Jefferson, T. (1802). *Letter to the Danbury Baptists.* Retrieved from http://www.loc.gov/loc/lcib/9806/danpre.html

Jefferson, T. (1805/2001). Second inaugural address. *The inaugural addresses of Thomas Jefferson, 1801 and 1805.* Columbia: University of Missouri Press.

Kramer, S. (Director). (1960). *Inherit the wind.* United States: United Artists.

Litynski, Z. (1961, January). Should we burn Darwin? *Science Digest, 51,* 61.

Miller, J., Scott, E., & Okamoto, S. (2005). Public acceptance of evolution. *Science, 313,* 765–766.

New York Times News Service. (1997, July 11). DNA analysis knocks Neanderthals out of the human evolutionary tree. Retrieved January 13, 2010, from http://articles.chicagotribune.com/1997-07-11/news/9707110084_1_humans-and-neanderthals-hominid-dna

Russo, C. J. (2002). Evolution v. creation science in the US: Can the courts divine a solution? *Education Law Journal, 3*(3), 152–158.

Serre, D., Langaney, A., Chech, M., Teschler-Nicola, M., Paunovic, M., Mennecier, P., et al. (2004). No evidence of Neandertal mtDNA contribution to early modern humans. *PLOS Biology, 2*, 313–317.

Wade, N. (2000, March 29). DNA tests cast doubt on link between Neanderthals and modern man. *The New York Times.* Retrieved January 13, 2010, from http://www.nytimes.com/2000/03/29/us/dna-tests-cast-doubt-on-link-between-neanderthals-and-modern-man.html

COURT CASES AND STATUTES

Butler Act. (1925). Retrieved from http://law2.umkc.edu/faculty/projects/ftrials/scopes/tennstat.htm

Edwards v. Aguillard, 482 U.S. 578 (1987).

Engel v. Vitale, 370 U.S. 421 (1962).

Epperson v. State of Arkansas, 393 U.S. 97 (1968).

Kitzmiller v. Dover Area School District, 400 F.Supp.2d 707 (M.D. Pa. 2005).

Lemon v. Kurtzman, 411 U.S. 6022 (1971).

School District of Abington Township v. Schempp, 374 U.S. 225 (1963).

School District of Abington Township v. Schempp and Murray v. Curlett, 374 U.S. 203 (1963).

Scopes v. State of Tennessee, 278 S.W. 57 (Tenn. Cir. Ct. 1925), *reversed* 289 S.W. 363 (Tenn. 1927).

State v. Epperson, 416 S.W.2d 322 (Ark. 1967).

Should school calendars take religious holidays into account?

POINT: Amy M. Steketee, *Baker & Daniels, South Bend, Indiana*
COUNTERPOINT: Allison S. Fetter-Harrott, *Franklin College*

OVERVIEW

As the United States becomes increasingly diversified religiously, the issue of whether school calendars should take religious holidays into account, an issue that has already generated legal controversy, is likely to become even more contentious. Put another way, as families that believe in minority religions move into neighborhoods that have largely been dominated by one or two specific faiths, questions are likely to arise about school calendars. More specifically, should school board officials accommodate the requests of parents who belong to minority religions to modify academic calendars to allow their children time off from class, like their peers who are members of the dominant religions, to celebrate the religious holidays of their faith traditions? The limited litigation on this issue has yielded mixed results.

Amid controversies over religious celebrations being observed as part of school calendars, the judiciary typically applies one or more of three tests that the Supreme Court has devised to evaluate the place of religion in schools. Under the most comprehensive of these standards, *Lemon v. Kurtzman* (1971), the Court declared, "First, the statute must have a secular legislative purpose; second, its principal or primary effect must be one that neither advances nor inhibits religion; finally, the statute must not foster an excessive government entanglement with religion" (pp. 612–613).

As the *Lemon* test, as it has come to be known, became increasingly unworkable, the Supreme Court devised two additional tests about the constitutionality of religion and public education. These tests ask whether the actions of school boards or officials endorse religious, or nonreligious, perspectives (*Lynch v. Donnelly*, 1984) or run the risk of coercing students to participate in religious activities other than their own traditions or lack thereof (*Lee v. Weisman*, 1992).

In a case directly addressing a school calendar, the federal trial court in New Jersey, in *Clever v. Cherry Hill Township Board of Education* (1993), rejected a challenge to a school board's policy of requiring classroom teachers to maintain calendars depicting an array of national, ethnic, and religious holidays while also permitting seasonal displays containing religious symbols. Applying the *Lemon* test, the court found that insofar as the policy had the purpose and effect of appropriately educating children about religious diversity, and was not entangled with religion, it satisfied the dictates of the Establishment Clause in the First Amendment to the Constitution.

In an earlier case where school calendars were not at the heart of the controversy, a school board in South Dakota enacted a set of guidelines designed to enable officials to develop a calendar that would have minimized conflicts with religious holidays of all faiths along with addressing the larger place of religion in its curriculum. The Eighth Circuit upheld the guidelines, including the calendar, because the religious themes that it addressed could be integrated into the curriculum as long as they were presented objectively as a traditional part of a holiday's cultural and religious heritage (*Florey v. Sioux Falls School District 49–5*, 1980a, 1980b).

Another issue impacting the formation of school calendars, albeit not as explicitly as the two previous cases, dealt with Good Friday, the day commemorating the death of Jesus Christ. Courts addressing concerns associated with the establishment of religion by recognizing a selected holy day in school calendars reached mixed results. For example, the Seventh Circuit affirmed that a law from Illinois making Good Friday a paid holiday for teachers and closing schools violated the Establishment Clause since it was a purely sectarian commemoration unaccompanied by any secular rituals (*Metzl v. Leininger*, 1995). Yet, in the first of three cases reaching the opposite result, the same Seventh Circuit later affirmed that Indiana's recognition of Good Friday as a legal holiday for state employees did not violate the Establishment Clause because it did so based on secular justifications that were supported by evidence including the provision of a spring holiday (*Bridenbaugh v. O'Bannon*, 1999). The Fourth (*Koenick v. Felton*, 1999) and Sixth (*Granzeier v. Middleton*, 1999) Circuits also upheld the status of Good Friday as a legal holiday.

Against this backdrop, the debates in this chapter rely largely on the same cases in reaching different outcomes over whether educational officials in public schools should take religious holidays into account when creating their school calendars. In the point essay, Amy M. Steketee, of Baker & Daniels (South Bend, Indiana), defends the affirmative position in declaring that taking religious holidays into account can, and does, satisfy First Amendment muster. She observes that as long as educational officials can demonstrate that their actions in taking religious holidays into account are meeting legitimate secular purposes such as fostering diversity, including religious diversity, then they should be legally acceptable under Establishment Clause analysis.

The counterpoint essay of Allison S. Fetter-Harrott (Franklin College) disagrees based on her concern that the modification of school calendars to accommodate religious holidays would violate the Establishment Clause. She asserts that insofar as educational officials in public schools need to be concerned primarily with their duty of educating students, coupled with the possibility that taking some, but not all, religions into account when setting school calendars, can lead to strife within communities, they are better off not taking religious holidays into account when devising school calendars.

As you read these debates, ask yourself the following questions. First, is it a good idea for officials to take religious holidays into account when creating their school calendars? Second, is the fear of strife, absent any real problems, over different religious holidays realistic? Put another way, does such fear offer a sufficient justification to exclude any consideration of religious holidays in developing academic calendars?

Charles J. Russo
University of Dayton

POINT: Amy M. Steketee
Baker & Daniels, South Bend, Indiana

Students in American public schools celebrate a wide variety of religious holidays. It is certainly impractical and likely impossible for school board officials to recognize and commemorate each and every one of these holidays. Even so, it is prudent for officials to identify the holidays that their students observe and to consider their dates when developing annual school calendars. Educational officials should be prepared to accommodate student requests to be absent on these days. Further, where a high percentage of student or employee absenteeism would cause administrative burdens and unnecessary expenses, boards should even consider school closings. This point essay thus provides an overview of relevant case law supporting the proposition that educational officials should take religious holidays into account when developing school calendars.

CONSTITUTIONAL PRINCIPLES AND LEGAL ANALYSIS

Three key clauses in the First Amendment to the Constitution, the Establishment, Free Exercise, and Free Speech Clauses, provide the framework for analysis relating to public schools' recognition of religious holidays as calendars impact the religious rights of students or employees.

The Establishment Clause

Courts have interpreted the Establishment Clause as prohibiting school boards from promoting, endorsing, or otherwise "establishing" any specific religion or religion in general. Courts apply any one or a combination of the following three tests in evaluating whether school boards violated the Establishment Clause. Under the most far-reaching standard, the *Lemon v. Kurtzman* (1971) test, a governmental action violates the Establishment Clause if it lacks a secular purpose; its principal or primary effect advances or inhibits religious belief or practice; or if it fosters excessive entanglement between the government and religion.

According to the endorsement test of *Lynch v. Donnelly* (1984), governmental action violates the Establishment Clause if it appears from the perspective of an objective observer to endorse a particular religious viewpoint or endorse religion over nonreligion. Under the coercion test enunciated in *Lee v. Weisman* (1992), governmental action violates the Establishment

Clause if it coerces individuals to support or participate in religious viewpoints or in religion over nonreligion.

Free Exercise Clause

Under the Free Exercise Clause, public school boards are prohibited from burdening individuals' ability to practice their religions. To succeed on Free Exercise claims, plaintiffs must show that school policies burden their religious beliefs or practice such as when they are forced to choose between their religious beliefs and complying with a policy and that the restriction outweighs the school's interest in the policy. Even if school board interests outweigh the restriction on the rights of students or employees, plaintiffs may prevail if they can show that less restrictive alternatives allow officials to achieve their goals without burdening religious beliefs.

Free Speech Clause

Pursuant to the Free Speech Clause, student or employee speech or conduct that is reasonably construed as speech that is made in the performance of official duties or speech in nonpublic fora such as classrooms may be subject to reasonable regulations. Courts have consistently held that avoidance of Establishment Clause violations is a reasonable regulation, and can, in some circumstances, constitute a narrowly tailored compelling state interest. For example, in *Lamb's Chapel v. Center Moriches Union Free School District* (1993), the Supreme Court noted that "the interest of the State in avoiding an Establishment Clause violation 'may be [a] compelling' one justifying an abridgement of free speech otherwise protected by the First Amendment (internal citations deleted)" (p. 39). However, the speech of individuals cannot be regulated due to their viewpoint absent a narrowly tailored compelling governmental interest.

To prevail on Free Speech claims, plaintiffs must prove one or more of the following: that school boards have created public fora; if the speech is in nonpublic fora, that officials are unable to demonstrate a legitimate pedagogical interest in regulating the speech; that the speech is a matter of public concern and has not jeopardized an employee's effectiveness or relationships with superiors or management; or that the regulation on the speech discriminates against certain viewpoints and that officials cannot demonstrate a narrowly tailored compelling interest sufficient to justify this regulation.

The inherent tension between these clauses should be obvious. For instance, when public school officials go too far in recognizing or promoting religious holidays, they may violate the Establishment Clause. Conversely, when officials refuse to accommodate the rights of students or employees to observe religious holidays, they may violate their Free Speech or Free Exercise rights. Boards must provide reasonable accommodations but are not required to offer accommodations that impose undue hardships on their operations (*Ansonia Board of Education v. Philbrook*, 1986).

With respect to calendar development, school boards that close for some, but not all, religious holidays risk facing Establishment Clause challenges. While school boards can avoid claims by never closing for religious holidays, they would risk infringing the Free Exercise rights of students or employees. Presumably, boards could also avoid claims by closing for every religious holiday, but this would be logistically impossible and impede their missions.

School officials charged with the duty to set the parameters for recognizing religious holidays must, therefore, be cognizant of the interrelationships between these clauses. Officials should further consider the effects of state constitutional principles, which may not mirror federal constitutional law, as well as state-specific religious freedom statutes.

SCHOOL POLICIES

School boards should avoid setting policies that penalize students who are absent due to a religious holiday. In *Church of God (Worldwide, Texas Region) v. Amarillo Independent School District* (1981), a federal trial court in Texas reviewed the constitutionality of a board policy that limited the number of excused absences students could take for religious holidays to 2 days per year. Students who were absent from school for more than two religious observances received zeroes on assignments. Students who were members of the Church of God were required to abstain from secular activity on 7 holy days and to attend a 7-day religious convocation. When these students received zeroes for assignments they missed on days they were observing these religious holidays, they challenged the policy, alleging that it violated their Free Exercise rights. Disagreeing, the school board argued that if it allowed an exception for these students, it would effectively promote their church in violation of the Establishment Clause.

The court rejected the board's argument in deciding that the policy violated the students' Free Exercise rights because it imposed a substantial burden on their right to exercise their religious beliefs. The court pointed out that its striking down the policy did not foster the establishment of religion and "reflects nothing more than the governmental obligation of neutrality in the face of religious differences" (p. 618). Thus, it is reasonable to infer that a policy of neutrality requires school boards to avoid penalizing students who exercise their religious rights and to accommodate requests to observe religious holidays.

SECULAR REASONS FOR SCHOOL HOLIDAYS

Courts agree that where there are secular reasons for declaring school holidays, officials may do so even when they coincide with religious holidays. For instance, in *Koenick v. Felton* (1999), the Fourth Circuit considered whether a Maryland statute that required a school holiday on Good Friday and Easter Monday was unconstitutional. A teacher challenging the statute argued that creating a 4-day holiday around Easter promoted Christianity over other religions. Disagreeing, the court explained,

> By simply giving students and teachers a school holiday around Easter, [the statute] does not mention or imply that the holiday is to be spent attending religious services in recognition of this Christian holy day. The statute merely gives people the days off to spend as they like. (p. 268)

The court thus observed that while the statute made it possible for students and teachers to attend services around the time of Easter, it neither promoted nor advanced this cause. The court added,

> Similarly, the Board has a policy of granting students and teachers excused absences to attend religious services in recognition of holy days in their own religions; however, by doing so there is no insinuation that such a policy advances any religion over another. (p. 268)

Also, the court found a secular purpose for the decision to close the school based on the "[b]oard's desire to economize resources that are wasted when classes are held on days with a high rate of absenteeism." Other courts reached like results as both the Ninth (*Cammack v. Waihee*, 1991) and Seventh (*Bridenbaugh v. O'Bannon*, 1999) Circuits refused to invalidate treating Good Friday as a holiday.

It should thus be clear that where there are secular reasons for closing schools on or around the time of religious holidays, boards should not avoid doing so for fear of violating the Establishment Clause. That decisions to close schools make it easier for students and staff to observe their religious holidays is simply an incidental benefit and not an endorsement of religion. In this regard, the Supreme Court noted in *Lynch v. Donnelly* (1984), a case about a Christmas display on public property, that not every law that confers an incidental benefit on religion is unconstitutional.

Case law suggests that school officials may schedule holidays on or near religious holidays when there are secular reasons for doing so. Yet, officials are not required to schedule holidays at those times. In fact, it would be entirely impractical for schools to close for each and every religious holiday. Still, on days of high rates of absenteeism due to religious holidays that would produce inefficiencies, it is prudent for boards to consider simply declaring holidays for all.

IDENTIFYING RELIGIOUS HOLIDAYS ON SCHOOL CALENDARS

At least one court reasoned that a policy of establishing calendars that identify a variety of religious holidays is constitutionally permissible. In *Clever v. Cherry Hill Township Board of Education* (1993), a board policy required elementary and junior high school teachers to maintain calendars including a wide variety of religious and cultural holidays. Opponents challenged the policy as a violation of the Establishment Clause.

The federal trial court in New Jersey rejected the challenge in noting that the policy had the purpose and effect of appropriately educating children about diversity because it "foster[ed] mutual understanding and respect for the rights of all individuals regarding their beliefs, values, and customs" (p. 942). Moreover, the court ruled that the policy neither fostered nor promoted religion and was not excessively entangled with religion.

CONCLUSION

The fears of the counterpoint essay notwithstanding, courts have agreed that religious neutrality does not require school boards to be insensitive to religious diversity. In fact, it is unnecessary, impractical, and perhaps even unconstitutional for school boards to promulgate calendars or policies that ignore religious holidays altogether and treat all students and staff identically. Nor should boards refuse to recognize one religious holiday for fear of having to then recognize each and every religious holiday. If anything, boards must be able to take pragmatic approaches to recognizing and accommodating religious diversity while providing sound and consistent educational programming.

To minimize conflicts relating to religious holiday accommodations, school boards should obtain information about students' and staff members' religious beliefs, identify religious holidays, engage in discussion with the relevant stakeholders, and then consider the most efficient strategies for allowing students and staff to observe these holidays. Boards can adopt different strategies. For example, if there is a strong likelihood that operations will be upset by a high rate of absenteeism due to religious observances, it may be most efficient to schedule the day off. Another approach is for boards to provide students with a set numbers of floating holidays, which may be redeemed as needed. Students simply would provide notes from their parents to redeem excused absences for religious purposes. In New Jersey, for instance, the state board of education has identified more than 100 religious holidays for which students may be excused from school and may not be penalized. Sometimes boards can identify "observance days" on which school meets, but teachers are prohibited from scheduling tests or special events. As communities become increasingly diverse, it is prudent for school boards to consider the religious diversity of their communities and to adopt calendars or policies designed to accommodate the differing needs of residents while affording students and employees opportunities to practice their religious beliefs freely.

COUNTERPOINT: Allison S. Fetter-Harrott
Franklin College

Simply put, calendars in public schools should not take religious holidays into account. Questions regarding the scheduling of school holidays and related vacations can raise tensions. Parents often have strong opinions about school schedules, especially with regard to such matters as scheduling family trips, coordinating work and school schedules, and the provision of childcare. Similarly, temperatures can run high when school boards and other public entities consider which, and to what extent, religious and secular holidays should be celebrated.

This debate raises questions of culture, tradition, and community relationships. Accordingly, the acknowledgment of specific religious holidays in public school calendars, even when well meaning, poses an untenable risk of divisiveness to school communities. Because school boards cannot accommodate all religious groups, their only choice would likely be to meet the needs of some and not others. Yet, adopting such an approach poses a risk of running afoul of the Establishment Clause in the First Amendment to the Constitution. Perhaps more importantly, efforts to accommodate some religions will necessarily favor those religions, invite additional requests for accommodations from other groups, and embroil school communities in unnecessarily divisive debates over the contents of school calendars. One of the strengths of American society is that it is increasingly diverse. To this end, our national sense of democratic pluralism dictates that educational leaders, respecting all religions and the nonreligious, must not take religious holidays into account in the creation of the school calendar.

POTENTIAL CONSTITUTIONAL CHALLENGES

The First Amendment, in relevant part, provides that "Congress shall make no law respecting an establishment of religion, or prohibiting the free exercise thereof." This language and the Supreme Court's subsequent interpretation of the meaning of the provision in the living history of our country rest on the understanding that "the premise that both religion and government can best work to achieve their lofty aims if each is left free from the other within its respective sphere" (*County of Allegheny v. American Civil Liberties Union*, 1989, pp. 590–591; internal citations omitted).

Individuals have challenged the actions of educational leaders to take religions into account in the creation of school calendars. These cases often allege that acknowledgment of religious holidays in public school schedules amount to the unconstitutional advancement of religion in violation of the Establishment Clause of the First Amendment. When reviewing disputes of this nature, courts consider whether observances have religious purposes, whether they have the principal or primary effect of advancing or inhibiting religion, and whether observances excessively entangle schools with religious entities. If the actions of governmental units such as public school boards fail any of these "prongs," they do not comport with the Establishment Clause as interpreted by *Lemon v. Kurtzman* (1971). Courts may also consider whether the actions of public school officials endorse religion (*Lynch v. Donnelly*, 1984) or coerce students to participate in religious activities (*Lee v. Weisman*, 1992).

If school leaders schedule the calendar observances of religious holidays for the purposes of facilitating or encouraging students and their families to commemorate those holidays, thereby advancing the associated religions, they are at significant risk of violating the first prong of the *Lemon* test and, therefore, running afoul of the Establishment Clause.

In *Metzl v. Leininger* (1995), by way of illustration, the Seventh Circuit affirmed the unconstitutionality of a law from Illinois that would have declared Good Friday, the day commemorating when Jesus of Nazareth was crucified and died, preceding the Christian holiday of Easter, a public school holiday. Citing the legislative history and the "purely religious" nature of the Good Friday holiday, the court agreed that the statute advanced a decidedly religious purpose, a factor that it could not reconcile with Establishment Clause analysis.

At the same time, if school calendars commemorate religious holidays in manners that have the primary effect of advancing or inhibiting religion, again, they are likely to be found to have violated the *Lemon* test. Yet, at least one court applied the *Lemon* test in holding that where a school calendar observed religious holidays from a diverse group of religious faiths, a reasonable observer would have viewed this observance not as the advancement of a given religion but rather as an educational lesson of various, diverse religious traditions (*Clever v. Cherry Hill Township Board of Education*, 1993).

Still, school board officials should tread very carefully because courts take special care to prevent coercion of school-age children, impressionable to the influence of school leaders, into the practice of religion. Likewise, courts are equally hesitant to approve policies that communicate preferences of one religion over another to children.

School calendars that take a variety of religious holidays into consideration may communicate an appreciation of religious diversity to students, an admittedly laudable aim. Still, by beginning to take religious holidays into account when scheduling school calendars, officials run the risk of traversing a very slippery and hopelessly irreversible slope. It may be possible for officials to accommodate one or two religious groups, but at some eventual point in time, they are unlikely to be unable to accommodate the religious holidays of every student and staff member in school calendars. There may simply not be enough weekdays or school days in the year to permit school officials to accommodate everyone with a day, a morning, or even a couple of hours off.

Elementary, middle, and secondary schools should be concerned with educating children, a task that is difficult to accomplish if students are not on task. Consequently, frequent interruptions or overall reductions in the number of days that students attend classes should not be tolerated. In addition, allowing some religious holidays to be commemorated but not others as part of school calendars presents the potential implication that highly impressionable school children may infer that some religions, those whose holidays are observed in their public school, are superior to others. Accordingly, the acknowledgment of religious holidays by public schools additionally poses a risk of unconstitutionally having the primary effect of advancing religion.

Finally, where the acknowledgment of one or more religious holidays in school calendars excessively entangles public school boards and leaders with religious entities, the practice fails the *Lemon* test and violates the Establishment Clause. Excessive entanglement typically rises as an issue in other kinds of school cases, such as where educational officials regulate prayers occurring at school events or fund teachers in religiously affiliated nonpublic schools. Admittedly, excessive entanglement seems less likely an issue in the religious holiday context. However, the more that public school officials choose to make recognizing and observing specific religious holidays their business, the more they risk excessive entanglement with religion. Imagine a scenario where two branches of the same religion observe their faith in differing ways or by observing it on different days. How are school officials to choose which one to integrate into its calendar? In so doing, do school boards risk regulating student practice of religion? Do board officials make judgments as to the rightness or appropriateness of one religious group's observance over the other? In determining which group's practices can be observed in schools, are educational leaders controlling the operations of the religious bodies? These are among the challenges that can be raised when school boards take religious holidays into account in establishing and observing their school calendars.

It is important to keep in mind that failure under any of the three prongs of the *Lemon* test results in a violation of the Establishment Clause. As such, school boards that take religious holidays into account in scheduling their calendars should be wary of challenges alleging that such actions have either the purpose or primary effect of advancing religion or that they excessively entangle themselves with religion. Accordingly, educational officials in public schools may discover that even well-meaning efforts to accommodate a variety of religions or to acknowledge religious diversity by taking religious holidays into account in scheduling their academic calendars may pose untenable risks of constitutional infirmity.

POTENTIAL LEADERSHIP AND COMMUNITY CHALLENGES

Even where the incorporation or observance of religious holidays into public school calendars would not run afoul of the Establishment Clause, adopting such an approach may create leadership and community challenges that outweigh the potential benefits of acknowledging such religious observances. One of the strengths of the United States in the 21st century is that we are an increasingly religiously diverse country. This diversity may even emerge in the same home or family, and virtually all community public schools should expect to serve students whose families adhere to a wide array of religious beliefs and traditions. By explicitly taking religious holidays into account in creating public school calendars, even if doing so in an attempt to accommodate the religious traditions of all members of communities, school officials risk outcomes that may undermine community cohesion.

If leaders recognize and observe the religious holidays of only a few faiths, they run the risk of breeding feelings of exclusion, frustration, or resentment between and among the groups whose holidays are recognized and those whose faith holidays are unobserved. Students of faiths that are unrecognized by official public school calendars may have to miss examinations or otherwise make difficult choices regarding attendance in class and at other school events or religious observances. The upshot is that the challenges of these choices may be all the more taxing to students if their peers of other faiths are unburdened by the same choices by virtue of special consideration in school calendar schedules. This resentment may grow between groups of parents as well, as some may feel free to organize family celebrations or trips around their faith holidays, while others must fit religious observances in between school classes, extracurricular events, and other school events. This same challenge may also arise among staff as some must take vacation days or plan for substitutes to observe their religious holidays, while others are free to observe these days based on the accommodation of their faith in their school calendars. As discussed, when school boards recognize some but not all religious holidays in their calendars, one potential inference that students, staff, parents, and community members may draw is a preference by the public school for some religions over others.

An alternative difficulty is that unrecognized groups may themselves seek to have their own holidays integrated into the religious holiday observances of the school calendar. When this occurs, school officials have options. If school officials grant such requests, they may do so without incident. However, there may be endpoints at which school board officials cannot accommodate the holiday observances of every religious group and still meet the needs of students and the expectations of the many federal and state authorities demanding ever increasing accountability in education. If school officials are unable to grant such requests for any reason, they have two options. First, if officials deny requests but continue to observe the religious holidays of other faiths, they run the risk of preferring one religious group and alienating another. Second, if educational leaders deny requests and discontinue the practice of observing other religious holidays in their calendars, they run the risk of breeding additional resentment between and among the groups. This brief discussion, demonstrating the potential for religious divisiveness that can pervade even the best-intentioned consideration of religious holidays in scheduling public school calendars, indicates that this is a practice to avoid.

CONCLUSION

The best practice is for school officials not to take specific religious observances into account in scheduling calendars. As noted in the point essay, and earlier, some may argue that school leaders can teach students about religious diversity and accommodate the faiths of various members of school communities by creating academic calendars that take various religious holidays into account. These are laudable goals indeed. Yet, in our increasingly diverse and pluralistic American society, there may be endpoints where accommodation of all religious holidays cannot be reconciled with the secular aims of keeping students in school and meeting instructional goals.

Perhaps more troublingly, the consideration of some religious holidays and not others in scheduling school calendars may pose a risk of religious divisiveness that would implicate both First Amendment concerns and disruptions to community cohesion. Accordingly, the best approach is for school officials to create school calendars by considering only secular aims such as testing and instructional goals, attendance, allocation of resources, and other educational interests. To do otherwise could pose risks that outweigh the potential well-intentioned benefits.

FURTHER READINGS AND RESOURCES

Chester, M. D. (2011, August 15). *Legal holidays; accommodation for religious observances.* Retrieved from Massachusetts Department of Elementary & Secondary Education website: http://www.doe.mass.edu/resources/holidaymemo.html?subsite=http://www.doe.mass.edu/nclb

Horner, J. (2006). Let's take the humbug out of Christmas: A guide to permissible activities at public schools during Christmas. *Education Law Reporter, 207,* 831–837.

Hutton, T. (2003, December). Help for the holidays: Where the courts haven't spoken, let community consensus be a guiding voice. *American School Board Journal,* pp. 19–21.

Imber, M. (2003, December). The Santa dilemma. *American School Board Journal,* pp. 16–18.

Mawdsley, R. D. (1994). *Clever v. Cherry Hill Township Board of Education:* Recognition of religious diversity in public schools. *Education Law Reporter, 90,* 533–545.

Mawdsley, R. D., & Russo, C. J. (2003). Religious holiday celebrations in public schools: What is permissible and what is prohibited? *Education Law Reporter, 182,* 1–6.

The Pew Forum on Religion and Public Life. (2008, February). *U.S. religious landscape survey: Religious affiliation: Diverse and dynamic.* Washington, DC: Author. Retrieved from http://religions.pewforum.org/pdf/report-religious-landscape-study-full.pdf

Russo, C. J., & Mawdsley, R. D. (2002). December dilemmas: The celebration of Christmas in American public schools. *Education and the Law, 13*(4), 381–387.

State of New Jersey Department of Education. (2011, February 16). *Resolution: The list of religious holidays permitting pupil absence from school.* Retrieved from http://www.state.nj.us/education/genfo/holidays1112.pdf

Yasus, J. (1996, Summer). What's in a name? Nothing good if it's Friday: The Seventh Circuit invalidates Good Friday public school holiday. *John Marshall Law Review, 29,* 1031.

COURT CASES AND STATUTES

Ansonia Board of Education v. Philbrook, 479 U.S. 60 (1986).
Bridenbaugh v. O'Bannon, 185 F.3d 796 (7th Cir. 1999), *cert. denied*, 529 U.S. 1003 (2000).
Cammack v. Waihee, 932 F.2d 765, 769 (9th Cir. 1991).
Church of God (Worldwide, Texas Region) v. Amarillo Indep. Sch. Dist., 511 F. Supp. 613 (N.D. Tex. 1981).
Clever v. Cherry Hill Township Board of Education, 838 F. Supp. 929 (D.N.J. 1993).
County of Allegheny v. American Civil Liberties Union, 492 U.S. 573 (1989).
Florey v. Sioux Falls School District 49–5, 619 F.2d 1311 (8th Cir. 1980a), *cert. denied*, 449 U.S. 987 (1980b).
Granzeier v. Middleton, 173 F.3d 568 (6th Cir. 1999).
Koenick v. Felton, 190 F.3d 259 (4th Cir. 1999), *cert. denied*, 528 U.S. 1118 (2000).
Lamb's Chapel v. Center Moriches Union Free School District, 508 U.S. 384 (1993).
Lee v. Weisman, 505 U.S. 577 (1992).
Lemon v. Kurtzman, 403 U.S. 602 (1971).
Lynch v. Donnelly, 465 U.S. 668 (1984).
Metzl v. Leininger, 57 F.3d 618 (7th Cir. 1995).

14

Does the Equal Access Act guarantee religious clubs equal access to public school facilities?

POINT: Michelle Gough McKeown, *Indiana University*
COUNTERPOINT: Allison S. Fetter-Harrott, *Franklin College*

OVERVIEW

Congress enacted the Equal Access Act in 1984 with broad bipartisan support, largely in response to two federal circuit court decisions in the Fifth (*Lubbock Civil Liberties Union v. Lubbock Independent School Dist.*, 1982) and Second (*Brandon v. Guilderland Board of Education*, 1980) Circuits that had prohibited student religious groups from meeting on school premises. Further, the Supreme Court's decision in *Widmar v. Vincent* (1981), allowing a religious group to have equal access to facilities, thereby affording them the opportunity to meet on the campus of a public university, also served as an impetus for the act's enactment.

Under the Equal Access Act, officials in public secondary schools with a "limited open forum" (20 U.S.C. § 4071(b)) are prohibited from discriminating against students who wish to conduct meeting within those fora on the basis of the "religious, political, philosophical, or other content of the speech at such meetings" (20 U.S.C. § 4071(a)). The legislative history of the act reveals that while it was designed in large part to protect the rights of religious groups, its reach has expanded to gay rights student groups (*East High School Prism Club v. Seidel*, 2000).

Pursuant to the Equal Access Act, a "limited open forum" exists whenever an official in a public secondary school "grants an offering to or opportunity for one or more noncurriculum related student groups to meet on school premises during noninstructional time" (20 U.S.C. § 4071(b)). "Noninstructional time" means "time set aside by the school before actual classroom instruction begins or after actual classroom instruction ends" (20 U.S.C. § 4072(4)).

As central as it is to its interpretation, the Equal Access Act does not define "noncurriculum related student group." However, in upholding the constitutionality of the act in *Board of Education of Westside Community Schools v. Mergens* (1990), the Supreme Court noted that

> even if a public secondary school allows only one [group] to meet, the Act's obligations are triggered and the school may not deny other clubs, on the basis of the content of their speech, equal access to meet on school premises during noninstructional time. (p. 236)

The immediate and dramatic impact of the Equal Access Act was that student religious groups that had been denied access to public school facilities in the past have federal statutory authority to claim the same access rights as other noncurriculum related student groups. At the same time, courts have extended the term "noninstructional time" not just to meeting times before or after school, but also to any meeting time during the school day.

In *Ceniceros v. Board of Trustees of San Diego School District* (1997), for example, the Ninth Circuit ruled that the lunch period during the school day when students were free to leave campus constituted noninstructional time as long as other student groups were permitted to meet. Five years later, in *Prince v. Jacoby* (2002), the same court found that a morning student/staff activity period also constituted a noninstructional time even though attendance was taken. As long as students had an option to meet with student-organized clubs during this time period, the court explained that religious clubs could not be excluded. In addition, the Ninth Circuit later reasoned that the reach of the act extended to providing the religious club equal access to funding, the yearbook, the public address system, and bulletin boards (*Truth v. Kent School District*, 2008).

At least one court further extended the provisions of the Equal Access Act, linking them to the Free Speech Clause. In *Donovan v. Punxsutawney Area School Board* (2003), the Third Circuit decided that the refusal of school officials to permit a religious club to meet during an activity period when attendance was taken and where other student groups were permitted to gather not only violated the act but also constituted viewpoint discrimination under the Free Speech Clause of the First Amendment.

Against this backdrop, the essays in this chapter debate whether the Equal Access Act has lived up to its promise in granting equal access to school facilities by religious groups in particular. In the point essay, Michelle Gough McKeown (Indiana University) takes the position that the act is working as it was designed. In her essay, she maintains that insofar as the intent of the act was to provide religious groups with access that was equal to, but not greater than, that of other organizations, it has lived up to its promise.

On the other hand, in the counterpoint essay, Allison S. Fetter-Harrott (Franklin College) examines seven gaps in the law, identifying ways in which the Equal Access Act fails to protect the rights of religious groups to equal access to school facilities. She thus posits that the access to school facility rights afforded religious groups under the act are significantly limited.

As you read these debates about access rights of religious groups to public school facilities, ask yourself the following questions. First, do you think that student religious groups lacking a curricular focus should have equal access to school facilities during noninstructional time? Second, as discussed in the ensuing debates, if so, what do you think about provisions in the act limiting the involvement of school officials or adults from outside of school communities? Third, has the Equal Access Act enhanced or diminished appreciation of religious diversity in public secondary schools with student-initiated clubs?

Charles J. Russo
University of Dayton

Ralph D. Mawdsley
Cleveland State University

POINT: Michelle Gough McKeown
Indiana University

In *Widmar v. Vincent* (1981), the Supreme Court ruled that officials at the University of Missouri–Kansas City could not deny a religious club access to facilities due to the religious content of the students' speech. Three years later, in essentially codifying *Widmar*, Congress enacted the Equal Access Act. Under the act, it is

> unlawful for any public secondary school which receives federal financial assistance and which has a limited open forum to deny equal access or a fair opportunity to, or discriminate against, any students who wish to conduct a meeting within that limited open forum on the basis of the religious, political, philosophical, or other content of the speech at such meetings. (20 U.S.C. §4071(a))

Among the exceptions to the act, officials are not required to recognize groups that might "materially and substantially interfere with the orderly conduct of educational activities within the school" (20 U.S.C. §4071(c)(4)).

The Equal Access Act survived a constitutional challenge in *Board of Education of Westside Community Schools v. Mergens* (1990). Even so, the act does little more than extend to public secondary schools what First Amendment case law, in particular *Widmar*, had already established—that viewpoint-based exclusion of religious groups from limited public fora is impermissible. The act is phrased to emphasize that religious groups, like others, may not be discriminated against on the basis of their viewpoints, unless the speech that would occur would interfere with school activities. Thus, the act merges the *Tinker v. Des Moines Independent Community School District* (1969) "material interference or substantial disruption" standard with limited public forum doctrine. In light of the preceding, then, this point essays stands for the position that insofar as the Equal Access Act is designed to provide equal, but not superior, access to limited public fora for religious student groups, it has achieved its goal.

JUDICIAL BACKGROUND

In the years since *Mergens*, an array of federal courts have held that under the Equal Access Act, student religious groups may require that their leaders fall within the club's religious standards (*Hsu v. Roslyn Union Free School District*,

1996a, 1996b), meet during lunch time (*Ceniceros v. Board of Trustees of the San Diego Unified School District*, 1997), and gather during a school's morning activity period at which attendance was taken, agreeing that such student activity periods are noninstructional time (*Donovan ex rel. Donovan v. Punxsutawney Area School Bd.*, 2003). Moreover, the Ninth Circuit was of the opinion that a school board violated the Equal Access Act when it denied a religious club access to funds and fund-raising activities, school supplies, audiovisual equipment, school vehicles, bulletin boards, the yearbook, and the public address system once it provided such access and supplies to other noncurriculuar student groups (*Prince v. Jacoby*, 2002, 2003). In a later case, the federal trial court in Arizona ruled that the Equal Access Act required school officials to grant religious clubs access to public address systems for announcements, to be permitted to distribute leaflets containing religious symbols, and to be allowed to broadcast a video with religious content that promoted the club during morning announcements to the extent such access was afforded noncurriculum student clubs (*Krestan v. Deer Valley Unified School District No. 97, of Maricopa County*, 2008).

At least one court rejected the claim that a school board created a limited open forum that would have permitted members of a religious club to make announcements involving prayers and Bible readings before classes on a school's public address system. Still, the court did permit voluntary student prayer before school to continue (*Herdahl v. Pontotoc County School District*, 1996).

The Ninth Circuit initially upheld a school board's motion for summary judgment after officials denied a request from a Christian group that it be granted Associated Student Body ("ASB") status. Officials denied the request not on account of the religious content of the group's speech, but rather because of what they described as its discriminatory membership criteria, fearing that it violated the district's nondiscrimination policies (*Truth v. Kent School District*, 2007). On further review, though, an en banc panel of the court reversed the decision in favor of the club's organizers (*Truth*, 2008). Describing the Christian student group's allegations that school officials arbitrarily granted waivers of the nondiscrimination policy to nonreligious groups, and explaining that such a practice would violate the act, the court concluded that the group had therefore raised a triable issue of fact.

THE EQUAL ACCESS ACT AS APPLIED

As demonstrated in the *Truth* decisions, although the Equal Access Act guarantees equal access to religious groups, such access need not be unqualified. In particular, the act does not require schools officials to provide unfettered access to groups that wish to discriminate in their membership or leadership policies on the basis of characteristics such as religion or sexual orientation. Indeed, the act may serve as a catalyst for educational leaders to be more deliberate and sophisticated in providing official recognition and benefits to student organizations to confer what amounts to school imprimatur on such practices.

School boards wishing to avoid the potentially divisive consequences of granting recognition or benefits to discriminatory student groups have essentially two options. First, school boards may simply close any limited open fora, thereby avoiding the requirements of the Equal Access Act altogether. However, because such an approach may undermine a school's educational mission, school officials are more likely to adopt the second approach, which involves conditioning access on compliance with nondiscrimination policies. Under the second approach, officials can grant recognition, financial assistance, or special access to groups that agree to abide by their nondiscrimination policies. It is under this latter approach, involving nondiscrimination policies, that controversies and litigation have arisen.

In the context of higher education, the Supreme Court's 2010 opinion in *Christian Legal Society Chapter of the University of California, Hastings College of the Law v. Martinez* illustrates how a nondiscrimination policy that served to condition access of a religious club to a limited public forum on compliance with a nondiscrimination policy led to controversy. *Christian Legal Society* was based on the First Amendment rather than the Equal Access Act, which does not apply in higher education. Yet, as discussed below, since the First Amendment and Equal Access Act analyses are largely similar, a review of this crucial case is instructive.

The Hastings law school had a policy under which groups seeking "Registered Student Organization" ("RSO") status were required to sign a nondiscrimination agreement that was consistent with state civil rights law as well as university policies. The parties jointly stipulated that the nondiscrimination policy was properly interpreted as an "all-comers" policy that prohibited any RSO from denying other students the opportunity to participate in its groups. RSO status provided groups with access to the RSO bulletin board and financial assistance. If a group chose not to agree to the nondiscrimination agreement, then it was not prohibited from existing on campus. Instead, such a group was simply unable to benefit from the financial assistance, bulletin boards, or other RSO perks. Accordingly, the Christian Legal Society was denied RSO status because its bylaws excluded from membership those who did not agree with the group's "Statement of Faith." Hastings maintained that the group's bylaws discriminated on the basis of religion and sexual orientation.

In a 5–4 decision, the Supreme Court upheld the all-comers policy as a content-neutral approach furthering the law school's policies aimed at cultivating a positive learning environment. The Court directly speaks to the issue of whether religious groups should and do have equal access to public school facilities. Under the case law and the Equal Access Act, religious groups do have equal access, but that access may be properly limited, in a viewpoint-neutral fashion, to protect the educational environment. School officials have only been able to prohibit access if they eliminate limited public fora altogether, through which practice all groups have an equal lack of access or they have generally applicable, viewpoint-neutral policies that in practice filter out groups whose activities violate the policy.

Some, including the Christian Legal Society, are of the view that conditioning access on compliance with a nondiscrimination policy has the effect of discriminating against religious organizations because those are the organizations whose tenets violate the policy. However, if the argument is that the only student groups restricted by such policies are those with religious backgrounds, then the argument seems disingenuous. It does not require much imagination to think of other potential groups that could be denied access or recognition due to their beliefs, and when lifted to these alternative contexts, the rationale for the Supreme Court's opinion finds support. For example, what should happen when White supremacist or Nazi groups seek access?

If the hands of school board officials are tied from restricting recognition and access to religious groups, as was urged by the Christian Legal Society, then groups whose belief systems disapprove of and discriminate against others would also have access to financial resources supplied by the very students against whom they discriminate (unless their activities meet the material disruption standard included in both *Tinker* and the Equal Access Act). Other approaches to distinguish between religious groups that require signed statements of disapproval of homosexual behavior and groups that discriminate on bases such as race or gender would likely involve the school in a line of inquiry that may lead to viewpoint discrimination.

Christian Legal Society sparked scholarly criticism regarding its restriction of liberty. William E. Thro and Charles J. Russo (2010) are convinced that the Supreme Court failed to follow its own precedent with regard to limited public forum precedent. They wrote that in so doing, the Court granted governmental officials the power to limit access based on membership policies by equating access to the forum with a subsidy. The authors added that the Court favored equality over the freedom of expression, freedom of religion, and the vital role of civil associations while modifying its "student organization jurisprudence by allowing indirect viewpoint discrimination and undermining the educational benefits of a diverse student body" (p. 496).

Yet, *Christian Legal Society* was written narrowly and emphasized the precise contours of the law school's policy. In practice, a policy that differs on any of the several factors considered by the Supreme Court may encounter a more hostile reception. The Court distinguished Hastings' all-comers policy from the policy in *Healy v. James* (1972), in which a university sought to place a complete ban on a group from campus. Here, the Court also emphasized the alternate methods of communication and alternate meeting locations available to non-RSOs. The Court also carefully distinguished *Rosenberger v. Rector and Visitors of University of Virginia* (1995), in which the university prohibited the publication of Christian content in a campus newspaper. The Court noted that Hastings denied RSO status to Christian Legal Society not because of its religious character but because of the group's discriminatory practices.

Finally, the decision in *Christian Legal Society* was framed to emphasize the deference consistently given to school administrators in developing policies to serve the special interests of the educational environment. "Cognizant that judges lack the on-the-ground expertise and experience of school administrators . . . [w]e have cautioned courts in various contests to resist substitut[ing] their own notions for those of the school authorities which they review" (p. 2988). Further, the law is applied with regard to the special considerations of the school: "First Amendment rights must be analyzed in light of the special characteristics of the school environment" (p. 2988, citing *Widmar*, 1981, at 268).

The lines drawn by the precedent and the language of the Equal Access Act create a jurisprudence that does provide religious groups with equal access to limited public fora. In this regard, equal access does not mean unlimited or superior access. Rather, so long as policies conditioning access are content neutral and justifiable without regard to the speech of a particular group, they should survive court review. In other words, school officials cannot grant access to one group but not another because of its viewpoints, but if an educational institution has a content-neutral policy aimed to further the school's educational mission, and the application of that policy results in the exclusion of a group whose views violate the policy, then that policy survives the Equal Access Act and the First Amendment even though the operation of the policy results in exclusion of a religious group.

The same rule would apply to other groups such as gay–straight alliance clubs. As noted in the *Christian Legal Society* opinion, all-comers policies do not single out religious clubs for application. Other groups whose beliefs operate to exclude others also are subject to the ultimatum of operating in a nonexclusionary manner—despite the potential for including those whose status or beliefs are at odds with the group's own—or forgoing the benefits of being a recognized student group. This is consistent with the rationale in the second Ninth Circuit opinion in *Truth*, in which the court reversed the grant of summary judgment in response to allegations that educational leaders inconsistently and arbitrarily applied the school board's nondiscrimination policy. For example, the *Christian Legal Society* analysis repeatedly made references to the parties' joint stipulation, which stated "for example, the Hastings Democratic Caucus cannot bar students holding Republican political beliefs from becoming members or seeking leadership positions in the organization" (p. 2982).

Finally, although *Christian Legal Society* focuses on the First Amendment decision and does not specifically address the Equal Access Act, no precedent has indicated that the act deviates significantly from First Amendment jurisprudence. If anything, in interpreting the Equal Access Act, the Second Circuit declared that "the Act creates an analog to the First Amendment's default rule banning content-based speech" (*Hsu v. Roslyn Union Free School District No. 3*, 1996, p. 856) but acknowledged that the Supreme Court has left the specific relationship between the two unaddressed, a situation that remains more than 15 years later. This relationship is underscored by comparison to the Ninth Circuit's opinion in *Truth*.

CONCLUSION

The Equal Access Act has achieved its goal of providing equal, but not superior, access to limited public fora for religious student groups. In doing so, the act leaves educational leaders free to implement generally applicable, viewpoint-neutral nondiscrimination policies to prevent student groups from engaging in discriminatory practices that may interfere with the educational missions of their schools. With the legal precedent supporting the ability of school boards to enforce nondiscrimination policies developed to safeguard students' learning environment, yet also enforcing students' rights to participate in and promote noncurricular groups on equal footing with nonreligious noncurricular groups, the Equal Access Act appears to have struck the appropriate balance.

COUNTERPOINT: Allison S. Fetter-Harrott
Franklin College

Enacted in 1984, the Equal Access Act generally forbids officials in public secondary schools from discriminating against religious and other student groups, requiring that they be afforded access to facilities on equal footing with other groups. As the Supreme Court observed in upholding the constitutionality of the Equal Access Act in *Board of Education of Westside Community Schools v. Mergens* (1990), "the [Equal Access] Act was intended to address perceived widespread discrimination against religious speech in U.S. public schools" (p. 239). Accordingly, the act was specifically aimed at defending the embattled rights of student religious groups to take part in the school community on equal footing with their peers.

While the Equal Access Act improved access for religious clubs to school facilities, in many aspects, religious clubs still face the challenges left by the significant gaps in its provisions. To this end, it is worth noting that the act applies only to specified kinds of schools, groups, meetings, and students. Given this, the act does not provide total access for religious groups' wish to use public school facilities. This counterpoint essay addresses the ways in which the Equal Access Act fails to protect the rights of religious groups to have access to school facilities, demonstrating that the "guarantee" of access by religious groups to school facilities under the act is significantly limited.

GAP 1: LIMITED OPEN FORUM

As an initial matter, it is important to recognize that the Equal Access Act does not apply to every school. More specifically, the act applies only to public secondary schools where officials have already created a "limited open forum" (20 U.S.C. § 4071(a)). Within the terms of the Equal Access Act, a limited open forum is created when officials permit student-initiated groups that are not school sponsored to meet in school buildings or otherwise on their grounds during noninstructional times (4071(b)). For example, by providing a noncurricular chess club access to cafeteria, classroom, or other meeting space in school buildings during lunchtime or after school, officials may have created a limited open forum for student clubs during that time, giving them the right to meet under the same terms as the chess club.

Insofar as the protections of the Equal Access Act only apply in public schools that have by their own will opened up limited open fora for student-initiated clubs to meet, there are many schools to which the act's protections simply do not apply. Additionally, except in rare cases where educational officials might have constitutionally impermissible motives, educators likewise may close limited open fora by prohibiting all non–school-sponsored groups from meeting at school facilities. For religious groups seeking access to meet in the facilities of schools with no limited open fora, therefore, the Equal Access Act provides absolutely no protection.

GAP 2: NO COVERAGE FOR PRIMARY SCHOOLS

In addition to applying its protections only to those public schools in which officials have created limited open fora, the Equal Access Act applies only to secondary schools receiving federal financial aid (20 U.S.C.S. § 4071(a)). Accordingly, student religious groups at the primary level have absolutely no protection for their rights to access school facilities under the Equal Access Act. This omission may affect more than just elementary school students. In defining the term *secondary school*, the Equal Access Act defers to state delineations of schools as primary or secondary (20 U.S.C.S. § 4072(1)). As such, in some states, middle schools are secondary schools whose student religious groups are entitled to protection of the Equal Access Act, while in other jurisdictions, middle school students—like their elementary school counterparts—enjoy no federal statutory protection to their access of school facilities.

GAP 3: NO COVERAGE FOR SCHOOL-SPONSORED, OUTSIDE, OR ADULT-LED GROUPS

Along with the other limitations discussed in this essay, the Equal Access Act additionally protects only the access to public school facilities of student-initiated religious groups (20 U.S.C.S. § 4071(c)(1)). This means that to gain access to school facilities under the act's auspices, religious groups cannot be school sponsored or otherwise led by educational personnel. Likewise, "nonschool persons may not direct, conduct, control, or regularly attend activities of student groups" (20 U.S.C.S. § 4071(c)(1)).

The application of the narrow scope of this protection to only specified and entirely student-run religious groups is demonstrated by *Sease v. School District of Philadelphia* (1993). In *Sease*, students challenged the actions of school officials who chose to discontinue granting them access to practice space and other school benefits for support of a student gospel group. The group began when two students approached a faculty member seeking support to begin a gospel choir at the school, further enlisting a school secretary to meet with the group during nonclass hours at school to direct the group's practices and performances. The group performed at the school, paying a rental fee for the school space it used, and performed in various other locales around the state. Moreover, the student gospel group involved other "nonschool" persons in its practices, including a person who was hired from the outside to accompany it on the piano and by inviting its alumni to continue to sing and perform in its performances. The group supported itself entirely with donations, admissions charged at performances, and by fund-raising carried out by its members. Given the nature of the student group as a decidedly gospel singing choir, its activities were distinctly religious.

When members of the school community raised concerns about the group's operations and endorsement of religion, and educational officials made efforts to require its leaders to make changes such as moving practices off of school grounds, transitioning away from the secretary's leadership, and other approaches, the students challenged their efforts. The school officials argued that they were merely attempting to bring the student gospel group's actions within the coverage of the Equal Access Act. A federal trial court in Pennsylvania agreed. Although the student gospel group was truly student initiated, begun at the request of a small group of children, the court refused to view it as a group whose meetings were protected by the Equal Access Act. It was undisputed that the school secretary led the group and that the group touted itself as representing the school. Likewise, the group involved the regular participation of outsiders. Given the involvement of these nonstudent school and nonschool adults in the group's functioning, the court explained, the gospel choir could not look to the Equal Access Act for protection of its right to meet on school grounds, even during noninstructional time.

GAP 4: NO PROTECTION FOR CURRICULAR GROUPS

At this point, it should be clear that the protection afforded for access to school facilities under the Equal Access Act applies only to student-initiated groups meeting in secondary schools operating limited open fora. Still, additional gaps exist in the protection that the act affords to religious groups. The act applies only to groups that are not related to school curricula (20 U.S.C.S. § 4071(b)). In other words, groups with significant overlap with curricular classes are not afforded protection for their desire to meet under the provisions of the act.

In most instances, the effect of this limitation will be somewhat muted, since school officials are generally prohibited from conducting religious curricular classes that proselytize to students. Even so, there may be instances, for example, where religious groups wish to form in conjunction with classes where students are studying world religions or reading the Bible as a literary or historical text. In light of the limit of the Equal Access Act's protections to purely noncurricular groups, it may be that such groups would encounter challenges in using the act to establish their right to meet on school grounds.

GAP 5: NO PROTECTION FOR GROUPS MEETING DURING INSTRUCTIONAL TIME

At the same time, the Equal Access Act protects only those secondary student-initiated religious groups wishing to meet during noninstructional time (20 U.S.C.S. § 4071(b)). The act, therefore, does not require officials in public schools to grant student religious groups access during times when attendance at school is required, further limiting the protection afforded under the statute.

GAP 6: NO PROTECTION FOR ACCESS TO ALL SCHOOL "FACILITIES"

By its own terms, the Equal Access Act requires school officials to permit secondary level student-led groups a fair opportunity to conduct meetings at school (20 U.S.C. § 4071(a)). By affording access to groups for meetings only, the act does not, therefore, guarantee necessarily unfettered access to all school facilities. In a 1992 judgment in *Clark v. Dallas Independent School District*, a federal trial court in Texas highlighted a limitation under the act. The court was of the opinion that the Equal Access Act's guarantee of meeting space did not afford a student group the right to gather in front of its public school and distribute religious readings to its peers.

Another provision states that the Equal Access Act specifically does not require public school officials to "to expend public funds beyond the incidental cost of providing the space for student-initiated meetings" (20 U.S.C.S. § 4071(d)(3)). In its 2002 decision in *Prince v. Jacoby*, the Ninth Circuit considered the contours of the right of access to student religious groups granted by the Equal Access Act. Members of a student religious club in *Prince* challenged, among other alleged wrongs, the decision of educational officials to deny it access to various school supplies, school audiovisual equipment, and school vehicles while providing access to those amenities to other groups. While the act required school officials to provide the student-led religious group access to school spaces to conduct its meetings, the court found that the act's provisions did not require educators to grant religious clubs access to school property that was not incidental to providing meeting space. Accordingly, the Ninth Circuit explained, the act did not protect the religious student group's right to access school supplies, audiovisual equipment, and school vehicles on equal footing with other nonreligious student groups.

Viewed together, *Clark* and *Prince* illustrate other potential gaps in the guarantees under the Equal Access Act for student religious groups. Put another way, while religious groups may be permitted to meet, school officials may, in some limited circumstances, still bar such groups from access to some school property without running afoul of the act's provisions. The result is that the Equal Access Act does not, in fact, provide a total guarantee of access to student religious groups.

GAP 7: THE SO-CALLED ORDER AND DISCIPLINE EXEMPTION

The Equal Access Act also includes what can be described as an *order and discipline* exception to its general requirement that student-led religious groups enjoy access to school facilities. This hails from language in the act mandating that nothing in its provisions can be interpreted as limiting "the authority of the school, its agents or employees, to maintain order and discipline on school premises, to protect the well-being of students and faculty, and to assure that attendance of students at meetings is voluntary" (20 U.S.C. § 4071(f)). Under this provision, at least one court has permitted further restriction of student access to school facilities.

Perhaps the most notable examples of the order and discipline exception in operation is the Seventh Circuit's decision in *Gernetzke v. Kenosha Unified School District No. 1* (2001). *Gernetzke* was an Equal Access Act challenge by two high school students who were members of their school's Bible Club. The controversy in *Gernetzke* arose when the principal invited all of the school's clubs to submit plans for murals for the school's hallway. The Bible Club submitted its plans, as did various other student groups, and the principal approved the club's plans generally but rejected its request to display a Christian cross in its piece of the mural, citing concerns about reactions, fears of litigation, and worry that including the cross would require him to permit other symbols by groups like neo-Nazis.

The members of the Bible Club unsuccessfully challenged the principal's decision as a violation of the Equal Access Act. However, the Seventh Circuit decided that the principal's action was justified by the maintenance of order provision in the act. The court conceded that by permitting the principal to limit the group's message due to fears of uproar in response was allowing the kind of impermissible "Heckler's veto" so disfavored under First Amendment jurisprudence. Stated differently, the court acknowledged that its judgment permitted the principal to limit the Bible Club's message simply because he feared the reactions of those who disagreed with the club, a reality that undermined the basic premise of the Equal Access Act that student groups be granted a fair opportunity at school access. Even so, the court concluded that the maintaining order provision in the act justified the principal's action and required such a finding.

What *Gernetzke* demonstrates is that even where a student religious club might have some protection for access to public school facilities under the Equal Access Act, school leaders may still stifle their access for fear of the reactions of other students. This poses a significant risk to the rights of student religious clubs, especially those whose students are members of religious minorities or whose observation of any religion make them a disfavored group in student bodies.

CONCLUSION

What the foregoing analysis makes clear is that while the Equal Access Act provides some protection for religious groups to access public school facilities, its promise is by no means a total guarantee. The Equal Access Act applies only to a limited range of activities and groups, excluding from its protection primary school groups, groups led by outside leaders, school-sponsored or curricular groups, groups of any kind in schools that choose not to operate limited open fora, and groups wishing to meet during instructional times.

Perhaps most notably, the Equal Access Act may additionally not protect the rights of student religious groups whose messages educational administrators view as inflammatory or otherwise posing threats to the maintenance of order in their school environments. While the maintenance of order in the school is important, applied too broadly, this order and discipline exception poses a significant threat to the rights of unpopular or minority religious student groups, thus undermining the intent of the Equal Access Act, which was to remove the barriers of discrimination against religious viewpoints in our nation's schools.

While there may be recourse for student religious groups that are denied access to facilities in public schools—the access they are due under constitutional doctrines, such as those interpreting the religion clauses or the Free Speech Clause of the First Amendment to the Constitution—it is unfortunate that the Equal Access Act does not go further in fulfilling its own intent and protecting the rights of religious groups. While constitutional principles can be murky and opaque, the subject of decades of disagreement between the most sophisticated constitutional scholars, the provisions of the Equal Access Act are relatively succinct and straightforward, far more accessible to laypersons or the already busy school administrators faced with having to make important decisions regarding access of student religious group to the facilities in their schools.

Be that as it may, the guarantee of access to school facilities for religious groups is not absolute under the Equal Access Act. While the statute may have broadened such groups' access to meeting spaces, its reach is limited.

Accordingly, school administrators, students, and community groups must be aware of the wider range of authorities governing student and community access to U.S. public school facilities in the hope that they will live up to the promise of the Equal Access Act.

FURTHER READINGS AND RESOURCES

Bjorklun, E. C. (1993). The Equal Access Act and state constitutions: The final chapter? *Education Law Reporter, 86,* 1–9.

Flemming, M. W., & Peeler, R. L. (1991). *Mergens*: The beginning, not the end, of questions arising under the Equal Access Act. *Education Law Reporter, 64,* 17–28.

Gregory, D. L., & Russo, C. J. (1991). Let us pray (but not "them"!): The troubled jurisprudence of religious liberty. *St. John's Law Review, 65*(1), 273–295.

Mawdsley, R. D. (1997). Noncurriculum related groups under the Equal Access Act. *Education Law Reporter, 137,* 865–873.

Mawdsley, R. D. (2003). Leveling the playing field for religious clubs: The interface of the Equal Access Act, free speech, and Establishment Clause. *Education Law Reporter, 174,* 809–824.

McKernan, T. B. (2009). Religious clubs and non-secondary schools: Expanding the scope of the Equal Access Act after *Good News. Rutgers Journal of Law and Religion, 14,* 14–42.

Russo, C. J., & Mawdsley, R. D. (1997). *Hsu v. Roslyn Union Free* School *District No. 3*: An update on the rights of high school students under the Equal Access Act. *Education Law Reporter, 114,* 359–371.

Schulze, E. W. (2005). Gay-related groups and the Equal Access Act. *Education Law Reporter, 196,* 369–383.

Thro, W., & Russo, C. (2010). A serious setback for freedom: The implications of *Christian Legal Society v. Martinez. Education Law Reporter, 261,* 473–496.

Woods, J. (2010). Gay–straight alliances and sanctioning pretextual discrimination under the Equal Access Act. *New York University Review of Law & Social Change, 34,* 373–422.

COURT CASES AND STATUTES

Board of Education of Westside Community Schools v. Mergens, 496 U.S. 226 (1990).
Brandon v. Guilderland Board of Education, 635 F.2d 971 (2d Cir. 1980).
Ceniceros v. Board of Trustees of San Diego School District, 106 F.3d 878 (9th Cir. 1997).
Christian Legal Society Chapter of the University of California, Hastings College of the Law v. Martinez, 130 S.Ct. 2971 (2010).
Clark v. Dallas Independent School District, 806 F. Supp. 116 (N.D. Tex. 1992).
Donovan ex rel. Donovan v. Punxsutawney Area School Board, 336 F.3d 211 (3d Cir. 2003).
East High School Prism Club v. Seidel, 95 F. Supp. 2d 1239 (D. Utah 2000).

Equal Access Act, 20 U.S.C. §§ 4071 *et seq.*
Gernetzke v. Kenosha Unified School District No. 1, 274 F.3d 464 (7th Cir. 2001).
Healy v. James, 408 U.S. 169 (1972).
Herdahl v. Pontotoc County School District, 933 F. Supp. 582 (N.D. Miss. 1996).
Hsu v. Roslyn Union Free School District No. 3, 85 F.3d 839 (2d Cir. 1996a), *cert. denied,* 519 U.S. 1040 (1996b).
Krestan v. Deer Valley Unified School District No. 97, of Maricopa County, 561 F. Supp. 2d 1078 (D. Ariz. 2008).
Lubbock Civil Liberties Union v. Lubbock Independent School District, 669 F.2d 1038 (5th Cir. 1982).
Prince v. Jacoby, 303 F.3d 1074 (9th Cir. 2002), *cert. denied,* 540 U.S. 813 (2003).
Rosenberger v. Rector and Visitors of University of Virginia, 515 U.S. 819 (1995).
Sease v. School District of Philadelphia, 811 F. Supp. 183 (E.D. Pa. 1993).
Tinker v. Des Moines Independent Community School District, 393 U.S. 503 (1969).
Truth v. Kent School District, 499 F.3d 999 (9th Cir. 2007).
Truth v. Kent School District, 524 F.3d 957 (9th Cir. 2008).
Widmar v. Vincent, 454 U.S. 263 (1981).

15

Should nonschool religious groups be allowed to use public school facilities?

POINT: Ralph D. Mawdsley, *Cleveland State University*
COUNTERPOINT: James L. Mawdsley, *Stark State College*

OVERVIEW

The Supreme Court's 1981 ruling in *Widmar v. Vincent* set in motion a series of cases that serve as the subject of three different debates in this volume on religion. These three essays focus on whether in-school religious clubs are guaranteed equal access to public school facilities under the Equal Access Act (Chapter 14), whether nonschool religious groups can be allowed to use public school facilities (this chapter), and whether students and others should be permitted to distribute religious materials in public schools (Chapter 16). Like the debaters, though, as litigation has continued, not all courts have agreed on these challenging questions.

In *Widmar*, the Supreme Court resolved a dispute wherein officials at a state university in Missouri excluded a religious group from using campus facilities. Ruling in favor of the religious group, the Court's First Amendment analysis noted that once officials made the facilities generally available for the activities of registered (secular) student groups, they could not deny access to other groups due to the religious content of their speech.

In 1984, based on its desire to expand the treatment of religious speech as a form of protected free speech, Congress essentially codified *Widmar* in enacting the Equal Access Act (EAA). According to the EAA, officials in public secondary schools receiving federal financial assistance and permitting non–curriculum-related student groups to meet during noninstructional time cannot deny access to groups due to the religious, political, philosophical, or other content of their speech. Although it was not at issue in any of the cases discussed in the debates in this chapter, the EAA does afford officials the discretion to exclude groups from using school facilities if there is a reasonable likelihood that their meetings may materially and substantially interfere with the orderly conduct of school activities. In 1990, the Supreme Court upheld the constitutionality of the EAA in *Board of Education of Westside Community Schools v. Mergens*. The Court found that in creating a limited open forum, officials could not exclude religious groups from meeting due to the religious content of their speech.

Later, in *Lamb's Chapel v. Center Moriches Union Free School District* (1993) and *Good News Club v. Milford Central School* (2001), the Supreme Court expanded the scope of access for nonschool groups to public school facilities. In another hybrid situation in which it treated religious speech as a form of free speech, in *Lamb's Chapel*, a rare unanimous decision, the justices essentially extended the rationale of *Mergens*, explaining that insofar as the board created a limited open forum by opening its facilities to an array of groups, it violated the free speech rights of a religious group that planned to show a religious film series on family values. The Court decided that the board engaged in impermissible viewpoint discrimination when it tried to exclude the religious group. Similarly, in *Good News Club*, the Court found that a school board violated the club's rights to free speech by engaging in impermissible viewpoint discrimination when it refused to permit it to use school facilities for its meetings, which were not religious services, even though three other groups could do so. The Court added that such a restriction was not justified by fears of violating the Establishment Clause of the First Amendment.

Of course, controversy continues post–*Lamb's Chapel* and *Good News Club*. To this end, as reflected in the following essays, some courts granted access on a equitable basis to outside religious groups (*Daugherty v. Vanguard Charter School Academy*, 2000; *Fairfax Covenant Church v. Fairfax County School Board*, 1994) while others refused to do so (*Campbell v. St. Tammany Parish School Board*, 2000; *Bronx Household of Faith v. Community School District #10*, 2011).

Against this backdrop, the essays in this chapter reach different outcomes over access to public school facilities by nonschool religious groups. The point essay by Ralph D. Mawdsley (Cleveland State University) takes the position that nonschool religious groups should have access to public school facilities. Based on his analysis of the case law as well as the Free Speech and Religion Clauses of the First Amendment, he concludes that such access is pedagogically important and constitutionally required because it helps to demonstrate that religious believers, including students, are not second-class citizens.

On the other side, the counterpoint essay by James L. Mawdsley (Stark State College) relies on much of the same case law in maintaining that nonschool groups should not be granted access to public school facilities. He voices the concern that pursuant to constitutional prohibitions, board officials must be careful not to appear to sanction religious activities lest they find themselves embroiled in unnecessary controversies, and litigation, from critics on both sides of the issue.

As you read these essays about the rights of nonschool religious groups to use public school facilities, ask yourself the following questions. First, do you think that nonschool religious groups should be granted access to public school facilities? Second, is granting nonschool religious groups access to facilities on the same bases as nonschool nonreligious organizations a violation of the Establishment Clause by aiding religion? Third, would excluding nonschool religious groups from schools violate their rights to freedom of religion and speech?

Charles J. Russo
University of Dayton

POINT: Ralph D. Mawdsley
Cleveland State University

As detailed below, since 1993, the Supreme Court has addressed two cases on whether nonschool religious groups should be allowed access to public school facilities. In both cases, *Lamb's Chapel v. Center Moriches Union Free School District* (1993) and *Good News Club v. Milford Central Schools* (2001), the Court found that granting access to the facilities afforded religious speech the same protection as other forms of speech under the First Amendment to the Constitution. As such, the Court concluded that the religious groups could not be denied the right to gather in public school facilities. However, not all lower courts have reached the same outcome. In light of ongoing litigation and the need to ensure that religious speech continues to be protected, this point essay stands for the proposition that nonschool religious groups should be allowed to use public school facilities.

SUPREME COURT CASES ALLOWING ACCESS

In its landmark decision in *Lamb's Chapel v. Center Moriches Union Free School District* (1993), the Supreme Court protected, under the Free Speech Clause of the First Amendment, a church's after-school access to a public school auditorium in New York for the purpose of showing a religious film series. In a unanimous judgment, the Court found that once a school board permits secular views of a subject (here, child rearing and family values), its refusal to permit a religious perspective constituted impermissible viewpoint discrimination under the Free Speech Clause. Having determined that the church's access was a protected form of free speech, the Court ruled that the board was not permitted, under the Establishment Clause of the First Amendment, to separate itself from all religious uses. In explaining its position, the Court observed that the religious group's presence could not reasonably have been interpreted as endorsing religion in violation of the Establishment Clause since the meetings occurred in the evenings when students were not present.

Eight years later, in *Good News Club v. Milford Central Schools* (2001), another case from New York, a divided Supreme Court ruled on behalf of an evangelical organization's use of elementary school facilities immediately after the end of the school day. As in *Lamb's Chapel*, the Court decided that insofar as the school board permitted secular, but not religious, groups to use its facilities for a subject matter area (in this case, character and moral development of children), its actions constituted impermissible viewpoint discrimination. The issue in *Good News*, more so than in *Lamb's Chapel*, became whether school officials exercised a sufficient degree of separation to avoid the perception of their endorsement of the club's meetings under the Establishment Clause.

In *Good News*, the Supreme Court reasoned that the two degrees of separation demonstrated by the school—evenhandedness in providing access for both religious and nonreligious groups, coupled with the requirement of parent permission—were sufficient to avoid impermissible school endorsement. The Court explained that requiring parental permission before permitting student participation in the after-school Good News Club meetings constituted a kind of "circuit breaker." This break, the Court thought, allowed student participation in the club to be perceived as due to prior parental permission not to the actions of school personnel. Yet, equally important, the Court rejected definitively the school board's efforts to distinguish between permitting meetings of the Boy Scouts, Girl Scouts, and 4-H Club on school premises while prohibiting the Good News Club from doing so by referring to the former as the teaching of character and morals and the latter as quintessentially religious activities. The Court pointed out, "We disagree that something that is 'quintessentially religious' or 'decidedly religious in nature' cannot also be characterized properly as the teaching of morals and character development from a particular viewpoint" (p. 111). The Court went on to declare,

> What matters for purposes of the Free Speech Clause is that we can see no logical difference in kind between the invocation of Christianity by the Club and the invocation of teamwork, loyalty, or patriotism by other associations to provide a foundation for their lessons. (p. 111)

Both *Lamb's Chapel* and *Good News* highlight the separation quandary facing public school boards when nonschool religious organizations request access to their premises. At stake, though, is more than meeting space. Religious organizations participate in activities that may be viewed as profoundly religious in nature. What is more important is that since these worship activities will occur on days and at times when children and members of the public would not be on school premises, access should be granted.

LOWER COURTS AND ACCESS

Daugherty v. Vanguard Charter School Academy (2000), a case that was post–*Lamb's Chapel* and pre–*Good News*, presents insights to the question of access. In *Daugherty*, a federal trial in Michigan upheld a public charter school's policies that permitted, as part of its overall Moral Focus Curriculum emphasis, a Moms' Prayer Group to use the Parents' Room for 90 minutes each week during school time. The Moms' Prayer Group was permitted to meet pursuant to a school policy that

> to enable "all students to reach their full academic potential and develop high moral character for becoming significant members of society," "the school board . . ." [makes] available for use by parents of students and parent groups during and after regular school hours, "a place to support the moral and academic excellence in the educational environment at the Academy." (p. 906)

The *Daugherty* court upheld the Moms' Prayer Group's access to school facilities under the Establishment Clause's *Lemon v. Kurtzman* (1971) test, finding that, by "refusing to discriminate against parents or parent groups who wish to use the parent room for prayer, [the policy] serve[d] the essential secular purpose of maintaining a governmental posture of neutrality toward religion" (pp. 907–908). More importantly, the court was of the opinion that "refusing to permit religious groups to use school facilities open to others would demonstrate hostility toward religion and create even greater risk of impermissible entanglement with religion" (p. 911). Insofar as the board made the Parents' Room available to any parents' groups, the court was satisfied that it was neutral on its face and "neither endorse[d] nor disapprove[d] of religion" (p. 908).

In *Daugherty*, the court disassembled in a most convincing manner the notion that impressionable elementary students would be influenced by having mothers meeting in a room at their school: "What the student 'audience' observes in this instance is simply the closed door of the parent room with knowledge that, during a ninety minute period each week, some students' mothers may be praying behind that door" (p. 908). The court further explained, "No student is confronted with an invitation to join in the prayer or even to observe it. No student is forced to assume special burdens to avoid the prayer."

Daugherty is a counterweight to cases involving the efforts of boards and their officials either to prohibit altogether or to significantly restrict access by religious groups to public schools. This case suggests that a lesser degree of separation is possible under the Establishment Clause as long as public school officials treat religious activities no differently than those that are not religious. Absent evidence that school personnel give preference to religious activities or emphasize them during instructional time, neutrality is a meaningful barrier to those challenging such evenhandedness. Indeed, lesser differential treatment of religious content by denying groups access runs the risk of projecting a message of hostility toward religion.

The most revealing litigation, though, is the long-running dispute involving the same parties, the New York City Board of Education and the Bronx Household of Faith (BHF), that has generated case law from 1996 through 2011. During these 15 years, rulings of the federal trial court and Second Circuit have sparred over whether prohibiting religious groups from renting school facilities during nonschool hours for worship services represented viewpoint discrimination under *Lamb's Chapel*.

In the most recent round of litigation, the Second Circuit, in *Bronx Household of Faith v. Board of Education of the City of New York* (2011), reversed an injunction granted to a group of pastors who wanted to rent public school facilities on Sunday for worship purposes. At issue were both a state statute and a school board operating policy. A New York State statute authorized school facilities

> to be used outside of school hours for purposes such as "social, civic and recreational meetings and entertainments, and other uses pertaining to the welfare of the community," as long as the uses are "nonexclusive and . . . open to the general public." (New York Educ. Code, § 414)

However, the board adopted a policy prohibiting the use of facilities for "religious services or religious instruction" (*Bronx*, 1997, p. 210). In its first review of the case, the Second Circuit affirmed the earlier order interpreting the policy of prohibiting religious services at school as reasonable and viewpoint neutral.

Following the Supreme Court's ruling in *Good News* in 2001, the BHF initiated another round of litigation, this time succeeding in both the federal trial court (*Bronx*, 2002) and Second Circuit (*Bronx*, 2003) in securing an injunction against the enforcement of the board policy. Both courts agreed that BHF had demonstrated a substantial likelihood of success in proving that the board's rejecting of their request to rent school facilities violated both the Free Speech and Establishment Clauses.

In 2005, the school board changed its policy to read as follows: "No permit shall be granted for the purpose of holding religious worship services, or otherwise using a school as a house of worship" (*Bronx*, 2005). On the basis of this new policy, school board officials refused to renew the BHF's permit to meet on school premises, prompting the most recent litigation. A federal trial court granted the BHF's request for an injunction, based on *Good News*, to prevent enforcement of the revised policy. On further review, the Second Circuit reversed, finding for purposes of the Free Speech Clause that the new school board policy did not constitute viewpoint discrimination. Instead, the court was satisfied that the policy represented a content-based exclusion. In addition, the Second Circuit held that permitting groups to meet on Sundays for religious worship could reasonably have been viewed as endorsing worship, thus violating the Establishment Clause (*Bronx*, 2011).

The string of litigation involving the BHF clearly reflects the fragility of the rights framed by Supreme Court decisions and their subsequent interpretations by lower courts. In the most recent round of litigation involving the BHF, the free speech issue hinged on the label that the courts attached to the school board's access policy. By identifying the board's policy as subject matter content rather than a viewpoint, the court side-stepped the precedent set by *Lamb's Chapel*. Likewise, by identifying the presence of a religious group in a public school as giving the appearance of sponsoring religion, the Second Circuit invoked the Establishment Clause, even though the religious group would have met on Sunday when no students would have been present.

Distinguishing between religious viewpoints, which are protected by free speech, and religious worship, which was not protected under the BHF litigation, was at issue in *Campbell v. St. Tammany Parish School Board* (2000). Here, a school board in Louisiana refused to permit a church to rent its facilities pursuant to a policy barring "religious services or religious instruction on school premises" (p. 943).

In *Campbell*, the Fifth Circuit affirmed that the board policy met the free speech requirements of *Lamb's Chapel* in its declaration that

> the use of school facilities by outside organizations or groups outside school hours for the purpose of discussing religious material or material which contains a religious viewpoint or for distributing such material is permissible if it does not interfere with one of the primary uses of such facilities. (p. 943)

The dissenting member of the panel called the legal soundness of this distinction into question by observing that the court

> would allow atheists to put on a program denouncing religion or anti-Semites to sponsor a rant against Judaism, but it would not allow religious believers of any stripe to convene or instruct the faithful in this forum. This is the very essence of viewpoint discrimination. (p. 949)

As reflected in another case, though, treating religious groups differently from nonreligious ones still presents risks. In a post–*Lamb's Chapel* case, *Fairfax Covenant Church v. Fairfax County School Board* (1994), the Fourth Circuit held that a board regulation allowing officials to charge churches an escalating rate for use of school facilities discriminated against religious speech in violation of the Free Speech Clause. The court also determined that the policy interfered with or burdened the church's right to speak and practice religion as protected by the Free Exercise Clause. Under the rental regulation, the court noted that cultural and civic groups, educational groups, and state and federal governmental groups paid a noncommercial rate designed to reimburse the county for the actual costs for the use of the facilities. Private organizations paid a commercial rate that was 5 times the noncommercial rate and was intended to approximate market rental rates. For churches, the regulation established a special escalating rate that allowed them to pay the noncommercial rate for the first 5 years but thereafter required the churches to pay the commercial rate over the next 4 years. In its analysis, the court recognized that the board "freely acknowledged that it has singled out churches for the escalating rental rate structure to encourage them to go elsewhere, out of a concern for violating the Establishment Clause of the U.S. Constitution" (p. 705).

Relying on *Lamb's Chapel*, in *Fairfax*, the Fourth Circuit held that the regulation discriminated against religious speech in violation of the Free Speech Clause. Absent evidence that the school board sought to advance a compelling state interest in justifying the regulation's discrimination against churches, the court wrote that, in addition to violating the church's free speech rights, the regulation violated its free exercise of religion rights. At the same time, the court roundly rejected the board's claim that charging churches the same rent as other cultural and civic groups amounted to a religious subsidy in violation of the Establishment Clause. Instead, the court found that rather than subsidizing a church user, the rent provided money to the board to offset its ongoing expenses for school facilities. Insofar as the court decided that the board acted inequitably toward the church, it permitted the latter to recover past rent overcharges of $280,000 plus interest, a warning that officials should act carefully when seeking to deny access to religious groups.

CONCLUSION

As reflected in the case law, the use of public school facilities by nonschool groups is both pedagogically important and constitutionally required. By excluding religious groups and individuals from public schools, educational officials, working as arms of the state, risk sending the message, however unintended it may be, that religious groups and individuals are unwelcomed, second-class citizens. The notion that nonschool religious organizations and their members, including school children, are second-class citizens is offensive. Yet, unfortunately, as is evident in cases such as *Bronx Household of Faith*, federal courts continue to fail to grasp the notion that the Supreme Court established in treating religious speech and activities such as worship as an expressive activity. This means that insofar as religious speech is a subset of free speech, it should be entitled to the full range of First Amendment protection as other forms of expression.

The failure of school officials and courts to protect the rights of nonschool religious groups is often treated as a matter of semantics, purportedly distinguishing between talking about religion and participating in religious activities, rather than being viewed as hostility toward religion. Insofar as this is a distinction that federal courts have no business trying to make, essentially violating the same principles of separation of church and state that they claim to be protecting, public school facilities should be accessible to non–school-related religious organizations as long as they are available to other groups. To treat religious groups in any other manner, essentially relegating them to the role of outsiders in the marketplace of ideas that is supposed to be present in American public schools, is to do a grave injustice to the very principles of religious freedom on which this nation was founded.

COUNTERPOINT: James L. Mawdsley
Stark State College

One of the most fundamental powers of public school boards and superintendents is the ability to decide to what purposes school facilities will be put. With limited space and limited time, not to mention limited money, officials must be able to prioritize those uses that will most benefit their students and their surrounding communities. At the same time, educational leaders must bear in mind that any use of school facilities will give the appearance of their approval, regardless of how much they may disclaim responsibility. For this reason, opening school buildings and grounds to nonschool religious groups is fraught with peril.

On the one hand, students and communities in general might well believe that the religious groups are in some way associated with and sanctioned by the school officials. This creates at least an appearance of a violation of the constitutional prohibition on an establishment of religion. On the other hand, to deny the religious groups access to school facilities when other outside organizations are permitted to use them creates the impression that the government is seeking to suppress religious expression. Moreover, since judicial opinions in recent decades have only served to make the job of educational leaders more difficult, educators are forced to steer between the Scylla of the Free Speech Clause and the

Charybdis of the Establishment Clause. Accordingly, as highlighted by the content of the cases reviewed herein, this counterpoint essay maintains that public school facilities should not be made accessible to nonschool religious groups.

NONSCHOOL RELIGIOUS GROUPS SHOULD BE DENIED ACCESS

The most direct genesis of the issue of access to public school facilities by nonschool groups can be traced to the Supreme Court's judgment in *Lamb's Chapel v. Center Moriches Union Free School District* (1993). In its unanimous decision, the Court reviewed the actions of officials who refused to allow a nonschool group to show a religious film on child rearing and family values in a public school auditorium even though they allowed nonreligious views on the same subject to be presented. The Court held that the actions of school officials amounted to impermissible viewpoint discrimination in violation of the Free Speech Clause of the First Amendment to the Constitution. On the surface, this was a reasonable outcome, one requiring only that officials be neutral with regard to religion. Even so, since *Lamb's Chapel* opened the door for further intrusion by religious groups onto public school grounds, some review of its facts is in order.

Over the course of 11 months, leaders of Lamb's Chapel, an evangelical Christian Church, sought to use facilities in the Center Moriches School District on at least four occasions. The first of these attempts was a formal application for permission to use facilities for Sunday morning services and a Sunday school, a fact that the Supreme Court, in its analysis, relegated to a footnote. As noted in the facts as reiterated by the Court, in a letter supporting the application, the pastor freely admitted that his church's "paramount objective [was] to share the love of Christ in very real and practical ways" (1992, p. 383). Not surprisingly, educational officials refused to sanction this attempt to turn public property into a church sanctuary.

After his first application was denied, the pastor twice asked permission to show a six-part film series by Dr. James Dobson on family life from a Christian perspective. The brochure that the pastor gave board officials described the film series as discussing "Dr. Dobson's views on the undermining influences of the media that could only be counterbalanced by returning to traditional, Christian family values instilled at an early stage" (1992, p. 388). Each time, board officials denied the pastor's request to use the rooms as a church, citing both a New York state law and a local rule forbidding the use of school facilities for religious purposes. Another important fact, which one may find in the Second Circuit's decision that was overturned by the Supreme Court, was that in his initial application to use the school's rooms for church services, the pastor expressly indicated that he did not intend to comply with the local rule against the use of school property for religious purposes.

There are two ways to interpret these facts. First, one might perceive this as a situation wherein church officials were simply looking for convenient facilities in which to conduct its activities and were heartlessly thwarted by educational bureaucrats who were hostile to religion. After all, between his first and second applications to show the film series, the pastor also asked if the church might use the elementary school or high school gymnasium for "for 'non-religious purposes' such as volley ball" (1992, p. 384), a request that was denied on the ground that the gymnasiums were not available on the nights he had requested. Under this interpretation, the request to use the gym might be seen as evidence that board officials regarded Lamb's Chapel with unreasonable hostility. After all, who could object to letting church members play an innocent game of volleyball?

In view of the first application to use school rooms as a church, though, board officials were arguably entitled to regard subsequent requests with a certain degree of suspicion. The second way to interpret the facts is to recognize that school officials made a rational deduction about the pastor's motives based on past experience. It did not take great detective work to discern that what the church really wanted was an opportunity to evangelize on school property. Indeed, the pastor already admitted that the church's "paramount objective" was proselytizing. One might argue that the Supreme Court ought to have taken judicial notice of the fact that the plaintiff was evidently determined to use public property for religious observances and recruitment.

The central problem with *Lamb's Chapel* and subsequent cases is that they take away the ability of school administrators to distinguish between religious groups that are simply looking for the best available facilities for activities and sports and those trying to make an end run around the Establishment Clause. This author readily concedes that, in this regard, the New York state law and the local rule that the school board attempted to follow were just as misguided as the Supreme Court was in *Lamb's Chapel*. If anything, both the courts and state legislatures should afford local officials leeway to make decisions that fit the beliefs and desires of their local communities, provided that these do not conflict with the Establishment Clause.

When school boards adopt policies seeming to favor religion, though, courts have sometimes upheld their actions even in the face of community disapproval. In *Rusk v. Clearview Local Schools* (2004), for example, the Sixth Circuit essentially ignored the concerns of a parent about distribution of literature advertising a meeting where proselytizing occurred. The board argued that the policy did not impermissibly advance religion since the flyers were not proselytizing but merely contained information about the upcoming meeting. The court adopted the board's logic in its rationale.

The Sixth Circuit thus followed analysis derived from the Supreme Court's ruling in *Good News Club v. Milford Central School* (2001), wherein the justices allowed a religious club to meet in a public school after the class day had ended. Yet, this kind of legal hairsplitting completely misses the point: The purpose of the Good News Club meetings, and, indeed, the entire club, is to proselytize. Whether flyers distributed at school contain adequate warnings of that fact would perhaps be relevant if they advertised a one-time event. However, the flyers were distributed by a regular club with news of its scheduled meetings, and if school officials, parents, and students were unaware of the nature of the Good News Club before the first meeting, they were surely aware of it afterward. For anyone who might miss the obvious reference in the club's name to the Christian Gospel, the group's website clearly and forthrightly sets out its purpose: "to evangelize boys and girls with the Gospel of the Lord Jesus Christ and establish (disciple) them in the Word of God and in a local church for Christian living." On the topic of the club's Good News Camps, the website assures parents that "trained staff maintain an exciting program focused on evangelism and discipleship" (Good News Club, n.d.).

Essentially, the board of the Clearview School District, supported by the Sixth Circuit, declared that proselytizing in its schools was to be banned, but handing out flyers that were invitations for students to be proselytized was protected. This is a distinction without a difference that educators must avoid. The clear purpose in both cases is to try to recruit new religious adherents on school property. The religious group, to its credit, had at no point attempted to dissemble or conceal its purpose, which was then and remains to this day to convert children to a particular strand of evangelical Christian belief. Instead of taking note of this, school officials and the court decided that as long as the actual business of proselytizing occurred safely off campus, they would ignore the religious group's activities on campus.

Defenders of *Rusk* might well point out the Sixth Circuit's insistence that parental approval for student attendance at the meetings prevents any reasonable perception that school officials or the board endorsed religion. Still, while it is admirable that the Good News Club admits only students whose parents have given the permission in advance, the issue of parental consent arguably ought to be immaterial to the question of the constitutionality of government action. If it is a violation of the Establishment Clause to have the Good News Club meet at a public school, then officials should forbid its meetings, and the courts should support the school board's decisions no matter how many parents sign permission slips.

The Ninth Circuit confronted similar questions in *Hills v. Scottsdale Unified School District* (2003), reaching the same conclusion. The Scottsdale schools had a policy allowing outside groups to leave flyers at the school for distribution to the students. The plaintiff, who operated a Christian summer camp for children, attempted to avail himself of this service. The flyers he submitted contained, among other things, the following exhortation to parents:

> Did you know that if a child does not come to the knowledge of JESUS CHRIST and learn of the importance of Bible reading by the age 12 chances are slim that they ever will in this life? We think it is important to start as young as possible! (p. 1048)

The school board understandably balked at having its students thus blatantly targeted for proselytizing on campus. Yet, despite this clear indication of Hills's intentions, the Ninth Circuit held that refusing to pass out his flyers amounted to impermissible viewpoint discrimination.

Supporters of access to schools, as demonstrated in the point essay, are likely to argue that the Sixth Circuit in *Rusk* and the Ninth Circuit in *Hills* merely followed the Supreme Court's precedent from *Good News*. In *Good News*, the Court asserted that school officials may not exercise a "modified heckler's veto" (p. 119), in which the deciding factor for Establishment Clause violations would be the misperceptions of children. In other words, under such an approach, educational officials cannot ban activities simply because young students might mistakenly believe that officials are endorsing the activities. Unfortunately, neither the Sixth Circuit nor the Supreme Court recognized that believing the Good News Club to be a proselytizing organization is not a misperception at all. Nor would it be a misperception if students came to the realization that officials in their schools were allowing the distribution of literature that promoted religion. The question that remains is whether it is fair to call the mistaken impressions of children—that is, that school officials are endorsing a religion—a "modified heckler's veto."

Young children frequently mistake permission for endorsement. It is precisely for this reason that both parents and educators usually take great care in selecting the books, TV shows, and movies that children are allowed to read and watch. Consider a video game in which graphic sex and violence are depicted. Few parents would knowingly allow their young children to play such games if they thought about how their children may be unduly influenced by the content. In a similar vein, if parents were aware that their children might confuse the actions of school boards that grant religious groups access to schools as an official endorsement of their teachings, perhaps in beliefs that conflict with familial values, it is unlikely that they would treat this as merely a childish mistake that can be easily rectified after the fact. This is by no means intending to equate religion with sex and violence, except insofar as all three are topics that many parents would not wish to have foisted on their unsuspecting children while attending public elementary schools.

The Third Circuit's judgment in *Walz v. Egg Harbor Township Board of Education* (2003) takes a more sensible approach than *Good News*, *Rusk*, and *Hills*. *Walz* did not involve the activities of an outside group, although the court noted that since the child was only in kindergarten when he started trying to hand out religious items to his classmates during instructional time, it was more than likely that his mother was the real driving force behind his efforts to evangelize on school property (p. 275). The case still has some bearing on the *Good News* line of cases. As the Third Circuit wrote in *Walz*,

> [I]n an elementary school classroom, the line between school-endorsed speech and merely allowable speech is blurred, not only for the young, impressionable students but also for their parents who trust the school to confine organized activities to legitimate and pedagogically-based goals. (p. 277)

One might add, though the Third Circuit did not, that this blurring effect does not magically disappear when the child leaves the confines of a classroom or when instructional time formally ends.

The reason for reviewing *Good News*, *Hills*, and *Rusk*, even though they were at least partially concerned with distribution, is that they also involved outside groups that attempted to use facilities of elementary schools to evangelize their young students. Instead of dismissing these children's impressions of endorsement as a "modified heckler's veto," courts and school boards ought to be sensitive to the fact that their impressions are neither simple nor necessarily easily corrected. Rather than addressing the issue, courts have simply dismissed it, occasionally in rather insulting terms. For example, the Sixth Circuit in *Rusk* quoted with approval the Seventh Circuit's assertion, in *Hedges v. Wauconda Community Unit School District No. 118* (1993), that "[s]chools may explain that they do not endorse speech by permitting it. If pupils do not comprehend so simple a lesson, then one wonders whether [their] schools can teach anything at all" (p. 422). Implying, as the Seventh Circuit did, that if students get the wrong idea about government endorsement of speech, it is either because they are stupid or because their teachers are incompetent, does nothing to solve the problem that the courts have created by granting nonschool religious groups access to school facilities.

CONCLUSION

Courts have erred in unnecessarily widening the scope of the "audience" for religious speech. In other words, even as courts have recognized that religious speech is a subset of free speech that is entitled to constitutional protection, this essay contends that jurists have failed to take the impact that religious speech in schools can have on the minds and attitudes of young children who may be swayed by it unduly. The crucial issue in both *Good News* and *Rusk* was precisely what the youngest members of the audience perceived, since they were the true intended audience.

If one follows the logic of these courts, then, one could reason that access to facilities to conduct meetings and to distribute flyers was intended for the parents, not the children, and that the adults could always refuse to give their children permission to attend the meetings. Yet, whether parents give permission is immaterial. The supposed parental firewall is simply a judicial slight of hand to avoid dealing with the central issues, particularly in elementary schools where officials and teachers ought to take into account the likely misperceptions of their impressionable students. As such, educators should steer well clear of anything that might give the impression of endorsing religion such as when nonschool groups are permitted to use their facilities. Courts, meanwhile, should not confuse the issues by focusing on parental permission and the free expression rights of groups that arguably should not be allowed on campuses in the first place.

FURTHER READINGS AND RESOURCES

Good News Club. (n.d.). *What Is a Good News Club?* Retrieved from the Child Evangelism Fellowship website: http://www.cefonline.com/index.php?option=com_content&view=category&id=13&Itemid=100049

Jenkins, J. K. (2002). Equal access to public school facilities by religious and other noncurricular groups. *Education Law Reporter, 170,* 439.

Mawdsley, R. D. (2005). Access by religious community organizations to public schools: A degrees of separation analysis. *Education Law Reporter, 193,* 633.

Mawdsley, R. D. (2007). Federal Court of Appeals decisions in Good News Club cases: Does this litigation represent good news for public schools? *Education Law Reporter, 220,* 1.

Mawdsley, R. D., & Russo, C. J. (2001). An update on religious liberty in the United States: *Good News Club v. Milford Central School. Australia and New Zealand Journal of Law and Education, 6,* 91–100.

Mawdsley, R. D., & Russo, C. J. (2009). Hostility toward religion and the rise and decline of constitutionally protected religious speech. *Education Law Reporter, 240,* 524.

Russo, C. J., & Gregory, D. L. (1990). *Board of Education of the Westside Community Schools v. Mergens:* A case analysis. *Religion & Public Education, 17,* 18–20.

Russo, C. J., & Mawdsley, R. D. (2001). And the wall keeps tumbling down: The Supreme Court upholds religious liberty in *Good News Club v. Milford Central School*. *Education Law Reporter, 157,* 1–14.

Russo, C. J., & Mawdsley, R. D. (2008). Religious events in public schools: Celebration or controversy? *School Business Affairs, 4*(11), 38–42.

Schimmel, D. (1993). Discrimination against religious viewpoints prohibited in public schools: Analysis of the *Lamb's Chapel* decision. *Education Law Reporter, 85,* 387.

Court Cases and Statutes

Board of Education of Westside Community Schools v. Mergens, 496 U.S. 226 (1990).

Bronx Household of Faith v. Board of Education of the CIty of New York, 650 F.3d 30 (2d Cir. 2011).

Bronx Household of Faith v. Community School District #10, 127 F.3d 207 (2d Cir. 1997); 226 F. Supp. 2d 401 (S.D.N.Y. 2002); 331 F.3d 342 (2d Cir. 2003); 400 F. Supp. 2d 581 (S.D.N.Y. 2005);—F.3d—, 2011 WL 2150974 (2d Cir. (2011).

Campbell v. St. Tammany Parish School Board, 231 F.3d 937 (5th Cir. 2000).

Daugherty v. Vanguard Charter School Academy, 116 F. Supp. 2d 897 (W.D. Mich. 2000).

Fairfax Covenant Church v. Fairfax County School Board, 17 F.3d 703 (4th Cir. 1994).

Good News Club v. Milford Central School, 533 U.S. 98 (2001).

Hedges v. Wauconda Community Unit School District No. 118, 9 F.3d 1295, 1300 (7th Cir. 1993).

Hills v. Scottsdale Unified School District, 329 F.3d 1044 (9th Cir. 2003).

Lamb's Chapel v. Center Moriches Union Free School District, 959 F.2d 381 (2nd Cir. 1992), 508 U.S. 384 (1993), *on remand,* 17 F.3d 1425 (2d Cir. 1994).

Lemon v. Kurtzman, 403 U.S. 602 (1971).

New York Educ. Code, § 414 (McKinney, 1995).

Rusk v. Clearview Local Schools, 379 F.3d 418 (6th Cir. 2004).

Walz v. Egg Harbor Township Board of Education, 342 F.3d 271 (3d Cir. 2003).

Widmar v. Vincent, 454 U.S. 263 (1981).

Should students and others be permitted to distribute religious materials in public schools?

POINT: Ralph D. Mawdsley, *Cleveland State University*
COUNTERPOINT: James L. Mawdsley, *Stark State College*

OVERVIEW

As detailed in the debate on access by religious groups to public school facilities in the previous chapter, a 1981 Supreme Court case set in higher education, *Widmar v. Vincent*, opened the door to protect religious speech as free speech. Not long thereafter, Congress extended the same protection to students in public high schools in the Equal Access Act (1984). The Court upheld the act in *Board of Education of Westside Community Schools v. Mergens* (1990). With these cases serving as the impetus, the Court went on to uphold the rights of a nonschool religious group to use public school facilities (*Lamb's Chapel v. Center Moriches Union Free School District*, 1993). Later, the Court also allowed a prayer club that was sponsored by a local mother to meet in a public school since other, secular, groups had the same right to do so (*Good News Club v. Milford Central School*, 2001). In all of these cases, the Court reasoned that insofar as religious speech is a subset of free speech, it was entitled to the same protection.

Not surprisingly, one of the related issues associated with access to facilities is the right of students and others to distribute religious materials in and around schools. Of course, as with the other issues on religion in this volume, and the many topics in this set, the courts fail to agree on the constitutionality of this practice. In fact, based on the unique facts of each case, two federal appellate courts, the Third and Sixth Circuits, rendered separate judgments both forbidding and permitting the distribution of religious literature in schools.

On the one hand, the Third (*Walz ex rel. Walz v. Egg Harbor Township Board of Education*, 2003, 2004,), Sixth (*Curry ex rel. Curry v. Hensiner*, 2008), and Seventh (*Berger v. Rensselaer Central School Corp.*, 1993a, 1993b) Circuits, along with other courts, agreed that students cannot distribute religious materials such as Bibles (*Roark v. South Iron R-1 School District*, 2008), religious newspapers (*Thompson v. Waynesboro Area School District*, 1987), and advertisements about religious activities (*Krestan v. Deer Valley Unified School Dist. No. 97, of Maricopa County*, 2008) or meetings (*Muller by Muller v. Jefferson Lighthouse School*, 1996, 1997). The courts agreed that if the materials to be distributed or the activities they addressed were religious in nature, and if officials set reasonable time, manner, and place restrictions, then they had the authority to forbid the distribution of religious materials at public schools.

On the other hand, the Third (*Child Evangelism Fellowship of New Jersey v. Stafford Township School District*, 2004), Fourth (*Child Evangelical Fellowship v. Montgomery County Public Schools*, 2006), Fifth (*Doe v. Duncanville Independent School District*, 1995), Sixth (*Rusk v. Crestview Local School District*, 2004), and Ninth (*Hills v. Scottsdale Unified School District No. 48*, 2003, 2004) Circuits, along with federal trial courts in Massachusetts (*Westfield High School L.I.F.E. Club v. City of Westfield*, 2003) and New York (*M.B. ex rel. Martin v. Liverpool Central School District*, 2007), permitted groups or individual students to distribute religious materials in schools on the basis that doing so did not violate the Establishment Clause of the First Amendment to the Constitution. These courts were satisfied that there were safeguards in place, such as educators reviewing material to ensure that they were not proselytizing and sending brochures home to parents who had to decide whether their children would participate in the activities.

Against this backdrop, the essays in this chapter highlight key selected cases in reaching different outcomes over whether students and other groups should be able to distribute religious materials in public schools. The point essay by Ralph D. Mawdsley (Cleveland State University) is of the opinion that students and others should be allowed to distribute religious materials in public schools. His analysis of the cases, focusing primarily on free speech, leads him to the conclusion that administrators should follow the line of cases recognizing that religious speech, including the distribution of religious materials, is entitled to the same protection as other kinds of speech.

On the other side, the counterpoint essay by James L. Mawdsley (Stark State College) relies on many of the same cases as the point essay in maintaining that students and others should be prohibited from being allowed to distribute religious materials in public school. His response focuses on the need of public schools to provide education to children rather than allow them to be treated as a captive audience for those wishing to distribute religious materials. In essence, he maintains that school officials should have authority to decide what is right for their communities, rather than having their hands tied.

As you read these essays, ask yourself the following related questions. First, do you think that it is permissible for public school officials to allow students and others to distribute religious materials? Second, is allowing such distributions a constitutional violation by aiding religion? Third, would forbidding the distribution of religious material violate the rights to freedom of religion and speech of those who wish to do so?

Charles J. Russo
University of Dayton

POINT: Ralph D. Mawdsley
Cleveland State University

The notion that public school students have free expression constitutional rights is well established. In 1969, the Supreme Court, in its groundbreaking decision *Tinker v. Des Moines Independent Community School District*, declared, "It can hardly be argued that either students or teachers shed their constitutional rights to freedom of speech or expression at the schoolhouse gate" (p. 506). Despite the arguments from such legal notables as Supreme Court Justice Clarence Thomas that *Tinker* should be reversed and public schools revert to *in loco parentis*, affording educators greater control over student actions, no one has taken seriously the argument that children should be divested of their constitutional rights, least of all to speech. Since students have such rights, the challenge is determining how those rights should be managed in public school settings.

Twenty-four years after *Tinker*, the Supreme Court, in *Lamb's Chapel v. Center Moriches Union Free Schools District* (1993), held that religious speech was a fully protected subset of the Free Speech Clause of the First Amendment to the Constitution. According to the Court, to prohibit the use of public school facilities by religious organizations solely on the basis of religion constituted impermissible viewpoint discrimination. Then, in *Good News Club v. Milford Central Schools* (2001), the Supreme Court ruled that a religious community organization had the right to send materials home with students on the same basis as nonreligious community groups and that the organization could meet in a public school.

As a corollary to *Lamb's Chapel* and *Good News Club*, disputes have arisen over whether students should be able to distribute religious literature in their public schools. Under the free speech principles established in *Tinker*, *Lamb's Chapel*, and *Good News Club*, this point essay adopts the position that students should have the right to distribute religious literature in their public schools.

LITIGATION ADDRESSING DISTRIBUTION

Distribution of religious materials in schools can occur by educators, students, or persons from the community. Support for the position that religious materials should be distributed in public schools requires a balancing of constitutional rights protecting free speech and preventing the establishment of religion. Courts agree that the application of constitutional rights depends very much on facts such as the sources of distribution, whether students or community organizations; the methods of distribution, whether hand delivered or via school intercoms; the places of distribution, whether in classrooms or hallways; the time of distribution, whether during noninstructional time or instructional hours; and, the content of distributed information, whether proselytizing or nonproselytizing in nature. In parsing the distribution rights of religious materials in public schools, then, much depends on the facts.

As an initial matter, as suggested in the counterpoint essay, distribution of religious materials by teachers in the classroom is all the more difficult after *Garcetti v. Ceballos* (2006), wherein the Supreme Court indicated that job-related speech activities are not entitled to free expression protection. However, this does not mean that teachers necessarily lose their rights as private citizens. In *Wigg v. Sioux Falls School District 49–5* (2004), admittedly pre-*Garcetti*, the Eighth Circuit found that an elementary teacher who was denied the opportunity to work with a Good News Club in her school after her contracted day ended was entitled to damages for the violation of her free speech rights. While one can argue that the rights of teachers as citizens to participate with students in religious activities are not inconsistent with *Garcetti*, it is not the main issue in this debate. Turning, then, to students and other groups, while it is not unanimous, the litigation is generally supportive that within the limits established in the cases, religious materials can be distributed in public schools.

Navigating the shifting sands between what is prohibited by the Establishment Clause and what is required under the Free Speech Clause has not always been an easy journey for public school officials who deal with student religion and speech rights. Although the Supreme Court has recognized that the Establishment Clause forbids public school endorsement of religion and religious messages, it conceded that private student speech is protected under the Free Speech Clause. Unfortunately, the mantra of separation of church and state has frequently skewed the definition of neutrality under the Establishment Clause in the direction of inappropriately prohibiting the dissemination of religious information in public schools. This essay decries the placing of restrictions on the distribution of religious materials since they should be entitled to the same protection as other speech.

As reflected in the litigation reviewed in this point essay, courts typically uphold the rights of students to distribute religious materials in their public schools. Yet, when children distribute religious materials or ask for permission to do so, public school officials have responded by punishing or threatening to punish children. In *Morgan v. Swanson* (2010), for example, the Fifth Circuit denied a request for qualified immunity that would have insulated two elementary school principals from liability. The educators forcefully refused to permit students to distribute pencils with religious messages at class parties but allowed other children to hand out pencils with nonreligious messages. At one point, one principal threatened a girl who was distributing a pencil on school property outside the school building with suspension, and her mother, who also was present, with criminal prosecution. In *Morgan*, officials categorically forbade only the distribution of religious materials anywhere within the school or on school property. The lesson from *Morgan* is that teachers, administrators, and boards that engage in such wholesale rejection of all requests to distribute religious material where other nonschool materials can be distributed run the risk of damages awards.

LITIGATION AGAINST DISTRIBUTION

A school's selective prohibition against distributing religious items will encounter substantial judicial scrutiny. In *Walz v. Egg Harbor Township Board of Education* (2003), a child sought to distribute religious materials in the form of pencils at a class party bearing the message, "Jesus [Loves] the Little Children." The Third Circuit upheld the teacher's confiscation of the pencils pursuant to an unwritten school board policy prohibiting "items with political, commercial, or religious references . . . be[ing] distributed in class during school hours" (p. 273).

Five years later, the Sixth Circuit, in *Curry v. Hensiner* (2008), held that officials did not violate a student's free speech rights when they forbade him from including religious materials, this time in the form of a card with pipe-cleaner candy canes, that he sold as part of the fifth-grade curriculum referred to as "Classroom City." However, officials "permitted the student to distribute the candy canes in the hallway outside the classroom, at recess, or after school as students were boarding buses" (p. 274). Although the student attempted to circumvent the curricular rules, he "received a grade of 'A' for his part of the Classroom City project, and was not disciplined for attempting to sell the candy canes with the religious cards" (p. 575). The court denied the child's claim that officials violated his rights, maintaining that they could control the curriculum under *Hazelwood School District v. Kuhlmeier* (1988), which allows educators discretion as long as their actions are rationally related to legitimate pedagogical concerns. In an attempt to mollify the situation, educators offered the student the opportunity to "sell the candy canes with the card . . . after school in the parking lot" (p. 576). *Walz* and *Curry* are distinguishable from *Morgan* since the principals in *Morgan* restricted the students' speech solely because of its religious character, not for pedagogical reasons or because of concern that the public might misperceive the speech as bearing the school's imprimatur.

Courts have distinguished between classrooms and other locations within schools in terms of free speech rights. Generally, classrooms can be reserved for curriculum-related information and are inaccessible to distribution of materials by either students or community organizations. In *Walz*, the Third Circuit carefully delineated between enforcement of a policy prohibiting distribution of materials with a wide range of personal messages in classrooms and student's rights "to speak to his classmates during snack time [which] he [is entitled to do] as an individual" (p. 280).

LITIGATION SUPPORTING DISTRIBUTION

Distribution of materials in nonclassroom areas such as hallways can depend on whether educators created limited public fora that allow distribution and whether doing so is considered disruptive under *Tinker*. In *Hills v. Scottsdale Unified School District No. 48* (2003), a local board permitted nonprofit organizations to distribute literature through its schools, promoting events and activities of interest to students, but it prohibited any flyers of a "commercial, political or religious nature" (p. 1046). The materials were "either made available for students to pick up or [were] placed in teachers' in-house mailboxes and then distributed by the teachers to their students" (p. 1047). Operating under a board policy that "[o]utside agencies must receive District Approval by the Superintendent or designee prior to distribution or display of any materials," the superintendent testified that distributing the flyers was a

> "community service" for parents and children, getting information to those who would be most interested in participating [with] [e]xamples of acceptable flyers [being] those promoting summer camps, art classes, sports leagues, artistic performances or exhibits, and various YMCA, boys and girls clubs, and scouting activities. (p. 1047)

The court observed that "if the District permits the distribution of similar secular programs by other non-profit organizations," then its place of distribution rules apply to literature advertising an off-campus summer program even though "it is taught from a Christian perspective" (p. 1053).

In a case dealing with the distribution of religious materials by community organizations involving students, the Third Circuit, in *Child Evangelism Fellowship of New Jersey v. Stafford Township School District* (2004), reasoned that a Good News Club was, like other groups, entitled to distribute promotional material in elementary schools at back-to-school nights and to post materials on a school bulletin board. Where the school had no part in writing, paying for, producing, or approving the materials, the latter constituted private speech and could not be regulated by the school under the theory that they were part of the school's "pedagogical concerns" under *Hazelwood*.

In *Child Fellowship of Maryland v. Montgomery County Public Schools* (2004), the Fourth Circuit held that officials in an elementary school engaged in viewpoint discrimination when they refused to include Good News Club flyers as part of their "take-home flyer forum." The forum permitted governmental and nonprofit organizations to submit materials to officials who had them placed in packets that the students would collect at the end of the day and take home to their parents. Reversing an earlier order to the contrary, the court ordered officials to include the nonproselytizing religious flyers in the folders because this did not violate the Establishment Clause.

The Sixth Circuit, in *Rusk v. Crestview Local School District* (2004), reached a similar result to *Montgomery County* regarding the Establishment Clause and distribution of Good News Club flyers. However, the notable difference between *Montgomery County* and *Stafford*, on the one hand, and *Rusk*, on the other, is that officials in the Crestview District wanted to include the Good News Club flyers in student folders. As a result, the *Rusk* court saw no need to evaluate whether distribution was required under the Free Speech Clause.

A federal trial court, in *Westfield High School L.I.F.E. Club v. City of Westfield* (2003), established perhaps the outer limits of student distribution rights in elementary schools. The court ruled that a student could distribute candy canes with proselytizing religious messages as part of "private, school-tolerated speech" (p. 114).

BURDEN ON SCHOOL OFFICIALS TO DENY DISTRIBUTION

When school officials prohibit the distribution of religious materials anywhere on school grounds or in schools, whether during recess or lunch or in hallways, they bear the burden of demonstrating that their actions fit within the permitted limitations on student speech. Officials need to ask whether distribution of the materials has or will be disruptive; whether excluding the distribution of religious materials and permitting nonreligious materials has a reasonable pedagogical justification; whether distributed religious materials are vulgar and lewd; and whether the materials promote the use of drugs in violation of school district policy. Since the latter two categories are highly unlikely, it is necessary to examine the first two, dealing with disruption and the school curriculum.

The Supreme Court observed in *Tinker* that "undifferentiated fear or apprehension of disturbance is not enough to overcome the right to freedom of expression" (p. 508). In *Westfield*, the court granted a preliminary injunction against a school official who refused to permit a student to distribute candy canes with a religious message. The court noted that nothing before it suggested that other children could not

> decline the candy canes, that the student plaintiffs coerced others into accept their message[,] invaded the rights of others not to receive literature ... or that the[y] blocked other[s] from entering class, actions which could constitute even substantial interference and justify restricting distribution to a more reasonable time, manner, and place. (p. 112)

Thus, the court allowed distribution to occur because it was not disruptive.

KEY QUESTIONS ABOUT DISTRIBUTION

Three key questions remain in support of allowing students to be able to distribute religious materials in schools just as other groups are free to do so. The first asks whether school policies permit nonreligious materials to be distributed. Officials may design policies prohibiting student distribution of all non–curriculum-related materials during the school day in hallways and at lunch or recess. Even so, courts are likely to find that distribution is protected by free speech under *Tinker* unless the method of distribution or the content is disruptive to the educational process.

The second question concerns whether distributions take place during noninstructional time. Noninstructional time includes any part of the school day when instruction does not occur, and includes homerooms at the beginning or end of the school day, as well as recess, lunchrooms, and passing periods.

The third question addresses whether materials are proselytizing in nature. Courts have not been especially helpful in defining what constitutes proselytizing material. Generally, nonproselytizing material announces an event such as a Good News Club meeting after school, while proselytizing material seeks to change student behavior such as an exhortation to accept Christ as one's personal Savior. Distribution of nonproselytizing material is probably protected under *Tinker*. Similarly, distribution of proselytizing materials may also be protected as long as the methods of distribution are not disruptive. Such an approach, though, suggests that the only sensitivities that matter in schools are those of the students who are to be the recipients of a proselytizing message. In response to these three queries, absent fear of disruption, as long as other groups are allowed to distribute their materials in schools, then religious groups should have the same rights.

CONCLUSION

Forbidding the distribution of religious materials from public schools amounts to hostility toward religion. Such is the intolerance toward religious views that we now permit application of an exclusionary principle, eliminating a religious practice such as school-sponsored prayer at graduations out of concern for the sensitivities of members of the public while excluding religious views of individual children in elementary schools, essentially deciding that their sensitivities or beliefs count for nothing. To quote Justice Samuel Alito (2004), in *Child Evangelism Fellowship of New Jersey v. Stafford Township School District*, when he was a member of the Third Circuit, "[W]e cannot say the danger that children would misperceive the endorsement of religion is any greater than the danger that they would perceive a hostility toward [religion] if [a classmate's views] were excluded from the public forum" (p. 532). Accordingly, students should have the right to distribute religious literature in their public schools.

COUNTERPOINT: James L. Mawdsley
Stark State College

In *Lamb's Chapel v. Center Moriches Union Free School District* (1993), the Supreme Court held that religious speech is protected expression under the First Amendment. *Lamb's Chapel* thus further complicated the lives of officials in public schools who before, and after, it was handed down faced the unenviable task of balancing the demands of two groups of parents and students. On the one hand are those for whom any appearance of religion within the confines of public school property is an impermissible establishment of religion. On the other are those for whom any restriction on religious activity is a violation of their freedom of speech and religion.

Administrators are faced with situations where any choices they make may raise parental ire and even end in litigation. School officials ought to be able to decide, on the basis of experience and familiarity with their local communities, which pamphlets and flyers are likely to cause offense. Accordingly, this counterpoint essay maintains that public school officials should have the authority to prevent students and others from distributing religious literature in their schools.

DISTRIBUTION IS A BAD IDEA

One may begin by identifying three groups whose attempts to distribute religious materials might cause trouble for school administrators: employees, outside groups (which may include the parents of students), and students. The first of these, employees, presents the least difficulty in terms of limiting their activities. Suppose teachers were to bring pamphlets to their classes advertising vacation bible schools at their churches. Does the Constitution require that the school administration allow the distribution? The Supreme Court, in *Tinker v. Des Moines Independent Community School District* (1969), expressly included teachers in its famous declaration that "[i]t can hardly be argued that either students or teachers shed their constitutional rights to freedom of speech or expression at the schoolhouse gate" (p. 506). Further, in *Pickering v. Board of Education* (1968), the Court decided that outside the school campus, teachers have the same free speech rights as everyone else to speak on matters of public interest.

As subsequent decisions have made clear, though, teachers shed a great deal more of their rights at the gate than students do. While teachers obviously retain certain of their rights while at school, *Tinker* does not require officials to indulge their every whim and desire. In *Garcetti v. Ceballos* (2006), for example, the Supreme Court pointed out that when public employees speak on matters pursuant to their official duties, an area that includes the distribution of religious literature, their government employers, including school boards, can restrict the content of their speech.

At the same time, the arguments of the point essay notwithstanding, public school officials may have an affirmative obligation to prohibit the distribution of religious literature given the likelihood that this would be seen as a violation of the Establishment Clause. In *Lemon v. Kurtzman* (1971), the Court set out what is now known as the three-pronged *Lemon* test: government action must have a secular purpose, must have the primary effect of neither advancing nor prohibiting religion, and must not result in an excessive entanglement with religion. Arguably, if teachers were to pass out religious tracts or even flyers for church youth group activities, the result would likely be a constitutional violation on all three prongs of the *Lemon* test.

There is no secular purpose to be served by educators distributing religious flyers to students while at school. To the contrary, the only purpose is the religious goal of attracting students to church activities. The primary effect of educators' handing out religious pamphlets would therefore be to advance religion. Moreover, since educators are state agents, their actions would arguably result in excessive government entanglement with religion. Students would be likely to conclude that officials and the state endorse the beliefs being promulgated in the pamphlet. Additionally, at least some students might be intimidated into taking the literature offered by their teachers or attending church events advertised in flyers under the reasonable belief that refusing to do so might have negative consequences for their grades.

Having established that teachers and other school employees can be prohibited from distributing religious materials on campus, the more difficult question involves outside groups including students. In light of a long line of cases involving Good News Clubs, the distribution of religious materials on campuses by outside groups presents challenges for public school administrators.

The Supreme Court, in *Good News Club v. Milford Central School* (2001), ruled that a religious group has the same rights to send literature home with students as any nonreligious group. In *Hills v. Scottsdale Unified School District No. 48* (2003), the Ninth Circuit held that religious groups must have the same access to students for their literature as nonreligious groups. However, nonreligious flyers are likely to attract considerably less controversy from parents.

School officials who wish to avoid controversy and possible litigation would thus do well to abide by the holdings of *Good News* and *Hills*. Thus, churches advertising summer camps must be allowed to distribute flyers in the same way as the Boy Scouts, Girl Scouts, or other groups. If, for instance, officials have allowed a special table to be set aside near the door of a school where outside groups can leave informational pamphlets and flyers, then space must be made available on that table for a religious group's flyers.

One can sympathize with the frustrations of parents whose children return home from school, fairly bursting with excitement at the prospect of attending a religious club or camp with their friends. The parents may feel that their own plans for their children's religious upbringing (or upbringing free from religion) have been undermined. And, what is more, the parents have been undermined at an allegedly secular public school, of all places. These parents are unlikely to feel placated by being told that, under *Good News*, the religious club or activity passes constitutional muster since they, the parents, are still free to say "no" to their children. One can also sympathize with school administrators who then have to deal with the complaints of these parents.

A simple, if somewhat draconian, solution presents itself when reading *Good News* and *Hills*: allow no outside, noncurricular material on campus at all. Rather than reserving a table near the front door for the distribution of pamphlets, administrators could simply refuse to allow literature from any groups to be handed out. Administrators could explain to any groups seeking to have their flyers handed out to the children that the school has a policy of only allowing the distribution of literature to students for school-sponsored events. If Boy Scouts and YMCA camps are not allowed to distribute flyers to students, then church camps cannot distribute flyers either. Such a decision is unlikely to prove popular in the wider community, but administrators could reasonably take the position that the primary function of public schools is to provide education to children, not to provide a captive audience for advertisers.

The most difficult case of all involves the distribution of religious materials on campus by students themselves. Since religious expression can be considered offensive by people who belong to different religions, or have no religion at all, the Supreme Court's decision in *Bethel School District v. Fraser* (1986) seems, at first glance, to offer some hope to administrators. In *Fraser*, which upheld the suspension of a high school student for delivering a lewd nominating speech, the Court explained that "it is a highly appropriate function of public school education to prohibit the use of vulgar and offensive terms in public discourse" (p. 683). But *Fraser* depended on the use of words and innuendo that were "vulgar and offensive." Further, while many people might be offended by proselytizing materials, such tracts and pamphlets are rarely, if ever, framed in the sort of terms that got the young orator in so much trouble in *Fraser*. *Fraser* therefore provides little guidance for school boards in formulating policies regarding the distribution of religious materials.

Returning to *Tinker*, the Supreme Court famously declared that students do not "shed their constitutional rights to freedom of speech or expression at the schoolhouse gate" (p. 506). Even so, there are limits to these expressive rights. In *Walz v. Egg Harbor Township Board of Education* (2003), by way of illustration, the Third Circuit affirmed an earlier order that declined to issue an injunction requiring school officials to allow a young student to distribute candy canes with a card bearing a religious message. Earlier, the student handed out pencils with the words "Jesus (Loves) the Little Children" (p. 773), which were confiscated by his teacher.

Walz turned on two significant factors, however. The first was the relative youth of the student and his classmates, who were only in kindergarten. As the Third Circuit pointed out, "as a general matter, the younger the students, the more control a school may exercise" (p. 276). The second, and perhaps more important, factor was that young Daniel Walz attempted to distribute candy canes during a structured school activity that was designed to teach the importance of sharing to the kindergarteners, not to promote religion. Therefore, the court had no difficulty in determining that the teacher had the authority to control the content of her own lesson by taking away the religious materials. From a constitutional perspective, the result was no different than if *Walz* had attempted to hand out baseball cards while the teacher was reading a book to the class during story time. In situations involving older students, though, or attempted distribution outside of classroom instructional time, the powers of school officials are severely and unnecessarily hampered by *Tinker*.

Under the *Tinker* standard, public school officials must reasonably anticipate a substantial disruption to the educational mission of their schools before they can limit or restrict student expressive activities, possibly including the distribution of religious materials. In general, courts have been unwilling to entertain the claim that the mere presence of religious materials in schools might bring about such disruptions.

In *Nixon v. Northern Local School District* (2005), a federal trial court granted an injunction allowing a student to wear a shirt at school that he purchased at a church camp. The shirt bore the words, "Homosexuality is a sin! Islam is a lie! Abortion is murder! Some issues are just black and white!" (p. 967). School officials were obliged to concede that no disruption had occurred as a result of the student's having worn the shirt and that there was no history of animosity toward or harassment of homosexuals or Muslims at the school.

This is not to say, though, that such a disruption could not have happened. It is an open question how such a case might be resolved if a student wore such a T-shirt, or brought pamphlets elaborating on the idea, explaining at length the falsity of a particular religion, from the perspective of those who prepared the materials, to a school where adherents to that religion made up a substantial minority, or even a majority, of the student body. It would seem that an administrator might then reasonably anticipate that a substantial disruption could occur, particularly if there is a history of animosity and conflict between groups of students of different faiths at that school. The situation is analogous to the many cases where courts forbid students from wearing Confederate paraphernalia to school based on the fear of substantial disruption that could be reasonably anticipated in light of opposition from other students.

Insofar as the *Tinker* standard of substantial disruption is almost impossible for most schools to meet, particularly with regard to religious messages, it should not be applied when dealing with religious literature because it is about how a message can be communicated, regardless of whether on a flyer or on a shirt. In *Zamecnik v. Indian Prairie School District* (2007), a federal trial court denied a request by two students for an injunction forcing their school's administration to allow them to wear a shirt bearing the message "Be Happy, Not Gay" (p. 520) since educators feared that their doing so would have been disruptive.

In fairness, *Zamecnik* was not about religious materials in schools per se but can be used by analogy or as a kind of persuasive precedent that can be relied on to prevent the distribution of religious materials in public schools. Even so, the plaintiff asserted that he wished to wear the T-shirt to "convey religious beliefs that are critical of homosexual conduct at school" (p. 522). Nonetheless, the trial court decision in *Zamenick* is relevant for school boards contemplating the creation of policies designed to restrict student speech, whether religious or nonreligious. Distinguishing the dispute before it from *Nixon*, the trial court found that school officials had a legitimate interest in promoting tolerance and preventing harassment of gay students. One might argue that school officials have a similar interest in promoting tolerance of differing religious beliefs and preventing the harassment of adherents to minority religions by banning the distribution of religious literature.

On appeal, though, under the name *Nuxoll ex rel. Nuxoll v. Indian Prairie School Dist. #204* (2008), the Seventh Circuit reversed the decision of the trial court in *Zamecnik* in describing the T-shirt's message as being "only tepidly negative." The court pointed out that the mere speculation about what kind of harassment of homosexuals at the school might possibly result from a student being allowed to wear the T-shirt was "too thin a reed on which to hang a prohibition of the exercise of a student's free speech" (p. 676). Therefore, it seems likely that, if a school's administration were to ban religious or antireligious statements in student-distributed literature, they would be unreasonably placed in the difficult position of having to be able to meet the difficult challenge of demonstrating that religious tensions were so severe in the school that a substantial disruption would result from allowing students to distribute the pamphlets or flyers.

Another difficulty that can arise is that controlling or supervising the distribution of religious material by students presents enormous—one might almost say insurmountable—practical challenges. School employees are adults and can usually be depended on to follow board policies. In limiting the distribution of religious materials, school officials can simply tell members of outside groups not to bring their flyers to campus anymore. Yet, no one can pretend that any school can hope to control what students say to each other in the hallways or what kind of papers or flyers a child brings to recess in his pocket. Nonetheless, school officials can and should have reasonable policies limiting the times and places at which such materials can be distributed. As noted throughout, simply removing all limitations on the distribution of religious materials is not a solution.

CONCLUSION

Educational leaders, rather than the courts, should be the ones who decide whether religious materials are appropriate for distribution in their schools and communities. However, a long series of court decisions at every level has tied the hands of administrators, obligating them to tolerate and accept religious materials for distribution that educators know will cause offense to some students and parents. Certainly, no one is entitled to a life free from being offended. Even so, educational officials need to be able to concentrate on their educational mission without worrying about the distraction that religious materials will inevitably cause. Courts should consider modifying the *Tinker* "substantial disruption" test, which would prevent distribution only if this were to occur, so as to allow administrators to do their jobs and ensure an inclusive and cooperative learning environment for all their students by keeping the distribution of religious materials from occurring in public school settings.

FURTHER READINGS AND REFERENCES

Bjorklun, E. (1991). Distribution of religious literature in the public schools. *Education Law Reporter, 68,* 957.

Clark, B. K. (2008). Filling the First Amendment gap: Can Gideons get away with in-school Bible distribution by exploiting the play in the joints between the Free Exercise and Establishment Clauses? *Washington University Journal of Law & Policy, 28,* 403.

Gey, S. G. (2000). When is religious speech not "free speech"? *University of Illinois Law Review, 2000,* 379.

Hardberger, R. (2006). Coercion, misperception and excessive entanglement with religion: A reexamination of *Child Evangelism Fellowship of Maryland, Inc. v. Montgomery County Public Schools*. *University of California Davis Law Review, 39,* 1941.

Mawdsley, R. D. (2005). The profane, the offensive, and the religious: The use of Hazelwood to prohibit religious activity in public schools. *Education Law Reporter, 195,* 425–441.

Mawdsley, R. D. (2011). Religious viewpoint discrimination in public elementary schools: Lessons from the Fifth Circuit. *Education Law Reporter, 269,* 29–45.

Mawdsley, R. D., Permuth, S., & Russo, C. J. (2005). Distribution of religious materials in public schools. *Education Law Reporter, 197,* 7–13.

McCarthy, M. M. (2004). Religious influences in public schools: The winding path toward accommodation. *Saint Louis University Public Law Review, 23,* 565.

COURT CASES AND STATUTES

Berger v. Rensselaer Central School Corp., 982 F.2d 1160 (7th Cir. 1993), *cert. denied*, 508 U.S. 911 (1993).

Bethel School District v. Fraser, 478 U.S. 675 (1986).

Board of Education of Westside Community Schools v. Mergens, 496 U.S. 226 (1990).

Bronx Household of Faith v. Community School District #10,—F.3d—, 2011 WL 2150974 (2d Cir. 2011).

Campbell v. St. Tammany Parish School Board, 231 F.3d 937 (5th Cir. 2000).

Child Evangelism Fellowship of New Jersey v. Stafford Township School District, 386 F.3d 514 (3d Cir. 2004).

Child Evangelical Fellowship v. Montgomery County Public Schools, 457 F.3d 376 (4th Cir. 2006).

Child Fellowship of Maryland v. Montgomery County Public Schools, 373 F.3d 589 (4th Cir. 2004).
Curry *ex rel.* Curry v. Hensiner, 513 F.3d 570 (6th Cir. 2008).
Doe v. Duncanville Independent School District, 70 F.3d 402 (5th Cir. 1995).
Garcetti v. Ceballos, 547 U.S. 410 (2006).
Good News Club v. Milford Central School, 533 U.S. 98 (2001).
Hazelwood School District v. Kuhlmeier, 484 U.S. 260 (1988).
Hills v. Scottsdale Unified School District No. 48, 329 F.3d 1044 (9th Cir. 2003), *cert. denied*, 540 U.S. 1149 (2004).
Krestan v. Deer Valley Unified School District No. 97, of Maricopa County, 561 F. Supp. 2d 1078 (D. Ariz. 2008).
Lamb's Chapel v. Center Moriches Union Free School District, 508 U.S. 384 (1993), *on remand*, 17 F.3d 1425 (2d Cir. 1994).
Lemon v. Kurtzman, 403 U.S. 602 (1971).
M.B. *ex rel.* Martin v. Liverpool Central School District, 487 F. Supp. 2d 117 (N.D.N.Y. 2007).
Morgan v. Swanson, 627 F.3d 170 (5th Cir. 2010).
Muller by Muller v. Jefferson Lighthouse School, 98 F.3d 1530 (7th Cir. 1996), *cert. denied*, 520 U.S. 1156 (1997).
Nixon v. Northern Local School District Board of Education, 383 F. Supp. 2d 965 (S.D. Ohio 2005).
Nuxoll v. Indian Prairie School District #204, 523 F.3d 668 (7th Cir. 2008).
Pickering v. Board of Education, 391 U.S. 563 (1968).
Roark v. South Iron R-1 School District, 540 F. Supp. 2d 1047 (E.D. Mo. 2008).
Rusk v. Crestview Local School District, 379 F.3d 418 (6th Cir. 2004).
Thompson v. Waynesboro Area School District, 673 F. Supp. 1379 (M.D. Pa. 1987).
Tinker v. Des Moines Independent Community School District, 393 U.S. 503 (1969).
Walz *ex rel.* Walz v. Egg Harbor Township Board of Education, 342 F.3d 271 (3d Cir. 2003), *cert. denied*, 541 U.S. 936 (2004).
Westfield High School L.I.F.E. Club v. City of Westfield, 249 F. Supp. 2d 98 (D. Mass. 2003).
Widmar v. Vincent, 454 U.S. 263 (1981).
Wigg v. Sioux Falls School District 49–5, 382 F.3d 807 (8th Cir. 2004).
Zamecnik v. Indian Prairie School District, 2007 WL 1141597 (N.D. Ill., 2007), *rev'd sub nom.* Nuxoll *ex rel.* Nuxoll v. Indian Prairie School District #204, 523 F.3d 668 (7th Cir. 2008).

17

Should students be allowed to wear distinctive religious garb in public schools?

POINT: Jane P. Novick, *University of Dayton*
COUNTERPOINT: Maureen Bridget Sexton, *University of Dayton*

OVERVIEW

As American schools, and society, become increasingly pluralistic with regard to such interrelated key demographic indicators as religion and ethnicity, an emerging controversy involves whether students should be permitted to wear distinctive religious clothing to public schools. Issues surrounding religious garb, involving the constitutional rights of students to freedom of religion and speech, not to mention the ability of the parents to direct the upbringing of their children, necessitate having to balance the rights of student against the duty of educational officials to maintain schools as safe and orderly leaning environments. The safety issue vis-à-vis religious dress has come to the fore in light of cases where students challenged prohibitions against wearing ceremonial daggers or rosary beads to their public schools in the face of policies dealing with zero-tolerance for weapons and fears that religious symbols can be used as forms of gang clothing, making identification of peers easier for other members.

Disagreements over religious dress have spawned legal controversy even though there has been relatively little reported litigation because disputes have tended to be resolved before they reached the trial stage. Yet, this does not mean that disputes over religious dress are any less intense or controversial.

In a case receiving a fair amount of attention, the Ninth Circuit ruled that school officials in California could not prevent male students who were Sikhs from wearing ceremonial daggers, or *kirpans*, in their belts despite the fact that the school had a zero-tolerance policy in place with regard to weapons (*Cheema v. Thompson*, 1995). The court held that educational officials exceeded their authority absent demonstrating proof that a total ban on weapons in schools was the least restrictive alternative way that they could have promoted campus safety.

Further, when students in Texas sought to wear rosary beads to school as necklaces, they challenged a board policy that forbade them from doing so since the rosaries were viewed as a form of gang clothing. A federal trial court struck down the policy on the basis that it violated the students' First Amendment right to pure speech, expression that is entitled to the highest level of protection. The court explained that insofar as the rosaries are a form of religious expression, they could not have been banned absent disruptions over their having been worn as necklaces (*Chalifoux v. New Caney Independent School District*, 1997).

At the same time, two federal courts upheld the rights of male students in Texas who are Native Americans to wear their hair long as a means of expressing their religious beliefs (*A.A. ex rel. Betenbaugh v. Needville Independent School District*, 2010; *Alabama and Coushatta Tribes of Texas v. Trustees of the Big Sandy Independent School District*, 1993, 1994). While these cases do not address religious clothing, they are informative nonetheless because they provide insights into judicial reasoning in disputes involving religious expression. Employing analysis similar to *Cheema*, the courts agreed that the restrictions were impermissible because they would have imposed substantial burdens on the students' sincerely held religious beliefs. Conversely, a federal trial court in Maryland, in another case not involving religion but also illustrative of the judicial thought process, upheld a ban preventing a student from wearing a head wrap to school to celebrate her cultural heritage (*Isaacs v. Board of Educ. of Howard County, Md.*, 1999). The court pointed out that the ban was permissible because the board had a preexisting policy in place forbidding students from wearing any type of headgear.

In a later incident that did not reach the courts, officials of an athletic association in Washington, D.C., forbade a Muslim female high school athlete from wearing a custom-made outfit during her track meets. The one-piece garment would have allowed the student to dress in a manner consistent with her Islamic beliefs, which forbid her from wearing clothing that displays any skin other than her face and hands. In barring the student from wearing the outfit during competition, officials avoided the religious controversy by relying solely on a rule that requires all competitors to dress in specified uniforms ("Muslim Track Athlete Disqualified," 2008).

Against this backdrop, the essays in this chapter take different approaches to whether students should be allowed to wear distinctively religious garb in public schools. In the point essay, Jane P. Novick (University of Dayton) maintains that students should be able to express their religious faiths in what they wear to their public schools. She presents the perspective that allowing students to come to schools dressed in religious clothes is consistent with the constitutional rights to freedom of religion and speech that go to the heart of what it means to be American.

Conversely, the counterpoint essay by Maureen Bridget Sexton (University of Dayton) asserts that students should not be able to wear religious clothes to public schools. Focusing on the fact that American schools have not always been welcoming to religions other than Christianity, coupled with the experiences of religious strife in other nations, she concludes that public schools should be religion-free zones because this would promote tolerance and respect while also helping ensure student safety.

As you read these essays, ask yourself the following questions. Do you think that students should be allowed to wear distinctively religious clothing to public schools? If students are allowed to wear religious garb to schools, will this help advance an understanding of religious diversity or is it more likely to result in greater separation or division along religious lines?

Charles J. Russo
University of Dayton

POINT: Jane P. Novick
University of Dayton

Allowing students to wear religious garb in public schools is consistent with the basic tenets of the public school concept. Although the Supreme Court has not yet ruled on this issue, the actions of the lower courts, Congress, and state legislatures indicate support for allowing students to wear religious garb in public schools.

Many of the disputes on this issue, which have typically been settled without litigation, have resulted in favorable outcomes for students. As such, in light of the history of American common schools, coupled with constitutional principles and relevant litigation, this point essay adopts the position that students should be allowed to wear religious clothing in public schools.

HISTORICAL CONTEXT AND LITIGATION

The common school movement, the precursor to the present public school system, appeared in the mid-1800s as its main proponents, Horace Mann and Samuel Lewis, articulated a philosophy of schools for all. These men believed that schools should be open to students of various ethnic, religious, and socioeconomic backgrounds since this would encourage mutual respect that would carry over into adulthood. Prior to this time, the colonial and early American schools emphasized homogeneity. Schools taught from the Protestant perspective, the religious belief of most early Americans. These schools were for White children and in some cases only for families with financial resources.

Following *Brown v. Board of Education* (1954), American public schools were forced to integrate. In attempting to make public schools reflect the makeup of all people living in the United States, the Supreme Court saw schools as a vehicle to introducing students to cultural values, a concept that is even more relevant today. While the purpose of public schools continues to be to educate children regardless of their backgrounds, exposing them to cultural values as expressed, for example, in dress is important in light of the increasing diversity of the American population.

The Constitution grants states the predominant power over public schools. More specifically, according to the Tenth Amendment, powers not granted to the federal government or prohibited to the states are reserved for the states. Education, of course, is among those powers. However, pursuant to Article VI, Sec. 2 of the Constitution, states may not create laws conflicting with any federal law. In other words, since state laws and school policies cannot trump federal laws, if students have rights to freedom of religion as expressed in their dress, then local school officials cannot impinge of the free exercise of their religious beliefs. School policies prohibiting students from wearing religious garb thus present potential conflicts to their First Amendment rights of religion and speech. These rights were especially important to our Founding Fathers because many of the colonists were escaping religious persecution in Europe.

If public schools are to educate all children, then they need to be both safe environments and respectful of diverse student bodies. This has been a major point in the controversy over school dress codes that infringe on some students' religious beliefs. On the one hand, the courts tend to agree that school boards do not have to tolerate student speech that is counter to a school's learning mission. On the other hand, boards cannot impose rules that violate students' constitutional rights. Since the Fourteenth Amendment protects the equal rights of all, state laws or policies must be consistent with this amendment.

As reflected in another debate in this series, school dress codes vary in their prohibitions and purposes. In the landmark Supreme Court case of *Tinker v. Des Moines Independent Community School District* (1969), officials sought to prohibit students from wearing black armbands to school to express their opposition to the Vietnam War. In finding that the conduct of the students was not disruptive, the Court treated this action as the same as if the students verbally articulated their opinion. Under the First Amendment, protected speech now includes verbal and written expression, as well as symbolic speech. Symbolic speech includes items such as a crucifix, a Star of David, or a swastika if the person displaying the symbol intends to convey a specific message that people would understand.

In reaching its judgment, the *Tinker* Court balanced the school's mission against students' rights to freedom of expression. Since the board was unable to prove that the students' symbolic speech caused a substantial disruption of, or material interference with, school activities, the Court invalidated the policy at issue. The Court aptly noted that it is all but impossible to prevent all types of controversies, nor can educators strive to always eliminate disagreements. The Court noted that controversy could erupt whenever any student spoke, a situation that would be especially true if the words spoken deviated from the general consensus of a particular group. The ability to express one's opinion, whether in speech or other forms, is a fundamental right of all Americans.

Also in *Tinker*, the Supreme Court recognized that students should not just passively receive information from teachers; rather, students should also be able to express their views. The Court understood that since schools should be places where there is an exchange of ideas, and that opinions can vary, students should be free to express their views by their manner of dress unless their doing so presents a reasonable forecast of material and substantial disruption to school activities. To this end, the Court indicated that free expression is an important aspect of the public school philosophy. Allowing students to express their beliefs through religious dress, then, fits squarely within this thinking.

Symbolic speech issues can be found in school dress codes that infringe on students' ability to wear religious garb. An incident involving symbolic speech took place in 1999 when a Jewish student in Gulfport, Mississippi, was prohibited from wearing a Star of David on the outside of his clothes. The school board's policy prohibited the wearing of some religious symbols because they could be construed as gang symbols. Yet, there was little evidence of gangs using the Star of David. Further, the student said he wore the Star of David as an affirmation of his religious heritage. Eventually the school board voted unanimously to exempt all religious symbols from its policy prohibiting students from wearing anything that could be viewed as a gang symbol (Preston, 1999). Consequently, the student dropped his case against the board.

Some dress codes that conflict with students' First Amendment rights involve both the free exercise of religion and the freedom of speech. At such times, courts use a standard different from the one articulated in *Tinker*. In 1990, the Supreme Court, in *Employment Division, Department of Human Resources of Oregon v. Smith*, decided that a law not designed specifically to target religious groups was permissible even if it inadvertently burdened religious freedoms. Such a law (or policy in a public school) would have to demonstrate that it was created to protect some important aspect of a school's mission. For example, a policy forbidding the wearing of headgear covering one's face may be able to pass this test because school officials could claim that safety and security issues preclude students from wearing veils covering their faces. However, there are exceptions to this standard, as some federal courts have taken a stricter approach to policies allegedly limiting the rights of students to freedom of expression and the free exercise of their religions via speech and conduct. Cases based on multiple First Amendment rights are called *hybrid claims*.

In *Chalifoux v. New Caney Independent School District* (1997), for instance, students in Texas raised free speech and free exercise of religion claims when told they could not wear their rosaries outside of their clothing. In response to a board policy prohibiting the wearing of what it described as gang-related apparel, including items such as rosaries, a federal trial court found that the *Tinker* standard was inappropriate because the intent of the policy was not to restrict the students' religious message. In deciding that the dispute was about speech and conduct when the students sought to wear the rosaries as symbolic speech, the court ruled in their favor. The court noted that there were no disruptions when the students wore their rosaries outside of their clothing, and only a small number of gang members actually wore rosaries. Consequently, the court concluded that school officials should have devised other ways to minimize gang-related behavior without having to violate the students' First Amendment rights.

Another example of a hybrid claim with regard to religious garb emerges over male students who are Native American and wish to wear their hair long. Although this does not implicate clothing per se, the reasoning of the court is useful. A common belief among many members of Native America tribes is that insofar as hair is equivalent to other body parts, cutting one's hair was tantamount to dismemberment of a body part. Courts have applied the hybrid standard to determine the constitutionality of a hair policy, roughly akin to a dress code, in cases where students have sincerely held religious beliefs since this protection covers more than majority or traditional religions. Further, religious expression, such as wearing hair long, need not be a mandatory practice of a religion. If students demonstrate sincerely held religious beliefs, school officials need to prove that their policies do not burden the free exercise of the students' religious beliefs even if dress codes are necessary regulations. As such, educators may have to find other ways to fulfill a policy's objective without burdening students' free exercise of religion.

In the first of two cases involving hair rather than dress, *Alabama and Coushatta Tribes of Texas v. Trustees of the Big Sandy Independent School District* (1993), the students claimed the school's policy violated their First Amendment rights to free exercise of religion and free speech. The policy prohibited boys from wearing their hair below the top of their shirt collars to foster respect for authority, to create a learning environment, and to foster a positive reflection of the school district and community during extracurricular activities. There was no apparent discriminatory purpose behind this law. In addition to their First Amendment claims, the parents alleged that the policy infringed on their rights to direct the upbringing of their children. This claim has played an important role in cases involving school policies that prohibit students from wearing religious clothing.

The court here pointed out that the general concept of parental rights was firmly established in *Wisconsin v. Yoder* (1972) wherein Amish families protested that the mandatory school attendance law was in direct conflict with their religious beliefs. The Supreme Court maintained that if the compulsory attendance laws prevailed and the Amish children had to attend school until the age of 16, the state would have been guiding the religious future and education of the children. Since the families and their communities would provide vocational training to their children, the Court agreed that the First and Fourteenth

Amendments precluded Wisconsin from requiring Amish students to remain in school until the age of 16. The issue of the rights of parents to direct the religious upbringing of their children was not new to the Supreme Court. Almost 50 years earlier, in 1925, the Court had reached essentially the same result in upholding parental rights in *Pierce v. Society of Sisters* (1925). The federal trial court in Texas, then, enjoined the enforcement of the hair policy because it would have violated the rights of both the students and their families.

In a more recent case of this nature from Texas, the Fifth Circuit struck down a board policy that prohibited students from having their hair touch their ears and that would have required a student who is a Native American to wear his long hair in a bun on top of his head or in a braid tucked into his shirt. The court affirmed that due to the student's sincere religious belief in wearing his hair visibly long, the policy would have imposed a substantial burden on his right to the free exercise of religion (*A.A. ex rel. Betenbaugh v. Needville Independent School District*, 2010).

ARGUMENT FOR PERMITTING STUDENTS TO WEAR RELIGIOUS GARB

Of course, public school officials may and should intercede if there are issues of health or safety of students at stake. At the same time, the Constitution prevents the government from favoring a particular religion, something that has not always been the case. In fact, historically, public schools demonstrated a clear preference to Protestant perspective. It is due to this governmental favoritism that separate religiously affiliated nonpublic schools were created. These schools helped to ensure religious freedom as well as opportunities for educational diversity and parental choice to educate their children in an environment that respected their religious beliefs.

One way educational officials have compromised on the dress code issue is by including exemption clauses in uniform policies that are designed to improve the overall learning environments of schools. Such opt-out provisions allow parents or students with legitimate religious or philosophical objections to uniform policies to apply for exemptions so that the students can dress as they wish. The use of exemptions thus seems to be an appropriate compromise between the right of school officials to provide adequate education for children and the rights of parents with regard to the religious beliefs they wish to instill in their children.

The issue of religious garb in the public schools appears to be increasing in frequency. The reactions of school boards as well as the federal and state governments seem to indicate a greater acceptance of students wearing religious clothing in public schools. By way of illustration, a dispute arose when a school board in Muskogee, Oklahoma, in an effort to reduce gang-related activity, instituted a dress code that prohibited hats and other head coverings and refused to grant exemptions for religious beliefs. After an 11-year-old Muslim student was advised that she could not continue to wear her headscarf to school, she was suspended for violating the policy that had been adopted 6 years earlier. However, after the U.S. Department of Justice participated in the settlement discussions, the school board agreed to allow exemptions for bona fide religious reasons ("Muslim Girl Suspended," 2003).

In a related issue, a rabbi serving as a chaplain in the U.S. Air Force unsuccessfully sought an exemption from a military rule prohibiting the wearing of headgear indoors. As a member of Orthodox Judaism, the rabbi wore a yarmulke (skullcap) at all times. In *Goldman v. Weinberger* (1986), the Supreme Court rejected the rabbi's request for an exemption since it was of the opinion that the military's purpose of national defense necessitated all soldiers to adhere to the strict military uniform guidelines. Interestingly, even though these guidelines are stricter than those in public schools, the U.S. Congress did not agree with the Court's decision and later enacted a law permitting military personnel to wear religious garb while on duty ("Religious Apparel," 1987). Thus, to the extent that Congress was willing to grant a faith-based exemption to accommodate the sincerely held beliefs of those in the U.S. military, then how much more should local school officials do the same for students in increasingly religiously diverse educational settings?

CONCLUSION

Many recent cases of school policies hindering students from wearing religious garb have been settled out of court. In numerous instances, school officials have compromised to allow students to wear their religious garb. The courts seem to want school officials to develop policies permitting students to wear religious dress in public schools. Ever since colonial times people fleeing persecution have come to the United States in pursuit of religious freedom, a tradition that should be extended to include allowing children to wear religious clothing to schools.

As the Constitution illustrates, the United States strongly supports religious freedom for all Americans. Allowing students to wear religious clothing in the public schools is one way to confirm those constitutional rights. Although the Supreme Court has not addressed this issue, the judicial trend seems to be to support the wearing of religious garb in the public schools. Since schools are the optimal setting to encourage respect for the different religious beliefs among Americans, educational officials should allow students to express their faiths by wearing the religious garb of their choice.

COUNTERPOINT: Maureen Bridget Sexton
University of Dayton

Educators are responsible for teaching tolerance and respect to all American school children, regardless of the students' religious beliefs or philosophical ideologies. One way of helping to teach tolerance and respect is for school officials to implement dress codes banning religious expressions on their campuses. This essay maintains that bans against religious garb are helpful because having students dress in a similar manner can encourage students to share common values rather than focus on religious separateness.

As reflected in court cases and incidents that stopped short of litigation involving religious dress, educators must take an even-handed approach. In other words, school officials cannot rely on policies that allow some students to wear religious symbols such as the Christian cross while banning others such as the Muslim hijab (the traditional female attire including veil), the Jewish Star of David, or Satanic pentagram. Therefore, public school officials must be consistent with regulations regarding students' wearing religious items. By implementing policies prohibiting all students from wearing religious garb to schools, educators seek to not only act consistently but also to safeguard all of their students, regardless of their beliefs, against bigotry, while affording them the freedom to practice their respective faiths, albeit outside of school.

LITIGATION

To date, most of the cases dealing with the wearing of religious garb in public schools have focused on forbidding teachers from wearing religious garb. For example, cases addressed whether Catholic nuns could wear habits in public schools (*O'Connor v. Hendrick*, 1906; *Gerhardt v. Heid*, 1936), whether a Sikh teacher could wear religious dress while teaching (*Cooper v. Eugene School District 4J*, 1986, 1987), whether a Muslim teacher could wear a hijab while teaching (*United States of America v. Board of Education for the School District of Philadelphia*, 1990), and whether a teacher could wear a T-shirt with a Christian message (*Downing v. West Haven Board of Education*, 2001). In all of these cases, the courts agreed that school boards were not violating the law by banning teachers from wearing religious garb while instructing class due to the need to maintain religious neutrality in public classrooms based on students' First Amendment rights guaranteed by the Establishment and Free Exercise Clauses of the Constitution.

Based on the First Amendment as applied in schools, students have the right to wear religious clothes to express their beliefs more freely than teachers. Yet, therein lies the basis for confusion—many cannot understand why students and teachers have different rights when it comes to wearing religious garb. Placing these differences aside, since teacher rights are subject to another debate in this volume (Chapter 18), schools should be religiously neutral zones for all people in today's world wherein educators and students alike should have to follow the same rules. It is interesting to note that to date, though, the Supreme Court has not heard a single dispute about students wearing religious garb in public schools.

In the limited number of cases involving students who sought to wear religious garb, courts have often entered judgments in their favor. One of the best-known disputes dealing with religious dress in public schools is *Cheema v. Thompson* (1995), a case about Sikh students in California who sought to wear to school ceremonial daggers under their clothing. The school board's defense was that it did not allow weapons on campus as part of a zero-tolerance policy. Even so, the Ninth Circuit ruled in favor of the students, arguing that First Amendment rights were violated and that the district needed a better zero-tolerance policy. In another case, a federal trial court in Texas decided that school officials violated the First Amendment rights of students to wear rosaries because they were a form of religious expression even though some in the school had worn them as a form of gang-related dress (*Chalifoux v. New Caney Independent School District*, 1997). These decisions aside, some have argued, as does this essay, that the courts in these cases should have deferred to the authority of local educational officials in allowing them to set standards for their own schools and districts.

ARGUMENTS AGAINST PERMITTING STUDENTS TO WEAR RELIGIOUS GARB
School Safety

In this post-Columbine and post-9/11 world, school safety, in particular in the context of these debates, is paramount. Sadly, some extremist groups across the globe have used religious garb to conceal weapons in clandestine attempts to hurt and kill innocent civilians, including school children. Just as the assailants in the Columbine school shooting wore trench coats to conceal guns, both foreign and domestic terrorists might seek to use religious garb to bring weapons on to school campuses. Thus, while in no way comparing religious garb with terror, any form of religious dress that could potentially conceal weapons, such as saris, cloaks, habits, robes, or burqas, should not be allowed in American public schools to ensure safety.

Against this backdrop, it is important to keep in mind that Americans have freedoms that are matched by relatively few nations; the two most important of these freedoms for this chapter deal with religion and speech. These freedoms are, after all, why the country was founded. As such, there has been much legislation in favor of maintaining students' religious rights as guaranteed by the First Amendment. For example, the Elementary and Secondary Education Act (ESEA), now the No Child Left Behind (NCLB) Act, addressed the constitutionality of students' right to religious expression in public schools that receive federal funding.

Both President Bill Clinton and President George W. Bush made public policy defending students' rights for freedom of religion and expression. During President Clinton's first term in office, in November 1993, Congress passed the Religious Freedom Restoration Act (RFRA) disallowing the government from limiting the religious expression rights of Americans. Although the Supreme Court ruled that the RFRA was unconstitutional in *City of Boerne, Texas v. Flores* (1997), Congress has since modified the statute to remedy the flaws that the justices pointed out. Moreover, states have enacted similar laws to protect religious freedom.

It is also worth noting that President Clinton made his decree in a pre-Columbine and pre-9/11 world. To put it simply, it was a less complex, perhaps safer, time. At their core, both tragedies encompassed intolerance. The Columbine massacre involved school bullying in a culture of violence, and 9/11 involved the continued Judeo-Christian/fundamental Islamic conflict, the Westernization of the globe, the economic dominance of capitalism, and the spread of democratic ideals around the world. Intolerance was at the center of the 9/11 tragedy and continues to live and grow in its aftermath.

Trying to combat the underpinnings of religious intolerance emerging in the American consciousness after the 9/11 attacks, while remaining true to the First Amendment, President George W. Bush, acting with congressional leaders, revised the ESEA and morphed it into the NCLB. The NCLB includes provisions that can remove federal funding from schools that infringe on students' religious rights. In March 2010, President Barack Obama laid out the blueprint to revise the ESEA/NCLB, but where the issue of religion in public school stands in this revision will not be known until the law moves further through the reauthorization process.

While Americans do not want to give up religious freedom, schools need to be safe for all students, teachers, staff, and administrators. Having campuses be religious-free zones is the only way to ensure safety and respect for all, regardless of beliefs, religion, or creed. That is, by seeking to exclude forms of religious dress or ornamentation that may divide students into different groups, thereby breeding the potential for violence and intolerance, educators can better keep schools as safe and orderly learning environments. In schools that are religious-free zones, educational officials can then focus their energies on education rather than regulating religious expressions that may lead to conflict between and among those with whom individuals or groups of students disagree.

Religious Neutrality and Tolerance

Today's schools face a significant dilemma. Educational institutions need to maintain safe campuses while respecting all religions, a daunting challenge in an increasingly diverse society. Given the reality of present-day America, many school boards outlaw religious clothing for students and faculty alike to maintain religiously neutral environments on campuses. The reality is that there are such diversities of opinion regarding religion in America that it can be difficult to accommodate all who are served by the public schools. School administrators face this challenge daily. By restricting religious garb on campuses, school officials are not practicing oppression but rather protecting individuals who wish to be free from religious symbolism and expression via dress. By keeping school campuses religiously neutral, school officials promote tolerance in the diverse American classrooms and campuses of the 21st century because they cannot be accused of favoring how students from one religious group dress when compared with others.

Sadly, religious differences have been the cause of many wars in history. Although some of the world's religions share core beliefs, religious intolerance is perpetuated throughout parts of the world. Even within mainstream religions, there are vast divisions of beliefs. According to the Central Intelligence Agency's *World Factbook*, as of 2007, a little over half of the American population was Protestant, and nearly a quarter was Roman Catholic. Jews made up fewer than 2% of the American population, and Buddhists and Muslims each made up less than 1% of the population. Additionally, close to 3% of Americans practiced some other, unspecified religion, a little over one tenth of Americans were unaffiliated with a religion, and slightly under 5% identified themselves as having no religion. Within the Christian religion alone, there are over 100 denominations with varying beliefs. Trying to accommodate the followers of all of these religions, even though they all fall under the general category of Christianity, is a difficult task. Further, in Islam, there are major theological differences between the Sunni and Shiite branches. Major wars are currently being fought over these theological divisions. Let one not forget agnosticism and atheism. There is no possible way that American schools can accommodate all religions within their walls. Since it does not appear to be feasible for public school officials to enact policies to accommodate the numerous religions observed by students, perhaps they should not even try to do so. Instead, they should just ban all religious garb.

In light of the rapidly increasing diversity in the American population, educational officials would be wise to preserve public schools as religious-free zones to respect all students' beliefs and promote an integrated society where no one group can stand out as more important than another, one wherein all students are treated equally.

Some students may wear religious items that others consider offensive, creating tension on school campuses. Administrators must then negotiate the legal rights of those students with the rights of those who are offended. Prohibiting all students from wearing all religious clothing to school should help to minimize or even eliminate such tensions on campuses.

As to a specific example, consider the Catholic rosary. To practicing Catholics, rosaries are prayer beads, religious items not used in many other Christian denominations. Moreover, rosaries may actually be offensive to some Christians who see their use as idolatry or worshiping a false god. Additionally, in recent years, rosaries have been affiliated with gangs because some gangs use them as symbols of membership. Thus, some school officials have sought to ban rosaries on campuses and have gone so far as suspending students for bringing them to school. However, as noted earlier, a federal trial court in Texas ruled that officials could not limit the rights of students to wear rosaries because they are religious symbols (*Chalifoux v. New Caney Independent School District*, 1997).

In recent years, students have been suspended for wearing crosses, having dreadlocks, donning African ethnic dress, and wearing gothic apparel—all for having violated school dress code policies, a subject of another debate in this series. School officials across the nation daily deal with the question of whether students have complied with dress code rules regardless of whether they are dressed in religious or other garb. Even so, when dealing with religious dress, in particular, what is offensive to one may be spiritual to another, so it is really a no-win situation. For this fact alone, educational officials should implement policies that place restrictions on wearing religious garb to school to limit conflict and intolerance of others in American public schools.

America could follow France's lead, where in 2004 Muslim girls and women were banned from wearing the hijab in public-sponsored organizations including schools. However, this regulation has been met with opposition. Muslims have claimed that they are being discriminated against because students are still allowed to wear Christian symbols such as the cross. Islamic girls have raised charges that they are ostracized and oppressed and go to such extremes as eating their lunches in secret places in the school, hidden from administrators, to wear their hijab to honor their religion and avoid punishment. Yet, America is not France. In America, all people are guaranteed the freedom of religion and expression. However, schools are not the platform for this expression. Schools must remain neutral to protect the religious freedoms of all students. Put another way, as noted, by having enacting policies requiring students dress in ways that do not highlight their religious differences, one can hope that schools can retain their neutrality by not favoring one religion over another. Such an approach may even help students better understand how they are more alike than different.

The list of controversial religious items is seemingly endless: crucifixes, crosses, fish, rosaries, prayer beads, yarmulkes, dreadlocks, pentagrams, Stars of David, hijabs, turbans, candy canes, Christmas trees, ankhs, pyramids, peace signs, zodiac constellations, wigs, tridents, bonnets, bindis, saris, prayer clothes, burqas, prayer shawls, totems, medicine wheels, medicine bags, bells, and shells. School officials cannot keep up with all of these and ways in which they may be displayed as parts of religious attire. Throw in tattooing, body piercing, body paint, and hairstyles, any and all of which can have religious connotations, and one can see that the various expressions of religions in America are far too vast for schools to regulate; therefore, school officials should not even attempt to do so. "Religion is too personal, too sacred, too holy, to permit" (*Engel*, 1962, p. 432) educational officials to decide which kinds of religious attire are acceptable. Accordingly, the only answer is to maintain public schools as religious neutral zones where all students are required to dress in nonreligious clothing.

CONCLUSION

In noting that Congress could neither pass laws about the establishment of a religion nor prohibit its free exercise, the Founders recognized the need for governmental neutrality with regard to matters of faith. Similarly, since the creation of public schools on a state-by-state basis in the mid-19th century, educational leaders realized early on that public schools must be religiously neutral. In adopting this approach, educational leaders, and eventually the courts, essentially adopted the Jeffersonian metaphor calling for a "wall of separation between church and state." This metaphor is important because Thomas Jefferson, founder of the University of Virginia, saw that in America, the government, now including public schools as an arm of the states, needed to stay out of religious affairs.

Educational theorists such as John Dewey in the early 20th century, a leader in the Progressive movement of education, prophesied the importance of tolerance in the pluralistic American classroom in his essay "Religion and Our Schools." Dewey understood that, ironically, to promote religious freedom and tolerance, religion had to stay out of the public domain. The wise educational philosopher saw that by removing religious division in the classrooms, American public schools had the opportunity not only to bring students from all religions together, but also to teach the highest moral values to students: that of unity, freedom of religion, and tolerance of all of people in the diverse American landscape. Thus, students should not be able to wear distinctive religious garb to public schools because it can have a divisive impact on all.

FURTHER READINGS AND RESOURCES

Central Intelligence Agency. (2007). *World factbook.* Retrieved from https://www.cia.gov/library/publications/the-world-factbook

Davis, D. H. (2004). Reacting to France's ban: Headscarves and other religious attire in American public schools. *Journal of Church and State, 43,* 221–233.

Dewey, J. (1908). Religion and our schools. *The Hibbert Journal, 6,* 800–807.

Gedicks, F. M. (2005). On the permissible scope of legal limitations on the freedom of religion or belief in the United States. *Emory International Law Review, 19,* 1187.

Jefferson, T. (1903). Letter to Danbury Baptist Association. In A. A. Lipscomb & A. E. Bergh (Eds.), *Writings of Thomas Jefferson* (Vol. 16, p. 281). Washington, DC: Issued under the auspices of the Thomas Jefferson Memorial Association of the United States. (Original work 1802)

Mazza, O. (2009). The right to wear headscarves and other religious symbols in Turkish, French, and American schools: How the government draws a veil on free expression of faith. *Journal of Catholic Legal Studies, 48,* 303–343.

Muslim girl suspended for head scarf. (2003, October 11). *CNN.com.* Retrieved from http://www.cnn.com/2003/EDUCATION/10/11/scarf.reut/index.html

Muslim track athlete disqualified over custom outfit. (2008, January 23). *Education Week,* p. 5.

Preston, J. (1999, August 25). Jewish boy can wear Star of David. *Pittsburgh Post Gazette,* p. A6.

Russo, C. J., & Hee, T. F. (2008). The right of students to wear religious garb in public schools: A comparative analysis of the United States and Malaysia. *Education and Law Journal, 18*(1), 1–19.

U.S. Department of Justice. (2004). *Justice Department reaches settlement agreement with Oklahoma school district in Muslim student headscarf case.* Retrieved from http://www.justice.gov/opa/pr/2004/May/04_crt_343.htm

U.S. Department of Justice. (2008). *Hate crime statistics, 2008.* Retrieved from http://www.fbi.gov/about-us/cjis/ucr/hate-crime/2008

Walterick, S. (2006) The prohibition of Muslim headscarves from French public schools and controversies surrounding the hijab in the Western world. *Temple International and Comparative Law Journal, 20,* 251–281.

COURT CASES AND STATUTES

A.A. *ex rel.* Betenbaugh v. Needville Independent School District, 611 F.3d 248 (5th Cir. 2010).
Alabama and Coushatta Tribes of Texas v. Trustees of the Big Sandy Independent School District, 817 F. Supp. 1319 (E.D. Tex. 1993), *remanded by* 20 F.3d 469 (5th Cir. 1994).
Brown v. Board of Education, 347 U.S. 483 (1954).
Chalifoux v. New Caney Independent School District, 976 F. Supp. 659 (S.D. Tex. 1997).
Cheema v. Thompson, 67 F.3d 883 (9th Cir. 1995).
City of Boerne, Texas v. Flores, 521 U.S. 507 (1997).
Cooper v. Eugene School District No. 4J, 723 P.2d 298 (Or. 1986), *appeal dismissed,* 480 U.S. 942 (1987).
Downing v. West Haven Board of Education, 163 F. Supp. 2d 19 (D. Conn. 2001).
Employment Division, Department of Human Resources of Oregon v. Smith, 494 U.S. 872 (1990).
Engel v. Vitale, 370 U.S. 432 (1962).
Gerhardt v. Heid, 267 N.W. 127 (N.D. 1936).
Goldman v. Weinberger, 475 U.S. 503 (1986).
Isaacs v. Board of Education of Howard County, Md., 40 F. Supp. 2d 335 (D. Md.1999).
No Child Left Behind Act, 20 U.S.C. §§ 6301 *et seq.*
O'Connor v. Hendrick, 184 N.Y. 421 (N.Y. 1906).
Pierce v. Society of Sisters, 268 U.S. 510 (1925).
Religious Apparel: Wearing While in Uniform, 10 U.S.C. § 774 (1987).
Religious Freedom Restoration Act, 42 U.S.C. §§ 2000bb *et seq.*
Tinker v. Des Moines Independent Community School District, 393 U.S. 503 (1969).
United States v. Board of Education for the School District of Philadelphia, 911 F.2d 882 (3d Cir. 1990).
Wisconsin v. Yoder, 406 U.S. 205 (1972).

18

Should teachers be allowed to wear distinctive religious garb in public schools?

POINT: Ally Ostrowski, *Rocky Mountain College of Art + Design*
COUNTERPOINT: Luke M. Cornelius, *University of North Florida*

OVERVIEW

Title VII of the Civil Rights Act and the First Amendment to the Constitution protect public school employees from religious discrimination. Religious discrimination occurs when employees are treated unfavorably due to their religious beliefs. Title VII protects individuals who belong to traditional, organized religions, such as Christianity, Judaism, Buddhism, Hinduism, and Islam, as well as those who have sincerely held religious, ethical, or moral beliefs but do not subscribe or belong to an organized religion.

Pursuant to Title VII, employers must make reasonable accommodations for the religious beliefs or practices of their employees unless doing so causes them significant difficulty or expense. In this way, school boards are required to make reasonable adjustments to work environments to allow employees to practice their religions. One frequently requested accommodation may entail the dress or grooming practices that employees follow for religious reasons. By way of example, some employees may don particular religious garments such as head coverings or wear certain hairstyles or facial hair for religious reasons. By the same token, some employees may be prohibited from wearing certain garments because of their religious dictates insofar as their clothing may unduly influence students. Yet, as evidenced in the following debates, some maintain that if it does not pose an undue hardship, it may not be unreasonable for school boards to grant employees certain requested dress or grooming accommodations.

Litigation on the question of whether teachers can wear religious garments, symbols, or emblems while teaching in the public schools has reached mixed results often depending on specific fact situations. In two early cases, state courts in North Dakota and Kentucky refused to prohibit public school teachers from wearing religious dress or emblems in their classrooms (*Gerhardt v. Heid*, 1936; *Rawlings v. Butler*, 1956). On the other hand, courts in Mississippi, New York, Oregon, and Pennsylvania upheld regulations banning public school teachers from wearing religious clothing while performing their official duties (*Commonwealth v. Herr*, 1910; *Cooper v. Eugene School District No. 4J*, 1986; *McGlothin v. Jackson Municipal Separate School District*, 1992; *O'Connor v. Hendrick*, 1906; *United States v. Board of Education of the School District of Pennsylvania*, 1990). These courts acknowledged that school officials need to be neutral when it comes to religion while recognizing that young children can be impressionable and could view the teachers' wearing of religious garments as a governmental endorsement of religion.

The essays in this chapter revolve around the concepts of separation of church and state and teachers' own First Amendment rights to practice their religions. It is well accepted today that teachers cannot use their official positions to proselytize or indoctrinate children with their own religious beliefs and concepts. On the other hand, many are of the opinion that teachers should be able to adhere to their religious tenets quietly while in their classroom and that being able to accept public employment should not mean that they must put aside important elements of their religious practices.

In the point essay, Ally Ostrowski (Rocky Mountain College of Art + Design) concedes that laws and judicial opinions prohibiting teachers from wearing religious garb in public schools have the noble purpose of protecting children while encouraging religious neutrality. Yet, she questions whether garb prohibitions really accomplish this goal and asks why teachers should not have the same right as students. In this respect, Ostrowski maintains that there is a difference between teachers simply wearing clothing that is emblematic of their religious beliefs and their explaining to their students why they wear specific garments or symbols. She suggests that school systems should not ban the wearing of religious garments simply because the potential exists that teachers may cross the line and take advantage of students' questions to explain their religious beliefs. Ostrowski concludes that bans on teachers' wearing religious garb in public school classrooms, based on the concept that students could be easily indoctrinated by such a practice, are antiquated and unsubstantiated.

In the counterpoint essay, Luke M. Cornelius (University of North Florida) argues that the need for school systems to maintain religious neutrality and nonendorsement restricts teachers from any activities that may tend to evangelize or proselytize specific faiths or creeds, including the wearing of religious garments or emblems. In this respect, Cornelius states that teachers' constitutional right to the free exercise of their religion must be subordinated in the classroom to protect the nonendorsement and religious neutrality of the school. He points out that insofar as public employment is a privilege, not a right, all teachers are free to accept or reject the terms of offered employment contracts but are not free to substitute their right of free expression and personal liberty for a school's overall mission of providing a religiously neutral public education. Further, he argues that teachers may use their positions to interfere with the rights of their students to an education free of religious indoctrination and sectarian influence.

In reading these essays, it may be helpful to reflect on the following questions: What constitutes religious garb? Does the fact that a public school teacher wears a religious garment or a symbol indicate that the school is endorsing that teacher's religion? Should teachers be required to give up some of their own religious freedom when they accept public employment? Should there be different rules for teachers and students regarding the display of religious symbols or emblems?

Allan G. Osborne, Jr.
Principal (Retired), Snug Harbor Community School,
Quincy, Massachusetts

POINT: Ally Ostrowski
Rocky Mountain College of Art + Design

American public school education often involves a delicate balance of conflicting issues, particularly concerning the dynamics between students and teachers in classrooms. Even an issue as basic as teacher attire or the right of teachers to wear religious garb in their classrooms has become a battleground between individual freedom of speech and expression with ensuring the separation between church and state. Currently, an array of states, including Nebraska, New York, and Pennsylvania, and Oregon, prohibit public school teachers from wearing religious garb in their classrooms. The purpose of these laws was to ensure religious neutrality in classrooms while making sure that no particular religious sect would control the education of American children. Although the initial intent of the laws was a noble concept, that is, protecting children from religious indoctrination in an atmosphere where they are vulnerable to authority, the continued applicability of the laws is debatable. As such, this essay stands for the proposition that public school teachers should be free to wear religious garb to work.

HISTORY AND BACKGROUND

The religious garb laws were written during the late 1800s specifically to restrict Catholic nuns who traditionally donned religious robes and habits while teaching in religious schools from taking positions in public schools. However, over time, as religious expression in the United States has evolved, the laws have been expanded beyond Catholicism and have been applied to teachers who wear headscarves or turbans and crucifixes or other attire with religious symbolism. In fact, a great deal of controversy has arisen regarding the rights of teachers to be able to express religiosity or affiliation through articles of clothing and the rights of students to receive a public education minus cues of religious expression from their teachers.

Historically, the religious garb laws were not shameful endeavors. The United States was firmly established on the division between issues of the church and issues of state, including the public education system. This separation allowed students from all religious traditions to receive a free and religiously unbiased general education to prepare them for future careers and lives as American citizens. Still, as American society continues to diversify, the antiquated laws designed to protect vulnerable children from religious indoctrination in school can now be interpreted as targeting teachers with strong religious beliefs as well as preventing the open discussion of diversity and difference in a time when these discussions are paramount to the nation's future.

THE RIGHTS OF TEACHERS

As reflected in another debate in this volume (Chapter 17), controversy has emerged over freedom of religious expression for students who seek to wear headscarves or other religious garb under an array of federal and state statutes. So, too, questions emerge over the rights of teachers to wear religious garb as they see fit. The prohibitions against permitting teachers to wear religious garb in their classrooms was meant to protect students and encourage religious neutrality in classrooms. Yet, in doing so, this provision violates the freedom of expression for teachers in a most profound and primal manner. The fact that public schools have so directly aimed their lens at teachers who wear religious garb could also be viewed as discrimination and an attack on certain religious traditions. Islam, for example, proscribes that women of faith dress modestly and cover their hair from public gaze. A Catholic woman of faith can likely feel that she is fulfilling the tenets of her tradition by wearing a small crucifix necklace that can even be hidden behind a shirt collar, but a practicing Muslim woman does not have this luxury. The Muslim woman either must choose between fulfilling what is expected of her religious faith and what is dictated to be appropriate by her employer.

Male teachers are faced with similar conundrums. An Orthodox Jewish man is required by Jewish law to wear a tzitzit, a religious undershirt with visible tassels, after reaching the age of 3. Conservative, Orthodox, and Hassidic Jewish men also typically cover their heads when outside their homes. Similarly, Sikh men cover their heads in a traditional turban, wear a silver bangle on their right wrist, and carry a small dagger as symbols of their religious tradition. These men of faith, again, must make the choice between fulfilling their religious obligations and being able to educate children in the American public school system, at least according to how the laws are currently interpreted. In the growing drought of qualified and passionate public school teachers, the American public school system cannot afford to continue to discriminate against prospective teachers who express their religious convictions through religious clothing.

Even though public school teachers perform their duty in service to the American educational system, they are still citizens who are entitled to the same laws protecting freedom of expression, as long as these liberties do not infringe on the rights of others. This raises two issues. The first question becomes partly whether teachers who wear religious garb actually do infringe on the separation of church and state and the ability of students to be free from religious coercion.

The other issue is whether it is constitutionally prudent to privilege the rights of students to be free of any religious paraphernalia in the classrooms over the rights of their teachers to express identifying symbols of religious faith through their clothing. Typically, individuals who choose to don religious apparel or symbolism do so because their religious beliefs are deeply ingrained into the individual's self-concept and identity. To some, asking teachers to remove religious garb so as not to bring religious symbolism and discourse into classrooms might seem trite. In this view, teachers are not being asked to abandon their adherence to a religious tradition, just the outward signs of sectarian affiliation. At the same time, to teachers with religious convictions that are integral to their sense of self, this is asking them to hide part of their identities under the guise of upholding the values of the American constitution. However, as religious strife, accompanied by significant violence, occurs in many parts of the world, it is arguable that keeping religious expression and religious symbolism out of classrooms simply perpetuates the ignorance and fear concerning religious difference instead of using the classrooms as a location to explore issues of diversity and tolerance.

Students in their American public educational systems are constitutionally protected from the infringement of religious doctrine or beliefs. In other words, parents can send their children to public schools without worrying that they are being introduced to or indoctrinated into a religious belief system. One of the prominent ways that state governments, at least a few, have conceptualized protecting this freedom is by preventing teachers from wearing religious paraphernalia in the classroom. Yet, do teachers donning hijabs or allowing the tzitzits to be exposed really equate to religious indoctrination? This line of inquiry assumes that mere exposure is equated with religious programming, and that is an unsubstantiated argument. These regulations were constructed without solid evidence that teachers' donning religious attire would actually have influence on student perceptions of religion and instead were based on conjecture and speculation, not to mention fear of rampant religious inoculation through the school system. It is certainly possible that teachers who wear religious garb might cross the line of merely wearing their religious symbols to explaining their origins and how they relate to the tenets of their particular faith. Still, it is the subsequent discussion regarding the religious tradition that becomes inappropriate rather than the donning of religious symbolism. This issue, then, falls under teacher conduct rather than teacher attire.

It can also be argued that the perceived power instructors have over students is age based. Put another way, while very young children typically look to adults as authority figures, teenagers are less likely to emulate behavior exhibited by teachers. Moreover, it is questionable whether teachers wearing religious symbolism actually have any effect at all on the religious liberties of students. In the modern area of mediated experiences, it is highly unlikely that children are merely captive audiences soaking up whatever teachers offer to them.

Children at even the youngest of ages are exposed to a wide array of stimuli and learn to filter content. If discussions concerning the religious attire do not occur in classrooms, it is more likely that students will direct questions regarding religious symbolism to their parents. It is then the prerogative of parents to direct how they desire their children to understand and interpret religious symbolism of religious traditions. It has been indicated that even discussing different religious beliefs might be impinging on the separation of church and state. In this vein, it is likely that very young children might ask teachers to explain why they are wearing religious garb with which they may not be familiar. Even so, this issue is highly dependent on the region of the country and diversified landscape with which students are already familiar.

Much of the violence across the world stems from misunderstandings and unawareness surrounding the religious beliefs of those of other faiths. Considering this, it is unethical to turn a blind eye to religious differences, particularly where the education of the future generation of citizens and leaders is concerned. Children need to be educated in environments where differences are not ignored. By allowing teachers of all religious backgrounds to express themselves through religious paraphernalia, it is likely that students will learn to appreciate and accept diverse points of view through mere exposure. Likewise, students should be afforded the opportunity to have religion be part of their educational environment without it being obliterated as a rampant infection. While religion has no direct role in public school education, the American public school system can no longer take a passive role in teaching the value of difference and diversity and should at least present religion as a "nonissue" for students and teachers rather than a prohibited element in the public school system.

This does not mean that religion should be brought into the daily conversation in American public schools, either. Yet, teachers, as individual citizens, should be allowed to wear religious garb to their place of employment. Teachers should be placed into their classrooms because of their qualifications to teach and not based on their clothing or their willingness to shed all outward signs of religious affiliation for employment. The presumption that students are captive audiences in public school classrooms, open and ready to be indoctrinated with religious beliefs through their teacher wearing a headscarf or a crucifix, is antiquated and unsubstantiated. Contemporary public school classrooms should move to the forefront of discussions concerning diversity and inclusivity, and these battles should include the expression of religion through religious garb.

RESPONSE TO COUNTERPOINT ESSAY

The counterpoint essay provides some excellent arguments from the perspective of jurisprudence but offers a limited perspective that does not take into account current research from the sociological and psychological perspectives on the American educational system. First, the young people of the modern era possess unique characteristics in their environment and social realm that combine to establish a distinct educational experience. It is inaccurate to presuppose that the psychological composition, maturity level, and exposure to stimuli of modern young people mirror those of children during the 1800s when many of these laws were originally fashioned. Contemporary youth rely on the Internet, television, radio, and social media for current affairs information and entertainment and through the glut of media are, when compared to past generations, exposed to levels of diversity and difference that were probably unthinkable not long ago. Thus, due to such far-ranging exposure, contemporary youth are not as readily influenced as students may have been in the past.

Second, this essay is not contending that discrimination has been banished from all public schools. To the contrary, this essay suggests that the American public school systems could and should play a more pivotal role in bringing issues of prejudice and intolerance to the forefront of discussion among youth. Modern American classrooms provide a fertile ground to raise issues of tolerance and discrimination, but champions of the garb laws would prevent the topic from being broached, even at the symbolic level through a religious symbol. Recent research proposes that by erasing all presence of any type of religious expression from an environment, the individuals, in this case children, are actually more likely to express less tolerance toward religion when it is expressed in other situations. This is not the original intent of the separation of church and state and, in fact, might actually be engendering the opposite effect in America's children.

Third, the supposed direct effects of teachers' wearing religious clothing on the opinions of their students have been relatively unsubstantiated and instead serve as relics from a time of fervent struggle over religious and secular education. Even if it can be assumed that teachers' wearing religious paraphernalia in their schools has the subliminal potential to indoctrinate the ripe minds of impressionable American youth, the age of the supposed victims and potential effects must be problematized. In legal discourse, the age of the student in question is also a significant variable for the application and interpretation of the religious garb laws. In *Board of Education of Westside Community Schools v. Mergens* (1990), the Supreme Court determined that there was indeed a distinction between the ability of younger children and older teens to distinguish between attempts of promoting a religious viewpoint and tolerating the presence of religious symbolism. Therefore, whether teachers should be able to wear clothing and artifacts of a religious nature should also be based on the age of the students and not be prohibited under the blanket assumption that all students are being subjected to religious coercion.

Additionally, the counterpoint essay strictly admonishes the rights of the teachers to express their religious inclinations as privileges, which are superseded by their role as an employee of the state. Yet, under the *Lemon* test that emerged in *Lemon v. Kurtzman* (1971), an interpretation of the religious garb laws suggests that, at least at the high school level, the intent behind wearing the symbolism in a public school setting is the key. The *Lemon* test basically suggests that students are more mature and able to distinguish between individual attitudes toward religion and a state-endorsed religiousness in high schools, and that as long as the teacher is not wearing the religious garb with the intent to promote a particular faith, then their individual ability to wear the artifact should be upheld. If the intent behind wearing religious garb is indeed to constantly engender religiously orientated conversations with students where one tradition is favored, then the teacher would be infringing on the students' rights to a public education free from religious programming. Yet, the *Lemon* test has been relegated to application at the local court level, and it is uncertain whether this perspective would be upheld if applied to a case at a higher court.

Finally, while the counterpoint essay provides excellent documentation to substantiate a legal rationale to prevent teachers from wearing religious symbolism in public schools, current literature from other, possibly related, disciplines questions the veracity of the original underpinnings of the law and suggests that prohibiting teachers from wearing religious garb is actually a much more complex issue that lies beyond the scope of legal theory alone. The world is changing, and with it the American educational system needs to evolve as well. American students need a safe place to learn, to grow, and to be taught how to function as the future American workforce and future American citizens. Included in both of these areas is the requirement of tolerance, exposure to diversity, and the ability to appreciate pluralism.

COUNTERPOINT: Luke M. Cornelius
University of North Florida

A major obstacle to supporting bans on conspicuous religious clothing for public school teachers is their rather dark origins in the Nativist Movement of the 1920s. Indeed, there is a great deal of irony in watching the last state laws formally banning such dress, which were adopted at the urging of anti-Catholic groups and the Ku Klux Klan, being defended by liberal pro-separation groups such as the American Civil Liberties Union. Additionally, it must be acknowledged that any limitations on dress of a religious nature can invoke great difficulties in not only defining clothing as pervasively religious but also in distinguishing such garments from nonreligious attire. For example, it may be hard for officials in American schools to uphold bans on hijabs, the head scarves worn by Muslim women, while allowing similar wrappings for teachers undergoing chemotherapy. Perhaps the best argument against such policies is the great difficulty in determining just what clothing constitutes distinctive religious garb as opposed to that which is either innocuous or worn for nonreligious purposes. This counterpoint essay recognizes that it can be difficult weighing conflicting understandings of exactly what constitutes religious garb. Even so, this essay agrees with the excellent arguments that remain in favor of imposing and retaining bans against allowing public school teachers to wear distinctive religious dress in the workplace.

ARGUMENTS IN FAVOR OF BANS

At the heart of the objections to teachers' wearing religious garb in public schools is the Establishment Clause of the First Amendment to the Constitution, which forbids state establishment or endorsement of religion. The Supreme Court and its subordinate tribunals have long held that activities such as school prayer, denominational instruction within public schools, and even the facilitation of student-led religious activities during school functions are unconstitutional. In essence, the need for schools to maintain religious neutrality and nonendorsement restricts them from any activities that may tend to evangelize or proselytize specific faiths or creeds. Even when teachers avoid any direct verbal or symbolic evangelism, certain highly distinctive types of religious clothing inevitably evokes student curiosity and even inspiration. It is not too much to suggest that impressionable children who greatly admire particular teachers dressed as nuns might aspire to that vocation, even if they are not in some cases Catholic. Likewise, teenagers who are rebelling against their parents, an archetype of American adolescence, might well take an interest in researching the meaning and beliefs embodied in a sympathetic teacher's pentacle or pentagram displayed on a necklace.

One thing that separates teachers from other adults and public employees is the expectation that they serve as role models for children and that they will model not only behavior but also proper dress and grooming to their students. Many federal circuit courts have recognized that while dress and grooming may represent protected personal liberty interests in general, school districts can generally supersede these rights by arguing the need for teachers to model appropriate professional appearance and behavior. Likewise, as the Supreme Court has clearly established in school prayer cases, the constitutional right to free exercise of religion by teachers as citizens must be subordinated in the workplace to protect the nonendorsement and religious neutrality of the schools themselves. Analogies cannot be drawn to other types of public employment. As recognized in nearly all constitutional rulings affecting public schools, schools are in special circumstances in which immature and often impressionable children are compelled by the power of the state to serve as captive audiences for their teachers and other school personnel. It is important to keep in mind that adults dealing with license examiners wearing hijabs cannot be remotely compared with impressionable fifth-graders who may be subjected daily to their teachers' burqa or Buddhist monastic robes.

Perhaps key to this issue has been the attitude of the courts. In *Roberts v. Madigan* (1990), the Tenth Circuit court held that a reading teacher who was expected to model reading during class time was in violation of the Establishment Clause as he usually read the Bible during reading time. If silently reading the Bible to oneself in front of students can be considered evangelism, then how much more so is the wearing of a nun's habit or a *thawb*, an ankle-length garment worn in many Arabic nations, in front of students 6 to 8 hours a day, 180 days a year? It is perhaps for this reason that, even as state statutes covering religious garb are repealed, courts generally uphold the authority of school boards to limit religious clothing that can be worn by staff in their classrooms and offices. Additionally, it should be noted here that a general ban on explicitly sectarian clothing saves school board officials and their administrators from charges of favoring one faith over another or trying to determine what religious attire is too distinctive. School administrators should not be put in the position of deciding that a hijab is permissible but a *dastar*, headgear worn by male members of the Sikh faith, is too much.

At the same time, it should be remembered that one of the key elements undergirding the separation of church and state is the protection of religious minorities. Perhaps the nun's habit or clerical collar would cause little disruption in a pervasively Catholic school system, but what of the effects on non-Catholics? In much the way segregated schools communicated a subtle, yet devastating, implication of inferiority to minority youth, might not the display of dominant religious affiliation send similar messages to noncongregant children? Given that religious minorities are often forced to resort to legal remedies to resist the unwelcome imposition of majority religious views in schools, permitting the increased introduction of distinctive religious elements into schools will, at the very least, do little to reduce First Amendment litigation against school districts.

Of course, there is then the question of fairness and potential disruption of the religious garb of teachers who espouse minority, esoteric, or controversial religions. Perhaps in the aforementioned predominantly Catholic school district, the presence of a Catholic priest wearing the distinctive white clerical collar and black suit would cause little or no disruption to the actual operation of the schools. Yet, what if a teacher in the same district were to don the black clerical collar adopted by some self-styled satanic high priests? Like nearly all well-intentioned ideas, the opening of schools to religious dress opens them as well to charges of favoritism, discrimination, and religious controversy. Given the outcry in some schools toward the hugely popular *Harry Potter* books, one can only imagine the reaction of some parents to an actual "Dumbledore" or "McGonagall" in their child's classroom.

This, in turn, leads to the question of disruption and fairness in regulating teacher religious dress. Leaving aside religions that require weapons as part of their garb or those that observe certain holy days in the nude, which invoke other areas of the law as barriers, there can be little doubt that some religious dress has the potential, depending on the student population, to cause disruption to the school and perhaps even undermine the teacher's authority. The maintenance of religious neutrality not only protects children and their families from unwanted religious messages but also protects the authority of school personnel from religious prejudice as well. Again, there are numerous possibilities to contemplate. It is hard enough for many educators to establish their authority in general. These difficulties would only multiply if a teacher in a yarmulke or tzitzit were confronted by several openly and aggressively anti-Semitic students.

Should school boards really attempt to create regimes in which they welcome summer Bible school golf shirts while trying to rationalize restrictions on Jewish, Druidic, or Muslim clothing as being too disruptive? As in all situations proposing greater public accommodation of religion, and especially in schools, it should always be remembered that there are very few constituents in the school community who truly want greater religious expression in schools. Many proponents of accommodation want only their own religious beliefs and traditions, or perhaps those that are relatively similar to their own, in the schools. When confronted by alternative or disliked faiths, such constituents are just as likely to fall back on strict separation and demand school authorities remove the offensive apparel, and possibly the offending teacher, from the classroom.

As previously mentioned, at present, few legal objections exist to maintaining a ban on teachers working in highly distinctive religious garb. Even in the absence of state statutes, federal and state courts have generally upheld the power of school boards to regulate employee dress in general and religious expression in particular. Numerous judicial opinions have found a reasonable basis for these restrictions based on many of the arguments laid out already. Indeed, in the well-known *East Hartford Education Association v. Board of Education* (1977) case, the Second Circuit established that teacher dress was a liberty interest that could be subordinated to the legitimate needs and interests of school boards in carrying out their primary mission of educating students. This case further serves as a reminder that public employment of any sort, including teaching, is a privilege, not a right. Prospective employees are free to accept or reject the terms of teacher contracts. These applicants are not free, though, to substitute their right of free expression and personal liberty for a board's overall mission of providing a religiously neutral public education, nor may they use their positions to interfere with the rights of their students to such an education free of religious indoctrination and sectarian influence.

To be certain, exceptions can and should be made. Not all religious clothing is distinctively sectarian. In Pennsylvania, by way of illustration, where much of the precedent upholding restrictions on teacher religious garb have been made, two relatively recent decisions stand out. In one, it was determined that a Muslim female teacher who wore a head scarf was not clearly in violation of state law or the Constitution as the mere wearing of a generic, brightly colored scarf was not sufficiently distinctive to indicate her religious motivation. Likewise, it was determined that the mere wearing of modest personal religious jewelry, such as a crucifix or Star of David pendant, was not so egregious as to constitute a violation of the separation of church and state. It is therefore still possible to accommodate some free exercise rights of public school teachers while still also protecting students from undue religious influence and indoctrination.

RESPONSE TO POINT ESSAY

The point essay raises some novel issues and arguments. The point essay raises the contention, without any apparent evidence, that restrictions on teacher religious garb are relics of a bygone era that are no longer needed as religious prejudice and intolerance have been successfully banished from American schools. The point essay also suggests that modern schoolchildren are more resistant to adult religious influence than those of a century ago. Further, the point essay suggests that rebellious adolescents are, by mere dint of their age, less suggestible than younger children. Yet, the point essay offers no basis for these claims, making their evaluation difficult.

Certainly, any review of recent First Amendment jurisprudence involving religion and schools suggests, if anything, that classrooms are increasingly becoming prime battlegrounds of the culture wars in this country. To posit that permitting teachers to model minority, and possibly esoteric, religious traditions will result in well-received lessons in diversity and tolerance appears, at the very least, somewhat naïve. Nor should it be the role of teachers who represent a majority or more widely accepted faiths to further marginalize the children of other religions by suggesting that their beliefs bear the imprimatur of their schools and the state. Legal experience suggests that such displays of religious faith in the classroom are more likely to result in litigation as opposed to tolerance.

In addition, the point essay suggests that these laws somehow deprive teachers of fundamental rights. This assertion ignores the distinction between teachers' rights as citizens and their responsibilities as agents of the state. As previously referenced, in the First Circuit ruling in *East Hartford Education Association*, the court clearly ruled that the expressive rights of teachers to dress as they wished were subordinate to the school board's needs. In that case, the reasoning that teachers should model professional dress and behavior was more than sufficient to outweigh any individual interests of the employees. The analogy of student to staff rights is clearly faulty. Students attend school, under legal compulsion, as citizens. Teachers are there, by their own choice, as employees with a duty to advance the employer's mission without bringing personal agendas into the classroom that distract from that mission. It must be restated that public employment, like all employment, is a privilege, not a right. Under the Constitution, no citizen is ever compelled to abandon his or her sincerely held beliefs. However, when the free exercise of those beliefs comes into conflict with her role as an agent of the state, then it may be that the employee's free exercise precludes her from a position in which her free exercise may conflict with the rights of others.

The point essay's argument acknowledges that what teachers wear can be as instructive as what they say. Applying this logic, why would it be any more permissible or constitutional for teachers to model their faith by their clothing as to incorporate it in their lesson plans? It must be stated at this point that these laws were enacted, for less than tolerant purposes, at a time when First Amendment law, especially in the area of church and state, was far less developed.

Modern jurisprudence suggests that even if Nativist Era state bans on religious garb were repealed, it is not at all clear that modern First Amendment precedents, such as the three-pronged *Lemon* test, would permit such religious clothing in the public sector. When one considers the constitutional restrictions that the Supreme Court has imposed on prayer, curriculum, and school events in public schools, there appears very little space for accommodating pervasively sectarian clothing worn by public school employees. For instance, a federal trial court in Texas, on remand from Fifth Circuit, found that a "Clergy in Schools" program, where members of the local clergy were invited to meet with students to provide generic counseling, was clearly unconstitutional (*Oxford v. Beaumont Independent School District*, 2002). The court reached this outcome despite the fact that the clergy in question were under instructions to neither proselytize their faith nor wear any religiously identifiable clothing. Given such precedent, it is hard to see where there would be any legal room for school board employees to wear pervasively religious garments on the job when the First Amendment restricts even the presence of nonemployee religious persons absent such wear.

Rather, the point essay suggests that these laws, regardless of their original intent, actually constitute a rational effort by states to help schools avoid complex First Amendment litigation that permitting such teacher garb is almost certain to generate. An excellent example of this principle can be found in the opinion of the Supreme Court of Oregon in *Cooper v. Eugene School District 4J* (1997). Here, the court considered a 1965 law banning religious dress when teachers were engaged in their public duties. The court upheld the law as a valid enactment designed to preserve religious neutrality in public schools and to avoid creating even an inadvertent suggestion that the school or the state endorsed the specific religious beliefs of some of its teachers by permitting them to dress in a pervasively sectarian manner. As has occurred in similar cases in other states, the court viewed the law as a legitimate and viewpoint-neutral enactment to avoid the very controversy that so often attends religious expression in public schools. *Cooper* reaffirms, explicitly, the oft-stated rationale for religious neutrality in recognizing the importance of leaving children's religious instruction and exposure to their families and not to public agencies and their employees. *Cooper* also reiterated the previously mentioned doctrine that restrictions on religious garb do not impair the free exercise rights of teachers as citizens, but rather only their personal expression when they accept a position of public trust and employment.

In this regard, it is important to remember the fundamental constitutional concepts that underpin the Bill of Rights in general and the separation of church and state in particular. In creating a regime of individual protections from the power and influence of government, it is not relevant whether the religious dress of teachers might engender a stimulating or useful discussion of diversity and tolerance. What matters is whether such attire improperly influences, offends, or distracts individual students or infringes on their parents' rights to control and direct the religious education of their children. It is for this reason that bans on religious clothing serve as a rational, and even constitutionally mandatory, policy to protect the rights of all students against even incidental improper influence from a handful of teachers who would seek to impose their rights as paramount to those of others within the school community.

Further Readings and Resources

Ado, A. (2008). Note: The legal status of hijab in the United States: A look at the sociopolitical influences on the legal right to wear the Muslim headscarf. *Hastings Race & Poverty Law Journal, 5,* 441.

Blum, V. C. (1955). Religious garb in the public schools: A study in conflicting liberties. *The University of Chicago Law Review, 22*(4), 888–895.

First Amendment Center. (2004). *A teacher's guide to religion in the public schools.* Nashville, TN: Author.

Holscher, K. (2011). Contesting the veil in America: Catholic habits and the controversy over religious clothing in the United States. *Journal of Church and State, 53*(4).

Kiracofe, C. R. (2010). Can teachers really wear that to school? Religious garb in public classrooms. *The Clearing House, 83,* 80–83.

MacMullen, I. (1997). *Faith in schools? Autonomy, citizenship, and religious education in the liberal state.* Princeton, NJ: Princeton University Press.

Swanson, R. A. (1994). The constitutionality of "garb laws" in the content of the public high school. *Journal of Law and Education, 23*(4), 549–569.

White, K. R. (2009). Connecting religion and teacher identity: The unexplored relationship between teachers and religion in public schools. *Teaching and Teacher Education, 25,* 857–866.

Court Cases and Statutes

Board of Education of Westside Community Schools v. Mergens, 496 U.S. 226 (1990).
Civil Rights Act of 1964, Title VII, 42 U.S.C. § 2000e *et seq.* (2006).
Commonwealth v. Herr, 78 A. 68 (Pa. 1910).
Cooper v. Eugene School District No. 4J, 723 P.2d 296 (Or. 1986), *appeal dismissed,* 480 U.S. 942 (1997).
Doe by Doe v. Beaumont Independent School District, 240 F.3d 462 (5th Cir. 2001).
East Hartford Education Association v. Board of Education, 562 F.2d 838 (2d Cir. 1977).
Gerhardt v. Heid, 267 N.W. 127 (N.D. 1936).
Lemon v. Kurtzman, 403 U.S. 602 (1971).
McGlothin v. Jackson Municipal Separate School District, 829 F. Supp. 853 (S.D. Mss. 1992).
Nichol v. Arin Intermediate Unit 28, 268 F. Supp. 2d 536 (W.D. Pa. 2003).
O'Connor v. Hendrick, 77 N.E. 612 (N.Y. 1906).
Oxford v. Beaumont Independent School District, 224 F. Supp. 2d 1099 (E.D. Tex. 2002).
Rawlings v. Butler, 290 S.W.2d 801 (Ky. 1956).
Roberts v. Madigan, 921 F.2d 1047 (10th Cir. 1990), *cert. denied,* 505 U.S. 1218 (1992).
United States v. Board of Education of the School District of Pennsylvania, 911 F.2d 882 (3d Cir. 1990).
Widmar v. Vincent, 454 U.S. 263 (1981).

INDEX

Note: Bolded numbers refer to volume numbers in the Debating Issues in American Education series.

AACTE. *See* American Association of Colleges for Teacher Education
Aaronson, Daniel, **9:**110
ABA. *See* Applied behavior analysis
Abbott v. Burke, **3:**182
Ability grouping, **3:**149–166
  achievement and, **3:**163–164
  alternatives to, **3:**157–158
  bases, **3:**149–150, **3:**158, **3:**164–165
  benefits of, **3:**150–151, **3:**153–154, **3:**159–160, **3:**164
  definition, **3:**152, **3:**159
  desegregation and, **3:**151, **3:**162
  distinction from tracking, **3:**149, **3:**152, **3:**159, **3:**165–166
  in elementary schools, **3:**152, **3:**155–156, **3:**160
  flexible, **3:**164, **3:**165
  history, **3:**152–153
  minority students and, **3:**155–156, **3:**162
  opposition, **3:**151, **3:**152, **3:**154–157, **3:**162–163
  research on, **3:**153–154, **3:**155–157, **3:**163–164
  types, **3:**160
  use of, **3:**149, **3:**152
  See also Tracking
Abuse and neglect
  definitions, **5:**92, **5:**96
  effects, **5:**92, **5:**93–94
  identifying, **5:**94, **5:**95, **5:**100, **5:**101
  investigations, **5:**94–95, **5:**97, **5:**102
  prevalence, **5:**90
  prevention, **5:**99, **5:**103
  in schools, **5:**95
  sexual abuse, **5:**92, **5:**95, **5:**97–98
Abuse and neglect reporting
  concerns about, **5:**96–97, **5:**100–101, **5:**102–103
  confidentiality, **5:**96–97
  failures to report, **5:**100–101, **5:**102
  federal laws, **5:**90, **5:**96, **5:**99
  frequency, **5:**99
  in good faith, **5:**90, **5:**97
  legal cases, **5:**97–98
  mandatory reporters, **5:**xxvi, **5:**89, **5:**91, **5:**93–94, **5:**96–97, **5:**99–104
  mistaken reports, **5:**90–91, **5:**102
  moral obligations, **5:**93–94, **5:**98–99
  obligations, **5:**xxvi, **5:**89–104
  overreporting, **5:**102
  state laws, **5:**89, **5:**96, **5:**98
ACA. *See* American Counseling Association
Academic calendars. *See* Holidays; School years
Academic dishonesty
  disciplinary process, **5:**127–132, **5:**134–135, **5:**136–138
  distinction from conduct violations, **5:**126–128, **5:**132, **5:**134–135
  offenses, **5:**126
  prevalence, **5:**126, **5:**132
  underlying factors, **5:**125, **5:**126, **5:**127–131, **5:**133–135
  See also Plagiarism
Academic freedom
  collective bargaining and, **8:**256–257
  curricular decisions and, **8:**xxi, **8:**1–19
  definition, **8:**1, **8:**4
  denial, **8:**2, **8:**11
  free speech and, **8:**1–3
  history, **8:**1, **8:**4, **8:**9–10
  legal cases, **8:**2–3, **8:**4
  societal value, **8:**5, **8:**204
  in teacher training programs, **2:**48–49
Academic integrity, promoting, **5:**127, **5:**132, **5:**135–138
Academic Integrity Framework (AIF), **5:**135–138
Academic performance
  ability grouping and, **3:**163–164
  accountability and, **9:**1–19
  arts education and, **2:**145–146, **2:**152
  of charter school students, **1:**10, **1:**11–14, **6:**279–280, **6:**289, **7:**137, **7:**215
  choice programs and, **1:**104–105, **6:**270
  effects of corporal punishment use, **5:**113
  gender of teacher and, **3:**269–270
  of homeless students, **8:**136–137, **8:**137, **8:**141

300

international comparisons, **6**:xxii, **7**:213,
    7:216–217, **7**:229, **7**:230
in Jewish day schools, **1**:131, **1**:132
in magnet schools, **1**:162–178
measuring, **6**:131–132
multicultural counseling and,
    3:24–25
in Native American schools, **1**:254–268
nonschool-related factors, **9**:140, **9**:143,
    9:229
in online courses, **10**:55–56, **10**:57
parental involvement and, **1**:131,
    5:207–208
pressures to succeed, **5**:128
in private schools, **1**:80, **1**:85–86,
    1:145–160, **3**:68, **6**:265
relationship to funding, **3**:175–176,
    6:188, **6**:208–209, **9**:221
in religious schools, **4**:14
in single-sex classes and schools, **1**:184,
    1:185, **1**:186–187, **1**:188, **1**:191
standards and, **9**:30–31
teachers evaluated on, **9**:84–85
uniform policies and, **8**:53
in virtual schools, **10**:71–73
voucher programs and, **6**:248–249
See also Achievement gaps;
    Assessments
Academy of Urban School Leadership,
    9:105
Access Now, Inc. v. Southwest Airlines,
    10:202
Accommodations, for assessments, **10**:8
Accountability
academic growth of students and,
    9:1–19
of administrators, **7**:xxiv, **7**:191–192,
    9:122–123, **9**:125–126
business support of increased, **7**:xxvi
of charter schools, **1**:9, **1**:11–17,
    1:24–25, **1**:106, **6**:284, **6**:286–288,
    6:289–291, **7**:133, **7**:145
choice programs and, **1**:106
of compensatory education, **3**:239,
    3:247
criticism of, **9**:2, **9**:10–11, **9**:49–52
educational malpractice claims,
    8:219–220, **8**:222
financing implementation of, **9**:
    190–213
of magnet schools, **1**:170
meanings, **9**:4, **9**:12, **9**:48–49
mitigating conditions for, **9**:xix–xxix

NCLB provisions, **6**:81–82, **7**:xxiv,
    7:xxviii, **7**:43–44, **7**:49, **7**:51–52,
    7:77, **7**:159, **7**:253, **9**:18, **9**:58,
    9:274
parental involvement in, **9**:263–280
professional, **9**:47–48, **9**:50–51
of school boards, **7**:9, **7**:121,
    7:124, **8**:13
school-level autonomy and,
    6:55, **6**:56
standards-based testing, **2**:26, **2**:94,
    7:229–230
of teacher training programs, **2**:39, **2**:43,
    9:71–93
unintended consequences, **9**:xix–xx
union roles in, **9**:156–173
See also Assessments; Electoral
    accountability; Standards
Accounting
school-based, **6**:57
See also Budgets
Accreditation
of administration preparation
    programs, **2**:40, **2**:42
assessments and, **2**:41–42
benefits of, **2**:37, **2**:40–44, **2**:50–51
costs, **2**:36, **2**:47
disadvantages, **2**:36–38, **2**:44–52
goals, **2**:45, **2**:46–47
issues in process, **2**:44, **2**:45–50,
    2:51–52, **9**:81, **9**:82, **9**:84
regional, **2**:39
of teacher training programs, **2**:35–52,
    9:79–83
unaccredited programs, **2**:49–50, **9**:81
See also Teacher licensing
Accreditation bodies
curriculum standards and, **2**:35–36
outcomes focus, **9**:89, **9**:91
regional, **9**:80
roles, **9**:79–83, **9**:93
standards, **2**:42, **2**:43, **9**:72, **9**:79–83,
    9:90, **9**:93
technology standards and, **10**:122
See also National Council for the
    Accreditation of Teacher
    Education; Teacher Education
    Accreditation Council
Achieve, Inc., **7**:175, **9**:5, **9**:10, **9**:32
Achievement gaps
benefits of preschool programs, **1**:198,
    1:204–207, **1**:209, **1**:212–213
choice movement and, **6**:268

consequences, **3:**xx, **6:**241, **7:**78, **9:**xxix, **9:**246–247
desegregation and, **3:**11, **7:**76–77
earnings gaps and, **9:**227–228
between economic classes, **3:**75–90
effects of NCLB, **3:**87–88, **3:**89, **7:**44, **7:**48, **7:**55
evidence of, **3:**80, **3:**104–105, **6:**xxii, **6:**199, **7:**75–76, **7:**85
explanations, **2:**69, **2:**152, **3:**xxii, **3:**94, **3:**96–97, **3:**98, **7:**51–52, **7:**82, **7:**86–88
factors influencing, **3:**80, **3:**176
financing adequacy and, **6:**202, **6:**206
financing inequities and, **6:**159
formative assessments and, **7:**154–156
gender, **3:**216–219
graduation rates, **3:**86, **7:**51, **7:**85
increases over time, **7:**51–52, **9:**242, **9:**244, **9:**245
in literacy skills, **2:**79–80, **2:**87
measurement, **3:**103–104, **7:**44–45
of Native American students, **1:**xviii, **1:**255, **1:**258, **1:**263, **1:**268, **3:**104
NCLB goals, **3:**84–85, **7:**44, **7:**48, **7:**49, **7:**77
obstacles to closing, **3:**105–109
pressures to reduce, **7:**76, **9:**6, **9:**41, **9:**228–229
between racial groups, **3:**xx, **3:**11
reductions, **3:**11, **9:**8, **9:**9, **9:**43
responsibility of school leaders in reducing, **7:**51–52, **7:**75–90
sociocultural factors, **3:**86–87, **7:**85, **7:**86–88, **7:**89, **7:**198
between states, **9:**57
strategies to address, **2:**79–80, **3:**90, **3:**97, **3:**175, **7:**79–84, **7:**86, **7:**87–90, **9:**6
summer learning losses, **1:**242, **1:**243–244, **3:**88
teacher performance and, **6:**137–138
trends, **1:**29, **3:**65, **3:**85–86, **3:**87–89, **3:**99–100, **3:**102, **3:**104–105, **7:**75, **9:**xxix, **9:**41
See also Compensatory education
ACLU. *See* American Civil Liberties Union
ACLU of Minnesota v. Tarek ibn Ziyad Academy, **1:**21
ACLU v. Black Horse Pike Regional Board of Education, **4:**40

ACLU v. McCreary County, **4:**125–126
Acosta, R. Vivian, **3:**209
ACT. *See* American College Testing
ACTE. *See* Association for Career and Technical Education
ADA. *See* Americans with Disabilities Act
Adams, Jacob, **7:**256
Adams, Jacob E., Jr., **9:**57
Adamson v. California, **4:**98
Adelman, Clifford, **9:**43
Adelman, Howard S., **5:**252
Adequacy suits
arguments, **6:**183–184, **6:**198, **6:**200, **6:**201–202
criticism of, **6:**198–201, **6:**204–205, **6:**209
defining adequacy, **6:**33, **6:**152, **6:**198, **6:**202, **6:**204–205, **6:**206–208
educational quality issue, **6:**xx–xxii, **6:**145
in federal courts, **3:**179, **6:**200
for gifted education, **6:**118
outcomes, **3:**173–174, **6:**153–154, **6:**198–199, **6:**200–201, **6:**209
property tax issues, **6:**64
in state courts, **3:**180–181, **6:**152, **6:**169, **6:**170–171, **6:**194–203, **6:**204–206, **6:**209, **9:**193–194, **9:**204
See also Financing adequacy
Adequate yearly progress (AYP)
assessments, **2:**9, **3:**99, **3:**103
NCLB provisions, **6:**103, **6:**106, **6:**127, **6:**131–132, **9:**6, **9:**61, **9:**277
special education and, **6:**104, **6:**106
Adler v. Duval County School Board, **4:**40, **4:**43, **4:**47
Administration
cost reductions, **9:**194–195
efficiency, **9:**15–16
governance and, **7:**xxiii
scientific methods, **9:**13, **9:**14, **9:**15
Administration preparation programs
accreditation, **2:**40, **2:**42
alternative programs, **9:**xxv, **9:**119–136
approaches, **3:**44, **7:**240–241
certification standards and, **7:**93, **7:**95, **7:**100
criticism of, **9:**119–120, **9:**126–127, **9:**134
curricula, **7:**100, **7:**107
curricular materials, **7:**105

diversity training, **3:**37–52
effects of NCLB, **9:**119–120
ethics in, **7:**99–100
evaluations, **7:**99
faculty, **7:**103, **7:**107, **7:**108, **9:**126–127
financial management skills, **6:**52–53, **6:**56
gender discrimination, **7:**94, **7:**106
gender issues addressed in, **3:**212, **7:**93–108
gender of students, **7:**104
graduate level, **7:**94, **7:**95, **7:**100
improving, **9:**131, **9:**136
for principals, **7:**95, **9:**125–127
required credentials, **7:**225
shortcomings, **7:**104–105, **7:**107–108
student loan forgiveness, **3:**255–272
for superintendents, **7:**95, **7:**233, **7:**237–238
Administrators
accountability, **7:**xxiv, **7:**191–192, **9:**122–123, **9:**125–126
budget maximization, **6:**7–8
bullying prevention responsibility, **5:**62–63
business degrees, **9:**120, **9:**128, **9:**129
career paths, **7:**105
certification standards, **7:**93, **7:**94, **7:**95, **7:**97, **7:**99
corporal punishment, **5:**205
cultural competence, **7:**196–197, **7:**199–200
effects of parental involvement in schools, **7:**187–205
expectations of, **7:**236, **9:**119–120, **9:**122–123
financial and business functions, **6:**45–46, **6:**52, **6:**56
flexibility limited by collective bargaining agreements, **7:**23, **7:**25–26, **7:**28–32, **7:**35–36
gender, **7:**94–95, **7:**97, **7:**100–101, **7:**102–103, **7:**104, **7:**105–106, **9:**15
gender issues, preparation for, **7:**93–108
gifted education and, **6:**121–122
liaison role, **7:**160
mandated reporting of abuse and neglect, **5:**96
mentoring, **7:**241
from non-educational backgrounds, **7:**225, **9:**xxv, **9:**125, **9:**133–134
performance, **9:**xxiv–xxv
priorities, **7:**190
professional development, **2:**8
professional status, **9:**132–133
qualifications, **7:**237–238
recruitment and retention, **9:**xxiv–xxv, **9:**125
relations with parents, **7:**xxvii, **7:**190–192, **7:**196, **7:**197, **7:**202–204
resistance to change, **7:**231
responsibilities under NCLB, **7:**xxiv, **7:**xxviii
roles, **7:**190, **7:**196, **7:**199
school resource officers and, **5:**164, **5:**173–174
shortages, **9:**133–134
skills and knowledge needed, **7:**238–240
socialization, **7:**227, **7:**238–239
technology standards, **10:**128
of virtual schools, **10:**92
voting in school board elections, **7:**9–10
women, **3:**219, **7:**94–95, **7:**100–101, **7:**104, **7:**105–106
See also Principals; Superintendents
Adolescent suicide. *See* Suicide, student
Adolescents. *See* High schools; LGBT youth; Teenagers
Advanced Placement (AP) courses
availability, **6:**121, **6:**228, **10:**56
class sizes, **6:**228–229
college credit, **6:**226, **6:**228, **6:**230, **6:**236–237, **10:**57
costs, **6:**226, **6:**228, **6:**229
exams, **6:**228, **6:**234–238
funding, **6:**xxvi–xxvii, **6:**229, **6:**232, **6:**236, **9:**198
grades, **6:**229
online, **10:**56–57, **10:**72
social mobility benefits, **6:**xxvi, **6:**226
student fees, **6:**225–238
teachers, **6:**229, **6:**236
topics, **6:**228
See also Gifted education
AEI. *See* American Enterprise Institute
Affirmative action, **1:**29, **2:**xxii
AFL-CIO. *See* American Federation of Labor-Congress of Industrial Organizations

AFRDS. *See* Association of Fund-Raising Distributors & Suppliers
African Americans
 ability grouping and, **3:**155–156, **3:**162
 achievement gaps, **3:**xx, **3:**88–89
 arrests, **5:**162
 churches, **1:**25, **3:**227
 civil rights, **3:**78
 Ebonics, **2:**109, **2:**125
 families, **3:**96
 graduation rates, **3:**86, **7:**51
 hip-hop culture, **3:**137–147
 identities, **3:**24–25
 juvenile crimes, **5:**47–48
 linguistic barriers, **3:**146
 male teachers, **3:**261
 NAEP scores, **3:**99–100, **3:**103–105, **3:**109, **7:**15, **7:**85
 parental involvement in schools, **3:**225
 in poverty, **3:**79–80
 in Reconstruction era, **7:**2
 school board members, **7:**118
 stereotypes of, **3:**147
 student population, **9:**241–242
 suspensions and expulsions, **5:**37, **5:**41–42, **5:**47, **5:**50
 teachers, **3:**259, **3:**261, **3:**263, **7:**23
 writers, **3:**146
 See also Achievement gaps; Minority students; Racial issues
Afrocentric charter schools, **1:**25
AFT. *See* American Federation of Teachers
Afterschool Alliance, **1:**242
Afterschool programs, **3:**225
Agar, Michael, **2:**129
Agostini v. Felton, **4:**7, **4:**19, **4:**24
Aguilar v. Felton, **4:**19, **4:**28
Aguillard v. Edwards, **8:**1, **8:**4, **8:**6
AIF. *See* Academic Integrity Framework
Aikin, Wilford M., **9:**16
AIM. *See* American Indian Movement
ALA. *See* American Library Association
Alabama
 moments of silence in schools, **4:**67, **4:**71–72, **4:**78
 prayer at graduation ceremonies, **4:**40
 suspensions and expulsions, **5:**43–44
Alabama and Coushatta Tribes of Texas v. Trustees of the Big Sandy Independent School District, **4:**268, **4:**273–274
Alaska, standards, **9:**26, **9:**40

Alcohol
 testing for, **8:**71
 use by students, **5:**26–27, **5:**29
 zero tolerance policies, **5:**19–22, **5:**26–27, **5:**29, **5:**31, **5:**204
Aldrich, Howard, **7:**172
Alex G. v. Board of Trustees of Davis Joint Unified School District, **5:**214
Alexander, Karl L., **1:**243–244
Alexander, Kern, **7:**68
Alexander, M. David, **7:**68
Alfred, Corinne, **1:**222
Algozzine, Bob, **1:**177
Alliance for Excellent Education, **3:**117
Almontaser v. New York City Department of Education, **1:**42
Alternative leadership programs
 admissions criteria, **9:**130
 compared to traditional programs, **9:**120–121
 criticism of, **9:**129–130, **9:**131–133
 models, **9:**127–129, **9:**130
 need for, **9:**119–136
Alternative licensure. *See* Teacher licensing, alternative routes
Alternative schooling. *See* Charter schools; Choice; Homeschooling; Private schools
Altman v. Bedford Central School District, **4:**110
Alumni, communication with, **10:**197
Amador, Paul, **3:**171
Amazon.com
 e-book sales, **10:**24
 Kindle, **10:**xx, **10:**16
American Academy of Pediatrics, **5:**109, **5:**110
American Association for the Advancement of Science, **2:**93
American Association of Colleges for Teacher Education (AACTE), **9:**75, **9:**91
American Association of School Administrators, **4:**13
American Association of University Women, **1:**187, **3:**267, **8:**150, **8:**156, **8:**157
American Bar Association, **5:**xx, **5:**46, **5:**202
American Civil Liberties Union (ACLU)
 Bible as literature classes and, **4:**173, **4:**179–180, **4:**181

extracurricular activity fee cases, **6:**230
free speech cases, **10:**179
gender discrimination issues, **1:**190
on immigration, **2:**212
on "official English" policies, **2:**118
online privacy and, **10:**140
on school discipline methods, **5:**33, **5:**110, **5:**206
on school resource officers, **5:**157–158, **5:**161–162
American College Testing (ACT) scores, **9:**32, **9:**220, **9:**253, **9:**254
American Counseling Association (ACA), **3:**23, **3:**24, **3:**25
American Enterprise Institute (AEI), **9:**125–126, **9:**127
American Federation of Labor-Congress of Industrial Organizations (AFL-CIO), **8:**249, **8:**254
American Federation of Teachers (AFT)
 affiliates, **7:**37
 history, **7:**34, **8:**249, **8:**254
 national standards and, **9:**33, **9:**34
 number of members, **7:**34, **8:**249
 policies, **7:**26, **7:**38, **8:**250
 structure, **9:**161–162
 zero tolerance policies and, **5:**xx
American Federation of Teachers v. Kanawha County Board of Education, **8:**75, **8:**80–81, **8:**86, **8:**87
American Indian Movement (AIM), **1:**257
American Indians. *See* Native Americans
American Library Association (ALA), **2:**207, **10:**140
American Psychological Association (APA), **3:**23, **3:**26
American Psychological Association Zero Tolerance Task Force, **5:**197–198, **5:**203
American Recovery and Reinvestment Act (ARRA), **2:**90, **2:**99–100, **3:**55–56, **3:**58, **6:**103, **6:**225, **8:**132
 See also Race to the Top; Teacher Incentive Fund
American School Counselor Association (ASCA), **3:**19, **3:**23, **3:**29
American Tort Reform Association, **5:**191
Americans with Disabilities Act (ADA), **6:**103, **8:**219, **10:**201–202
Amish, **1:**xx–xxi, **1:**112–113, **1:**123, **4:**74, **4:**273–274

Anderson, A., **10:**88, **10:**89
Anderson, Benedict, **2:**130
Anderson, Lee, **6:**288
Anderson, Nick, **1:**222
Anderson, Stephen E., **7:**80–81
Anderson, Wendell, **5:**12
Andrews v. Drew Municipal Separate School District, **8:**235
Andrews v. Independent School District, **8:**161
Ansalone, George, **3:**153–154, **3:**156
Ansonia Board of Education v. Philbrook, **4:**206
Anthony, Mitch, **6:**230–231
Antibullying legislation, **5:**56, **5:**63, **5:**64, **5:**65, **10:**154, **10:**155, **10:**162–163, **10:**165–166
 See also Bullying
Anti-Federalists, **4:**96–97, **4:**101
Anxiety
 interventions, **5:**252–254
 prevalence, **5:**251
 symptoms, **5:**xxi, **5:**248, **5:**255, **5:**257, **5:**258–259, **5:**260
 See also Internalizing disorders
AP courses. *See* Advanced Placement courses
APA. *See* American Psychological Association
Apple, **10:**2, **10:**33
 See also iPads
Apple, M. W., **7:**219
Applied behavior analysis (ABA), **5:**231, **5:**234
Applied Technology Education Act, **3:**127–128
Apprenticeships. *See* Vocational education
Apps, **10:**1–2, **10:**24, **10:**46
Arab Americans, **2:**129–130
Arabic language schools, **1:**21, **1:**25–26, **1:**50
Archer, Deborah, **5:**202
Arendt, Hannah, **2:**94
Arias, M. Beatriz, **3:**45
Arieti, Silvano, **2:**170
Aristotle, **2:**174, **6:**220, **10:**171
Arizona
 charter schools, **6:**287, **6:**289
 education tax credits, **1:**98–100, **1:**104, **6:**269
 for-profit schools, **1:**85–86
 immigration laws, **2:**134–135, **2:**139, **3:**193

Arizona Christian School Tuition Organization v. Winn, **1:**99–100, **1:**104
Arkansas
  evolution instruction prohibited, **4:**185, **4:**196
  school desegregation, **3:**15
Arkansas Supreme Court, **6:**148
Armijo v. Wagon Mound Public Schools, **5:**81–82
Armor, David J., **3:**4
ARRA. *See* American Recovery and Reinvestment Act
Articles of Confederation, **7:**41
Artificial intelligence, **10:**210
Arts
  benefits for students, **2:**142–143, **2:**145–150, **2:**155, **6:**221
  budget cuts in, **2:**144, **2:**154, **9:**xxvi
  in curriculum, **2:**142–156
  distinction from craft, **2:**151–152, **2:**153–154
  as distraction, **2:**143, **2:**150, **2:**152–153, **2:**154, **2:**156
  gifted students, **2:**160, **2:**163
  in interdisciplinary courses, **2:**143, **2:**154
  popular culture and, **2:**214
  as separate subjects, **2:**142–143, **2:**145
  skill transfer, **2:**145–149, **2:**150
  technology and, **2:**230
  virtual worlds, **2:**229–230
  in year-round schools, **1:**244
  See also Humanities; Music
ASCA. *See* American School Counselor Association
Asian American students, **3:**115, **9:**242
  See also Minority students
Asquith, Christina, **3:**7
Assessed curriculum, **2:**60
Assessments
  accommodations, **10:**8
  alternative methods, **1:**262
  businesses providing, **7:**166
  of college students, **9:**68–69
  Common Core standards, **2:**57, **2:**62, **9:**xxi, **9:**40, **9:**59–60, **9:**187–188, **9:**224
  computerized, **2:**238–239
  data, **7:**80–81
  high stakes, **2:**xxv, **2:**26
  improving, **9:**224
  international comparisons, **7:**213
  media publication of results, **2:**26, **9:**xx
  performance-based, **9:**180, **9:**187
  as political objects, **2:**94–95
  standards-based, **2:**21, **2:**61–62, **6:**80–81, **7:**229–230, **10:**127–128, **10:**130
  See also Formative assessments; Standardized tests
Assistive technology (AT)
  advantages, **2:**237–238, **10:**2, **10:**4, **10:**6, **10:**9
  compared to universal design, **10:**xix, **10:**1–14
  definition, **10:**4
  educational benefits, **10:**32–48
  effectiveness, **10:**5–6
  evaluations, **10:**7, **10:**11
  examples, **10:**6, **10:**11
  IDEA provisions, **2:**189, **10:**2, **10:**4, **10:**7–9, **10:**10–11
  links to universal design, **2:**238, **10:**3, **10:**4–5, **10:**8–9, **10:**13–14
  types, **10:**1–2
Association for Career and Technical Education (ACTE), **3:**128–129
Association for the Gifted, **6:**121
Association of Fund-Raising Distributors & Suppliers (AFRDS), **6:**302
Association of Multicultural Counseling and Development, **3:**32
Association of Trial Lawyers of America, **5:**191
AT. *See* Assistive technology
Athletics
  booster clubs, **6:**217–218, **6:**294, **6:**296
  coaches, **6:**299–300
  drug testing, **5:**26, **8:**57–58, **8:**63–64, **8:**66, **8:**84, **10:**104–105
  gender equity and Title IX, **3:**210–211
  history, **6:**220
  Muslim garb, **4:**268
  prayers before events, **4:**xxi, **4:**36, **4:**39, **4:**46–47, **4:**62–63, **4:**73
  public funding, **6:**216–217
  women's participation, **3:**210–211, **3:**219, **4:**268
  year-round schedules and, **1:**245, **1:**250
  See also Extracurricular activities
At-risk students
  credit recovery courses, **10:**51, **10:**57–58, **10:**73, **10:**77
  families, **1:**201, **1:**211
  in Head Start, **1:**197–199, **1:**200–201, **1:**204–205, **1:**209

needs, **1:**204–205, **1:**208
positive behavior intervention supports, **5:**236–238
in single-sex classes and schools, **1:**186
stereotypes of, **2:**226
suspensions under zero-tolerance policies, **5:**32–33
voucher use, **6:**247–248
in year-round schools, **1:**241–244, **1:**245–246
See also Compensatory education; Full-service community schools; Homeless students; Low socioeconomic groups; Minority students
AT&T, **9:**246
Au, Kathryn, **3:**142, **3:**145
Aubrey v. School Board of Lafayette Parish, **8:**75, **8:**77, **8:**82, **8:**84
Augenblick, Palaich, and Associates, **10:**88
Australia, single-sex schools, **1:**186
Austria, tracking system, **3:**150
Authentic Israel, **1:**141
Authenticity
  mentors and, **2:**xxiii
  in reading instruction, **2:**76–78, **2:**80, **2:**81
Authoritative disciplinarians, **5:**207
Autism, **8:**114, **8:**118
Autonomy, of teachers, **3:**71, **8:**5, **8:**8–9
Autonomy, school-level
  accountability and, **6:**55, **6:**56
  of charter schools, **1:**7–8, **1:**11, **1:**24, **1:**36, **6:**xxiv, **6:**48–49, **6:**53, **6:**279
  financial, **6:**41–57
  of Jewish day schools, **1:**131–132
Autonomy Zone, **6:**48
Avery v. Homewood City Board of Education, **8:**234–235

Bailey, Marcia Harr, **1:**40, **1:**43
Bailey, T. M., **9:**110
Baker, Bruce D., **6:**114, **6:**116, **6:**118, **6:**120
Baker, Keith, **2:**112
Baker, L. A., **6:**90
Baker v. Owen, **5:**106, **5:**111, **5:**195
Baltimore, mayoral control of schools, **7:**15–16, **7:**18, **7:**19
Band. *See* Music
Bankston, Carla L., **3:**12
Bannon v. School District of Palm Beach County, **4:**121–122

Barksdale-Ladd, Mary Alice, **2:**23
Barnes, Robin D., **6:**xxii
Barrea-Marlys, Mirta, **2:**51
Barton, Paul E., **3:**85, **3:**104–105
Basford, Letitia, **1:**60–61
Battelle, **9:**250
Battelle for Kids, **9:**145
Bauchman v. West High School, **4:**104, **4:**107–108, **4:**110
Bauries, Scott R., **6:**185, **6:**186
BBYO (B'nai B'rith Youth Organization), **1:**141
Beach, Richard, **2:**218
Beare, Hedley, **7:**134
Bearne, Eve, **2:**215
Beghetto, Ronald A., **2:**166
Behavior intervention plans (BIPs), **5:**210–211, **8:**95, **8:**102, **8:**103
Behavior modification programs, **5:**210, **5:**221
Behavioral disorders, **5:**231–245
  See also Emotional and behavioral disorders; Internalizing disorders
Behavioral interventions. *See* Positive behavior intervention supports
Behavioral report cards, **5:**236–237
Behaviors
  changes in, **5:**255
  maladaptive, **5:**xxi
  signs of abuse, **5:**95
Belk v. Charlotte-Mecklenburg Board of Education, **3:**2–3
Bell, Colleen, **7:**105–106
Bell, Courtney, **9:**142
Bell, Derrick, **3:**5
Bell, T. H., **9:**237
Bell, Vaughan, **10:**36–37
Bellevue John Does v. Bellevue School District # 405, **8:**161, **8:**164, **8:**169, **8:**172
BellSouth Foundation, **10:**88
Ben Gamla Charter School, **1:**25, **1:**50
Benbow, Camilla P., **2:**165
Bennet, Michael, **9:**130
Bennett, Randy Elliot, **2:**99
Bennett, William, **3:**192, **9:**33
Benton, Thomas Hart, **2:**174
Berliner, David C., **7:**115
Berne, Robert, **3:**173
Berry, Barnett, **9:**116
Berry, Thomas, **2:**240, **2:**244
BES. *See* Building Excellent Schools

Bethel School District No. 403 v. Fraser,
   2:201, **4:**262, **5:**8, **5:**198, **8:**50, **8:**177, **8:**181, **8:**186–187, **10:**166–167, **10:**170, **10:**179, **10:**186
Bezdicheck v. State, **3:**181–182
BIA. *See* Bureau of Indian Affairs
Bible
   creation account, **4:**184, **4:**188
   cultural importance, **4:**89–90, **4:**124, **4:**171, **4:**172
   as literature, **4:**xxiv–xxv, **4:**50, **4:**92–93, **4:**168–182, **4:**227
   required reading in schools, **4:**35–36, **4:**45, **4:**62, **4:**176–177
   in school libraries, **4:**63, **4:**86
   silent reading by teachers, **4:**xxii, **4:**53, **4:**63, **4:**85–101
   Ten Commandments, **4:**xxii–xxiii, **4:**113, **4:**120–121, **4:**126, **4:**131–132, **4:**133
   versions, **4:**179, **4:**181
   See also Religious texts
Biddle, Bruce J., **7:**115
BIE. *See* Bureau of Indian Education
Bifulco, Robert, **3:**70
Bilingual education
   advantages, **2:**109, **3:**187, **3:**205
   costs, **3:**195–196
   curricular models, **2:**112
   dual immersion model, **3:**187–188
   instructional approaches, **2:**115–116, **3:**187–188
   legal requirements, **1:**xviii
   for Native Americans, **1:**260
   opponents, **2:**118, **3:**191–194, **3:**195–196
   research on, **2:**112–114, **3:**195, **3:**196
   teachers, **3:**196
   transitional, **3:**187, **3:**191, **3:**194, **3:**195, **3:**199
Bilingual Education Act, **3:**192
Bilingual students, **2:**109, **2:**111, **2:**112–116, **2:**237, **3:**190, **7:**xxviii
   See also Achievement gaps; English Language Learners; Immigrants
Bill and Melinda Gates Foundation. *See* Gates Foundation
Bill of Rights, **4:**96–98
Billings, Robert, **2:**205
Biloxi Public School District, Mississippi, **10:**98
Bin Laden, Osama, **4:**174

Biology. *See* Evolution; Science
BIPs. *See* Behavior intervention plans
Birkby, Robert H., **4:**72
Bisexuals, **8:**233–234
   See also LGBT youth
Bivens v. Albuquerque Public Schools, **5:**5, **8:**181
Black, Cathie, **7:**177
Black, Hugo, **4:**1–2
Blacks. *See* African Americans
Blackstone, William, **5:**194, **5:**204, **5:**205, **5:**206
Blackwelder v. Safnauer, **1:**113–114, **1:**120
Blaine, James G., **2:**199, **4:**7
Blaine Amendment, **2:**199, **4:**7
Blau v. Fort Thomas Public School District, **8:**44–45, **8:**181–182
Blogs, **2:**219, **8:**180, **8:**188, **10:**139, **10:**149
Blonigen, Bruce A., **5:**243
Bloom, Benjamin, **2:**158–159
Bloomberg, Michael, **7:**257
Blount, Jackie, **7:**107
BLS. *See* Boston Latin School; Bureau of Labor Statistics
Blumenson, Eric, **5:**43, **5:**44
B'nai B'rith Youth Organization (BBYO), **1:**141
Board of Education of Central School District No. 1 v. Allen, **4:**xx, **4:**6, **4:**21, **4:**27
Board of Education of Cincinnati v. Minor, **4:**168
Board of Education of Hendrick Hudson Central School District v. Rowley, **8:**91, **8:**109
Board of Education of Independent School District No. 92 of Pottawatomie County v. Earls, **5:**26, **8:**57–58, **8:**60, **8:**61, **8:**63, **8:**64–65, **8:**66–67, **8:**77, **8:**84, **10:**104–105
Board of Education of Oklahoma v. Dowell, **3:**7
Board of Education of the City School District of Cincinnati v. Walter, **9:**191, **9:**204, **9:**210–211
Board of Education of Westside Community Schools v. Mergens, **4:**xxvi, **4:**23, **4:**74, **4:**81, **4:**217, **4:**219, **4:**225, **4:**234, **4:**291
Board of Regents of the University of Wisconsin System v. Southworth, **6:**218
Board of Regents v. Roth, **8:**229, **8:**240
Boger, John C., **3:**5

Index **309**

Bolick, Clint, **6**:xxii
Bollinger, Lee, **7**:78, **7**:90
Bolman, Lee G., **3**:49
Bonds
  costs, **6**:27
  debt limits, **6**:21–38
  foreign investors, **6**:27
  interest rates, **6**:21, **6**:22, **6**:26, **6**:31, **6**:36
  issuance, **6**:21–22
  purposes, **6**:22, **6**:25, **6**:32, **6**:37
  state oversight, **6**:28
  voter approval, **6**:28, **6**:32, **6**:36–37
Bonner v. Daniels, **3**:182
Books
  banned, **2**:207, **7**:188
  virtual worlds, **2**:229
  See also e-books; Religious texts; Textbooks
Borman Geoffrey D., **3**:89
Boston
  arts education, **2**:146–149
  charter schools, **6**:280
  court takeover of schools, **7**:14
  school committees, **7**:12
  school desegregation controversy, **7**:14
  segregated schools, **7**:62
  transportation of religious school students, **4**:8
Boston Excels, **3**:226
Boston Latin School (BLS), **1**:xvi, **2**:xxi–xxii
Boston Teacher Residency (BTR), **9**:104–105
Bott v. Board of Education, Deposit Central School District, **5**:107
Bourdieu, Pierre, **3**:79, **3**:83–84
Bowe, Frank, **10**:13
Bowles, Samuel, **3**:70
Boyd, William L., **7**:258
Boyer, Ernest, **2**:24, **9**:177
BR. *See* Business Roundtable
Bracey, Gerald, **1**:86, **1**:88, **7**:15, **9**:32
Braddock, Jomills Henry, II, **3**:155–156
Bradford v. Roberts, **4**:5
Bradley v. Missouri, **3**:9
Branch, Gregory, **3**:69
Brand, Myles, **3**:51
Brannen v. Kings Local School District Board of Education, **10**:102–103
Brannum v. Overton County School Board, **10**:109

Bransford, John, **3**:42–43, **3**:45, **3**:46
Breault, Donna A., **9**:18
Bridgeland, J. M., **3**:86
Brigham v. State, **6**:158
Brimley, Vern, Jr., **6**:36
Broad Center, **7**:233
Broad Foundation, **3**:38–39
Broader, Bolder Approach to Education, **7**:52
Bronx Household of Faith v. Board of Education of the City of New York, **4**:239–240, **4**:241
Brown, Elissa F., **6**:122
Brown v. Board of Education
  Brown II, **3**:5, **3**:13
  cases included, **3**:2
  consequences, **3**:242, **6**:99, **6**:268, **7**:76–77, **8**:xvi
  criticism of, **3**:5
  enforcement, **2**:19, **3**:xxi, **3**:2, **3**:5, **3**:13, **3**:15, **7**:250
  equal protection, **7**:62, **7**:66, **7**:70
  impact on students with disabilities, **8**:120
  importance of education, **1**:xviii, **5**:44, **6**:16, **6**:185, **9**:213
  majority opinion, **3**:13, **3**:248
  plaintiffs' strategy, **3**:10
  "separate, but equal" doctrine overturned, **1**:22–23, **3**:1, **3**:5, **7**:xix
  See also Desegregation
Brown v. Ramsey, **5**:211
Brunsma, David L., **5**:2, **8**:53
Bryan, William Jennings, **9**:67
Bryant, Anne, **2**:18
Bryk, Anthony, **7**:174
BTR. *See* Boston Teacher Residency
Buber, Martin, **2**:244
Bubis, Gerald, **1**:134
Bucci, Terri Teal, **10**:123–124
Buchanan, NiCole T., **8**:149
Buchanan, Nina, **1**:20
Buckingham, David, **2**:218
Buddin, Richard, **3**:67
Budget-maximizing educational bureaus, **6**:7–8
Budgets
  cuts, **4**:12–13
  residual, **9**:206
  of school districts, **6**:44, **7**:239, **9**:222
  See also Financing

Budig, Gene A., **3:**259, **3:**264
Building Excellent Schools (BES), **9:**128–129
Bullough, R. V., Jr., **2:**48
Bully Police USA, **5:**63
Bullying
  antibullying policies, **5:**56
  awareness of issue, **5:**64
  in classrooms, **5:**59, **5:**60–61, **5:**65, **5:**66
  counselor interventions, **5:**61–62
  differences from cyberbullying, **10:**157–158
  educator responsibility for prevention, **5:**xxiii, **5:**55–69
  effects, **5:**59–60
  federal laws, **5:**63
  incidence, **5:**xxiii, **5:**55
  lawsuits, **5:**55–56, **5:**65–67, **5:**68
  locations, **5:**59
  prevention, **4:**263–264, **5:**56–57, **5:**60–63, **5:**64, **5:**65, **5:**66, **10:**156, **10:**170–171
  state laws, **5:**56, **5:**63, **5:**64, **5:**65, **10:**154, **10:**155, **10:**162–163, **10:**165–166
  suicides related to, **5:**xxiii, **5:**55, **5:**64, **5:**86, **10:**147, **10:**157
  targeted students, **5:**xxiii, **5:**55
  underlying causes, **5:**64–65, **5:**68–69
  See also Cyberbullying
Burch, Patricia, **3:**68, **7:**178
Bureau of Indian Affairs (BIA), **1:**257–258
Bureau of Indian Education (BIE), **1:**xxviii, **1:**254–255
  See also Native American schools
Bureau of Justice Statistics, **5:**24
Bureau of Labor Statistics (BLS), **3:**118, **3:**255
Bureaucracies, **6:**7–8
  See also Administration
Burn, Andrew, **2:**218
Burns, David, **1:**219
Burpee v. Burton, State ex rel., **5:**195
Bush, George H. W., **9:**xxvii, **9:**24
Bush, George W., **1:**49, **2:**130–131, **2:**205, **5:**190, **9:**60
Bush, George W., administration
  church-school partnerships, **3:**228
  community policing, **5:**168
  education policies, **6:**56
  Teacher Incentive Fund, **7:**36
  teacher training programs, **3:**xxiii
  Title IX amendments, **3:**210
  See also No Child Left Behind Act
Bush v. Holmes, **1:**95, **1:**97–98
Business interests
  charter school operators, **1:**10, **1:**13, **1:**82–87, **6:**279, **6:**287, **6:**288, **7:**144, **7:**179–180, **9:**225
  cyberschool operators, **10:**81, **10:**84–85, **10:**87
  educational services, **7:**10, **7:**166–167, **7:**178, **7:**184
  effects on school governance, **7:**165–184
  efficiency, **9:**12–13, **9:**15–16
  engagement in education, **9:**236
  fund-raising services, **6:**294, **6:**296, **6:**304
  influence on public education, **7:**xxvi, **7:**6, **9:**15, **9:**32
  investment in education, **9:**233–260
  outsourcing to, **7:**166–167
  participative management, **2:**23–24
  performance pay, **6:**130, **6:**132–134
  profits, **9:**256, **9:**258
  school board elections and, **7:**10
  school improvement industry, **7:**170–171, **7:**173–174
  social obligations, **9:**258–259
  taxes, **6:**74, **6:**269, **9:**259
  technology funding, **10:**xvii
  technology skills needed by, **2:**237
  textbook publishers, **2:**29, **2:**32, **7:**166, **9:**18, **10:**21, **10:**22, **10:**93
  vocational education and, **1:**216–217, **1:**232
  See also Educational management organizations; Proprietary for-profit schools; Public-private partnerships
Business leaders, **7:**237, **7:**238–239, **7:**242
Business model
  in education reform, **7:**xxviii, **7:**47, **7:**247
  in private schools, **1:**72, **1:**78–79, **1:**81, **1:**82, **1:**88–89, **3:**68, **6:**266
  of Race to the Top, **7:**47, **7:**55, **7:**116
  See also Market competition
Business Roundtable (BR), **9:**247
Busing. *See* Transportation services
Butts, Calvin, **3:**138
Bybee, Deborah, **3:**24

CAEP. *See* Council for the Accreditation of Educator Preparation
Caldarella, Paul, **5:**243
Caldas, Stephen J., **3:**12
Calendars. *See* Holidays; School years
California
  Advanced Placement fees, **6:**230
  charter schools, **1:**15, **6:**xxiv, **6:**282, **6:**287
  constitution, **3:**179, **6:**202, **10:**108
  discipline policies, **10:**161–162
  diversity, **9:**58
  "English-only" curriculum, **3:**190
  extracurricular activity fees, **6:**218
  finance litigation, **3:**179, **6:**168–169
  for-profit schools, **1:**83, **1:**86, **1:**88
  property tax limits, **6:**27–28, **9:**202
  school district financial management, **6:**46
  school funding, **3:**177, **6:**27–28, **6:**64, **6:**99, **6:**200, **6:**202, **9:**191
  school shootings, **5:**24
  teacher compensation, **7:**210
  teacher licensing exams, **9:**85
  teacher training regulations, **9:**79
  year-round schools, **1:**237
California Charter Academy (CCA), **6:**287
California Supreme Court, **3:**179, **6:**168–169, **8:**2, **8:**233
Callahan, Raymond E., **9:**16–17, **9:**135
Cameras. *See* Video surveillance cameras
Camp Modin, **1:**139
Campaign for Fiscal Equity (CFE) Inc. v. State, **3:**182
Campbell, Amy L., **5:**237, **5:**242
Campbell v. St. Tammany Parish School Board, **4:**234, **4:**240
Camps, Jewish, **1:**126, **1:**132–133, **1:**136, **1:**139
Canada
  corporal punishment ban, **5:**110
  higher education, **6:**235
  Muslim students, **1:**59
Canada, Geoffrey, **9:**62, **9:**234
Canady v. Bossier Parish School Board, **5:**8, **8:**42–43, **8:**50
Cannan, John, **10:**180–181
Cannon v. University of Chicago, **8:**144–145
Cantwell v. Connecticut, **4:**xvii, **4:**44–45, **4:**98

Capper, Colleen A., **3:**249, **3:**251, **7:**106
CAPTA. *See* Child Abuse Prevention and Treatment Act
Care
  duty of, **5:**66
  ethic of, **5:**76
  meaning, **5:**100–101
  shown by teachers, **5:**150
  warm demanders, **5:**150–151
Career and technical education (CTE). *See* Vocational education
Carl D. Perkins Vocational and Applied Technology Education Act of 1990, **3:**127
Carlin, George, **2:**207
Carmichael, Sheila Byrd, **9:**26
Carnegie, Andrew, **9:**64, **9:**65–66, **9:**67–68, **9:**70
Carnegie Corporation of New York (CCNY), **9:**67–69
Carnegie Foundation for the Advancement of Teaching, **7:**174, **9:**65–67, **9:**177–178, **9:**183–184, **9:**185
Carnegie Units
  advantages, **9:**176, **9:**184–185
  alternatives to, **9:**176, **9:**181–182
  Common Core standards and, **9:**186, **9:**187–188
  creation, **9:**66–67, **9:**175, **9:**177–178, **9:**183–184
  criticism of, **9:**177, **9:**178–181, **9:**185, **9:**187
  definition, **9:**178
  potential elimination of, **9:**175–188
  proposed changes, **9:**181, **9:**185–188
  states abolishing, **9:**181–182
Carnoy, Martin, **1:**42, **3:**68
Carolina Abecedarian Project, **1:**202–203, **1:**205–206, **1:**213
Carparts Distribution Center, Inc. v. Automotive Wholesaler's Association, **10:**201
Carpenter, Linda Jean, **3:**209
Carrell, Scott, **7:**194
Carroll, Lewis, **7:**155
Carroll, Thomas, **9:**113, **9:**114
Carter, Deborah R., **5:**242
Carter, Jimmy, **7:**41, **7:**77, **9:**55
Carter, Stephen L., **10:**164
Catholic Church. *See* Roman Catholics
Cavalluzzo, Linda, **10:**90
Cavanaugh, Cathy, **10:**55

CBAs. *See* Collective bargaining agreements
CCA. *See* California Charter Academy
CCCR. *See* Citizens' Commission on Civil Rights
CCNY. *See* Carnegie Corporation of New York
CCSSI. *See* Common Core State Standards Initiative
CCSSO. *See* Council of Chief State School Officers
Cell phones. *See* Mobile technologies
Ceniceros v. Board of Trustees of San Diego School District, **4:**217, **4:**220
Censorship, **2:**207–208
Census Bureau, U.S., **2:**116–117, **3:**23, **9:**219
Center for Applied Special Technology, **10:**12
Center for Education Reform (CER), **1:**3, **1:**8, **1:**11, **6:**6, **7:**133, **7:**145
Center for Effective Discipline, **5:**113
Center for Talented Youth (CTY), Johns Hopkins University, **2:**164, **2:**165, **2:**167
Center for Teaching Quality, **6:**134, **9:**164
Center for the Prevention of School Violence (CPSV), **5:**169, **5:**170, **5:**173
Center on Education Policy (CEP), **3:**88, **3:**103, **3:**104, **7:**44, **7:**45, **7:**50, **9:**5, **9:**8, **9:**9, **9:**11
Centers for Disease Control and Prevention, **5:**29, **5:**74, **5:**78
CEP. *See* Center on Education Policy
CER. *See* Center for Education Reform
CFT. *See* Cincinnati Federation of Teachers
Chae, Mark H., **3:**26, **3:**27
Chae, Sung Y., **3:**26, **3:**27
Chalifoux v. New Caney Independent School District, **4:**268, **4:**272–273, **4:**277, **4:**280, **5:**13–14
Chall, Jeanne S., **2:**74, **2:**82–84, **2:**86–87, **2:**152, **2:**154
Chamberlin v. Dade County Board of Public Instruction, **4:**36, **4:**104, **4:**111
Chambers, Jay G., **6:**97
Chance, Cindi, **7:**53
Chandler v. James, **4:**40
Chandler v. Siegelman, **4:**47
Change
  failed efforts, **2:**236
  leadership of, **7:**80, **7:**232
  resistance to, **7:**212, **7:**231, **7:**255
  teachers' adaptation to, **2:**28–29
  See also Innovation; Reform proposals
Charles Hamilton Houston Institute for Race and Justice (CHHIRJ), **5:**163
Charlotte-Mecklenburg Board of Education, **6:**253
Charter school governance
  autonomy, **1:**7–8, **1:**11, **1:**24, **1:**36, **6:**xxiv, **6:**48–49, **6:**53, **6:**279
  differences from other public schools, **7:**140–142, **7:**145–146
  local control, **1:**1–2
  models, **7:**134–135
  reporting requirements, **6:**289–290
  state regulations, **1:**xxii, **1:**15, **1:**23–24, **6:**276–291, **7:**138–139, **7:**140–142
  in Washington, D.C., **7:**10–11
Charter school performance
  compared to public schools, **1:**9–10, **3:**56, **3:**67, **3:**69
  disclosure, **6:**290
  failures, **3:**70, **6:**53, **6:**287, **7:**145
  inconsistency, **6:**xxiv, **6:**277, **7:**139, **7:**143–145
  market forces and, **6:**284
  research on, **1:**11–14, **6:**279–280, **6:**282, **6:**289, **7:**215, **7:**220–221
  student achievement, **1:**10, **1:**11–14, **6:**279–280, **6:**289, **7:**137, **7:**215
Charter schools
  accountability, **1:**9, **1:**11–17, **1:**24–25, **1:**106, **6:**284, **6:**286–288, **6:**289–291, **7:**133, **7:**145
  advantages, **1:**4–10
  advocates, **1:**4–10, **1:**11, **1:**49, **6:**279–285, **6:**286, **7:**131, **7:**133
  approval agencies, **6:**287–288, **6:**290, **7:**131
  closures, **1:**15–16, **1:**17, **6:**284, **6:**287, **7:**145
  collective bargaining agreements and, **6:**xxiv, **6:**281, **7:**132, **7:**140–141, **9:**168–169
  competition with traditional schools, **1:**14, **6:**xxiv, **6:**270, **7:**142–143, **7:**214–215, **9:**230
  culturally specific, **1:**xxiii, **1:**54–70
  curricula, **1:**5, **1:**6–7
  cyber, **10:**77, **10:**87, **10:**88
  definition, **1:**xxii, **7:**130

enrollment, **1:**8–9, **1:**11, **1:**35, **7:**141
equity and diversity issues, **1:**16, **1:**24, **6:**282–283, **7:**144
ethnocentric, **1:**xxiii, **1:**6–7, **1:**19–33, **1:**49, **1:**133–134
financial management, **1:**14, **6:**48–49, **6:**53, **6:**284, **6:**287
for-profit management, **1:**10, **1:**13, **1:**82–87, **6:**279, **6:**287, **6:**288, **7:**144, **7:**179–180, **9:**225
funding, **1:**9, **1:**10, **1:**49, **6:**261, **6:**281–282, **6:**284–285, **6:**287, **9:**224–225
future of, **1:**10
goals, **1:**47, **1:**49, **1:**51–52, **7:**133
governance impact, **7:**xxvi–xxvii, **7:**130–146
growth, **1:**4, **1:**11, **1:**35, **1:**80–81
history, **1:**xxii, **1:**2, **6:**xxiii–xxiv, **6:**268, **7:**130–131
hybrid nature, **1:**2
instructional methods, **1:**5, **1:**6, **6:**291
leader development, **9:**124, **9:**127, **9:**128–129
learning communities, **6:**280–281
legislation, **6:**xxiv, **6:**279, **6:**286, **6:**290–291, **7:**130–132, **7:**133–134
lotteries, **1:**12, **6:**280
management problems, **1:**15, **1:**23
NCLB and, **1:**24–25, **6:**286, **6:**291, **7:**133
niche, **1:**xxii–xxiii, **1:**19
opposition, **1:**11–17, **6:**279, **6:**284
parental involvement, **6:**xxiv, **7:**189
politics and, **6:**290
privatization proposal, **1:**47–48
Race to the Top and, **3:**56, **3:**63
research on, **1:**10, **1:**17, **6:**279–280, **6:**282, **6:**288, **6:**289
segregated, **1:**16, **1:**24, **1:**31–32, **1:**51, **3:**56, **3:**70, **6:**254, **6:**277, **7:**52–53
sizes, **1:**8–9
students with disabilities, **1:**14, **1:**16
target populations, **1:**6–7
teacher firing, **1:**6, **1:**17
teacher hiring, **1:**17, **6:**281, **7:**132, **7:**140–141
teacher salaries, **1:**14
teacher turnover, **1:**17, **6:**281, **7:**143
teachers, **1:**17, **6:**xxiv, **6:**291
union policies, **1:**2, **6:**284, **7:**38
variations, **7:**131–132, **7:**134–135
viability as alternative, **1:**1–17

virtual, **1:**5, **1:**13, **10:**77
in Washington, D.C., **7:**10–11, **7:**131
See also Faith-based charter schools
Charters, W. W., **9:**14
Chase, Susan, **7:**105–106
Chávez-Eakle, Rosa Aurora, **2:**170, **2:**171–172
Cheating. *See* Academic dishonesty
Check-in/check-out (CICO) systems, **5:**236–237
Cheema v. Thompson, **4:**267–268, **4:**277
Cheney, Lynne, **2:**155
CHHIRJ. *See* Charles Hamilton Houston Institute for Race and Justice
Chicago Public Schools
charter schools, **1:**13
mayoral control, **7:**15, **7:**18, **7:**226
NAEP scores, **7:**15
performance pay, **7:**37
school councils, **7:**15
schools chancellor, **7:**226
teacher salaries, **6:**140, **9:**172
teacher turnover, **9:**114
video surveillance, **10:**xxiv
Chicago School Reform Act of 1988, **7:**15
Chicago Teacher Advancement Program, **3:**270
Child abuse. *See* Abuse and neglect
Child Abuse Prevention and Treatment Act of 1974 (CAPTA), **5:**90, **5:**96, **5:**99
Child Evangelical Fellowship v. Montgomery County Public Schools, **4:**251
Child Evangelism Fellowship of New Jersey v. Stafford Township School District, **4:**251, **4:**256–257, **4:**259
Child Fellowship of Maryland v. Montgomery County Public Schools, **4:**257
Child labor laws, **7:**3, **7:**149
Child pornography, **10:**148
Child Protective Services (CPS) agencies, **5:**94–95, **5:**96, **5:**97, **5:**102
Children's Internet Protection Act (CIPA), **10:**140
Children's Law Center, **5:**xx–xxi
Chile, school system, **7:**47
China
Christianity in, **4:**175
economic power, **7:**76
one child policy, **7:**53
school year lengths, **1:**248

Choi, Daniel, **2:**119
Choice
  benefits of, **1:**150–151, **7:**137, **7:**214–215, **7:**219
  constitutional issues, **6:**242, **6:**244, **6:**250–251
  debates on, **1:**92–107, **6:**xxiii, **6:**249–250, **6:**283–284
  effects on academic performance, **1:**104–105, **6:**270
  future issues, **1:**107
  governance issues, **1:**105–106
  history, **6:**268
  legal basis, **1:**xix–xxi
  local school funding and, **6:**15–16
  options, **1:**xxi, **1:**101
  private funding, **7:**179
  public funding, **1:**92–107
  religious schools included in, **6:**xxiii, **6:**241–242
  results, **1:**102–104
  rights and, **1:**27
  state programs, **9:**224–225
  tax credits for tuition, **1:**92, **6:**258, **6:**261, **6:**263–265
  tracking students, **7:**210
  See also Charter schools; Homeschooling; Magnet schools; Market competition; Private schools; Vouchers
Christensen, Clayton M., **10:**xviii, **10:**xxv–xxvi, **10:**115
Christensen, Lynnette, **5:**243
Christenson, Bruce, **1:**170, **1:**177
Christian Coalition, **1:**48
Christian Legal Society Chapter of the University of California, Hastings College of the Law v. Martinez, **2:**201, **4:**221–223, **4:**224
Christian Right, **7:**218
Christianity
  African American churches, **1:**25, **3:**227
  Amish, **1:**xx–xxi, **1:**112–113, **1:**123, **4:**74, **4:**273–274
  global spread, **4:**174, **4:**175
  nondenominational churches, **1:**149
  Protestants, **1:**22, **2:**198, **4:**274
  Puritans, **4:**172, **4:**176
  See also Religions; Religious symbols; Roman Catholics
Christie, Chris, **3:**58, **3:**63
Christmas. *See* Religious holidays

Chubb, John E., **1:**150–151, **7:**178
Church of God (Worldwide, Texas Region) v. Amarillo Independent School District, **4:**206
Churches. *See* Christianity; Religious groups
Church-state separation
  charter schools and, **1:**xxiii, **1:**21, **1:**25, **1:**29–31, **1:**57, **1:**65
  Jefferson on, **2:**204, **4:**xvii, **4:**17–18, **4:**45, **4:**100, **4:**130, **4:**194, **4:**281
  Madison on, **1:**46
  neutrality of government, **4:**44, **4:**56, **4:**57–58, **4:**85–86
  neutrality of schools, **4:**xxviii, **4:**91, **4:**279, **4:**280, **4:**281, **4:**287, **4:**293
  released time programs and, **4:**153, **4:**158, **4:**163–164
  religious music and, **4:**104, **4:**114–116
  religious schools and, **1:**40–41, **1:**46, **4:**xviii, **4:**1–2, **6:**267–268, **6:**272–273
  science curriculum and, **4:**196–197
  in state constitutions, **6:**250–251, **6:**267–268
  Supreme Court invocation of, **4:**xix, **4:**1–2, **4:**18, **4:**45, **4:**130–131
  vouchers and, **1:**30–31, **1:**40–41, **1:**93, **1:**95–96, **6:**xxiii, **6:**242, **6:**244, **6:**255, **6:**272
  wall metaphor, **4:**1–2, **4:**130–131, **4:**194, **4:**281
  See also Endorsement test; Establishment Clause; First Amendment; *Lemon* (tripartite) test; Religions
CICO systems. *See* Check-in/check-out systems
Cincinnati Federation of Teachers (CFT), **7:**37
Cincinnati Public Schools (CPS), **1:**229–230, **6:**45
Cincinnati v. Walter, **9:**191, **9:**204, **9:**210–211
CIPA. *See* Children's Internet Protection Act
Circle Schools v. Pappert, **4:**138–139, **4:**149
Cities. *See* Local governments; Urban school districts
Citizens' Commission on Civil Rights (CCCR), **7:**27–28
Citizens for Strong Schools v. Florida State Board of Education, **6:**171–172

Citizenship, **9**:219, **9**:220, **9**:231
  See also Digital citizenship
City of Boerne, Texas v. Flores, **4**:278
Civil rights. *See* Due process; Rights
Civil Rights Act of 1964
  desegregation and, **3**:2, **3**:13, **3**:15
  equal pay and, **3**:207
  passage, **3**:78, **3**:242, **7**:250
  Title IV, **3**:13
  Title VI, **1**:xviii, **3**:13, **3**:15
  Title VII, **4**:284, **7**:xix, **7**:93–94, **8**:147, **8**:241
  Title IX, **7**:xxviii, **7**:93–94, **7**:104
Civil rights movement, **3**:78
CLA. *See* Collegiate Learning Assessment
Clark, D. C., **2**:48
Clark County School District (CCSD), Nevada, **5**:160, **7**:137–138
Clark v. Crues, **8**:22
Clark v. Dallas Independent School District, **4**:228
CLASS. *See* Classroom Assessment Scoring System
Class differences. *See* Economic classes; Low socioeconomic groups
Class sizes
  efficiency considerations, **9**:16
  in for-profit schools, **1**:83
  legislated maximum, **6**:228
  student achievement and, **1**:131, **9**:198–199
Classroom Assessment Scoring System (CLASS), **9**:152–153
Classroom management
  bullying prevention, **5**:61, **5**:65
  collaborative learning environments, **5**:xxiv, **5**:141–142
  engaging students, **5**:154–155
  extrinsic motivators, **5**:141–155
  importance, **5**:xxiv, **5**:141, **5**:144
  instructional plans and, **5**:151–152
  rules, **5**:144, **5**:148, **5**:149, **5**:151
  skills, **5**:xxiv, **5**:142–143, **5**:144
Clergy, **4**:297–298
  See also Religious groups
Cleveland, Ohio
  court takeover of schools, **7**:14
  mayoral control of schools, **7**:15, **7**:126
  public-private partnerships, **9**:249–250
  voucher program, **1**:95–97, **6**:244, **6**:245–247

Cleveland Board of Education v. Loudermill, **8**:230
Clever v. Cherry Hill Township Board of Education, **4**:104, **4**:109–110, **4**:202, **4**:208, **4**:211
Clinton, Bill, **1**:49, **3**:14, **4**:278, **5**:2, **9**:xviii, **9**:xxvii, **9**:24
Clothing
  cultural differences, **2**:130
  gang-related, **4**:268, **5**:1, **5**:5, **5**:11–15, **8**:50
  messages on, **4**:263, **4**:264, **5**:5, **5**:6–10, **5**:15–16, **8**:50, **8**:182, **8**:190
  See also Dress code policies; Religious garb; Uniforms
Clubs
  gay rights groups, **4**:216
  student-led, **4**:217
  See also Religious clubs
C.N. v. Willmar Public Schools, **5**:225, **5**:226
Coaching, of teachers, **2**:4–5
  See also Athletics
Coalition for Adequacy and Fairness in School Funding v. Chiles, **3**:181, **6**:202–203
Coalition for Educational Equity and Adequacy v. Heineman, **3**:182
Coalition of Essential Schools, **9**:42
Cobb, Casey, **5**:11, **8**:53, **8**:54–55
Cobb, Edith, **2**:244
Cochran v. Louisiana State Board of Education, **4**:5, **4**:26
Cochran-Smith, Marilyn, **9**:115
Cocteau, Jean, **2**:230
Coeducation
  advantages, **1**:192–195
  history, **1**:189–190
  See also Single-sex schools and classes
Coercion test
  prayer in schools and, **4**:xix, **4**:38, **4**:40, **4**:46, **4**:99
  religious holidays and, **4**:202, **4**:204–205, **4**:210, **4**:211
  religious music and, **4**:114, **4**:116
  See also Establishment Clause
Cognitive skills, **2**:169–170, **2**:172–173
Cohen, David K., **7**:171
Cohen-Vogel, Lora, **9**:136
Coklar, Ahmet Naci, **10**:123
Coleman, James, **1**:148, **3**:98, **9**:263
Coleman Report, **3**:80, **3**:98

Coley, Richard J., **3**:85, **3**:104–105
Collaboration
  among teachers, **7**:81, **7**:83
  with community agencies, **9**:201
  with parents, **9**:269, **9**:271–272
  in science, **2**:91
  use of technology, **10**:198–199
Collaborative learning environments
  engaging students, **5**:141–142
  establishing, **7**:152
  importance, **5**:xxiv
  technology used, **10**:40, **10**:214, **10**:217, **10**:223
Collective bargaining
  criticism of, **7**:26, **7**:34
  legislation, **7**:23, **7**:33, **7**:34
  by public employees, **8**:244, **8**:245, **8**:248, **8**:258
  resistance to reforms, **7**:27–32
  topics, **7**:33
  See also Unions
Collective bargaining agreements (CBAs)
  academic freedom and, **8**:256–257
  charter schools and, **6**:xxiv, **6**:281, **7**:132, **7**:140–141, **9**:168–169
  criticism of, **8**:xxiv, **8**:255–257
  effects, **9**:167, **9**:168
  effects on reform process, **7**:27–32
  employment protections, **8**:239–240
  financial provisions, **7**:29, **7**:36–37, **8**:255–256, **9**:169, **9**:171–172
  grievance procedures, **8**:239–240
  limits on administrative flexibility, **7**:23, **7**:25–26, **7**:28–32, **7**:35–36
  negotiations, **1**:77, **8**:245, **8**:255, **8**:256, **8**:257
  performance-based pay and, **6**:137
  public views of, **8**:245
  seniority provisions, **9**:168–170
  work rules, **7**:30–31, **7**:35, **8**:256–257
College Board, **3**:162, **3**:259, **3**:260, **6**:221, **6**:234, **6**:235, **6**:237–238, **9**:29, **9**:32, **9**:253
  See also Advanced Placement courses
Colleges and universities. *See* Higher education
Collegiate Learning Assessment (CLA), **9**:68–69
Colonial governments
  control of schools, **7**:xvii
  religion and, **4**:88–89
  school systems, **1**:xvi–xvii, **7**:6, **7**:115–116
  See also Massachusetts Bay Colony
Colorado
  charter schools, **6**:xxiv, **6**:277, **7**:131, **10**:88
  debt limits, **6**:35
  finance litigation, **3**:180
  Pledge of Allegiance law, **4**:147
  virtual schools, **10**:88, **10**:89
Colorado Education Association, **7**:36
Colorado Supreme Court, **8**:58, **8**:69
Columbine shootings, **4**:277, **4**:278, **5**:xxii, **5**:16, **5**:24, **5**:28, **5**:64, **5**:190
Columbus City Schools, **9**:164, **9**:248
Colvin ex rel. Colvin v. Lowndes County, Mississippi, School District, **5**:20
Colwell, Brad, **1**:118
Committee for Educational Rights v. Edgar, **6**:158
Committee for Public Education and Religion Liberty v. Regan, **4**:6
Committee for Public Education v. Nyquist, **4**:11–12
Committee of Ten, **3**:153
Common Core State Standards Initiative (CCSSI), **9**:20–35
  adoption, **2**:62, **6**:14, **6**:82, **9**:39, **9**:40, **9**:62
  assessments, **2**:57, **2**:62, **9**:xxi, **9**:40, **9**:59–60, **9**:187–188, **9**:224
  assumptions, **9**:40
  Carnegie Units and, **9**:186, **9**:187–188
  criticism of, **9**:30, **9**:60
  development of, **2**:31, **6**:82, **9**:5, **9**:11, **9**:31–32, **9**:33–34, **9**:59
  failure predicted, **9**:35
  federal support, **3**:63, **6**:82, **9**:59, **9**:62
  funding tied to, **6**:82
  goals, **2**:31–32, **3**:63, **9**:xxi, **9**:20, **9**:34–35, **9**:230–231
  literacy standards, **2**:105
  need for, **2**:62, **9**:29–30, **9**:224
  technology standards, **10**:217–218
Common school movement, **4**:270
Communication
  with alumni, **10**:197
  cultural differences and, **2**:128–130, **2**:132–134
  between schools and parents, **3**:xxiv, **9**:268, **9**:269–270, **10**:195–197

Communications technology, **2:**240–241, **7:**213, **10:**32, **10:**199–200, **10:**220–221
 See also Mobile technologies; Technology
Communities
 influences on bullying behaviors, **5:**69
 local history, **2:**70
 relations with schools, **6:**304, **7:**236, **9:**201
 segregated, **1:**31–32, **3:**16, **3:**86, **6:**18–19, **7:**61, **7:**63
 suicide prevention, **5:**74–75
 See also Local control of schools; Local governments
Communities of practice, **2:**133, **3:**44, **3:**45
Community colleges
 cooperative programs with high schools, **1:**231, **9:**44–45
 programs, **3:**122, **3:**123
 remedial classes, **6:**237, **6:**303–304
Community policing, **5:**167–168, **5:**174
Community schools. *See* Full-service community schools
Compensatory education
 accountability, **3:**239, **3:**247
 alternative models, **3:**249–250, **3:**251
 closing achievement gaps, **3:**75–90, **3:**93–110
 definition, **3:**237
 eligibility, **3:**239, **3:**249
 goals, **3:**241–242
 grade levels, **3:**250
 overrepresentation of minority students, **3:**169
 pull-out programs, **3:**239, **3:**243–245, **3:**247–248, **3:**249–250, **3:**251–252
 schoolwide model, **3:**239
 state-funded, **3:**6–7
 stigma of pull-out programs, **3:**239, **3:**249, **3:**253
 target populations, **3:**237–238, **3:**242, **3:**243
 Title I funding, **3:**56, **3:**75, **3:**82, **3:**93–94, **3:**98, **3:**238, **3:**243, **3:**251
 See also Head Start
Competition. *See* Global competition; Market competition
Compton, Robert, **7:**54
Compulsory education laws
 constitutionality, **1:**119
 financing obligations of states, **6:**13
 for high school, **3:**114, **6:**215, **7:**149
 history, **1:**xvii, **6:**182, **6:**221, **7:**149
 homeschooling and, **1:**114, **1:**116, **1:**118, **1:**121, **1:**122
 in loco parentis doctrine and, **5:**205
 purpose, **6:**215, **6:**221
 released time programs and, **4:**164
 religious exemptions, **1:**xx–xxi, **1:**112–113, **1:**114, **1:**123, **4:**74, **4:**273–274
Computers
 digital consciousness, **2:**241–242
 educational benefits, **10:**212–215, **10:**222–223
 laptops, **10:**39, **10:**41, **10:**111
 ratio to students, **10:**xvi, **10:**215
 See also Technology
Congress
 Child Abuse Prevention and Treatment Act, **5:**90, **5:**96, **5:**99
 conditional spending legislation, **6:**87–92
 Drug-Free Schools and Campuses Act of 1989, **5:**22
 education funding, **6:**77–78
 education legislation, **6:**86, **6:**102, **7:**xxv, **7:**41, **7:**76–77
 Keep America's Students Safe Act, **5:**219, **5:**223, **5:**224, **5:**227, **5:**228
 powers, **6:**77–78, **6:**85–87
 See also Gun-Free Schools Act; Individuals with Disabilities Education Act
Conn, Kathleen, **8:**156
Connecticut
 constitution, **6:**233
 magnet schools, **1:**169
 New Haven, **9:**164
 school resource officers, **5:**161–162
 teacher assessments, **9:**90
Conner, Erin, **3:**139
Connick v. Myers, **8:**193–194, **8:**199–200, **8:**205–206
Conservatives, **1:**47–48, **1:**50–51, **2:**154–155, **2:**203–205, **3:**244, **4:**31, **7:**252
Constitution, U.S.
 Bill of Rights, **4:**96–98
 Commerce Clause, **6:**164
 congressional powers, **6:**77–78, **6:**85–87
 copyright clause, **8:**31
 Eighteenth Amendment, **2:**204

Eighth Amendment, **5**:xviii, **5**:49, **5**:107, **5**:111, **5**:116, **5**:199, **5**:218
federalism, **7**:61–62
Founders' debates, **4**:96–97
as living document, **7**:62–63
Nineteenth Amendment, **3**:207–208
originalism, **7**:61–62
privacy protection, **8**:160, **8**:165–166, **10**:103–104, **10**:108
Privileges and Immunities Clause, **7**:66
Spending Clause, **6**:77–78, **6**:86–88, **6**:89–90, **7**:42
state powers, **6**:76–77, **7**:1–2
Tenth Amendment, **6**:86, **6**:114, **7**:1–2, **7**:40, **7**:68, **9**:28
See also First Amendment; Fourteenth Amendment; Fourth Amendment
Constitutions, state. *See* State constitutions
Constructivist curriculum and instruction, **2**:xxiii, **2**:235
Contemplation and Education Initiative, **2**:245
Continuous improvement, **9**:201
Cooper, Bruce S., **1**:40, **1**:43, **10**:16
Cooper v. Aaron, **3**:15
Cooper v. Eugene School District 4J, **4**:276, **4**:285, **4**:298
Cooperative learning, **1**:266, **3**:157
COPS. *See* Office of Community Policing Services
Copyright Act, **8**:21–22, **8**:32, **8**:34
Copyright law
constitutional provision, **8**:31
copyrightable works, **8**:21–23
e-book issues, **10**:22
fair use in education, **8**:xxv, **8**:21–36
fair use tests, **8**:26–28, **8**:32, **8**:34
length of protection, **8**:25
new technology and, **8**:31, **8**:35, **10**:22
potential changes, **8**:30
practical application, **8**:28–29, **8**:31
purpose, **8**:24–25
student ignorance of, **5**:129, **5**:130, **5**:133–134
"works for hire," **8**:22–23
See also Plagiarism
Copyright Term Extension Act (CTEA), **8**:25
Corales v. Bennett, **5**:84
Corbell, Kristen A., **10**:123
Cordeiro, Paula A., **7**:13

Corder v. Lewis Palmer School District No. 38, **4**:41, **4**:42, **4**:43, **4**:46
Cornell University, **9**:65
Corporal punishment
abolition of, **5**:106–121
by administrators, **5**:205
alternatives, **5**:114–115, **5**:119
current use, **5**:110–111, **5**:116, **5**:199, **5**:206
definition, **5**:109
educational benefits, **5**:119–120
effectiveness, **5**:112–113, **5**:119
excessive, **5**:95, **5**:117
federal ban issue, **5**:115, **5**:118, **5**:120–121
history of use, **5**:xviii, **5**:107, **5**:110
inequities, **5**:113–114
in loco parentis doctrine and, **5**:195, **5**:199, **5**:204–206
legal cases, **5**:106, **5**:107, **5**:111–112, **5**:117, **5**:195, **5**:204–206
legal status, **5**:106–107, **5**:110–112, **5**:115–117, **5**:199, **5**:218
negative consequences, **5**:109–110, **5**:112–114
state bans, **5**:xviii, **5**:107, **5**:110, **5**:111–112, **5**:116–117
by teachers, **5**:107, **5**:195, **5**:204–206
See also Ingraham v. Wright; Physical restraints
Corporation of Presiding Bishop of Church of Jesus Christ of Latter-day Saints v. Amos, **4**:23, **4**:24, **4**:57
Corporations. *See* Business interests; Educational management organizations
Corruption, **7**:xix, **7**:xx, **7**:3
Co-teaching, **7**:46
Cottle, Thomas J., **3**:156
Council for Exceptional Children, **6**:121
Council for the Accreditation of Educator Preparation (CAEP), **2**:44
Council of Chief State School Officers (CCSSO), **7**:155, **7**:175, **9**:31–32, **9**:89, **9**:91
See also Common Core State Standards Initiative
Counselors
bullying prevention and interventions, **5**:61–62
communication with parents, **3**:xxiv
dismissals, **8**:233–234

effectiveness, **3:**30
ethics codes, **3:**23, **3:**24, **3:**25
mandated reporting of abuse and neglect, **5:**96
mental health interventions, **5:**253–254
multicultural education for, **3:**19–35
popular culture use by, **3:**143
prejudices, **3:**25, **3:**28
professionalization, **3:**19–20
roles and responsibilities, **3:**19–20
suicide prevention efforts, **5:**78, **5:**80, **5:**85, **5:**254
See also Psychologists
Counts, George, **9:**15
County governments. *See* Local governments
County of Allegheny v. American Civil Liberties Union, **4:**22, **4:**121, **4:**132–133, **4:**210
Courts. *See* Judicial branch
Coutts, Larry M., **1:**192
Couture v. Board of Education of Albuquerque Public Schools, **5:**215
Coventry, Rhode Island, **5:**15–16
Coverdell Teacher Protection Act of 2001 (TPA), **5:**xxv, **5:**177–178, **5:**180, **5:**183, **5:**190–191
Covey, Stephen, **7:**196
Cowan v. Strafford R-VI School District, **8:**235–236
Cox, Chikako I., **3:**32–33
Coy v. Board of Education of Canton City Schools, **10:**186–187
CPS. *See* Child Protective Services; Cincinnati Public Schools; Creative problem solving
CPSV. *See* Center for the Prevention of School Violence
Craft
distinction from art, **2:**151–152, **2:**153–154
instruction as, **2:**151, **2:**153
Crawford, Matthew B., **1:**230
Creation science, **4:**xxv, **4:**184, **4:**185, **4:**193, **4:**196–197
See also Intelligent design
Creative Commons licensing, **10:**22
Creative problem solving (CPS), **2:**172–173
Creativity
cognitive processes, **2:**169–170, **2:**172–173
cosmic consciousness and, **2:**244
cultivating, **2:**xxii–xxiii, **2:**155
of gifted students, **2:**165, **2:**166–167, **2:**168–169, **2:**171–172
play and, **2:**174–175
skills learned in arts education, **2:**145–149
Credit recovery courses, **10:**51, **10:**57–58, **10:**73, **10:**77
Crime
involvement of suspended students, **5:**32
overrepresentation of minorities, **5:**47–48
in schools, **5:**24, **5:**25, **5:**48, **5:**160, **5:**161–162, **5:**180–181
school-to-prison pipeline, **5:**33–34, **5:**44–45, **5:**162
sexual assault, **10:**202
theft, **2:**208
violent, **5:**24
white collar, **2:**208
See also Abuse and neglect; Safety
Crimmins, Daniel, **5:**233
Crist v. Alpine Union School District, **10:**102
Crockett, Lee, **1:**229
Croft v. Governor of Texas, **4:**68, **4:**74–75
Cross, Frank, **6:**174
CRT. *See* Culturally responsive teaching
Crucial conversations, **7:**88
Cruz, Carlos, **2:**171–172
CTE. *See* Career and technical education
CTEA. *See* Copyright Term Extension Act
CTY. *See* Center for Talented Youth
Cubism, **2:**94–95, **2:**155
Cullen, Julie B., **6:**106
Cultural capital, **2:**108–109
Cultural competence
of administrators, **7:**196–197, **7:**199–200
definition, **3:**51
of teachers, **3:**51, **3:**144–145, **7:**82
Cultural differences
aspects, **2:**124–126
communication and, **2:**128–130, **2:**132–134
counselors and, **3:**19–35
in curriculum, **2:**136–137, **3:**21
languages and, **3:**198–199
in learning styles, **3:**165
Muslim students and mainstream culture, **1:**59–61, **1:**63
stereotypes, **2:**128–130, **3:**147

between teachers and students, **2:**136, **2:**137–138, **5:**100
See also Diversity; Ethnocentric charter schools; Immigrants; Languages; Minority students; Native American schools
Cultural relativism, **3:**33–34
Cultural tolerance
  holiday celebrations, **7:**188
  learning and, **7:**201
  moral development and, **2:**197
  See also Religious tolerance
Culturally responsive learning, **7:**199–200
Culturally responsive teaching (CRT), **1:**258–261, **1:**265–266, **1:**267, **3:**134–135, **3:**137, **3:**141, **3:**143–145
  See also Popular culture
Culture
  Eurocentrism, **2:**134–137
  high vs. low, **2:**214
  See also Arts; Popular culture
Cunningham, William G., **7:**13
Curricula
  arts in, **2:**142–156
  of charter schools, **1:**5, **1:**6–7
  constructivist, **2:**xxiii
  definition, **2:**xvii
  discipline and control model, **2:**xxii–xxv
  discretion of teachers, **7:**158–161, **7:**161, **8:**7–9, **8:**10–11, **8:**13, **8:**14–15
  diversity in, **1:**203–204, **2:**136–137, **3:**xxi–xxii, **3:**21, **3:**70, **3:**134–135
  English language arts, **2:**32, **7:**45, **7:**50, **9:**14
  in for-profit schools, **1:**79, **1:**83
  gatekeeper subjects, **9:**11
  gifted education, **2:**158–175, **6:**122
  hidden, **7:**80
  history, **6:**220
  homeschooling, **1:**110, **1:**116, **1:**120–121
  liberal arts, **2:**xxi–xxii, **2:**152
  of magnet schools, **1:**161, **1:**166, **1:**171, **1:**175
  materials publishers, **2:**29, **7:**166
  mathematics, **2:**32, **3:**154–155, **7:**45, **7:**50
  narrowing due to NCLB, **7:**45, **7:**50–51, **7:**55, **9:**10–11, **9:**29
  parental objections to content, **2:**202
  popular culture in, **2:**211–226, **3:**133–147
  programmatic, **1:**83, **2:**1–2, **2:**4–10, **2:**14–17, **2:**19, **8:**8
  reading, **6:**79–80
  research on, **2:**29
  research-based, **1:**79, **2:**5–6, **6:**85
  Science, Technology, Engineering, and Mathematics, **9:**225
  science controversies, **1:**116, **4:**xxv, **4:**31, **4:**184–199
  social studies, **8:**6
  soft skills, **7:**54
  student relationships to, **2:**12–13, **2:**15
  student-centered, **2:**152
  for students with disabilities, **2:**181–186, **2:**187, **2:**192–193
  teacher relationships to, **2:**13–15, **3:**42–43
  technology integration, **2:**234–236, **2:**239, **10:**131–132
  theories, **2:**xvii–xxv
  tracking and, **3:**154–155, **3:**161–162
  traditional, **2:**xxiii–xxiv, **2:**56, **2:**152
  trends, **2:**xxiii–xxiv, **2:**55–56
  universal design in, **10:**13–14
  See also Carnegie Units; "English-only" curriculum; Instruction; Textbooks
Curriculum development and adoption
  academic freedom and, **8:**xxi, **8:**1–19
  alignment to standards, **2:**55–70, **6:**80–81, **8:**13, **8:**14, **9:**5
  assessed curriculum, **2:**60
  centralized control, **2:**xxiv, **2:**1, **2:**4–6, **2:**19, **2:**21, **7:**258–259
  challenges, **2:**5–6, **2:**13–14
  commercial interests and, **2:**29, **2:**32
  conceptual framework, **2:**60–61
  enacted curriculum, **2:**60, **2:**63
  federal mandates, **6:**76–92
  implementation, **6:**82–83
  instructional practices and, **6:**81, **6:**82–83
  intended curriculum, **2:**58–59, **2:**60
  local control, **2:**30–31, **2:**64, **8:**6, **8:**10, **8:**12, **9:**59–60, **10:**131–132
  political agendas, **8:**5–6
  professional development, **6:**122
  standards-based reform and, **2:**58–59
  teacher roles, **2:**18–33, **3:**42–43, **8:**4–9
  uniformity, **8:**14–15

Curriculum standards
  disadvantages, **2:**64, **2:**66–67, **2:**69, **2:**70
  English language arts, **2:**221, **6:**82, **9:**5,
    9:25, **9:**26–27, **9:**40, **9:**59
  granularity, **10:**128
  for history, **9:**32–33
  influence of accreditation bodies, **2:**35–36
  NCLB requirements, **2:**184
  purposes, **10:**127
  of states, **2:**21, **2:**61–62, **8:**12–13, **8:**14,
    8:17, **9:**5, **10:**128
  See also Common Core State Standards
    Initiative
Curry v. Hensiner, **4:**251, **4:**255
Customs Service, U.S., **8:**78
Cutter v. Wilkinson, **4:**22, **4:**56–57
Cyberbullying
  activities, **10:**154
  definition, **10:**153, **10:**157
  differences from traditional bullying,
    10:157–158
  discipline authority of schools, **8:**184,
    10:xxv, **10:**153–171, **10:**189
  effects, **10:**157, **10:**158
  incidence, **10:**xxv, **10:**37–38, **10:**153,
    10:154, **10:**203
  legal cases, **10:**159–160, **10:**168–170
  prevention, **10:**156, **10:**170–171
  sexual, **8:**157
  on social networking sites, **5:**63–64,
    10:xxv, **10:**147, **10:**205
  state laws, **10:**154, **10:**155, **10:**162–163,
    10:165–166
  See also Bullying
Cyberbullying Research Center, **10:**153
Cyberharassment
  discipline policies, **10:**153–171
  incidence, **10:**xxv, **10:**153, **10:**157
  state laws, **10:**154, **10:**155
Cyberschools
  cost-effectiveness, **10:**87–88
  costs, **10:**81–82, **10:**84–85, **10:**89
  definition, **10:**81
  for-profit management, **10:**81,
    10:84–85, **10:**87
  See also Online courses; Virtual schools
Czerniak, Charlene, **2:**96

Dabrowski, Kazimierz, **2:**171
Dade County Schools (DCS), **5:**160
Daggett, Willard R., **1:**222, **1:**229, **1:**233
D'Agostino, Jerome V., **3:**89

Dalai Lama, **2:**245
Dale, Reginald, **1:**192
Daley, Richard, **7:**15, **7:**18
Daniel R.R. v. State Board of Education,
  8:114–115, **8:**121
Danzberger, Jacqueline P., **7:**13–14
Darling-Hammond, Linda, **2:**40, **2:**245,
  3:42–43, **3:**45, **3:**46, **3:**86, **7:**114,
  9:xxii–xxiii, **9:**89, **9:**112, **9:**115–116
Darrow, R., **10:**84
Darwin, Charles, **4:**187–188, **4:**190, **4:**191,
  4:195–196
Data leaders, principals as, **7:**80–81, **9:**120
Data Quality Campaign, **9:**223–224
*Daugherty v. Vanguard Charter School
  Academy*, **4:**234, **4:**237–238
Daughtrey, A., **9:**116
*Davis v. Monroe County Board of
  Education*, **5:**55–56, **5:**67–68, **8:**145,
  8:147, **8:**148–149, **8:**151, **8:**154–155
Dayton Early College Academy (DECA),
  9:168–169, **9:**171
Dayton Leadership Academies, **1:**86
DCPCSB. *See* District of Columbia Public
  Charter School Board
DCPS. *See* District of Columbia Public
  Schools
DCS. *See* Dade County Schools
de Broglie, Louis, **2:**170
De Luca, Barbara M., **6:**73–74
Deal, Terrence E., **3:**49
Debt
  limits on, **6:**21–38
  market forces and, **6:**31, **6:**36–37
  short-term, **6:**27
  See also Bonds
DECA. *See* Dayton Early College Academy
Decentralized governance, **6:**76–77, **7:**246,
  7:255–256, **9:**124–125
  See also Autonomy
Deci, Edward L., **5:**152, **5:**153
Decision output theory, **7:**256
Decker, Janet R., **5:**186–187
Declaration of Independence, **4:**144
Dede, Chris, **2:**235
Deetz, Stanley, **9:**268, **9:**272
deKlerk, Gerda, **2:**119
del Carmen Lara, M, **2:**171–172
Delaware, finance litigation, **3:**182
Delconte v. State of North Carolina, **1:**121
Deleuze, Gilles, **2:**230
Delpit, Lisa, **9:**270

DeMitchell, Todd A., **5**:11, **8**:47, **8**:53, **8**:54–55
Demmert, William G., Jr., **1**:260
Democracy
 in curriculum, **2**:18
 public education and, **2**:xviii–xxi, **2**:20, **6**:268
 school governance and, **2**:18, **2**:24–25, **7**:178, **7**:257–258, **9**:17
 theories, **7**:256
 See also Elections; Equality; Rights
Demographics
 of school board members, **7**:118, **7**:124
 of teachers, **2**:22
 See also Diversity
Denver Classroom Teachers Association, **7**:36
Denver Public Schools, **7**:36, **9**:16
Department of Education, U.S.
 attempts to abolish, **7**:252
 budgets, **6**:107, **9**:252
 charter school research, **1**:12
 church-school partnerships, **3**:228
 Common Core standards and, **9**:24, **9**:59–60
 crime reports, **5**:180, **5**:181
 data system improvements, **9**:223–224
 desegregation efforts, **3**:16
 evidence-based practices, **5**:243
 GFSA reports, **5**:23, **5**:26
 history, **7**:2, **7**:41, **7**:77, **9**:55
 IDEA implementation reports, **2**:190
 Institute of Education Sciences, **1**:131, **2**:10
 Magnet Schools Assistance Program, **1**:166, **1**:167, **1**:169, **1**:170, **1**:175
 National Educational Technology Plan, **10**:55, **10**:130, **10**:132, **10**:218–219
 National Household Education Surveys Program, **1**:112
 National Indian Education Study, **1**:263
 National School Civil Rights Survey, **5**:31
 Office of Civil Rights, **5**:111, **5**:114, **8**:149, **8**:152, **8**:153–154
 privacy protection, **10**:109
 roles, **7**:2
 school improvement grants, **9**:123–124
 school uniform policies, **8**:38, **8**:47
 technology funding, **10**:xvii
 technology research, **10**:xix

Third International Mathematics and Science Study, **1**:241
Title I implementation reports, **3**:103
Department of Health and Human Services, U.S., **5**:26, **5**:90
See also Head Start
Department of Justice, U.S., **5**:166
Depression
 interventions, **5**:253
 prevalence, **5**:xxi, **5**:251
 symptoms, **5**:xxi, **5**:248, **5**:251, **5**:255, **5**:257, **5**:258–259
 See also Internalizing disorders
Deregulation. *See* Teacher licensing, alternative routes
DeRolph v. State, **3**:181, **6**:25, **6**:27, **6**:200, **6**:201, **9**:204, **9**:207, **9**:211–212
Desegregation
 ability grouping and, **3**:151, **3**:162
 achievement gap and, **3**:11, **7**:76–77
 in Boston, **7**:14
 challenges in, **3**:xxvi, **7**:xxvii–xxviii
 compensatory education and, **3**:7, **3**:237
 court rulings, **3**:xxvi, **3**:1–17, **6**:253, **7**:62–63
 court supervision, **3**:2, **3**:6, **3**:15
 in Detroit, **3**:6, **7**:67
 federal role, **3**:15, **3**:16, **6**:99, **6**:253, **7**:250
 financial leverage, **3**:15
 forced busing, **3**:2–3, **6**:253
 Green factors, **3**:2, **3**:6
 of higher education, **3**:4–5
 implementation, **3**:xxi, **3**:2, **3**:261
 importance, **3**:8–9
 legislated policies, **3**:11–12, **3**:13–14, **3**:17
 magnet schools and, **1**:xxvi, **1**:163, **1**:166, **1**:168, **1**:171–172, **1**:174, **1**:175, **1**:177, **3**:8
 resegregation, **7**:61, **7**:63
 resistance to, **3**:xix, **3**:2–3, **3**:11, **3**:15, **3**:16, **6**:254, **7**:14, **7**:71, **7**:251
 results, **3**:10–11, **3**:97
 sources of policy, **3**:4
 strategies, **3**:14–15
 unitary status, **3**:2, **3**:6, **3**:7, **3**:9
 See also Brown v. Board of Education; Diversity; Segregated schools
Detroit
 desegregation plans, **3**:6, **7**:67
 suburbs, **7**:67

Dewey, John, **2:**xviii, **2:**xxiii, **2:**199, **3:**126–127, **4:**282, **9:**14, **9:**231
Diagnostic and Statistical Manual on Mental Disorders (4th edition), **5:**251
Diamond, Alex, **9:**113
Differentiated instruction, **1:**231–232, **1:**266, **2:**179, **2:**191–192
Digital citizenship, **10:**34, **10:**38, **10:**143–144, **10:**176–177, **10:**190, **10:**221
Digital divide, **2:**237, **10:**xvi–xvii, **10:**20, **10:**38–39, **10:**65, **10:**198, **10:**210–211, **10:**215
Digital media. *See* e-books
Diiulio, John J., Jr., **3:**86
Disabilities, students with
  accessible technology, **2:**237–238, **10:**65, **10:**201–202
  accommodations for assessments, **10:**8
  appropriate education, **2:**178–179, **2:**181–183, **2:**186, **2:**190
  behavior intervention plans, **5:**210–211, **8:**95, **8:**102, **8:**103
  bullying victims, **5:**xxxiii, **5:**55
  in charter schools, **1:**14, **1:**16
  curricular needs, **2:**181–186, **2:**187, **2:**192–193
  disciplinary measures, **5:**xix, **5:**113–114, **5:**206, **5:**210–211, **5:**214–215
  discipline issues, **5:**xxi–xxii, **5:**162
  discipline policies for, **5:**20–21, **5:**212, **5:**218–219, **5:**227–228
  early intervention, **1:**201–203
  educational goals, **2:**191
  functional capabilities, **10:**5–6, **10:**13
  future employment, **2:**184–185
  in general education classrooms, **2:**178, **2:**179, **2:**185, **2:**187–193, **3:**215–216, **3:**218, **3:**244–245, **3:**253
  identifying, **6:**100, **6:**101, **6:**104–107
  instructional approaches, **8:**118, **8:**123–124
  mainstreaming vs. separate special education classes, **2:**177–193, **8:**108–125
  NCLB and, **2:**178, **2:**184, **2:**190–192, **3:**218
  online course accessibility, **10:**65
  parents' rights, **1:**xix, **8:**98
  placement changes, **8:**91, **8:**93–94, **8:**96–97, **8:**99
  in religious schools, **4:**18, **4:**24
  responsibilities, **8:**105–106
  restraints and seclusion as disciplinary measures, **5:**210–229
  rights of, **5:**xix, **5:**216–219, **5:**222–223, **8:**xvii–xviii, **8:**90, **8:**99, **8:**100–101, **8:**108
  transition planning, **2:**185
  vouchers for, **1:**43–44
  year-round schools and, **1:**243
  zero tolerance policies and, **5:**20–21, **5:**23, **5:**25
  See also Assistive technology; Free appropriate public education; Individualized education programs; Learning disabilities; Least restrictive environment; Special education
Disciples, **2:**xxiv
Disciplinary measures
  abuses, **5:**215–219, **5:**221–223, **8:**16
  behavior management challenges, **5:**220
  control methods, **2:**2–3
  GAO report, **5:**211–212, **5:**215–216, **5:**221–222
  in individualized education programs, **5:**210, **5:**211, **5:**225–226, **5:**227, **5:**228–229, **8:**102, **8:**103
  inequities, **5:**113–114
  law enforcement involvement, **5:**33–34
  liability issues, **5:**177–178, **5:**205
  for minority students, **5:**162, **5:**206
  office referrals, **5:**241–242
  options, **5:**201
  physical restraints and seclusion, **5:**210–229
  preventive, **5:**201
  in private schools, **5:**216
  racial disparities, **5:**32–33, **5:**37, **5:**40–44, **5:**47, **5:**50, **5:**113–114
  for students with disabilities, **5:**xix, **5:**113–114, **5:**206, **5:**210–211, **5:**214–215, **8:**xvii, **8:**90–106
  time-outs, **5:**210–211, **5:**214–216, **5:**218–219, **5:**221–226, **5:**227, **5:**228–229
  training in, **5:**221, **5:**228
  See also Corporal punishment; Expulsions; Suspensions
Discipline policies
  for academic dishonesty, **5:**127–132, **5:**134–135, **5:**136–138

for activity on social networking sites, **8**:180, **8**:183, **8**:184–185, **10**:174–190, **10**:204–205
authoritative, **5**:207
behavior codes, **5**:63
bullying prevention, **5**:62–63, **10**:156, **10**:170–171
corporal punishment bans, **5**:107
criminalization, **5**:158, **5**:162, **5**:163, **5**:202
for cyberbullying and harassment, **10**:xxv, **10**:153–171
due process and, **5**:xviii–xix, **5**:133, **5**:200, **5**:217–218, **5**:223
enforcement, **5**:181
fairness, **5**:42, **5**:135
federal laws and policies, **5**:218–219, **5**:223–224
goals, **5**:197–198, **5**:200
history, **5**:xvii
liability protection, **5**:xxiv–xxv, **5**:177–191
preventive, **5**:34, **5**:234
restorative justice, **5**:45
school board responsibilities, **5**:xvii, **5**:118–119
state laws and regulations, **5**:xviii, **5**:xix, **5**:xx, **5**:219, **5**:222, **5**:224
for students with disabilities, **5**:20–21, **5**:212, **5**:218–219, **5**:227–228
See also In loco parentis doctrine; Zero tolerance policies
Discrimination
by ethnocentric charter schools, **1**:19–33
laws addressing, **3**:13, **7**:70, **7**:93–94
policies prohibiting, **4**:221–224
religious, **1**:42, **2**:198–199, **4**:219, **4**:220–222, **4**:284, **4**:288, **4**:292–293
by religious schools, **4**:32
scientific arguments, **2**:65
See also Gender discrimination
Distance learning
conflicts with Carnegie Units, **9**:180–181
copyright issues, **8**:35
student performance, **10**:55–56
See also Online learning
District of Columbia Public Charter School Board (DCPCSB), **7**:10–11

District of Columbia Public Schools (DCPS)
charter schools, **7**:10–11, **7**:131
enrollment, **7**:10
mayoral appointment of superintendent, **7**:226
Race to the Top and, **3**:62–63
Rhee as superintendent, **7**:10, **7**:19, **7**:23
special education, **6**:101
standards, **9**:26–27
voucher program, **7**:226
Divergent thinking, **2**:169, **2**:172–173
Diversity
administrator training for, **3**:37–52
challenges and opportunities, **2**:124–141, **3**:xix
in charter schools, **1**:16
counselors and, **3**:19–35
in curriculum, **1**:203–204, **2**:136–137, **3**:xxi–xxii, **3**:21, **3**:70, **3**:134–135
effects of tax credits, **6**:266–267
equity audits, **7**:108
ethics and, **7**:99–100
ethnic studies courses, **2**:134–135
impact on education system, **7**:217
increase in, **3**:23, **3**:259, **9**:58, **9**:241–242
increasing through school assignments, **3**:xxi, **3**:2, **3**:3, **3**:7, **3**:8, **7**:61, **7**:63–64
legal cases, **7**:xxvii, **7**:61, **7**:63–64, **7**:65–66, **7**:72
in magnet schools, **1**:162–163, **1**:175
multicultural education, **2**:137–141
parental involvement and, **7**:197–198, **7**:204–205
popular culture use and, **3**:133–147
religious, **1**:26, **4**:59, **4**:89, **4**:179, **4**:212, **4**:279–280
strategies, **3**:8
as strength, **9**:45–47
support services and, **3**:xxiv
of teacher candidates, **3**:260, **3**:262–263, **9**:89
of teacher training faculty, **3**:50
teacher training for, **2**:43, **3**:37–52
of teachers, **3**:xxvi–xxvii, **3**:259–262, **4**:59
valorization, **2**:138–141
See also Cultural differences; Desegregation; Disabilities, students with; Gender; Minority students; Racial issues

Dixon v. Alabama State Board of Education, **5**:xix, **5**:133, **5**:195
D.K. ex rel. Kennedy v. District School Board Indian River County, **5**:20
Dlugosh, Larry L., **7**:12
Dobson, James, **4**:243
Dockery v. Barnett, **5**:211
Doe v. Duncanville Independent School District, **4**:104, **4**:108
Doe v. Human, **4**:169, **4**:178, **4**:180–181
Doe v. Koger, **8**:94
Doe v. Madison School District No. 321, **4**:40, **4**:43, **4**:46
Doe v. S & S Consolidated Independent School District, **5**:211
Doe v. Santa Fe Independent School District, **4**:xxi
Doe v. School District of City of Norfolk, **4**:47
Dohrn, Bernadine, **5**:42
Donelan, R. W., **3**:156
Doninger v. Niehoff, **8**:188–189, **10**:160
Donovan v. Punxsutawney Area School Board, **4**:217, **4**:220
Dothan, Michael, **6**:35
Doubet, Kristina, **3**:165
Draper, Andrew, **9**:132
Dress code policies
 conflicts with freedom of expression, **5**:5–10, **5**:13, **5**:14, **8**:181–182, **8**:190
 controversies, **5**:xxv–xxvi, **5**:2
 effects, **5**:1–3, **5**:4, **5**:9
 enforcement, **5**:7, **5**:13–16, **5**:17
 gang-related clothing restrictions, **5**:1, **5**:5, **5**:11–15
 grooming policies, **5**:6
 legal cases, **8**:41–48, **8**:49–51, **8**:190
 limits, **4**:272, **5**:17
 messages on clothing, **5**:5, **5**:6–10, **5**:15–16
 religious symbols prohibited, **4**:272, **4**:280
 safety concerns, **5**:xxv, **5**:1–17, **8**:38–39, **8**:48
 as school board responsibility, **5**:8–10
 state laws, **5**:11–12, **8**:42, **8**:43, **8**:45
 zero tolerance, **5**:204
 See also Clothing; Uniforms
Driscoll, David P., **9**:27
Driscoll, Marcy P., **5**:154–155

Dropouts
 bullying victims, **5**:60
 causes, **3**:124–125, **3**:126
 consequences, **3**:113–114, **3**:118–119, **9**:219–220
 credit recovery courses, **10**:51, **10**:57–58
 minority students, **3**:113, **3**:117, **5**:33, **5**:43–44, **5**:45, **6**:199, **6**:241
 rates, **3**:113, **3**:117, **6**:199
 in urban school districts, **2**:208, **6**:xxii, **6**:241
 of virtual schools, **10**:77–78
Drug testing
 arguments against random, **8**:67–68, **8**:69–72, **8**:85
 arguments for, **8**:60–61, **8**:65, **8**:82
 of athletes, **5**:26, **8**:57–58, **8**:63–64, **8**:66, **8**:84, **10**:104–105
 costs, **8**:65, **8**:69–70
 of employees, **8**:62–63, **8**:74–75, **8**:77, **8**:78, **8**:83–84
 privacy rights and, **8**:58, **8**:63–65, **8**:75, **8**:79, **8**:85–86
 random, **8**:58, **8**:67, **8**:75, **8**:77, **8**:80–82, **8**:85, **8**:86–87
 of students, **8**:xix–xx, **8**:57–72, **8**:84
 of teachers, **8**:xxii, **8**:74–88
 use of results, **8**:70–71, **8**:72
Drug-Free Schools and Campuses Act of 1989, **5**:22
Drugs
 availability in schools, **5**:29
 use by students, **5**:26–27, **5**:29, **8**:58, **8**:68, **8**:71
 war on, **5**:22, **8**:63
 zero tolerance policies, **5**:19–22, **5**:26–27, **5**:29, **5**:31, **5**:204
Du Bois, W. E. B., **3**:126, **9**:231
Due process
 corporal punishment and, **5**:111, **5**:116, **5**:117
 IDEA provisions, **5**:210, **5**:224, **5**:226, **8**:90, **8**:93, **8**:97–98
 in loco parentis doctrine and, **5**:200, **5**:204
 procedural, **5**:xviii, **5**:xix, **5**:111, **5**:116, **5**:133, **5**:223, **6**:174
 in student discipline cases, **5**:xviii–xix, **5**:133, **5**:200, **5**:217–218, **5**:223
 substantive, **5**:xviii, **5**:13–14, **5**:17, **5**:111, **5**:117, **5**:223

in teacher dismissals, **8:**xxiii–xxiv, **8:**228–243
vague rules and, **5:**13–15
zero tolerance policies and, **5:**xx, **5:**20, **5:**49, **5:**50
See also Goss v. Lopez
Dumay, Xavier, **7:**259
Duncan, Arne
  on common standards, **3:**63, **9:**24, **9:**59
  letter to states on discipline policies, **5:**219, **5:**221, **5:**222
  on male teacher shortage, **3:**261
  on mayoral school takeovers, **7:**18
  on performance pay, **6:**134, **7:**37
  Race to the Top and, **3:**62
  reform efforts, **7:**52
  school improvement grants, **9:**123–124
  on STEM education, **2:**93
  on teacher training programs, **9:**101
Dupriez, Vincent, **7:**259

EAA. *See* Equal Access Act
Eagly, Alice, **7:**100
Early childhood education. *See* Head Start; Preschool programs
Early College High School Initiative (ECHSI), **9:**42, **9:**43
Earthman, Glen I., **6:**37
East Hartford Education Association v. Board of Education, **4:**295–296, **4:**297
EBDs. *See* Emotional and behavioral disorders
Eber, Lucille, **5:**232
EBM. *See* Evidence-based model
Ebonics, **2:**109, **2:**125
e-books
  advantages, **10:**16–17, **10:**19–21, **10:**24–25
  annotating, **10:**24
  concerns about, **10:**22–23, **10:**25–30
  definition, **10:**16
  enhanced, **10:**21
  impact on instruction, **10:**19–21, **10:**23–24, **10:**27–28, **10:**29–30
  impact on libraries, **10:**18, **10:**22–23, **10:**25, **10:**28–29
  increased availability, **10:**xx, **10:**16, **10:**19–20
  limitations, **10:**18, **10:**22
  for online courses, **10:**93

  public domain, **10:**20
  as replacement for traditional books, **10:**xx, **10:**16–30
EBP. *See* Evidence-based practices
ECHSI. *See* Early College High School Initiative
Eckert, Penelope, **2:**133
Eckes, Suzanne S., **5:**179, **5:**186–187
ECM. *See* Every Child Matters
Economic classes
  achievement gaps, **3:**75–90
  divisions among, **2:**125, **2:**154
  elites, **2:**xxi–xxii, **2:**xxiv
  increasing diversity by school assignments, **3:**3, **3:**8
  magnet school segregation, **1:**175
  private school students, **1:**157
  race and, **3:**3, **3:**8
  reproduced by schools, **3:**70
  segregation, **3:**248
  standardized test scores and, **1:**157
  tracking and, **3:**155–156, **3:**162
  See also Inequities; Low socioeconomic groups; Middle class
Economic development, education and, **7:**76
Economic success
  educational attainment and, **9:**xxix, **9:**219, **9:**220, **9:**225–228, **9:**231
  preparation of students for, **7:**208–223
ED. *See* Department of Education; Emotional disturbances
Edgewood Independent School District v. Kirby, **6:**185
Edison Schools, **1:**13, **1:**83–85, **1:**86, **1:**88–89, **7:**179
Edmodo, **10:**xxiv, **10:**198–199, **10:**214
Edmunds, J. A., **9:**43
Education
  as art, **2:**151
  purpose, **3:**72
  theories, **2:**xvii–xxv
  See also Public education
Education Amendments of 1972. *See* Title IX
Education Department. *See* Department of Education
Education for All Handicapped Children Act of 1975 (EHCA), **1:**xviii, **2:**177, **3:**243, **6:**96, **6:**97, **6:**99, **6:**103, **8:**100
  See also Individuals with Disabilities Education Act

Education law. *See* School law
Education policies
 of executive branch, **7:**41
 issues, **7:**xxiv–xxv
 of Progressive reformers, **7:**xix, **7:**xx, **7:**3, **7:**246
 See also Governance; Reform proposals
Education schools. *See* Teacher training programs
Education Sciences Reform Act of 2002, **3:**99
Education special purpose local option sales taxes (E-SPLOST), **6:**27
Education Support Professionals (ESP), **5:**171–172
Education tax credits. *See* Tax credits
Education Trust–West, **6:**46
Educational Alternatives, Inc., **7:**179
Educational attainment
 economic success and, **3:**118–121, **9:**xxix, **9:**219, **9:**220, **9:**225–228, **9:**231
 racial and class disparities, **3:**115, **9:**xxix
 trends, **3:**114
 See also Dropouts; Graduation rates
Educational excellence movement, **6:**5–6
Educational Leadership Constituent Council (ELCC), **7:**99
 Standards for Advanced Programs in Educational Leadership, **7:**124
Educational malpractice
 NCLB and, **8:**219–220, **8:**221
 objections, **8:**221–226
 obstacles, **8:**220–221
 rejected claims, **5:**83, **8:**213–214, **8:**217–218, **8:**221, **8:**222
 remedies, **8:**216–217, **8:**225–226
 school board liability, **8:**xxv, **8:**213–226
Educational management organizations (EMOs), **1:**13, **1:**82–89, **6:**288, **7:**144, **7:**167, **7:**178–183
 See also Proprietary for-profit schools
Educational Testing Service (ETS), **2:**51
EDUCAUSE Learning Initiative, **10:**120
Edutrain Charter School, **6:**287
Edwards v. Aguillard, **4:**xxv, **4:**185, **4:**196–197
Effective schools research, **6:**6
Efficiency, in education systems, **6:**4–6, **6:**10–11, **6:**17–18

EHCA. *See* Education for All Handicapped Children Act
Ehri, Linnea, **2:**88
Einstein, Albert, **2:**170, **4:**191, **9:**145
Eisel, Nicole, **5:**80–81
Eisel v. Board of Education of Montgomery County, **5:**80–81
Eisenhower, Dwight D., **1:**xvii, **3:**15, **9:**24
Eisner, Elliot W., **2:**142
ELCC. *See* Educational Leadership Constituent Council
Elected officials, women, **7:**103
 See also Mayors; School boards
Elected political leaders, control of schools, **7:**1–20
 criticism of, **7:**9, **7:**15, **7:**16–17, **7:**18–20
 mayors, **7:**5–6, **7:**7, **7:**10, **7:**14–18, **7:**19, **7:**126, **7:**226, **7:**257, **7:**258
 performance of schools, **7:**15, **7:**17, **7:**18–19
 positive effects, **7:**5–6, **7:**17–18
 school takeovers, **7:**xxiii–xxiv, **7:**3, **7:**7, **7:**14–15, **7:**17–19
 superintendent's role, **7:**xxi
 support for, **7:**5–11, **7:**257, **7:**258
Elections
 bond referenda, **6:**28, **6:**32, **6:**36–37
 of school board members, **7:**9–10, **7:**13, **7:**111, **7:**113, **7:**118, **7:**136–137
Electoral accountability, of school boards, **7:**9, **7:**121, **7:**124, **7:**256
Electronic books. *See* e-books
Elementary and Secondary Education Act of 1965 (ESEA)
 antidiscrimination measures, **7:**70
 effects, **7:**xix
 funding conditionality, **3:**15
 future reauthorizations, **6:**84, **6:**92, **7:**46–47
 goals, **1:**xvii, **3:**xxiii, **3:**13–14, **3:**97–98, **6:**197
 Gun-Free Schools Act, **5:**197, **5:**203–204
 Jacob Javits Gifted and Talented grants, **6:**120
 passage, **1:**xvii, **1:**39–40, **3:**78, **3:**98, **3:**242–243, **7:**43
 private schools and, **1:**39–40
 provisions, **1:**xviii, **6:**102, **7:**44, **7:**76, **9:**58
 reauthorizations, **3:**14, **6:**120
 See also No Child Left Behind Act; Title I

Elementary schools
  ability grouping, **3:**152, **3:**155–156, **3:**160
  charter schools, **1:**6–7, **1:**13
  counselors, **3:**20
  gifted students, **6:**121, **6:**122
  parental involvement, **7:**195
  private, **1:**145, **1:**156
  teacher salaries, **7:**36
  year-round schedules, **1:**245
Eliot, Charles W., **9:**28–29, **9:**65, **9:**178, **9:**183
Elk Grove Unified School District v. Newdow, **4:**xxxiii, **4:**25, **4:**50, **4:**138
ELL. *See* English Language Learners
Ellison, Ralph, **3:**146
Elmore, Richard, **7:**172
E-mail, disciplining students for activity on, **8:**180
Emmett v. Kent School District, **10:**187
EMOs. *See* Educational management organizations
Emotional and behavioral disorders (EBDs)
  interventions, **5:**xxi–xxii, **5:**232–233
  negative effects of corporal punishment, **5:**114
  positive behavioral interventions, **5:**231–245
  symptoms, **6:**105
  See also Positive behavior intervention supports
Emotional disturbances (ED), **5:**254
Emotions
  in open education, **2:**2
  overexcitability, **2:**171
Employee unions. *See* Unions
Employees
  drug testing, **8:**77, **8:**78
  employment protections, **8:**230
  religious materials distributed by, **4:**260–261
  video surveillance, **10:**102–103, **10:**109, **10:**112
  See also Public employees
Employment
  of dropouts, **3:**114, **3:**118–119
  educational requirements, **3:**119–120
  gender discrimination, **2:**126
  of individuals with disabilities, **2:**184–185
  See also Economic success; Vocational education

Employment Division, Department of Human Resources of Oregon v. Smith, **4:**57, **4:**91, **4:**272
Empowerment Schools Program, New York State, **6:**48, **6:**53
Enacted curriculum, **2:**60, **2:**63
Endorsement test
  graduation speeches and, **4:**43
  religious garb and, **4:**293
  religious group access to public schools, **4:**239–240, **4:**247
  religious holidays and, **4:**202, **4:**204, **4:**210
  religious music and, **4:**113, **4:**115
  religious symbols and, **4:**xviii–xix, **4:**120, **4:**121, **4:**123, **4:**126–127, **4:**128, **4:**132
  See also Establishment Clause
Engagement. *See* Student engagement
Engberg, Mark E., **3:**34
Engel v. Vitale, **4:**35, **4:**45, **4:**61–62, **4:**98, **4:**194–195
Engels, Frederick, **8:**247
Engineering. *See* Science, Technology, Engineering, and Mathematics
English as a Second Language (ESL)
  instructional approaches, **3:**187, **3:**191, **3:**199–205
  program funding, **3:**171, **3:**172
  teachers, **2:**120
  See also English Language Learners
English language
  communications styles and, **3:**146
  hegemonic spread, **2:**128
  metaphors, **2:**128, **2:**131
  as official language, **2:**118, **3:**190, **3:**192
  orthography, **2:**85–87, **2:**112–113
  social and academic language, **3:**198
English language arts
  Bible as literature, **4:**xxiv–xxv, **4:**50, **4:**92–93, **4:**168–182, **4:**227
  curricula, **2:**32, **7:**45, **7:**50, **9:**14
  impact of digital technology, **10:**26–28
  popular culture use, **3:**139, **3:**146
  popular texts, **2:**215–216, **2:**221
  standards, **2:**221, **6:**82, **9:**5, **9:**25, **9:**26–27, **9:**40, **9:**59
  token diversity, **2:**136–137
  tracking, **3:**154
  vocabulary, **2:**86–87, **2:**88, **2:**114
  See also Reading

Index **329**

English Language Learners (ELL)
  heritage language maintenance, **3:**187–188, **3:**190, **3:**192, **3:**193–194
  individual differences, **3:**199, **3:**201
  instructional approaches, **3:**160, **3:**186–205
  See also Achievement gaps; Bilingual education; "English-only" curriculum; Immigrants
"English-only" curriculum
  advantages, **2:**109, **3:**188, **3:**193, **3:**194–195
  cost-effectiveness, **3:**188
  criticism of, **2:**111–116, **2:**118, **3:**188, **3:**197–201
  implementation, **2:**111
  instructional approaches, **2:**120–122
  legal mandates, **2:**119, **2:**122, **3:**191, **3:**192, **3:**193, **3:**200
  models, **2:**119–120, **3:**191, **3:**203–204
  political issues, **2:**111–112, **2:**118, **3:**190, **3:**191–194, **3:**200, **3:**202
  pull-out programs, **2:**119, **2:**120, **3:**191, **3:**195
  research on, **2:**112–114, **3:**195
  supporters, **2:**109, **2:**110, **2:**117–122, **3:**190, **3:**193–194
Entwisle, Doris R., **1:**243–244
Epperson v. Arkansas, **4:**xxv, **4:**22, **4:**185, **4:**196
Epstein, Joyce L., **7:**88–89, **7:**90
Equal Access Act (EAA)
  application, **4:**220–224
  effectiveness, **4:**216–231
  enactment, **4:**216, **4:**219, **4:**233
  gaps, **4:**225–230
  goals, **4:**225
  impact, **4:**74
  legal cases, **4:**xxvi, **4:**217, **4:**219–220, **4:**225, **4:**226–227, **4:**228, **4:**229–230, **4:**234
  limitations, **4:**xxvi, **4:**50, **4:**220–224, **4:**227–231
  order and discipline exception, **4:**229–230
  provisions, **2:**201, **4:**216–217, **4:**219, **4:**225, **4:**229, **4:**233–234
Equal Pay Act, **3:**207
Equality
  in curriculum and instruction, **2:**xix–xx
  distinction from equity, **6:**179
  of educational opportunity, **6:**15–16, **6:**148, **6:**152, **6:**264–265
  state constitutional requirements, **6:**xviii–xix, **6:**1–2, **6:**22, **6:**148, **6:**152
  tension with local control, **6:**xxv, **6:**2–3, **6:**110–111
  See also Fourteenth Amendment
Equity
  charter schools and, **1:**16, **6:**282–283, **7:**144
  choice programs and, **1:**106–107
  digital divide, **10:**xvi–xvii, **10:**20, **10:**38–39, **10:**65, **10:**198, **10:**210–211, **10:**215
  distinction from equality, **6:**179
  gender, **1:**190, **7:**xxviii
  in gifted education, **6:**116–117
  horizontal, **3:**173, **6:**66, **6:**116, **6:**152, **6:**179, **6:**188
  increasing, **3:**xix, **7:**248, **7:**250–251, **7:**261, **9:**xxvii–xxix, **9:**227–228
  of inputs or outcomes, **9:**196–197
  in special education, **6:**95, **6:**98–99
  in tax systems, **6:**66–67
  vertical, **3:**173, **6:**6, **6:**66, **6:**116, **6:**152, **6:**180, **6:**188
  See also Discrimination; Financing equity; Inequities
Equity audits, **7:**108
Equity suits
  arguments, **3:**15–16, **6:**xx, **6:**144–145, **6:**183
  in federal courts, **3:**xxvi, **6:**xxi, **6:**14, **6:**193, **9:**191
  goals, **7:**253
  outcomes, **3:**xxvi, **3:**169–170, **3:**174, **6:**153, **6:**200
  property tax issues, **3:**173, **6:**63–64, **6:**72, **6:**168–169
  in state courts, **3:**xxvi, **3:**170, **3:**180–182, **6:**xxi, **6:**14, **6:**25, **6:**152, **6:**194, **9:**191
  See also San Antonio Independent School District v. Rodriguez
Erastians, **4:**95
e-readers. *See* e-books
Ericsson, K. Anders, **9:**146
ESEA. *See* Elementary and Secondary Education Act
ESL. *See* English as a Second Language
ESP. *See* Education Support Professionals

Espelage, Dorothy L., **5**:69
E-SPLOST. *See* Education special purpose local option sales taxes
Establishment Clause
  accommodationist approach, **4**:123, **4**:124, **4**:131, **4**:132
  ethnocentric charter schools and, **1**:21, **1**:29–31
  extension to states, **1**:xvii, **4**:44–45, **4**:71, **4**:98
  government aid to religious schools and, **4**:4, **6**:255
  interpretations, **4**:21–22, **4**:98–99, **4**:159–160
  moments of silence as violations, **4**:67
  motives, **4**:44, **4**:82, **4**:97
  prayer in schools as violation of, **4**:35–36, **4**:45–47, **4**:48, **4**:49, **4**:61–62
  released time programs and, **4**:xxiv
  religious holidays and, **4**:204–207, **4**:210–212
  religious materials distribution in public schools, **4**:251, **4**:257
  See also Church-state separation; Coercion test; Endorsement test; First Amendment; *Lemon* (tripartite) test
Ethics
  academic integrity, **5**:127, **5**:132, **5**:135–138
  of administrators, **7**:99–100
  of counselors, **3**:23
  digital citizenship, **10**:34, **10**:38, **10**:143–144, **10**:176–177, **10**:190, **10**:221
  diversity and, **7**:99–100
  expectations of teachers, **10**:147, **10**:148–151
  moral education and, **10**:170–171
  new models, **2**:208–209
  in school cultures, **10**:156, **10**:171
  See also Academic dishonesty; Moral values
Ethnic identities, **1**:28, **1**:32, **3**:24–25
  See also Cultural differences; Minority students
Ethnic minorities. *See* Achievement gaps; Diversity; Minority students
Ethnocentric charter schools, **1**:19–33
  advantages, **1**:20–21, **1**:28, **1**:32
  Afrocentric, **1**:25
  constitutionality, **1**:xxiii, **1**:20, **1**:21, **1**:25–26, **1**:29–32
  criticism of, **1**:21, **1**:49, **1**:50
  curricula, **1**:6–7
  reasons for choosing, **1**:20–21
  religious groups and, **1**:25–26, **1**:29–30, **1**:50, **1**:133–134
  segregated, **1**:31–32
Ethnocentric schools, **1**:21, **1**:25–26
  See also Native American schools
ETS. *See* Educational Testing Service
Eugenics movement, **2**:65
Eurocentrism, **2**:134–137
Europe
  immigrants in, **2**:131–132
  public and private school comparisons, **1**:154, **1**:158–159
  school governance in, **7**:259
  school year lengths, **1**:248
European Union, Year of Creativity and Innovation, **2**:155
Evans, Katherine, **10**:205
Everson v. Board of Education of Ewing Township
  child benefit test, **4**:xix, **4**:6, **4**:11, **4**:18
  dissent, **4**:10
  Establishment Clause extension to states, **4**:xvii, **4**:98
  legacy, **1**:31, **4**:27–28, **6**:272
  majority opinion, **4**:xviii, **4**:1–2, **4**:5–6, **4**:9–10, **4**:21
  wall metaphor, **4**:1–2, **4**:27, **4**:45
Evertson, Carolyn M., **5**:150
Every Child Matters (ECM; U.K.), **7**:53
Evidence-based model (EBM) of school funding, **6**:206–207, **6**:208, **9**:207–208
Evidence-based practices (EBP), **5**:243, **5**:244, **8**:117, **8**:118
Evolution
  Darwinian theory, **4**:187–188, **4**:190, **4**:191, **4**:195–196
  instruction in, **4**:187
  public views of, **4**:197–198
  Scopes Monkey Trial, **4**:xxv, **4**:185, **4**:196
  state laws on teaching, **4**:185, **4**:196–197
  weaknesses of theory, **4**:187–191
A.A. ex rel. Betenbaugh v. Needville Independent School District, **4**:268, **4**:274
Excessive entanglement. *See Lemon* (tripartite) test

Executive branch
  education policies, **7**:41
  Interagency Council on Homelessness, **8**:127
  privacy protection, **10**:109
  role in education, **7**:xxv
  See also Department of Education
Expenditures. *See* Budgets; Per pupil expenditures
Expulsions
  due process requirements, **5**:xviii, **5**:xix
  negative consequences, **5**:199–200, **5**:202–203
  racial disparities, **5**:37, **5**:40–42, **5**:43–44, **5**:47, **5**:50
  of students with disabilities, **8**:93–94, **8**:95, **8**:103–104
  for weapons possession, **5**:23, **5**:25–26
  See also Zero tolerance policies
Extracurricular activities
  benefits, **6**:xxvi–xxvii, **6**:212, **6**:219–220, **6**:221, **6**:222, **6**:223
  costs, **6**:xxvii, **6**:213, **6**:216–217, **9**:198
  fund-raising for, **6**:217–218, **6**:222, **6**:293–294, **6**:296
  in gifted education, **6**:110
  nonparticipants, **6**:218
  public funding, **6**:212–213, **6**:216–217, **6**:219, **6**:223–224
  student fees, **6**:212–224, **6**:234
  See also Athletics; Clubs; Music
Extrinsic motivators
  examples, **5**:145, **5**:146–149
  negative effects, **5**:142, **5**:153
  reward systems, **5**:147–149, **6**:139–140
  support for use of, **5**:142, **5**:148–149, **5**:153

Facebook
  alternatives to, **10**:xxiv, **10**:198–199
  policies, **10**:147
  student use of, **10**:169
  usage, **10**:135–136, **10**:182, **10**:195, **10**:202
  See also Social networking sites
Fair use. *See* Copyright law
Fairfax Covenant Church v. Fairfax County School Board, **4**:234, **4**:240–241
Fairness. *See* Equity
Faith-based charter schools
  arguments for, **1**:38–45
  constitutionality, **1**:35–52
  cultural focus, **1**:25–26, **1**:40, **1**:49, **1**:50
  curricula, **1**:50–51
  funding, **1**:43–44
  Jewish, **1**:25
  limits on religious activity, **1**:57
  Muslim culture, **1**:25–26, **1**:42, **1**:54–70
  opposition, **1**:xxiii, **1**:36, **1**:37, **1**:45–52
  religious values promoted, **1**:36–37, **1**:38, **1**:42–43
  See also Religious schools
Falwell, Jerry, **2**:204
Families
  bilingual, **2**:122
  domestic violence, **7**:194
  emotional influences on students, **5**:69
  immigrant, **2**:122
  importance, **9**:263
  poor, **2**:68, **3**:79–80, **3**:222, **5**:207, **9**:58, **9**:239, **9**:279
  of school age children, **7**:192–193
  structures, **7**:193
  See also Abuse and neglect; Homeschooling; Parents
Family and Medical Leave Act, **8**:241
Family Educational Rights and Privacy Act (FERPA), **10**:106, **10**:108, **10**:109, **10**:140
FAPE. *See* Free appropriate public education
Farrell, Anne F., **5**:233
Farrington v. Tokushige, **1**:xx, **1**:73, **1**:146
FBAs. *See* Functional behavioral assessments
FBI (Federal Bureau of Investigation), **5**:47–48, **10**:103
Federal courts. *See* Judicial branch; Supreme Court
Federal government
  arts funding, **2**:154, **2**:155
  tax reductions, **7**:209
  See also Congress; Executive branch; Judicial branch
Federal government role in education
  appropriateness, **9**:54–70
  benefits of, **7**:248, **7**:250–251, **7**:261, **9**:60, **9**:62–63
  during Cold War, **7**:xix
  constitutional basis, **6**:77–78, **6**:86–90, **7**:70
  constitutional limits, **6**:76–77, **6**:85–86, **6**:91, **7**:1–2, **7**:40, **9**:28

desegregation and, **6:**99, **7:**250
executive branch, **7:**xxv, **7:**41
expansion, **1:**xviii–xix, **2:**19, **7:**xix–xx, **7:**43, **7:**114–115, **7:**248, **7:**252–253, **9:**54, **9:**55
in future, **7:**253–254
history, **1:**xvii–xix, **7:**40–41, **7:**250–253, **9:**55
legislation, **7:**xxv, **9:**55, **9:**58
limiting, **7:**68
religious schools and, **1:**39–40
resistance to expansion, **7:**116–117
school governance role, **7:**xix–xx, **7:**xxi, **7:**40–56, **7:**112, **7:**248–250
teacher training standards, **9:**75
See also Department of Education; Financing, federal; No Child Left Behind Act; Race to the Top
Federalism
cooperative, **7:**253–254
judiciary and, **7:**64, **7:**65, **7:**68
state roles, **6:**76–77, **6:**114–115, **7:**61–62, **7:**64
Federalist No. 51, **4:**182
Federalists, **4:**96
Fees
for academic programs, **6:**225–238
for extracurricular activities, **6:**212–224, **6:**234
for transportation, **6:**230
FEFP. *See* Florida Education Finance Plan
Feinberg, Mike, **9:**23
Fennimore, Beatrice S., **3:**174
Fenstermacher, Gary D., **9:**xix
Fenty, Adrian, **7:**10
FERA. *See* New York Foundation for Education Reform and Accountability
FERPA. *See* Family Educational Rights and Privacy Act
Field trips
fund-raising for, **6:**293–294
government aid to religious schools, **4:**xx, **4:**2, **4:**6
learning opportunities, **9:**179–180, **9:**187
virtual, **7:**213
Figlio, David N., **6:**37
Finance litigation
complexity, **6:**147, **6:**150, **6:**152, **6:**153, **6:**157, **6:**160–161, **6:**169, **6:**171
justiciability, **6:**143–161, **6:**164, **6:**167–168, **6:**173
local control issue, **9:**210–212

results, **3:**173–174, **3:**178–180
waves, **3:**179, **6:**xxi, **6:**168–169, **6:**184
See also Adequacy suits; Equity suits
Financing
accountability and, **9:**203
allocation to schools, **6:**44, **10:**84
alternative models, **9:**197–199, **9:**207–208
bonds, **6:**21–38
of charter schools, **6:**261, **6:**281–282, **9:**224–225
cost reductions, **9:**194–195, **9:**198–200, **9:**222
debt limits, **6:**21–38
donations, **7:**179
economic pressures, **4:**12–13, **7:**247, **9:**xxvi–xxvii, **9:**193, **9:**222, **9:**244
educational benefits, **6:**17, **9:**221
evidence-based model, **6:**206–207, **6:**208, **9:**207–208
expenditure totals, **6:**107
growth, **9:**251–252
history, **1:**xvii, **6:**215, **7:**6
individual students as focus, **3:**176–177
international comparisons, **6:**235, **7:**209, **9:**239, **9:**240, **9:**252
local role, **3:**168–169, **6:**1–19, **6:**62, **6:**70, **6:**180
in mayor-controlled systems, **7:**17
minority student marginalization and, **3:**168–183
revenue declines, **7:**209, **9:**193, **9:**209
revenue sources, **6:**62, **6:**64–65
revenue totals, **7:**165
school-based accounting, **6:**57
short-term debt, **6:**27
student achievement relationship, **3:**175–176, **6:**188, **6:**208–209, **9:**221
student needs and, **6:**44, **9:**203–204, **9:**206–207
sufficiency, **9:**204, **9:**205, **9:**212–213
of urban school districts, **7:**17
values and, **6:**15–19, **6:**21–23
of virtual schools, **10:**xxi–xxii, **10:**81, **10:**84, **10:**86, **10:**88–90, **10:**95–96
See also Budgets; Fund-raising; Per pupil expenditures; Property taxes; Public-private partnerships; Vouchers

Financing, federal
  of charter schools, **6:**285
  conditional, **3:**15, **6:**79, **6:**87–92,
    6:96–97, **7:**42, **9:**29, **9:**62
  curriculum mandates and, **6:**82,
    6:83–84
  of gifted education, **6:**120
  of magnet schools, **1:**163, **1:**166, **1:**167,
    1:170, **1:**175
  mandated curricula and, **6:**76–92
  obligations, **9:**60, **9:**61–62
  reductions, **7:**252
  refusal of, **6:**99
  regulatory, **6:**90–91
  reimbursement-based, **6:**90–91
  share of total revenue, **3:**xxv, **3:**169, **6:**62,
    6:70, **6:**107, **7:**252, **9:**243
  social impact, **6:**99–101, **7:**250–251
  of special education services,
    6:93–108, **6:**248
  targeted to neediest schools, **6:**80
  unfunded mandates, **6:**99, **9:**200–201
  of vocational education, **1:**228,
    3:127–128
  See also Race to the Top; Title I
Financing, state
  bans on aid to religious schools, **1:**95,
    1:96, **2:**199, **4:**4
  categorical funding, **3:**171–172
  of charter schools, **6:**284–285
  conflict with local control, **6:**187
  court roles, **6:**143–161, **6:**191
  economic pressures, **6:**99–100,
    6:209–210, **6:**251–252
  fluctuations, **6:**73, **6:**209–210
  foundation programs, **3:**171, **3:**172,
    3:178, **6:**26
  funding formulas, **3:**xxv, **3:**169, **6:**62–63,
    6:70–71, **6:**154–155, **6:**159,
    6:179–180, **6:**188, **6:**190–191
  of gifted education, **6:**110–124
  history, **3:**172, **6:**13–14, **6:**62, **6:**182,
    9:208–209
  needs and, **3:**178
  for performance pay, **6:**127–128, **6:**137
  political issues, **6:**149, **6:**160–161, **6:**164
  per pupil allocations, **6:**13, **6:**62, **6:**70,
    6:119–120, **6:**180, **9:**205, **9:**228
  reforms, **9:**207–208
  residual budgeting, **9:**206
  revenue declines, **9:**xxvi, **9:**193,
    9:208
  share of state spending, **6:**167
  share of total revenue, **3:**168–169,
    6:13–14, **6:**62, **6:**69–70, **6:**107,
    9:243
  of special education, **6:**98–99, **6:**100,
    6:108, **6:**188
  unfunded mandates, **9:**200–201
  of vocational education, **1:**228
  weighted student funding, **3:**171, **3:**172,
    3:175–177, **6:**180,
    6:190–191, **9:**197–198
  See also Financing adequacy; Financing
    equity; Religious schools,
    government aid to
Financing adequacy
  for accountability implementation,
    3:172–173, **9:**190–213
  costs and, **6:**207, **9:**xxv–xxvi, **9:**207
  costs of not achieving, **3:**173–174,
    6:199–200, **6:**202
  debt limits and, **6:**33–34
  defining, **6:**33, **6:**117–118, **6:**198, **6:**202,
    6:204–205, **6:**206–208, **9:**xxvi
  educational quality and, **6:**xx–xxii,
    6:145, **6:**198–200, **6:**201, **6:**204
  measuring, **6:**155–156
  for minority students, **3:**175–177
  models, **6:**200–201, **6:**206–208
  needs and, **3:**176, **6:**44, **9:**xxvii,
    9:206–207
  research on, **6:**204–205, **6:**206–208
  by states, **6:**145, **6:**155–156, **6:**157,
    6:170–171, **6:**173, **6:**181,
    6:193–210
  See also Adequacy suits
Financing equity
  achievement gaps and, **6:**159
  consequences of inequities, **6:**xvii, **6:**144,
    7:221, **7:**222–223
  debt limits and, **6:**21–38
  defining, **3:**173
  differences between states, **7:**253, **9:**233
  within districts, **3:**81
  efficiency and, **6:**4–6, **6:**10–11,
    6:17–18
  ethical arguments, **6:**16–17
  gifted education and, **6:**119–120
  increasing, **7:**221, **9:**222, **9:**228
  inputs and outcomes, **9:**196–197
  local control and, **9:**210–211
  property taxes and, **6:**60, **7:**222–223,
    9:204–205

school-level autonomy and, **6:**41–42
segregated schools, **3:**5
as state goal, **3:**xxv, **3:**171, **6:**xviii–xix, **6:**2, **6:**13, **6:**19, **6:**30–31, **6:**155, **6:**179–191
between states, **3:**xx
teacher salaries, **6:**46
Title I and, **3:**81
unintended results of increasing, **6:**187–190
See also Equity suits
Finkelstein, Martin J., **3:**50
Finland
  achievement gap, **9:**263–264
  curricula and instruction, **2:**30–31, **2:**33
  teachers, **2:**30–31, **6:**140, **9:**xxii, **9:**xxiii
Finn, Chester E., Jr., **9:**25, **9:**26, **9:**33–34, **9:**111, **9:**112
Finnigan, Kara, **6:**288
Fiorina, Carly, **7:**237
First Amendment
  adoption, **4:**193
  balancing freedoms of speech and religion, **4:**93–94
  extension to states, **4:**xvii, **4:**17, **4:**44–45, **4:**71, **4:**97–98
  Free Exercise Clause, **4:**xvii, **4:**9, **4:**56–57, **4:**73–74, **4:**88, **4:**91, **4:**110–111, **4:**205–207
  interpretations, **4:**193–194
  See also Church-state separation; Establishment Clause; Free speech rights; Religious freedom
First Step to Success Program, **5:**237–238
Fischel, William A., **6:**73
Fisman, Raymond, **10:**170
Flag, American, **4:**143, **4:**147
  See also Pledge of Allegiance
Fleishman, E. A., **7:**98
Flesch, Rudolf, **8:**213
Flexible credit, **9:**181–182
Florey v. Sioux Falls School District, **4:**104, **4:**109, **4:**202
Florida
  A++ Plan, **6:**127–128
  Advanced Placement classes, **6:**229
  charter schools, **1:**25, **1:**50, **6:**280, **6:**290–291
  class sizes, **6:**228
  constitution, **1:**97–98, **6:**170–171, **6:**173, **6:**203, **6:**228, **6:**251, **6:**252–253

education tax credits, **6:**269
finance litigation, **3:**181
homeschooling, **1:**122
magnet schools, **1:**169
Opportunity Scholarship Program, **1:**97–98, **6:**252–253
Pledge of Allegiance law, **4:**148–149
school districts, **6:**44
school funding, **6:**170–172, **6:**202–203, **6:**252
special education, **6:**106–107
voucher programs, **6:**106–107, **6:**251, **6:**252–253
See also Dade County Schools
Florida Education Finance Plan (FEFP), **6:**229
Florida Supreme Court, **1:**97–98, **4:**111, **6:**170, **6:**251, **6:**252–253
Florida TaxWatch Center, **10:**86
Florida Virtual School (FLVS), **10:**68, **10:**86–87
FLVS. *See* Florida Virtual School
Foley, Pamela F., **3:**26, **3:**27
Fonagy, Peter, **2:**174
Food, fund-raising sales, **6:**300, **6:**302, **6:**304–306
Force. *See* Corporal punishment; Physical restraints
Ford, Gerald, **8:**100
Ford Foundation, **3:**xxii
Fordham Foundation, **9:**30, **9:**31, **9:**33, **9:**112, **9:**197, **9:**201
Fordham Institute, **9:**7, **9:**24, **9:**25, **9:**26
Foreign languages. *See* Bilingual education; English as a Second Language; Languages
Formative assessments
  benefits of, **7:**151
  for Native Americans, **1:**266–267
  principals' support of, **7:**84, **7:**154–156
  purpose, **1:**266, **7:**153
  technology used, **2:**238
  use of, **1:**232, **7:**152–156, **7:**162–163, **9:**187–188, **9:**223
  See also Assessments
For-profit private schools. *See* Proprietary for-profit schools
For-profit school managers. *See* Educational management organizations
Fossey, Richard, **8:**53, **8:**54–55

Foster, Elizabeth, **9:**113, **9:**114
Foucault, Michel, **2:**2, **2:**153
Foundations
    reform funding, **7:**227, **9:**56
    school funding, **7:**179
    school leadership training, **7:**233
    See also Gates Foundation;
        Philanthropy
Fourteenth Amendment
    equal protection, **1:**25, **1:**31, **5:**49, **5:**50,
        6:xxi, **6:**xxiv–xxv, **6:**168, **7:**62,
        7:66–67, **7:**70–71
    First Amendment and, **4:**17, **4:**44–45,
        4:71, **4:**97–98
    privacy rights, **8:**165–166
    school finance and, **6:**168, **7:**66–67
    segregation and, **1:**25, **3:**13, **7:**70–71
    See also Due process
Fourth Amendment
    drug testing and, **8:**xix–xx, **8:**57,
        8:61–63, **8:**78, **8:**79–80, **8:**81–82,
        8:83–84, **8:**87
    seclusion cases, **5:**223
    surveillance technologies and, **10:**101,
        10:102–104
    violations of rights, **5:**164, **5:**217
    See also Searches
Fowler v. Szostek, **5:**82
Fox, Robert, **1:**20
France, hijab ban, **4:**280–281
Franchises, charter schools, **7:**180, **7:**182
Frankenberg, Erica, **7:**52
Franklin, Benjamin, **2:**xxii, **7:**149
Franklin v. Gwinnett County Public Schools,
    8:145, **8:**147, **8:**151,
    8:152–153
Fraser, James W., **4:**70
Frattura, Elise, **3:**249, **3:**251
Frazier v. Winn, **4:**148–149
Free appropriate public education
    (FAPE)
    background, **8:**108–109
    definition, **8:**91, **8:**109
    federal funding, **6:**93, **6:**96–97, **6:**103
    for gifted students, **6:**232
    IDEA provisions, **6:**96–97, **8:**90, **8:**109
    inclusion vs. pullout programs,
        8:108–125
    individualized, **2:**186
    rights to, **8:**xvii–xviii, **8:**108
    standards, **8:**109–110
    See also Least restrictive environment

Free Exercise Clause, **4:**xvii, **4:**9, **4:**56–57,
    4:73–74, **4:**88, **4:**91, **4:**110–111,
    4:205–207
    See also First Amendment; Religious
        freedom
Free market. *See* Choice; Market
    competition
Free speech rights
    censorship, **2:**207–208
    distribution of religious materials in
        public schools, **4:**xxvii, **4:**250–265
    of employees, **8:**234
    fora, **4:**121, **4:**205
    online, **10:**186–188
    religious speech, **4:**92, **4:**93, **4:**121,
        4:128–129, **4:**205–206, **4:**236,
        4:240–242, **4:**248, **4:**253
    in school environments,
        8:206–209
    on social networking sites, **8:**182–183,
        10:178, **10:**180–182, **10:**187,
        10:204–206
    See also First Amendment
Free speech rights of students
    cyberbullying and, **10:**159–160,
        10:168–170
    dress code policies and, **5:**5–10, **5:**13,
        5:14, **8:**181–182, **8:**190
    expansion, **5:**xviii, **5:**4–5
    historical basis, **8:**179–180
    inconsistent jurisprudence, **8:**183–184
    legal cases, **8:**176–177, **8:**181–191,
        10:166–169, **10:**179–180
    limits on, **4:**135, **4:**149, **8:**50,
        8:176–191
    in newspapers, **8:**177, **8:**187,
        8:206–207
    offensive language, **8:**177, **8:**186–187
    online, **10:**179–183, **10:**185–189
    parental support, **8:**189–190
    Pledge of Allegiance recitation and,
        4:145, **4:**146–147, **4:**148,
        4:149–150
    political process and, **8:**181
    political speech, **5:**5, **8:**176–177,
        8:188–189
    religious clubs and, **4:**217
    religious garb and, **4:**xxvii, **4:**271–272
    religious speech, **4:**40–42, **4:**47, **4:**48–49,
        4:205–206, **4:**255–258, **4:**262–263
    in school environments, **8:**xx–xxi, **8:**181,
        8:206–207

substantial disruption standard, **10:**155, **10:**158–160, **10:**179, **10:**181–182
symbolic speech, **4:**271–273
trivial cases, **8:**180, **8:**181–182
uniforms and, **8:**xix, **8:**42, **8:**43, **8:**44–45, **8:**46, **8:**49–51
See also First Amendment; *Tinker v. Des Moines Independent Community School District*
Free speech rights of teachers
control of curriculum, **8:**6–7
limits on, **4:**91, **4:**260, **8:**xxii, **8:**193–211
online, **10:**205–206
political views, **8:**2, **8:**7, **8:**208
as private citizens or public employees, **4:**254, **4:**260, **8:**xxi–xxii, **8:**194
religious clubs and, **4:**53–54, **4:**93, **4:**254
religious speech, **4:**92
See also Academic freedom
Freedom, **2:**95–96, **2:**99, **7:**218–219
See also Academic freedom; Religious freedom
Freeman v. Pitts, **7:**63, **7:**64
Freire, Paulo, **2:**121, **3:**143
Freund, Paul, **4:**10
Friedman, Milton, **1:**93, **1:**150, **3:**244, **4:**5, **6:**262–263, **7:**137, **9:**258, **9:**259
Friedman, Thomas, **1:**222, **2:**233, **7:**54, **7:**213, **9:**163
Friedman-Nimz, Reva, **6:**116, **6:**118, **6:**120
Fries, Mary Kim, **9:**115
Fullan, Michael, **2:**236, **7:**155
Fuller, Howard, **1:**102, **1:**106–107
Fuller v. Decatur Public School Board of Education, **5:**50
Full-service community schools
afterschool programs, **3:**225
definition, **3:**223, **3:**224
drawbacks, **3:**233–235
effectiveness, **3:**221–235
examples, **3:**225, **3:**226, **3:**232–233
goals, **3:**224–225
implementation, **3:**225–226, **3:**228–229, **3:**231–233
interest in, **3:**222
models, **3:**224–225
parental involvement, **3:**225
partnerships, **3:**225, **3:**226–228, **3:**232
services, **3:**xxv, **3:**223, **3:**224–225

staff, **3:**225
supporters, **3:**224–229, **3:**230
Functional behavioral assessments (FBAs), **5:**238, **8:**95, **8:**103
Fund-raising
alternatives to, **6:**305–306
amounts raised, **6:**301–302, **6:**303
benefits for students, **6:**298–300
business services, **6:**294, **6:**296, **6:**304
competitions, **6:**298–300
educational outcomes, **6:**303–304
for extracurricular activities, **6:**217–218, **6:**222, **6:**293–294, **6:**296
food sales, **6:**300, **6:**302, **6:**304–306
frequency, **6:**302
negative return on investment, **6:**304–305
organizing, **6:**297
parental involvement, **6:**217–218, **6:**296, **6:**301
by religious schools, **1:**39
requiring student participation, **6:**293–306
school policies, **6:**297, **6:**298
Futterman, David, **4:**28

Gabler, Neal, **2:**214
Gaines, Ernest, **3:**146
Gallagher, Patricia, **5:**238
Gallimore, Ronald, **1:**260–261, **1:**266
Gamoran, Adam, **1:**168–169, **3:**62
Gang-related clothing, **4:**268, **4:**272–273, **4:**280, **5:**1, **5:**5, **5:**11–15, **8:**50
GAO. *See* Government Accountability Office
Garber, Barry, **10:**187
Garcetti v. Ceballos, **4:**254, **4:**260, **8:**194, **8:**200–201, **8:**203, **8:**206, **8:**208, **8:**209
Garcia, David R., **1:**85
Garcia, Eugene, **3:**45
Gardner, Howard, **2:**xxiii, **7:**255
Garfield, Rulon R., **6:**36
Garrison Institute, **2:**245
Gates, Bill, **10:**210
Gates Foundation, **3:**63, **9:**32, **9:**33, **9:**56, **9:**85, **9:**145, **9:**248–249, **10:**xvii
Gatlin, S., **9:**112
Gau, Rebecca, **6:**288
Gay rights student groups, **4:**216
See also LGBT youth

G.C. v. School Board of Seminole County, **5:**215
GE Lighting, **9:**249–250
Gebser v. Lago Vista Independent School District, **8:**145, **8:**147, **8:**148, **8:**151, **8:**153
Gee, James P., **10:**210
Gemin, Butch, **10:**77, **10:**89
Gender
   of administrators, **3:**219, **9:**15
   career associations, **3:**257
   as diversity criterion, **3:**206–219
   leadership style differences, **7:**98–99, **7:**100–102
   learning style differences, **1:**180, **1:**185, **3:**216–217
   meaning, **7:**97
   of principals, **7:**xxii, **7:**94, **7:**100, **7:**101, **7:**103, **7:**104
   roles, **1:**189–190, **1:**192
   stereotypes, **1:**190
   student loan forgiveness based on, **3:**255–272
   of superintendents, **7:**104
   suspensions and expulsions by, **5:**41
   of teachers, **3:**255–272, **7:**94, **7:**97, **7:**101, **7:**104
   See also Men; Single-sex schools and classes; Women
Gender discrimination
   in administrator hiring, **7:**94–95, **7:**103, **7:**105, **7:**106
   in administrator preparation programs, **7:**94, **7:**106
   antidiscrimination laws, **3:**208
   in education, **3:**208, **3:**209, **3:**211–214
   in employment, **2:**126
   forms, **3:**206–208
   in higher education, **3:**208, **3:**213–214, **8:**144–145
   laws addressing, **3:**207, **3:**213, **7:**93–94
   in military, **3:**207
   persistence, **3:**206, **3:**209, **3:**212–214
   pregnancy discrimination, **8:**234, **8:**241
   by researchers, **9:**15
   reverse, **3:**209
   single-sex schools and classes, **1:**181, **1:**183, **1:**190–191, **1:**194
   in teacher pay, **7:**36
   by teachers, **1:**187, **3:**212
   violence and, **3:**206–207
   in wages, **3:**207
   against women of childbearing age, **7:**23
   See also Title IX
Gender issues
   achievement gaps, **3:**216–219
   equity, **1:**190, **3:**206–214, **7:**xxviii
   lack of attention to, **7:**104–105
   preparation of school administrators for, **3:**212, **7:**93–108
Gender-based education. *See* Single-sex schools and classes
General Accounting Office, **1:**254, **1:**255
General education classrooms. *See* Inclusion classrooms
Generalized anxiety disorder, **5:**251
   See also Anxiety; Internalizing disorders
George, Michael, **5:**238
Georgia
   antibullying legislation, **5:**63
   charter schools, **7:**131–132, **10:**87
   constitution, **1:**47, **6:**173
   discipline policies, **5:**224
   education tax credits, **6:**269
   moments of silence in schools, **4:**78–79, **4:**80
   virtual schools, **10:**87
Georgia Cyber Academy, **10:**87
Germany
   Nazi regime, **4:**142
   tracking system, **3:**150
Gernetzke v. Kenosha Unified School District No. 1, **4:**229–230
Gessner, Conrad, **10:**36
GFSA. *See* Gun-Free Schools Act
Gibbons v. Ogden, **6:**164
Gibbs, Nancy, **7:**193–194
Gifted education
   acceleration, **2:**159, **2:**160, **2:**162, **2:**166–168, **6:**121–122
   best practices, **6:**121–123
   creative methods and processes, **2:**168, **2:**169, **2:**172–175
   creative skills, **2:**162
   curricula, **2:**158–175, **6:**122
   enrichment, **2:**160, **2:**162, **2:**163
   equity, **6:**116–117
   expenditures on, **6:**114
   extracurricular activities, **6:**110
   forms, **6:**119
   full state funding, **6:**110–124
   funding, **6:**xxv–xxvii, **6:**120, **6:**123, **6:**232
   goals, **2:**162, **2:**172

identification of students, 2:163–166,
    2:168–169, 6:105–106
  individualized, 2:159, 2:163–164, 2:166,
    2:167
  legal requirements, 6:xxiv–xxv
  mandates, 6:110, 6:113, 6:115–116,
    6:117, 6:119
  need for, 2:163, 2:165
  response to intervention model,
    2:163–164
  school sizes and, 6:116–117
  societal benefits, 6:237–238
  teachers, 2:159, 6:122–123
  See also Advanced Placement courses;
    International Baccalaureate
    courses; Magnet schools
Gifted students
  ability grouping, 3:150, 3:163, 3:164
  in arts, 2:160, 2:163
  career choices, 2:159–160, 2:165
  creativity, 2:165, 2:166–167,
    2:168–169, 2:171–172
  definition, 2:162–163
  differences among, 2:164–165
  in general education, 2:163
  identification of, 2:163–166,
    2:168–169, 6:105–106
  mentoring of, 2:159, 2:174
  number of, 6:113–114
  overexcitabilities, 2:171
  private services, 6:114
  in Science, Technology, Engineering,
    and Mathematics, 2:159–160,
    2:164–166, 2:167
  talent development, 2:158–159,
    2:164–165
Gilbert, David, 1:59
Gillespie, Lauren Nicole, 3:179
Gilligan, Carol, 2:196
Gillis, Lisa, 10:87
Gimbert, Belinda, 10:124
Gintis, Herbert, 3:70
Gitomer, Drew H., 2:99
*Givhan v. Western Line Consolidated School
    District*, 8:199
Glennan, Thomas, 7:170
Global competition
  in education, 9:57–58, 9:218,
    9:226–227, 9:236–239
  impact on education, 7:213,
    7:215–216, 7:247
  impact on school funding, 7:209

increase in, 7:213
  in science, technology, engineering, and
    mathematics, 2:90–106
  standards and, 9:20–35
  vocational education and, 1:217
  See also International comparisons;
    Market competition
Globalization, definition, 2:131
Goe, Laura, 9:142
Goetz v. Ansell, 4:147
Gogol Bordello, 2:211–213
Goldman, Daniel, 2:245
Goldman Sachs, 9:111, 9:234
Goldman v. Weinberger, 4:275
Goldstein, Dan, 10:201
Goldstein, Thalia, 2:150
Golly, Annemieke, 5:237
Good News Club, 4:53–54
*Good News Club v. Milford Central School
    District*, 2:202, 4:xxvi–xxvii, 4:49,
    4:81, 4:234, 4:236–237, 4:245, 4:246,
    4:253, 4:261
Goodman, Ken, 2:73
Goodman, Yetta, 2:73
Google, 10:16
Gordon, June, 3:262, 3:263
Gordon, Rebecca, 5:41
Goss v. Lopez, 5:xviii–xix, 5:49, 5:195,
    5:200, 5:204, 5:206
Governance
  administration and, 7:xxiii
  centralized, 2:19, 2:24, 7:178, 7:246,
    7:255–260, 7:261–262
  choice programs and, 1:105–106
  decentralized, 6:76–77, 7:246,
    7:255–256, 9:124–125
  definition, 7:249
  democratic, 2:18, 2:24–25, 7:178,
    7:257–258, 9:17
  effects of business interests,
    7:165–184
  effects of charter schools, 7:xxvi–xxvii,
    7:130–146
  federal role, 7:xix–xx, 7:xxi, 7:40–56,
    7:112, 7:248–250
  history, 7:xvii–xxiii, 7:1–3, 7:6–7,
    7:12–13, 7:255–256
  issues, 7:xxiii–xxviii
  managerial, 7:180–182
  parental involvement, 9:267, 9:270,
    9:271–274
  politicization, 7:xxiii

reform efforts, **7:**14, **7:**172, **7:**246–247
school improvement and, **7:**169–172
structural changes, **7:**245–262
teachers' roles, **2:**21–25, **7:**xxii, **7:**27
See also Charter school governance; Elected political leaders, control of schools; Local control; Principals; School boards; Superintendents
Government Accountability Office (GAO), **3:**211, **5:**211–212, **5:**215–216, **5:**221–222
Governmental immunity, **5:**82, **5:**189
Governments. *See* Federal government; Local governments; State governments
Grable, Lisa Leonor, **10:**123
Graduation ceremonies
music, **4:**47–48, **4:**116–117
prayers, **4:**xix, **4:**xxi, **4:**35–51, **4:**62, **4:**73, **4:**99, **4:**114
student speeches, **4:**41–44
Graduation rates
calculating, **6:**127
declines, **7:**51
from higher education, **3:**100, **3:**114–115, **6:**235, **9:**xxix, **9:**220, **9:**221
international comparisons, **9:**57, **9:**219, **9:**220
at Native American schools, **1:**258
as performance measure, **6:**127
racial disparities, **3:**86, **7:**51, **7:**85
trends, **9:**254
See also Dropouts; Educational attainment
Graham, Frank Porter, **1:**202
Graham, Patricia, **2:**46–47
Gramsci, Antonio, **2:**20
Greece, ancient, **2:**xviii–xix, **6:**220
Green v. County School Board, **3:**2, **3:**6
Greene, Jay P., **6:**106–107
Greene County Career Center, Ohio, **1:**223–224
Greenleaf, Robert, **7:**101
Greenshields v. Independent School District I-1016 of Payne County, Oklahoma, **8:**8–9
Gregory, A., **5:**207
Grenny, Joseph, **7:**88
Griffin v. County School Board, **3:**15
Griffith v. Butte School District, **4:**41–42, **4:**43
Grigg v. Commonwealth of Virginia, **1:**121

Grove, Andrew, **9:**227
Grubb, Erica B., **6:**170
Guaranteed tax base (GTB) programs, **6:**63, **6:**64
Guggenheim, Davis, **2:**132
Guidance counselors. *See* Counselors
Guilford, J. P., **2:**169
Gun-Free Schools Act (GFSA)
of 1994, **5:**22–23, **5:**197, **5:**203
of 1995, **5:**xx, **5:**23, **5:**197, **5:**203–204
of 2004, **5:**28
impact, **5:**26
provisions, **5:**25, **5:**30, **5:**33
scope, **5:**203–204
See also Zero tolerance policies for weapons
Guthrie, James W., **3:**174, **9:**244
Guthrie, John T., **2:**15

Haberman, Martin, **3:**124
Hackney, Catherine, **7:**100–101
Haft, William, **5:**39, **5:**45
Hall, Daria, **3:**103
Hall, Stuart, **2:**216–217
Hall v. Tawney, **5:**117
Hallinan, Maurice, **3:**96
Hamilton, Alexander, **6:**86–87, **6:**89–90, **6:**91
Hamilton, Laura, **2:**58
Hamilton, Marci A., **4:**28, **4:**29
Hancock v. Commissioner of Education, **3:**182
Hanson, Avarita L., **5:**45
Hanushek, Eric, **3:**69
Harassment. *See* Bullying; Cyberharassment; Sexual harassment
Harbison, Victor, **1:**174
Harlem Children's Zone, **3:**64, **3:**68, **9:**62, **9:**234
Harr, Jenifer J., **6:**97
Harrelson, Woody, **8:**6
Harris, Charlotte, **7:**101
Harris, Eric, **5:**24
See also Columbine shootings
Harris-Murri, Nancy J., **3:**45
Harrison, Kathy, **3:**24
Hartzell v. Connell, **6:**218
Hausner, Lucy, **10:**88
Havighurst, Robert, **1:**259
Hawaii Board of Education, **7:**8, **7:**9
Hawaii education system
governance, **7:**8, **7:**126

performance, 7:8–9
reading instruction, 3:145
regulations, 1:xx, 1:73
Hawthorne, Nathaniel, 3:145, 3:146
Haycock, Kati, 3:87, 3:103, 7:79–80, 7:86, 7:87
Hazelwood School District v. Kuhlmeier, 2:201, 4:42, 4:92, 4:255, 5:8, 8:177, 8:181, 8:187, 8:206–207, 10:167, 10:179–180
Head Start
   benefits of, 1:xxvii, 1:197–199, 1:200–201, 1:203–208
   criticism of, 1:xxvii, 1:208–214
   curriculum, 1:197, 1:203–204
   effectiveness, 1:197–214
   enrollments, 1:198
   establishment, 1:xviii, 1:197
   funding, 1:209–211
   history, 1:197, 3:238
   management issues, 1:210–211
   parental involvement, 1:211–212, 1:213
   teachers, 1:204, 1:206–207, 1:213
Health services, 3:222, 3:223, 3:225
Healy v. James, 4:223
Hebrew Charter School Center, 1:133
Hebrew language schools, 1:25, 1:50, 1:131, 1:133–134
   See also Jewish education
Hechinger, John, 7:19
Hedges v. Wauconda Community Unit School District No. 118, 4:247
Heebner, Amy, 1:169
Heilig, J., 9:110, 9:112
Helicopter parents, 7:193–194
Helms, Jesse, 2:155, 2:205
Hennessy, Judy, 9:171
Herrnstein, Richard J., 3:96
Herold, Jeffrey R., 2:3
Herrington, Carolyn D., 6:118
Hess, F. M., 9:xxi, 9:119, 9:131
Hess, Rick, 9:xx
H.H. v. Moffett, 5:218
HHS. *See* Department of Health and Human Services
Hibbs v. Winn, 1:95, 1:99
Hickman, Wesley, 5:238
Hiebert, Elfrieda H., 3:163
Higgins, Michael, 10:90
High schools
   Carnegie Units, 9:66–67, 9:175–188
   charter schools, 1:12–13
   class rankings, 6:229
   comprehensive, 7:259
   cooperative programs with community colleges, 1:231, 9:44–45
   counselors, 3:20
   early college design, 9:41–44, 9:168
   flexible credit, 9:181–182, 9:187
   flexible scheduling, 7:151, 7:154, 7:155
   gifted education, 6:121
   governance, 7:7
   history, 1:xvi, 2:xxi–xxii, 7:7, 7:148–149, 9:175–176
   immigrant students, 2:132, 2:134, 2:138
   innovation in, 9:41–45
   leadership of, 7:148–163
   parental involvement, 7:195
   preparation for college, 3:121–122, 3:154, 6:303–304, 7:150, 9:40–43, 9:66, 9:183–184, 9:220
   private, 1:145, 1:156
   roles, 7:149–150
   science textbooks, 2:104–105
   sports schedules, 1:245, 1:250
   standardized tests, 2:67
   standards-based reform, 9:40–41
   students with disabilities, 2:185
   teachers, 7:36, 7:157–158
   universal, 3:114
   virtual, 10:72
   See also Advanced Placement courses; Dropouts; Equal Access Act; International Baccalaureate courses; Tracking students; Vocational education
Higher education
   admissions standards, 9:28–29, 9:67, 9:183
   application process, 3:20
   credits for Advanced Placement courses, 6:226, 6:228, 6:230, 6:236–237
   desegregation, 3:4–5
   earnings of graduates, 3:120–121, 3:256, 6:233, 9:219, 9:220
   employment of graduates, 3:119–120
   faculty pensions, 9:65–67, 9:183
   faculty research, 3:51–52
   funding, 6:237
   gender discrimination, 3:208, 3:213–214, 8:144–145
   graduation rates, 3:100, 3:114–115, 6:235, 9:xxix, 9:220, 9:221

historically Black institutions, **3:**262
international rankings, **1:**150–151
land grant universities, **1:**216, **1:**219
minority students, **3:**113–129, **3:**262–263
Morrill Acts, **7:**149
as norm, **3:**113–129
preparation of students for, **2:**xxii, **3:**121–122, **3:**154, **6:**303–304, **7:**150, **9:**40–43, **9:**66, **9:**177–178, **9:**183–184, **9:**220
remedial classes, **6:**237, **6:**303–304
student fees, **6:**218
student's share of costs, **6:**230–231
women's athletics programs, **3:**210–211, **3:**219
See also Administration preparation programs; Teacher training programs
Higher Education Act, Title IV, **3:**265
Highlen, Pamela S., **3:**32–33
Hill, Cynthia D., **1:**85
Hill, Paul, **7:**70, **9:**125, **9:**169, **9:**170, **9:**172
Hills v. Scottsdale Unified School District, **4:**246, **4:**256, **4:**261
Hinduja, Sameer, **10:**153
Hinshaw, Steven A., **6:**73–74
Hip-hop culture, **3:**137–147
Hirsch, E. D., Jr.,**9:**33, **9:**34
Hispanic Americans. *See* Latino Americans
History
curricula, **6:**220
local, **2:**70
standards, **9:**32–33
Hitler, Adolf, **4:**142
Hoekstra, Mark, **7:**194
Hogard, Elaine, **7:**100–101
Holdtzman, D., **9:**112
Holidays
public, **4:**128, **4:**202
secular purposes, **4:**207–208
See also Religious holidays
Hollifield, John, **3:**164
Holme, Jennifer Jellison, **1:**157, **1:**159
Holmes, Donald, **4:**71
Holmes v. Bush, **6:**251
HomeBase, **5:**237
Homeless students
challenges, **8:**136–137, **8:**141
identifying, **8:**140
number of, **8:**127, **8:**137
of preschool age, **8:**140

rights of, **8:**xx, **8:**127–142
school enrollments, **8:**131–132, **8:**133–134, **8:**136, **8:**138
services, **8:**133, **8:**134–135, **8:**138
standardized test scores, **8:**141
See also McKinney-Vento Homeless Assistance Act
Homeschooling
competition with traditional schools, **7:**214–215
curricula, **1:**110, **1:**116, **1:**120–121
equivalence to public education, **1:**110, **1:**113–117
growth, **1:**109, **1:**112, **1:**118
history, **1:**xxiv, **1:**109
legal cases, **1:**110, **1:**112–114, **1:**115, **1:**116, **1:**118, **1:**119–122
online courses, **1:**110
reasons for choosing, **1:**110, **1:**112, **1:**122–123
regulations, **1:**xxv, **1:**109–123
religious reasons, **1:**112, **1:**115–116, **1:**119, **1:**121, **4:**74
teacher qualifications, **1:**114–115, **1:**116–117, **1:**118, **1:**119–120
Homosexuality, **4:**263–264
See also LGBT youth
Honig v. Doe, **8:**91, **8:**94, **8:**97–98, **8:**100–101
Honor codes, **5:**128
See also Academic integrity
hooks, bell, **3:**143
Horn, Michael B., **10:**xviii, **10:**xxv–xxvi, **10:**115
Horner, Robert H., **5:**234, **5:**237
Hospitals, religious affiliations, **4:**5
Houang, Richard, **9:**31
Houston, Eric, **5:**24
Houston Independent School District, **9:**145
Howard, Jeff, **3:**174
Howard, Tyrone C., **3:**144
Hoxby, Caroline M., **1:**42
Hsu v. Roslyn Union Free School District No. 3, **4:**219–220, **4:**224
Huang, Francis L., **9:**113
Huang, Jingzi, **2:**51
Hughes, Bob, **10:**124–125, **10:**126
Human capital, **9:**218, **9:**226
Human Rights Watch, **5:**206
Humanities
budget cuts in, **9:**xxvi

curricula focused on, **2:**xxi–xxii, **2:**152
impact of digital technology, **10:**25, **10:**26–29
Hussar, William J., **9:**110
Husserl, Edmund, **2:**241
Hutton, Thomas, **10:**188
Hyland, Tim, **5:**178–179

Iacocca, Lee, **7:**237
Iannaccone, Lawrence, **7:**256, **7:**257, **7:**258
IASA. *See* Illinois Association of School Administrators
IB. *See* International Baccalaureate
IBM, **10:**144, **10:**210
ICS. *See* Integrated Comprehensive Services
Idaho
  charter schools, **1:**50–51
  finance litigation, **3:**180
  homeschooling laws, **1:**113
  prayer at graduation ceremonies, **4:**40
  suicide prevention programs, **5:**72
  virtual school funding, **10:**86
Idaho Digital Learning Academy (IDLA), **10:**86
Idaho Schools for Equal Educational Opportunity v. Evans, **3:**180
IDEA. *See* Individuals with Disabilities Education Act
Identity construction, **1:**64, **1:**65–70, **2:**218–219, **2:**222, **2:**225
  See also Ethnic identities; Religious identities
IDLA. *See* Idaho Digital Learning Academy
IEPs. *See* Individualized education programs
Illback, Robert J., **7:**255
Illinois
  moments of silence in schools, **4:**49–50, **4:**68, **4:**72–73, **4:**75, **4:**79
  school transportation funding, **4:**13
  See also Chicago
Illinois Association of School Administrators (IASA), **10:**199
Illinois Supreme Court, **1:**121, **6:**158
Illinois Virtual High School (IVHS), **10:**72
Imagine Schools, **1:**89
Imazeki, Jennifer, **6:**117–118
Imber, Mickey, **2:**122
Immigrants
  cultural capital, **2:**108–109

English language instruction, **2:**119, **2:**120, **2:**122, **3:**186–187, **3:**192, **3:**193–194
in Europe, **2:**131–132
families, **7:**194, **7:**204
frustrations, **2:**212
illegal, **7:**194, **7:**204
Muslim, **1:**57–58, **1:**59, **1:**60–61, **1:**63–64, **1:**69
nationalism, **2:**130
in public schools, **2:**132, **2:**134, **2:**138, **3:**152–153, **3:**161, **3:**186
See also Cultural differences; English Language Learners
Immigration laws, state, **2:**134–135, **2:**139, **3:**193
Immunity, governmental, **5:**82, **5:**189
iNACOL. *See* International Association for K-12 Online Learning
Incentive pay. *See* Performance pay
Inclusion classrooms
  accommodations, **8:**113–114
  co-teaching, **2:**178, **7:**46
  as default placement, **8:**113, **8:**121, **8:**124
  disadvantages, **3:**215–216, **3:**244–245
  discipline problems, **8:**101–102
  gifted students in, **2:**163
  instruction, **2:**179, **2:**185, **2:**191–193
  special education compared to, **2:**177–193, **8:**108–125
  student achievement, **8:**123–124
  students with disabilities in, **2:**178, **2:**179, **2:**185, **2:**187–193, **3:**215–216, **3:**218, **3:**244–245, **3:**253, **8:**110, **8:**112
  supporters, **8:**112, **8:**119–125
Inclusive learning communities, **7:**79–80
Income inequality, **9:**229
  See also Inequities
Income taxes
  corporate, **6:**74, **6:**269, **9:**259
  deductions, **1:**92, **6:**259, **6:**261–262
  equity, **6:**66
  federal, **6:**64, **6:**65
  local, **6:**65, **6:**71
  state, **6:**64, **6:**65, **6:**67, **6:**68, **6:**74
  See also Tax credits, educational; Taxes
Incomes. *See* Economic success; Teacher salaries and benefits
Incubation Model of Teaching, **2:**173
Indebtedness limits, **6:**21–38
Independent schools. *See* Private schools

India, schools, **1**:54
Indian Education Act (IEA), **1**:257
Indian Nations at Risk Task Force, **1**:265
Indian Self-Determination and Education Assistance Act (ISDEAA), **1**:257–258
Indiana
   Advanced Placement fees, **6**:230
   Teacher Protection Act, **5**:178, **5**:183–184, **5**:187
Indiana University High School, **6**:230
Indians. *See* Native Americans
Individualized education programs (IEPs)
   accommodations, **2**:188
   contents, **2**:188
   disciplinary measures, **5**:210, **5**:211, **5**:225–226, **5**:227, **5**:228–229, **8**:102, **8**:103
   legal requirements, **2**:183, **2**:188, **8**:91
   parental involvement, **8**:91
   placement decisions, **2**:177–178, **8**:118–119, **8**:121
   for students with internalizing disorders, **5**:254–255, **5**:257–258
   supplementary aids and services, **2**:178, **2**:188, **2**:189–190, **8**:119, **8**:121
   writing, **2**:183, **2**:187, **2**:188
   See also Disabilities, students with; Least restrictive environment
Individuals with Disabilities Education Act (IDEA)
   amendments (1997), **6**:103, **8**:91, **8**:94
   amendments (2004), **8**:91, **8**:94, **8**:95
   assistive technology provisions, **10**:2, **10**:4, **10**:7–9, **10**:10–11
   charter schools and, **1**:16
   continuum of placements, **2**:177, **2**:178, **2**:190, **8**:xviii, **8**:109, **8**:112, **8**:121
   disciplinary measures, **5**:218–219, **5**:223–224, **8**:xvii, **8**:90–106
   due process provisions, **5**:210, **5**:224, **5**:226, **8**:90, **8**:93, **8**:97–98, **8**:101
   educational malpractice claims, **8**:214, **8**:219, **8**:220
   funding, **6**:97, **6**:98, **6**:101–102, **6**:248
   implementation costs, **6**:xxv
   internalizing disorders and, **5**:254–255, **5**:257–258
   least restrictive environment, **2**:177–178, **2**:189, **2**:193, **3**:250, **8**:109, **8**:112, **8**:113, **8**:119
   NCLB and, **2**:184, **2**:190–192
   passage, **1**:xviii, **6**:103
   positive behavior intervention supports, **5**:xxii, **5**:231, **5**:232
   preventing overrepresentation of students of color in special education, **5**:38
   provisions, **1**:xviii–xix, **2**:177, **2**:183, **6**:93, **6**:96–97
   purpose, **2**:181, **2**:185–186, **8**:112
   reauthorizations, **2**:189, **6**:101
   scope, **6**:93
   supplementary services, **2**:189–190
   transition planning, **2**:185
   zero tolerance policies and, **5**:20–21, **5**:23, **5**:25
   See also Individualized education programs
Inequities
   effects of tax credits, **6**:266–267
   in gifted education, **6**:115–117
   income inequality, **9**:229
   local control and, **6**:xix, **6**:2–3
   in past, **9**:xxviii–xxix
   in Science, Technology, Engineering, and Mathematics, **2**:93
   in special education, **6**:98–99
   See also Equity; Financing equity; Segregated schools
INET. *See* International Networking for Education Transformation
Informal learning, **2**:214–215, **2**:219–220
Information literacy, **5**:133, **5**:135–136
Infrastructure, educational, **7**:171–172, **7**:175, **7**:183–184
Ingraham v. Wright, **5**:xviii, **5**:49, **5**:107, **5**:111, **5**:116, **5**:117, **5**:199, **5**:200, **5**:203, **5**:204–206, **5**:218
Injuries of students
   in discipline process, **5**:xxv, **5**:117, **5**:205, **5**:224
   effects, **5**:214
Injury, in negligence cases, **5**:66–67, **5**:185, **5**:188, **5**:189
In loco parentis doctrine
   corporal punishment, **5**:106, **5**:115–116
   custodial powers, **5**:xvii, **5**:198, **5**:202
   discipline policies and, **5**:xvii, **5**:194–208
   history of, **5**:194–195, **5**:198, **5**:203
   implementation, **5**:200–202, **5**:204, **5**:206
   legal cases, **5**:198–199, **5**:203, **5**:204–206
   new applications, **2**:203, **5**:206–208

student rights and, **5:**195, **5:**198–199, **5:**200, **5:**203, **5:**204–206
suicide prevention responsibility, **5:**73
Innovation
  in charter schools, **1:**4–7, **1:**10
  choice programs and, **1:**106
  diffusion of, **10:**139
  disruptive, **10:**xviii, **10:**43
  in high schools, **9:**41–45
  in magnet schools, **1:**167–168, **1:**169
  standards-based reform and, **9:**37–52
  in teacher training programs, **2:**48, **2:**52
  See also Reform proposals; Technology
Inquiry learning, **2:**13, **2:**121, **10:**40, **10:**212–213
Insight Schools Inc., **10:**87
Institutes of higher education (IHEs). *See* Higher education; Teacher training programs
Institutionalization, **7:**136–137
Instruction
  authentic, **2:**xxiii, **2:**76–78
  characteristics of high quality teaching, **1:**264–265, **8:**15–16, **8:**220, **9:**151–153
  in charter schools, **1:**5, **1:**6
  conditions supporting, **9:**153–154
  conflicts with Carnegie Units, **9:**179–181
  constructivist, **2:**xxiii, **2:**235
  as craft, **2:**151, **2:**153
  cultural relevance, **1:**258–261, **1:**265–266, **1:**267, **3:**70, **3:**71–72, **3:**134–135, **7:**81–82
  differentiated, **1:**231–232, **1:**266, **2:**179, **2:**191–192
  direct, **2:**19, **2:**74
  discipleship models, **2:**xxiv
  discipline and control model, **2:**xxii–xxv, **2:**1, **2:**2–3
  freedom in, **2:**95–96, **2:**99
  impact of e-books, **10:**19–21, **10:**23–24, **10:**27–28, **10:**29–30
  impact of standards-based reforms, **2:**59, **9:**xix
  improving quality, **2:**63–64, **6:**82–83, **7:**83, **7:**84
  key factors, **10:**223–224
  in learning skills, **9:**18–19
  links to out-of-school experiences, **2:**219
  new models, **10:**132–133
  performance-based assignments, **9:**180, **9:**187
  programmatic, **2:**1–17, **2:**29
  in reading, **2:**7, **2:**72–89, **2:**115–116, **9:**83, **9:**84
  scripted, **2:**1, **2:**7, **2:**10, **2:**19, **2:**69
  student-centered, **2:**xxv, **2:**159, **2:**163–164, **2:**166, **2:**167
  teacher-centered, **2:**xxiii–xxiv, **2:**1
  teaching to tests, **1:**249, **2:**59–61, **6:**139, **7:**45, **7:**51, **7:**218, **9:**10, **9:**59
  transformative potential of technology, **10:**208–224
  See also Assistive technology; Curricula; Learning; Online learning; Teachers; *and specific subject areas*
Instructional leadership, **7:**151–152, **7:**162, **7:**199–201
Insurance, liability, **5:**182, **5:**187–188
INTASC. *See* Interstate New Teacher Assessment and Support Consortium
Integrated Comprehensive Services (ICS) model, **3:**251
Integrity. *See* Academic integrity
Intellectual property, **10:**22
  See also Copyright law
Intelligence tests, **2:**65
Intelligent design
  coexistence with evolutionary theory, **4:**188–189, **4:**190–191
  criticism of, **4:**xxv, **4:**188
  instruction in, **4:**187, **4:**188, **4:**197
  proponents, **4:**184, **4:**188–189, **4:**191
  See also Creation science
Intended curriculum, **2:**58–59, **2:**60
Interagency Council on Homelessness, **8:**127
Internalizing disorders
  impact on academic performance, **5:**251, **5:**255–256, **5:**257–260
  individualized education programs, **5:**254–255, **5:**257–258
  interventions, **5:**252–254, **5:**256–257, **5:**259, **5:**260–263
  prevalence, **5:**248, **5:**251
  symptoms, **5:**248, **5:**251, **5:**255, **5:**258–259, **5:**260
  teachers' roles in identification and treatment, **5:**xxi, **5:**248–263
International Association for K-12 Online Learning (iNACOL), **10:**80, **10:**88–89, **10:**94, **10:**95, **10:**96, **10:**119, **10:**129
International Baccalaureate (IB) courses
  college credit, **6:**226

costs, **6:**226
funding, **6:**xxvi, **6:**xxvii, **6:**232
introduction of, **3:**161
online, **10:**57
social mobility benefits, **6:**xxvi, **6:**226
student fees, **6:**225–238
International comparisons
  academic performance, **6:**xxii, **7:**213, **7:**216–217, **7:**229, **7:**230
  achievement gaps, **7:**75, **7:**76
  complicating factors, **7:**217
  education funding, **7:**209
  graduation rates, **9:**57, **9:**219, **9:**220
  higher education institutions, **1:**150–151
  impact of reforms, **7:**53
  measures, **2:**100–103
  national curricula, **9:**29–30
  per pupil expenditures, **6:**235, **9:**239, **9:**240, **9:**252
  quality of schools, **7:**209
  school year lengths, **1:**248
  standardized test scores, **2:**102–103, **9:**29–30, **9:**57, **9:**220, **9:**237–239, **9:**254–255
  teacher salaries, **6:**140
  See also Global competition
International Networking for Education Transformation (iNet), **7:**53–54
International Society for Technology in Education (ISTE), **10:**xxii, **10:**48, **10:**119, **10:**123, **10:**127, **10:**128, **10:**130
Internet
  ADA-compliant sites, **10:**201–202
  blogs, **2:**219, **8:**180, **8:**188, **10:**139, **10:**149
  censorship, **2:**207–208
  disciplining students for activity on, **8:**180, **8:**184–185, **8:**188–189
  educational use, **2:**234–236, **10:**212–215, **10:**222–223
  e-mail, **8:**180
  games, **2:**214–215, **2:**219
  increased access in schools, **2:**237, **10:**xvi, **10:**139
  interactivity, **2:**217, **2:**219
  research methods, **5:**128–129, **5:**133–134, **5:**135–136, **10:**213
  safety concerns, **10:**xxiii, **10:**147–148
  school websites, **10:**206
  student use of, **2:**226

virtual worlds, **2:**217, **2:**230–231, **2:**241
See also Cyberbullying; Online courses; Social networking sites
Interstate New Teacher Assessment and Support Consortium (INTASC), **9:**79, **9:**88, **9:**89–91
Interstate School Leaders Licensure Consortium (ISLLC) Standards, **7:**78, **7:**89–90, **7:**97, **7:**124, **7:**191
Intrinsic motivation, **5:**142, **5:**145–147, **5:**148–149, **5:**152–153, **5:**154–155
Investment in education
  by business interests, **9:**233–260
  by philanthropies, **9:**55–56
  by state governments, **9:**216, **9:**218–225
Iowa
  charter schools, **7:**132
  disciplinary measures, **5:**222
  dress code laws, **5:**11–12
  education tax credits, **6:**269
Iowa Association of School Boards, **7:**125–126
iPads, **10:**xix, **10:**2
  See also Mobile technologies
iPhone, **10:**33
iPod Touch, **10:**39
IQ tests, **2:**65
Isaacson, Walter, **9:**25
ISDEAA. *See* Indian Self-Determination and Education Assistance Act
Islam
  Arab American communities, **2:**129–130
  attitudes and perceptions in United States, **1:**42, **1:**67, **2:**134, **2:**137, **2:**205
  cultural differences, **1:**58
  culturally specific charter schools, **1:**xxiii, **1:**54–70
  extremism, **4:**174
  female clothing, **4:**268, **4:**275, **4:**276, **4:**280–281, **4:**288, **4:**296
  increasing understanding of, **4:**174–175
  Koran, **1:**55, **4:**170, **4:**171–172, **4:**179
  mosques, **6:**254–255
  schools, **1:**54, **1:**55, **1:**66, **6:**255–256
  See also Religions
Islamic Cultural Center, New York City, **2:**134, **2:**137
ISLLC. *See* Interstate School Leaders Licensure Consortium

ISTE. *See* International Society for Technology in Education
IVHS. *See* Illinois Virtual High School

Jackson, Jesse, **5:**50
Jackson v. Benson, **1:**95, **1:**96
Jacobs v. Clark County School District, **8:**45–47
Jacobsen, Rebecca, **1:**42, **3:**68
Jacullo-Noto, Joann, **3:**262
James, Tim, **3:**193
James Madison University, **2:**18
Jamie S. v. Milwaukee Public Schools, **6:**100
Japan
  immigrants in, **2:**132
  school year lengths, **1:**248
J.C. v. Beverly Hills Unified School District, **8:**183
Jefferson, Thomas
  on church-state separation, **2:**204, **4:**xvii, **4:**17–18, **4:**45, **4:**100, **4:**130, **4:**194, **4:**281
  Declaration of Independence, **4:**144
  public education and, **7:**xvii, **7:**xxii, **7:**116, **7:**255
  second inaugural address, **4:**191–192
Jeglin v. San Jacinto Unified School District, **5:**5
Jehovah's Witnesses, **4:**xvii, **4:**xxiii
Jenson, Susan, **1:**222
Jernigan v. State of Alabama, **1:**119
Jewish day schools
  affordability, **1:**134, **1:**136, **1:**137
  alternatives to, **1:**126, **1:**132–134, **1:**136–137, **1:**138–142
  arguments for universality, **1:**130–135
  definition, **1:**125
  enrollments, **1:**126, **1:**128, **1:**136
  growth, **1:**128–130
  Jewish identity and, **1:**xxv, **1:**125–143
  number of, **1:**126, **1:**129–130, **1:**136
  student achievement, **1:**131, **1:**132
  supporters, **1:**125–126, **1:**128–135
  variety, **1:**129–130, **1:**134
Jewish education
  availability, **1:**141–142
  debates on, **1:**126–127
  Hebrew language schools, **1:**25, **1:**50, **1:**131, **1:**133–134
  history, **1:**128

  part-time programs (after-school/ summer), **1:**126, **1:**128, **1:**132–133, **1:**136–137, **1:**138–142
  released time programs, **4:**162
  texts, **4:**170, **4:**179
Jewish religious garb and symbols, **4:**272, **4:**275, **4:**288
Jeynes, William H., **1:**153, **5:**207
Jez, Su Jin, **9:**110, **9:**112
Joanou, Jamie, **6:**289
Jobs. *See* Employment; Teacher hiring
Jobs for the Future, **9:**38, **9:**43
Jocson, Korina M., **3:**139
Johns Hopkins University
  Center for Talented Youth, **2:**164, **2:**165, **2:**167
  psychology lab, **2:**xxiii
  Talent Development Middle Grades and High Schools programs, **2:**7
Johnson, Andrew, **7:**41
Johnson, Curtis W., **10:**xviii, **10:**xxv–xxvi, **10:**115
Johnson, Lyndon B., **1:**39–40, **1:**197, **3:**14, **3:**78, **3:**97, **3:**242, **7:**76, **7:**251
Jones, Deneese L., **3:**156
Jones, John T., **6:**38
Jones v. Clear Creek Independent School District, **4:**39–40, **4:**43
Jones v. Graham County Board of Education, **8:**75, **8:**81, **8:**86–88
Jones v. McKenzie, **8:**77, **8:**84
Jordan, Cathie, **3:**142, **3:**145
Jordan, Teresa S., **3:**171
J.S. v. Blue Mountain School District, **8:**184, **10:**159, **10:**169, **10:**177, **10:**180–181, **10:**183, **10:**187, **10:**204
Judd, Charles H., **9:**14
Judicial branch
  analysis and decision making, **6:**150–151, **6:**171
  appointments, **7:**59, **7:**71–72
  constitutional interpretation, **6:**163–164
  criticism of, **7:**59–60
  debates on education role, **6:**143–161, **6:**150–154, **7:**64–65, **7:**68–73
  desegregation role, **3:**xxvi, **3:**1–17, **6:**253, **7:**62–63
  education cases, **5:**133, **7:**62–64, **7:**66–67, **7:**69
  interpretations of role, **7:**61–63
  issues affected by, **7:**xxv–xxvi, **7:**69, **7:**71

political process and, **6:**149, **6:**160–161, **6:**164, **7:**58–59, **7:**71–72
positive influence, **7:**60
power, **7:**59
role in school governance, **7:**58–73
school takeovers, **6:**xxii, **7:**xxiii, **7:**14, **7:**63
uncertainty created by, **7:**66, **7:**68
See also Finance litigation; State courts; Supreme Court
Judicial review, **6:**148, **6:**156–157, **7:**69–70, **7:**73
Jukes, Ian, **1:**229
Julian, Liam, **9:**25, **9:**33–34
Jurgensen, Jerry, **9:**248
Justice, restorative, **5:**45
Justice Policy Institute, **5:**xx–xxi

K12 Inc., **10:**84–85
Kaboolian, Linda, **8:**249
Kafka, Franz, **2:**212
Kahlenberg, Richard, **1:**48
Kaiser Family Foundation, **2:**219
Kalin, John, **3:**69
Kane, Thomas, **9:**85
Kansas, charter schools, **7:**132
Kansas City, Mo.
  magnet schools, **1:**168
  school system, **7:**63
Kanstoroom, M., **9:**112
Karr, Chesley, **5:**6
KASSA. *See* Keep America's Students Safe Act
Katnami, Samar, **2:**xxii
Katz, Lisa, **1:**139
Katz v. United States, **10:**103–104
Kaufman, James C., **2:**166
Keep America's Students Safe Act (KASSA), **5:**219, **5:**223, **5:**224, **5:**227, **5:**228
Keeping Children and Families Safe Act of 2003, **5:**90, **5:**99
Kekulé, August, **2:**170
Keleher, Terry, **5:**41
Kelly, Andrew P., **9:**131
Kempe, C. Henry, **5:**89
Kennedy, Anthony, **3:**8
Kennedy, John F., **2:**204, **8:**244
Kentucky
  constitution, **6:**169, **6:**173
  finance litigation, **3:**181, **6:**33, **6:**64, **6:**149, **6:**169, **6:**198, **6:**201

privacy rights, **10:**108
school funding, **6:**64, **6:**149, **6:**169, **6:**184–185, **6:**194, **6:**198, **6:**201
school resource officers, **5:**165
school shootings, **5:**24
school takeovers by courts, **6:**xxii
standardized test scores, **6:**199
Ten Commandments displays, **4:**xxii–xxiii, **4:**113, **4:**120, **4:**131–132, **4:**133
Kentucky Supreme Court, **6:**194
Kenyon, Daphne A., **6:**69
Kerchner, Charles Taylor, **8:**250
Kern, Lee, **5:**238
Kerr, Donna H., **8:**52–53
Kerry, John, **2:**130–131
Keyes, Maureen W., **3:**251
Keyishian v. Board of Regents, **8:**204, **8:**208
Khalil Gibran International Academy, **1:**50
Killen, Rob, **8:**50
Killion v. Franklin Regional School District, **10:**168–169
Kimmich, Madeleine, **5:**237
Kindergarten, early entry, **6:**121
Kindle, **10:**xx, **10:**16
  See also e-books
King, Keith A., **5:**73
KIPP. *See* Knowledge Is Power Program
Kiracofe, Christine, **6:**215–216, **6:**218
Kirkland, David E., **3:**145
Kirst, Michael, **7:**256
Kitwana, Bakari, **3:**138
Kitzmiller v. Dover, **4:**193, **4:**197
Klauke, Amy, **1:**175, **1:**177
Klebold, Dylan, **5:**24
  See also Columbine shootings
Klein, Joel, **7:**177
Kloo, Amanda, **2:**179
Klopfer, Eric, **10:**46
Knowledge Is Power Program (KIPP), **1:**10, **3:**64, **3:**68, **9:**23, **9:**42, **9:**225
KnowledgeWorks Foundation, **9:**165
Knox County Education Association v. Knox County Board of Education, **8:**74, **8:**75, **8:**77, **8:**80, **8:**82–83, **8:**85
Koehler, Matthew J., **10:**124
Koenick v. Felton, **4:**202, **4:**207
Koerner, James, **3:**48
Koestler, Arthur, **2:**169
Koestner, R., **5:**153
Kohl, Herb, **2:**2
Kohlberg, Lawrence, **2:**196

Kohn, Alfie, **9:**29–30, **9:**34
Koppich, Julia E., **8:**250
Koran, **1:**55, **4:**170, **4:**171–172, **4:**179
Koretz, Daniel, **9:**230
Korzybski, Alfred, **2:**241
Kotterman v. Killian, **1:**99
Kozol, Jonathan, **7:**139, **7:**248
Krajcik, Joseph, **2:**96
Kridel, Craig, **9:**16
Krishnamurti schools, **2:**246
Ku Klux Klan, **4:**2, **4:**293
Kukulska-Hulme, Agnes, **10:**43
Kyllo v. United States, **10:**104

Labaree, David F., **3:**48
Labbo, Linda, **2:**215
Labor unions. *See* Unions
Ladd, Helen F., **3:**70, **3:**173, **3:**176
Ladson-Billings, Gloria, **3:**70, **3:**137, **3:**143, **3:**146
LaForest, Edmond, **2:**128
Lagerman, Ellen Condliffe, **9:**14–15
Lam, Linda D., **4:**76
Lamb's Chapel v. Center Moriches Union Free School District, **2:**202, **4:**xxvi–xxvii, **4:**42, **4:**205, **4:**234, **4:**236, **4:**243–244, **4:**253, **4:**259
Land, Anna, **10:**146
Lander v. Seaver, **5:**107, **5:**195
Lane v. Owens, **4:**147
Languages
  Arabic, **1:**21, **1:**25–26, **1:**50
  as cultural capital, **2:**108–109
  cultural identities and, **2:**128, **3:**193–194
  Ebonics, **2:**109, **2:**125
  Hebrew, **1:**25, **1:**50, **1:**131, **1:**133–134
  Native American, **1:**260
  second language acquisition, **3:**198–200, **3:**204–205
  in United States, **2:**117, **2:**124–125, **3:**196
  See also Bilingual students; English language; Spanish language
Lantieri, Linda, **2:**245
Lareau, Annette, **3:**96
Las Virgenes Educators Association v. Las Virgenes Unified School District, **10:**162
Lasley, Thomas J., **9:**271
LASPD, **5:**160
Lassonde v. Pleasanton Unified School District, **4:**46

Latino Americans
  ability grouping and, **3:**155–156, **3:**162
  arrests of students, **5:**162
  graduation rates, **7:**51
  migrant workers, **1:**246
  NAEP scores, **3:**100, **3:**109
  poor, **3:**79
  population growth, **9:**58
  proportion of student bodies, **3:**104
  school board members, **7:**118
  Spanish-speaking, **2:**109, **2:**117, **2:**125
  student population, **9:**241–242
  suspensions and expulsions, **5:**37, **5:**41–42, **5:**47
  See also Achievement gaps; Minority students
Lau v. Nichols, **1:**xviii, **3:**191, **3:**197
Lave, Jean, **2:**133
Law. *See* School law; State laws
Law enforcement. *See* Police; School resource officers
Lawsuits
  bullying-related, **5:**55–56, **5:**65–67, **5:**68
  costs, **5:**182, **5:**186, **5:**187–188
  educational malpractice, **5:**83
  fear of, **5:**186–187
  governmental immunity, **5:**82, **5:**189
  settlements, **5:**183
  See also Finance litigation; Liability; Negligence; Teacher protection acts; Tort law
Layshock v. Hermitage School District
  disruption test applied, **10:**159, **10:**169, **10:**180–181
  parody profile, **8:**182–183, **10:**182, **10:**183
  ruling, **8:**184, **10:**177, **10:**187, **10:**204
Leadership
  of change, **7:**80, **7:**232
  collaborative, **7:**89
  effective, **7:**231–232
  gender differences in styles, **7:**98–99, **7:**100–102
  instructional, **7:**151–152, **7:**162, **7:**199–201
  intrinsic motivation, **5:**148–149
  of principals, **7:**80–82, **7:**89–90
  servant, **7:**101
  of teachers, **1:**76–77
  trait approach, **7:**98
  transformational, **7:**99

turnover, **7:**143–144
See also Alternative leadership programs; Interstate School Leaders Licensure Consortium Standards; Principals; Superintendents
Leander, Kevin, **2:**215
Learning
  behavioral theories, **6:**133
  cooperative approaches, **1:**266, **3:**157
  cultural tolerance and, **7:**201
  culturally responsive, **7:**199–200
  cultural-specific styles, **3:**165
  extrinsic motivators and, **5:**142
  gender differences in styles, **1:**80, **1:**85, **3:**216–217
  informal vs. formal, **2:**214–215, **2:**219–220
  inquiry, **2:**13, **2:**121, **10:**40, **10:**212–213
  intrinsic motivation, **5:**142, **5:**145–147, **5:**152–153, **5:**154–155
  scaffolding, **2:**11–12, **2:**15
  sociocultural theory, **2:**11–14
  summer losses, **1:**241, **1:**242, **1:**243–244, **1:**250–251, **3:**88
  teacher expectations of students, **5:**150–151, **5:**155
  theories, **3:**42
  See also Instruction
Learning communities
  in charter schools, **1:**8–9, **6:**280–281
  inclusive, **7:**79–80
  school sizes and, **1:**8–9
Learning disabilities
  assistive technologies, **10:**5
  diagnosis, **6:**105, **6:**106, **6:**107
  individualized instruction and, **5:**249
  See also Disabilities, students with
Learning environments
  collaborative, **5:**xxiv, **5:**141–142, **7:**152, **10:**40, **10:**214, **10:**217, **10:**223
  ecosystems of relationships, **2:**11–16
  establishing, **5:**150–152, **7:**152
  informal, **2:**xxv, **2:**214–215
  new models, **10:**132–133
  research on, **10:**50–52
  virtual schools, **10:**xxi, **10:**68–78
  See also Universal Design for Learning
Learning management systems (LMS), **10:**64, **10:**91, **10:**94

"Learning to read" vs. "reading to learn," **2:**72–89
LEAs (local education agencies). *See* School districts
Least restrictive environment (LRE)
  continuum of placements, **2:**178, **2:**189, **2:**190, **2:**193, **8:**xviii, **8:**109, **8:**112
  implications, **8:**121, **8:**124–125
  legal requirements, **8:**109, **8:**112, **8:**113, **8:**119
  placement decisions, **1:**202, **2:**177–178, **8:**118–119, **8:**121
  teachers in, **3:**250
  tests, **8:**114–115
  See also Free appropriate public education; Inclusion classrooms
Ledbetter, Lilly, **3:**207
Ledbetter v. Goodyear Tire & Rubber Company, **3:**207
Lee, Chungmei, **3:**108
Lee, Jaekyung, **3:**69
Lee, Valerie, **1:**192
Lee v. Weisman, **1:**25, **1:**29–30, **4:**xix, **4:**xxi, **4:**36, **4:**38, **4:**46, **4:**62, **4:**73, **4:**99, **4:**114, **4:**116
Lefstein, Adam, **2:**220
Leithwood, Kenneth, **7:**80–81
Lemon (tripartite) test
  development of, **4:**xviii, **4:**6
  government aid to religious schools and, **4:**xviii, **4:**xxv, **4:**6, **4:**18, **4:**22–24, **4:**27
  moments of silence and, **4:**68, **4:**71, **4:**79, **4:**82
  prayer in schools and, **4:**48, **4:**49–50, **4:**62
  released time religious instruction and, **4:**159
  religious garb and, **4:**292
  religious groups meeting in public schools, **4:**238
  religious holidays and, **4:**201–202, **4:**204, **4:**210–212
  religious instruction in schools and, **4:**168–169, **4:**177–178
  religious materials distribution and, **4:**260–261
  religious music and, **4:**104, **4:**107–110, **4:**113, **4:**114–115
  religious symbols and, **4:**123, **4:**124–127, **4:**131
  science curricula and, **4:**195

teachers reading sacred texts and, **4**:99
See also Establishment Clause
Lemon v. Kurtzman, **1**:31, **4**:12, **4**:18, **4**:22–23, **4**:27, **4**:62, **4**:86, **4**:99, **4**:107
Lennon, John, **2**:131
LePage, Pamela, **3**:42–43, **3**:45, **3**:46
Lesbians. *See* LGBT youth
Levin, D., **9**:23
Levin, Henry M., **1**:103, **1**:105, **6**:15
Levine, Arthur, **2**:40, **9**:81, **9**:126, **9**:127, **9**:135
Levitt v. Committee for Public Education and Religious Liberty, **4**:6
Levittown v. Nyquist, **3**:182, **3**:183
Lewis, Chance W., **3**:264
Lewis, Morgan, **1**:222
Lewis, Samuel, **4**:270
Lewis, Wayne D., **3**:218, **3**:219
Lewis-Palmer, Teri, **5**:232
LGBT youth
 attitudes toward, **4**:263–264
 bullying victims, **4**:263–264, **5**:xxiii, **5**:55
 gay rights student groups, **4**:216
Liability
 protection, **5**:xxiv–xxv, **5**:177–191
 released time programs and, **4**:165–166
 for suicide, **5**:83–84
 of teachers, **5**:xxiv–xxv, **5**:204–205
 See also Teacher protection acts
Liability insurance, **5**:182, **5**:187–188
Liberals, **2**:204
Librarians, **10**:23
Libraries
 Bibles, **4**:63, **4**:86
 digital, **10**:22
 e-reader lending, **10**:19–20
 impact of e-books, **10**:18, **10**:22–23, **10**:25, **10**:28–29
 information literacy courses, **5**:135–136
 Internet access, **2**:237
 media specialists, **2**:216, **10**:23
 traditional, **10**:19, **10**:29
Licensing. *See* Teacher licensing
Lichty, Lauren F., **8**:149
Lincoln Institute of Land Policy, **9**:202
Lingle, Linda, **7**:8, **7**:9
Lipp v. Morris, **4**:147
Literacy
 achievement gaps, **2**:79–80, **2**:87
 information, **5**:133, **5**:135–136

 instructional focus, **2**:72–89
 popular culture and, **2**:222–223
 rates, **3**:114
 technology and, **10**:220–221
 See also Reading
Little, Olivia, **9**:142
Littlefield v. Forney Independent School District, **8**:43–44
Litynski, Zygmunt, **4**:191
Liu, Keke, **3**:174
LMS. *See* Learning management systems
Loans. *See* Student loan forgiveness programs
Lobato v. State, **3**:180
Local control of schools
 balance with federal role, **2**:19, **6**:xxv, **7**:248, **7**:254, **7**:261
 of charter schools, **7**:136
 corporal punishment policies, **5**:118–119
 of curricula, **2**:30–31, **2**:64, **8**:6, **8**:10, **8**:12, **9**:59–60, **10**:131–132
 disadvantages, **8**:10, **9**:59–60
 financing and, **6**:xviii, **6**:xix, **6**:1–19, **6**:22–23, **6**:60–61, **9**:210–211
 history, **6**:12–14, **7**:xvii–xxiii, **7**:115–116, **9**:28
 increasing, **6**:6–10
 by local governments, **6**:158–159, **7**:xvii–xviii, **7**:xix, **7**:3, **7**:7
 property taxes and, **6**:73
 refusal of federal funds, **6**:99
 state financing and, **6**:187
 state mandates and, **6**:110–111
 teacher performance measures, **6**:132
 tension with equality, **6**:xxv, **6**:2–3, **6**:110–111
 See also Autonomy; School boards
Local education agencies (LEAs). *See* School districts
Local governments
 collaboration with school districts, **9**:201
 control of schools, **6**:158–159, **7**:xvii–xviii, **7**:xix, **7**:3, **7**:7
 relationship to school superintendents, **7**:xx–xxi
 revenue sources, **6**:71
 taxes, **6**:71, **6**:74, **6**:158–159, **7**:209
 See also Communities; Mayors; Property taxes
Lombardi, Vince, **6**:299–300

Long Beach Unified School District, California, dress code policies, **5:**1–2
Los Angeles
  charter schools, **6:**287
  school construction, **6:**28
Los Angeles School Police Department (LASPD), **5:**160
Los Angeles Times, **9:**xx
Lospennato, Ronald K., **5:**43–45
Louis, Karen Seashore, **7:**80–81
Louisiana
  Creationism Act, **4:**185, **4:**196–197
  religious groups meeting in public schools, **4:**240
  See also New Orleans
Louv, Richard, **2:**240
Lovvorn, Jason, **2:**215
Low socioeconomic groups
  ability grouping and, **3:**162
  academic performance, **3:**86–87
  activity fee payments, **6:**217, **6:**221–222
  AP exam fees, **6:**234, **6:**236
  benefits of school uniforms, **5:**2
  disciplinary measures, **5:**113–114
  dropout rates, **2:**208, **3:**117
  educational attainment, **9:**xxix
  educational opportunities, **7:**220, **9:**223
  families, **1:**201, **2:**68, **5:**207, **7:**194, **9:**58, **9:**239, **9:**279
  minority groups, **3:**xxiv–xxv, **3:**76, **3:**79–80, **3:**94
  parental involvement, **6:**253–254
  private school scholarships, **6:**262, **6:**267
  proportion of students, **3:**107
  religious identities, **1:**62
  in segregated schools, **3:**108
  services for, **3:**222
  social mobility, **6:**xxvi, **6:**226, **6:**263–264
  standardized test scores, **2:**68, **2:**102–103
  Title I programs, **3:**75–90
  tuition tax credits, **6:**271–272
  voucher programs, **1:**100–101, **6:**240–256
  year-round schools and, **1:**242–244, **1:**248
  See also Achievement gaps; At-risk students; Head Start; Homeless students
Lowry v. Watson Chapel School District, **8:**47, **8:**51

LRE. *See* Least restrictive environment
Lubienski, Christopher, **7:**221
Lubienski, Sarah, **7:**221
Lubinski, David, **2:**165
Lucy Stone Elementary School, **3:**226, **3:**232–233
Lujan v. Colorado State Board of Education, **3:**180
Lumina Foundation, **9:**xxix, **9:**216, **9:**221
Luther, Martin, **6:**220–221, **6:**223
Lutz, Frank, **7:**256, **7:**257, **7:**258
Lyman, Richard, **2:**46–47
Lynch v. Donnelly, **4:**xviii–xix, **4:**23, **4:**113, **4:**115, **4:**121, **4:**123, **4:**126–127, **4:**132
Lyons v. Penn Hills School District, **5:**20

Maag, John W., **5:**253
MacGregor, Douglas, **7:**122
Madison, James, **1:**46, **4:**182, **6:**86, **6:**89
Mael, Fred A., **1:**193
Magnet schools
  accountability, **1:**170
  admissions processes, **1:**167, **1:**172–175
  criticism of, **1:**165, **1:**166–167, **1:**170, **1:**172–178
  curricula, **1:**161, **1:**166, **1:**171, **1:**175
  definition, **1:**xxvi, **1:**162
  desegregation and, **1:**xxvi, **1:**163, **1:**166, **1:**168, **1:**171–172, **1:**174, **1:**175, **1:**177, **3:**8
  diversity, **1:**162–163, **1:**175
  federal funding, **1:**163, **1:**166, **1:**167, **1:**170, **1:**175
  growth, **1:**165
  history, **1:**166–167, **1:**171–172
  innovation in, **1:**167–168, **1:**169
  principals, **1:**177
  per pupil expenditures, **1:**176
  reasons for choosing, **1:**162, **1:**167, **1:**172–173
  research on, **1:**168–171, **1:**177
  segregation by ability, **1:**174–175
  student achievement, **1:**162–178
  teachers, **1:**170, **1:**175
  transportation costs, **1:**176
  year-round schools, **1:**246
Magnet Schools Assistance Program (MSAP), **1:**166, **1:**167, **1:**169, **1:**170, **1:**175
Mahiri, Jabari, **3:**139
Mainstreaming. *See* Inclusion classrooms

Malpractice, **8:**216, **8:**223
See also Educational malpractice
Managerial governance, **7:**180–182
Manhattan Institute, **6:**106–107
Mann, Horace, **4:**177, **4:**270, **6:**221, **6:**223, **6:**282–283
Marbury v. Madison, **6:**148, **6:**156–157, **7:**69
Marcus v. Rowley, **8:**22
Marina, Brenda, **7:**53
Market competition
  advocates, **6:**32, **7:**209–210, **7:**218–219
  benefits of, **7:**137, **7:**212, **7:**214–215
  effects on educational performance, **7:**208–23
  factors in increase in, **7:**218
  financing issues, **6:**34–35
  inequality and, **7:**219, **7:**220
  private schools and, **6:**262–264, **6:**266, **6:**269–270
  in public sector, **6:**29–30
  research on, **7:**220–221
  See also Choice
Marks, Helen M., **1:**192
Marshall, Catherine, **3:**212, **7:**103, **7:**104, **7:**105
Marshall, John, **6:**164
Marshall, Thurgood, **3:**5, **3:**10
Martindale, Colin, **2:**170, **2:**171
Martino, Gabrielle, **9:**26
Marx, Karl, **8:**247, **8:**248
Maryland
  AP Access and Success plan, **6:**237
  takeover of Baltimore schools, **7:**18
  teacher training regulations, **9:**77–79
  year-round schools, **1:**242
Marzano, R., **5:**142
Massachusetts
  antibullying law, **10:**162–163, **10:**164
  charter schools, **1:**16
  compulsory education law, **1:**xvii, **6:**221, **7:**149
  education department, **7:**xviii
  finance litigation, **3:**182
  full-service community schools, **3:**226, **3:**232–233
  property tax limits, **9:**202
  school funding, **3:**182
  school governance, **7:**12
  school laws, **1:**113, **6:**182, **9:**215
  special education, **6:**94, **6:**105, **6:**107–108
  standards, **9:**23, **9:**27
  See also Boston
Massachusetts Bay Colony, **1:**xvi–xvii, **4:**176–177, **6:**62, **6:**182, **7:**xvii
Mastropieri, Margo, **2:**179
Matczynski, Thomas J., **9:**271
Mathematica Policy Research, **6:**140
Mathematics
  curricula, **2:**32, **3:**154–155, **7:**45, **7:**50
  as gatekeeper subject, **9:**11
  gifted students, **2:**164–166
  instructional approaches, **2:**96
  science and, **2:**104, **2:**105
  single-sex classes, **1:**183, **1:**185, **1:**186, **1:**188
  standardized test scores, **2:**104–105, **9:**8–9, **9:**237, **9:**238, **9:**239, **9:**241, **9:**242, **9:**253, **9:**255
  standards, **6:**82, **9:**5, **9:**25, **9:**59
  teacher education programs, **9:**77, **9:**78
  teachers, **3:**269–270
  tracking, **3:**154–155
  Trends in International Math and Science Study, **7:**213, **7:**259, **9:**23, **9:**30, **9:**255
  in vocational education, **1:**222
  See also Science, Technology, Engineering, and Mathematics
Mathis, William, **9:**29–30, **9:**32
May v. Cooperman, **4:**67
Mayer v. Monroe County Community School Corporation, **8:**194, **8:**208–209
Mayors
  control of schools, **7:**5–6, **7:**10, **7:**14–18, **7:**19, **7:**126, **7:**226, **7:**257, **7:**258
  school takeovers, **7:**7, **7:**14–15, **7:**19
  See also Elected political leaders; Local governments
McArdle, Nancy, **3:**84
McCain, Ted D., **1:**229
McCluskey, Neal, **9:**29–30, **9:**31
McCollum v. Board of Education of School District No. 71, **4:**93
McConnell-Ginet, Sally, **2:**133
McCormick, Alexander, **3:**51
McCreary County, Kentucky v. American Civil Liberties Union of Kentucky, **4:**23, **4:**120, **4:**133
McDuffy v. Secretary, **3:**182
McGrath v. Dominican College, **5:**86
McIntosh, Kent, **5:**242

McKinney-Vento Homeless Assistance Act
  effectiveness, **8:**xx, **8:**127–142
  enforcement, **8:**138–139
  funding, **8:**127, **8:**132–133
  homelessness definition, **8:**130–131, **8:**138
  implementation costs, **8:**134
  parental notification, **8:**132, **8:**138–139
  passage, **8:**127
  problems with, **8:**138–141
  provisions, **8:**127–128, **8:**130–132, **8:**135, **8:**138
  Title VII, **8:**128
McKinsey & Company, **9:**246–247
McLane, Janae Zolna, **5:**237
McLaren, Peter, **3:**124
McLuhan, Marshall, **10:**45
McMillan, Ron, **7:**88
McNamara, Robert, **2:**206–207
McUsic, Molly, **6:**176
M.D. v. St. Johns County School District, **4:**104, **4:**117
Meckel, Katherine, **9:**110
Media
  coverage of schools, **3:**256, **7:**115, **7:**117–118, **7:**237, **9:**xx, **9:**156
  democratic role, **7:**127
  entertainment, **2:**219
  images of Muslims, **1:**67
  student exposure, **4:**291
  See also Popular culture
Media specialists, **2:**216, **10:**23
  See also Libraries
Medical model, **2:**152–153
Meek v. Pittenger, **4:**xx, **4:**27
Meier, Deborah, **1:**51
Meier, Megan, **10:**147
Melissa v. School District, **5:**215
Men
  career opportunities, **3:**263
  career paths, **7:**105
  earnings, **3:**120–121
  gender discrimination, **3:**209
  principals, **7:**xxii, **7:**94
  school board members, **7:**118
  shortages of teachers, **3:**261–265
  student loan forgiveness, **3:**255–272
  teachers, **3:**259, **3:**261, **3:**263, **3:**270–271
  See also Gender
Mencken, H. L., **9:**109–110
Mensinger, Janell, **1:**191

Mental health
  negative effects of corporal punishment, **5:**114
  professional teams, **5:**262–263
  teachers' roles in diagnosis and treatment, **5:**249–250, **5:**255–257, **5:**258–263
  See also Emotional and behavioral disorders; Internalizing disorders
Mentoring
  of administrators, **7:**241
  of gifted students, **2:**159, **2:**174
  by school resource officers, **5:**169
  of teachers, **2:**xxiii, **7:**243, **9:**223
Meredith v. Jefferson County Public Schools (Louisville), **3:**7
Merit-based pay. *See* Performance pay
Metacognition, **2:**73
Metz, Mary Harwood, **1:**177
Metzl v. Leininger, **4:**210
Mexico, poor students in, **2:**103
Meyer, Gwen G., **5:**237
M.H. by Mr. and Mrs. H. v. Bristol Board of Education, **5:**211
Michaelsen, Robert, **1:**40
Michigan
  Arab American communities, **2:**129–130
  charter schools, **1:**85, **1:**88, **7:**179
  compensatory education funding, **3:**6
  homeschooling regulations, **1:**115, **1:**119
  school funding, **6:**68
  virtual schools, **10:**84–85, **10:**87–88
  See also Detroit
Michigan Virtual Charter Academy (MVCA), **10:**84–85
Microsoft Corporation, **9:**249, **10:**210
Middle class
  achievement gaps, **3:**65
  cultural capital, **3:**96
  social mobility, **6:**263–264
Middle schools
  charter schools, **1:**12–13
  counselors, **3:**20
  gifted students, **6:**121, **6:**122
  parental involvement, **7:**195
  Science, Technology, Engineering, and Mathematics instruction, **2:**96–98
  teacher credentials, **9:**75, **9:**76, **9:**83
  year-round schedules, **1:**245
Migration. *See* Immigrants
Miles, Michael L., **10:**16
Military, **3:**114, **3:**207, **4:**275

Milken Family Foundation, **6:**131
Milliken v. Bradley, **3:**6, **6:**60, **7:**63, **7:**67
Mills v. Board of Education of the District of Columbia, **8:**90, **8:**100, **8:**108
Milwaukee
　special education, **6:**100
　voucher program, **1:**95–96, **1:**102, **6:**249
Mind and Life Institute, **2:**245
Minersville School District v. Gobitis, **4:**xxiii, **4:**137, **4:**140, **4:**146
Minnesota
　charter schools, **1:**2, **1:**50, **1:**57, **1:**60–61, **1:**66, **6:**xxiv, **6:**270, **7:**130–131
　education tax credits, **1:**95, **4:**7, **6:**262, **6:**269
　ethnocentric schools, **1:**21, **1:**25–26
　open enrollment policy, **7:**226
Minority students
　ability grouping and, **3:**155–156, **3:**162
　affirmative action, **1:**29, **2:**xxii
　arrests, **5:**162
　crime victims, **5:**48
　cultural differences in schools, **2:**130, **7:**198
　cultural relevance, **3:**70, **3:**71–72, **3:**137–147, **7:**81–82
　disciplinary measures, **5:**40–43, **5:**47, **5:**113–114, **5:**162, **5:**206
　dropout rates, **1:**263, **3:**113, **3:**117, **5:**33, **5:**43–44, **5:**45, **6:**199, **6:**241
　educational opportunities, **2:**68, **7:**220, **7:**251
　ethnocentric charter schools, **1:**xxiii, **1:**6–7, **1:**19–33, **1:**49, **1:**133–134
　experiences ignored in curriculum, **2:**70, **2:**135–136
　families, **3:**xxiv, **3:**96–97, **5:**207
　higher education, **3:**113–129, **3:**262–263
　history, **2:**65
　identities, **1:**28, **1:**32, **3:**24–25
　increased number, **9:**241–242, **9:**243
　as majority, **3:**108, **3:**259, **9:**58
　marginalization of, **3:**174–177
　middle class, **3:**65
　NCLB performance measures, **3:**85, **3:**88–89, **3:**94–95, **3:**99, **3:**102–103, **3:**218
　overrepresentation in office discipline referrals, **5:**242
　overrepresentation in special education programs, **3:**169, **5:**38, **7:**81
　overrepresentation in zero tolerance enforcement, **5:**32–33, **5:**36–52
　poor, **3:**xxiv–xxv, **3:**76, **3:**79–80, **3:**94
　quotas for, **2:**xxii
　in religious schools, **4:**14
　school finance and, **3:**168–183
　school-to-prison pipeline, **5:**33–34, **5:**44–45, **5:**162
　stereotypes of, **3:**32, **3:**147, **3:**156
　support services, **3:**xxiv
　suspensions and expulsions, **5:**37, **5:**40–42, **5:**47
　teachers' expectations of, **3:**xxii
　year-round schools and, **1:**242–243, **1:**245–246
　See also Achievement gaps; African Americans; Compensatory education; Diversity; Equity; Latino Americans; Native Americans
Minow, Martha, **7:**184
Mintrom, Michael, **7:**133
Mintrop, Heinrich, **7:**51
Miron, Gary, **1:**14, **7:**179
Mishel, Lawrence, **1:**42, **3:**68
Mishra, Punya, **10:**124
Mississippi
　Biloxi Public School District, **10:**98
　charter schools, **6:**xxiv
　compulsory education law, **7:**149
　constitution, **6:**170, **6:**197
　school system, **7:**64–65
Missouri v. Jenkins, **1:**168, **3:**6–7, **8:**226
Missouri v. Jenkins III, **7:**63, **7:**64
Mitchell v. Helms, **4:**xx, **4:**7, **4:**28, **4:**29, **4:**30–31, **4:**32
Mixell v. School Administrative Unit No. 33, **5:**84–85
Mobile technologies
　apps, **10:**1–2, **10:**24, **10:**46
　as distraction, **2:**211, **10:**37, **10:**46–47
　educational benefits, **10:**32–48, **10:**65, **10:**222
　history, **10:**32
　limitations, **10:**43–44, **10:**47–48
　online courses accessed through, **10:**61, **10:**62–63, **10:**65
　policies on use in schools, **10:**36, **10:**38–40, **10:**41, **10:**48, **10:**65
　trade-offs, **10:**33–34, **10:**44–45, **10:**46
　use in schools, **10:**xxiii, **10:**39–40, **10:**197
　See also Technology

Moe, T. M., **1:**150–151, **7:**178, **8:**251, **9:**167
Moffett, Isaac, **1:**51
Moffitt, Susan L., **7:**171
Molnar, Alex, **6:**289
Moments of silence
   arguments against allowing, **4:**76–77, **4:**79–83
   arguments for allowing, **4:**75–76
   legal cases, **4:**xxi–xxii, **4:**49–50, **4:**67–68, **4:**71–75, **4:**78, **4:**79
   secular purposes, **4:**68, **4:**71–72, **4:**74–76, **4:**78–79, **4:**81
   state laws, **4:**49–50, **4:**67, **4:**68, **4:**71–73, **4:**74–75, **4:**78–79
   See also Prayer in schools
Monolingual education. *See* "English-only" curriculum
Montana Supreme Court, **4:**41–42
Montessori schools, **2:**155, **2:**245
Moral education
   bullying prevention, **10:**170–171
   character development, **2:**199, **2:**200, **2:**201
   legal cases, **2:**201–202, **2:**203
   nonsectarian, **2:**198
   parental roles, **2:**201–202
   Progressive approach, **2:**199–201, **2:**202
   Protestant, **2:**198
   in public schools, **2:**195–209, **10:**170–171
   religious groups meeting in public schools, **4:**237–238
   returning to schools, **2:**201–203
Moral Majority, **2:**204–205
Moral values
   behaviors contradicting, **2:**205–208
   conservative/liberal divide, **2:**203–205, **2:**206
   definitions, **2:**195–196
   development of, **2:**196–197
   Jewish, **1:**131
   new models, **2:**208–209
   Protestant, **2:**198, **4:**274
   taught in faith-based charter schools, **1:**42–43
   See also Ethics
Morales, David, **5:**15–16
Morgan v. Swanson, **4:**254–255
Morrell, Ernest, **2:**215
Morrill Acts, **1:**216, **7:**149
Morrison v. State Board of Education, **8:**233, **8:**237

Morse v. Frederick
   arguments, **10:**167–168
   background, **8:**177, **8:**182
   impact, **2:**201, **4:**42, **5:**8
   in loco parentis doctrine, **5:**195
   majority opinion, **8:**181, **8:**187, **8:**188, **10:**168
   Thomas concurrence, **2:**203, **5:**199, **8:**179
Moss v. Spartanburg County School District No. 7, **4:**181
Motivation
   factors influencing, **5:**153–154
   of individual students, **2:**15, **5:**142, **5:**144–146, **5:**152, **5:**153–154
   intrinsic, **5:**142, **5:**145–147, **5:**148–149, **5:**152–153, **5:**154–155, **6:**139
   in reading instruction, **2:**78–80
   of teachers, **3:**269
   See also Extrinsic motivators
Motorola, **10:**32
MSAP. *See* Magnet Schools Assistance Program
Mt. Healthy City School District v. Doyle, **8:**198
Mueller v. Allen, **1:**95, **1:**99, **4:**7, **4:**23, **4:**28
Multicultural counseling
   academic performance and, **3:**24–25
   definition, **3:**26
   effectiveness of training, **3:**30–34
   need for, **3:**19–35
   rationale for, **3:**23, **3:**24–26
   research on, **3:**34
   training models, **3:**26–28
Multicultural education, **2:**137–141
Multiethnic societies. *See* Diversity; Immigrants
Municipal bonds. *See* Bonds
Municipal governments. *See* Local governments
Munroe, Natalie, **10:**149
Murphy, Joseph, **3:**175, **7:**78, **7:**83
Murphy v. State of Arkansas, **1:**120, **1:**122
Murray, Charles, **3:**96, **6:**xxii
Murray, Frank B., **2:**47
Murray, Richard, **5:**2–3
Murray v. Curlett, **4:**xxiv, **4:**62, **4:**72, **4:**85, **4:**98, **4:**177, **4:**195
Music
   academic benefits of study of, **2:**145, **6:**221
   budget cuts in, **9:**xxvi

drug testing of band members, **8:**58
hip-hop, **3:**137–147
popular, **2:**211–213
religious, **4:**xxii, **4:**47–48, **4:**103–118
song lyrics, **2:**211–212, **2:**223, **2:**225
student-led groups, **4:**226–227
virtual worlds, **2:**229
See also Arts; Extracurricular activities; Humanities
Music Educators National Conference, **2:**145
Muslims. *See* Islam
MVCA. *See* Michigan Virtual Charter Academy
Myers, Linda J., **3:**32–33
Myers v. Loudoun County Public Schools, **4:**138
Myspace
alternatives to, **10:**xxiv
cyberbullying, **10:**147
parody profiles, **8:**182–183, **8:**184, **10:**159, **10:**169, **10:**180–181, **10:**183, **10:**204
student use of, **10:**159, **10:**169, **10:**205
teachers' use of, **10:**205
usage, **10:**136
See also Social networking sites

NAACP Advancement Project, **5:**33–34
NAEP. *See* National Assessments of Educational Progress
NAEYC. *See* National Association for the Education of Young Children
Nalepa v. Plymouth-Canton Community School District, **5:**83
Nampa Classical Academy, **1:**50–51
Nampa Classical Academy v. Goesling, **4:**170, **4:**173, **4:**178
Nashville, performance pay, **6:**139–140
NASRO. *See* National Association of School Resource Officers
NASSP. *See* National Association of Secondary School Principals
NASSPE. *See* National Association for Single Sex Public Education
A Nation at Risk
criticism of schools, **6:**241, **7:**212, **7:**229, **9:**xviii, **9:**39, **9:**40
equity and efficiency, **6:**4–5
impact, **1:**xix, **6:**6, **7:**27, **7:**114
international comparisons, **6:**xxii, **7:**75, **7:**212, **7:**216–217

recommendations, **2:**56, **3:**16–17, **7:**252, **9:**237
National Alliance for Public Charter Schools, **1:**49, **9:**124
National Assessment of Vocational Education, **1:**228
National Assessments of Educational Progress (NAEP)
achievement gaps, **3:**89, **3:**99–100, **3:**103, **7:**44–45, **7:**85, **9:**6, **9:**9, **9:**41, **9:**242, **9:**244, **9:**245
charter school scores, **1:**10, **1:**12
correlations among science, reading, and math scores, **2:**104–105
education spending and scores, **9:**221
performance of mayor-controlled school districts, **7:**15
private school student scores, **6:**265
proficiency requirements, **9:**xxi
scores in for-profit schools, **1:**86
state differences, **6:**199, **9:**57
state standards and, **9:**30
trends, **3:**99–100, **9:**9, **9:**239, **9:**241, **9:**242, **9:**253
National Association for Gifted Children, **6:**113, **6:**121, **6:**123
National Association for Single Sex Public Education (NASSPE), **1:**181, **1:**186
National Association for the Education of Young Children (NAEYC), **2:**36
National Association for Year-Round Education (NAYRE), **1:**236–237, **1:**240, **1:**241
National Association of Colleges and Employers, **3:**119
National Association of Elementary School Principals, **6:**302, **8:**53
National Association of School Nurses, **5:**109
National Association of School Resource Officers (NASRO), **5:**166, **5:**170, **5:**171, **5:**172
National Association of Secondary School Principals (NASSP), **5:**2, **5:**110, **9:**186
National Caucus of Native American State Legislators, **1:**263
National Center for Alternative Certification, **9:**108, **9:**110
National Center for Education Information, **9:**104
National Center for Educational Statistics (NCES), **1:**xxiv, **3:**117, **3:**259, **5:**25,

5:29, **5:**31, **5:**37, **5:**41, **5:**113, **5:**114, **6:**62, **6:**100, **6:**113, **6:**199, **6:**235, **6:**262, **7:**104, **9:**209, **10:**xvi, **10:**56
National Center for School Safety, **5:**24
National Center on Child Abuse and Neglect, **5:**89, **5:**90
National Center on School Choice, **1:**17
National Commission on Excellence in Education, **2:**56, **7:**229
See also A Nation at Risk
National Commission on Teaching and America's Future (NCTAF), **9:**68, **9:**114
National Council for the Accreditation of Teacher Education (NCATE)
  accreditation process, **2:**39, **2:**43, **2:**44, **2:**45, **9:**93
  administrator preparation standards, **7:**99
  benefits of accreditation, **2:**51
  changes recommended, **2:**37
  criticism of, **9:**81, **9:**82
  impact, **9:**81
  merger with TEAC, **9:**80, **9:**91
  outcomes focus, **9:**89
  standards, **9:**90
  state relationships with, **9:**80–81
  teacher training standards, **2:**40, **2:**42, **2:**46, **2:**48, **2:**49, **2:**51, **9:**72, **9:**82–83
National Council of State Legislators, **9:**193
National Council of Teachers of English (NCTE), **2:**221, **3:**162, **10:**127
National Council of Teachers of Mathematics (NCTM), **2:**36, **2:**148, **10:**119, **10:**124, **10:**125, **10:**127
National Council on Teacher Quality (NCTQ), **9:**xxii, **9:**74–79, **9:**86, **9:**95–96
National Crime Prevention Council (NCPC), **5:**169, **5:**171
National Defense Education Act of 1958 (NDEA), **1:**xvii–xviii, **3:**265–266, **6:**197, **7:**xix
National Defense Student Loan Program, **3:**265
National Disability Rights Network, **5:**224
National Education Association (NEA)
  Committee of Fifteen report, **9:**13
  Committee of Ten on Secondary School Studies, **9:**175, **9:**183
  Committee on College Entrance Requirements, **9:**29
  criticism of Coverdell Act, **5:**xxv
  cultural competence definition, **3:**51
  Economy of Time in Education committees, **9:**14
  history, **7:**34, **8:**249, **8:**254, **9:**166
  on male teacher shortage, **3:**260–261, **3:**263, **3:**264
  number of members, **7:**34, **8:**249
  policies, **7:**26, **7:**38, **8:**250
  school funding data, **9:**205–206
  on school resource officers, **5:**166, **5:**170–171
  structure, **9:**161–162
  teacher demographic surveys, **2:**22, **3:**48, **3:**49–50
  on teacher protection acts, **5:**178
National Education Commission on Time and Learning, **1:**240–241
National Educational Technology Plan (NETP), **10:**55, **10:**130, **10:**132, **10:**218–219
National Educational Technology Standards for School Administrators (NETS-A), **10:**128
National Educational Technology Standards for Teachers (NETS-T), **10:**119–120, **10:**123, **10:**124, **10:**125, **10:**126, **10:**128, **10:**129–131
National Endowment for the Arts (NEA), **2:**155, **2:**205
National Federation of the Blind v. Target, **10:**201–202
National Governors Association (NGA), **3:**162, **7:**85, **7:**175, **9:**31–32
  See also Common Core State Standards Initiative
National Institute on Drug Abuse, **8:**58
National Labor Relations Act (NLRA), **8:**248
National Parent Teacher Association, **7:**188
National Policy Board for Educational Administration (NPBEA), **7:**89, **7:**97, **7:**99
National Research Council, **1:**213
National School Boards Association (NSBA), **2:**18, **7:**9, **7:**117, **7:**118, **7:**121, **7:**123, **7:**124, **7:**127, **10:**xxiii, **10:**174, **10:**195
National School Safety and Security Services (NSSSS), **5:**59, **5:**170, **5:**171, **5:**172

National Science Education Standards, **2:**148
National Science Foundation, **3:**xxii
National Student Clearinghouse, **9:**249
National Survey on Drug Use and Health, **5:**251–252
National Taxpayers Union, **9:**202
National Treasury Employees Union v. Von Raab, **8:**63, **8:**77, **8:**78
Nationwide Insurance, **9:**248
Native American schools
  achievement gaps, **1:**xviii, **1:**255
  advantages, **1:**258–262
  alternative assessments, **1:**262, **1:**266–267
  charter schools, **1:**20
  culturally based instruction, **1:**260–261
  culturally sensitive environment, **1:**258–259
  curricula, **1:**xviii, **1:**258, **1:**259–260
  funding, **1:**257–258
  graduation rates, **1:**258
  legal basis, **1:**257–258
  legal requirements, **1:**xxviii, **1:**254–255, **1:**263
  number of, **1:**254
  parental and community involvement, **1:**259
  student outcomes, **1:**254–268
  teachers, **1:**254, **1:**259
Native Americans
  activism, **1:**257
  dropout rates, **1:**263
  graduation rates, **7:**51
  languages, **1:**260
  learning needs, **1:**260–261, **1:**265, **1:**266
  public school students, **1:**xviii, **1:**257, **1:**262–268, **9:**242
  religious freedom, **4:**91, **4:**268, **4:**273, **4:**274
  See also Achievement gaps; Minority students
Natural world
  human relationships with, **2:**240–241, **2:**242–246
  isolation from, **2:**239–240
  scientific view, **2:**240
Navarre v. South Washington County Schools, **8:**162
NAYRE. *See* National Association for Year-Round Education

NCATE. *See* National Council for the Accreditation of Teacher Education
NCERF. *See* North Carolina Education Reform Foundation
NCES. *See* National Center for Educational Statistics
NCLB. *See* No Child Left Behind Act
NCPC. *See* National Crime Prevention Council
NCTAF. *See* National Commission on Teaching and America's Future
NCTE. *See* National Council of Teachers of English
NCTM. *See* National Council of Teachers of Mathematics
NCTQ. *See* National Council on Teacher Quality
NDEA. *See* National Defense Education Act
NEA. *See* National Education Association; National Endowment for the Arts
Neal, Gerald A., **3:**156
Neal v. Fulton County Board of Education, **5:**117
Neanderthals, **4:**189–190, **4:**199
Nebraska, finance litigation, **3:**182
Neeley v. West Orange-Cove Consolidated Independent School District, **3:**181
Neglect. *See* Abuse and neglect
Negligence
  lawsuits against teachers, **5:**181–183, **5:**186, **5:**188–189
  suicide and, **5:**83, **5:**84
  in tort law, **5:**65–67, **5:**181–183, **5:**188–189
  See also Educational malpractice
Nelson, Brandi, **5:**82
Nelson, Christopher, **7:**179
Nelson, Wayne A., **10:**124
Neoliberals, **7:**218–219
  See also Choice
NETP. *See* National Educational Technology Plan
NETS-A. *See* National Educational Technology Standards for School Administrators
NETS-T. *See* National Educational Technology Standards for Teachers
Neuman, Susan, **2:**79
Neumann, Richard A., **9:**136
Nevada, charter schools, **7:**137–138
New American Foundation, **3:**83

New Hampshire, constitution, **6:**173
New Hampshire State Board of Education, **9:**181
New Jersey
  alternative teaching certification, **9:**100
  constitution, **6:**173
  education debates, **3:**58
  finance litigation, **3:**182, **6:**xxi, **6:**64, **6:**184, **6:**200, **9:**191
  full-service community schools, **3:**225
  prayer at graduation ceremonies, **4:**40
  Race to the Top and, **3:**63
  school funding, **3:**182, **6:**xxi, **6:**64, **6:**101, **6:**184, **9:**191
  special education, **6:**101
  See also Everson v. Board of Education of Ewing Township
New Jersey Professional Standards for Teachers and School Leaders, **10:**148–149
New Jersey Supreme Court, **3:**182, **6:**xxi, **6:**64, **6:**184, **6:**200
New Jersey v. T.L.O., **5:**195, **5:**198, **8:**57, **8:**60, **8:**62, **8:**67–68, **10:**101, **10:**102
New Leaders for New Schools (NLNS), **3:**38, **3:**39, **3:**51, **9:**128
New Media Consortium, **10:**120
New Mexico, charter schools, **7:**132
New Orleans
  charter schools, **6:**48–49, **6:**53
  privatization of schools, **7:**55–56
The New Teacher Project (TNTP), **9:**xxiii, **9:**103, **9:**106
New York City
  alternative licensing routes, **9:**103
  arts funding, **2:**154
  charter schools, **1:**42, **1:**50, **6:**279–280
  education policies, **7:**183
  fiscal crises, **8:**252
  Harlem Children's Zone, **9:**62, **9:**234
  Islamic Cultural Center, **2:**134, **2:**137
  mayoral control of schools, **7:**7, **7:**15, **7:**257
  NAEP scores, **7:**15
  Panel for Educational Policy, **7:**7, **7:**257
  public transit system, **4:**8
  school district governance, **7:**226
  school facility rental by religious groups, **4:**239–240
  school reforms, **7:**177
  school resource officers, **5:**164–165
  school-level autonomy, **6:**48, **6:**53
  schools chancellor, **7:**7, **7:**131, **7:**177, **7:**226
  special education students, **6:**100
  teachers' unions, **8:**244, **8:**252
  Teaching Fellows, **9:**103, **9:**108
New York Foundation for Education Reform and Accountability (FERA), **1:**43
New York Police Department, **5:**164–165
New York State
  charter schools, **1:**16, **1:**42, **1:**48–49, **1:**50
  constitution, **3:**182
  education oversight, **7:**xx, **7:**6, **7:**7
  Empowerment Schools Program, **6:**48, **6:**53
  finance litigation, **3:**182
  magnet schools, **1:**169
  prayer in schools, **4:**35, **4:**61–62
  Race to the Top and, **3:**62
  school laws, **6:**182
Newdow v. Rio Linda Union School District, **4:**xxiii, **4:**138
Newell, Markeda L., **3:**30
Newlon, Jesse, **9:**16
Newsom, Alan, **5:**16
NGA. *See* National Governors Association
Niemöller, Martin, **4:**141–142
Nieto, Sonia, **2:**108
Nietzsche, Friedrich, **2:**206
Nilson, Eva S., **5:**43, **5:**44
Ninth Amendment, **4:**97
Nixon, Richard M., **7:**251
Nixon v. Northern Local School District, **4:**263
NLNS. *See* New Leaders for New Schools
NLRA. *See* National Labor Relations Act
No Child Left Behind Act of 2001 (NCLB)
  accountability measures, **6:**81–82, **7:**xxiv, **7:**xxviii, **7:**43–44, **7:**49, **7:**51–52, **7:**77, **7:**159, **7:**253, **9:**18, **9:**58, **9:**274
  achievement gap monitoring, **7:**xxviii, **9:**6
  adequate yearly progress assessments, **6:**103, **6:**106, **6:**127, **6:**131–132, **9:**6, **9:**61, **9:**277
  assessment and standards, **2:**184, **3:**94–95, **6:**127, **7:**158–159, **9:**xix–xxi, **9:**39–40, **10:**8
  charter schools and, **1:**24–25, **6:**286, **6:**291, **7:**133
  compared to Race to the Top, **3:**61, **3:**63

Coverdell Teacher Protection Act, **5:**xxv, **5:**177–178, **5:**180, **5:**183, **5:**190–191
criticism of, **3:**58, **3:**69, **6:**103–104, **7:**45, **7:**54, **7:**260, **9:**xix–xxi, **9:**11
curriculum adoption and, **2:**21, **7:**166
educational malpractice claims, **8:**219–220, **8:**221
effects, **3:**17, **3:**89, **7:**xx, **7:**44–47, **7:**49–53, **7:**54, **7:**55, **7:**56, **7:**218, **9:**41
effects on administration preparation programs, **9:**119–120
effects on administrators, **7:**xxiv, **7:**xxviii, **9:**125–126
English-language learners, **2:**119, **3:**191, **3:**200
faith-based organization funding, **2:**205
funding, **3:**58, **3:**106, **6:**91, **6:**99, **7:**112, **7:**176, **9:**29
gifted student definition, **2:**162–163
goals, **1:**xix, **3:**85, **3:**102, **6:**197, **7:**43–44, **7:**48, **7:**49, **9:**6
impact on governance, **7:**252–253
magnet schools, **1:**162, **1:**163
narrowing of curriculum, **7:**45, **7:**50–51, **7:**55
Native American education, **1:**263
performance of student subgroups, **3:**85, **3:**88–89, **3:**94–95, **3:**99, **3:**102–103, **3:**218, **8:**141
problems with, **7:**44, **7:**48, **7:**49–53, **9:**29
proficiency requirements, **9:**xix–xxi
provisions, **7:**43, **7:**44, **7:**45, **9:**18
religious freedom protection, **4:**278
school restructuring options, **7:**8–9, **9:**6, **9:**224, **9:**230
single-sex schools, **1:**181
special education students and, **6:**104
standards-based reform, **2:**56–57, **2:**58, **3:**98–99, **7:**43–45, **7:**114, **7:**253, **9:**xxvii–xxviii, **9:**18
students with disabilities and, **2:**178, **2:**184, **2:**190–192
teacher credentials, **3:**256, **6:**132, **9:**75, **9:**76
See also Title I
Noddings, Nel, **2:**xx
Noguera, Pedro, **3:**125
Nonprofit organizations. *See* Foundations; Philanthropy

Nonpublic schools. *See* Homeschooling; Private schools; Religious schools
Nonschool religious groups. *See* Religious groups
Nonsectarian private schools. *See* Private schools
North Carolina
charter schools, **1:**16, **3:**70
constitution, **6:**233–234
Innovative Education Initiatives Act of 2003, **9:**44–45
New Schools Project, **9:**42–43, **9:**44
school laws, **1:**121
segregated schools, **3:**2–3, **3:**6, **3:**8
year-round schools, **1:**239, **1:**240
North Carolina Education Reform Foundation (NCERF), **1:**47
North Dakota, school laws, **1:**116, **1:**119
Norton, M. Scott, **7:**12
Norway, education policies, **2:**30–31
Norwood v. Harrison, **1:**23, **1:**29, **4:**32
Notre Dame University, Educational Leadership Program, **9:**129
NPBEA. *See* National Policy Board for Educational Administration
NSBA. *See* National School Boards Association
NSSSS. *See* National School Safety and Security Services
Null v. Board of Education of County of Jackson, **1:**120
Nurre v. Whitehead, **4:**48, **4:**104, **4:**116–117
Nussbaum, Hedda, **5:**90
Nuxoll ex rel. Nuxoll v. Indian Prairie School Dist. #204, **4:**264
Nuxoll v. Indian Prairie School District, **8:**180

Oakes, Jeannie, **3:**154–155, **3:**156, **3:**161, **3:**162, **3:**163
Obama, Barack, **1:**49, **1:**52, **1:**248, **2:**131, **3:**207, **3:**261, **6:**134, **9:**xxix, **9:**31
Obama administration
arts education and, **2:**154
higher education policies, **6:**235
Native American education, **1:**264
No Child Left Behind Act amendments, **4:**278
Promise Neighborhood Initiative, **9:**62
school improvement grants, **9:**123–124

stimulus package, **1**:209
Teacher Incentive Fund, **6**:134, **7**:36–37
Title IX policies, **3**:210
See also Department of Education; Race to the Top
Oberti v. Board of Education of the Borough of Clementon School District, **8**:115, **8**:121
O'Brien, David, **2**:218
OCR. *See* Office of Civil Rights
OCTCA. *See* Ohio Career Technical Competency Assessment
Odabasi, Hatice Ferhan, **10**:123
O'Day, Jennifer, **7**:172
Odden, Allan R., **6**:202, **9**:xxvi
ODRs. *See* Office discipline referrals
OEA. *See* Ohio Education Association
OECD. *See* Organisation for Economic Co-operation and Development
Office discipline referrals (ODRs), **5**:241–242
Office of Civil Rights (OCR), Department of Education, **5**:111, **5**:114, **8**:149, **8**:152, **8**:153–154
Office of Community Policing Services (COPS), **5**:166, **5**:167–168
Ohio
 antibullying law, **10**:165–166
 charter schools, **1**:13, **7**:132
 Columbus City Schools, **9**:164, **9**:248
 constitution, **6**:197, **9**:207
 credit flexibility plan, **9**:182
 educational service centers, **9**:194
 finance litigation, **3**:181, **6**:25, **6**:27, **6**:200, **6**:201, **9**:204, **9**:207, **9**:211–212
 for-profit schools, **1**:86
 mandatory reporting law, **5**:96
 Novice Teacher Study, **9**:151–153
 property tax limits, **9**:202
 public-private partnerships, **9**:248
 per pupil expenditures, **6**:246
 school funding, **6**:25, **6**:27, **6**:68, **6**:71, **6**:74, **6**:200, **6**:201, **9**:193, **9**:204, **9**:205–213
 vocational education, **1**:220–221, **1**:222, **1**:223–225, **1**:229–232
 voucher programs, **1**:30–31, **1**:95–97
 See also Cincinnati; Cleveland
Ohio Board of Education of Cincinnati v. Walter, **3**:181

Ohio Career Technical Competency Assessment (OCTCA), **1**:222, **1**:224
Ohio Education Association (OEA), **9**:160, **10**:205
Ohio State University school, **9**:17, **9**:18
Ohio STEM Learning Network (OSLN), **9**:250
Oklahoma City, segregated schools, **7**:63
Oklahoma City v. Dowell, **7**:63, **7**:64
Old Order Amish. *See* Amish
Olsen v. State, **3**:180
Olson, Linda S., **1**:243–244
O'Malley, Martin, **6**:237
Oncale v. Sundowner Offshore Services, **8**:155
Online courses
 access to, **10**:xvii–xviii, **10**:65
 Advanced Placement, **10**:56–57, **10**:72
 advantages, **2**:237–238, **10**:51, **10**:54–55, **10**:58–59, **10**:60, **10**:61–62
 availability, **9**:196, **10**:54
 copyright issues, **8**:35
 costs, **10**:93–94
 credit recovery, **10**:51, **10**:57–58, **10**:73, **10**:77
 demand for, **10**:59
 development of, **10**:93–94
 effectiveness, **10**:51–52, **10**:55–56, **10**:60
 enrollment growth, **9**:200, **10**:51, **10**:54, **10**:75
 flexibility, **10**:55, **10**:58, **10**:60, **10**:61, **10**:64, **10**:68, **10**:73–74
 homeschooling use, **1**:110
 implementation challenges, **10**:xviii–xix, **10**:63–65
 policies and procedures, **10**:xx–xxi, **10**:50–66
 for professional development, **10**:64
 standards, **10**:119, **10**:125, **10**:129
 teachers, **10**:64, **10**:92, **10**:119, **10**:125
 technology standards and, **10**:xxii
 tools, **10**:64, **10**:91, **10**:94
 universal design in, **10**:129
 See also Virtual schools
Online learning
 changes caused by, **2**:235
 combined with traditional instruction, **10**:xviii
 concerns about, **10**:26, **10**:30
Open school movement, **2**:xix–xx, **2**:2
Oregon
 finance litigation, **3**:180

First Step to Success Program, **5**:237–238
school laws, **1**:xix–xx, **1**:39, **1**:46, **1**:73, **1**:146
Oregon Supreme Court, **4**:298
Orfield, Gary, **1**:51, **3**:5, **3**:84, **3**:108
Organisation for Economic Co-operation and Development (OECD), **6**:235, **7**:209, **7**:213, **9**:220, **9**:237, **9**:252
See also Programme for International Student Assessment
Originalism, **7**:61–62
Osborne, Jason W., **10**:123
OSLN. *See* Ohio STEM Learning Network
Outsourcing. *See* Privatization
Oxford v. Beaumont Independent School District, **4**:297–298
Oyserman, Daphna, **3**:24

P21. *See* Partnership for 21st Century Skills
Pääbo, Svante, **4**:190
Pacchiano, Debra, **5**:232
PACT. *See* Performance Assessment for California Teachers
Paideia curriculum, **2**:xviii–xix
Paige, Mark A., **8**:47
Palmer, Parker, **2**:14
Palmer, Paul, **5**:6–8, **5**:9
Palmer v. Waxahachie Independent School District, **5**:4, **5**:6–10, **8**:190
Panel for Educational Policy (PEP), New York City, **7**:7, **7**:257
PAR. *See* Peer assistance and review
PARCC. *See* Partnership for Assessment of Readiness for College and Careers
Paredes Scribner, Kent, **3**:245
Parental choice. *See* Choice
Parental involvement in schools
    academic outcomes and, **1**:131, **5**:207–208
    accountability and, **9**:263–280
    of African Americans, **3**:225
    amount of, **7**:189
    appropriate, **7**:195–196
    in bilingual education, **3**:194
    in charter schools, **6**:xxiv, **7**:189
    committees, **7**:202
    complaints, **7**:190–191, **7**:192
    effects on administrators' leadership, **7**:187–205
    in elementary, middle, and high schools, **7**:195, **9**:268
    in extracurricular activities, **6**:217–218
    financial donations, **6**:305–306
    for-profit management and, **7**:181, **7**:183
    in full-service community schools, **3**:225
    fund-raising, **6**:217–218, **6**:296, **6**:301
    governance roles, **7**:xxvii, **9**:267, **9**:270, **9**:271–274
    in Head Start, **1**:211–212, **1**:213
    importance, **7**:197–205, **9**:275
    increasing, **7**:176, **9**:267, **9**:271–272, **9**:273–274
    in individualized education programs, **8**:91
    influence, **5**:207–208, **7**:187–188, **9**:264, **9**:266
    in Native American schools, **1**:259
    obstacles, **6**:253–254, **9**:278, **9**:279
    parameters and restrictions, **7**:188–189, **7**:204–205
    partnerships, **7**:200–201, **7**:202–204
    of poor families, **6**:253–254
    in private schools, **1**:154
    in school choice, **7**:181
    as social capital, **7**:202–204
    spending decisions, **6**:42
    use of data, **9**:277
Parents
    collaboration with, **9**:269, **9**:271–272
    communications from schools, **3**:xxiv, **9**:268, **9**:269–270, **10**:195–197
    conferences with, **7**:84
    as consumers, **7**:181
    decisions on charter or private schools, **6**:280–281
    duties, **5**:200
    educational roles, **7**:127, **7**:194, **7**:195–196
    emotional influences on students, **5**:69
    engaging, **7**:83–84
    impact of NCLB, **7**:46
    lawsuits, **7**:xxvii, **7**:188, **7**:191
    monitoring Internet use of children, **10**:188
    moral education roles, **2**:201–202
    overprotective, **7**:193–194
    prayer groups, **4**:237–238
    relations with administrators, **7**:xxvii, **7**:190–192, **7**:196, **7**:197, **7**:202–204

religious instruction by, **4:**181
single-parent households, **3:**97, **3:**222, **9:**241
special interests, **7:**193–195
as stakeholders, **9:**268–269, **9:**271–273
voting in school board elections, **7:**10
See also Abuse and neglect; Families; Homeschooling
Parents Involved in Community Schools v. Seattle School District No. 1 [PICS v. Seattle], **1:**20, **3:**xxi, **3:**xxvi, **3:**2, **3:**7, **7:**xxvii, **7:**61, **7:**63–64, **7:**65–66, **7:**72
Parents' rights
to choose private schools, **1:**xix–xx, **1:**146
to choose religious schools, **1:**39, **1:**46, **1:**73
to control child's upbringing, **4:**149, **8:**44, **8:**45, **8:**189
to direct religious education of children, **4:**156, **4:**273–274
due process, **8:**98
to homeschool, **1:**112–113
religious freedom, **1:**xx–xxi
Parent-teacher associations, **6:**296, **7:**188
Paris, Scott G., **2:**77
Park, C., **5:**137
Park, Yeonjeong, **10:**43, **10:**44, **10:**46, **10:**47
Parker, Larry, **3:**212
Parma City School District, Ohio, **5:**12
Parochial schools. *See* Religious schools
Parrish, Thomas B., **6:**97
Parry, Becky, **2:**218
Partnership for 21st Century Skills (P21), **2:**32, **2:**237
Partnership for Assessment of Readiness for College and Careers (PARCC), **9:**xxi, **9:**22
Passeron, Jean-Claude, **3:**79, **3:**83–84
Patchin, Justin W., **10:**153
Patchogue-Medford Congress of Teachers v. Board of Education of Patchogue-Medford Union Free School District, **8:**75, **8:**79–80, **8:**85, **8:**86
Paterson, F. R. A., **4:**31
Patrick, Susan, **10:**129
Patterson, C. H., **3:**31
Patterson, Kerry, **7:**88
Patterson, R. S., **2:**48
Paul D. Coverdell Teacher Protection Act. *See* Coverdell Teacher Protection Act

Pavel, D. Michael, **1:**258
Pavlica v. Behr, **8:**22–23
Pay-for-performance. *See* Performance pay
Payne v. Peninsula School District, **5:**225–226
PBIS. *See* Positive behavior intervention supports
PBS. *See* Project-based science
PEA. *See* Progressive Education Association
Pearson, Donna, **1:**222
Pedagogy. *See* Instruction
Peebles-Wilkins, Wilma, **3:**226
Peer assistance and review (PAR), **7:**37
Peer tutoring, **3:**150
Pendleton School District v. State of Oregon, **3:**180
Peng, Arthur, **9:**244
Pennsylvania
charter schools, **1:**13, **1:**16, **7:**132
Code of Professional Practice and Conduct for Educators, **10:**149–150
disciplinary measures, **5:**217–218
education tax credits, **6:**269
for-profit schools, **1:**83–84
Pittsburgh Public Schools, **7:**36–37
school board association, **7:**xviii
special education, **6:**108
See also J.S. v. Blue Mountain School District; Layshock v. Hermitage School District
Pennsylvania Association for Retarded Children v. Pennsylvania, **8:**90, **8:**100, **8:**108
People of Illinois v. Levisen, **1:**121
People of the State of Illinois ex rel. McCollum v. Board of Education of School District No. 71, Champaign County, **4:**xviii, **4:**xxiv, **4:**110, **4:**152–153, **4:**154, **4:**161–163, **4:**173
People v. DeJonge, **1:**115, **1:**119
People v. Federman, **5:**164–165
PEP. *See* Panel for Educational Policy
Per pupil expenditures
at charter schools, **1:**9, **6:**285
district differences, **9:**210, **9:**211
effects of tax credits, **6:**266
increases, **1:**xvi, **6:**265–266, **9:**221, **9:**243, **9:**245, **9:**252
international comparisons, **6:**235, **9:**239, **9:**240, **9:**252

of magnet schools, **1:**176
state allocations, **6:**13, **6:**62, **6:**70,
6:119–120, **6:**180, **9:**207, **9:**228
state differences, **9:**205–206, **9:**233
Performance Assessment for California
Teachers (PACT), **9:**85, **9:**91
Performance evaluations. *See* Teacher
performance evaluations
Performance pay
for Advanced Placement teachers, **6:**229
at charter schools, **6:**281
cheating in system, **6:**138–139
funding, **3:**56, **6:**127–128, **6:**137, **6:**140
implementation challenges, **6:**126–129,
6:131, **6:**136–139
knowledge- and skill-based, **6:**131,
6:136
motivation and morale effects,
6:133–134, **6:**138, **9:**172
in other fields, **6:**130, **6:**132–134
performance measures, **6:**127, **6:**130,
6:131–132, **6:**136–137, **9:**173
recruitment and retention benefits,
6:132–133, **9:**223
research on, **6:**130, **6:**139–140
school-based, **6:**136
as short-term strategy, **6:**126
student achievement effects,
6:139–140
supporters, **6:**126, **6:**128, **6:**130–135
types, **6:**136
unintended consequences, **6:**137–138,
6:139
union views of, **7:**36–37, **9:**173
Performance-based assignments, **9:**180,
9:187
Perry v. Sindermann, **8:**229
*Peter W. v. San Francisco Unified School
District*, **8:**222
Peterson, Kent, **3:**40
Peterson, Paul, **7:**137
Peterson, Paul E., **9:**xxi
Petrilli, Michael J., **9:**25, **9:**33–34
Petrosino, Anthony J., **10:**123–124
Peyser, James A., **6:**xxii
PFPSs. *See* Proprietary for-profit
schools
P.H. v. School District of Kansas City,
5:97–98
Philadelphia
charter schools, **1:**13
for-profit schools, **1:**83–84

Philanthropy
criticism of, **9:**67
definition, **9:**63–64
educational impact, **9:**66–67, **9:**68–70
independence, **9:**63
investment in education, **9:**55–56
scholarship funds, **6:**262, **6:**267, **6:**269,
6:273
strategic, **9:**64–65
See also Foundations
Phonics, **2:**74, **2:**77, **2:**84–85
Physical punishment. *See* Corporal
punishment
Physical restraints
appropriate use, **5:**214–215, **5:**216,
5:221, **5:**222
lack of statistics on use, **5:**215–216
misuse of, **5:**215–216, **5:**217–218,
5:221–226, **5:**227
notification and documentation,
5:228–229
policies on use of, **5:**221
Piana, Libero Della, **5:**41
Pianta, Robert C., **9:**152
Pickering v. Board of Education, **4:**92, **4:**260,
8:196–198, **8:**202, **8:**205, **8:**209, **8:**240
PICS v. Seattle. *See Parents Involved in
Community Schools v. Seattle School
District No. 1*
Picus, Lawrence O., **6:**56, **6:**57, **6:**202,
9:xxvi
*Pierce ex rel. Pierce v. Sullivan West Central
School District*, **4:**154, **4:**157
Pierce v. Society of Sisters, **1:**xix–xx, **1:**39,
1:46, **1:**73, **1:**146, **2:**202, **4:**25, **4:**274,
8:60, **8:**79
Pink, Daniel, **9:**146
PISA. *See* Programme for International
Student Assessment
Pitt, Elizabeth, **5:**16
Pittsburgh Federation of Teachers,
7:36–37
Pittsburgh Public Schools, **7:**36–37
Pixley, Christopher J., **6:**xxii
Plagiarism
definition, **5:**123, **5:**124, **5:**134
detection software, **5:**123
disciplinary process, **5:**136, **5:**137
forms, **5:**130
legal cases, **5:**123–125
by teachers, **8:**22
technology used, **5:**128–129, **5:**133–134

underlying factors, **5:**125, **5:**128–129
See also Academic dishonesty;
Copyright law
Platt, Tony, **3:**31
Play, **2:**174–175, **2:**214–215
Pledge of Allegiance
addition of "under God" clause, **4:**138
interpretation of "under God" clause, **4:**143–144
legal cases, **4:**137–138, **4:**140, **4:**146, **4:**147–150
meaning, **4:**140–145
objections to "under God" clause, **4:**xxiii–xxiv, **4:**50, **4:**138, **4:**146, **4:**150
opting out by students, **4:**145–146, **4:**147, **4:**150
parental notification of nonparticipation, **4:**138–139, **4:**145–146, **4:**148–149
required recitation, **4:**137, **4:**138, **4:**146, **4:**147, **4:**148
teachers opting out of, **4:**92
voluntary participation, **4:**140, **4:**144–145, **4:**147
Plessy v. Ferguson, **3:**xxi, **3:**1, **3:**4, **3:**5, **3:**9, **3:**10, **3:**12, **7:**2, **7:**62
Pluralism, **2:**137
Plyler v. Doe, **3:**191, **6:**185
Pocket assistive technologies. *See* Assistive technology; Mobile technologies
Podgursky, Michael, **6:**134
Police
community policing, **5:**167–168, **5:**174
relations with school districts, **5:**160
school district forces, **5:**160
students reported to, **5:**33
surveillance cameras in schools linked to, **10:**xxiv, **10:**109
See also School resource officers
Policy entrepreneurs, **2:**29
Political campaigns, **2:**130–131
Political leaders. *See* Elected political leaders; Mayors
Political values, **2:**125
Politics
assessments and, **2:**94–95
charter schools and, **6:**290
in curriculum adoption, **8:**5–6
"English-only" curriculum issue, **2:**111–112, **2:**118, **3:**190, **3:**191–194, **3:**200, **3:**202

governance and, **7:**xxiii
judicial branch and, **6:**149, **6:**160–161, **6:**164, **7:**58–59, **7:**71–72
Race to the Top and, **2:**91, **2:**95, **2:**100
social networking sites and, **2:**233, **10:**145
state education financing and, **6:**148–149, **6:**160–161, **6:**164
student free speech rights, **5:**5, **8:**176–177, **8:**181, **8:**188–189
teacher free speech rights, **8:**2, **8:**7, **8:**194, **8:**208
teacher protection acts, **5:**190–191
teachers' unions and, **8:**245, **8:**249
Pollock, Jackson, **2:**174
Popham, W. James, **2:**59
Popper, Karl, **2:**xxiv
Popular culture
biblical references, **4:**89–90
concerns about, **2:**221, **2:**222
in curricula, **2:**211–226, **3:**133–147
definition, **2:**214
as distraction, **2:**219
hip-hop, **3:**137–147
identity construction and, **2:**218–219, **2:**222, **2:**225
leading to traditional content, **2:**222–223
music, **2:**211–213
postmodern view, **2:**214
production-in-use theory, **2:**217
reservations on use of, **2:**221–226
texts, **2:**215–220, **2:**223, **2:**225
time spent with, **2:**219
Pornography
child, **10:**148
online, **2:**207–208
Porter, Andrew, **2:**60
Porter, Rosalie Pedalino, **3:**195
Portfolio-based assignments, **9:**180, **9:**187
Positive behavior intervention supports (PBIS)
components, **5:**232, **5:**234–239
effectiveness, **5:**232, **5:**233, **5:**234, **5:**237–238, **5:**239, **5:**244–245
foundation, **5:**234
in IDEA reauthorization, **5:**231, **5:**232
implementation costs, **5:**242–243
individualized, **5:**233, **5:**238–239
limitations and criticisms, **5:**233, **5:**240–245
primary interventions, **5:**234–236, **5:**240, **5:**241

schoolwide, **5:**234–236, **5:**240, **5:**241
secondary interventions, **5:**236–238
targeted groups, **5:**236–238
tertiary interventions, **5:**238–239
treatment fidelity, **5:**240–241
use of, **5:**xxii, **5:**231–232, **8:**102
Posner, Richard, **8:**180
Postmodernism, **3:**33–34
Postsecondary education, **3:**118–121, **3:**128
  See also Community colleges; Higher education; Vocational education
Poverty. *See* Low socioeconomic groups
Powell, Mandy, **2:**218
Prayer in schools
  arguments against allowing, **4:**45–51, **4:**61–65
  arguments for allowing, **4:**42–43, **4:**56–60
  Equal Access Act and, **4:**50
  at graduation ceremonies, **4:**xix, **4:**xxi, **4:**35–51, **4:**62, **4:**73, **4:**99, **4:**114
  legal cases, **1:**29–30, **4:**xxi–xxii, **4:**35–36, **4:**38–42, **4:**45, **4:**46–47, **4:**51, **4:**61–63, **4:**73, **4:**77
  moments of silence, **4:**xxi–xxii, **4:**49–50, **4:**67–83
  nondenominational, **4:**35, **4:**36, **4:**39–40
  psychological coercion test, **4:**xix, **4:**38, **4:**40, **4:**46, **4:**99
  school-sponsored, **4:**45, **4:**46, **4:**47, **4:**61–62, **4:**64, **4:**77–78, **4:**98–99
  silent, **4:**49
  at sports events, **4:**xxi, **4:**36, **4:**39, **4:**46–47, **4:**62–63, **4:**73
  state laws, **4:**35–36, **4:**49–50, **4:**61–62
  student-led, **4:**35–51, **4:**77–78, **4:**80, **4:**220
  supporters, **2:**205
  by teachers, **4:**xxi, **4:**53–65
  traditions, **1:**30, **4:**78
  See also Religious clubs
Pregnancy discrimination, **8:**234, **8:**241
Pregnancy Discrimination Act of 1978, **7:**xxviii, **8:**241
Premont, Roxanne, **1:**47–48
Prendergrast v. Masterson, **5:**205
Preschool programs, **1:**198, **1:**200–203, **1:**213, **3:**101, **8:**140, **9:**223, **9:**278–279
  See also Head Start
Presidents. *See* Executive branch; *and individual presidents*

Price, Peter, **5:**166
Prince v. Jacoby, **4:**217, **4:**220, **4:**228
Principals
  administration preparation programs, **3:**44, **7:**95, **9:**125–127
  bullying prevention responsibility, **5:**62–63
  constraints due to collective bargaining agreements, **7:**25–26, **7:**28–32, **7:**35–36
  cultural competence, **7:**196–197, **7:**199–200
  as data leaders, **7:**80–81, **9:**120
  of high schools, **7:**148–163
  hiring authority, **6:**47, **7:**30
  history, **6:**54, **7:**xxi–xxii
  influence on student achievement, **6:**48, **7:**78
  instructional leadership, **7:**151–152, **7:**162, **7:**199–201
  knowledge domains, **3:**43
  of magnet schools, **1:**177
  male, **7:**xxii, **7:**94
  mobility, **6:**47–48, **6:**54–55
  performance pay, **7:**36
  programmatic instruction and, **2:**8
  responsibility for reducing achievement gap, **7:**51–52, **7:**75–90
  roles and responsibilities, **6:**54, **7:**xxii, **7:**77, **7:**78–84, **7:**238–240, **7:**246
  school turnaround specialists, **9:**129
  shortages of qualified candidates, **3:**40–41
  sociopolitical identities, **7:**80
  spending authority, **6:**41–57
  support for teachers, **7:**81, **7:**82, **7:**83
  turnover, **6:**48, **6:**54–55
  women, **7:**100, **7:**101, **7:**103, **7:**104
  See also Administrators
Prisons, school-to-prison pipeline, **5:**33–34, **5:**44–45, **5:**162
Pritchett, Henry S., **9:**65
Privacy
  drug testing, **10:**104–105
  issues with surveillance cameras in schools, **10:**xxiv, **10:**98–113
  laws, **10:**106, **10:**108
  reasonable expectation, **10:**103–104, **10:**108
  students' rights, **10:**xxiv, **10:**103–106, **10:**108
  teachers' rights, **10:**140

Privacy rights
  constitutional provisions, **8:**160, **8:**165–166, **10:**108
  of students, **8:**58, **8:**62, **8:**63–65, **10:**xxiv, **10:**103–106, **10:**108
  of teachers, **8:**75, **8:**79, **8:**85–86, **8:**160–162, **8:**164, **8:**165–167, **8:**168–169, **8:**172, **10:**140
Private goods, **6:**273–274
Private schools
  academic performance, **1:**80, **1:**85–86, **1:**145–160, **3:**68, **6:**265
  advantages, **6:**265
  characteristics, **1:**xxiv, **1:**156
  competition with public schools, **1:**72, **1:**78–79, **1:**150–153, **6:**262–263, **7:**10, **7:**214–215
  disciplinary measures, **5:**216
  diverse student bodies, **6:**267
  enrollments, **1:**39, **1:**41, **1:**156
  for-profit, **1:**xxiv–xxv, **1:**72–89, **3:**68, **6:**266
  funding, **1:**145
  home schools as, **1:**121
  need for, **1:**41–42, **1:**44–45
  nonsectarian, **1:**xxiv, **1:**xxvi, **1:**145–160
  number of, **1:**xxiv, **1:**72, **1:**145
  parental involvement, **1:**154
  parents' rights to choose, **1:**xix–xx, **1:**146
  performance, **7:**220–221
  reasons for choosing, **1:**145–146, **1:**157, **1:**159
  rights to operate, **1:**xix–xx, **1:**73
  scholarships, **1:**97–98, **6:**262, **6:**267, **6:**269, **6:**273
  segregated, **6:**254
  selection of, **2:**xxi, **6:**280–281
  selective admissions, **1:**149, **1:**156, **1:**157
  single-sex, **1:**181
  special education, **6:**101, **6:**106–107, **6:**247–248
  tax credits for tuition, **1:**92, **1:**150, **6:**258–274
  teachers, **1:**77, **1:**157–158
  tuition levels, **1:**148, **6:**264–265, **6:**271
  uniforms, **8:**38, **8:**41, **8:**49
  vouchers, **1:**150, **6:**xxiii, **6:**106–107, **6:**240–256
  See also Religious schools
Private sector. *See* Business interests; Philanthropy; Public-private partnerships

Privatization
  advocates, **3:**68, **7:**178
  of charter schools, **1:**47–48
  definition, **7:**166–167
  research on effects, **7:**184
  of school systems, **1:**47–48, **7:**55–56, **7:**172
  See also Educational management organizations
Procter & Gamble, **9:**250
ProEnglish, **2:**118
Professional associations, of teachers, **7:**33
Professional development
  for administrators, **2:**8
  culturally relevant instruction, **1:**267
  financial rewards, **6:**131
  for gifted education, **6:**119, **6:**121, **6:**122
  importance, **9:**146–147
  learning communities, **9:**8
  learning networks, **10:**140–141, **10:**198–199
  online courses, **10:**64
  in popular text use, **2:**215–216, **2:**225
  in private schools, **1:**77–78
  programmatic instruction and, **2:**8
  school-based, **2:**8
  in social media use, **10:**193
  for teachers, **2:**62–63, **6:**83, **7:**46, **7:**156, **7:**158, **7:**243, **9:**153–154
  for teachers of online courses, **10:**92, **10:**95
  in technology, **10:**122, **10:**124, **10:**216, **10:**224
  technology used in, **10:**198–200
  See also Teacher training
Professionals
  administrators as, **9:**132–133
  characteristics, **3:**41, **7:**159–160
  licensing boards, **2:**25–26
  malpractice liabilities, **8:**216, **8:**223
  standards of conduct, **8:**218
  See also Teaching profession
Programmatic instruction and curriculum
  advantages, **2:**1, **2:**4–10
  disadvantages, **2:**1–2, **2:**10, **2:**14–17, **8:**8
  disruptions caused by, **2:**10, **2:**14–16
  research on, **2:**10
Programme for International Student Assessment (PISA), **1:**158–159, **2:**30, **2:**102–103, **7:**213, **7:**259, **9:**220, **9:**237, **9:**238, **9:**239, **9:**254

Progressive Education Association (PEA), Eight-Year Study, **9:**16–18
Progressive reformers
 business regulations, **9:**13
 child labor laws, **7:**3, **7:**149
 education policies, **2:**65, **3:**153, **7:**xix, **7:**xx, **7:**3, **7:**246
 moral education and, **2:**199–201, **2:**202
Project-based science (PBS), **2:**96
Property taxes
 additional, **6:**1–19, **6:**180
 administration and compliance, **6:**66, **6:**71
 alternatives to, **6:**68, **6:**73–74
 capacity, **6:**63
 debt servicing and, **6:**25, **6:**26
 dependence on, **6:**59–75, **9:**204–205, **9:**209
 equity suits, **6:**63–64, **6:**72, **6:**168–169
 increasing, **6:**222, **6:**223
 inequities from dependence on, **6:**60, **6:**71, **6:**72, **6:**183, **7:**66–67, **7:**222–223, **9:**204–205
 limits, **6:**27–28, **6:**67, **6:**70, **9:**202
 rates, **6:**25, **6:**67, **6:**74–75, **6:**158–159, **9:**202
 reductions, **6:**74–75, **7:**209
 relief programs, **6:**67
 revenue declines, **7:**209, **9:**193, **9:**209
 share of total revenue, **6:**62, **6:**69
 stability of revenue, **6:**65, **6:**68, **6:**73, **6:**209–210
 state, **6:**72
 state supplementation, **6:**13–14, **6:**26, **6:**62–63, **9:**222
 tax base, **6:**63, **6:**65, **6:**72
 taxpayer compact with schools, **6:**222
 See also Taxes
Proprietary for-profit schools (PFPSs), **1:**72–89
 business model, **1:**72, **1:**78–79, **1:**81, **1:**82, **1:**88–89, **3:**68, **6:**266
 concerns, **1:**79–80, **1:**82–89
 costs, **1:**82–85, **1:**88
 curricula, **1:**79, **1:**83, **1:**85–86
 definition, **1:**72
 education reform and, **1:**75–77
 professional development, **1:**77–78
 pros and cons, **1:**xxiv–xxv, **1:**73–74, **3:**68
 segregated, **1:**87
 student performance, **1:**80, **1:**85–86
 teachers, **1:**77–78, **1:**79, **1:**83

virtual schools, **1:**89
 See also Private schools
Prosser, Charles, **3:**126–127
Protestants
 moral values, **2:**198, **4:**274
 schools, **1:**22
 See also Christianity; Religious schools
Psychological coercion test. *See* Coercion test
Psychologists, school, **5:**253–254, **5:**256, **5:**262
Psychology
 moral development, **2:**196–197
 reading research, **2:**72, **2:**73
Public Agenda, **5:**181
Public education
 democracy and, **2:**xviii–xxi, **2:**20, **6:**268
 failures, **6:**241
 free, **6:**215–216, **6:**221, **6:**222, **6:**225–226, **6:**231–234, **6:**240
 growth, **1:**xvi
 history, **1:**xvi–xvii, **4:**176–177, **4:**270, **7:**xvii–xix, **7:**6–7, **7:**115–116
 as monopoly, **1:**78, **1:**151, **6:**249–250, **6:**263, **6:**269–270
 positive externalities, **6:**274
 privatization proposals, **1:**47–48, **7:**55–56, **7:**172
 privilege in, **2:**xxi–xxii, **2:**xxiv
 public views of, **7:**229–230, **7:**249–250
 societal benefits, **6:**233, **6:**268, **6:**274
Public employees
 collective bargaining, **8:**244, **8:**245, **8:**248, **8:**258
 drug testing, **8:**63, **8:**77, **8:**78, **8:**83–84
 employment protections, **8:**230
 free speech rights, **8:**193–194, **8:**198, **8:**199–201, **8:**202, **8:**205–206
 See also Employees; Teachers
Public goods, education as, **6:**262–263, **6:**273, **6:**274
Public school governance. *See* Governance
Public-private partnerships
 advantages, **9:**236, **9:**246–251
 alternatives to, **9:**259–260
 data projects, **9:**248–249
 effects, **9:**255–258
 need for, **9:**245–246
 in policy and research, **9:**246–248
 See also Business interests
Publishers. *See* Textbook publishers

Pull-out programs. *See* Compensatory education; "English-only" curriculum; Special education
Punishment. *See* Corporal punishment; Discipline policies
Puritans, **4:**172, **4:**176

Quaid, Libby, **7:**18
Quakers, **2:**246, **4:**172
Quality of education
 defining, **7:**219–220
 equality of, **6:**1–2
 factors influencing, **2:**105
 financing adequacy and, **6:**xx–xxii, **6:**145, **6:**198–200, **6:**201, **6:**204
 financing inequities and, **6:**xvii, **6:**xxi–xxii, **7:**221
 improving, **7:**220, **7:**221–222
 instructional quality, **6:**82–83, **7:**83, **7:**84
 international rankings, **7:**209
 for minority students, **3:**xx
Quinby, Robert F., **3:**30
Quitman Street Community School, **3:**225

Race to the Top (RTT)
 alternative certification programs, **3:**56
 announcement, **3:**58, **3:**59–60
 business model, **7:**47, **7:**55, **7:**116
 charter schools, **3:**56, **3:**63
 common standards, **2:**21, **9:**25, **9:**31–32, **9:**62
 compared to NCLB, **3:**61, **3:**63
 competition for funding, **2:**90–92, **2:**94, **2:**100, **6:**284, **7:**47, **7:**116, **7:**253
 conditions, **3:**56, **6:**84, **9:**62
 context, **3:**67–68
 corporations and, **9:**247–248
 criticism of, **3:**63–64, **3:**65–72, **9:**xxviii
 data systems, **3:**61
 effects, **3:**62–63, **3:**64–65
 funding, **2:**99–100
 goals, **3:**60–61
 grants, **2:**91, **2:**100, **3:**55–56, **3:**58, **3:**60, **3:**61–62, **3:**65
 legislation, **3:**55–56
 obstacles, **3:**56–57
 performance pay for teachers, **3:**56, **6:**134
 political aspects, **2:**91, **2:**95, **2:**100
 potential results, **3:**55–72
 process, **3:**61–62, **3:**67
 programs supported, **3:**xxiii
 school turnarounds, **3:**56–57, **3:**61, **9:**123
 STEM education and, **2:**90–106
 supporters, **3:**58–65
 teacher evaluations, **3:**62, **3:**63, **3:**66, **9:**xxviii, **9:**75
Racial ethnic identities (REI), **3:**24–25
 See also Ethnic identities
Racial issues
 categorizations, **2:**124
 continuing, **7:**xxvii
 discrimination in teacher pay, **7:**23
 disparities in disciplinary measures, **5:**32–33, **5:**37, **5:**40–44, **5:**47, **5:**50, **5:**113–114
 evolutionary theory and, **4:**190
 institutional racism, **7:**82
 Jim Crow system, **3:**12
 socially constructed attitudes, **7:**80
 See also Achievement gaps; Desegregation; Minority students; Segregated schools
RAND Corporation, **1:**12–13, **1:**14, **1:**86, **6:**139–140
Ranker, Jason, **2:**215
Rap music, **3:**138–139
 See also Hip-hop culture
Ratner, Gershon, **6:**170
Ratner v. Loudoun County Public Schools, **5:**20, **5:**49
Ravitch, Diane, **1:**102–103, **2:**58, **3:**69, **7:**54, **7:**182, **7:**192, **7:**195, **7:**197, **9:**33, **9:**34, **9:**41, **9:**135, **9:**230
RAVSAK: The Jewish Community Day School Network, **1:**129
Rayner, Eric, **2:**175
Raytheon, **9:**250
Reading
 achievement gaps, **3:**99–100, **9:**242, **9:**244, **9:**245
 culturally relevant instruction, **3:**145
 curricula, **6:**79–80
 federally mandated curriculum, **2:**6, **6:**79–80
 as gatekeeper subject, **9:**11
 impact of digital technology, **2:**73, **10:**26–28
 instructional approaches, **2:**7, **2:**72–89, **2:**115–116, **9:**83, **9:**84
 research on, **2:**72, **2:**73, **2:**74, **2:**113–115, **9:**83
 in second language, **2:**112–116

stages, **2:**82–84, **2:**87–89
standardized test scores, **2:**102–103, **2:**104–105, **9:**8–9, **9:**239, **9:**241, **9:**242, **9:**253
strategy instruction, **2:**77–78, **2:**80–81
summer setbacks, **3:**88
textbooks, **2:**72–73, **2:**75, **2:**76, **2:**80, **2:**86, **3:**133–134
written word knowledge, **2:**84–87, **2:**88
See also e-books; English language arts; Literacy
Reading First program, **2:**6, **6:**79–80, **6:**91
"Reading to learn" vs. "learning to read," **2:**72–89
Readings, Bill, **10:**27
Reagan, Ronald, **2:**56, **2:**205, **3:**16, **3:**192, **4:**142, **7:**252
Rebell, Michael A., **6:**174
REEP. *See* Rice Education Entrepreneurship Program
Reflection, **2:**149
Reform proposals
  bipartisan, **6:**284
  Broader, Bolder Approach to Education, **7:**52
  business model, **7:**xxviii, **7:**47, **7:**247
  collective bargaining agreements and, **7:**27–32
  effects of unions, **7:**22–38, **9:**156, **9:**163, **9:**164–166, **9:**167, **9:**173
  full-service community schools, **3:**xxv, **3:**221–235
  funding, **9:**222–223
  funding formulas, **6:**63, **7:**221
  in governance, **7:**14, **7:**172, **7:**246–247
  quality improvements, **7:**221–222
  single-sex classes and schools, **1:**180–195
  teacher involvement, **2:**23, **7:**27
  teacher training, **9:**xxii, **9:**xxiii–xxiv, **9:**69, **9:**84–85
  teachers' unions and, **9:**160, **9:**161, **9:**164–166
  technology use and, **10:**209–210
  See also Market competition; Performance pay; Standards-based reform
Regents of the University of California v. Bakke, **7:**70–71
Rehabilitation Act of 1973, Section 504
  damage claims, **8:**219
  right to education, **6:**102–103
  rights of students with disabilities, **5:**219, **5:**226, **6:**232
  supplementary services, **2:**189
  teacher rights, **8:**241
REI. *See* Racial ethnic identities
Released time religious instruction
  alternatives to, **4:**166
  arguments against allowing, **4:**163–167
  arguments for allowing, **4:**158–161
  benefits of, **4:**160–161
  constitutionality, **4:**153–154, **4:**156, **4:**157, **4:**161–164
  current programs, **4:**157, **4:**162, **4:**166–167
  definition, **4:**152
  funding, **4:**158–159, **4:**164
  history, **4:**156–157, **4:**162
  legal cases, **4:**152–154, **4:**157–158, **4:**161–163
  Lemon test and, **4:**159
  off campus, **4:**152, **4:**153–154, **4:**157, **4:**165–166
  opposition, **4:**158
  on school property, **4:**xxiv, **4:**152–153, **4:**154, **4:**163
  See also Religious instruction in schools
Religions
  as academic topic, **4:**89, **4:**92–93, **4:**109, **4:**134, **4:**171, **4:**174–175, **4:**202, **4:**208
  activities in public settings, **4:**xviii–xix
  cultural influence, **2:**126
  distinction from culture, **1:**26
  diversity, **1:**26, **4:**59, **4:**89, **4:**179, **4:**212, **4:**279–280
  historical role in United States, **4:**70, **4:**88–89, **4:**144
  hostility toward, **4:**44, **4:**259
  minority, **4:**49, **4:**117–118, **4:**134, **4:**201, **4:**294–295
  Sikh, **4:**267–268, **4:**276, **4:**277, **4:**288
  values, **2:**126, **2:**155, **2:**198, **4:**274
  Wiccan, **4:**134, **4:**293
  See also Christianity; Church-state separation; Islam; Jewish education; Moral values; Prayer in schools
Religious clubs
  access to school buildings, **4:**xxvi–xxvii, **4:**50, **4:**74, **4:**81, **4:**216–231, **4:**236–237

discriminatory, **4:**220–222
free speech rights of students, **4:**217
leaflet distribution, **4:**220, **4:**245, **4:**256–257
meeting times, **4:**217
moral education and, **2:**201, **2:**202
rights of, **4:**229–230
teacher participation, **4:**53–54, **4:**93, **4:**254
Religious discrimination, **1:**42, **2:**198–199, **4:**219, **4:**220–222, **4:**284, **4:**288, **4:**292–293
Religious education, **4:**156, **4:**273–274
See also Released time religious instruction; Religious instruction in schools
Religious freedom
compulsory education and, **1:**xx–xxi, **1:**112–113, **1:**114, **1:**123
educational choices and, **1:**xxiii, **1:**36
limits on, **4:**91
motives for American settlement, **4:**176
religious garb and, **4:**267–282, **4:**284–298
school uniform policies and, **8:**43, **8:**44, **8:**46, **8:**47
in state constitutions, **1:**47, **4:**58, **4:**111
of students, **2:**202, **4:**81, **4:**110–111, **4:**159, **4:**271–273, **4:**277, **4:**278
of teachers, **4:**56–59, **4:**91, **4:**92, **4:**93–94, **4:**284–285, **4:**288–289, **4:**294
in U.S. society, **1:**39, **4:**88–89, **4:**95
violations, **4:**240–241
See also First Amendment
Religious Freedom Restoration Act (RFRA), **4:**278
Religious garb
acceptance, **4:**274–275
arguments against allowing, **4:**277–282, **4:**292–298
arguments for allowing, **4:**270–276, **4:**288–292
of Catholic nuns, **4:**276, **4:**287
dress code policies on, **4:**272, **4:**274–275, **4:**276, **4:**280
endorsement test and, **4:**293
French law, **4:**280–281
Jewish, **4:**275, **4:**288
legal cases, **4:**267–268, **4:**272–273, **4:**276–277, **4:**285, **4:**295–296, **4:**297–298
Muslim, **4:**268, **4:**275, **4:**280–281, **4:**288, **4:**296

safety issues, **4:**267–268, **4:**277–279
Sikh, **4:**267–268, **4:**276, **4:**277, **4:**288
student reactions, **4:**289–290, **4:**291–292, **4:**294, **4:**298
of students, **4:**xxvii, **4:**267–282
of teachers, **4:**xxvii–xxviii, **4:**92, **4:**93, **4:**276–277, **4:**284–298
Religious groups
access to school buildings, **4:**xxvi–xxvii, **4:**216, **4:**226, **4:**233–248
exemptions from compulsory education, **1:**xx–xxi, **1:**112–113, **1:**123
materials distributed at public schools, **4:**xxvii, **4:**246, **4:**247, **4:**250–265
partnerships with full-service community schools, **3:**226–228
Religious holidays
absenteeism, **4:**207, **4:**208–209
on classroom calendars, **4:**202, **4:**208
coercion test and, **4:**202, **4:**204–205, **4:**210, **4:**211
endorsement test and, **4:**202, **4:**204, **4:**210
Good Friday and Easter, **4:**115, **4:**202, **4:**207, **4:**210
legal cases, **4:**202, **4:**206–208, **4:**210
Lemon test and, **4:**201–202, **4:**204, **4:**210–212
of minority religions, **4:**201, **4:**211, **4:**212–213
music, **4:**109–110, **4:**114–115, **4:**118
reasonable accommodations, **4:**206, **4:**209, **4:**213
in school calendars, **4:**xxvi, **4:**201–214
seasonal displays with religious symbols, **1:**26, **4:**121, **4:**126–127, **4:**128, **4:**132–133, **4:**202
Religious identities
benefits of, **1:**61–63
development of, **1:**64, **1:**65–70
Jewish, **1:**xxv, **1:**50, **1:**125–143
Muslim, **1:**54–70
Religious instruction in schools
benefits of, **4:**160
Bible study, **4:**169–170, **4:**178, **4:**180–181
history, **2:**198–199, **4:**176–177
legal cases, **4:**93, **4:**169–170, **4:**177–178, **4:**180–181
Lemon test and, **4:**168–169, **4:**177–178
released time, **4:**xxiv, **4:**152–167
See also Religious texts

Religious music
  arguments against allowing, **4**:114–118
  arguments for allowing, **4**:106–112
  educational value, **4**:106, **4**:107–110, **4**:111–112
  Establishment clause violations, **4**:104, **4**:114–116
  at graduation ceremonies, **4**:47–48, **4**:116–117
  at holidays, **4**:109–110, **4**:114–115, **4**:118
  legal cases, **4**:104, **4**:107–110, **4**:111, **4**:116–117
  Lemon test and, **4**:104, **4**:107–110, **4**:113, **4**:114–115
  opting out of performing, **4**:110–111, **4**:116, **4**:118
  policy arguments against using, **4**:117–118
  in public schools, **4**:xxii, **4**:47–48, **4**:103–118
Religious schools
  academic performance, **4**:14
  admissions, **1**:149–150
  advantages, **4**:4, **4**:5, **4**:13–14
  affordability, **1**:148
  church-state separation issue, **1**:40–41, **1**:46, **1**:93, **4**:xviii, **4**:1–2, **6**:267–268, **6**:272–273
  curricula, **1**:54
  federal government and, **1**:39–40
  funding, **1**:29–30, **1**:39, **2**:199, **6**:246, **6**:283
  history, **1**:xxiii–xxiv, **1**:72–73
  Islamic, **1**:54, **1**:55, **1**:66, **6**:255–256
  Jewish, **1**:xxv, **1**:125–143
  nonsectarian approach, **1**:149
  parents' rights to choose, **1**:39, **1**:46, **1**:73, **4**:25
  Protestant, **1**:22
  Quaker, **2**:246
  racial discrimination by, **4**:32
  Roman Catholic, **1**:xxiii–xxiv, **1**:22, **1**:39–40, **1**:44, **1**:98–99, **2**:199, **4**:294–295, **8**:38
  scholarships, **1**:95, **1**:98–100, **1**:104, **6**:262
  science curricula, **1**:116, **4**:31
  tuition levels, **6**:262
  See also Faith-based charter schools
Religious schools, government aid to
  arguments against, **4**:9–14, **4**:19, **4**:26–32
  arguments for, **4**:7–9, **4**:19, **4**:21–26
  bans on state aid, **1**:95, **1**:96, **2**:199
  child benefit test, **4**:xix, **4**:6, **4**:11, **4**:18
  ethnocentric charter schools, **1**:29–30
  for field trips, **4**:xx, **4**:2, **4**:6
  indirect, **4**:11–12, **4**:26, **4**:27, **4**:28, **4**:29, **4**:30
  for instructional materials, **4**:7, **4**:27, **4**:28
  legal cases, **4**:xviii, **4**:1–2, **4**:4–7, **4**:18, **4**:27–29
  Lemon test for, **4**:xviii, **4**:xxv, **4**:6, **4**:18, **4**:22–24, **4**:27
  prohibitions, **4**:2, **4**:11–12
  for special education, **4**:7, **4**:19, **4**:28
  state aid types, **4**:4, **4**:11–12, **4**:18
  state bans, **1**:95, **1**:96, **2**:199, **4**:4
  for students with disabilities, **4**:18, **4**:24
  tax credits for tuition, **1**:92, **1**:150, **6**:267–268, **6**:272–273
  for textbooks, **4**:xx, **4**:5, **4**:17–32
  for transportation, **4**:xix–xx, **4**:1–14
  See also Vouchers
Religious symbols
  arguments against allowing, **4**:129–135
  arguments for allowing, **4**:123–129
  contexts of displays, **4**:127–128
  educational value, **4**:124–125, **4**:128–129, **4**:134
  endorsement test and, **4**:xviii–xix, **4**:120, **4**:121, **4**:123, **4**:126–127, **4**:128, **4**:132
  Equal Access Act and, **4**:229
  free speech rights and, **4**:128–129
  gang use of, **4**:268, **4**:272–273, **4**:280
  Jewish, **4**:272
  legal cases, **1**:26, **4**:120–122, **4**:124–127, **4**:131–133
  Lemon test and, **4**:123, **4**:124–127, **4**:131
  Nativity scenes, **4**:121, **4**:126–127, **4**:128, **4**:132
  in public schools, **1**:26, **4**:xxii–xxiii, **4**:120–135
  secular purposes of displays, **4**:123–126, **4**:128–129, **4**:132–133, **4**:134
  Ten Commandments, **4**:xxii–xxiii, **4**:113, **4**:120–121, **4**:124, **4**:126, **4**:131–132, **4**:133
  wearing, **4**:93, **4**:272, **4**:296
  See also Religious garb
Religious texts
  cultural importance, **4**:171–172
  as literature, **4**:xxiv–xxv, **4**:168–182

silent reading by teachers in public schools, **4**:xxii, **4**:85–101
teacher knowledge of, **4**:179–180, **4**:181
See also Bible; Koran
Religious tolerance
definition, **4**:134
holiday celebrations, **4**:109, **7**:188
for minority religions, **4**:49
need for, **4**:90
prayer at graduation ceremonies and, **4**:38, **4**:43, **4**:44
promoting, **4**:50, **4**:59, **4**:63–64, **4**:135, **4**:276, **4**:279–280, **4**:290, **4**:291
in United States, **4**:129, **4**:134–135, **4**:192, **4**:282
See also First Amendment
Remedial education. *See* Compensatory education
Renshaw, Tyler L., **5**:243
Renzulli, Joseph S., **6**:120, **6**:123
Reschovsky, Andrew, **6**:117–118
Residual budgeting, **9**:206
Resnick, Michael, **2**:18
Resource rooms, **8**:122–123
See also Special education
Response to intervention (RTI) model, **2**:163–164, **5**:252–254, **5**:259–261
Restorative justice, **5**:45
Restraints. *See* Physical restraints
Reward systems, **5**:147–149
See also Extrinsic motivators; Teacher salaries and benefits
Reynolds v. United States, **4**:100
RFRA. *See* Religious Freedom Restoration Act
Rhee, Michelle, **7**:10, **7**:19, **7**:23
Rhode Island
education tax credits, **6**:269
prayer at graduation ceremonies, **4**:36, **4**:38, **4**:62
per pupil expenditures, **9**:205
Rice Education Entrepreneurship Program (REEP), **9**:128
Richards, Craig E., **6**:114
Richardson, Virginia, **9**:xix
Rights
choice programs and, **1**:27
of minorities, **6**:149–150
negative, **6**:174
See also Due process; Parents' rights; Privacy rights; Religious freedom; Teacher rights

Rights of students
balance with safety, **8**:65–66
kto education, **5**:xviii–xix, **6**:14, **6**:102, **6**:144, **6**:148, **6**:185, **9**:191, **9**:213
freedom from unreasonable restraint or seclusion, **5**:216–219, **5**:223, **5**:226
of homeless students, **8**:xx, **8**:127–142
in loco parentis doctrine and, **5**:195, **5**:198–199, **5**:200, **5**:203, **5**:204–206
privacy, **8**:58, **8**:62, **8**:63–65, **10**:xxiv, **10**:103–106, **10**:108
religious freedom, **4**:81, **4**:110–111, **4**:159, **4**:271–273, **4**:277, **4**:278
school resource officers and, **5**:158
of students with disabilities, **5**:xix, **5**:216–219, **5**:222–223, **8**:xvii–xviii, **8**:90, **8**:99, **8**:100–101, **8**:108
uniforms and, **8**:41, **8**:42
See also Free speech rights of students
Riley, Richard, **7**:249
Riordan, Cornelius, **1**:195
Rivkin, Steven, **3**:69
Robbins v. Lower Merion School District, **10**:111
Robert, Peter, **1**:158–159
Roberts, Mark, **1**:219
Roberts v. City of Boston, **7**:62
Roberts v. Houston Independent School District, **10**:102
Roberts v. Madigan, **4**:xxii, **4**:53, **4**:54, **4**:63, **4**:65, **4**:86, **4**:94, **4**:100, **4**:294
Robinson, Kimberly, **7**:253
Robinson v. Cahill, **3**:182, **6**:xxi, **6**:64, **6**:184, **6**:200, **9**:191
Robles-Wong et al. v. State of California, **3**:179, **6**:202
Robots, **2**:3, **10**:210
Rochin v. California, **5**:217
Rockquemore, Kerry A., **5**:2, **8**:53
Rodriguez, Gloria M., **3**:176
Rodriguez v. San Antonio Independent School District, **3**:181
Roemer, John E., **3**:173
Roman Catholics
discrimination against, **2**:198–199, **4**:7, **4**:292–293
hospitals, **4**:5
nuns, **4**:276, **4**:287
rosaries, **4**:268, **4**:272–273, **4**:277, **4**:280, **5**:13–14

schools, **1:**xxiii–xxiv, **1:**22, **1:**39–40, **1:**44, **1:**98–99, **2:**199, **4:**294–295, **8:**38
See also Christianity
Roosevelt, Franklin D., **8:**248
Root-Bernstein, Michelle M., **2:**160
Root-Bernstein, Robert S., **2:**160
Rose v. Council for Better Education, **3:**181, **6:**33, **6:**64, **6:**149, **6:**169, **6:**198, **6:**201
Rosenberger v. Rector and Visitors of University of Virginia, **4:**223
Rossell, Christine H., **2:**112
Rothenberg, Albert, **2:**170
Rothstein, Richard, **1:**42, **3:**68, **3:**71, **7:**86, **7:**88, **9:**228–229
Rowan, Anna Habash, **3:**103
Rowan, Brian, **7:**170–171
Rowland v. Mad River Local School District, **8:**233–234
Rowley, James B., **9:**271
RTI. *See* Response to intervention model
RTT. *See* Race to the Top
Rusch, Edith, **7:**104
Rusk v. Clearview Local Schools, **4:**244–245, **4:**247, **4:**257
Russell, Bertrand, **9:**51
Russo, Charles J., **4:**222
Ryan, James E., **3:**172
Ryan, Jennifer, **10:**77
Ryan, Richard M., **5:**152, **5:**153

S-1 v. Turlington, **8:**94
Sacramento City Unified School District Board of Education v. Rachel H., **8:**115, **8:**121
Sacred texts. *See* Bible; Religious texts
Sadker, David, **3:**212
Safety
classroom management and, **5:**141–142, **5:**144
concerns in schools, **5:**11, **5:**24–25
dress codes and, **5:**xxv, **5:**1–17, **8:**38–39, **8:**48
drug testing and, **8:**xix, **8:**60–61, **8:**65–66, **8:**77, **8:**78, **8:**79, **8:**80–81, **8:**82–83, **8:**86
goals of disciplinary policies, **5:**197–198
on Internet, **10:**xxiii, **10:**147–148
rationale for zero tolerance policies, **5:**19–34, **5:**39, **5:**40
released time programs and, **4:**165–166

religious garb issues, **4:**267–268, **4:**277–279
on social networking sites, **10:**xxiii, **10:**xxiv, **10:**xxv, **10:**174, **10:**202–203
video surveillance and, **10:**99, **10:**101–102, **10:**107, **10:**110, **10:**112
See also Abuse and neglect; Bullying; School resource officers; Zero tolerance policies
Safford Unified School District #1 v. Redding, **5:**195, **5:**199, **8:**67, **8:**68
Salaries. *See* Teacher salaries and benefits
Sales taxes, **6:**27, **6:**64, **6:**65, **6:**66, **6:**67, **6:**68, **6:**73
Samuels v. Independent School District 279, **5:**163–164
San Antonio Independent School District v. Rodriguez
background, **9:**191
funding disparities allowed, **3:**181
impact, **3:**xxvi, **6:**147, **6:**168, **6:**172–173, **6:**184, **7:**66
plaintiffs' arguments, **6:**xxi, **6:**184
right to education not found in Constitution, **6:**14, **9:**191, **9:**213
See also Financing equity
San Diego Unified School District, **6:**230
Sanders, William, **9:**139
Sankofa symbol, **3:**241, **3:**252
Santa Fe Independent School District v. Doe, **1:**25, **1:**30, **4:**36, **4:**39, **4:**46–47, **4:**62–63, **4:**73
Santayana, George, **9:**136
Sasso, Gary M., **3:**32, **3:**33–34
SAT. *See* Scholastic Aptitude Test
Sataline, Suzanne, **7:**19
SBM. *See* School-based management
Scaffolding, **2:**11–12, **2:**15
Schaill v. Tippecanoe County School Corp., **8:**57
Schema theory, **2:**73
Schmidt, William, **9:**31
Schmoker, Michael, **1:**264
Schneider, Frank W., **1:**192
Scholastic Aptitude Test (SAT) scores, **2:**66, **9:**253
School boards
accountability, **7:**9, **7:**121, **7:**124, **8:**13
advantages, **7:**19
alternative models, **7:**10–11, **7:**121–122, **7:**126–127
antibullying policies, **5:**56

appointed, **7:**111, **7:**112, **7:**118
declining authority, **7:**xix, **7:**xxiv, **7:**xxv, **7:**114–115
demographics of members, **7:**118, **7:**124
discipline policies, **5:**xvii, **5:**118–119
educational malpractice liability, **8:**xxv, **8:**213–226
elections, **7:**9–10, **7:**13, **7:**111, **7:**113, **7:**118, **7:**136–137
electoral accountability, **7:**9, **7:**121, **7:**124, **7:**256
female members, **7:**103, **7:**118, **9:**15
governmental immunity, **5:**82, **5:**189
graduation ceremony speech policies, **4:**41–44, **4:**46–47
harassment prevention responsibility, **5:**55–56, **5:**67–68
hiring procedures, **7:**93, **7:**125
history, **7:**xvii–xx, **7:**6, **7:**13
influence on student achievement, **7:**125–126
interest group influence, **7:**9–10, **7:**113, **7:**123–124
misinformation about, **7:**117–118
motives of members, **7:**117, **7:**122–124
need for, **7:**111–127
problems with, **7:**13–14, **7:**121–127, **7:**141
proposals to eliminate, **7:**255
relations with superintendents, **7:**13, **7:**125
responsibilities under NCLB, **7:**xxviii
roles and responsibilities, **6:**xviii–xix, **7:**13–14, **7:**119–120, **7:**121, **7:**123, **7:**125, **7:**127, **7:**246
social composition, **9:**15
suicide prevention responsibility, **5:**80–82, **5:**85
training, **7:**121
in urban districts, **7:**112, **7:**255, **7:**258
See also Local control of schools
School choice. *See* Choice
School committees, **7:**12
School counselors. *See* Counselors
School days
of charter schools, **1:**5
of full-service community schools, **3:**225
lengths, **7:**35, **7:**222
School District No. 8 v. Superior Court, **8:**229

School District of Abington Township v. Schempp, **4:**xxiv, **4:**xxv, **4:**22, **4:**35–36, **4:**45, **4:**50, **4:**62, **4:**72, **4:**85–86, **4:**98–99, **4:**168–169, **4:**173, **4:**177, **4:**195
School districts
additional taxes, **6:**1–19, **6:**180
budgets, **6:**44, **7:**239, **9:**222
capital improvements, **3:**6–7
centralized financial management, **6:**45–46, **6:**49–50, **6:**56
consolidation, **7:**246, **9:**54–55
debt limits, **6:**21–38
NCLB report cards, **7:**46
number of, **1:**xvi, **7:**13
online learning policies, **10:**xx–xxi, **10:**60–66
organization of, **7:**111–112
sizes, **9:**194–195
unitary status, **3:**2, **3:**6, **3:**7, **3:**9
See also Financing; School boards; Superintendents; Urban school districts
School finance. *See* Financing
School governance. *See* Governance
School improvement industry, **7:**170–171, **7:**173–174
School improvement networks, **7:**167–168, **7:**174
School law
applied, **8:**xv–xviii
evolving nature, **8:**xv, **8:**xviii, **8:**xxv–xxvi
future of, **8:**xxv–xxvi
precedents, **8:**xviii
research methods, **8:**xv
See also Rights; State laws
School Ministries, Inc., **4:**162
School resource officers (SROs)
activities, **5:**170, **5:**171
administrators and, **5:**164, **5:**173–174
arrests made, **5:**158, **5:**161–162
concerns about, **5:**157–158, **5:**161–165, **5:**174
increased number, **5:**xxii–xxiii, **5:**168
law enforcement function, **5:**157–174
multiple roles, **5:**160, **5:**166–174
supervision, **5:**157, **5:**173
teaching role, **5:**169
training, **5:**163, **5:**164, **5:**165, **5:**166, **5:**170–173
triad model, **5:**160, **5:**165, **5:**166–167, **5:**168–169

School takeovers
  by courts, **6**:xxii, **7**:xxiii, **7**:14, **7**:63
  increase in, **7**:xxiii–xxiv
  by mayors, **7**:7, **7**:14–15, **7**:19
  by state governments, **7**:3, **7**:14, **7**:17–19, **9**:224
School turnaround specialists, **9**:129
School years
  of charter schools, **1**:5
  extending, **1**:237, **1**:240–241, **1**:248
  four-day weeks, **9**:200
  lengths, **1**:237, **7**:35, **7**:222
  of private schools, **1**:78–79
  traditional calendar, **1**:xvii, **1**:236, **1**:250–251
  year-round schools, **1**:xxvii–xxviii, **1**:5, **1**:236–253
  See also Holidays
School-based accounting, **6**:57
School-based management (SBM), **6**:50–52, **6**:55–56
  See also Autonomy
Schoolmasters, **7**:xxii
Schools
  adequate yearly progress assessments, **2**:9, **3**:99, **3**:103, **9**:6, **9**:61, **9**:277
  capital improvements, **3**:6–7
  construction bonds, **6**:22, **6**:25, **6**:32, **6**:37
  equal access to buildings, **2**:201, **2**:202, **4**:xxvi–xxvii, **4**:50, **4**:74, **4**:81, **4**:216–231, **4**:233–248
  See also Autonomy; Charter schools; Magnet schools; Private schools
School-to-prison pipeline, **5**:33–34, **5**:44–45, **5**:162
Schott Foundation for Public Education, **3**:86
Schuster, Jack H., **3**:50
Schwartz, Brian, **1**:118
Science
  collaboration in, **2**:91
  creative thinking, **2**:170
  curricula, **4**:31
  evolution, **1**:116, **4**:xxv, **4**:184–199
  instructional approaches, **2**:96–97
  project-based, **2**:96
  standardized test scores, **2**:104–105, **9**:237, **9**:238, **9**:239, **9**:255
  standards, **9**:59
  textbooks, **2**:104–105
  view of natural world, **2**:240
Science, Technology, Engineering, and Mathematics (STEM)
  career education, **1**:217, **1**:225, **1**:231–232
  corporate investments, **9**:246, **9**:247, **9**:249–250
  curricula, **9**:225
  female students, **3**:211, **3**:213
  freedom in instruction, **2**:95–96, **2**:99
  gifted students, **2**:159–160, **2**:164–166, **2**:167
  global leadership in, **2**:103–105
  high schools focused on, **9**:42, **9**:225, **9**:249–250
  improving instruction in, **2**:32, **2**:92, **2**:106, **9**:225
  instructional approaches, **2**:96–98
  international competition, **2**:90–106
  Race to the Top and, **2**:90–106
  single-sex classes, **1**:183, **1**:185, **1**:186, **1**:187, **1**:188
  teacher training, **3**:xxii–xxiii
  Trends in International Math and Science Study, **7**:213, **7**:259, **9**:23, **9**:30, **9**:255
  unequal access to education in, **2**:93
  virtual simulations, **2**:235
  See also Mathematics; Technology
Sclar, Elliot, **7**:184
Scopes Monkey Trial, **4**:xxv, **4**:185, **4**:196
Scott, Rick, **6**:252, **6**:253
Scott v. Montgomery County Board of Education, **5**:83
Scruggs, Thomas, **2**:179
Seal v. Morgan, **5**:20
Searches, reasonable, **8**:57, **8**:61–62, **8**:67–68, **10**:101, **10**:102–104
  See also Drug testing; Fourth Amendment; Video surveillance cameras
Sease v. School District of Philadelphia, **4**:226–227
Sebastian, James, **7**:106
SEC. *See* Surveys of the Enacted Curriculum
Sechler v. State College Area School District, **4**:115, **4**:118
Seclusion. *See* Time-outs
Second language acquisition (SLA), **3**:198–200, **3**:204–205
Second Life, **2**:217, **2**:231

Secondary schools. *See* High schools; Middle schools
Sectarian schools. *See* Faith-based charter schools; Religious schools
Security, **5:**11
  See also Safety; Video surveillance cameras
Security officers, **5:**163
  See also School resource officers
Sefton-Green, Julian, **2:**214–215
Segregated schools
  charter schools, **1:**16, **1:**24, **1:**31–32, **1:**51, **3:**56, **3:**70, **6:**254, **6:**277, **7:**52–53
  closures, **3:**261
  consequences, **3:**230, **7:**62
  court rulings, **3:**xxi, **3:**1–17, **7:**61, **7:**62–64, **7:**66
  de jure, **3:**13, **7:**67
  for-profit schools, **1:**87
  history, **1:**22, **3:**xxi, **3:**1, **3:**4, **3:**12
  lower quality, **3:**4
  magnet schools, **1:**174–175
  poor students, **3:**108
  private, **6:**254
  in Reconstruction era, **7:**2
  resegregation, **1:**51, **3:**7, **3:**8, **3:**11, **3:**14–15, **3:**231, **3:**248, **7:**61, **7:**63
  segregated communities and, **1:**31–32, **3:**16, **3:**86, **7:**61, **7:**63
  self-segregation, **1:**20
  "separate, but equal" doctrine, **1:**20, **1:**23, **3:**xxi, **3:**4, **3:**5, **3:**10, **3:**12, **7:**2, **7:**62, **7:**70–71
  in southern states, **1:**22, **3:**1, **3:**4, **3:**5, **3:**12, **7:**xviii–xix, **7:**2
  in suburbs, **3:**9, **3:**16
  teachers, **3:**261
  See also Desegregation; Ethnocentric charter schools; Native American schools; Single-sex schools and classes
Segregation, residential, **1:**31–32, **3:**16, **3:**86, **6:**18–19, **7:**61, **7:**63
SEI. *See* Structured English Immersion
Senge, Peter, **7:**79
Separation of powers, **6:**151–152, **6:**168, **6:**201, **6:**202–203
Serna, Carolina, **3:**45
Serrano v. Priest, **3:**179, **6:**28, **6:**64, **6:**168–169, **6:**200, **9:**191
Servant leadership, **7:**101

Sex. *See* Gender; Single-sex schools and classes
Sex discrimination. *See* Gender discrimination
Sexting, **2:**208, **8:**157, **10:**xxiii, **10:**147–148
Sexton, Robert, **7:**256
Sexual abuse
  effects, **5:**92
  in schools, **5:**95, **5:**97–98, **8:**166
  signs of, **5:**95
  See also Abuse and neglect; Sexual misconduct charges
Sexual assault, by teachers, **10:**202
Sexual harassment
  definition, **8:**149–150, **8:**155–156
  deliberate indifference standard, **5:**67
  impact, **8:**150–151
  legal cases, **8:**145–146, **8:**147–148, **8:**152–153, **8:**154–155
  peer-to-peer, **8:**145, **8:**148, **8:**154–155, **8:**157
  policies on, **8:**149–150, **8:**153–154
  prevalence, **8:**150, **8:**156–157
  prevention responsibility, **5:**55–56, **5:**67–68, **5:**86
  on social media, **8:**157
  teacher-on-student, **8:**145, **8:**147–148, **8:**152–154, **8:**156–157
  tests for liability, **8:**xvii, **8:**144–158
  zero tolerance policies, **10:**161
Sexual misconduct charges
  false, **8:**xxiii, **8:**160–161, **8:**162, **8:**169–170, **8:**172–174
  investigations, **8:**xxiii, **8:**164–165, **8:**168, **8:**170–172
  as public records, **8:**xxiii, **8:**160–174
  reasons for disclosure, **8:**164–169, **8:**170
  reasons for nondisclosure, **8:**165, **8:**169–174
  student complaints, **8:**166–167, **8:**168
  teacher dismissals, **8:**161, **8:**165
  types of conduct, **8:**166
Sexuality, **2:**202, **2:**207
  See also LGBT youth
Shakeshaft, Charol, **7:**103, **7:**105, **10:**202
Shakespeare, William, **4:**172
Shakrani, Sharif, **9:**31
Shanker, Albert, **1:**2, **9:**33
Shapiro, Svi, **2:**xxi
Shariff, Abusaleh, **1:**56
Shariff, Shaheen, **10:**189–190
Shelton v. Tucker, **4:**128

Shen, Francis X., **7**:5, **7**:7, **7**:17, **7**:258
Sherman v. Community Consolidated School District 21 of Wheeling Township, **4**:138
Sherman v. Koch, **4**:49–50, **4**:68, **4**:75, **4**:79
Shift age, **9**:195–196
Shmurak, Carole, **1**:192
Shreve, David, **9**:25
Shulman, L., **3**:44
Siddiqui, Shahid, **1**:56
Siegel-Hawley, Genevieve, **7**:52
Sielke, Catherine C., **6**:37
Sikhs, **4**:267–268, **4**:276, **4**:277, **4**:288
Singer, Alan, **8**:252
Single-sex schools and classes
 benefits of, **1**:180, **1**:184–188
 history, **1**:184
 interest in, **1**:xxvi
 learning styles and, **1**:180, **1**:185
 legal issues, **1**:181, **1**:183–184, **1**:190–191
 number of, **1**:181
 opposition, **1**:xxvi, **1**:189–195
 private schools, **1**:181
 public schools, **1**:180–195
 research on, **1**:184–188, **1**:191–193
 school climates, **1**:192–193
 teacher preparation, **1**:188
SIS. *See* Student information systems
Skiba, R. J., **5**:206
Skills
 arts education and, **2**:145–149, **2**:150
 creative thinking, **2**:169–170, **2**:172–173
 critical thinking, **9**:18–19
 needed for future, **1**:xxvii, **1**:229, **7**:54
 technology-related, **2**:237, **2**:40, **10**:64, **10**:216, **10**:217–218, **10**:220, **10**:221–222
Skinner v. Labor Railway Executives' Association, **8**:63, **8**:77, **8**:78, **8**:83, **8**:84
Skoros v. City of New York, **1**:26, **1**:31
Skype, **10**:199
SLA. *See* Second language acquisition
Slaughterhouse Cases, **7**:66
Slavin, Robert E., **2**:112, **3**:155–156, **3**:163–164
SLD. *See* Specific learning disabled students
Sloan Consortium, **10**:xviii
Smartphones. *See* Mobile technologies
Smith, Adam, **6**:29–30, **6**:32, **6**:34, **6**:268

Smith, Marshall S., **7**:172
Smith, Thomas M., **9**:136
Smith-Hughes Act, **1**:216, **1**:219, **3**:127
SMPY. *See* Study of Mathematically Precocious Youth
Smuts, Gary, **9**:164–165
Snell, Julia, **2**:220
Snyder, Rick, **10**:61
Social capital, **7**:202–204
Social cohesion, **6**:18–19
Social Darwinism, **3**:153
Social justice, **7**:106–107
Social media. *See* Social networking sites
Social mobility, **6**:xxvi, **6**:226, **6**:263–264, **7**:222–223
Social networking sites
 ADA compliance, **10**:201–202
 cyberbullying, **5**:63–64, **10**:xxv, **10**:147, **10**:203, **10**:205
 definition, **10**:135, **10**:175, **10**:192
 disciplining students for activity on, **8**:180, **8**:183, **8**:184–185, **10**:174–190, **10**:204–205
 educating students on use of, **10**:176–177, **10**:184, **10**:190
 educational benefits, **10**:xxiii–xxiv, **10**:40
 free speech rights on, **8**:182–183, **10**:178, **10**:180–182, **10**:187, **10**:204–206
 legal issues, **10**:203–206
 misuse of, **10**:142–143, **10**:147–149, **10**:159, **10**:201, **10**:202, **10**:203
 parody profiles, **8**:182–183, **8**:184, **10**:159, **10**:169, **10**:180–181, **10**:183, **10**:187, **10**:190, **10**:204
 permanence of information, **10**:176, **10**:182–183
 policies on teachers' use, **10**:137, **10**:138, **10**:140–146, **10**:150–151, **10**:202–203, **10**:205
 political impact, **2**:233, **10**:145
 restrictions on use in schools, **10**:xxiii, **10**:174–175
 safety concerns, **10**:xxiii, **10**:xxiv, **10**:xxv, **10**:174, **10**:202–203
 school promotion on, **10**:192–206
 sexting, **2**:208, **8**:157, **10**:xxiii, **10**:147–148
 sexual harassment, **8**:157
 student use of, **2**:219, **10**:62, **10**:159, **10**:169, **10**:174–190, **10**:192, **10**:197, **10**:204–206

teachers' use of, **10:**135–151, **10:**198–200, **10:**202–203, **10:**205–206
usage, **10:**136, **10:**178, **10:**182, **10:**195
Social networks
  face-to-face, **10:**139
  learning networks, **10:**140–141, **10:**198–199
Social services agencies, **8:**135, **8:**165
Social studies curricula, **8:**6
Sociocultural learning theory, **2:**11–14
Socioeconomic classes. *See* Economic classes; Low socioeconomic groups; Middle class
Soft skills, **7:**54
Soltero, Anthony, **5:**84
Sonny Bono Copyright Term Extension Act, **8:**25
South Dakota, finance litigation, **3:**181–182
South Dakota v. Dole, **6:**77, **6:**87–88, **6:**89, **6:**90, **6:**91, **6:**92
Southern Education Foundation, **3:**107
Southern Regional Education Board (SREB), **10:**119, **10:**125
Southern states
  education systems, **7:**xviii, **7:**2, **7:**64–65
  school districts, **7:**112
  segregated schools, **7:**xviii–xix, **7:**2
Southern University, **3:**262, **3:**264
Southwest Airlines, **10:**202
Soviet Union, Sputnik launch, **1:**xvii, **1:**1, **6:**197, **7:**216, **7:**217
Spanierman v. Hughes, **10:**205
Spanish language, **1:**50, **2:**109, **2:**110, **2:**112–113, **2:**114, **2:**117, **2:**125
  See also Bilingual education
Spanos, William V., **10:**26
Speak Up National Research Project, **10:**xviii–xix
Special education
  adequate yearly progress goals and, **6:**104, **6:**106
  in charter schools, **1:**16
  costs, **6:**xxv, **6:**93–95, **6:**97–98, **6:**100–101, **6:**102, **6:**107–108
  definition, **2:**183, **6:**96
  educational malpractice claims, **8:**214
  equity, **6:**95, **6:**98–99
  funding, **6:**xxv–xxvi, **6:**93–108, **6:**248
  general education compared to, **2:**177–193, **8:**108–125
  goals, **2:**191

history, **6:**102–103
instructional approaches, **2:**178–179
legal requirements, **2:**183, **6:**xxiv–xxv
local funding, **6:**97–98, **6:**99
mental health interventions, **5:**253–254, **5:**260
need for, **8:**113–114, **8:**115–116, **8:**117
number of students, **6:**100, **6:**104–107
overrepresentation of minority students, **3:**169, **5:**38, **7:**81
in private schools, **6:**101, **6:**106–107, **6:**247–248
in religious schools, **4:**7, **4:**19, **4:**28
resource rooms, **8:**122–123
separate classes, **2:**181–186, **8:**113–116, **8:**117, **8:**119–120, **8:**121
service reductions, **6:**100–101
state funding, **6:**98–99, **6:**100, **6:**108, **6:**188
teachers, **2:**178, **2:**179, **3:**247, **7:**46, **8:**115, **8:**122
voucher programs and, **6:**247–248
  See also Assistive technology
Special populations. *See* Disabilities, students with; Emotional and behavioral disorders; Internalizing disorders
Specialized schools. *See* Magnet schools
Specific learning disabled (SLD) students, **6:**105, **6:**107
  See also Learning disabilities
Speight, Suzette L., **3:**32–33
Spelling, **2:**85–87, **2:**112–113
  See also English language arts; Literacy
Spellings, Margaret, **1:**183–184
Sports. *See* Athletics
Springer, Matthew G., **3:**174, **6:**134
Springfield Township v. Quick, **6:**182
Sputnik, **1:**xvii, **1:**1, **6:**197, **7:**216, **7:**217
Squire, Kurt, **10:**46
SROs. *See* School resource officers
Stakeholders, parents as, **9:**268–269, **9:**271–273
Standardized Testing and Reporting (STAR) research project, **9:**199
Standardized tests
  bias in, **2:**65–67
  charter school scores, **1:**10, **1:**12, **6:**289
  computerized, **2:**238–239
  criticism of, **2:**64, **2:**65–70, **9:**2
  curricular alignment, **2:**55–70, **6:**80–81, **8:**13, **8:**14, **9:**5

goals, **2:**59
history, **2:**65
improved scores, **9:**8–9, **9:**23
inflated scores, **9:**24, **9:**230
international comparisons,
  2:102–103, **9:**29–30, **9:**57, **9:**220,
  9:237–239, **9:**254–255
magnet school student scores, **1:**169,
  1:170
NCLB requirements, **6:**127, **7:**44
overuse of scores, **9:**230
special education student performance,
  6:104
as teacher effectiveness measures,
  2:59–60, **2:**63–64, **2:**69,
  9:139–140, **9:**143
for teacher licensing, **3:**262
teaching to tests, **1:**249, **2:**55–70, **6:**139,
  7:45, **7:**51, **7:**218, **9:**10, **9:**59
test-taking skills, **2:**67–68, **9:**10
tracking based on, **3:**150, **3:**161
See also Achievement gaps; National
  Assessments of Educational
  Progress
Standards
  academic performance and, **9:**30–31
  dumbed down, **9:**11
  global competitiveness and, **9:**20–35
  for online courses, **10:**119, **10:**125,
    10:129
  parental involvement, **9:**266,
    9:267–271, **9:**273, **9:**275–278
  state, **6:**81–82, **6:**177, **9:**xx–xxi, **9:**5,
    9:23–24, **9:**26–27, **9:**30
  for teacher qualifications, **9:**xxii, **9:**61
  teacher support, **2:**23
  for teacher training programs, **2:**40,
    2:42, **2:**43, **2:**51, **3:**262
  for teachers, **9:**59
  value of, **2:**55
  See also Curriculum standards; Teacher
    training standards; Technology
    standards
Standards for Advanced Programs in
  Educational Leadership, **7:**97
Standards-based reform
  components, **2:**58–59
  contradiction with culturally relevant
    instruction, **3:**70, **3:**71–72
  criticism of, **9:**18–19
  increasing expectations, **9:**58–59
  innovation and, **9:**37–52

instructional impact, **2:**59, **9:**xix
NCLB provisions, **2:**56–57, **2:**58,
  3:98–99, **7:**43–45, **7:**114, **7:**253,
  9:xxvii–xxviii, **9:**18
in past, **2:**xxvi–xxvii, **2:**56–57, **9:**xviii,
  9:xxvii–xxviii, **9:**28–29, **9:**39
positive effects on academic
  performance, **9:**4–5
proponents, **9:**xviii–xix
unintended consequences, **9:**xix–xx
value-added measures, **9:**7–8, **9:**85
See also Accountability
Standards-based testing
  accountability and, **2:**26, **2:**94
  advantages, **9:**10
  assumptions, **2:**153
  developing, **6:**80–81, **7:**229–230
  limitations, **2:**98–99, **10:**127–128,
    10:130
Stanford University, **1:**12, **9:**91
Stanford–Binet IQ test, **2:**65
Stanley, Julian C., **2:**164
STAR. *See* Standardized Testing and
  Reporting research project
Stark, Andrew, **4:**12
Starosta, Kristin, **5:**238
State constitutions
  bans on aid to religious schools, **1:**95,
    1:96, **2:**199, **4:**4
  church-state separation, **6:**250–251,
    6:267–268
  differences from U.S. Constitution,
    6:156–157
  equal protection, **6:**168, **6:**172
  interpretations, **6:**156–158, **6:**163–177
  religious freedom, **1:**47, **4:**58, **4:**111
State constitutions, education clauses
  adequacy, **6:**152, **6:**170–171, **6:**184,
    6:202–203
  basic principles, **6:**1–2, **7:**68
  efficiency, **6:**169
  enforceability, **6:**163–177
  equality, **6:**xviii–xix, **6:**xxiv–xxv, **6:**1–2,
    6:22, **6:**60, **6:**148, **6:**152
  equity suits and, **6:**xxi, **6:**152
  free public education, **6:**144,
    6:233–234
  interpretations, **6:**157–158, **6:**164,
    6:167–168, **6:**169–170, **6:**173, **6:**203
  limits on legislative discretion,
    6:185–186
  local control, **6:**xix, **6:**2, **6:**22–23, **6:**60

Index **381**

right to education, **3:**179, **6:**144, **6:**148, **6:**185
uniformity requirement, **6:**251, **6:**252–253
variations, **6:**xx, **6:**156, **6:**170, **6:**197
State courts
  adequacy suits, **3:**180–181, **6:**152, **6:**169, **6:**170–171, **6:**194–203, **6:**204–206, **6:**209, **9:**193–194, **9:**204
  compliance with rulings, **6:**153
  constitutional interpretation, **6:**152, **6:**156–158, **6:**163–177
  education role, **6:**150–154, **6:**160, **7:**69
  equity suits, **3:**xxxvi, **3:**170, **3:**180–182, **6:**xxi, **6:**14, **6:**25, **6:**152, **6:**194, **9:**191
  extracurricular activity fee cases, **6:**218
  judicial review, **6:**156
  jurisdictions, **8:**xviii
  school financing cases, **6:**143–161, **6:**184–185
  See also Judicial branch
State governments
  administrator certification, **7:**93, **7:**94, **7:**95, **7:**99
  charter school regulations, **1:**xxii, **1:**15, **1:**23–24, **6:**276–291, **7:**138–139, **7:**140–142
  control of schools, **6:**xviii, **6:**xx, **7:**xxiv–xxv, **7:**7, **7:**8, **7:**9, **7:**68–69
  curriculum decisions, **2:**18–33
  curriculum standards, **2:**21, **2:**61–62, **8:**12–13, **8:**14, **8:**17, **9:**5, **10:**128
  debt limits on school districts, **6:**21–38
  discipline regulations, **5:**xix, **5:**219, **5:**222
  education agencies, **7:**172–173
  education oversight, **6:**13, **6:**14, **6:**28–29, **6:**114–115, **7:**xviii–xix, **7:**1–2, **9:**54
  education standards, **6:**81–82, **6:**177, **9:**xx–xxi, **9:**23–24, **9:**26–27, **9:**30
  education tax credits, **6:**258–274
  in federal system, **6:**76–77, **6:**114–115, **7:**61–62, **7:**64
  free appropriate public education standards, **8:**109–110
  gifted education mandates, **6:**110, **6:**113, **6:**115–116, **6:**117, **6:**119
  governance roles, **2:**19, **7:**245–246, **7:**250
  higher education funding, **6:**237
  holidays, **4:**202

homeschooling regulations, **1:**xxv, **1:**109–123
interventions in low-performing schools, **9:**224
investment in education, **9:**216, **9:**218–225
NCLB report cards, **7:**46, **9:**xix–xxi
online learning policies, **10:**xx–xxi, **10:**62
property taxes, **6:**72
roles in education system, **6:**13–14, **9:**215–232
school boards and, **7:**111, **7:**112
school takeovers, **7:**3, **7:**14, **7:**17–19, **9:**224
school uniform policies, **8:**38
sovereign powers, **6:**76–77
suicide prevention programs, **5:**72
taxes, **6:**64, **6:**65, **6:**67, **6:**68, **6:**74, **6:**189–190, **7:**209
teacher licensing, **9:**85
teacher training regulations, **2:**39–40, **2:**43–44, **9:**72, **9:**77–79, **9:**80, **9:**88–89
Tenth Amendment and, **6:**86, **6:**114, **7:**1–2, **7:**40, **7:**68
See also Financing, state
State laws
  abuse and neglect reporting, **5:**89, **5:**96, **5:**98
  adequate education, **6:**205–206
  antibullying, **5:**56, **5:**63, **5:**64, **5:**65, **10:**147, **10:**154, **10:**155, **10:**162–163, **10:**165–166
  charter schools, **1:**19, **1:**24, **1:**35–36, **1:**48–49, **6:**xxiv, **6:**279, **6:**286, **6:**290–291, **7:**130–132, **7:**133–134
  corporal punishment bans, **5:**xviii, **5:**107, **5:**110, **5:**111–112, **5:**116–117
  on discipline policies, **5:**xviii, **5:**xix, **5:**xx, **5:**xxv, **5:**219, **5:**222, **5:**224, **10:**161–162
  on dress codes, **5:**11–12, **8:**42, **8:**43, **8:**45
  on "English-only" instruction, **2:**119, **2:**122, **3:**190, **3:**192, **3:**193, **3:**200
  on evolution instruction, **4:**185, **4:**196–197
  on homeschooling, **1:**113–114, **1:**118, **1:**121
  on immigration, **2:**134–135, **2:**139
  on maximum class sizes, **6:**228

on moments of silence, **4:**49–50, **4:**67, **4:**68, **4:**71–73, **4:**74–75, **4:**78–79
privacy protection, **10:**108
on private schools, **1:**73
public employment relations, **8:**245, **8:**248, **8:**258
on public records, **8:**161
teacher protection, **5:**178–179, **5:**183–184, **5:**191
on teacher tenure, **8:**228–229, **8:**232–233
See also Compulsory education laws
State legislatures
education funding process, **3:**172, **3:**178
education governance role, **7:**68, **9:**215–216
educational failures, **6:**148–149
judicial branch and, **6:**168, **6:**175
school finance obligations, **6:**164, **6:**185–186
state content standards, **6:**177
See also Financing, state
State of Indiana ex rel. Anderson v. Brand, **8:**229
State superintendents, **7:**xx
State v. Epperson, **4:**196
State v. Mizner, **5:**107
State v. Patzer, **1:**116, **1:**119
Stecher, Brian, **2:**58
Steifel, Leanna, **3:**173
Steinberg, Joel, **5:**90
Steinberg, Lawrence, **9:**268
Steiner, Rudolf, **2:**155
STEM. *See* Science, Technology, Engineering, and Mathematics
Stephenson, Brianna, **5:**14
Stephenson v. Davenport Community School District, **5:**14–15
Stereotypes
of at-risk students, **2:**226
cultural differences, **2:**128–130, **3:**147
gender-based, **1:**190
of gifted students, **6:**119
of minority students, **3:**32, **3:**147, **3:**156
of Muslims, **1:**67
of student technology use, **2:**226
Stern, Sol, **1:**102
Sterzing v. Fort Bend Independent School District, **8:**7
Stevenson, Adlai, **6:**232–233
Stone, Addison, **2:**12

Stone, Deborah, **7:**183
Stone, James, **1:**222
Stone v. Graham, **4:**xxii–xxiii, **4:**113, **4:**120, **4:**124, **4:**131–132
STOs. *See* Student tuition organizations
Stout, Robert T., **3:**245
Stovall, David, **3:**140, **3:**142
Strasser, Mark, **4:**28, **4:**31
Stratechuk v. Board of Education, South Orange-Maplewood School District, **4:**47–48, **4:**104, **4:**116
Street, Brian, **2:**xxvi
Strickland, Ted, **10:**87
Strong American Schools, **6:**303
Structured English Immersion (SEI), **2:**112, **2:**119–120
Stuart v. Nappi, **8:**93–94
Student achievement. *See* Academic performance
Student engagement
ability grouping and, **3:**155
cultural relevance and, **3:**145
curricula and, **2:**15
levels, **10:**37
popular culture use and, **3:**141
in reading instruction, **2:**78–79
technology use and, **10:**41, **10:**47
Student information systems (SIS), **10:**94
Student loan forgiveness programs
arguments against gender-based, **3:**266–271
conditions, **3:**265–266
criteria, **3:**266, **3:**267, **3:**268
gender-based, **3:**255–272
Higher Education Act, **3:**265
history, **3:**265
National Defense Student Loan Program, **3:**265–266
Teacher Recruitment and Retention Act, **3:**264
Student teachers, **9:**82, **9:**105
See also Teacher training
Student tuition organizations (STOs), **1:**98–100
Students, relationships to curricula, **2:**12–13, **2:**15
See also Disabilities, students with; Gifted students
Students of color. *See* Minority students

Study of Mathematically Precocious Youth (SMPY), **2:**164–165
StumbleUpon, **10:**195, **10:**199
Suárez-Orozco, Marcelo M., **2:**131
Substance abuse. *See* Alcohol; Drugs
Suburban school districts
   flight to, **3:**16
   gifted education, **6:**117
   revenue sources, **6:**74
   segregated schools, **3:**9, **3:**16
Success for All, **1:**83, **2:**19, **2:**112, **3:**239
Successful schools studies, **6:**207–208
Sugai, George, **5:**234
Suicide, student
   internalizing disorders and, **5:**251
   litigation on, **5:**80–85
   prevalence, **5:**74, **5:**252
   related to bullying, **5:**xxiii, **5:**55, **5:**64, **5:**86, **10:**147, **10:**157
   students considering, **5:**251–252, **10:**157
Suicide prevention
   community-based efforts, **5:**74–75
   district policies, **5:**72, **5:**77, **5:**80
   educator responsibility, **5:**xxii, **5:**71–86
   legal duty, **5:**76–78, **5:**80–82
   moral duty, **5:**75–76, **5:**80, **5:**85–86
   school-based programs, **5:**76, **5:**78, **5:**254
   strategies, **5:**78–79
   warning signs, **5:**76, **5:**78–79
Summer school, **3:**88
Summers
   enrichment activities, **1:**251, **1:**252
   Jewish camps, **1:**126, **1:**132–133, **1:**136, **1:**139
   learning losses, **1:**241, **1:**242, **1:**243–244, **1:**250–251, **3:**88
Sunderman, Gail, **7:**51
Superintendents
   administration preparation programs, **7:**95, **7:**233, **7:**237–238
   changes affecting, **7:**xxi
   hiring of, **7:**93, **7:**125
   history, **7:**xx–xxi, **7:**6, **7:**12–13, **9:**13
   from non-educational backgrounds, **7:**xxi, **7:**xxiv, **7:**225–243, **9:**133–134
   relations with local governments, **7:**xx–xxi
   relations with school boards, **7:**13, **7:**125
   roles and responsibilities, **7:**xx, **7:**232–233, **7:**236

shortage of qualified candidates, **7:**226, **7:**232, **7:**241
   skills and knowledge needed, **7:**124–125, **7:**227, **7:**231, **7:**232–233, **7:**235
   state, **7:**xx
   women, **7:**104
   See also Administrators
Support services. *See* Counselors; Full-service community schools
Supreme Court, U.S.
   appointments, **7:**71–72
   constitutional interpretation, **6:**164
   desegregation views, **3:**7–8, **3:**10
   judicial review, **6:**148, **6:**156–157, **7:**69–70, **7:**73
   rulings, **8:**xviii
   sexual harassment liability tests, **8:**xvii, **8:**144–158
Supreme courts, state. *See* State courts
Surowiecki, James, **9:**229
Surveillance technology, **10:**103–104, **10:**111
   See also Video surveillance cameras
Surveys of the Enacted Curriculum (SEC), **2:**63
Suspensions
   due process requirements, **5:**xviii–xix, **5:**49–50
   increased number, **5:**31–32, **5:**199, **5:**202
   negative consequences, **5:**32, **5:**199–200, **5:**202–203
   racial disparities, **5:**32–33, **5:**37, **5:**40–42, **5:**43–44, **5:**47
   of students with disabilities, **8:**93–94, **8:**95, **8:**96–97, **8:**103
   See also Zero tolerance policies
Sutherland, Paul, **8:**249
Swann v. Charlotte-Mecklenburg Board of Education, **3:**xxvi, **3:**6, **6:**253
Swanson, Christopher B., **7:**51
Swanson, Elizabeth A., **2:**179
Swearer, Susan M., **5:**69, **5:**253
Switzer, Al, **7:**88
Sybouts, Ward, **7:**12
Symbolic speech, **4:**271–273
Symbols, religious. *See* Religious symbols
Systems theory, **7:**210
Systems thinking, **7:**200–201

Tallerico, Marilyn, **3:**245
Tanner, Daniel, **9:**17–18
Tanner, Laurel, **9:**17–18

Tao, Terence, **2:**159, **2:**165–166
TAP. *See* Teacher Advancement Program
Tarek ibn Ziyad Academy (TiZA), **1:**21, **1:**25–26, **1:**50
Tattoos, **5:**14–15
Tax credits, educational
  arguments for, **6:**258, **6:**261–268, **6:**269–270, **6:**271
  church-state separation issue, **6:**267–268, **6:**272–273
  criticism of, **6:**266–267, **6:**271–274
  deductions, **6:**259, **6:**261–262
  effects on state budgets, **6:**266
  legal cases, **1:**95, **1:**99–100, **1:**104, **4:**7
  for private school tuition, **1:**92, **1:**150, **4:**28, **6:**258–274
  qualified expenses, **6:**259, **6:**261–262
  restrictions and caps, **6:**266, **6:**271
  for scholarship fund donations, **1:**95, **1:**98–100, **1:**104, **6:**262, **6:**267, **6:**269, **6:**273
  target groups, **6:**259
  variations, **6:**259, **6:**269, **6:**271
Taxes
  additional local, **6:**1–19, **6:**27, **6:**180
  administration and compliance, **6:**65–66
  equity, **6:**66–67
  local, **6:**71, **6:**74, **6:**158–159, **7:**209
  sales, **6:**27, **6:**64, **6:**65, **6:**66, **6:**67, **6:**68, **6:**73
  variations among states, **6:**189–190
  yields, **6:**67–68
  See also Income taxes; Property taxes
Taylor, Carl S., **3:**138
Taylor, Linda, **5:**252
Taylor, Virgil, **3:**138
TBEA (test-based educational accountability). *See* Accountability; Standardized tests
TEAC. *See* Teacher Education Accreditation Council
TEACH Act. *See* Technology, Education and Copyright Harmonization Act
Teach For America (TFA)
  as alternative certification route, **9:**108
  evaluations, **9:**xxiv, **9:**112
  fees, **9:**114
  funding, **3:**38, **9:**68
  mission, **3:**xxiii, **9:**111
  number of participants, **9:**110
  operation of, **3:**51, **9:**102–103
  performance of teachers, **9:**xxii, **9:**xxiv, **9:**106, **9:**112–113
  retention, **9:**xxiv, **9:**111, **9:**113–114
  training approach, **9:**xxiii
Teacher Advancement Program (TAP), **6:**131
Teacher dismissals
  barriers, **8:**237–238, **8:**240–242
  in charter schools, **1:**6, **1:**17
  due process protection, **8:**xxiii–xxiv, **8:**228–243
  immorality charges, **8:**233–235
  of low performers, **9:**xxviii, **9:**170
  of nontenured teachers, **8:**232, **8:**235–236, **8:**239
  obstacles, **7:**25–26, **9:**xxiv–xxv, **9:**170, **9:**171
  for sexual misconduct, **8:**161, **8:**165
  speech-related issues, **8:**196, **8:**198, **8:**199, **8:**240
  of tenured teachers, **7:**25–26, **8:**228–230, **8:**232–235, **8:**238, **8:**240–241
  violations of teacher rights, **8:**233–236
Teacher education. *See* Teacher training
Teacher Education Accreditation Council (TEAC)
  accreditation process, **2:**40, **2:**44, **2:**46, **2:**47, **9:**72, **9:**90, **9:**93
  benefits of accreditation, **2:**50
  establishment, **2:**40, **2:**45–46
  merger with NCATE, **9:**80, **9:**91
  outcomes focus, **9:**89
  standards, **2:**42, **2:**46, **2:**51
Teacher hiring
  at charter schools, **1:**17, **7:**132, **7:**140–141
  criteria, **7:**84, **9:**168, **9:**169
  number needed, **9:**110
  by principals, **6:**47, **7:**30
  at private schools, **1:**77, **1:**158
  qualifications, **9:**xxiii–xxiv, **9:**13, **9:**61
  recruitment, **3:**38, **3:**260, **3:**264, **3:**271, **6:**132, **6:**137, **6:**139, **9:**xxiii–xxiv, **9:**223
  rules in collective bargaining agreements, **7:**35
  shortages of qualified candidates, **3:**40
  technology standards used in, **10:**122
  See also Teacher salaries and benefits
Teacher Incentive Fund (TIF), **6:**134, **7:**36–37
Teacher licensing
  exams, **2:**51

homeschooling and, **1:**109–110, **1:**115, **1:**119
standardized tests, **3:**262
standards, **2:**39, **9:**87
state requirements, **2:**49, **9:**85
Teacher licensing, alternative routes
criticism of, **9:**xxiv, **9:**96–97, **9:**110–111, **9:**112–114, **9:**136
definition, **9:**107–108
history, **9:**99–101
models, **3:**40, **9:**102–104, **9:**106, **9:**108
number of hires, **3:**56, **9:**101
Race to the Top funding, **3:**56
rationale for, **9:**99–101, **9:**109–110
results, **8:**16, **9:**95–116
supporters, **2:**49, **3:**38–39, **9:**xxii, **9:**xxiii, **9:**71–72, **9:**96, **9:**98–107, **9:**111–112
See also Teach For America
Teacher Performance Assessment Consortium (TPAC), **9:**91–92
Teacher performance evaluations
in alternative licensing programs, **9:**105–106
certification based on, **9:**106
characteristics of high quality teaching, **9:**151–153
collective bargaining agreements and, **8:**239
financial rewards, **9:**171, **9:**173
ineffective, **9:**170
measures, **9:**106, **9:**139, **9:**142, **9:**144–145, **9:**151–153
merit pay and, **6:**136–137
Race to the Top, **3:**62, **3:**63, **3:**66, **9:**xxviii, **9:**75
standards, **3:**63, **9:**91
student achievement measures, **2:**69, **9:**xx, **9:**62, **9:**84–85, **9:**139–140
technology standards and, **10:**116–117
value-added models, **9:**7–8, **9:**139–155
Teacher Protection Act. *See* Coverdell Teacher Protection Act
Teacher protection acts (TPAs)
effects, **5:**179, **5:**184–185
federal, **5:**177–178, **5:**183, **5:**190–191
limitations, **5:**178, **5:**183, **5:**186, **5:**187, **5:**190–191
need for, **5:**177–191
state, **5:**178–179, **5:**183–184, **5:**191
Teacher Recruitment and Retention Act, **3:**264

Teacher rights
antidiscrimination laws, **8:**241
due process, **8:**xxiii–xxiv, **8:**228–243
limits on, **4:**54, **4:**260, **4:**295–296, **4:**297
privacy, **8:**75, **8:**79, **8:**85–86, **8:**160–162, **8:**164, **8:**165–167, **8:**168–169, **8:**172, **10:**140
religious freedom, **4:**56–59, **4:**91, **4:**92, **4:**93–94, **4:**284–285, **4:**288–289, **4:**294
See also Academic freedom; Free speech rights of teachers
Teacher salaries and benefits
averages, **9:**206
in charter schools, **1:**14
collective bargaining agreements, **7:**29, **7:**36–37, **8:**255–256, **9:**171–172
decline in, **6:**46–47, **7:**210
disparities between schools, **6:**46–47
in for-profit schools, **1:**83
gender and, **3:**256, **3:**263, **3:**264, **7:**36
in Head Start, **1:**213
increasing, **3:**xxiii, **3:**38, **3:**264, **3:**271
international comparisons, **6:**140
public views of, **8:**245
racial discrimination in, **7:**23
retirement plans, **7:**210
teacher quality and, **7:**210
See also Performance pay
Teacher training
in Bible as literature, **4:**179–180, **4:**181
cooperating teacher quality, **9:**82
disciplinary measures, **5:**221, **5:**228
for diversity, **2:**43
effectiveness, **9:**xxi–xxiv
evolution, **7:**94, **9:**13–15
for gifted education, **6:**121, **6:**122–123
identifying and reporting abuse and neglect, **5:**94, **5:**101–102
identifying internalizing disorders, **5:**249, **5:**256
reform proposals, **9:**xxii, **9:**xxiii–xxiv, **9:**69, **9:**84–85
shortcomings, **9:**74, **9:**75, **9:**82–84, **9:**86, **9:**99–100, **9:**101, **9:**111
in technology, **2:**235–236, **10:**121–122, **10:**123–124, **10:**216, **10:**224
See also Professional development
Teacher training programs
accountability, **2:**39, **2:**43, **9:**71–93
admissions standards, **9:**72, **9:**82, **9:**89, **9:**95–96, **9:**101

advanced degrees, 2:43, 3:49
assessments, 2:41–42
calls for reform, 2:37, 7:221, 9:115–116, 9:195
characteristics, 3:44–45
clinical experiences, 2:42
compared to alternative licensing routes, 3:46–47, 9:96–97, 9:108–109, 9:112
criticism of, 3:48–49, 3:50–52
curricula, 2:36, 2:43
diversity of faculty, 3:50
diversity of students, 3:260, 3:262–263
diversity training, 3:37–52
at elite institutions, 3:xxii–xxiii
at historically Black institutions, 3:262
improvements, 2:40–42, 2:44, 2:50–51
innovation in, 2:48, 2:52
institutional oversight, 9:83–84
instructional approaches, 3:50–51
men in, 3:256, 3:257
mentoring, 9:223
multiple approaches, 9:82
number of, 9:74, 9:75, 9:93
performance measures, 2:51, 9:84–85
rankings, 3:47
recruitment, 3:256, 3:257, 3:260
reporting by, 2:47, 2:48, 2:50, 9:75
research and development, 3:45–46, 3:50–51
standards, 2:40, 2:42, 2:43, 2:51, 3:262
state oversight, 2:39–40, 2:43–44, 9:72, 9:77–79, 9:80, 9:88–89
STEM programs, 3:xxii–xxiii
student loan forgiveness, 3:255–272
See also Accreditation
Teacher training standards, 9:71–93
of accreditation bodies, 2:42, 2:43, 9:72, 9:79–83, 9:90, 9:93
definition, 9:87
history, 9:88–90
outcome measures, 9:85, 9:88–89, 9:115
proposals, 9:84–85, 9:86, 9:90–92
of states, 9:72, 9:77–79
variability, 9:77–79, 9:83–84
Teachers
academic backgrounds, 2:22, 9:95–96, 9:99–100
accountability, 2:26
attracting talented candidates, 3:xxii–xxiii, 3:xxvi
autonomy, 3:71, 8:5, 8:8–9
bullying prevention responsibility, 5:xxiii, 5:56–57, 5:60–61, 5:64, 5:65, 5:66
at charter schools, 1:6, 1:17, 7:132, 7:140–141, 7:143
collaboration, 7:81, 7:83
conferences with parents, 7:84
crime victims, 5:24
cultural competence, 3:51, 3:144–145, 3:262–263, 7:82
curriculum development roles, 2:18–33, 3:42–43, 8:4–9
deprofessionalization, 2:69
diversity, 3:xxxvi–xxxvii, 3:259–262, 4:59
drug testing, 8:xxii, 8:74–88
in elementary schools, 7:36
for-profit management and, 7:181–182
in gifted education, 2:159
governance roles, 2:21–25, 7:xxii, 7:27
in high schools, 7:36, 7:157–158
highly-qualified, 2:178, 6:132, 7:45–46, 7:55, 7:82, 8:219, 8:222, 9:xxii, 9:86
in high-poverty schools, 3:107–108
impact of NCLB, 3:256, 7:45–46, 7:51–52
inexperienced, 2:4–5, 9:223
instructional discretion, 7:158–161
instructional leadership and, 7:152
job security, 8:232, 8:233, 8:241–242, 9:172–173
judgment, 8:16–17
leadership of, 1:76–77
liability protection, 5:xxiv–xxv, 5:177–191
limitations of, 2:28–30
at magnet schools, 1:170, 1:175
as mandated reporters of abuse and neglect, 5:xxvi, 5:91, 5:93–94, 5:96–97, 5:99–104
men, 3:259, 3:261, 3:263, 3:270–271
mentoring, 2:xxiii, 7:243, 9:223
minority group members, 7:23
motivations, 3:269
of online courses, 10:64, 10:92, 10:119, 10:125
peer assistance and review, 7:37
personal learning networks, 10:140–141, 10:198–199
personal records, 8:161–162
political views, 8:2, 8:7, 8:194, 8:208

practices of effective, **9**:145–146
prayer in schools, **4**:xxi, **4**:53–65
preschool, **1**:213
principals' support of, **7**:81, **7**:82, **7**:83
at private schools, **1**:77, **1**:157–158
public perceptions, **3**:256, **3**:257
relationships to curricula, **2**:13–15
religious activities, **4**:53–54, **4**:63, **4**:92, **4**:93, **4**:99
religious garb, **4**:xxvii–xxviii, **4**:92, **4**:93, **4**:276–277, **4**:284–298
religious materials distributed by, **4**:254, **4**:260–261
religious texts read by, **4**:xxii, **4**:85–101
replaced by technology, **10**:210
responsibility for achievement gap, **7**:51–52
retention, **3**:xxiii, **3**:270–271, **6**:132–133, **9**:223
roles in identifying internalizing disorders, **5**:248–263
schoolmasters, **7**:xxii
seniority, **7**:26, **7**:30
sexual harassment by, **8**:145, **8**:147–148, **8**:152–154, **8**:156–157
sexual misconduct by, **8**:xxiii, **8**:160–174
social media use, **10**:135–151, **10**:198–200, **10**:202–203, **10**:205–206
in special education, **2**:178, **2**:179, **3**:247, **7**:45, **8**:115, **8**:122
subject area knowledge, **2**:14, **2**:22, **2**:25
suicide prevention responsibility, **5**:xxii, **5**:71–72, **5**:78–79
transmission of knowledge, **2**:3
turnover, **1**:17, **1**:79, **1**:83, **6**:281, **7**:143, **9**:113–114
videotaping of in classrooms, **10**:102, **10**:112
voting in school board elections, **7**:9–10
women, **3**:255–257, **3**:259, **3**:269–270, **7**:94, **7**:97, **7**:101, **7**:104
See also Classroom management; Disciplinary measures; Instruction; Tenure
Teachers for a New Era (TNE), **9**:69
Teachers Insurance Annuity Association (TIAA), **9**:66, **9**:67
Teachers Union Reform Network (TURN), **7**:34
Teachers' unions
criticism of, **3**:58, **8**:xxiv, **8**:252–258
curriculum development roles, **2**:22
declining influence, **2**:19–20, **8**:245
differences from industrial unions, **7**:26
financing of school board elections, **7**:10
involvement in reform efforts, **8**:250, **9**:160, **9**:161, **9**:164–166
liability insurance, **5**:187
national standards and, **9**:29, **9**:34
political influence, **8**:245, **8**:249
positive impact, **8**:xxiv, **8**:247–252
Race to the Top and, **3**:63
roles, **8**:255, **9**:162, **9**:163–165, **9**:167
strength, **8**:244–245, **9**:160–161
strikes, **8**:255
structure, **9**:161–162
See also American Federation of Teachers; Collective bargaining; National Education Association; Unions
Teacher-student relationships
communications styles, **3**:146
expectations of students, **3**:87
inappropriate online, **10**:202, **10**:203
learning and, **2**:11–12, **2**:15–16
popular culture use and, **2**:220, **2**:223
role models, **4**:65, **4**:293–294
sexual harassment, **8**:145, **8**:147–148, **8**:152–154, **8**:156–157
in virtual schools, **10**:73–74, **10**:92
See also Sexual misconduct charges
Teaching profession
application of knowledge, **3**:43, **7**:161, **9**:264
communities of practice, **3**:44, **3**:45
differences from other professions, **8**:224
enhancing, **7**:221, **9**:115, **9**:172–173
knowledge domains, **3**:42–43, **7**:160–161
respect for, **2**:25, **6**:140
service to society, **3**:41–42
standards of conduct, **8**:218–219, **8**:220
unions and, **8**:254–255, **8**:258
Technical education. *See* Vocational education
Technology
accessibility, **2**:237–238, **10**:65, **10**:201–202
adoption decisions, **10**:33, **10**:36, **10**:42–44
arts and, **2**:230
assessment systems, **2**:238–239

communications, 2:240–241, 7:213,
  10:32, 10:199–200, 10:220–221
concerns about, 2:236, 2:239–246
copyright issues, 8:31, 8:35, 10:22
digital citizenship, 10:34, 10:38,
  10:143–144, 10:176–177, 10:190,
  10:221
digital divide, 2:237, 10:xvi–xvii,
  10:20, 10:38–39, 10:65, 10:198,
  10:210–211, 10:215
fear of new, 10:22–23, 10:25–30, 10:33,
  10:36–37
future educational uses, 2:229–246,
  9:196, 10:xxv–xxvi, 10:115, 10:210,
  10:212–223
increased access in schools, 2:237, 10:xvi
information systems, 9:60–61,
  9:223–224, 9:248
instructional approaches, 2:97–98
integration into curriculum,
  2:234–236, 2:239, 10:131–132
music players, 2:211
overreliance of students on,
  5:128–129, 5:133
perspectives on, 10:208–209
potential to transform instruction,
  10:208–224
private funding, 10:xvii
shift age, 9:195–196
stereotypes of student use, 2:226
teacher training in, 2:235–236,
  10:121–122, 10:123–124, 10:216,
  10:224
values and, 10:45–46
video games, 2:214–215, 2:219
virtual field trips, 7:213
virtual simulations of real life,
  2:230–231, 2:235, 2:241
See also Assistive technology; Computers;
  e-books; Internet; Mobile
  technologies; Science, Technology,
  Engineering, and Mathematics
Technology, Education and Copyright
  Harmonization (TEACH) Act, 8:31,
  8:35
Technology standards
  application of, 10:123–124, 10:127
  assessments, 10:122–123, 10:130–131
  benefits of, 10:116–118, 10:121–122,
    10:124, 10:126
  criticism of, 10:117, 10:124–126,
    10:127–131

examples, 10:119–121
generality, 10:120–121, 10:124–125,
  10:128
high-stakes testing and, 10:117,
  10:127–128, 10:130
local definition, 10:125, 10:131–132
professional, 10:119
purpose, 10:126–127, 10:130
as requirement for teachers, 10:xxii,
  10:115–133
for students, 10:48, 10:217–218
Teenagers, popular culture, 3:134
See also High schools
Telecommunications Act of 1996, 2:237
Templeton, Shane, 2:88
Ten Commandments displays,
  4:xxii–xxiii, 4:113, 4:120–121, 4:124,
  4:126, 4:131–132, 4:133
Tennessee
  prayer in schools, 4:72
  Scopes Monkey Trial, 4:xxv, 4:185, 4:196
  Standardized Testing and Reporting
    research project, 9:199
  video surveillance cameras in schools,
    10:103, 10:109
Tennessee Value-Added Assessment System
  (TVAAS), 9:139
Tenth Amendment, 6:86, 6:114, 7:1–2,
  7:40, 7:68, 9:28
Tenure, of teachers
  criticism of, 8:229–230
  definition, 8:232
  dismissal procedures, 7:25–26,
    8:228–230, 8:232–235, 8:238,
    8:240–241, 9:xxiv–xxv, 9:171
  elimination, 7:23
  employment rights, 9:169–170
  procedures, 8:238–239, 9:170
  property interest, 8:229
  purpose, 8:229
  state laws, 8:228–229, 8:232–233,
    8:236–239, 8:240–241
Test-based educational accountability
  (TBEA). *See* Accountability;
  Standardized tests
Testing. *See* Assessments; Standardized
  tests
Texas
  charter schools, 3:69
  curriculum development, 8:6
  discipline problems in schools, 5:162
  for-profit schools, 1:84, 1:85, 1:86

homeschooling laws, **1:**113
Islamic schools, **1:**66
moments of silence in schools, **4:**74–75
Race to the Top and, **3:**63–64
reported restraint use, **5:**216
school funding, **6:**185
school resource officers, **5:**165
school shootings, **5:**24
school takeovers by courts, **6:**xxii
special education, **6:**106
standards, **9:**26, **9:**40
student-led prayer in schools, **4:**39–40
teacher speech rights, **8:**7
teacher training programs, **9:**77, **9:**78, **9:**83
Ten Commandments displays, **4:**120–121, **4:**126, **4:**133
See also San Antonio Independent School District v. Rodriguez
Texas Appleseed, **5:**162, **5:**165
Texas Education Agency, **8:**156–157
Texas High School Project, **9:**42, **9:**44
Texas Supreme Court, **6:**xxii, **6:**185
Textbook publishers
    curriculum development and, **2:**29, **2:**32
    e-books, **10:**21, **10:**22, **10:**93
    influence, **2:**29, **7:**166
    NCLB requirements, **9:**18
Textbooks
    for Advanced Placement courses, **6:**229
    authentic, **2:**76, **2:**80
    drawbacks, **10:**213–214
    government aid to religious schools, **4:**xx, **4:**5, **4:**17–32
    readers, **2:**72–73, **2:**75, **2:**76, **2:**80, **2:**86, **3:**133–134
    religious content, **4:**31
    science, **2:**104–105
    token diversity, **2:**136–137
    See also e-books
TFA. *See* Teach For America
Tharp, Roland G., **1:**260–261, **1:**266
Theocrats, **4:**95
Theoharis, George, **3:**212, **7:**106
Theriot, Matthew T., **5:**158
Thomas, Clarence, **1:**30, **1:**31, **2:**203, **4:**31, **4:**253, **8:**67, **8:**179–180
Thomas, E., **9:**170
Thomas, K. R., **3:**31, **3:**32
Thomas, Karen F., **2:**23
Thomeczek, Melissa, **10:**124

Thompson, Fred, **6:**35
Thompson v. Engelking, **3:**180
Thorndike, Edward Lee, **2:**72, **9:**14–15
Thro, William E., **4:**222, **6:**168, **6:**175, **6:**186
TIAA. *See* Teachers Insurance Annuity Association
Tieken, Christopher, **9:**30
Tieso, Carol L., **3:**163–164
TIF. *See* Teacher Incentive Fund
Tillman, Linda, **3:**261
Time Warner Cable, **9:**246, **9:**250
Time-outs
    appropriate use, **5:**215, **5:**216, **5:**221, **5:**222
    lack of statistics on, **5:**215–216
    misuse of, **5:**215–216, **5:**218–219, **5:**221–226, **5:**227
    notification and documentation, **5:**228–229
    policies on use of, **5:**221
    for students with disabilities, **5:**210–211, **5:**214–215
    See also Disciplinary measures
TIMSS. *See* Trends in International Math and Science Study
Tinker v. Des Moines Independent Community School District
    academic freedom and, **8:**1–2
    application of substantial disruption standard, **4:**262–263, **8:**xx–xxi, **8:**183, **8:**184, **8:**188–189, **10:**166–169, **10:**178
    criticism of decision, **8:**179–180
    dissent, **5:**199
    dress codes and, **5:**6, **5:**8, **8:**49–50, **8:**51
    impact, **2:**201, **4:**253
    majority opinion, **8:**181
    narrowing, **4:**149
    religious speech and, **4:**42, **4:**49, **4:**262–263, **4:**265
    rights of students affirmed, **4:**271–272, **5:**xviii, **5:**4–5, **5:**195, **5:**198, **8:**185, **10:**166
    substantial disruption standard, **8:**176–177, **8:**180, **8:**186, **10:**158–159, **10:**180, **10:**185
    symbolic speech, **4:**271
Title I, Elementary and Secondary Education Act of 1965
    aid types, **3:**81–82
    amendments, **3:**76, **3:**84–85
    benefits of, **3:**79, **3:**81, **3:**83, **3:**243

criticism of, **3:**82–83, **3:**89–90
effectiveness, **3:**76, **3:**84, **3:**89,
  3:99–102, **3:**105, **3:**246–247
funding approach, **3:**83–84,
  3:106–107, **3:**238, **3:**249
goals, **3:**57, **3:**75–76, **3:**78, **3:**81, **3:**98,
  3:249
history, **3:**241–243, **7:**250–251
implementation, **3:**76, **3:**78–79,
  3:83–84, **3:**103, **3:**250
improving, **3:**83–84, **3:**90
obstacles, **3:**105–109
programs supported, **3:**xxiii–xxiv, **3:**xxv,
  3:14, **3:**81–83, **3:**93–94
Reading First program, **2:**6, **6:**79–80, **6:**91
schools accepting funds, **3:**56
students with disabilities and, **3:**243
supporters, **3:**78–84
unintended consequences, **3:**248
See also Compensatory education
Title I Comparability Law, **3:**79
Title VII, Civil Rights Act of 1964, **4:**284,
  7:xix, **7:**93–94, **8:**147, **8:**241
Title IX, Civil Rights Act of 1964, **7:**xxxviii,
  7:93–94, **7:**104
Title IX, Education Amendments of 1972
  amendments (2005), **3:**210
  athletics regulations, **3:**210–211
  compliance process, **3:**210, **3:**211
  harassment prevention and liability,
    5:55–56, **5:**60, **5:**67–68, **5:**86
  influence, **3:**209–211, **3:**213, **8:**xvi–xvii
  legal cases, **8:**144–145
  provisions, **3:**208, **3:**210, **7:**xxviii
  sexual harassment cases, **8:**144, **8:**145,
    8:147–148, **8:**152–153
  sexual harassment policies, **8:**149
  single-sex schools and, **1:**181, **1:**183,
    1:190
TiZA. *See* Tarek ibn Ziyad Academy
TNE. *See* Teachers for a New Era
TNTP. *See* New Teacher Project
Todd, Anne W., **5:**237
Tolerance. *See* Cultural tolerance; Religious
  tolerance
Tomain, Joseph A., **10:**186
Tomlinson, Carol, **3:**165
Torrance, E. Paul, **2:**168–169, **2:**173
Torres, Jennifer M. C., **8:**149
Tort law
  bullying and, **5:**65–67
  definitions, **5:**185

liability for suicide, **5:**83–84
negligence, **5:**65–67, **5:**181–183,
  5:188–189
political issues, **5:**190, **5:**191
See also Lawsuits
Towner, John C., **1:**260
TPA. *See* Coverdell Teacher Protection
  Act
TPAC. *See* Teacher Performance
  Assessment Consortium
TPAs. *See* Teacher protection acts
Tracking students
  curricular differences, **3:**154–155,
    3:161–162
  definition, **3:**159
  disadvantages, **3:**151, **3:**156, **3:**161–162,
    3:165–166
  distinction from ability grouping, **3:**149,
    3:152, **3:**159, **3:**165–166
  history, **3:**152–153, **3:**161
  market competition and, **7:**210
  in middle and high schools, **3:**152,
    3:156, **3:**161–162
  in other countries, **3:**150
  stereotypes in assignments, **3:**156
  use of, **3:**149, **3:**152, **3:**160
  See also Ability grouping; Gifted
    education
Training
  of school board members, **7:**121
  of school resource officers,
    5:163, **5:**164, **5:**165, **5:**166,
    5:170–173
  See also Administration preparation
    programs; Professional
    development; Teacher training;
    Vocational education
Transformational leadership, **7:**99
Transgender youth. *See* LGBT youth
Transportation services
  cost reductions, **9:**199–200
  driver drug testing, **8:**77, **8:**84
  fees, **6:**230
  for field trips, **4:**xx, **4:**2, **4:**6
  forced busing, **6:**253
  government aid to religious schools,
    4:xix–xx, **4:**1–14
  for homeless students, **8:**128, **8:**131,
    8:132, **8:**138
  to magnet schools, **1:**176
  outsourcing, **7:**167
  safety concerns, **10:**110–111

Trends in International Math and Science Study (TIMSS), **7:**213, **7:**259, **9:**23, **9:**30, **9:**255
Tribal schools. *See* Native American schools
Trow, Martin, **2:**46–47
Troxel v. Granville, **8:**189
Truth v. Kent School District, **4:**217, **4:**220, **4:**223–224
Tuition tax credits. *See* Tax credits
TURN. *See* Teachers Union Reform Network
Turner, Julianne, **2:**77
Turney, A. H., **3:**153–154
TVAS. *See* Tennessee Value-Added Assessment System
T.W. v. School Board, **5:**224–225
Twain, Mark, **9:**50
Twining v. State of New Jersey, **4:**98
Twitter, **10:**136, **10:**145, **10:**182, **10:**195, **10:**199
    See also Social networking sites
Tyler, Ralph, **9:**17

UCEA. *See* University Council for Educational Administration
UDL. *See* Universal Design for Learning
UK. *See* United Kingdom
Underkuffler, Laura S., **4:**30, **4:**32
UNESCO Information, Communication, Technology (ICT) competency framework, **10:**119–120, **10:**124, **10:**125, **10:**126
Uniforms
    criticism of, **8:**39
    effectiveness, **8:**48–49, **8:**52–54, **8:**55
    free speech rights and, **8:**xix, **8:**42, **8:**43, **8:**44–45, **8:**46, **8:**49–51
    legal cases, **8:**39, **8:**41–48, **8:**51–52
    opt-out provisions, **8:**43, **8:**44, **8:**46, **8:**54
    in private schools, **8:**38, **8:**41, **8:**49
    in public schools, **5:**1–3, **8:**xix, **8:**38–55
    rationales for, **5:**1–3, **8:**38–39, **8:**41, **8:**42–43, **8:**45, **8:**46–47, **8:**48
    tolerability questions, **8:**54–55
    See also Dress code policies
Unions
    accountability and, **9:**156–173
    charter schools and, **1:**2, **6:**284, **7:**38
    conflicts with reformers, **7:**27–32
    cooperation with administration, **9:**202–203
    criticism of, **7:**23, **7:**28–32, **8:**252–258, **8:**254, **9:**156, **9:**157, **9:**159, **9:**166–173
    definition, **7:**33
    effects on reform process, **7:**22–38, **9:**156, **9:**163, **9:**164–166, **9:**167, **9:**173
    industrial model, **8:**247–248, **8:**253–254
    influence on school governance, **7:**xxvi
    local, **7:**28–29, **7:**32, **7:**34, **7:**35–38
    national, **7:**34, **7:**38, **9:**161–162
    political edge, **7:**25–26
    positive effects, **7:**32, **8:**247–252
    purpose, **8:**245
    state, **7:**32, **7:**36, **7:**38
    support of reforms, **7:**32–33, **7:**34, **7:**36–38, **9:**164–166
    See also Collective bargaining; Teachers' unions
United Kingdom, Every Child Matters, **7:**53
United States v. Butler, **6:**77, **6:**87, **6:**89, **6:**90, **6:**91
United States v. O'Brien, **8:**51, **8:**52
United States v. Virginia, **1:**181
United Teachers of New Orleans v. Orleans Parish School Board, **8:**75, **8:**80, **8:**85–86
Universal design, in building design, **10:**11, **10:**12
Universal Design for Learning (UDL)
    advantages, **6:**83, **10:**2–3, **10:**10
    assumptions, **10:**11–12
    compared to assistive technology, **10:**xix, **10:**1–14
    definition, **10:**11, **10:**12
    elements, **10:**4
    links to assistive technology, **2:**238, **10:**3, **10:**4–5, **10:**8–9, **10:**13–14
    in online courses, **10:**129
    principles, **10:**12–13
    scope, **10:**12
    training and support, **10:**13
Universities and colleges. *See* Higher education
University Council for Educational Administration (UCEA), **7:**100
University of California, **4:**31, **4:**221–223
University of Missouri–Kansas City, **4:**219, **4:**233
University of Texas, **9:**83

University of Virginia
  Carnegie pensions, **9:**66
  School Turnaround Specialist Program, **9:**129
Urban school districts
  achievement gaps, **6:**241
  administrators with non-educational backgrounds, **7:**225–226
  alternative teacher licensing routes, **3:**56, **9:**103–105, **9:**111, **9:**113–114
  charter schools, **1:**23–25, **1:**27, **1:**80–81, **3:**67
  dropout rates, **2:**208, **6:**xxii, **6:**241
  families leaving, **6:**245, **8:**134
  gifted education, **6:**117
  governance, **7:**255, **7:**258, **9:**15
  leadership development, **9:**128
  magnet schools, **1:**162–163, **1:**166, **1:**171–172
  poor students, **3:**86, **3:**108
  problems, **2:**68
  reform efforts, **3:**65–72, **7:**226–227
  revenue sources, **6:**74
  segregated schools, **3:**108, **3:**231
  special provisions, **7:**112
  standardized test scores, **2:**68, **9:**8
  stereotypes of students, **2:**226
  teacher recruitment, **3:**260
  video surveillance cameras, **10:**109
  See also Elected political leaders, control of schools; Financing adequacy; *and specific cities*
Urschel, Jessica, **1:**14
Utah
  education funding, **9:**205, **9:**233
  virtual schools, **10:**74–75

Valenti, Maria T., **8:**149
Value-added modeling (VAM)
  background, **9:**139–140
  benefits of, **9:**142, **9:**143–144, **9:**147–148
  concerns about, **9:**149–151, **9:**156
  use of data, **9:**7–8, **9:**140–141, **9:**147, **9:**149, **9:**154
  variations, **9:**150
Values
  political, **2:**125
  religious, **2:**126, **2:**155, **2:**198
  See also Moral values
VAM. *See* Value-added modeling
Van Biema, David, **4:**172

van Geel, Tyl, **2:**122
Van Orden v. Perry, **4:**22–23, **4:**120–121, **4:**126, **4:**133
Vanderbilt University, **6:**139–140
Vandiver v. Hardin County Board of Education, **1:**120–121
Vann v. Stewart, **5:**49
VanTassel-Baska, Joyce, **6:**122
Velton, Barbara, **9:**xxii, **9:**xxiii
Veltri, B. T, **9:**112
Vergari, S., **7:**133
Vergon, Charles B., **5:**26
Vermont, education funding, **9:**233
Vermont Supreme Court, **6:**158
Vernonia School District 47J v. Acton, **5:**198, **5:**203, **8:**57–58, **8:**60–61, **8:**62, **8:**63–64, **8:**66–67, **8:**68, **8:**84
Verstegen, Deborah A., **3:**171, **3:**179
VHS. *See* Virtual High School
Vicky M. v. Northeastern Education Intermediate Unit 19, **5:**217–218
Video surveillance cameras in schools
  benefits, **10:**99–100, **10:**110–112
  deterrent effect, **10:**101–102, **10:**107, **10:**110
  employee surveillance, **10:**99, **10:**102–103, **10:**112
  flexibility, **10:**111
  guidelines, **10:**105–106
  linked to police stations, **10:**xxiv, **10:**109
  notification, **10:**106
  placement, **10:**103, **10:**105, **10:**109–111
  privacy concerns, **10:**xxiv, **10:**98–113
  protection of data, **10:**99, **10:**111
  public support, **10:**110–111
  use of, **10:**xxiv, **10:**98, **10:**101, **10:**106–107, **10:**112–113
Violence
  clothing messages and, **5:**15–16
  hip-hop culture and, **3:**138–140, **3:**147
  incidents in schools, **5:**24, **5:**25, **5:**27, **5:**28
  in popular culture, **2:**222
  school shootings, **4:**277, **4:**278, **5:**xxii, **5:**16, **5:**24, **5:**28, **5:**64, **5:**190
  against women, **3:**206–207
  See also Crime; Gang-related clothing; Safety; Zero tolerance policies
Virginia
  charter schools, **6:**254
  constitution, **6:**170
  "English-only" law, **3:**192

homeschooling laws, **1:**121
moments of silence in schools, **4:**73
Race to the Top and, **3:**63–64
racial discrimination in teacher pay, **7:**23
resistance to desegregation, **6:**254, **7:**251
school desegregation, **3:**2, **3:**6
school system, **7:**xvii–xviii
segregated schools, **3:**15
standards, **9:**26
Virginia Military Institute (VMI), **1:**181
Virtual High School (VHS), **10:**72
Virtual schools
  administrators, **10:**92
  attrition, **10:**76, **10:**77–78
  benefits of, **10:**xxi, **10:**68–69, **10:**71–74, **10:**90
  charter schools, **1:**5, **1:**13, **10:**77
  cost-effectiveness, **10:**xxi–xxii, **10:**80–96
  costs, **10:**81, **10:**84–85, **10:**89, **10:**91–95, **10:**96
  definition, **10:**71, **10:**80
  development of, **10:**68
  effectiveness, **10:**xxi, **10:**68–78
  enrollment growth, **10:**70, **10:**71, **10:**74–75, **10:**80
  for-profit, **1:**89
  funding, **10:**xxi–xxii, **10:**81, **10:**84, **10:**86, **10:**88–90, **10:**95–96
  research on, **10:**69, **10:**71–73, **10:**75–78
  teacher-student relationships, **10:**73–74, **10:**92
  technology, **10:**94–95
  See also Cyberschools; Online courses
Visual arts. *See* Arts
Visualization skills, **2:**147–148
VMI. *See* Virginia Military Institute
Vocational education
  academic subjects and, **1:**219, **1:**222, **1:**225, **1:**230, **3:**127
  availability, **3:**122–123
  benefits of, **1:**221, **1:**225–227, **3:**125–126, **3:**128–129
  challenges, **1:**xxvii, **1:**224–225, **1:**228–230
  criticism of separate, **1:**227–233, **3:**126–127
  enrollments, **1:**220
  funding, **1:**228, **3:**127–128
  history, **1:**216, **1:**219, **3:**125–127
  new models, **1:**229–233

  programs, **1:**220–221, **1:**223–225
  relations with business and industry, **1:**216–217, **1:**232
  student organizations, **1:**222–223
  value of, **1:**xxvii, **1:**216–233
Vocational Education Act of 1963, **1:**219, **1:**233
Vockell, E. L., **5:**120
Volonino, Victoria, **2:**179
Voting rights, of women, **3:**207–208
Vouchers
  advantages, **6:**244–247, **6:**248–249
  amounts, **6:**246–247, **6:**248
  constitutional issues, **1:**xxv, **1:**30–31, **1:**93, **1:**96–97
  cost-effectiveness, **6:**246–247
  criticism of, **1:**93, **6:**242, **6:**247–248, **6:**250–256, **6:**270
  definition, **6:**xxiii
  examples, **1:**95–98, **7:**226
  funding, **6:**251–252, **9:**224–225
  governance impact, **7:**xxvi–xxvii
  history, **1:**93, **6:**268
  legal obstacles, **6:**250–251
  means testing, **6:**244, **6:**247
  research on, **6:**106–107, **6:**248–249
  for special needs students, **6:**106–107, **6:**247–248
  supporters, **1:**47–48, **1:**93, **1:**102
  use at private schools, **1:**150, **6:**xxiii, **6:**106–107, **6:**240–256
  See also Choice
Vouchers for religious schools
  benefits of, **6:**241–242
  constitutionality, **1:**xxv, **1:**40–41, **1:**93, **6:**xxiii, **6:**255
  examples, **1:**95–97, **6:**244
  opposition, **6:**254–256
  prohibited by state constitutions, **6:**xxiii
  states offering, **1:**43–44
  supporters, **1:**93, **4:**5, **6:**272
  See also Zelman v. Simmons-Harris
Vygotsky, Lev S., **2:**234, **2:**235

Wagner Act, **8:**248
Wahlstrom, Kyla L., **7:**80–81
Waiting for Superman, **3:**68
Wake County Public School District, North Carolina, **7:**226
Waldorf Education, **2:**xx, **2:**155, **2:**245–246
Walker, Hill M., **5:**237, **5:**241
Walker, Vanessa Siddle, **7:**182

Wallace, Alfred Russell, **4:**190
Wallace Foundation, **6:**48
Wallace v. Jaffree, **4:**xxi, **4:**23, **4:**49, **4:**67, **4:**71–72, **4:**78, **4:**113
Walton Family Foundation, **7:**179
Walz v. Egg Harbor Township Board of Education, **4:**247, **4:**251, **4:**255, **4:**256, **4:**262
Wang, Jia, **7:**52
Warhol, Andy, **2:**230
Warnock, Mary, **3:**215
Wars, casualties, **2:**206–207
Washegesic v. Bloomingdale Public Schools, **4:**122
Washington, Booker T., **3:**126
Washington, D.C.
   languages spoken, **2:**110
   private schools, **7:**10
   See also District of Columbia Public Schools
Washington, George, **4:**142, **4:**172
Waters, Maxine, **3:**138–139
Waters v. Churchill, **8:**202
Watson, John, **10:**77, **10:**89
Weapons
   ceremonial daggers, **4:**267–268, **4:**277, **4:**288
   guns, **5:**20, **5:**28–29, **8:**16
   knives, **5:**20, **5:**46, **5:**49
   pictures on T-shirts, **5:**15–16
   See also Violence; Zero tolerance policies for weapons
Webb, L. Dean, **7:**12
Websites. *See* Internet; Social networking sites
Weider, Virginia, **6:**118
Weighted student funding (WSF), **3:**171, **3:**172, **3:**175–177, **6:**180, **6:**190–191, **9:**197–198
Weinrach, S. G., **3:**31, **3:**32
Weinstein, Carol Simon, **5:**150
Weinstein, R. S., **5:**207
Weintraub v. Board of Education, **8:**209
Weisberg, Daniel, **9:**172
Wells, Amy Stuart, **6:**288
Wells, Stuart, **1:**107
Welner, Kevin, **6:**272
Welsch, David M., **1:**85
Wenger, Etienne, **2:**133
West, Martin R., **7:**137
West Publishing Co. v. Mead Data Center, **8:**21

West Virginia State Board of Education v. Barnette, **4:**xxiii, **4:**50, **4:**137–138, **4:**140, **4:**146, **4:**147, **4:**148
Westfield High School L.I.F.E. Club v. City of Westfield, **4:**257–258
Wheelock, Anne, **3:**155
Wherry, John, **7:**193
Whiston, Susan C., **3:**30
Whitehurst, George, **9:**30
Whites
   arrests of students, **5:**162
   cultural socialization, **2:**137–138
   dropouts, **6:**199
   educational attainment, **3:**115
   NAEP scores, **3:**89, **3:**99–100, **3:**103–105, **7:**85
   privileges, **3:**17
   school board members, **7:**118
   school choice and, **7:**220
   student population, **9:**241
   suspensions and expulsions, **5:**32, **5:**37, **5:**41–42, **5:**47
   teachers, **2:**135, **2:**137–138
   See also Achievement gaps; Racial issues; Segregated schools
Whole language movement, **2:**73, **2:**74
Wiccan religion, **4:**134, **4:**293
Wicks, Mathew, **10:**77
Widmar v. Vincent, **4:**216, **4:**219, **4:**233
Wieder, A., **9:**116
Wigfield, Allan, **2:**15
Wigg v. Sioux Falls School District 49–5, **4:**53–54, **4:**93, **4:**254
Wiley, Terrence G., **2:**119
Willard, Nancy, **10:**178
Wilson, August, **3:**146
Wilson, E. O., **2:**138
Wilson, Rita, **3:**58
Wilson, W. Stephen, **9:**26
Winn v. Arizona Christian School Tuition Organization, **1:**99
Winters, Marcus A., **6:**106–107
Wirt, Frederick, **7:**256
Wirt, William, **4:**157
Wisconsin
   collective bargaining by public employees, **8:**244, **8:**245, **8:**258
   compulsory education law, **1:**xx–xxi
   constitution, **1:**96
   school funding, **9:**193
   special education students, **6:**100

teacher training programs, **9:**88–89
See also Milwaukee
Wisconsin Center for Educational Reform, **2:**63
Wisconsin v. Yoder, **1:**xx–xxi, **1:**112–113, **1:**114, **1:**123, **4:**74, **4:**273–274
Woessmann, Ludger, **7:**137
Woida, Chloe, **2:**207–208
Wolf, Patrick, **6:**248
Wolman v. Walter, **4:**xx, **4:**2, **4:**6, **4:**18, **4:**27
Wolstencroft, Helen, **2:**215
Women
　administrators, **3:**219, **7:**94–95, **7:**100–101, **7:**104, **7:**105–106
　career paths, **7:**105
　Catholic nuns, **4:**276, **4:**287
　earnings, **3:**120–121
　elected officials, **7:**103
　higher education graduates, **3:**114–115
　Muslim garb, **4:**268, **4:**275, **4:**276, **4:**280–281, **4:**288, **4:**296
　principals, **7:**100, **7:**101, **7:**103, **7:**104
　school board members, **7:**103, **7:**118, **9:**15
　superintendents, **7:**104
　teachers, **3:**255–257, **3:**259, **3:**269–270, **7:**94, **7:**97, **7:**101, **7:**104
　violence against, **3:**206–207
　voting rights, **3:**207–208
　See also Gender
Wong, Kenneth K., **7:**5, **7:**7, **7:**17, **7:**258
Wood, R. Craig, **6:**206–207
World Health Organization, **2:**169
Wright, Wayne E., **2:**119
WSF. *See* Weighted student funding
Wyke v. Polk County School Board, **5:**81
Wyner, Joshua S., **3:**86
Wyoming, charter schools, **7:**132

Yahoo Groups, **10:**199
Year-round schools
　alternative reforms, **1:**251–252
　benefits of, **1:**xxvii–xxviii, **1:**236, **1:**239–246
　charter schools, **1:**5
　cost savings, **1:**245, **1:**252
　as distraction from reform efforts, **1:**246–253
　intersession activities, **1:**239–240, **1:**241–242, **1:**244, **1:**246
　models, **1:**239, **1:**242
　number of, **1:**236–237, **1:**239, **1:**245
　planning, **1:**243, **1:**244
　research on, **1:**239, **1:**240–244, **1:**245, **1:**246
　schedules, **1:**236, **1:**237, **1:**239, **1:**241–242
　student outcomes, **1:**236–253
　See also School years
Yemeni Americans, **2:**129–130
Yeung, Ryan, **3:**177, **8:**53
Young, K. Richard, **5:**243
Youth culture. *See* Popular culture
Youth Risk Behavior Survey, **5:**29
YouTube, **2:**217, **8:**183, **10:**169, **10:**182
Yuan, Kun, **2:**58

Zamecnik v. Indian Prairie School District, **4:**263–264
Zeichner, Kenneth, **3:**41
Zelman, Susan Tave, **1:**221
Zelman v. Simmons-Harris
　arguments, **6:**244
　conditions for voucher constitutionality, **1:**30–31
　criticism of public schools, **6:**245–246
　dissents, **6:**255
　impact, **6:**242, **6:**250, **6:**283
　majority opinion, **1:**93, **1:**95, **1:**96–97, **4:**7, **4:**23–24, **6:**xxiii
　vouchers seen to benefit families, **1:**40–41
Zero tolerance policies
　alternatives to, **5:**45
　case-by-case reviews, **5:**25–26, **5:**30
　criticism of, **5:**xx–xxi, **5:**27–34
　for cyberbullying, **10:**155, **10:**161
　definition, **5:**xx, **5:**22
　for drugs and alcohol, **5:**19–22, **5:**26–27, **5:**29, **5:**31, **5:**204
　due process and, **5:**xx, **5:**20, **5:**49, **5:**50
　effectiveness, **5:**25, **5:**43
　enforcement, **5:**25–26, **5:**30–33, **5:**43, **5:**44, **5:**51
　historical background, **5:**22–23, **5:**24–25, **5:**39–40
　impact, **5:**23–27, **5:**28–34, **5:**43–45
　introduction of, **5:**xviii, **5:**xix–xx, **5:**22, **5:**23
　legal challenges, **5:**xx, **5:**19–20, **5:**49–50
　objectives, **5:**22, **5:**25
　other offenses included, **5:**32, **5:**33, **5:**40, **5:**204

overrepresentation of students of color, **5**:32–33, **5**:36–52
safety rationale, **5**:19–34, **5**:39, **5**:40
state laws, **5**:xx, **10**:161–162
students with disabilities and, **5**:20–21, **5**:23, **5**:25
unintended consequences, **5**:29–34, **5**:36, **5**:44–45
Zero tolerance policies for weapons
background, **5**:24–25, **5**:203–204
case-by-case reviews, **5**:25–26
enforcement, **5**:25–26, **5**:30, **5**:39, **5**:46, **5**:49
expulsions, **5**:23, **5**:25–26
federal laws and policies, **5**:22–23
impact, **5**:25, **5**:28–29
legal cases, **5**:20
police referrals, **5**:33
religious garb issues, **4**:267–268, **4**:277
See also Gun-Free Schools Act
Zhao, Chun-Mei, **3**:51
Zhao, Yong, **7**:54
Zigmond, Naomi, **2**:179
Zimmer, Ron, **3**:67, **6**:38
Zins, Joseph E., **7**:255
Zobrest v. Catalina Foothills School District, **4**:18–19, **4**:24
Zorach v. Clauson, **4**:153–154, **4**:156, **4**:157, **4**:161–162, **4**:163
Zumbo, Bruno D., **5**:242